Beginning C++17

From Novice to Professional

Fifth Edition

Ivor Horton
Peter Van Weert

Beginning C++17: From Novice to Professional

Ivor Horton
Stratford-upon-Avon, Warwickshire, United Kingdom

Peter Van Weert
Kessel-Lo, Belgium

ISBN-13 (pbk): 978-1-4842-3365-8
https://doi.org/10.1007/978-1-4842-3366-5

ISBN-13 (electronic): 978-1-4842-3366-5

Library of Congress Control Number: 2018936369

Managing Director, Apress Media LLC: Welmoed Spahr
Acquisitions Editor: Steve Anglin
Development Editor: Matthew Moodie
Coordinating Editor: Mark Powers

Cover designed by eStudioCalamar

Cover image designed by Freepik (`www.freepik.com`)

Distributed to the book trade worldwide by Springer Science+Business Media New York, 233 Spring Street, 6th Floor, New York, NY 10013. Phone 1-800-SPRINGER, fax (201) 348-4505, e-mail orders-ny@springer-sbm.com, or visit `www.springeronline.com`. Apress Media, LLC is a California LLC and the sole member (owner) is Springer Science + Business Media Finance Inc (SSBM Finance Inc). SSBM Finance Inc is a **Delaware** corporation.

For information on translations, please e-mail editorial@apress.com; for reprint, paperback, or audio rights, please email bookpermissions@springernature.com.

Apress titles may be purchased in bulk for academic, corporate, or promotional use. eBook versions and licenses are also available for most titles. For more information, reference our Print and eBook Bulk Sales web page at `www.apress.com/bulk-sales`.

Any source code or other supplementary material referenced by the author in this book is available to readers on GitHub via the book's product page, located at `www.apress.com/9781484233658`. For more detailed information, please visit `www.apress.com/source-code`.

This is for Alexander and Henry who are both going to learn programming soon.
If their amazing expertise with Minecraft is anything to go by,
they will be brilliant at it.

—Ivor Horton

For my wonderful family. For all your love and support. For putting up with
me never having the time to help out around the house or to play
with the train set I got you for Christmas.

—Peter Van Weert

Contents

viii

About the Authors

Ivor Horton graduated as a mathematician and was lured into information technology with promises of great rewards for very little work. In spite of the reality being a great deal of work for relatively modest rewards, he has continued to work with computers to the present day. He has been engaged at various times in programming, systems design, consultancy, and the management and implementation of projects of considerable complexity.

Ivor has many years of experience in designing and implementing systems for engineering design and manufacturing control. He has developed occasionally useful applications in a wide variety of programming languages and has taught primarily scientists and engineers to do likewise. His currently published works include tutorials on C, C++, and Java. At the present time, when he is not writing programming books or providing advice to others, he spends his time fishing, traveling, and enjoying life in general.

Peter Van Weert is a Belgian software engineer whose main interests and expertise are application software development, programming languages, algorithms, and data structures.

He received his master of science degree in computer science *summa cum laude* with congratulations of the Board of Examiners from the University of Leuven. In 2010, he completed his PhD thesis there on the design and efficient compilation of rule-based programming languages at the research group for declarative programming languages and artificial intelligence. During his doctoral studies, he was a teaching assistant for object-oriented programming (Java), software analysis and design, and declarative programming.

After graduating, Peter worked at Nikon Metrology for more than six years on large-scale, industrial application software in the area of 3D laser scanning and point cloud inspection. He learned to master C++ and refactoring and debugging of very large code bases, and he gained further proficiency in all aspects of the software development process, including the analysis of functional and technical requirements, and agile and scrum-based project and team management.

Today, Peter works for Danaher in its R&D unit for digital dentistry software, developing software for the dental practice of tomorrow.

In his spare time, he has co-authored two books on C++ and two award-winning Windows 8 apps and is a regular expert speaker at, and board member of, the Belgian C++ Users Group.

About the Technical Reviewer

Marc Gregoire is a software engineer from Belgium. He graduated from the University of Leuven, Belgium, with a degree in "Burgerlijk ingenieur in de computer wetenschappen" (equivalent to a master of science degree in computer engineering). The year after, he received the *cum laude* degree of master in artificial intelligence at the same university. After his studies, Marc started working for a software consultancy company called Ordina Belgium. As a consultant, he worked for Siemens and Nokia Siemens Networks on critical 2G and 3G software running on Solaris for telecom operators. This required working on international teams stretching from South America and the United States to Europe, the Middle East, and Asia. Currently, Marc works for Nikon Metrology on industrial 3D laser scanning software.

Introduction

Welcome to *Beginning C++17*. This is a revised and updated version of Ivor Horton's original book called *Beginning ANSI C++*. The C++ language has been extended and improved considerably since then, so much so that it was no longer possible to squeeze detailed explanations of all of C++ into a single book. This tutorial will teach the essentials of the C++ language and Standard Library features, which will be more than enough for you to write your own C++ applications. With the knowledge from this book, you should have no difficulty in extending the depth and scope of your C++ expertise.

We have assumed no prior programming knowledge. If you are keen to learn and have an aptitude for thinking logically, getting a grip on C++ will be easier than you might imagine. By developing C++ skills, you'll be learning a language that is already used by millions and that provides the capability for application development in just about any context.

C++ is very powerful. Arguably, it's more powerful than most programming languages. So, yes, like with any powerful tool you can wield some considerable damage if you use it without proper training. We often compare C++ to a Swiss Army knife: age-old, trusted, incredibly versatile, yet potentially mind-boggling and full of pointy things that could really hurt you. Once someone clearly explains to you what all the different tools are meant for, however, and teaches you some elementary knife safety rules, then you'll never have to look for another pocketknife again.

C++ does not need to be dangerous or difficult at all either. C++ today is much more accessible than many people assume. The language has come a long way since its conception nearly 40 years ago. In essence, we have learned how to wield all its mighty blades and tools in the safest and most effective way possible. And, more importantly perhaps, the C++ language and its Standard Library have evolved accordingly to facilitate this. The past decade in particular has seen the rise of what is now known as "modern C++." Modern C++ emphasizes the use of newer, more expressive, safer language features, combined with tried and tested best practices and coding guidelines. Once you know and apply a handful of simple rules and techniques, C++ loses much of its complexity. Key is that someone properly and gradually explains not simply what you *can* do with C++ but rather what you *should* do with C++. And that's where this book comes in!

In this latest revision of the book, we have gone through great lengths to bring it back in line with the new, modern era of C++ programming we're living in. As before, we of course do so in the form of a gradual, informal tutorial. We'll introduce to you all the shiny blades and pointy things C++ has to offer—both old and new—using many hands-on coding samples and exercises. But that's not all: more than ever before we've made sure to always explain which tool is best to use for which purpose, why that is the case, and how to avoid getting cut. We've made sure that you will begin C++, from day one, using the safe, productive, modern programming style that employers will expect from you tomorrow.

The C++ language in this book corresponds to the latest International Organization for Standardization (ISO) standard, commonly referred to as C++17. Not everything of C++17 is covered, since many of the extensions compared to previous versions of the language are targeted toward more advanced use. All the examples in the book can be compiled and executed using C++17-conforming compilers that are available now.

Using the Book

To learn C++ with this book, you'll need a compiler that conforms to the C++17 standard and a text editor suitable for working with program code. Several compilers are available currently that are C++17 compliant, some of which are free.

The GCC and Clang compilers have comprehensive support for C++17 and are both open source and free to download. Installing them and putting them together with a suitable editor can be a little tricky if you are new to this kind of thing. An easy way to install GCC along with a suitable editor is to download Code::Blocks or Qt Creator. Both are free integrated development environments (IDEs) for Linux, Apple macOS, and Microsoft Windows. They support a complete program development for several compilers, including GCC and Clang. This implies you get support for both C and C++.

Another possibility is to use Microsoft Visual C++ that runs under Microsoft Windows. It is nearly fully compliant with C++17 as well; all examples in this book should compile with the latest version just fine. The Community and Express editions are free for individual use or even small professional teams. With Visual Studio you get a comprehensive professional editor and support for other languages such as C# and Basic.

There are other compilers that support C++17 as well, which you can find with a quick online search. The online download section for this book also contains a list of further useful resources on how to get started.

We've organized the material in this book to be read sequentially, so you should start at the beginning and keep going until you reach the end. However, no one ever learned programming by just reading a book. You'll only learn how to program in C++ by writing code, so make sure you key in all the examples—don't just copy them from the download files—and compile and execute the code that you've keyed in. This might seem tedious at times, but it's surprising how much just typing in C++ statements will help your understanding, especially when you may feel you're struggling with some of the ideas. If an example doesn't work, resist the temptation to go straight back to the book to see why. Try to figure out from your code what is wrong. This is good practice for what you'll have to do when you are developing C++ applications for real.

Making mistakes is a fundamental part of the learning process, and the exercises should provide you with ample opportunity for that. It's a good idea to dream up a few exercises of your own. If you are not sure about how to do something, just have a go before looking it up. The more mistakes you make, the greater the insight you'll have into what can, and does, go wrong. Make sure you attempt all the exercises, and remember, don't look at the solutions until you're sure that you can't work them out yourself. Most of these exercises just involve a direct application of what's covered in a chapter—they're just practice, in other words—but some also require a bit of thought or maybe even inspiration.

We wish you every success with C++. Above all, enjoy it!

Ivor Horton
Peter Van Weert

CHAPTER 1

Basic Ideas

In this book we sometimes will use certain code in the examples before having explained it in detail. This chapter is intended to help you when this occurs by giving presenting an overview of the major elements of C++ and how they hang together. We'll also explain a few concepts relating to the representation of numbers and characters in your computer.

In this chapter, you'll learn:

- What is meant by *modern C++*

- What the terms *C++11*, *C++14*, and *C++17* mean

- What the C++ Standard Library is

- What are the elements of a C++ program

- How to document your program code

- How your C++ code becomes an executable program

- How object-oriented programming differs from procedural programming

- What binary, hexadecimal, and octal number systems are

- What floating-point numbers are

- How a computer represents numbers using nothing but bits and bytes

- What Unicode is

Modern C++

The C++ programming language was originally developed in the early 1980s by Danish computer scientist Bjarne Stroustrup. That makes C++ one of the older programming languages still in active use—very old, in fact, in the fast-paced world of computer programming. Despite its age, though, C++ is still standing strong, steadily maintaining its top-five position in most popularity rankings for programming languages. There's no doubt whatsoever that C++ still is one of the most widely used and most powerful programming language in the world today.

Just about any kind of program can be written in C++, from device drivers to operating systems and from payroll and administrative programs to games. Major operating systems, browsers, office suites, email clients, multimedia players, database systems—name one and chances are it's written at least partly in C++. Above all else, C++ is perhaps best suited for applications where performance matters, such as applications that have to process large amounts of data, modern games with high-end graphics, or apps that target embedded or mobile devices. Programs written in C++ are still easily many times faster than those

© Ivor Horton and Peter Van Weert 2018
I. Horton and P. Van Weert, *Beginning C++17*, https://doi.org/10.1007/978-1-4842-3366-5_1

written in other popular languages. Also, C++ is far more effective than most other languages for developing applications across an enormous range of computing devices and environments, including for personal computers, workstations, mainframe computers, tablets, and mobile phones.

The C++ programming language may be old, but it's still very much alive and kicking. Or, better yet: it's *again* very much alive and kicking. After its initial development and standardization in the 1980s, C++ evolved slowly—until 2011, that is, when the International Organization for Standardization (ISO) released a new version of the standard that formally defines the C++ programming language. This edition of the standard, commonly referred to as *C++11*, revived C++ and catapulted the somewhat dated language right back into the 21st century. It modernized the language and the way we use it so profoundly that you could almost call C++11 a completely new language.

Programming using the features of C++11 and beyond is referred to as *modern C++*. In this book, we'll show you that modern C++ is about more than simply embracing the language's new features—lambda expressions, auto type deduction, and range-based for loops, to name a few. More than anything else, modern C++ is about modern ways of programming, the consensus of what constitutes good programming style. It's about applying an implicit set of guidelines and best practices, all designed to make C++ programming easier, less error-prone, and more productive. A modern, safe C++ programming style replaces traditional low-level language constructs with the use of containers (Chapters 5 and 19), smart pointers (Chapter 6), or other RAII techniques (Chapter 15), and it emphasizes exceptions to report errors (Chapter 15), passing objects by value through move semantics (Chapter 17), writing algorithms instead of loops (Chapter 19), and so on. Of course, all this probably means little to nothing to you yet. But not to worry: in this book, we'll gradually introduce everything you need to know to program in C++ today!

The C++11 standard appears to have revived the C++ community, which has been actively working hard on extending and further improving the language ever since. Every three years, a new version of the standard is published. In 2014, the *C++14* standard was finalized, and in 2017 the *C++17* edition. This book relates to C++ as defined by C++17. All code should work on any compiler that complies with the C++17 edition of the standard. The good news is that most major compilers have been keeping up with the latest developments, so if your compiler does not support a particular feature yet, it soon will.

Standard Libraries

If you had to create everything from scratch every time you wrote a program, it would be tedious indeed. The same functionality is required in many programs—reading data from the keyboard, calculating a square root, and sorting data records into a particular sequence are examples. C++ comes with a large amount of prewritten code that provides facilities such as these so you don't have to write the code yourself. All this standard code is defined in the *Standard Library*.

The Standard Library is a huge collection of routines and definitions that provide functionality that is required by many programs. Examples are numerical calculations, string processing, sorting and searching, organizing and managing data, and input and output. We'll introduce major Standard Library functionalities in virtually every chapter and will later zoom in a bit more specifically on some key data structures and algorithms in Chapter 19. Nevertheless, the Standard Library is so vast that we will only scratch the surface of what is available in this book. It really needs several books to fully elaborate all the capabilities it provides. *Beginning STL* (Apress, 2015) is a companion book that is a tutorial on using the Standard Template Library, which is the subset of the C++ Standard Library for managing and processing data in various ways. For a compact yet complete overview of everything the modern Standard Library has to offer, we also recommend the book C++ *Standard Library Quick Reference* (Apress, 2016).

Given the scope of the language and the extent of the library, it's not unusual for a beginner to find C++ somewhat daunting. It is too extensive to learn in its entirety from a single book. However, you don't need to learn all of C++ to be able to write substantial programs. You can approach the language step-by-step, in which case it really isn't difficult. An analogy might be learning to drive a car. You can certainly become a competent and safe driver without necessarily having the expertise, knowledge, and experience to drive in the Indianapolis 500. With this book you can learn everything you need to program effectively in C++. By the time you reach the end, you'll be confidently writing your own applications. You'll also be well equipped to explore the full extent of C++ and its Standard Library.

C++ Program Concepts

There will be much more detail on everything we discuss in this section later in the book. We'll jump straight in with the complete, fully working C++ program shown in Figure 1-1, which also explains what the various bits are. We'll use the example as a base for discussing some more general aspects of C++.

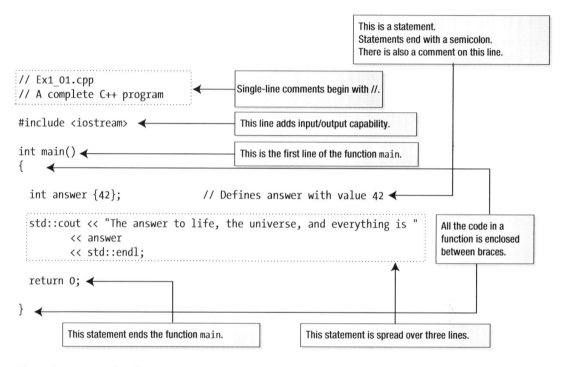

Figure 1-1. *A complete C++ program*

Source Files and Header Files

The file depicted in Figure 1-1, Ex1_01.cpp, is in the code download for the book. The file extension, .cpp, indicates that this is a C++ *source file*. Source files contain functions and thus all the executable code in a program. The names of source files usually have the extension .cpp, although other extensions such as .cc, .cxx, or .c++ are sometimes used to identify a C++ source file.

C++ code is actually stored in two kinds of files. Next to source files, there're also so-called header files. Header files contain, among other things, *function prototypes* and *definitions* for classes and templates that are used by the executable code in a .cpp file. The names of header files usually have the extension .h, although other extensions such as .hpp are also used. You'll create your first very own header files in Chapter 10; until then all your programs will be small enough to be defined in a single source file.

Comments and Whitespace

The first two lines in Figure 1-1 are *comments*. You add comments that document your program code to make it easier to understand how it works. The compiler ignores everything that follows two successive forward slashes on a line, so this kind of comment can follow code on a line. In our example, the first line is a comment that indicates the name of the file containing this code. We'll identify the file for each working example in the same way.

■ **Note**   The comment with the file name in each header or source file is only there for your convenience. In normal coding there is no need to add such comments; it only introduces an unnecessary maintenance overhead when renaming files.

There's another form of comment that you can use when you need to spread a comment over several lines. Here's an example:

```
/* This comment is
   over two lines.  */
```

Everything between /* and */ will be ignored by the compiler. You can embellish this sort of comment to make it stand out. For instance:

```
/******************\
 * This comment is  *
 * over two lines.  *
\******************/
```

Whitespace is any sequence of spaces, tabs, newlines, or form feed characters. Whitespace is generally ignored by the compiler, except when it is necessary for syntactic reasons to distinguish one element from another.

Preprocessing Directives and Standard Library Headers

The third line in Figure 1-1 is a *preprocessing directive*. Preprocessing directives cause the source code to be modified in some way before it is compiled to executable form. This preprocessing directive adds the contents of the Standard Library header file with the name iostream to this source file, Ex1_01.cpp. The header file contents are inserted in place of the #include directive.

Header files, which are sometimes referred to just as *headers*, contain definitions to be used in a source file. iostream contains definitions that are needed to perform input from the keyboard and text output to the screen using Standard Library routines. In particular, it defines std::cout and std::endl among many other things. If the preprocessing directive to include the iostream header was omitted from Ex1_01.cpp, the source file wouldn't compile because the compiler would not know what std::cout or std::endl is. The contents of header files are included into a source file before it is compiled. You'll be including the contents of one or more Standard Library header files into nearly every program, and you'll also be creating and using your own header files that contain definitions that you construct later in the book.

▓ **Caution**   There are no spaces between the angle brackets and the standard header file name. With some compilers, spaces are significant between the angle brackets, < and >; if you insert spaces here, the program may not compile.

Functions

Every C++ program consists of at least one and usually many more *functions*. A function is a named block of code that carries out a well-defined operation such as "read the input data" or "calculate the average value" or "output the results." You execute, or *call*, a function in a program using its name. All the executable code in a program appears within functions. There must be one function with the name main, and execution always starts automatically with this function. The main() function usually calls other functions, which in turn can call other functions, and so on. Functions provide several important advantages:

- A program that is broken down into discrete functions is easier to develop and test.

- You can reuse a function in several different places in a program, which makes the program smaller than if you coded the operation in each place that it is needed.

- You can often reuse a function in many different programs, thus saving time and effort.

- Large programs are typically developed by a team of programmers. Each team member is responsible for programming a set of functions that are a well-defined subset of the whole program. Without a functional structure, this would be impractical.

The program in Figure 1-1 consists of just the function main(). The first line of the function is as follows:

```
int main()
```

This is called the *function header*, which identifies the function. Here, int is a type name that defines the type of value that the main() function returns when it finishes execution—an integer. An integer is a number without a fractional component; that is, 23 and -2048 are integers, while 3.1415 and ¼ are not. In general, the parentheses following a name in a function definition enclose the specification for information to be passed to the function when you call it. There's nothing between the parentheses in this instance, but there could be. You'll learn how you specify the type of information to be passed to a function when it is executed in Chapter 8. We'll always put parentheses after a function name in the text—like we did with main()—to distinguish it from other things that are code.

The executable code for a function is always enclosed between curly braces. The opening brace follows the function header.

Statements

A *statement* is a basic unit in a C++ program. A statement always ends with a semicolon, and it's the semicolon that marks the end of a statement, not the end of the line. A statement defines something, such as a computation, or an action that is to be performed. Everything a program does is specified by statements. Statements are executed in sequence until there is a statement that causes the sequence to be altered. You'll learn about statements that can change the execution sequence in Chapter 4. There are three statements in `main()` in Figure 1-1. The first defines a variable, which is a named bit of memory for storing data of some kind. In this case, the variable has the name `answer` and can store integer values:

```
int answer {42};                          // Defines answer with the value 42
```

The type, `int`, appears first, preceding the name. This specifies the kind of data that can be stored—integers. Note the space between `int` and `answer`. One or more whitespace characters is essential here to separate the type name from the variable name; without the space, the compiler would see the name `intanswer`, which it would not understand. An initial value for `answer` appears between the braces following the variable name, so it starts out storing 42. There's a space between `answer` and {42}, but it's not essential. Any of the following definitions are valid as well:

```
int one{ 1 };
int two{2};
int three{
    3
};
```

The compiler mostly ignores superfluous whitespace. However, you should use whitespace in a consistent fashion to make your code more readable.

There's a somewhat redundant comment at the end of the first statement explaining what we just described, but it does demonstrate that you can add a comment to a statement. The whitespace preceding the // is also not mandatory, but it is desirable.

You can enclose several statements between a pair of curly braces, { }, in which case they're referred to as a *statement block*. The body of a function is an example of a block, as you saw in Figure 1-1 where the statements in the `main()` function appear between curly braces. A statement block is also referred to as a *compound statement* because in most circumstances it can be considered as a single statement, as you'll see when we look at decision-making capabilities in Chapter 4, and loops in Chapter 5. Wherever you can put a single statement, you can equally well put a block of statements between braces. As a consequence, blocks can be placed inside other blocks—this concept is called *nesting*. Blocks can be nested, one within another, to any depth.

Data Input and Output

Input and output are performed using *streams* in C++. To output something, you write it to an output stream, and to input data, you read it from an input stream. A *stream* is an abstract representation of a source of data or a data sink. When your program executes, each stream is tied to a specific device that is the source of data in the case of an input stream and the destination for data in the case of an output stream. The advantage of having an abstract representation of a source or sink for data is that the programming is then the same regardless of the device the stream represents. You can read a disk file in essentially the same way as you read from the keyboard. The standard output and input streams in C++ are called `cout` and `cin`, respectively, and by default they correspond to your computer's screen and keyboard. You'll be reading input from `cin` in Chapter 2.

The next statement in `main()` in Figure 1-1 outputs text to the screen:

```
std::cout << "The answer to life, the universe, and everything is "
          << answer
          << std::endl;
```

The statement is spread over three lines, just to show that it's possible. The names `cout` and `endl` are defined in the `iostream` header file. We'll explain about the `std::` prefix a little later in this chapter. << is the insertion operator that transfers data to a stream. In Chapter 2 you'll meet the extraction operator, >>, that reads data from a stream. Whatever appears to the right of each << is transferred to cout. Inserting endl to std::cout causes a new line to be written to the stream and the output buffer to be flushed. Flushing the output buffer ensures that the output appears immediately. The statement will produce the following output:

```
The answer to life, the universe, and everything is 42
```

You can add comments to each line of a statement. Here's an example:

```
std::cout << "The answer to life, the universe, and everything is "  // This statement
          << answer                                                  // occupies
          << std::endl;                                              // three lines
```

You don't have to align the double slashes, but it's common to do so because it looks tidier and makes the code easier to read. Of course, you should not start writing comments just to write them. A comment normally contains useful information that is not immediately obvious from the code.

return Statements

The last statement in main() is a return statement. A return statement ends a function and returns control to where the function was called. In this case, it ends the function and returns control to the operating system. A return statement may or may not return a value. This particular return statement returns 0 to the operating system. Returning 0 to the operating system indicates that the program ended normally. You can return nonzero values such as 1, 2, etc., to indicate different abnormal end conditions. The return statement in Ex1_01.cpp is optional, so you could omit it. This is because if execution runs past the last statement in main(), it is equivalent to executing return 0.

■ **Note** main() is the only function for which omitting return is equivalent to returning zero. Any other function with return type int always has to end with an explicit return statement—the compiler shall never presume to know which value an arbitrary function should return by default.

Namespaces

A large project will involve several programmers working concurrently. This potentially creates a problem with names. The same name might be used by different programmers for different things, which could at least cause some confusion and may cause things to go wrong. The Standard Library defines a lot of names, more than you can possibly remember. Accidental use of Standard Library names could also cause problems. *Namespaces* are designed to overcome this difficulty.

A *namespace* is a sort of family name that prefixes all the names declared within the namespace. The names in the Standard Library are all defined within a namespace that has the name std. cout and endl are names from the Standard Library, so the full names are std::cout and std::endl. Those two colons together, ::, have a fancy title: *the scope resolution operator*. We'll have more to say about it later. Here, it serves to separate the namespace name, std, from the names in the Standard Library such as cout and endl. Almost all names from the Standard Library are prefixed with std.

The code for a namespace looks like this:

```
namespace my_space {

  // All names declared in here need to be prefixed
  // with my_space when they are reference from outside.
  // For example, a min() function defined in here
  // would be referred to outside this namespace as my_space::min()

}
```

Everything between the braces is within the my_space namespace. You'll find out more about defining your own namespaces in Chapter 10.

■ **Caution**   The main() function must not be defined within a namespace. Things that are not defined in a namespace exist in the *global namespace*, which has no name.

Names and Keywords

Ex1_01.cpp contains a definition for a variable with the name answer, and it uses the names cout and endl that are defined in the iostream Standard Library header. Lots of things need names in a program, and there are precise rules for defining names:

- A name can be any sequence of upper or lowercase letters A to Z or a to z, the digits 0 to 9, and the underscore character, _.

- A name must begin with either a letter or an underscore.

- Names are case sensitive.

The C++ standard allows names to be of any length, but typically a particular compiler will impose some sort of limit. However, this is normally sufficiently large that it doesn't represent a serious constraint. Most of the time you won't need to use names of more than 12 to 15 characters.

Here are some valid C++ names:

```
toe_count    shoeSize    Box    democrat    Democrat    number1    x2    y2    pValue    out_of_range
```

Uppercase and lowercase are differentiated, so democrat is not the same name as Democrat. You can see a couple examples of conventions for writing names that consist of two or more words; you can capitalize the second and subsequent words or just separate them with underscores.

Keywords are reserved words that have a specific meaning in C++, so you must not use them for other purposes. class, double, throw, and catch are examples of keywords. Other names that you are not supposed to use include the following:

- Names that begin with two consecutive underscores

- Names that begin with an underscore followed by an uppercase letter

- Within the global namespace: all names that begin with an underscore

While compilers often won't really complain if you use these, the problem is that such names might clash either with those that are generated by the compiler or with names that are used internally by your Standard Library implementation. Notice that the common denominator with these *reserved names* is that they all start with an underscore. Thus, our advice is this:

░ **Tip**   Do not use names that start with an underscore.

Classes and Objects

A *class* is a block of code that defines a data type. A class has a name that is the name for the type. An item of data of a class type is referred to as an *object*. You use the class type name when you create variables that can store objects of your data type. Being able to define your own data types enables you to specify a solution to a problem in terms of the problem. If you were writing a program processing information about students, for example, you could define a Student type. Your Student type could incorporate all the characteristic of a student—such as age, gender, or school record—that was required by the program.

You will learn all about creating your own classes and programming with objects in Chapters 11 through 14. Nevertheless, you'll be using objects of specific Standard Library types long before that. Examples include vectors in Chapter 5 and strings in Chapter 7. Even the std::cout and std::cin streams are technically objects. But not to worry: you'll find that working with objects is easy enough, much easier than creating your own classes, for instance. Objects are mostly intuitive in use because they're mostly designed to behave like real-life entities (although some do model more abstract concepts, such as input or output streams, or low-level C++ constructs, such as data arrays and character sequences).

Templates

You sometimes need several similar classes or functions in a program where the code differs only in the kind of data that is processed. A *template* is a recipe that you create to be used by the compiler to generate code automatically for a class or function customized for a particular type or types. The compiler uses a *class template* to generate one or more of a family of classes. It uses a *function template* to generate functions. Each template has a name that you use when you want the compiler to create an instance of it. The Standard Library uses templates extensively.

Defining function templates is the subject of Chapter 9, and defining class templates is covered in Chapter 16. But, again, you'll be using some concrete Standard Library templates throughout earlier chapters, such as instantiations of the container class templates in Chapter 5 or certain elementary utility function templates such as std::min() and max().

Code Appearance and Programming Style

The way in which you arrange your code can have a significant effect on how easy it is to understand. There are two basic aspects to this. First, you can use tabs and/or spaces to indent program statements in a manner that provides visual cues to their logic, and you can arrange matching braces that define program blocks in a consistent way so that the relationships between the blocks are apparent. Second, you can spread a single statement over two or more lines when that will improve the readability of your program.

There are many different styles for code. The following table shows three of many possible options for how a code sample could be arranged:

Style 1	Style 2	Style 3
``namespace mine
{
bool has_factor(int x, int y)
{
int factor{ hcf(x, y) };
if (factor > 1)
{
return true;
}
else
{
return false;
}
}
}```	```namespace mine {
bool has_factor(int x, int y)
{
int factor{ hcf(x,y) };
if (factor>1) {
return true;
} else {
return false;
}
}
}```	```namespace mine {
bool has_factor(int x, int y) {
int factor{ hcf(x, y) };
if (factor > 1)
return true;
else
return false;
}
}```

We will use Style 1 for examples in the book. Over time, you will surely develop your own, based either on personal preferences or on company policies. It is recommended to, at some point, pick one style that suits you and then use this consistently throughout your code. Not only does a consistent code presentation style look good, but it also makes your code easier to read.

A particular convention for arranging matching braces and indenting statements is only one of several aspects of one's *programming style*. Other important aspects include conventions for naming variables, types, and functions, and the use of (structured) comments. The question of what constitutes a good programming style can be highly subjective at times, though some guidelines and conventions are objectively superior. The general idea, though, is that code that conforms to a consistent style is easier to read and understand, which helps to avoid introducing errors. Throughout the book we'll regularly give you advice as you fashion your own programming style.

■ **Tip**   One of the best tips we can give you regarding good programming style is no doubt to choose clear, descriptive names for all your variables, functions, and types.

Creating an Executable

Creating an executable module from your C++ source code is basically a three-step process. In the first step, the *preprocessor* processes all preprocessing directives. One of its key tasks is to, at least in principle, copy the entire contents of all #included headers into your .cpp files. Other preprocessing directives are discussed in Chapter 10. In the second step, your *compiler* processes each .cpp file to produce an *object file* that contains the machine code equivalent of the source file. In the third step, the *linker* combines the object files for a program into a file containing the complete executable program.

Figure 1-2 shows three source files being compiled to produce three corresponding object files (the preprocessing stage is not shown explicitly). The filename extension that's used to identify object files varies between different machine environments, so it isn't shown here. The source files that make up your program may be compiled independently in separate compiler runs, or most compilers will allow you to compile them in a single run. Either way, the compiler treats each source file as a separate entity and produces one object file for each .cpp file. The link step then combines the object files for a program, along with any library functions that are necessary, into a single executable file.

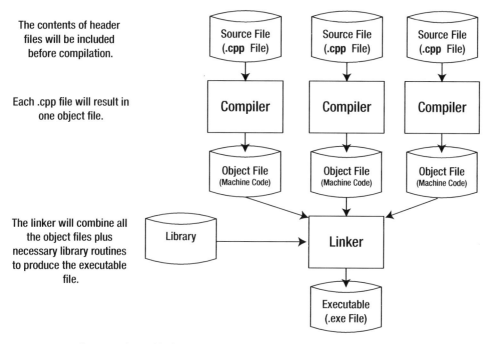

The contents of header files will be included before compilation.

Each .cpp file will result in one object file.

The linker will combine all the object files plus necessary library routines to produce the executable file.

Figure 1-2. *The compile and link process*

In the first half of the book, your programs will consist of a single source file. In Chapter 10 we will show you how to compose a larger program, consisting of multiple header and source files.

░ **Note**   The concrete steps you have to follow to get from your source code to a functioning executable differ from compiler to compiler. While most of our examples are small enough to compile and link through a series of command-line instructions, it is probably easier to use a so-called *integrated development environment* (IDE) instead. Modern IDEs offer a very user-friendly graphical user interface to edit, compile, link, run, and debug your programs. References to the most popular compilers and IDEs as well as pointers on how to get started are available from the Apress website (www.apress.com/book/download.html) together with the source code of all examples and the solutions to all exercises.

In practice, compilation is an iterative process because you're almost certain to have made typographical and other errors in the code. Once you've eliminated these from each source file, you can progress to the link step, where you may find that yet more errors surface. Even when the link step produces an executable module, your program may still contain logical errors; that is, it doesn't produce the results you expect. To fix these, you must go back and modify the source code and try to compile it once more. You continue this process until your program works as you think it should. As soon as you declare to the world at large that your program works, someone will discover a number of obvious errors that you should have found. It hasn't been proven beyond doubt so far as we know, but it's widely believed that any program larger than a given size will always contain errors. It's best not to dwell on this thought when flying....

Procedural and Object-Oriented Programming

Historically, procedural programming is the way almost all programs were written. To create a procedural programming solution to a problem, you focus on the process that your program must implement to solve the problem. Here is a rough outline of what you do, once the requirements have been defined precisely:

- You create a clear, high-level definition of the overall process that your program will implement.

- You segment the overall process into workable units of computation that are, as much as possible, self-contained. These will usually correspond to functions.

- You code the functions in terms of processing basic types of data: numerical data, single characters, and character strings.

Apart from the common requirement of starting out with a clear specification of what the problem is, the object-oriented approach to solving the same problem is quite different:

- From the problem specification, you determine what types of *objects* the problem is concerned with. For example, if your program deals with baseball players, you're likely to identify BaseballPlayer as one of the types of data your program will work with. If your program is an accounting package, you may well want to define objects of type Account and type Transaction. You also identify the set of *operations* that the program will need to carry out on each type of object. This will result in a set of application-specific data types that you will use in writing your program.

- You produce a detailed design for each of the new data types that your problem requires, including the operations that can be carried out with each object type.

- You express the logic of the program in terms of the new data types you've defined and the kinds of operations they allow.

The program code for an object-oriented solution to a problem will be completely unlike that for a procedural solution and almost certainly easier to understand. It will also be a lot easier to maintain. The amount of design time required for an object-oriented solution tends to be greater than for a procedural solution. However, the coding and testing phase of an object-oriented program tends to be shorter and less troublesome, so the overall development time is likely to be roughly the same in either case.

To get an inkling of what an objected-oriented approach implies, suppose you're implementing a program that deals with boxes of various kinds. A feasible requirement of such a program would be to package several smaller boxes inside another, larger box. In a procedural program, you would need to store the length, width, and height of each box in a separate group of variables. The dimensions of a new box that could contain several other boxes would need to be calculated explicitly in terms of the dimensions of each of the contained boxes, according to whatever rules you had defined for packaging a set of boxes.

An object-oriented solution might involve first defining a Box data type. This would enable you to create variables that can reference objects of type Box and, of course, create Box objects. You could then define an operation that would add two Box objects together and produce a new Box object that could contain them. Using this operation, you could write statements like this:

```
bigBox = box1 + box2 + box3;
```

In this context, the + operation means much more than simple addition. The + operator applied to numerical values will work exactly as before, but for Box objects it has a special meaning. Each of the variables in this statement is of type Box. The statement would create a new Box object big enough to contain box1, box2, and box3.

Being able to write statements like this is clearly much easier than having to deal with all the box dimensions separately, and the more complex the operations on boxes you take on, the greater the advantage is going to be. This is a trivial illustration, though, and there's a great deal more to the power of objects than you can see here. The purpose of this discussion is just to give you an idea of how readily problems solved using an object-oriented approach can be understood. Object-oriented programming is essentially about solving problems in terms of the entities to which the problems relates rather than in terms of the entities that computers are happy with: numbers and characters.

Representing Numbers

Numbers are represented in a variety of ways in a C++ program, and you need to have an understanding of the possibilities. If you are comfortable with binary, hexadecimal, and floating-point number representations, you can safely skip this bit.

Binary Numbers

First, let's consider exactly what a common, everyday decimal number, such as 324 or 911, means. Obviously, what we mean here is "three hundred and twenty-four" or "nine hundred and eleven." These are shorthand ways of saying "three hundreds" plus "two tens" plus "four," as well as "nine hundred" plus "one ten" plus "one." Putting this more precisely, we really mean this:

- 324 is $3 \times 10^2 + 2 \times 10^1 + 4 \times 10^0$, which is $3 \times 100 + 2 \times 10 + 4 \times 1$.

- 911 is $9 \times 10^2 + 1 \times 10^1 + 1 \times 10^0$, which is $9 \times 100 + 1 \times 10 + 1 \times 1$.

This is called *decimal notation* because it's built around powers of 10. We also say that we are representing numbers to *base 10* here because each digit position is a power of 10. Representing numbers in this way is handy for beings with ten fingers and/or ten toes, or indeed ten of any kind of appendage that can be used for counting. Your PC is rather less handy, being built mainly of switches that are either on or off. Your PC is OK for counting in twos but not spectacular at counting in tens. You're probably aware that this is why your computer represents numbers using base 2, rather than base 10. Representing numbers using base 2 is called the *binary system* of counting. Numbers in base 10 have digits that can be from 0 to 9. In general, for numbers in an arbitrary base, n, the digit in each position in a number can be from 0 to n-1. Thus, binary digits can be only 0 or 1. A binary number such as 1101 breaks down like this:

- $1 \times 2^3 + 1 \times 2^2 + 0 \times 2^1 + 1 \times 2^0$, which is $1 \times 8 + 1 \times 4 + 0 \times 2 + 1 \times 1$

This is 13 in the decimal system. In Table 1-1, you can see the decimal equivalents of all the numbers you can represent using eight binary digits. A binary digit is more commonly known as a *bit*.

Table 1-1. *Decimal Equivalents of 8-Bit Binary Values*

Binary	Decimal	Binary	Decimal
0000 0000	0	1000 0000	128
0000 0001	1	1000 0001	129
0000 0010	2	1000 0010	130
. . .	. . .	. . .	. . .
0001 0000	16	1001 0000	144
0001 0001	17	1001 0001	145
. . .	. . .	. . .	. . .
0111 1100	124	1111 1100	252
0111 1101	125	1111 1101	253
0111 1110	126	1111 1110	254
0111 1111	127	1111 1111	255

Using the first seven bits, you can represent positive numbers from 0 to 127, which is a total of 128 different numbers. Using all eight bits, you get 256, or 2^8, numbers. In general, if you have n bits available, you can represent 2^n integers, with positive values from 0 to $2^n - 1$.

Adding binary numbers inside your computer is a piece of cake because the "carry" from adding corresponding digits can be only 0 or 1. This means that very simple—and thus excruciatingly fast—circuitry can handle the process. Figure 1-3 shows how the addition of two 8-bit binary values would work.

```
      Binary          Decimal
     0001 1101           29
 +   0010 1011         + 43
     ---------          ----
     0100 1000           72
      ↑↑↑↑↑↑            ----
      carries
```

Figure 1-3. *Adding binary values*

The addition operation adds corresponding bits in the operands, starting with the rightmost. Figure 1-3 shows that there is a "carry" of 1 to the next bit position for each of the first six bit positions. This is because each digit can be only 0 or 1. When you add 1 + 1, the result cannot be stored in the current bit position and is equivalent to adding 1 in the next bit position to the left.

Hexadecimal Numbers

When you are dealing with larger binary numbers, a small problem arises with writing them. Look at this:

• 1111 0101 1011 1001 1110 0001

Binary notation here starts to be more than a little cumbersome for practical use, particularly when you consider that this in decimal is only 16,103,905—a miserable eight decimal digits. You can sit more angels on the head of a pin than that! Clearly you need a more economical way of writing this, but decimal isn't always appropriate. You might want to specify that the 10th and 24th bits from the right in a number are 1, for example. Figuring out the decimal integer for this is hard work, and there's a good chance you'll get it wrong anyway. An easier solution is to use *hexadecimal notation*, in which the numbers are represented using base 16.

Arithmetic to base 16 is a much more convenient option, and it fits rather well with binary. Each hexadecimal digit can have values from 0 to 15 and the digits from 10 to 15 are represented by the letters A to F (or a to f), as shown in Table 1-2. Values from 0 to 15 happen to correspond nicely with the range of values that four binary digits can represent.

Table 1-2. *Hexadecimal Digits and Their Values in Decimal and Binary*

Hexadecimal	Decimal	Binary
0	0	0000
1	1	0001
2	2	0010
3	3	0011
4	4	0100
5	5	0101
6	6	0110
7	7	0111
8	8	1000
9	9	1001
A or a	10	1010
B or b	11	1011
C or c	12	1100
D or d	13	1101
E or e	14	1110
F or f	15	1111

Because a hexadecimal digit corresponds to four binary digits, you can represent any binary number in hexadecimal simply by taking groups of four binary digits starting from the right and writing the equivalent hexadecimal digit for each group. Look at the following binary number:

- 1111 0101 1011 1001 1110 0001

Taking each group of four bits and replacing it with the corresponding hexadecimal digit from the table produces the following:

- F   5   B   9   E   1

You have six hexadecimal digits corresponding to the six groups of four binary digits. Just to prove that it all works out with no cheating, you can convert this number directly from hexadecimal to decimal by again using the analogy with the meaning of a decimal number. The value of this hexadecimal number therefore works out as follows: F5B9E1 as a decimal value is given by the following:

- $15 \times 16^5 + 5 \times 16^4 + 11 \times 16^3 + 9 \times 16^2 + 14 \times 16^1 + 1 \times 16^0$

Thankfully, this adds up to the same number you got when converting the equivalent binary number to a decimal value: 16,103,905. In C++, hexadecimal values are written with 0x or 0X as a prefix, so in code the value would be written as 0xF5B9E1. Obviously, this means that 99 is not at all the same as 0x99.

The other handy coincidence with hexadecimal numbers is that modern computers store integers in words that are an even number of bytes, typically 2, 4, 8, or 16 so-called bytes. A *byte* is 8 bits, which is exactly two hexadecimal digits, so any binary integer word in memory always corresponds to an exact number of hexadecimal digits.

Negative Binary Numbers

There's another aspect to binary arithmetic that you need to understand: negative numbers. So far, we've assumed that everything is positive—the optimist's view—and so the glass is still half-full. But you can't avoid the negative side of life—the pessimist's perspective—that the glass is already half-empty. But how is a negative number represented in a modern computer? You'll see shortly that the answer to this seemingly easy question is actually far from obvious....

Integers that can be both positive and negative are referred to as *signed integers*. Naturally, you only have binary digits at your disposal to represent numbers. At the end of the day, any language your computer speaks shall consist solely of bits and bytes. As you know, your computer's memory is generally composed of 8-bit bytes, so all binary numbers are going to be stored in some multiple (usually a power of 2) of 8 bits. Thus, you can also only have signed integers with 8 bits, 16 bits, 32 bits, or whatever.

A straightforward representation of signed integers therefore consists of a fixed number of binary digits, where one of these bits is designated as a so-called sign bit. In practice, the sign bit is always chosen to be the leftmost bit. Say we fix the size of all our signed integers to 8 bits; then the number 6 could be represented as 00000110, and -6 could be represented as 10000110. Changing +6 to –6 just involves flipping the sign bit from 0 to 1. This is called a *signed magnitude* representation: each number consists of a sign bit that is 0 for positive values and 1 for negative values, plus a given number of other bits that specify the *magnitude* or absolute value of the number (the value without the sign in other words).

While signed magnitude representations are easy to work with for humans, they have one unfortunate downside: they are not at all easy to work with for computers! More specifically, they carry a lot of overhead in terms of the complexity of the circuits that are needed to perform arithmetic. When two signed integers are added, for instance, you don't want the computer to be messing about, checking whether either or both of the numbers are negative. What you really want is to use the same simple and very fast "add" circuitry regardless of the signs of the operands.

Let's see what happens when we naively add together the signed magnitude representations of 12 and -8. You almost know in advance that it won't work, but we'll carry on regardless:

12 in binary is	00001100
–8 in binary (you suppose) is	10001000
If you now "add" these together, you get	10010100

This seems to give –20, which of course isn't what you wanted at all. It's definitely not +4, which you know is 00000100. "Ah," we hear you say, "you can't treat a sign just like another digit." But that is just what you *do* want to do to speed up binary computations!

Virtually all modern computers therefore take a different approach: they use the so-called *2's complement representation* of negative binary numbers. With this representation, you can produce the negative of any positive binary number by a simple procedure that you can perform in your head. At this point, we need to ask you to have a little faith because we'll avoid getting into explanations of why it works.

Like a true magician, we won't explain our magic. We'll show you how you can create the 2's complement form of a negative number from a positive value, and you can prove to yourself that it does work. For this, let's return to the previous example, in which you need the 2's complement representation of –8:

1. You start with +8 in binary: 00001000.

2. You then "flip" each binary digit, changing 0s to 1s, and vice versa: 11110111.

   This is called the *1's complement* form.

3. If you now add 1 to this, you get the 2's complement form of -8: 11111000.

Note that this works both ways. To convert the 2's complement representation of a negative number back into the corresponding positive binary number, you again flip all bits and add one. For our example, flipping 11111000 gives 00000111, adding one to this gives 00001000, or +8 in decimal. Magic!

But of course, the proof of the pudding is in the eating. The 2's complement representation would just be a fun parlor trick if it didn't facilitate binary arithmetic. So, let's see how 11111000 fares with your computer's elementary add circuitry:

+12 in binary is	00001100
The 2's complement representation of –8 is	11111000
If you add these together, you get	00000100

The answer is 4—it works! The "carry" propagates through all the leftmost 1s, setting them back to 0. One fell off the end, but you shouldn't worry about that—it's probably compensating for the one you borrowed from the end in the subtraction you did to get –8. In fact, what's happening is that you're implicitly assuming that the sign bit, 1 or 0, repeats forever to the left. Try a few examples of your own; you'll find it always works, like magic. The great thing about the 2's complement representation of negative numbers is that it makes arithmetic—and not just addition, by the way—very easy for your computer. And that accounts for one of the reasons computers are so good at crunching numbers.

Octal Values

Octal integers are numbers expressed with base 8. Digits in an octal value can only be from 0 to 7. Octal is used rarely these days. It was useful in the days when computer memory was measured in terms of 36-bit words because you could specify a 36-bit binary value by 12 octal digits. Those days are long gone, so why are we introducing it? The answer is the potential confusion it can cause. You can still write octal constants in C++. Octal values are written with a leading zero, so while 76 is a decimal value, 076 is an octal value that corresponds to 62 in decimal. So, here's a golden rule:

▓ **Caution**   Never write decimal integers in your source code with a leading zero. You'll get a value different from what you intended!

Bi-Endian and Little-Endian Systems

Integers are stored in memory as binary values in a contiguous sequence of bytes, commonly groups of 2, 4, 8, or 16 bytes. The question of the sequence in which the bytes appear can be important—it's one of those things that doesn't matter until it matters, and then it *really* matters.

Let's consider the decimal value 262,657 stored as a 4-byte binary value. We chose this value because in binary each byte happens to have a pattern of bits that is easily distinguished from the others:

00000000 00000100 00000010 00000001

If you're using a PC with an Intel processor, the number will be stored as follows:

Byte address:	00	01	02	03
Data bits:	00000001	00000010	00000100	00000000

As you can see, the most significant eight bits of the value—the one that's all 0s—are stored in the byte with the highest address (last, in other words), and the least significant eight bits are stored in the byte with the lowest address, which is the leftmost byte. This arrangement is described as *little-endian*. Why on earth, you wonder, would a computer reverse the order of these bytes? The motivation, as always, is rooted in the fact that it allows for more efficient calculations and simpler hardware. The details don't matter much; the main thing is that you're aware that most modern computers these days use this counterintuitive encoding.

Most, but not all computers, do, though. If you're using a machine based on a Motorola processor, the same data is likely to be arranged in memory in a more logical manner, like this:

Byte address:	00	01	02	03
Data bits:	00000000	00000100	00000010	00000001

Now the bytes are in reverse sequence with the most significant eight bits stored in the leftmost byte, which is the one with the lowest address. This arrangement is described as *bi-endian*. Some processors such as PowerPC and all recent ARM processors are *bi-endian*, which means that the byte order for data is switchable between bi-endian and little-endian.

▓ **Note**   Regardless of whether the byte order is bi-endian or little-endian, the bits within each byte are arranged with the most significant bit on the left and the least significant bit on the right.

This is all very interesting, you may say, but when does it matter? Most of the time, it doesn't. More often than not, you can happily write a program without knowing whether the computer on which the code will execute is bi-endian or little-endian. It does matter, however, when you're processing binary data that comes from another machine. You need to know the endianness. Binary data is written to a file or transmitted over a network as a sequence of bytes. It's up to you how you interpret it. If the source of the data is a machine with a different endianness from the machine on which your code is running, you must reverse the order of the bytes in each binary value. If you don't, you have garbage.

For those who collect curious background information, the terms *bi-endian* and *little-endian* are drawn from the book *Gulliver's Travels* by Jonathan Swift. In the story, the emperor of Lilliput commanded all his subjects to always crack their eggs at the smaller end. This was a consequence of the emperor's son having cut his finger following the traditional approach of cracking his egg at the big end. Ordinary, law-abiding

Lilliputian subjects who cracked their eggs at the smaller end were described as Little Endians. The Big Endians were a rebellious group of traditionalists in the Lilliputian kingdom who insisted on continuing to crack their eggs at the big end. Many were put to death as a result.

Floating-Point Numbers

All integers are numbers, but of course not all numbers are integers: 3.1415 is no integer, and neither is -0.00001. Many applications will have to deal with fractional numbers at one point or another. So clearly you need a way to represent such numbers on your computer as well, complemented with the ability to efficiently perform computations with them. The mechanism nearly all computers support for handling fractional numbers, as you may have guessed from the section title, is called *floating-point* numbers.

Floating-point numbers do not just represent fractional numbers, though. As an added bonus, they are able to deal with very large numbers as well. They allow you to represent, for instance, the number of protons in the universe, which needs around 79 decimal digits (though of course not accurate within one particle, but that's OK—who has the time to count them all anyway?). Granted, the latter is perhaps somewhat extreme, but clearly there are situations in which you'll need more than the ten decimal digits you get from a 32-bit binary integer, or even more than the 19 you can get from a 64-bit integer. Equally, there are lots of very small numbers, for example, the amount of time in minutes it takes the typical car salesperson to accept your generous offer on a 2001 Honda (and it's covered only 480,000 miles...). Floating-point numbers are a mechanism that can represent both these classes of numbers quite effectively.

We'll first explain the basic principles using decimal floating-point numbers. Of course, your computer will again use a binary representation instead, but things are just so much easier to understand for us humans when we use decimal numbers. A so-called normalized number consists of two parts: a *mantissa* or *fraction* and an *exponent*. Both can be either positive or negative. The magnitude of the number is the mantissa multiplied by 10 to the power of the exponent. In analogy with the binary floating-point number representations of your computer, we'll moreover fix the number of decimal digits of both the mantissa and the exponent.

It's easier to demonstrate this than to describe it, so let's look at some examples. The number 365 could be written in a floating-point form, as follows:

```
3.650000E02
```

The mantissa here has seven decimal digits, the exponent two. The E stands for "exponent" and precedes the power of 10 that the 3.650000 (the mantissa) part is multiplied by to get the required value. That is, to get back to the regular decimal notation, you simply have to compute the following product: 3.650000×10^2. This is clearly 365.

Now let's look at a small number:

```
-3.650000E-03
```

This is evaluated as -3.65×10^{-3}, which is -0.00365. They're called floating-point numbers for the fairly obvious reason that the decimal point "floats" and its position depends on the exponent value.

Now suppose you have a larger number such as 2,134,311,179. Using the same amount of digits, this number looks like this:

```
2.134311E09
```

It's not quite the same. You've lost three low-order digits, and you've approximated your original value as 2,134,311,000. This is the price to pay for being able to handle such a vast range of numbers: not all these numbers can be represented with full precision; floating-point numbers in general are only approximate representations of the exact number.

Aside from the fixed-precision limitation in terms of accuracy, there's another aspect you may need to be conscious of. You need to take great care when adding or subtracting numbers of significantly different magnitudes. A simple example will demonstrate the problem. Consider adding `1.23E-4` to `3.65E+6`. The exact result, of course, is 3,650,000 + 0.000123, or 3,650,000.000123. But when converted to floating-point with seven digits of precision, this becomes the following:

```
3.650000E+06  + 1.230000E-04  =  3.650000E+06
```

Adding the latter, smaller number to the former has had no effect whatsoever, so you might as well not have bothered. The problem lies directly with the fact that you carry only seven digits of precision. The digits of the larger number aren't affected by any of the digits of the smaller number because they're all further to the right.

Funnily enough, you must also take care when the numbers are nearly equal. If you compute the difference between such numbers, most numbers may cancel each other out, and you may end up with a result that has only one or two digits of precision. This is referred to as *catastrophic cancellation*, and it's quite easy in such circumstances to end up computing with numbers that are totally garbage.

While floating-point numbers enable you to carry out calculations that would be impossible without them, you must always keep their limitations in mind if you want to be sure your results are valid. This means considering the range of values that you are likely to be working with and their relative values. The field that deals with analyzing and maximizing the precision—or *numerical stability*—of mathematical computations and algorithms is called *numerical analysis*. This is an advanced topic, though, and well outside the scope of this book. Suffice to say that the precision of floating-point numbers is limited and that the order and nature of arithmetic operations you perform with them can have a significant impact on the accuracy of your results.

Your computer, of course, again does not work with decimal numbers; rather, it works with binary floating-point representations. Bits and bytes, remember? Concretely, nearly all computers today use the encoding and computation rules specified by the IEEE 754 standard. Left to right, each floating-point number then consists of a single sign bit, followed by a fixed number of bits for the exponent, and finally another series of bits that encode the mantissa. The most common floating-point numbers representations are the so-called *single precision* (1 sign bit, 8 bits for the exponent, and 23 for the mantissa, adding up to 32 bits in total) and *double precision* (1 + 11 + 52 = 64 bits) floating-point numbers.

Floating-point numbers can represent huge ranges of numbers. A single-precision floating-point number, for instance, can already represent numbers ranging from 10^{-38} to 10^{+38}. Of course, there's a price to pay for this flexibility: the number of digits of precision is limited. You know this already from before, and it's also only logical; of course not all 38 digits of all numbers in the order of 10^{+38} can be represented exactly using 32 bits. After all, the largest signed integer a 32-bit binary integer can represent exactly is only $2^{31} - 1$, which is about $2 \times 10^{+9}$. The number of decimal digits of precision in a floating-point number depends on how much memory is allocated for its mantissa. A single-precision floating-point value, for instance, provides approximately seven decimal digits accuracy. We say "approximately" because a binary fraction with 23 bits doesn't exactly correspond to a decimal fraction with seven decimal digits. A double-precision floating-point value corresponds to around 16 decimal digits accuracy.

Representing Characters

Data inside your computer has no intrinsic meaning. Machine code instructions are just numbers: of course numbers are just numbers, but so are, for instance, characters. Each character is assigned a unique integer value called its *code* or *code point*. The value 42 can be the atomic number of molybdenum; the answer to life, the universe, and everything; or an asterisk character. It all depends on how you choose to interpret it. You can write a single character in C++ between single quotes, such as `'a'` or `'?'` or `'*'`, and the compiler will generate the code value for these.

ASCII Codes

Way back in the 1960s, the American Standard Code for Information Interchange (ASCII) was defined for representing characters. This is a 7-bit code, so there are 128 different code values. ASCII values 0 to 31 represent various nonprinting control characters such as carriage return (code 15) and line feed (code 12). Code values 65 to 90 inclusive are the uppercase letters *A* to *Z*, and 97 to 122 correspond to lowercase *a* to *z*. If you look at the binary values corresponding to the code values for letters, you'll see that the codes for lowercase and uppercase letters differ only in the sixth bit; lowercase letters have the sixth bit as 0, and uppercase letters have the sixth bit as 1. Other codes represent digits 0 to 9, punctuation, and other characters.

The original 7-bit ASCII is fine if you are American or British, but if you are French or German, you need things like accents and umlauts in text, which are not included in the 128 characters that 7-bit ASCII encodes. To overcome the limitations imposed by a 7-bit code, extended versions of ASCII were defined with 8-bit codes. Values from 0 to 127 represent the same characters as 7-bit ASCII, and values from 128 to 255 are variable. One variant of 8-bit ASCII that you have probably met is called Latin-1, which provides characters for most European languages, but there are others for languages such as Russian.

If you speak Korean, Japanese, Chinese, or Arabic, an 8-bit coding is totally inadequate. To give you an idea, modern encodings of Chinese, Japanese, and Korean scripts (which share a common background) cover nearly 88,000 characters—a tiny bit more than the 256 characters you're able to get out of 8 bits! To overcome the limitations of extended ASCII, the *Universal Character Set* (UCS) emerged in the 1990s. UCS is defined by the standard ISO 10646 and has codes with up to 32 bits. This provides the potential for hundreds of millions of unique code values.

UCS and Unicode

UCS defines a mapping between characters and integer code values, called *code points*. It is important to realize that a *code point* is not the same as an *encoding*. A code point is an integer; an encoding specifies a way of representing a given code point as a series of bytes or words. Code values of less than 256 are popular and can be represented in one byte. It would be inefficient to use four bytes to store code values that require just one byte just because there are other codes that require several bytes. Encodings are ways of representing code points that allow them to be stored more efficiently.

Unicode is a standard that defines a set of characters and their code points identical to those in UCS. Unicode also defines several different encodings for these code points and includes additional mechanisms for dealing with such things as right-to-left languages such as Arabic. The range of code points is more than enough to accommodate the character sets for all the languages in the world, as well as many different sets of graphical characters such as mathematical symbols, or even emoticons and emojis. Regardless, the codes are arranged such that strings in the majority of languages can be represented as a sequence of single 16-bit codes.

One aspect of Unicode that can be confusing is that it provides more than one *character encoding method*. The most commonly used encodings are referred to as UTF-8, UTF-16, and UTF-32, either of which can represent all the characters in the Unicode set. The difference between them is in how a given character code point is presented; the numerical code value for any given character is the same in either representation. Here's how these encodings represent characters:

- *UTF-8* represents a character as a variable-length sequence of between 1 and 4 bytes. The ASCII character set appears in UTF-8 as single byte codes that have the same codes values as ASCII. Most web pages use UTF-8 to encode text.

- *UTF-16* represents characters as one or two 16-bit values. UTF-16 includes UTF-8. Because a single 16-bit value accommodates all of code plane 0, UTF-16 covers most situations in programming for a multilingual context.

- *UTF-32*, you guessed it, simply represents all characters as 32-bit values.

You have four integer types that store Unicode characters. These are types char, wchar_t, char16_t, and char32_t. You'll learn more about these in Chapter 2.

C++ Source Characters

You write C++ statements using a *basic source character set*. This is the set of characters that you're allowed to use explicitly in a C++ source file. The character set that you can use to define a name is a subset of this. Of course, the basic source character set in no way constrains the character data that you work with in your code. Your program can create strings consisting of characters outside this set in various ways, as you'll see. The basic source character set consists of the following characters:

- The letters *a* to *z* and *A* to *Z*
- The digits 0 to 9
- The whitespace characters space, horizontal tab, vertical tab, form feed, and newline
- The characters _ { } [ ] # ( ) < > % : ; . ? * + - / ^ & | ~ ! = , \ " '

This is easy and straightforward. You have 96 characters that you can use, and it's likely that these will accommodate your needs most of the time. Most of the time the basic source character set will be adequate, but occasionally you'll need characters that aren't in it. You can, at least in theory, include Unicode characters in a name. You specify a Unicode character in the form of a hexadecimal representation of its code point, either as \udddd or as \Udddddddd, where d is a hexadecimal digit. Note the lowercase u in the first case and the uppercase U in the second; either is acceptable. Compiler support for Unicode characters in names is limited, though. Both character and string data can include Unicode characters.

Escape Sequences

When you want to use *character constants* such as a single character or a character string in a program, certain characters are problematic. Obviously, you can't enter characters such as newline directly as character constants, as they'll just do what they're supposed to do: go to a new line in your source code file (the only exception to this rule are raw string literals, which are covered in Chapter 7). You can enter these problem characters in character constants by means of an *escape sequence*. An escape sequence is an indirect way of specifying a character, and it always begins with a backslash. Table 1-3 shows the escape sequences that represent control characters.

Table 1-3. *Escape Sequences That Represent Control Characters*

Escape Sequence	Control Character
\n	Newline
\t	Horizontal tab
\v	Vertical tab
\b	Backspace
\r	Carriage return
\f	Form feed
\a	Alert/bell

There are some other characters that are a problem to represent directly. Clearly, the backslash character itself is difficult because it signals the start of an escape sequence. The single and double quote characters that are used as delimiters, as in the constant 'A' or the string "text", can also be a problem (it depends on the context; more on this later). Table 1-4 shows the escape sequences for these.

Table 1-4. *Escape Sequences That Represent "Problem" Characters*

Escape Sequence	"Problem" Character
\\	Backslash
\'	Single quote
\"	Double quote

Because the backslash signals the start of an escape sequence, the only way to enter a backslash as a character constant is by using two successive backslashes (\\).

This program that uses escape sequences outputs a message to the screen. To see it, you'll need to enter, compile, link, and execute the code:

```
// Ex1_02.cpp
// Using escape sequences
#include <iostream>

int main()
{
  std::cout << "\"Least \'said\' \\\n\t\tsoonest \'mended\'.\"" << std::endl;
}
```

When you manage to compile, link, and run this program, you should see the following output displayed:

```
"Least 'said' \
            soonest 'mended'."
```

The output is determined by what's between the outermost double quotes in the following statement:

```
  std::cout << "\"Least \'said\' \\\n\t\tsoonest \'mended\'.\"" << std::endl;
```

In principle, *everything* between the outer double quotes in the preceding statement gets sent to cout. A string of characters between a pair of double quotes is called a *string literal*. The double quote characters are *delimiters* that identify the beginning and end of the string literal; they aren't part of the string. Each escape sequence in the string literal will be converted to the character it represents by the compiler, so the character will be sent to cout, not the escape sequence itself. A backslash in a string literal *always* indicates the start of an escape sequence, so the first character that's sent to cout is a double quote character.

Least followed by a space is output next. This is followed by a single quote character, then said, followed by another single quote. Next is a space, followed by the backslash specified by \\. Then a newline character corresponding to \n is written to the stream so the cursor moves to the beginning of the next line. You then send two tab characters to cout with \t\t, so the cursor will be moved two tab positions to the right. The word soonest is output next followed by a space and then mended between single quotes. Finally, a period is output followed by a double quote.

■ **Note**   If you're no fan of escape sequences, Chapter 7 will introduce a possible alternative to them called *raw string literals*.

The truth is, in our enthusiasm for showcasing character escaping, we may have gone a bit overboard in Ex1_02.cpp. You actually do not have to escape the single quote character, ', inside string literals; there's already no possibility for confusion. So, the following statement would have worked just fine already:

```
std::cout << "\"Least 'said' \\\n\t\tsoonest 'mended'.\"" << std::endl;
```

It's only when within a character literal of the form '\'' that a single quote really needs escaping. Conversely, double quotes, of course, won't need a backslash then; your compiler will happily accept both '\"' and '"'. But we're getting ahead of ourselves: character literals are more a topic of the next chapter.

▒ **Note** The \t\t escape sequences in Ex1_02 are, strictly speaking, not required either—you could in principle type tabs in a string literal as well (as in "\"Least 'said' \\\n   soonest 'mended'.\""). Using \t\t is nevertheless recommended; the problem with tabs is that one generally cannot tell the difference between a tab, "   ", and a number of spaces, "   ", let alone properly count the number of tabs. Also, some text editors tend to convert tabs into spaces upon saving. It's therefore not uncommon for style guides to require the use of the \t escape sequence in string literals.

Summary

This chapter's content has been a broad overview to give you a feel for some of the general concepts of C++. You'll encounter everything discussed in this chapter again, and in much more detail, in subsequent chapters. However, some of the basics that this chapter covered are as follows:

- A C++ program consists of one or more functions, one of which is called main(). Execution always starts with main().

- The executable part of a function is made up of statements contained between braces.

- A pair of curly braces is used to enclose a statement block.

- A statement is terminated by a semicolon.

- Keywords are reserved words that have specific meanings in C++. No entity in your program can have a name that coincides with a keyword.

- A C++ program will be contained in one or more files. Source files contain the executable code, and header files contain definitions used by the executable code.

- The source files that contain the code defining functions typically have the extension .cpp.

- Header files that contain definitions that are used by a source file typically have the extension .h.

- Preprocessor directives specify operations to be performed on the code in a file. All preprocessor directives execute before the code in a file is compiled.

- The contents of a header file are added into a source file by an #include preprocessor directive.

- The Standard Library provides an extensive range of capabilities that supports and extends the C++ language.

- Access to Standard Library functions and definitions is enabled through including Standard Library header files in a source file.

- Input and output are performed using streams and involve the use of the insertion and extraction operators, << and >>. std::cin is a standard input stream that corresponds to the keyboard. std::cout is a standard output stream for writing text to the screen. Both are defined in the iostream Standard Library header.

- Object-oriented programming involves defining new data types that are specific to your problem. Once you've defined the data types that you need, a program can be written in terms of the new data types.

- Unicode defines unique integer code values that represent characters for virtually all of the languages in the world as well as many specialized character sets. Code values are referred to as *code points*. Unicode also defines how these code points may be encoded as byte sequences.

EXERCISES

The following exercises enable you to try what you've learned in this chapter. If you get stuck, look back over the chapter for help. If you're still stuck after that, you can download the solutions from the Apress website (www.apress.com/book/download.html), but that really should be a last resort.

Exercise 1-1: Create, compile, link, and execute a program that will display the text "Hello World" on your screen.

Exercise 1-2: Create and execute a program that outputs your name on one line and your age on the next line.

Exercise 1-3: The following program produces several compiler errors. Find these errors and correct them so the program can compile cleanly and run.

```
include <iostream>

Int main()
{
  std:cout << "Hello World" << std:endl
)
```

■ ■ ■

Introducing Fundamental Types of Data

In this chapter, we'll explain the fundamental data types that are built into C++. You'll need these in every program. All of the object-oriented capabilities are founded on these fundamental data types because all the data types that you create are ultimately defined in terms of the basic numerical data your computer works with. By the end of the chapter, you'll be able to write a simple C++ program of the traditional form: input – process – output.

In this chapter, you'll learn

- What a fundamental data type is in C++

- How you declare and initialize variables

- How you can fix the value of a variable

- What integer literals are and how you define them

- How calculations work

- How to define variables that contain floating-point values

- How to create variables that store characters

- What the auto keyword does

Variables, Data, and Data Types

A *variable* is a named piece of memory that you define. Each variable stores data only of a particular type. Every variable has a *type* that defines the kind of data it can store. Each fundamental type is identified by a unique type name that consists of one or more *keywords*. Keywords are reserved words in C++ that you cannot use for anything else.

The compiler makes extensive checks to ensure that you use the right data type in any given context. It will also ensure that when you combine different types in an operation such as adding two values, for example, either they are of the same type or they can be made to be compatible by converting one value to the type of the other. The compiler detects and reports attempts to combine data of different types that are incompatible.

Numerical values fall into two broad categories: integers, which are whole numbers, and floating-point values, which can be nonintegral. There are several fundamental C++ types in each category, each of which can store a specific range of values. We'll start with integer types.

© Ivor Horton and Peter Van Weert 2018
I. Horton and P. Van Weert, *Beginning C++17*, https://doi.org/10.1007/978-1-4842-3366-5_2

Defining Integer Variables

Here's a statement that defines an integer variable:

```
int apple_count;
```

This defines a variable of type `int` with the name `apple_count`. The variable will contain some arbitrary junk value. You can and should specify an initial value when you define the variable, like this:

```
int apple_count {15};                              // Number of apples
```

The initial value for `apple_count` appears between the braces following the name so it has the value 15. The braces enclosing the initial value are called a *braced initializer*. You'll meet situations later in the book where a braced initializer will have several values between the braces. You don't have to initialize variables when you define them, but it's a good idea to do so. Ensuring variables start out with known values makes it easier to work out what is wrong when the code doesn't work as you expect.

The size of variables of type `int` is typically 4 bytes, so they can store integers from -2,147,483,648 to +2,147,483,647. This covers most situations, which is why `int` is the integer type that is used most frequently.

Here are definitions for three variables of type `int`:

```
int apple_count {15};                              // Number of apples
int orange_count {5};                              // Number of oranges
int total_fruit {apple_count + orange_count};      // Total number of fruit
```

The initial value for `total_fruit` is the sum of the values of two variables defined previously. This demonstrates that the initial value for a variable can be an expression. The statements that define the two variables in the expression for the initial value for `total_fruit` must appear earlier in the source file; otherwise, the definition for `total_fruit` won't compile.

The initial value between the braces should be of the same type as the variable you are defining. If it isn't, the compiler will try to convert it to the required type. If the conversion is to a type with a more limited range of values, the conversion has the potential to lose information. An example would be if you specified the initial value for an integer variable that is not an integer—1.5, for example. A conversion to a type with a more limited range of values is called a *narrowing conversion*. If you use curly braces to initialize your variables, the compiler will always issue either a warning or an error whenever it detects a narrowing conversion.

There are two other ways for initializing a variable. *Functional notation* looks like this:

```
int orange_count(5);
int total_fruit(apple_count + orange_count);
```

A second alternative is the so-called assignment notation:

```
int orange_count = 5;
int total_fruit = apple_count + orange_count;
```

Both these possibilities are equally valid as the braced initializer form and mostly completely equivalent. Both are therefore used extensively in existing code as well. In this book, however, we'll adopt the braced initializer syntax. This is the most recent syntax that was introduced in C++11 specifically to standardize initialization. Its main advantage is that it enables you to initialize just about everything in the same way—which is why it is also commonly referred to as *uniform initialization*. Another advantage is that the braced initializer form is slightly safer when it comes to narrowing conversions:

```
int banana_count(7.5);        // May compile without warning
int coconut_count = 5.3;      // May compile without warning
int papaya_count{0.3};        // At least a compiler warning, often an error
```

All three definitions clearly contain a narrowing conversion. We'll have more to say about floating-point to integer conversions later, but for now believe us when we say that after these variable definitions banana_count will contain the integer value 7, coconut_count will initialize to 5, and papaya_count will initialize to 0—provided compilation does not fail with an error because of the third statement, of course. It's unlikely that this is what the author had in mind. Definitions with narrowing conversions such as these are therefore almost always mistakes.

Nevertheless, as far as the C++ standard is concerned, our first two definitions are perfectly legal C++. They are allowed to compile without even the slightest warning. While some compilers do issue a warning about such flagrant narrowing conversions, definitely not all of them do. If you use the braced initializer form, however, a conforming compiler is required to at least issue a diagnostic message. Some compilers will even issue an error and refuse to compile such definitions altogether. We believe inadvertent narrowing conversions do not deserve to go unnoticed, which is why we favor the braced initializer form.

▓ **Note**   To represent fractional numbers, you typically use floating-point variables rather than integers. We'll describe these later in this chapter.

Prior to C++17, there was one relatively common case where uniform initialization could not be used. We'll return to this exception near the end of this chapter when we discuss the auto keyword. But since this quirk will soon be nothing more than a bad memory, we believe there's little objective reason left not to embrace the new syntax. Uniformity and predictability, on the other hand, are desirable traits—especially for you, someone who's taking the first steps in C++. In this book, we'll therefore consistently use braced initializers.

You can define and initialize more than one variable of a given type in a single statement. Here's an example:

```
int foot_count {2}, toe_count {10}, head_count {1};
```

While this is legal, it's often considered best to define each variable in a separate statement. This makes the code more readable, and you can explain the purpose of each variable in a comment.

You can write the value of any variable of a fundamental type to the standard output stream. Here's a program that does that with a couple of integers:

```
// Ex2_01.cpp
// Writing values of variables to cout
#include <iostream>

int main()
{
  int apple_count {15};                       // Number of apples
  int orange_count {5};                       // Number of oranges
  int total_fruit {apple_count + orange_count};   // Total number of fruit

  std::cout << "The value of apple_count is "  << apple_count  << std::endl;
  std::cout << "The value of orange_count is " << orange_count << std::endl;
  std::cout << "The value of total_fruit is "  << total_fruit  << std::endl;
}
```

If you compile and execute this, you'll see that it outputs the values of the three variables following some text explaining what they are. The integer values are automatically converted to a character representation for output by the insertion operator, <<. This works for values of any of the fundamental types.

■ **Tip** The three variables in Ex2_01.cpp, of course, do not really need any comments explaining what they represent. Their variable names already make that crystal clear—as they should! In contrast, a lesser programmer might have produced the following, for instance:

```
int n {15};

int m {5};

int t {n + m};
```

Without extra context or explanation, no one would ever be able to guess this code is about counting fruit. You should therefore always choose your variable names as self-descriptive as possible. Properly named variables and functions mostly need no additional explanation in the form of a comment at all, by which we of course do not mean you should never add comments to declarations. You cannot always capture everything in a single name. A few words or, if need be, a little paragraph of comments can then do wonders in helping someone understand the code. A little extra effort at the time of writing can considerably speed up future development!

Signed Integer Types

Table 2-1 shows the complete set of fundamental types that store signed integers—that is, both positive and negative values. The memory allocated for each type, and hence the range of values it can store, may vary between different compilers. Table 2-1 shows the sizes and ranges used by compilers for all common platforms and computer architectures.

Table 2-1. *Signed Integer Types*

Type Name	Typical Size (Bytes)	Range of Values
signed char	1	-128 to +127
short short int signed short signed short int	2	-256 to +255
int signed signed int	4	-2,147,483,648 to +2,147,483,647
long long int signed long signed long int	4 or 8	Same as either int or long long
long long long long int signed long long singed long long int	8	-9,223,372,036,854,775,808 to +9,223,372,036,854,775,807

Type signed char is always 1 byte (which in turn nearly always is 8 bits); the number of bytes occupied by the others depends on the compiler. Each type will always have at least as much memory as the one that precedes it in the list, though.

Where two type names appear in the left column, the abbreviated name that comes first is more commonly used. That is, you will usually see long used rather than long int or signed long int.

The signed modifier is mostly optional; if omitted, your type will be signed by default. The only exception to this rule is char. While the unmodified type char does exist, it is compiler-dependant whether it is signed or unsigned. We'll discuss this further in the next subsection. For all integer types other than char, however, you are free to choose whether you add the signed modifier. Personally, we normally do so only when we really want to stress that a particular variable is signed.

Unsigned Integer Types

Of course, there are circumstances where you don't need to store negative numbers. The number of students in a class or the number of parts in an assembly is always a positive integer. You can specify integer types that only store non-negative values by prefixing any of the names of the signed integer types with the unsigned keyword—types unsigned char or unsigned short or unsigned long long, for example. Each unsigned type is a different type from the signed type but occupies the same amount of memory.

Type char is a different integer type from both signed char and unsigned char. The char type is intended only for variables that store character codes and can be a signed or unsigned type depending on your compiler. If the constant CHAR_MIN in the climits header is 0, then char is an unsigned type with your compiler. We'll have more to say about variables that store characters later in this chapter.

■ **Tip**   Only use variables of the unmodified `char` type to store characters. For `char` variables that store other data such as plain integer numbers, you should always add the appropriate sign modifier.

With the possible exception of `unsigned char`, increasing the range of representable numbers is rarely the main motivator for adding the `unsigned` modifier—it rarely matters, for instance, whether you can represent numbers up to +2,147,483,647 or up to +4,294,967,295 (the maximum values for `signed` and `unsigned int`, respectively). No. Instead, you mostly add the `unsigned` modifier to make your code more self-documenting, that is, to make it more predictable what values a given variable will or should contain.

■ **Note**   You can also use the keywords `signed` and `unsigned` on their own. As Table 2-1 shows, the type `signed` is considered shorthand for `signed int`. So naturally, `unsigned` is short for `unsigned int`.

Zero Initialization

The following statement defines an integer variable with an initial value equal to zero:

```
int counter {0};          // counter starts at zero
```

You could omit the 0 in the braced initializer here, and the effect would be the same. The statement that defines counter could thus be written like this:

```
int counter {};          // counter starts at zero
```

The empty curly braces somewhat resemble the number zero, which makes this syntax easy to remember. *Zero initialization* works for any fundamental type. For all fundamental numeric types, for instance, an empty braced initializer is always assumed to contain the number zero.

Defining Variables with Fixed Values

Sometimes you'll want to define variables with values that are fixed and must not be changed. You use the `const` keyword in the definition of a variable that must not be changed. Such variables are often referred to as *constants*. Here's an example:

```
const unsigned toe_count {10};          // An unsigned integer with fixed value 10
```

The `const` keyword tells the compiler that the value of toe_count must not be changed. Any statement that attempts to modify this value will be flagged as an error during compilation; cutting off someone's toe is a definite no-no! You can use the `const` keyword to fix the value of variables of any type.

■ **Tip**   If nothing else, knowing which variables can and cannot change their values along the way makes your code easier to follow. So, we recommend you add the `const` specifier whenever applicable.

Integer Literals

Constant values of any kind, such as 42, 2.71828, 'Z', or "Mark Twain", are referred to as *literals*. These examples are, in sequence, an *integer literal*, a *floating-point literal*, a *character literal*, and a *string literal*. Every literal will be of some type. We'll first explain integer literals and introduce the other kinds of literals in context later.

Decimal Integer Literals

You can write integer literals in a very straightforward way. Here are some examples of decimal integers:

```
-123L     +123     123     22333     98U -1234LL   12345ULL
```

Unsigned integer literals have u or U appended. Literals of types long and type long long have L or LL appended, respectively, and if they are unsigned, they also have u or U appended. If there is no suffix, an integer constant is of type int. The U and L or LL can be in either sequence. You can use lowercase for the L and LL suffixes, but we recommend that you don't because lowercase L is easily confused with the digit 1.

You could omit the + in the second example, as it's implied by default, but if you think putting it in makes things clearer, that's not a problem. The literal +123 is the same as 123 and is of type int because there is no suffix.

The fourth example, 22333, is the number that you, depending on local conventions, might write as either 22,333; 22 333; or 22.333 (though other formatting conventions exist as well). You must not use commas or spaces in a C++ integer literal, though, and adding a dot would turn it into a floating-point literal (as discussed later). Ever since C++14, however, you can use the single quote character, ', to make numeric literals more readable. Here's an example:

```
22'333     -1'234LL    12'345ULL
```

Here are some statements using some of these literals:

```
unsigned long age {99UL};              // 99ul or 99LU would be OK too
unsigned short price {10u};            // There is no specific literal type for short
long long distance {15'000'000LL};     // Common digit grouping of the number 15 million
```

Note that there are no restrictions on how to group the digits. Most Western conventions tend to group digits per three, but this is not universal. Natives of the subcontinent of India, for instance, would typically write the literal for 15 million as follows (using groups of two digits except for the rightmost group of three digits):

```
1'50'00'000LL
```

So far we have been very diligent in adding our literal suffixes—u or U for unsigned literals, L for literals of type long, and so on. In practice, however, you'll rarely add these in variable initializers of this form. The reason is that no compiler will ever complain if you simply type this:

```
unsigned long age {99};
unsigned short price {10};           // There is no specific literal type for short
long long distance {15'000'000};     // Common digit grouping of the number 15 million
```

While all these literals are technically of type (signed) int, your compiler will happily convert them to the correct type for you. As long as the target type can represent the given values without loss of information, there's no need to issue a warning.

▧ **Note**   While mostly optional, there are situations where you do need to add the correct literal suffixes, such as when you initialize a variable with type auto (as explained near the end of this chapter) or when calling overloaded functions with literal arguments (as covered in Chapter 8).

An initializing value should always be within the permitted range for the type of variable, as well as from the correct type. The following two statements violate these restrictions. They require, in other words, what you know to be narrowing conversions:

```
unsigned char high_score { 513U };    // The valid range for unsigned char is [0,255]
unsigned int high_score { -1 };       // -1 is a literal of type signed int
```

As we explained earlier, depending on which compiler you use, these braced initializations will result in at least a compiler warning, if not a compilation error.

Hexadecimal Literals

You can write integer literals as hexadecimal values. You prefix a hexadecimal literal with 0x or 0X, so 0x999 is a hexadecimal number of type int with three hexadecimal digits. Plain old 999, on the other hand, is a decimal value of type int with decimal digits, so the value will be completely different. Here are some more examples of hexadecimal literals:

Hexadecimal literals:	0x1AF	0x123U	0xAL	0xcad	0xFF
Decimal literals:	431	291U	10L	3245	255

A major use for hexadecimal literals is to define particular patterns of bits. Each hexadecimal digit corresponds to 4 bits, so it's easy to express a pattern of bits as a hexadecimal literal. The red, blue, and green components (RGB values) of a pixel color, for instance, are often expressed as three bytes packed into a 32-bit word. The color white can be specified as 0xFFFFFF because the intensity of each of the three components in white have the same maximum value of 255, which is 0xFF. The color red would be 0xff0000. Here are some examples:

```
unsigned int color {0x0f0d0e};    // Unsigned int hexadecimal constant - decimal 986,382
int mask {0XFF00FF00};            // Four bytes specified as FF, 00, FF, 00
unsigned long value {0xDEADlu};   // Unsigned long hexadecimal literal - decimal 57,005
```

Octal Literals

You can also write integer literals xas octal values—that is, using base 8. You identify a number as octal by writing it with a leading zero.

Octal literals:	0657	0443U	012L	06255	0377
Decimal literals:	431	291U	10L	3245	255

░ **Caution** Don't write decimal integer values with a leading zero. The compiler will interpret such values as octal (base 8), so a value written as 065 will be the equivalent of 53 in decimal notation.

Binary Literals

Binary literals were introduced by the C++14 standard. You write a binary integer literal as a sequence of binary digits (0 or 1) prefixed by either 0b or 0B. As always, a binary literal can have L or LL as a suffix to indicate it is type long or long long, and u or U if it is an unsigned literal. Here's an example:

Binary literals:	0B110101111	0b100100011U	0b1010L	0B110010101101	0b11111111
Decimal literals:	431	291U	10L	3245	255

We have illustrated in the code fragments how you can write various combinations for the prefixes and suffixes such as 0x or 0X and UL, LU, or Lu, but of course it's best to stick to a consistent way of writing integer literals.

As far as your compiler is concerned, it doesn't matter which number base you choose when you write an integer value. Ultimately it will be stored as a binary number. The different ways for writing an integer are there just for your convenience. You choose one or other of the possible representations to suit the context.

░ **Note** You can use a single quote as a separator in any integer literal to make it easier to read. This includes hexadecimal or binary literals. Here's an example: 0xFF00'00FF'0001UL or 0b1100'1010'1101.

Calculations with Integers

To begin with, let's get some bits of terminology out of the way. An operation such as addition or multiplication is defined by an *operator*—the operators for addition and multiplication are + and *, respectively. The values that an operator acts upon are called *operands*, so in an expression such as 2*3, the operands are 2 and 3. Operators such as multiplication that require two operands are called *binary operators*. Operators that require one operand are called *unary operators*. An example of a unary operator is the minus sign in the expression -width. The minus sign negates the value of width, so the result of the expression is a value with the opposite sign to that of its operand. This contrasts with the binary multiplication operator in expressions such as width * height, which acts on two operands, width and height.

Table 2-2 shows the basic arithmetic operations that you can carry out on integers.

Table 2-2. *Basic Arithmetic Operations*

Operator	Operation
+	Addition
-	Subtraction
*	Multiplication
/	Division
%	Modulus (the remainder after division)

The operators in Table 2-2 are all binary operators and work largely in the way you would expect. There are two operators that may need a little word of explanation, though: the somewhat lesser-known modulus operator, of course, but also the division operator. Integer division is slightly idiosyncratic in C++. When applied to two integer operands, the result of a division operation is always again an integer. Suppose, for instance, that you write the following:

```
int numerator = 11;
int quotient = numerator / 4;
```

Mathematically speaking, the result of the division 11/4 is of course 2.75 or 2¾, that is, 2 and three quarters. But 2.75 is clearly no integer, so what to do? Any sane mathematician would suggest that you round the quotient to the nearest integer, so 3. But, alas, that is *not* what your computer will do. Instead, your computer will simply discard the fractional part, 0.75, altogether. No doubt this is because proper rounding would require more complicated circuitry and hence also more time to evaluate. This means that, in C++, 11/4 will always give the integer value 2. Figure 2-1 illustrates the effects of the division and modulus operators on our example.

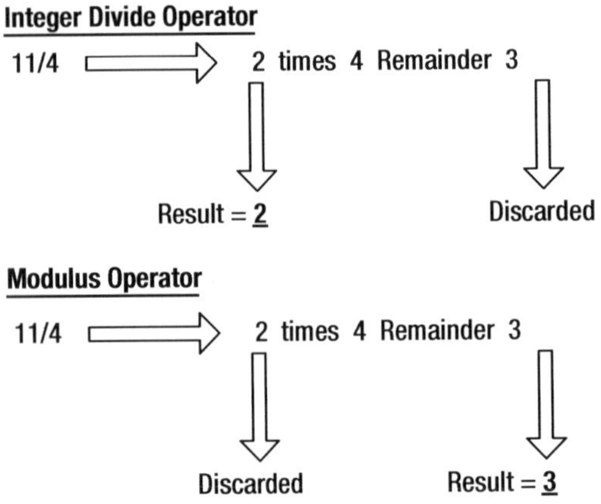

Integer Divide Operator

11/4 ⟹ 2 times 4 Remainder 3

Result = **2**   Discarded

Modulus Operator

11/4 ⟹ 2 times 4 Remainder 3

Discarded   Result = **3**

Figure 2-1. *Contrasting the division and modulus operators*

Integer division returns the number of times that the denominator divides into the numerator. Any remainder is discarded. The modulus operator, %, complements the division operator in that it produces the *remainder after integer division*. It is defined such that, for all integers x and y, (x / y) * y + (x % y) equals x. Using this formula, you can easily deduce what the modulus operand will do for negative operands.

The result of both the division and modulus operator is undefined when the right operand is zero—what'll happen depends, in other words, on your compiler and computer architecture.

Compound Arithmetic Expressions

If multiple operators appear in the same expression, multiplication, division, and modulus operations always execute before addition and subtraction. Here's an example of such a case:

```
long width {4};
long length {5};
long area { width * length };        // Result is 20
long perimeter {2*width + 2*length}; // Result is 18
```

You can control the order in which more complicated expressions are executed using parentheses. You could write the statement that calculates a value for `perimeter` as follows:

```
long perimeter{ (width + length) * 2 };   // Result is 18
```

The subexpression within the parentheses is evaluated first. The result then is multiplied by two, which produces the same end result as before. If you omit the parentheses here, however, the result would no longer be 18. The result, instead, would become 14:

```
long perimeter{ width + length * 2 };     // Result is 14
```

The reason is that multiplication is always evaluated before addition. So, the previous statement is actually equivalent to the following one:

```
long perimeter{ width + (length * 2) };
```

Parentheses can be nested, in which case subexpressions between parentheses are executed in sequence from the innermost pair of parentheses to the outermost. This example of an expression with nested parentheses will show how it works:

```
2*(a + 3*(b + 4*(c + 5*d)))
```

The expression `5*d` is evaluated first, and `c` is added to the result. That result is multiplied by 4, and `b` is added. That result is multiplied by 3, and `a` is added. Finally, that result is multiplied by 2 to produce the result of the complete expression.

We will have more to say about the order in which such *compound expressions* are evaluated in the next chapter. The main thing to remember is that whatever the default evaluation order is, you can always override it by adding parentheses. And even if the default order happens to be what you want, it never hurts to add some extra parentheses just for the sake of clarity:

```
long perimeter{ (2*width) + (2*length) };   // Result is 18
```

Assignment Operations

In C++, the value of a variable is fixed only if you use the `const` qualifier. In all other cases, the value of a variable can always be overwritten with a new value:

```
long perimeter {};
// ...
perimeter = 2 * (width + length);
```

This last line is an *assignment statement*, and the = is the *assignment operator*. The arithmetic expression on the right of the assignment operator is evaluated, and the result is stored in the variable on the left. Initializing the `perimeter` variable upon declaration may not be strictly necessary—as long as the variable is not read prior to the assignment, that is—but it's considered good practice to always initialize your variables nevertheless. And zero is often as good a value as any.

You can assign a value to more than one variable in a single statement. Here's an example:

```
int a {}, b {}, c {5}, d{4};
a = b = c*c - d*d;
```

The second statement calculates the value of the expression c*c - d*d and stores the result in b, so b will be set to 9. Next the value of b is stored in a, so a will also be set to 9. You can have as many repeated assignments like this as you want.

It's important to appreciate that an assignment operator is quite different from an = sign in an algebraic equation. The latter implies equality, whereas the former is specifying an action—specifically, the act of overwriting a given memory location. A variable can be overwritten as many times as you want, each time with different, mathematically nonequal values. Consider the assignment statement in the following:

```cpp
int y {5};
y = y + 1;
```

The variable y is initialized with 5, so the expression y + 1 produces 6. This result is stored back in y, so the effect is to increment y by 1. This last line makes no sense in common math: as any mathematician will tell you, y can never equal y + 1 (except of course when y equals infinity...). But in programming languages such as C++ repeatedly incrementing a variable with one is actually extremely common. In Chapter 5, you'll find that equivalent expressions are, for instance, ubiquitous in loops.

Let's see some of the arithmetic operators in action in an example. This program converts distances that you enter from the keyboard and in the process illustrates using the arithmetic operators:

```cpp
// Ex2_02.cpp
// Converting distances
#include <iostream>                    // For output to the screen

int main()
{
  unsigned int yards {}, feet {}, inches {};

  // Convert a distance in yards, feet, and inches to inches
  std::cout << "Enter a distance as yards, feet, and inches "
            << "with the three values separated by spaces:"
            << std::endl;
  std::cin >> yards >> feet >> inches;

  const unsigned feet_per_yard {3};
  const unsigned inches_per_foot {12};

  unsigned total_inches {};
  total_inches = inches + inches_per_foot * (yards*feet_per_yard + feet);
  std::cout << "The distances corresponds to " << total_inches << " inches.\n";

  // Convert a distance in inches to yards feet and inches
  std::cout << "Enter a distance in inches: ";
  std::cin >> total_inches;
  feet   = total_inches / inches_per_foot;
  inches = total_inches % inches_per_foot;
  yards  = feet / feet_per_yard;
  feet   = feet % feet_per_yard;
  std::cout << "The distances corresponds to "
            << yards  << " yards "
            << feet   << " feet "
            << inches << " inches." << std::endl;
}
```

The following is an example of typical output from this program:

```
Enter a distance as yards, feet, and inches with the three values separated by spaces:
9 2 11
The distances corresponds to 359 inches.
Enter a distance in inches: 359
The distances corresponds to 9 yards 2 feet 11 inches.
```

The first statement in main() defines three integer variables and initializes them with zero. They are type unsigned int because in this example the distance values cannot be negative. This is an instance where defining three variables in a single statement is reasonable because they are closely related.

The next statement outputs a prompt to std::cout for the input. We used a single statement spread over three lines, but it could be written as three separate statements as well:

```
std::cout << "Enter a distance as yards, feet, and inches";
std::cout << "with the three values separated by spaces:";
std::cout << std::endl;
```

When you have a sequence of << operators as in the original statement, they execute from left to right so the output from the previous three statements will be the same as the original.

The next statement reads values from cin and stores them in the variables yards, feet, and inches. The type of value that the >> operator expects to read is determined by the type of variable in which the value is to be stored. So, in this case, unsigned integers are expected to be entered. The >> operator ignores spaces, and the first space following a value terminates the operation. This implies that you cannot read and store spaces using the >> operator for a stream, even when you store them in variables that store characters. The input statement in the example could again also be written as three separate statements:

```
std::cin >> yards;
std::cin >> feet;
std::cin >> inches;
```

The effect of these statements is the same as the original.

You define two variables, inches_per_foot and feet_per_yard, that you need to convert from yards, feet, and inches to just inches, and vice versa. The values for these are fixed, so you specify the variables as const. You could use explicit values for conversion factors in the code, but using const variables is much better because it is then clearer what you are doing. The const variables are also positive values, so you define them as type unsigned int. You could add U modifiers to the integer literals if you prefer, but there's no need. The conversion to inches is done is a single assignment statement:

```
total_inches = inches + inches_per_foot * (yards*feet_per_yard + feet);
```

The expression between parentheses executes first. This converts the yards value to feet and adds the feet value to produce the total number of feet. Multiplying this result by inches_per_foot obtains the total number of inches for the values of yards and feet. Adding inches to that produces the final total number of inches, which you output using this statement:

```
std::cout << "The distances corresponds to " << total_inches << " inches.\n";
```

The first string is transferred to the standard output stream, cout, followed by the value of total_inches. The string that is transferred to cout next has \n as the last character, which will cause the next output to start on the next line.

Converting a value from inches to yards, feet, and inches requires four statements:

```
feet   = total_inches / inches_per_foot;
inches = total_inches % inches_per_foot;
yards  = feet / feet_per_yard;
feet   = feet % feet_per_yard;
```

You reuse the variables that stored the input for the previous conversion to store the results of this conversion. Dividing the value of total_inches by inches_per_foot produces the number of whole feet, which you store in feet. The % operator produces the remainder after division, so the next statement calculates the number of residual inches, which is stored in inches. The same process is used to calculate the number of yards and the final number of feet.

Notice the use of whitespace to nicely outline these assignment statements. You could've written the same statements without spaces as well, but that simply does not read very fluently:

```
feet=total_inches/inches_per_foot;
inches=total_inches%inches_per_foot;
yards=feet/feet_per_yard;
feet=feet%feet_per_yard;
```

We generally add a single space before and after each binary operator, as it promotes code readability. Adding extra spaces to outline related assignments in a semitabular form doesn't harm either.

There's no return statement after the final output statement because it isn't necessary. When the execution sequence runs beyond the end of main(), it is equivalent to executing return 0.

The op= Assignment Operators

In Ex2_02.cpp, there was a statement that you could write more economically:

```
feet = feet % feet_per_yard;
```

This statement could be written using an op= assignment operator. The op= *assignment operators*, or also *compound assignment operators*, are so called because they're composed of an operator and an assignment operator =. You could use one to write the previous statement as follows:

```
feet %= feet_per_yard;
```

This is the same operation as the previous statement.

In general, an op= assignment is of the following form:

```
lhs op= rhs;
```

lhs represents a variable of some kind that is the destination for the result of the operator. rhs is any expression. This is equivalent to the following statement:

```
lhs = lhs op (rhs);
```

The parentheses are important because you can write statements such as the following:

```
x *= y + 1;
```

This is equivalent to the following:

```
x = x * (y + 1);
```

Without the implied parentheses, the value stored in x would be the result of x * y + 1, which is quite different.

You can use a range of operators for op in the op= form of assignment. Table 2-3 shows the complete set, including some operators you'll meet in Chapter 3.

Table 2-3. *op= Assignment Operators*

Operation	Operator	Operation	Operator
Addition	+=	Bitwise AND	&=
Subtraction	-=	Bitwise OR	|=
Multiplication	*=	Bitwise exclusive OR	^=
Division	/=	Shift left	<<=
Modulus	%=	Shift right	>>=

Note that there can be no spaces between op and the =. If you include a space, it will be flagged as an error. You can use += when you want to increment a variable by some amount. For example, the following two statements have the same effect:

```
y = y + 1;
y += 1;
```

The shift operators that appear in the table, << and >>, look the same as the insertion and extraction operators that you have been using with streams. The compiler can figure out what << or >> means in a statement from the context. You'll understand how it is possible that the same operator can mean different things in different situations later in the book.

SIDEBAR: USING DECLARATIONS AND DIRECTIVES

There were a lot of occurrences of std::cin and std::cout in Ex2_02.cpp. You can eliminate the need to qualify a name with the namespace name in a source file with a using *declaration*. Here's an example:

```
using std::cout;
```

This tells the compiler that when you write cout, it should be interpreted as std::cout. With this declaration before the main() function definition, you can write cout instead of std::cout, which saves typing and makes the code look a little less cluttered.

You could include two using declarations at the beginning of Ex2_02.cpp and avoid the need to qualify cin and cout:

```
using std::cin;
using std::cout;
```

Of course, you still have to qualify endl with std, although you could add a using declaration for that too. You can apply using declarations to names from any namespace, not just std.

A using *directive* imports all the names from a namespace. Here's how you could use any name from the std namespace without the need to qualify it:

```
using namespace std;        // Make all names in std available without qualification
```

With this at the beginning of a source file, you don't have to qualify any name that is defined in the std namespace. At first sight this seems an attractive idea. The problem is it defeats a major reason for having namespaces. It is unlikely that you know all the names that are defined in std, and with this using directive you have increased the probability of accidentally using a name from std.

We'll use a using directive for the std namespace occasionally in examples in the book where the number of using declarations that would otherwise be required is excessive. We recommend that you make use of using directives only when there's a good reason to do so.

The sizeof Operator

You use the sizeof operator to obtain the number of bytes occupied by a type, by a variable, or by the result of an expression. Here are some examples of its use:

```
int height {74};
std::cout << "The height variable occupies " << sizeof height << " bytes." << std::endl;
std::cout << "Type \"long long\" occupies " << sizeof(long long) << " bytes." << std::endl;
std::cout << "The result of the expression height * height/2 occupies "
          << sizeof(height * height/2) << " bytes." << std::endl;
```

These statements show how you can output the size of a variable, the size of a type, and the size of the result of an expression. To use sizeof to obtain the memory occupied by a type, the type name must be between parentheses. You also need parentheses around an expression with sizeof. You don't need parentheses around a variable name, but there's no harm in putting them in. Thus, if you always use parentheses with sizeof, you can't go wrong.

You can apply sizeof to any fundamental type, class type, or pointer type (you'll learn about pointers in Chapter 5). The result that sizeof produces is of type size_t, which is an unsigned integer type that is defined in the Standard Library header cstddef. Type size_t is implementation defined, but if you use size_t, your code will work with any compiler.

Now you should be able to create your own program to list the sizes of the fundamental integer types with your compiler.

Incrementing and Decrementing Integers

You've seen how you can increment a variable with the += operator and we're sure you've deduced that you can decrement a variable with -=. There are two other operators that can perform the same tasks. They're called the *increment operator* and the *decrement operator*, ++ and --, respectively.

These operators are more than just other options. You'll see a lot more of them, and you'll find them to be quite an asset once you get further into C++. In particular, you'll use them all the time when working with arrays and loops in Chapter 5. The increment and decrement operators are unary operators that you can apply to an integer variable. The following three statements that modify count have exactly the same effect:

```
int count {5};
count = count + 1;
count += 1;
++count;
```

Each statement increments count by 1. Using the increment operator is clearly the most concise. The action of this operator is different from other operators that you've seen in that it directly modifies the value of its operand. The effect in an expression is to increment the value of the variable and then to use the incremented value in the expression. For example, suppose count has the value 5 and you execute this statement:

```
total = ++count + 6;
```

The increment and decrement operators execute before any other binary arithmetic operators in an expression. Thus, count will be incremented to 6, and then this value will be used in the evaluation of the expression on the right of the assignment. total will therefore be assigned the value 12.

You use the decrement operator in the same way:

```
total = --count + 6;
```

Assuming count is 6 before this statement, the -- operator will decrement it to 5, and then this value will be used to calculate the value to be stored in total, which will be 11.

You've seen how you place a ++ or -- operator before the variable to which it applies. This is called the *prefix form* of these operators. You can also place them after a variable, which is called the *postfix form*. The effect is a little different.

Postfix Increment and Decrement Operations

The postfix form of ++ increments the variable to which it applies *after* its value is used in context. For example, you can rewrite the earlier example as follows:

```
total = count++ + 6;
```

With an initial value of 5 for count, total is assigned the value 11. In this case, count will be incremented to 6 only *after* being used in the surrounding expression. The preceding statement is thus equivalent to the following two statements:

```
total = count + 6;
++count;
```

In an expression such as a++ + b, or even a+++b, it's less than obvious what you mean, or indeed what the compiler will do. These two expressions are actually the same, but in the second case you might have meant a + ++b, which is different—it evaluates to one more than the other two expressions. It would be clearer to write the preceding statement as follows:

```
total = 6 + count++;
```

Alternatively, you can use parentheses:

```
total = (count++) + 6;
```

The rules that we've discussed in relation to the increment operator also apply to the decrement operator. For example, suppose count has the initial value 5 and you write this statement:

```
total = --count + 6;
```

This results in total having the value 10 assigned. However, consider this statement:

```
total = 6 + count--;
```

In this instance, total is set to 11.

You should take care applying these operators to a given variable more than once in an expression. Suppose count has the value 5 and you write this:

```
total = ++count * 3 + count++ * 5;
```

The result of this statement is undefined because the statement modifies the value of count more than once using increment operators. Even though this expression is undefined according to the C++ standard, this doesn't mean that compilers won't compile them. It just means that there is no guarantee at all of consistency in the results.

The effects of statements such as the following used to be undefined as well:

```
k = k++ + 1;
```

Here you're incrementing the value of the variable that appears on the left of the assignment operator in the expression on the right, so you're again modifying the value of k twice. Starting with C++17, however, the latter expression has become well-defined. Informally, the C++17 edition of the standard added the rule that all side effects of the right side of an assignment (and this includes compound assignments, increments, and decrements) are fully committed before evaluating the left side and the actual assignment. Nevertheless, the precise rules of when precisely an expression is defined or undefined remain subtle, even in C++17, so our advice remains unchanged:

▪ **Tip** Modify a variable only once as a result of evaluating a single expression and access the prior value of the variable only to determine its new value—that is, do not attempt to read a variable again after it has been modified in the same expression.

The increment and decrement operators are usually applied to integers, particularly in the context of loops, as you'll see in Chapter 5. You'll see later in this chapter that you can apply them to floating-point variables too. In later chapters, you'll explore how they can also be applied to certain other data types, in some cases with rather specialized (but very useful) effects.

Defining Floating-Point Variables

You use floating-point variables whenever you want to work with values that are not integral. There are three floating-point data types, as shown in Table 2-4.

Table 2-4. *Floating-Point Data Types*

Data Type	Description
float	Single precision floating-point values
double	Double precision floating-point values
long double	Double-extended precision floating-point values

▓ **Note**   You cannot use the unsigned or signed modifiers with floating-point types; floating-point types are always signed.

As explained in Chapter 1, the term *precision* refers to the number of significant digits in the mantissa. The types are in order of increasing precision, with float providing the lowest number of digits in the mantissa and long double the highest. The precision only determines the number of digits in the mantissa. The range of numbers that can be represented by a particular type is determined by the range of possible exponents.

The precision and range of values aren't prescribed by the C++ standard, so what you get with each type depends on your compiler. And this, in turn, will depend on what kind of processor is used by your computer and the floating-point representation it uses. The standard does guarantee that type long double will provide a precision that's no less than that of type double, and type double will provide a precision that is no less than that of type float.

Today, virtually all compilers and computer architectures use floating-point numbers and arithmetic as specified by the IEEE standard we introduced in Chapter 1. Typically, float thus provides 7 decimal digits of precision (with a mantissa of 23 bits), double nearly 16 digits (52 bit mantissa), and long double provides about 18 to 19 digits of precision (64-bit mantissa). With some major compilers, however, long double only has the same precision as double. Table 2-5 shows typical ranges of values that you can represent with the floating-point types on an Intel processor.

Table 2-5. *Floating-Point Type Ranges*

Type	Precision (Decimal Digits)	Range (+ or –)
float	7	$\pm 1.18 \times 10^{-38}$ to $\pm 3.4 \times 10^{38}$
double	15 (nearly 16)	$\pm 2.22 \times 10^{-308}$ to $\pm 1.8 \times 10^{308}$
long double	18-19	$\pm 3.65 \times 10^{-4932}$ to $\pm 1.18 \times 10^{4932}$

The numbers of digits of precision in Table 2-5 are approximate. Zero can be represented exactly with each type, but values between zero and the lower limit in the positive or negative range can't be represented, so the lower limits are the smallest possible nonzero values.

Here are some statements that define floating-point variables:

```
float pi {3.1415926f};                          // Ratio of circle circumference to diameter
double inches_to_mm {25.4};
long double root2  {1.41421356237309050488L};  // Square root of 2
```

As you see, you define floating-point variables just like integer variables. Type double is more than adequate in the majority of circumstances. You typically use float only when speed or data size is truly of the essence. If you do use float, though, you always need to remain vigilant that the loss of precision is acceptable for your application.

Floating-Point Literals

You can see from the code fragment in the previous section that float literals have f (or F) appended and long double literals have L (or l) appended. Floating-point literals without a suffix are of type double. A floating-point literal includes either a decimal point or an exponent, or both; a numeric literal with neither is an integer.

An exponent is optional in a floating-point literal and represents a power of 10 that multiplies the value. An exponent must be prefixed with e or E and follows the value. Here are some floating-point literals that include an exponent:

5E3 (5000.0)   100.5E2 (10050.0)   2.5e-3 (0.0025)   -0.1E-3L (-0.0001L)   .345e1F (3.45F)

The value between parentheses following each literal with an exponent is the equivalent literal without the exponent. Exponents are particularly useful when you need to express very small or very large values.

As always, your compiler will happily initialize floating-point variables with literals that lack a proper F or L suffix, or even with integer literals. If the literal value falls outside the representable range of the variable's type, though, your compiler should at least issue a warning regarding a narrowing conversion.

Floating-Point Calculations

You write floating-point calculations in the same way as integer calculations. Here's an example:

```
const double pi {3.141592653589793};  // Circumference of a circle divided by its diameter
double a {0.2};          // Thickness of proper New York-style pizza (in inches)
double z {9};            // Radius of large New York-style pizza (in inches)
double volume {};        // Volume of pizza - to be calculated
volume = pi*z*z*a;
```

The modulus operator, %, can't be used with floating-point operands, but all the other binary arithmetic operators that you have seen, +, -, *, and /, can be. You can also apply the prefix and postfix increment and decrement operators, ++ and --, to a floating-point variable with essentially the same effect as for an integer; the variable will be incremented or decremented by 1.0.

Pitfalls

You need to be aware of the limitations of working with floating-point values. It's not difficult for the unwary to produce results that may be inaccurate or even incorrect. As you'll recall from Chapter 1, common sources of errors when using floating-point values include the following:

- Many decimal values don't convert exactly to binary floating-point values. The small errors that occur can easily be amplified in your calculations to produce large errors.

- Taking the difference between two nearly identical values will lose precision. If you take the difference between two values of type float that differ in the sixth significant digit, you'll produce a result that will have only one or two digits of accuracy. The other digits in the mantissa will be garbage. In Chapter 1, we already named this phenomenon *catastrophic cancellation*.

- Working with values that differ by several orders of magnitude can lead to errors. An elementary example of this is adding two values stored as type float with 7 digits of precision where one value is 10^8 times larger than the other. You can add the smaller value to the larger as many times as you like, and the larger value will be unchanged.

Invalid Floating-Point Results

So far as the C++ standard is concerned, the result of division by zero is undefined. Nevertheless, floating-point operations in most computers are implemented according to the IEEE 754 standard (also known as IEC 559). So in practice, compilers generally behave quite similarly when dividing floating-point numbers by zero. Details may differ across specific compilers, so consult your product documentation.

The IEEE floating-point standard defines special values having a binary mantissa of all zeroes and an exponent of all ones to represent +infinity or -infinity, depending on the sign. When you divide a positive nonzero value by zero, the result will be +infinity, and dividing a negative value by zero will result in -infinity.

Another special floating-point value defined by this standard is called *not-a-number*, usually abbreviated to NaN. This represents a result that isn't mathematically defined, such as when you divide zero by zero or infinity by infinity. Any operation in which either or both operands are NaN results in NaN. Once an operation results in ±infinity, this will pollute all subsequent operations in which it participates as well. Table 2-6 summarizes all the possibilities.

Table 2-6. *Floating-Point Operations with NaN and ±infinity Operands*

Operation	Result	Operation	Result
±value / 0	±infinity	0 / 0	NaN
±infinity ± value	±infinity	±infinity / ±infinity	NaN
±infinity * value	±infinity	infinity - infinity	NaN
±infinity / value	±infinity	infinity * 0	NaN

value in the table is any nonzero value. You can discover how your compiler presents these values by plugging the following code into main():

```
double a{ 1.5 }, b{}, c{};
double result { a / b };
std::cout << a << "/" << b << " = " << result << std::endl;
std::cout << result << " + " << a << " = " << result + a << std::endl;
result = b / c;
std::cout << b << "/" << c << " = " << result << std::endl;
```

You'll see from the output when you run this how ±infinity and NaN look. One possible outcome is this:

```
1.5/0 = inf
inf + 1.5 = inf
0/0 = -nan
```

▓ **Tip**   The easiest way to obtain a floating-point value that represents either infinity or NaN is using the facilities of the limits header of the Standard Library, which we discuss later in this chapter. That way you do not really have to remember the rules of how to obtain them through divisions by zero. To check whether a given number is either infinity or NaN, you should use the std::isinf() and std::isnan() functions provided by the cmath header—what to do with the results of these functions will only become clear in Chapter 4, though.

Mathematical Functions

The cmath Standard Library header file defines a large selection of trigonometric and numerical functions that you can use in your programs. In this section, we'll only discuss some of the functions that you are likely to use on a regular basis, but there are many, many more. The functions defined by cmath today truly range from the very basic to some of the most advanced mathematical functions (in the latter category, the C++17 standard, for instance, has recently added beauties such as cylindrical Neumann functions, associated Laguerre polynomials, and the Riemann zeta function). You can consult your favorite Standard Library reference for the complete list.

Table 2-7 presents some of the most useful functions from this header. As always, all the function names defined are in the std namespace. Unless otherwise noted, all functions of cmath accept arguments that can be of any floating-point or integral type. The outcome will always be of the same type as the given floating-point arguments and of type double for integer arguments.

Table 2-7. *Numerical Functions in the cmath Header*

Function	Description
abs(arg)	Computes the absolute value of arg. Unlike most cmath functions, abs() returns an integer type if arg is integer.
ceil(arg)	Computes a floating-point value that is the smallest integer greater than or equal to arg, so std::ceil(2.5) produces 3.0 and std::ceil(-2.5) produces -2.0.
floor(arg)	Computes a floating-point value that is the largest integer less than or equal to arg, so std::floor(2.5) results in 2.0 and std::floor(-2.5) results in -3.0.
exp(arg)	Computes the value of e^arg.
log(arg)	Computes the natural logarithm (to base e) of arg.
log10(arg)	Computes the logarithm to base 10 of arg.
pow(arg1, arg2)	Computes the value of arg1 raised to the power arg2, or arg1arg2. arg1 and arg2 can be integer or floating-point types. The result of std::pow(2, 3) is 8.0, std::pow(1.5f, 3) equals 3.375f, and std::pow(4, 0.5) is equal to 2.
sqrt(arg)	Computes the square root of arg.
round(arg)	Rounds arg to the nearest integer. The result is a floating-point number though, even for integer inputs. The cmath header also defines lround() and llround() that evaluate to the nearest integer of type long and long long, respectively. Halfway cases are rounded away from zero. In other words, std::lround(0.5) gives 1L, whereas std::round(-1.5f) gives -2.0f.

Besides these, the cmath header provides all basic trigonometric functions (std::cos(), sin(), and tan()), as well as their inverse functions (std::acos(), asin(), and atan()). Angles are always expressed in radians.

Let's look at some examples of how these are used. Here's how you can calculate the cosine of an angle in radians:

```
double angle {1.5};                    // In radians
double cosine_value {std::cos(angle)};
```

If the angle is in degrees, you can calculate the tangent by using a value for π to convert to radians:

```
float angle_deg {60.0f};                      // Angle in degrees
const float pi { 3.14159265f };
const float pi_degrees {180.0f};
float tangent {std::tan(pi * angle_deg/pi_degrees)};
```

If you know the height of a church steeple is 100 feet and you're standing 50 feet from its base, you can calculate the angle in radians of the top of the steeple like this:

```
double height {100.0};                      // Steeple height- feet
double distance {50.0};                      // Distance from base
double angle {std::atan(distance / height)}; // Result in radians
```

You can use this value in angle and the value of distance to calculate the distance from your toe to the top of the steeple:

```
double toe_to_tip {distance / std::sin(angle)};
```

Of course, fans of Pythagoras of Samos could obtain the result much more easily, like this:

```
double toe_to_tip {std::sqrt(std::pow(distance,2) + std::pow(height, 2))};
```

■ **Tip** The problem with an expression of form std::atan(a / b) is that by evaluating the division a / b, you lose information about the sign of a and b. In our example this does not matter much, as both distance and height are positive, but in general you may be better off calling std::atan2(a, b). The atan2() function is defined by the cmath header as well. Because it knows the signs of both a and b, it is capable of properly reflecting this in the resulting angle. You can consult a Standard Library reference for the detailed specification.

Let's try a floating-point example. Suppose that you want to construct a circular pond in which you will keep fish. Having looked into the matter, you know that you must allow 2 square feet of pond surface area for every 6 inches of fish length. You need to figure out the diameter of the pond that will keep the fish happy. Here's how you can do it:

```
// Ex2_03.cpp
// Sizing a pond for happy fish
#include <iostream>
#include <cmath>                      // For square root function

int main()
{
  // 2 square feet pond surface for every 6 inches of fish
  const double fish_factor { 2.0/0.5 };  // Area per unit length of fish
  const double inches_per_foot { 12.0 };
  const double pi { 3.141592653589793238 };

  double fish_count {};               // Number of fish
  double fish_length {};              // Average length of fish
```

```
std::cout << "Enter the number of fish you want to keep: ";
std::cin >> fish_count;
std::cout << "Enter the average fish length in inches: ";
std::cin >> fish_length;
fish_length /= inches_per_foot;   // Convert to feet

// Calculate the required surface area
const double pond_area {fish_count * fish_length * fish_factor};

// Calculate the pond diameter from the area
const double pond_diameter {2.0 * std::sqrt(pond_area/pi)};

std::cout << "\nPond diameter required for " << fish_count << " fish is "
          << pond_diameter << " feet.\n";
}
```

With input values of 20 fish with an average length of 9 inches, this example produces the following output:

```
Enter the number of fish you want to keep: 20
Enter the average fish length in inches: 9
Pond diameter required for 20 fish is 8.74039 feet.
```

You first define three const variables in main() that you'll use in the calculation. Notice the use of a constant expression to specify the initial value for fish_factor. You can use any expression for an initial value that produces a result of the appropriate type. You specify fish_factor, inches_per_foot, and pi as const because their values are fixed and should not be altered.

Next, you define the fish_count and fish_length variables in which you'll store the user input. Both have an initial value of zero. The input for the fish length is in inches, so you convert it to feet before you use it in the calculation for the pond. You use the /= operator to convert the original value to feet.

You define a variable for the area for the pond and initialize it with an expression that produces the required value:

```
const double pond_area {fish_count * fish_length * fish_factor};
```

The product of fish_count and fish_length gives the total length of all the fish in feet, and multiplying this by fish_factor gives the required area for the pond in square feet. Once computed and initialized, the value of pond_area will and should not be changed anymore, so you might as well declare the variable const to make that clear.

The area of a circle is given by the formula πr^2, where r is the radius. You can therefore calculate the radius of the circular pond by dividing the area by π and calculating the square root of the result. The diameter is twice the radius, so the whole calculation is carried out by this statement:

```
const double pond_diameter {2.0 * std::sqrt(pond_area / pi)};
```

You obtain the square root using the sqrt() function from the cmath header.

Of course, you could calculate the pond diameter in a single statement like this:

```
const double pond_diameter {2.0 * std::sqrt(fish_count * fish_length * fish_factor / pi)};
```

This eliminates the need for the pond_area variable so the program will be smaller and shorter. It's debatable whether this is better than the original, though, because it's far less obvious what is going on.

The last statement in main() outputs the result. Unless you're an exceptionally meticulous pond enthusiast, however, the pond diameter has more decimal places than you need. Let's look into how you can fix that.

Formatting Stream Output

You can change how data is formatted when it is written to an output stream using *stream manipulators*, which are declared in the iomanip and ios Standard Library headers. You apply a stream manipulator to an output stream with the insert operator, <<. We'll just introduce the most useful manipulators. You should consult a Standard Library reference if you want to get to know the others.

All manipulators declared by ios are automatically available if you include the familiar iostream header. Unlike those of the iomanip header, these stream manipulators do not require an argument:

std::fixed	Output floating-point data in fixed-point notation.
std::scientific	Output all subsequent floating-point data in scientific notation, which always includes an exponent and one digit before the decimal point.
std::defaultfloat	Revert to the default floating-point data presentation.
std::dec	All subsequent integer output is decimal.
std::hex	All subsequent integer output is hexadecimal.
std::oct	All subsequent integer output is octal.
std::showbase	Outputs the base prefix for hexadecimal and octal integer values. Inserting std::noshowbase in a stream will switch this off.
std::left	Output is left-justified in the field.
std::right	Output is right-justified in the field. This is the default.

The iomanip header provides useful parametric manipulators as well, some of which are listed next. To use them, you need to include the iomanip header in your source file first.

std::setprecision(n)	Sets the floating-point precision or the number of decimal places to n digits. If the default floating-point output presentation is in effect, n specifies the number of digits in the output value. If fixed or scientific format has been set, n is the number of digits following the decimal point. The default precision is 6.
std::setw(n)	Sets the output field width to n characters, but only for the next output data item. Subsequent output reverts to the default where the field width is set to the number of output character needed to accommodate the data.
std::setfill(ch)	When the field width has more characters than the output value, excess characters in the field will be the default fill character, which is a space. This sets the fill character to be ch for all subsequent output.

When you insert a manipulator in an output stream, it normally remains in effect until you change it. The only exception is std::setw(), which only influences the width of the next field that is output.

Let's see how some of these work in practice. Replace the output statement at the end of Ex2_03.cpp with the following, and enter, for instance, 20 and 9 as input again:

```
std::cout << "\nPond diameter required for " << fish_count << " fish is "
          << std::setprecision(2)                    // Output value is 8.7
          << pond_diameter << " feet.\n";
```

You'll get the floating-point value presented with 2 digits of precision, which will correspond to 1 decimal place in this case. Because the default handling of floating-point output is in effect, the integer between the parentheses in setprecision() specifies the output precision for floating-point values, which is the total number of digits before and after the decimal point. You can make the parameter specify the number of digits after the decimal point—the number of decimal places in other words—by setting the mode as fixed. For example, try this in Ex2_03.cpp:

```
std::cout << "\nPond diameter required for " << fish_count << " fish is "
          << std::fixed << std::setprecision(2)
          << pond_diameter << " feet.\n";              // Output value is 8.74
```

Setting the mode as fixed or as scientific causes the setprecision() parameter to be interpreted as the number of decimal places in the output value. Setting scientific mode causes floating-point output to be in scientific notation, which is with an exponent:

```
std::cout << "\nPond diameter required for " << fish_count << " fish is "
          << std::scientific << std::setprecision(2)
          << pond_diameter << " feet.\n";              // Output value is 8.74e+00
```

In scientific notation there is always one digit before the decimal point. The value set by setprecision() is still the number of digits following the decimal point. There's always a two-digit exponent value, even when the exponent is zero.

The following statements illustrate some of the formatting possible with integer values:

```
int a{16}, b{66};
std::cout << std::setw(5) << a << std::setw(5) << b << std::endl;
std::cout << std::left << std::setw(5) << a << std::setw(5) << b << std::endl;
std::cout << " a = " << std::setbase(16) << std::setw(6) << std::showbase << a
          << " b = " << std::setw(6) << b << std::endl;
std::cout << std::setw(10) << a << std::setw(10) << b << std::endl;
```

The output from these statements is as follows:

```
16    66
16    66
a = 0x10    b = 0x42
0x10       0x42
```

It's a good idea to insert showbase in the stream when you output integers as hexadecimal or octal so the output won't be misinterpreted as decimal values. We recommend you try various combinations of these manipulators and stream constants to get a feel for how they all work.

Mixed Expressions and Type Conversion

You can write expressions involving operands of different types. For example, you could have defined the variable to store the number of fish in Ex2_03 like this:

```
unsigned int fish_count {};          // Number of fish
```

The number of fish is certainly an integer, so this makes sense. The number of inches in a foot is also integral, so you would want to define the variable like this:

```
const unsigned int inches_per_foot {12};
```

The calculation would still work OK in spite of the variables now being of differing types. Here's an example:

```
fish_length /= inches_per_foot;         // Convert to feet
double pond_area{fish_count * fish_length * fish_factor};
```

Technically, all binary arithmetic operands require both operands to be of the same type. Where this is not the case, however, the compiler will arrange to convert one of the operand values to the same type as the other. These are called *implicit conversions*. The way this works is that the variable of a type with the more limited range is converted to the type of the other. The fish_length variable in the first statement is of type double. Type double has a greater range than type unsigned int, so the compiler will insert a conversion for the value of inches_per_foot to type double to allow the division to be carried out. In the second statement, the value of fish_count will be converted to type double to make it the same type as fish_length before the multiply operation executes.

With each operation with operands of different types, the compiler chooses the operand with the type that has the more limited range of values as the one to be converted to the type of the other. In effect, it ranks the types in the following sequence, from high to low:

1. long double	2. double	3. float
4. unsigned long long	5. long long	6. unsigned long
7. long	8. unsigned int	9. int

The operand to be converted will be the one with the lower rank. Thus, in an operation with operands of type long long and type unsigned int, the latter will be converted to type long long. An operand of type char, signed char, unsigned char, short, or unsigned short is always converted to at least type int.

Implicit conversions can produce unexpected results. Consider these statements:

```
unsigned int x {20u};
int y {30};
std::cout << x - y << std::endl;
```

You might expect the output to be -10, but it isn't. The output will most likely be 4294967286! This is because the value of y is converted to unsigned int to match the type of x, so the result of the subtraction is an unsigned integer value. And -10 cannot be represented by an unsigned type. For unsigned integer types, going below zero always wraps around to the largest possible integer value. That is, for a 32-bit unsigned int type, -1 becomes 2^{32} - 1 or 4294967295, -2 becomes 2^{32} - 2 or 4294967293, and so on. This of course means that -10 indeed becomes 2^{32} - 10, or 4294967286.

■ **Note** The phenomenon where the result of a subtraction of unsigned integers wraps around to very large positive numbers is sometimes called *underflow*. In general, underflow is something to watch out for (we'll encounter examples of this in later chapters). Naturally, the converse phenomenon exists as well and is called *overflow*. Adding the unsigned char values 253 and 5, for instance, will not give 258—the largest value a variable of type unsigned char can hold is 255! Instead, the result will be 2, or 258 modulo 256. The outcome of overflow and underflow with signed integer types is undefined—that is, it depends on the compiler and computer architecture you are using.

The compiler will also insert an implicit conversion when the expression on the right of an assignment produces a value that is of a different type from the variable on the left. Here's an example:

```
int y {};
double z {5.0};
y = z;                    // Requires an implicit narrowing conversion
```

The last statement requires a conversion of the value of the expression on the right of the assignment to allow it to be stored as type int. The compiler will insert a conversion to do this, but since this is a narrowing conversion, it may issue a warning message about possible loss of data.

You need to take care when writing integer operations with operands of different types. Don't rely on implicit type conversion to produce the result you want unless you are certain it will do so. If you are not sure, what you need is an *explicit type conversion*, also called an *explicit cast*.

Explicit Type Conversion

To explicitly convert the value of an expression to a given type, you write the following:

```
static_cast<type_to_convert_to>(expression)
```

The static_cast keyword reflects the fact that the cast is checked statically, that is, when the code is compiled. Later, when you get to deal with classes, you'll meet *dynamic casts*, where the conversion is checked dynamically, that is, when the program is executing. The effect of the cast is to convert the value that results from evaluating expression to the type that you specify between the angle brackets. The expression can be anything from a single variable to a complex expression involving lots of nested parentheses. You could eliminate the warning that arises from the assignment in the previous section by writing it as follows:

```
y = static_cast<int>(z);      // Never a compiler warning this time...
```

By adding an explicit cast, you signal the compiler that a narrowing conversion is intentional. If the conversion is not narrowing, you'd rarely add an explicit cast. Here's another example of the use of static_cast<>():

```
double value1 {10.9};
double value2 {15.9};
int whole_number {static_cast<int>(value1) + static_cast<int>(value2)};
```

The initializing value for whole_number is the sum of the integral parts of value1 and value2, so they're each explicitly cast to type int. whole_number will therefore have the initial value 25. Note that as with integer division, casting from a floating-point type to an integral type uses *truncation*. That is, it simply discards the entire fractional part of the floating-point number.

■ **Tip**　As seen earlier in this chapter, the std::round(), lround(), and llround() functions from the cmath header allow you to round floating-point numbers to the nearest integer. In many cases, this is better than (implicit or explicit) casting, where truncation is used instead.

The casts do not affect the values stored in value1 and value2, which will remain as 10.9 and 15.9, respectively. The values 10 and 15 produced by the casts are just stored temporarily for use in the calculation and then discarded. Although both casts cause a loss of information, the compiler always assumes you know what you're doing when you explicitly specify a cast.

Of course, the value of whole_number would be different if you wrote this:

```
int whole_number {static_cast<int>(value1 + value2)};
```

The result of adding value1 and value2 will be 26.8, which results in 26 when converted to type int. As always with braced initializers, without the explicit type conversion in this statement, the compiler will either refuse to insert or at least warn about inserting implicit narrowing conversions.

Generally, the need for explicit casts should be rare, particularly with basic types of data. If you have to include a lot of explicit conversions in your code, it's often a sign that you could choose more suitable types for your variables. Still, there are circumstances when casting is necessary, so let's look at a simple example. This example converts a length in yards as a decimal value to yards, feet, and inches:

```
// Ex2_04.cpp
// Using explicit type conversions
#include <iostream>

int main()
{
  const unsigned feet_per_yard {3};
  const unsigned inches_per_foot {12};

  double length {};                    // Length as decimal yards
  unsigned int yards{};                // Whole yards
  unsigned int feet {};                // Whole feet
  unsigned int inches {};              // Whole inches

  std::cout << "Enter a length in yards as a decimal: ";
  std::cin >> length;

  // Get the length as yards, feet, and inches
  yards  = static_cast<unsigned int>(length);
  feet   = static_cast<unsigned int>((length - yards) * feet_per_yard);
  inches = static_cast<unsigned int>
                    (length * feet_per_yard * inches_per_foot) % inches_per_foot;
```

```
  std::cout << length << " yards converts to "
            << yards  << " yards "
            << feet   << " feet "
            << inches << " inches." << std:: endl;
}
```

This is typical output from this program:

```
Enter a length in yards as a decimal:  2.75
2.75 yards converts to 2 yards 2 feet 3 inches.
```

The first two statements in main() define conversion constants feet_per_yard and inches_per_foot as integers. You declare these as const to prevent them from being modified accidentally. The variables that will store the results of converting the input to yards, feet, and inches are of type unsigned int and initialized with zero.

The statement that computes the whole number of yards from the input value is as follows:

```
  yards = static_cast<unsigned int>(length);
```

The cast discards the fractional part of the value in length and stores the integral result in yards. You could omit the explicit cast here and leave it to the compiler to take care of, but it's always better to write an explicit cast in such cases. If you don't, it's not obvious that you realized the need for the conversion and the potential loss of data. Many compilers will then issue a warning as well.

You obtain the number of whole feet with this statement:

```
  feet = static_cast<unsigned int>((length - yards) * feet_per_yard);
```

Subtracting yards from length produces the fraction of a yard in the length as a double value. The compiler will arrange for the value in yards to be converted to type double for the subtraction. The value of feet_per_yard will then be converted to double to allow the multiplication to take place, and finally the explicit cast converts the result from type double to type unsigned int.

The final part of the calculation obtains the residual number of whole inches:

```
  inches = static_cast<unsigned int>
                     (length * feet_per_yard * inches_per_foot) % inches_per_foot;
```

The explicit cast applies to the total number of inches in length, which results from the product of length, feet_per_yard, and inches_per_foot. Because length is type double, both const values will be converted implicitly to type double to allow the product to be calculated. The remainder after dividing the integral number of inches in length by the number of inches in a foot is the number of residual inches.

Old-Style Casts

Prior to the introduction of static_cast<> into C++ around 1998—so a very, very long time ago—an explicit cast of the result of an expression was written like this:

```
(type_to_convert_to)expression
```

The result of `expression` is cast to the type between the parentheses. For example, the statement to calculate `inches` in the previous example could be written like this:

```
inches  = (unsigned int)(length * feet_per_yard * inches_per_foot) % inches_per_foot;
```

This type of cast is a remnant of the C language and is therefore also referred to as a *C-style cast*. There are several kinds of casts in C++ that are now differentiated, but the old-style casting syntax covers them all. Because of this, code using the old-style casts is more prone to errors. It isn't always clear what you intended, and you may not get the result you expected. Therefore:

▓ **Tip**   You'll still see old-style casting used because it's still part of the language, but we strongly recommend that you use only the new casts in your code. One should never use C-style casts in C++ code anymore. Period. That is why this is also the last time that we mention this syntax in this book....

Finding the Limits

You have seen typical examples of the upper and lower limits for various types. The `limits` Standard Library header makes this information available for all the fundamental data types so you can access this for your compiler. Let's look at an example. To display the maximum value you can store in a variable of type `double`, you could write this:

```
std::cout << "Maximum value of type double is " << std::numeric_limits<double>::max();
```

The expression `std::numeric_limits<double>::max()` produces the value you want. By putting different type names between the angled brackets, you can obtain the maximum values for other data types. You can also replace `max()` with `min()` to get the minimum value that can be stored, but the meaning of minimum is different for integer and floating-point types. For an integer type, `min()` results in the true minimum, which will be a negative number for a signed integer type. For a floating-point type, `min()` returns the minimum positive value that can be stored.

▓ **Caution**   `std::numeric_limits<double>::min()` typically equals `2.225e-308`, an extremely tiny *positive* number. So, for floating-point types, `min()` does not give you the complement of `max()`. To get the lowest *negative* value a type can represent, you should use `lowest()` instead. For instance, `std::numeric_limits<double>::lowest()` equals `-1.798e+308`, a hugely negative number. For integer types, `min()` and `lowest()` always evaluate to the same number.

The following program will display the maximums and minimums for some of the numerical data types:

```
// Ex2_05.cpp
// Finding maximum and minimum values for data types
#include <limits>
#include <iostream>
```

```
int main()
{
  std::cout << "The range for type short is from "
            << std::numeric_limits<short>::min() << " to "
            << std::numeric_limits<short>::max()  << std::endl;
  std::cout << "The range for type int is from "
            << std::numeric_limits<int>::min() << " to "
            << std::numeric_limits<int>::max() << std::endl;
  std::cout << "The range for type long is from "
            << std::numeric_limits<long>::min()<< " to "
            << std::numeric_limits<long>::max() << std::endl;
  std::cout << "The range for type float is from "
            << std::numeric_limits<float>::min() << " to "
            << std::numeric_limits<float>::max() << std::endl;
  std::cout << "The positive range for type double is from "
            << std::numeric_limits<double>::min() << " to "
            << std::numeric_limits<double>::max() << std::endl;
  std::cout << "The positive range for type long double is from "
            << std::numeric_limits<long double>::min() << " to "
            << std::numeric_limits<long double>::max() << std::endl;
}
```

You can easily extend this to include unsigned integer types and types that store characters. On our test system, the results of running the program are as follows:

```
The range for type short is from -32768 to 32767
The range for type int is from -2147483648 to 2147483647
The range for type long is from -9223372036854775808 to 9223372036854775807
The range for type float is from 1.17549e-38 to 3.40282e+38
The positive range for type double is from 2.22507e-308 to 1.79769e+308
The positive range for type long double is from 3.3621e-4932 to 1.18973e+4932
```

Finding Other Properties of Fundamental Types

You can retrieve many other items of information about various types. The number of binary digits, or bits, for example, is returned by this expression:

```
std::numeric_limits<type_name>::digits
```

type_name is the type in which you're interested. For floating-point types, you'll get the number of bits in the mantissa. For signed integer types, you'll get the number of bits in the value, that is, excluding the sign bit. You can also find out what the range of the exponent component of floating-point values is, whether a type is signed or not, and so on. You can consult a Standard Library reference for the complete list.

Before we move on, there are two more numeric_limits<> functions we still want to introduce. We promised you earlier that we would. To obtain the special floating-point values for infinity and not-a-number (NaN), you should use expressions of the following form:

```
float positive_infinity = std::numeric_limits<float>::infinity();
double negative_infinity = -std::numeric_limits<double>::infinity();
long double not_a_number = std::numeric_limits<long double>::quiet_NaN();
```

None of these expressions would compile for integer types, nor would they compile in the unlikely event that the floating-point types that your compiler uses do not support these special values. Besides `quiet_NaN()`, there's a function called `signaling_NaN()`—and not `loud_NaN()` or `noisy_NaN()`. The difference between the two is outside the scope of this brief introduction, though: if you're interested, you can always consult your Standard Library documentation.

Working with Character Variables

Variables of type char are used primarily to store a code for a single character and occupy 1 byte. The C++ standard doesn't specify the character encoding to be used for the basic character set, so in principle this is down to the particular compiler, but it's usually ASCII.

You define variables of type char in the same way as variables of the other types that you've seen. Here's an example:

```
char letter;              // Uninitialized - so junk value
char yes {'Y'},no {'N'};  // Initialized with character literals
char ch {33};             // Integer initializer equivalent to '!'
```

You can initialize a variable of type char with a character literal between single quotes or by an integer. An integer initializer must be within the range of type char—remember, it depends on the compiler whether it is a signed or unsigned type. Of course, you can specify a character as one of the escape sequences you saw in Chapter 1.

There are also escape sequences that specify a character by its code expressed as either an octal or a hexadecimal value. The escape sequence for an octal character code is one to three octal digits preceded by a backslash. The escape sequence for a hexadecimal character code is one or more hexadecimal digits preceded by \x. You write either form between single quotes when you want to define a character literal. For example, the letter 'A' could be written as hexadecimal '\x41' in ASCII. Obviously, you could write codes that won't fit within a single byte, in which case the result is implementation defined.

Variables of type char are numeric; after all, they store integer codes that represent characters. They can therefore participate in arithmetic expressions, just like variables of type int or long. Here's an example:

```
char ch {'A'};
char letter {ch + 5};     // letter is 'F'
++ch;                     // ch is now 'B'
ch += 3;                  // ch is now 'E'
```

When you write a char variable to cout, it is output as a character, not as an integer. If you want to see it as a numerical value, you can cast it to another integer type. Here's an example:

```
std::cout << "ch is '" << ch
          << "' which is code " << std::hex << std::showbase
          << static_cast<int>(ch) << std::endl;
```

This produces the following output:

```
ch is 'E' which is code 0x45
```

When you use >> to read from a stream into a variable of type char, the first nonwhitespace character will be stored. This means you can't read whitespace characters in this way; they're simply ignored. Further, you can't read a numerical value into a variable of type char; if you try, the character code for the first digit will be stored.

Working with Unicode Characters

ASCII is generally adequate for national language character sets that use Latin characters. However, if you want to work with characters for multiple languages simultaneously or if you want to handle character sets for many non-English languages, 256 character codes doesn't go nearly far enough, and Unicode is the answer. You can refer to Chapter 1 for a brief introduction on Unicode and character encodings.

Type wchar_t is a fundamental type that can store all members of the largest extended character set that's supported by an implementation. The type name derives from *wide char*acters because the character is "wider" than the usual single-byte character. By contrast, type char is referred to as "narrow" because of the limited range of character codes that are available.

You define wide-character literals in a similar way to literals of type char, but you prefix them with L. Here's an example:

```
wchar_t wch {L'Z'};
```

This defines wch as type wchar_t and initializes it to the wide-character representation for Z.

Your keyboard may not have keys for representing other national language characters, but you can still create them using hexadecimal notation. Here's an example:

```
wchar_t wch {L'\x0438'};      // Cyrillic и
```

The value between the single quotes is an escape sequence that specifies the hexadecimal representation of the character code. The backslash indicates the start of the escape sequence, and x or X after the backslash signifies that the code is hexadecimal.

Type wchar_t does not handle international character sets very well. It's much better to use type char16_t, which stores characters encoded as UTF-16, or char32_t, which stores UTF-32 encoded characters. Here's an example of defining a variable of type char16_t:

```
char16_t letter {u'B'};               // Initialized with UTF-16 code for B
char16_t cyr {u'\x0438'};             // Initialized with UTF-16 code for cyrillic и
```

The lowercase u prefix to the literals indicates that they are UTF-16. You prefix UTF-32 literals with uppercase U. Here's an example:

```
char32_t letter {U'B'};               // Initialized with UTF-32 code for B
char32_t cyr {U'\x044f'};             // Initialized with UTF-32 code for cyrillic я
```

Of course, if your editor and compiler have the capability to accept and display the characters, you can define cyr like this:

```
char32_t cyr {U'я'};
```

The Standard Library provides standard input and output streams wcin and wcout for reading and writing characters of type wchar_t, but there is no provision with the library for handling char16_t and char32_t character data.

■ **Caution**   You should not mix output operations on wcout with output operations on cout. The first output operation on either stream sets an orientation for the standard output stream that is either *narrow* or *wide*, depending on whether the operation is to cout or wcout. The orientation will carry forward to subsequent output operations for either cout or wcout.

The auto Keyword

You use the auto keyword to indicate that the compiler should deduce the type. Here are some examples:

```
auto m {10};            // m has type int
auto n {200UL};         // n has type unsigned long
auto pi {3.14159};      // pi has type double
```

The compiler will deduce the types for m, n, and pi from the initial values you supply. You can use functional or assignment notation with auto for the initial value as well:

```
auto m = 10;            // m has type int
auto n = 200UL;         // n has type unsigned long
auto pi(3.14159);       // pi has type double
```

Having said that, this is not really how the auto keyword is intended to be used. Typically, when defining variables of fundamental types, you might as well specify the type explicitly so you know for sure what it is. You'll meet the auto keyword again later in the book where it is more appropriately and much more usefully applied.

■ **Caution**   You need to be careful when using braced initializers with the auto keyword. For example, suppose you write this (notice the equal sign!):

```
auto m = {10};
```

Then the type deduced for m will not be int, but instead will be std::initializer_list<int>. To give you some context, this is the same type you would get if you'd use a list of elements between the braces:

```
auto list = {1, 2, 3};    // list has type std::initializer_list<int>
```

You will see later that such lists are typically used to specify the initial values of containers such as std::vector<>. To make matters worse, the type deduction rules have changed in C++17. If you are using an older compiler, the type the compiler deduces in place of auto may not at all be what you'd expect in many more cases. Here's an overview:

```
/* C++11 and C++14 */
auto i {10};            // i has type std::initializer_list<int> !!!
auto pi = {3.14159};    // pi has type std::initializer_list<double>
auto list1{1, 2, 3};    // list1 has type std::initializer_list<int>
auto list2 = {4, 5, 6}; // list2 has type std::initializer_list<int>

/* C++17 and later */
auto i {10};            // i has type int
auto pi = {3.14159};    // pi has type std::initializer_list<double>
auto list1{1, 2, 3};    // error: does not compile!
auto list2 = {4, 5, 6}; // list2 has type std::initializer_list<int>
```

To summarize, if your compiler properly supports C++17, you can use braced initialization to initialize any variable with a single value, provided you do not combine it with an assignment. This also is the guideline we'll follow in this book. If your compiler is not fully up-to-date yet, however, you should simply never use braced initializers with `auto`. Instead, either explicitly state the type or use assignment or functional notation.

Summary

In this chapter, we covered the basics of computation in C++. You learned about most of the fundamental types of data that are provided for in the language. The essentials of what we've discussed up to now are as follows:

- Constants of any kind are called literals. All literals have a type.

- You can define integer literals as decimal, hexadecimal, octal, or binary values.

- A floating-point literal must contain a decimal point or an exponent or both. If there is neither, you have specified an integer.

- The fundamental types that store integers are `short`, `int`, `long`, and `long long`. These store signed integers, but you can also use the type modifier `unsigned` preceding any of these type names to produce a type that occupies the same number of bytes but stores unsigned integers.

- The floating-point data types are `float`, `double`, and `long double`.

- Uninitialized variables generally contain garbage values. Variables may be given initial values when they're defined, and it's good programming practice to do so. A braced initializer is the preferred way of specifying initial values.

- A variable of type `char` can store a single character and occupies one byte. Type `char` may be `signed` or `unsigned`, depending on your compiler. You can also use variables of the types `signed char` and `unsigned char` to store integers. Types `char`, `signed char`, and `unsigned char` are different types.

- Type `wchar_t` stores a wide character and occupies either two or four bytes, depending on your compiler. Types `char16_t` and `char32_t` may be better for handling Unicode characters in a cross-platform manner.

- You can fix the value of a variable by using the `const` modifier. The compiler will check for any attempts within the program source file to modify a variable defined as `const`.

- The four main mathematic operations correspond to the binary +, -, *, and / operators. For integers, the modulus operator % gives you the remainder after integer division.

- The ++ and -- operators are special shorthand for adding or subtracting one from a numeric variable. Both exist in postfix and prefix forms.

- You can mix different types of variables and constants in an expression. The compiler will arrange for one operand in a binary operation to be automatically converted to the type of the other operand when they differ.

- The compiler will automatically convert the type of the result of an expression on the right of an assignment to the type of the variable on the left where these are different. This can cause loss of information when the left-side type isn't able to contain the same information as the right-side type—double converted to int, for example, or long converted to short.

- You can explicitly convert a value of one type to another using the static_cast<>() operator.

EXERCISES

The following exercises enable you to try what you've learned in this chapter. If you get stuck, look back over the chapter for help. If you're still stuck after that, you can download the solutions from the Apress website (www.apress.com/book/download.html), but that really should be a last resort.

Exercise 2-1. Write a program that will compute the area of a circle. The program should prompt for the radius of the circle to be entered from the keyboard, calculate the area using the formula area = pi * radius * radius, and then display the result.

Exercise 2-2. Using your solution for Exercise 2-1, improve the code so that the user can control the precision of the output by entering the number of digits required. To really show off how accurate floating-point numbers can be, you can perhaps switch to double-precision floating-point arithmetic as well. You'll need a more precise approximation of π. 3.141592653589793238 will do fine.

Exercise 2-3. Create a program that converts inches to feet and inches. In case you're unfamiliar with imperial units: 1 foot equals 12 inches. An input of 77 inches, for instance, should thus produce an output of 6 feet and 5 inches. Prompt the user to enter an integer value corresponding to the number of inches and then make the conversion and output the result.

Exercise 2-4. For your birthday you've been given a long tape measure and an instrument that measures angles (the angle between the horizontal and a line to the top of a tree, for instance). If you know the distance, d, you are from a tree, and the height, h, of your eye when peering into your angle-measuring device, you can calculate the height of the tree with the formula h + d*tan(angle). Create a program to read h in inches, d in feet and inches, and angle in degrees from the keyboard, and output the height of the tree in feet.

▓ **Note** There is no need to chop down any trees to verify the accuracy of your program. Just check the solutions on the Apress website!

Exercise 2-5. Your body mass index (BMI) is your weight, w, in kilograms divided by the square of your height, h, in meters (w/(h*h)). Write a program to calculate the BMI from a weight entered in pounds and a height entered in feet and inches. A kilogram is 2.2 pounds, and a foot is 0.3048 meters.

Exercise 2-6. Here's an extra exercise for puzzle fans. Write a program that will prompt the user to enter two different positive integers. Identify in the output the value of the larger integer and the value of the smaller integer. Using the decision-making facilities of Chapter 5, this would be like stealing a piece of cake from a baby while walking in the park. What makes this a brain teaser, though, is that this *can* be done solely with the operators you've learned about in this chapter!

Working with Fundamental Data Types

In this chapter, we expand on the types that we discussed in the previous chapter and explain how variables of the basic types interact in more complicated situations. We also introduce some new features of C++ and discuss some of the ways that these are used.

In this chapter, you'll learn

- How the execution order in an expression is determined

- What the bitwise operators are and how you use them

- How you can define a new type that limits variables to a fixed range of possible values

- How you can define alternative names for existing data types

- What the storage duration of a variable is and what determines it

- What variable scope is and what its effects are

Operator Precedence and Associativity

You already know that there is a priority sequence for executing arithmetic operators in an expression. You'll meet many more operators throughout the book, including a few in this chapter. In general, the sequence in which operators in an expression are executed is determined by the *precedence* of the operators. Operator precedence is just a fancy term for the priority of an operator.

Some operators, such as addition and subtraction, have the same precedence. That raises the question of how an expression such as a+b-c+d is evaluated. When several operators from a group with the same precedence appear in an expression, in the absence of parentheses, the execution order is determined by the *associativity* of the group. A group of operators can be *left-associative*, which means operators execute from left to right, or they can be *right-associative*, which means they execute from right to left.

Nearly all operator groups are left-associative, so most expressions involving operators of equal precedence are evaluated from left to right. The only right-associative operators are the unary operators, assignment operators, and conditional operator. Table 3-1 shows the precedence and associativity of all the operators in C++.

© Ivor Horton and Peter Van Weert 2018
I. Horton and P. Van Weert, *Beginning C++17*, https://doi.org/10.1007/978-1-4842-3366-5_3

Table 3-1. *The Precedence and Associativity of C++ Operators*

Precedence	Operators	Associativity
1	`::`	Left
2	`()` `[]` `->` `.` postfix `++` and `--`	Left

3	`!` `~`
	unary `+` and `-`
	prefix `++` and `--`
	address-of `&` indirection `*`
	C-style cast `(type)`
	`sizeof`
	`new` `new[]` `delete` `delete[]`
		Right

4	`.*` `->*`	Left
5	`*` `/` `%`	Left
6	`+` `-`	Left
7	`<<` `>>`	Left
8	`<` `<=` `>` `>=`	Left
9	`==` `!=`	Left
10	`&`	Left
11	`^`	Left
12	`|`	Left
13	`&&`	Left
14	`||`	Left

15	`?:` (conditional operator)
	`=` `*=` `/=` `%=` `+=` `-=` `&=` `^=` `|=` `<<=` `>>=`
	`throw`
		Right

16	`,` (comma)	Left

You haven't met most of these operators yet, but when you need to know the precedence and associativity of any operator, you'll know where to find it. Each row in Table 3-1 is a group of operators of equal precedence, and the rows are in precedence sequence, from highest to lowest. Let's see a simple example to make sure that it's clear how all this works. Consider this expression:

```
x*y/z - b + c - d
```

The * and / operators are in the same group with precedence that is higher than the group containing + and -, so the expression x*y/z is evaluated first, with a result of r, say. The operators in the group containing * and / are left-associative, so the expression is evaluated as though it was (x*y)/z. The next step is the evaluation of r - b + c - d. The group containing the + and - operators is also left-associative, so this will be evaluated as ((r - b) + c) - d. Thus, the whole expression is evaluated as though it was written as follows:

```
((((x*y)/z) - b) + c) - d
```

Remember, nested parentheses are evaluated in sequence from the innermost to the outermost. You probably won't be able to remember the precedence and associativity of every operator, at least not until you have spent a lot of time writing C++ code. Whenever you are uncertain, you can always add parentheses to make sure things execute in the sequence you want. And even when you *are* certain (because you happen to be a precedence guru), it never hurts to add some extra parentheses to clarify a complex expression.

Bitwise Operators

As their name suggests, *bitwise operators* enable you to operate on an integer variable at the bit level. You can apply the bitwise operators to any type of integer, both `signed` and `unsigned`, including type `char`. However, they're usually applied to `unsigned` integer types. A typical application is to set individual bits in an integer variable. Individual bits are often used as *flags*, which is the term used to describe binary state indicators. You can use a single bit to store any value that has two states: on or off, male or female, true or false.

You can also use the bitwise operators to work with several items of information stored in a single variable. For instance, color values are usually recorded as three 8-bit values for the intensities of the red, green, and blue components in the color. These are typically packed into 3 bytes of a 4-byte word. The fourth byte is not wasted either; it usually contains a value for the transparency of the color. This transparency value is called the color's *alpha* component. Such color encodings are commonly denoted by letter quadruples such as RGBA or ARGB. The order of these letters then corresponds to the order in which the red (R), green (G), blue (B), and alpha (A) components appear in the 32-bit integer, with each component encoded as a single byte. To work with individual color components, you need to be able to separate out the individual bytes from a word, and the bitwise operators are just the tool for this.

Let's consider another example. Suppose you need to record information about fonts. You might want to store the style and the size of each font and whether it's bold or italic. You could pack all of this information into a 2-byte integer variable, as shown in Figure 3-1.

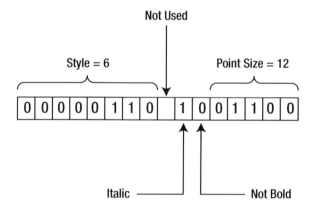

Using Bits to Store Font Data

Figure 3-1. Packing font data into 2 bytes

Here one bit records whether the font is italic—1 signifies italic, and 0 signifies normal. Another bit specifies whether the font is bold. One byte selects one of up to 256 different styles. Five bits could record the point size up to 31 (or 32, if you disallow letters of size zero). Thus, in one 16-bit word you have four separate pieces of data. The bitwise operators provide you with the means of accessing and modifying the individual bits and groups of bits from an integer very easily so they provide you with the means of assembling and disassembling the 16-bit word.

The Bitwise Shift Operators

The bitwise *shift operators* shift the contents of an integer variable by a specified number of bits to the left or right. These are used in combination with the other bitwise operators to achieve the kind of operations we described in the previous section. The >> operator shifts bits to the right, and the << operator shifts bits to the left. Bits that fall off either end of the variable are lost.

All the bitwise operations work with integers of any type, but we'll use type short, which is usually 2 bytes, to keep the illustrations simple. Suppose you define and initialize a variable, number, with this statement:

```
unsigned short number {16387};
```

You can shift the contents of this variable with this statement:

```
auto result{ static_cast<unsigned short>(number << 2) };   // Shift left two bit positions
```

■ **Caution**   The static_cast<> part of the previous statement is required because the expression number << 2 evaluates to a value of type int. This despite the fact that both number is of type short. The reason is that there are technically no mathematical or bitwise operators for integer types smaller than int. If their operands are either char or short, they are always implicitly converted to int first. Signedness is not preserved during this conversion either. Without static_cast<>, your compiler would issue at least a compiler warning to signal the narrowing conversion, or it might even refuse to compile the assignment altogether.

The left operand of the left shift operator, <<, is the value to be shifted, and the right operand specifies the number of bit positions by which the value is to be shifted. Figure 3-2 shows the effect.

Decimal 16,387 in binary is: | 0 | 1 | 0 | 0 | 0 | 0 | 0 | 0 | 0 | 0 | 0 | 0 | 0 | 0 | 1 | 1 |

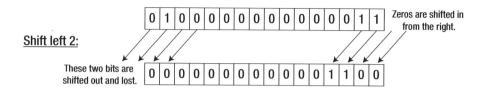

Shift left 2:

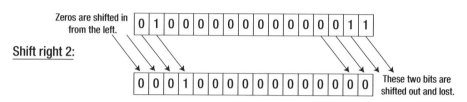

Shift right 2:

Figure 3-2. *Shift operations*

As you can see from Figure 3-2, shifting 16,387 two positions to the left produces the value 12. The rather drastic change in the value is the result of losing the high order bit. This statement shifts the value right two bit positions:

```
result = static_cast<unsigned short>(number >> 2); // Shift right two bit positions
```

The result is 4,096, so shifting right two bits effectively divides the value by 4. As long as bits aren't lost, shifting *n* bits to the left is equivalent to multiplying by 2, *n* times. In other words, it's equivalent to multiplying by 2*n*. Similarly, shifting right *n* bits is equivalent to dividing by 2*n*. But beware: as you saw with the left shift of number, if significant bits are lost, the result is nothing like what you would expect. However, this is not different from the "real" multiply operation. If you multiplied the 2-byte number by 4, you would get the same result, so shifting left and multiplying are still equivalent. The incorrect result arises because the result of the multiplication is outside the range of a 2-byte integer.

When you want to modify the original value of a variable using a shift operation, you can do so by using a >>= or <<= operator. Here's an example:

```
number >>= 2;                                    // Shift right two bit positions
```

This is equivalent to the following:

```
number = static_cast<unsigned short>(number >> 2);  // Shift right two bit positions
```

There's no confusion between these shift operators and the insertion and extraction operators for input and output. As far as the compiler is concerned, the meaning is clear from the context. If it isn't, the compiler will generate a message in most cases, but you do need to be careful. For example, to output the result of shifting number left by two bits, you could write this:

```
std::cout << (number << 2) << std::endl;     // Prints 65548
```

The parentheses are essential here. Without them, the compiler would interpret the shift operator as a stream insertion operator, so you wouldn't get the result that you intended:

```
std::cout << number << 2 << std::endl;      // Prints 163872 (16387 followed by 2)
```

Note that if number starts out as 16,387 like before in Figure 3-2, the former statement does not print out 12. Instead, it prints 65,548, which happens to be 16,387 times 4. The reason again is that number is implicitly promoted to a value of type int prior to shifting its bits to the left by two positions, and int is more than large enough to represent the exact result: 65,548. To obtain 12 instead, you could add static_cast<> to explicitly cast the result back to unsigned short:

```
std::cout << static_cast<unsigned short>(number << 2) << std::endl;
```

Shifting Signed Integers

You can apply the bitwise shift operators to signed and unsigned integers. However, the effect of the right shift operator on signed integer types depends on your compiler and computer architecture. In some cases, a right shift on negative integers will introduce "0" bits at the left to fill vacated bit positions. In other cases, the sign bit is propagated, so "1" bits fill the vacated bit positions to the left. Which of the two happens depends on the binary encoding that your compiler uses for negative integers (the most common encoding schemes were discussed in Chapter 1).

The reason for propagating the sign bit, where this occurs, is to maintain consistency between a right shift and a divide operation. We can illustrate this with a variable of type signed char, just to show how it works. Suppose you define value like this:

```
signed char value {-104};      // Value is 10011000
```

104 in binary is 01101000, so assuming your computer employs a two's complement notation for negative integers, -104 becomes 10011000 (remember, to obtain the two's complement binary encoding, you have to first flip all bits of the positive binary value and then add one). You can shift value two bits to the right with this operation:

```
value >>= 2;                // Result is 11100110
```

The binary result when the sign is propagated is shown in the comment. Two 0s are shifted out at the right end, and because the sign bit is 1, further 1s are inserted on the left. The decimal value of the result is –26 (flipping the bits of 11100110 and adding one gives 00011010 in binary, which is 26 in decimal notation). And -26 is the same as if you had divided by 4, as you would expect. With operations on unsigned integer types, of course, the sign bit isn't propagated, and 0s are always inserted on the left.

As we said, what *actually* happens when you right-shift negative integers is implementation defined. Because for the most part you'll be using these operators for operating at the bit level—where maintaining the integrity of the bit pattern is important—you should always use unsigned integers to ensure that you avoid the high-order bit being propagated.

Logical Operations on Bit Patterns

Table 3-2 shows the four bitwise operators that modify bits in an integer value.

Table 3-2. *Bitwise Operators*

Operator	Description
~	The *bitwise complement operator* is a unary operator that inverts the bits in its operand, so 1 becomes 0, and 0 becomes 1.
&	The *bitwise AND operator* ANDs corresponding bits in its operands. If the corresponding bits are both 1, then the resulting bit is 1; otherwise, it's 0.
^	The *bitwise exclusive OR operator* or *XOR operator* exclusive-ORs corresponding bits in its operands. If the corresponding bits are different, then the result is 1. If the corresponding bits are the same, the result is 0.
|	The *bitwise OR operator* ORs corresponding bits in its operands. If either bit is 1, then the result is 1. If both bits are 0, then the result is 0.

The operators appear in Table 3-2 in order of precedence, so the bitwise complement operator has the highest precedence, and the bitwise OR operator has the lowest. The shift operators << and >> are of equal precedence, and they're below the ~ operator but above the & operator.

Using the Bitwise AND

You'll typically use the bitwise AND operator to select particular bits or groups of bits in an integer value. Suppose you are using a 16-bit integer to store the point size, the style of a font, and whether it is bold and/or italic, as we illustrated in Figure 3-1. Suppose further that you want to define and initialize a variable to specify a 12-point, italic, style 6 font (in fact, the very same one illustrated in Figure 3-1). In binary, the style will be 00000110 (binary 6), the italic bit will be 1, the bold bit will be 0, and the size will be 01100 (binary 12). Remembering that there's an unused bit as well, you need to initialize the value of the font variable to the binary number 0000 0110 0100 1100. Because groups of four bits correspond to a hexadecimal digit, the most compact way to do this is to specify the initial value in hexadecimal notation:

```
unsigned short font {0x064C};                    // Style 6, italic, 12 point
```

Of course, ever since C++14 you also have the option to simply use a binary literal instead:

```
unsigned short font {0b00000110'0'10'01100};     // Style 6, italic, 12 point
```

Note the creative use of the digit grouping character here to signal the borders of the style, italic/bold, and point size components.

To work with the size afterward, you need to extract it from the font variable; the bitwise AND operator will enable you to do this. Because bitwise AND produces 1 bit only when both bits are 1, you can define a value that will "select" the bits defining the size when you AND it with font. You need to define a value that contains 1s in the bit positions that you're interested in and 0s in all the others. This kind of value is called a *mask*, and you can define such a mask with one of these statements (both are equivalent):

```
unsigned short size_mask {0x1F};
// unsigned short size_mask {0b11111};
```

The five low-order bits of font represent its size, so you set these bits to 1. The remaining bits are 0, so they will be discarded. (Binary 0000 0000 0001 1111 is hexadecimal 1F.)

You can now extract the point size from font with the following statement:

```
auto size {static_cast<unsigned short>( font & size_mask )};
```

Where both corresponding bits are 1 in an & operation, the resultant bit is 1. Any other combination of bits results in 0. The values therefore combine like this:

font	0000 0110 0100 1100
size_mask	0000 0000 0001 1111
font & size_mask	0000 0000 0000 1100

We have shown the binary values in groups of four bits just to make it easy to identify the hexadecimal equivalent; it also makes it easier to see how many bits there are in total. The effect of the mask is to separate out the five rightmost bits, which represent the point size.

You can use the same mechanism to select the font style, but you'll also need to use a shift operator to move the style value to the right. You can define a mask to select the left eight bits as follows:

```
unsigned short style_mask {0xFF00};       // Mask for style is 1111 1111 0000 0000
```

You can obtain the style value with this statement:

```
auto style {static_cast<unsigned short>( (font & style_mask) >> 8 )};
```

The effect of this statement is as follows:

font	0000 0110 0100 1100
style_mask	1111 1111 0000 0000
font & style_mask	0000 0110 0000 0000
(font & style_mask) >> 8	0000 0000 0000 0110

You should be able to see that you could just as easily isolate the bits indicating italic and bold by defining a mask for each. Of course, you still need a way to test whether the resulting bit is 1 or 0, and you'll see how to do that in the next chapter.

Another use for the bitwise AND operator is to turn bits off. You saw previously that a 0 bit in a mask will produce 0 in the result of the AND operator. To just turn the italic bit off in font, for example, you bitwise-AND font with a mask that has the italic bit as 0 and all other bits as 1. We'll show you the code to do this after we've shown you how to use the bitwise OR operator, which is next.

Using the Bitwise OR

You can use the bitwise OR operator for setting one or more bits to 1. Continuing with your manipulations of the font variable, it's conceivable that you would want to set the italic and bold bits on. You can define masks to select these bits with these statements:

```
unsigned short italic {0x40};       // Seventh bit from the right
unsigned short bold    {0x20};       // Sixth bit from the right
```

Naturally, you could again use binary literals to specify these masks. In this case, however, using the left-shift operator is probably easiest:

```
auto italic {static_cast<unsigned short>( 1u << 6 )};    // Seventh bit from the right
auto bold   {static_cast<unsigned short>( 1u << 5 )};    // Sixth bit from the right
```

■ **Caution**   Do remember, though, that, to turn on the *n*th bit, you have to shift the value 1 to the left by *n*-1! To see this, it's always easiest to think about what happens if you shift with smaller values: shifting by *zero* gives you the *first* bit, shifting by *one* the *second*, and so on.

This statement then sets the bold bit to 1:

```
font |= bold;                          // Set bold
```

The bits combine like this:

font	0000 0110 0100 1100
bold	0000 0000 0010 0000
font | bold	0000 0110 0110 1100

Now font specifies that the font is bold as well as italic. Note that this operation will set the bit on regardless of its previous state. If it was on, it remains on.

You can also OR masks together to set multiple bits. The following statement sets both the bold and italics bits:

```
font |= bold | italic;                 // Set bold and italic
```

■ **Caution**   It's easy to fall into the trap of allowing language to make you select the wrong operator. Because you say "Set italic *and* bold," there's a temptation to use the & operator, but this would be wrong. ANDing the two masks would result in a value with all bits 0, so you wouldn't change anything.

Using the Bitwise Complement Operator

As we said, you can use the & operator to turn bits off—you just need a mask that contains 0 at the bit position you want to turn off and 1 everywhere else. However, this raises the question of how best to specify such a mask. To specify it explicitly, you need to know how many bytes there are in the variable you want to change (not exactly convenient if you want the program to be in any way portable). However, you can obtain the mask that you want using the bitwise complement operator on the mask that you would use to turn the bit on. You can obtain the mask to turn bold off from the bold mask that turns it on:

bold	0000 0000 0010 0000
~bold	1111 1111 1101 1111

The effect of the complement operator is to flip each bit, 0 to 1 or 1 to 0. This will produce the result you're looking for, regardless of whether bold occupies 2, 4, or 8 bytes.

▓ **Note**   The bitwise complement operator is sometimes called the *bitwise NOT operator* because for every bit it operates on, what you get is not what you started with.

Thus, all you need to do to turn bold off is to bitwise-AND the complement of the bold mask with font. The following statement will do it:

```
font &= ~bold;                    // Turn bold off
```

You can set multiple bits to 0 by combining several inverted masks using the & operator and bitwise-ANDing the result with the variable you want to modify:

```
font &= ~bold & ~italic;          // Turn bold and italic off
```

This sets both the italic and bold bits to 0 in font. No parentheses are necessary here because ~ has a higher precedence than &. However, if you're ever uncertain about operator precedence, put parentheses in to express what you want. It certainly does no harm, and it really does good when they're necessary. Note that you can accomplish the same effect using the following statement:

```
font &= ~(bold | italic);         // Turn bold and italic off
```

Here the parentheses are required. We recommend you take a second to convince yourself that both statements are equivalent. If this doesn't come natural yet, rest assured: you'll get more practice working with similar logic when learning about so-called Boolean expressions in the next chapter.

Using the Bitwise Exclusive OR

The outcome of the bitwise *exclusive OR operator*—or *XOR operator* for short—contains a 1 if and only if precisely one of the corresponding input bits is equal to 1, while the other equals 0. Whenever both input bits are equal, even if both are 1, the resulting bit is 0. The latter is where the XOR operator differs from the regular OR operator. Table 3-3 summarizes the effect of all three binary bitwise operators:

Table 3-3. *Truth Table of Binary Bitwise Operators*

x	y	x & y	x | y	x ^ y
0	0	0	0	0
1	0	0	1	1
0	1	0	1	1
1	1	1	1	0

One interesting property of the XOR operator is that it may be used to *toggle* or *flip* the state of individual bits. With the font variable and the bold mask defined as before, the following toggles the bold bit—that is, if the bit was 0 before, it will now become 1, and vice versa:

```
font ^= bold;                     // Toggles bold
```

This implements the notion of clicking the Bold button in a typical word processor. If the selected text is not bold yet, it then simply becomes bold. If the selection is already bold, however, its font reverts to the regular, nonbold style. Let's take a closer look at how this works:

font	0000 0110 0100 1100
bold	0000 0000 0010 0000
font ^ bold	0000 0110 0010 1100

If the input is a font that is not bold, the result thus contains 0 ^ 1, or 1. Conversely, if the input already would be bold, the outcome would contain 1 ^ 1, or 0.

The XOR operator is used less frequently than the & and | operators. Important applications arise, however, in for instance cryptography, random number generation, and computer graphics. XOR is also used for the backup of hard disk data by certain RAID technologies. Suppose you have three similar hard drives, two with data and one to serve as backup. The basic idea is to ensure that the third drive at all times contains the XOR'ed bits of all contents of the two other drives, like so:

Drive one	... 1010 0111 0110 0011 ...
Drive two	... 0110 1100 0010 1000 ...
XOR drive (backup)	... 1100 1011 0100 1011 ...

If either of these three drives is then lost, its contents can be recovered by XOR'ing that of both other drives. Suppose, for instance, that you lose your second drive because of some critical hardware failure. Then its contents are easily recovered as follows:

Drive one	... 1010 0111 0110 0011 ...
XOR drive (backup)	... 1100 1011 0100 1011 ...
Recovered data (XOR)	... 0110 1100 0010 1000 ...

Notice that even with such a relatively simple trick, you already need only *one* extra drive to back up *two* others. The naïve approach would be to simply copy the contents of each drive onto another, meaning you'd need not three but four drives. The XOR technique is thus already a tremendous cost saver!

Using the Bitwise Operators: An Example

It's time we looked at some of this stuff in action. This example exercises bitwise operators:

```
// Ex3_01.cpp
// Using the bitwise operators
#include <iostream>
#include <iomanip>

int main()
{
  unsigned int red {0xFF0000u};          // Color red
  unsigned int white {0xFFFFFFu};        // Color white - RGB all maximum
```

```cpp
    std::cout << std::hex                     // Hexadecimal output
              << std::setfill('0');           // Fill character 0

    std::cout << "Try out bitwise complement, AND and OR operators:";
    std::cout << "\nInitial value:      red = " << std::setw(8) << red;
    std::cout << "\nComplement:        ~red = " << std::setw(8) << ~red;

    std::cout << "\nInitial value:    white = " << std::setw(8) << white;
    std::cout << "\nComplement:      ~white = " << std::setw(8) << ~white;

    std::cout << "\nBitwise AND: red & white = " << std::setw(8)  << (red & white);
    std::cout << "\nBitwise  OR: red | white = " << std::setw(8)  << (red | white);

    std::cout << "\n\nNow try successive exclusive OR operations:";
    unsigned int mask {red ^ white};
    std::cout << "\nmask = red ^ white = " << std::setw(8) << mask;
    std::cout << "\n         mask ^ red = " << std::setw(8) << (mask ^ red);
    std::cout << "\n       mask ^ white = " << std::setw(8) << (mask ^ white);

    unsigned int flags {0xFF};                 // Flags variable
    unsigned int bit1mask {0x1};               // Selects bit 1
    unsigned int bit6mask {0b100000};          // Selects bit 6
    unsigned int bit20mask {1u << 19};         // Selects bit 20

    std::cout << "\n\nUse masks to select or set a particular flag bit:";
    std::cout << "\nSelect bit 1 from flags  : " << std::setw(8) << (flags & bit1mask);
    std::cout << "\nSelect bit 6 from flags  : " << std::setw(8) << (flags & bit6mask);
    std::cout << "\nSwitch off bit 6 in flags: " << std::setw(8) << (flags &= ~bit6mask);
    std::cout << "\nSwitch on bit 20 in flags: " << std::setw(8) << (flags |= bit20mask)
              << std::endl;
}
```

If you typed the code correctly, the output is as follows:

```
Try out bitwise complement, AND and OR operators:
Initial value:        red = 00ff0000
Complement:          ~red = ff00ffff
Initial value:      white = 00ffffff
Complement:        ~white = ff000000
Bitwise AND: red & white = 00ff0000
Bitwise  OR: red | white = 00ffffff

Now try successive exclusive OR operations:
mask = red ^ white = 0000ffff
         mask ^ red = 00ffffff
       mask ^ white = 00ff0000

Use masks to select or set a particular flag bit:
Select bit 1 from flags  : 00000001
Select bit 6 from flags  : 00000020
Switch off bit 6 in flags: 000000df
Switch on bit 20 in flags: 000800df
```

There's an `#include` directive for the `iomanip` header because the code uses manipulators to control the formatting of the output. You define variables `red` and `white` as unsigned integers and initialize them with hexadecimal color values.

It will be convenient to display the data as hexadecimal values, and inserting `std::hex` in the output stream does this. The `hex` is modal, so all subsequent integer output will be in hexadecimal format. It will be easier to compare output values if they have the same number of digits and leading zeros. You can arrange for this by setting the fill character as 0 using the `std::setfill()` manipulator and ensuring the field width for each output value is the number of hexadecimal digits, which is 8. The `setfill()` manipulator is modal, so it remains in effect until you reset it. The `std::setw()` manipulator is not modal; you have to insert it into the stream before each output value.

You combine `red` and `white` using the bitwise AND and OR operators with these statements:

```
std::cout << "\nBitwise AND red & white = " << std::setw(8)  << (red & white);
std::cout << "\nBitwise  OR red | white = " << std::setw(8)  << (red | white);
```

The parentheses around the expressions are necessary here because the precedence of `<<` is higher than `&` and `|`. Without the parentheses, the statements wouldn't compile. If you check the output, you'll see that it's precisely as discussed. The result of ANDing two bits is 1 if both bits are 1; otherwise, the result is 0. When you bitwise-OR two bits, the result is 1 unless both bits are 0.

Next, you create a mask to use to flip between the values `red` and `white` by combining the two values with the XOR operator. The output for the value of `mask` shows that the exclusive OR of two bits is 1 when the bits are different and 0 when they're the same. By combining `mask` with either color values using exclusive OR, you obtain the other. This means that by repeatedly applying exclusive OR with a well-chosen mask, you can toggle between two different colors. Applying the mask once gives one color, and applying it a second time reverts to the original color. This property is often exploited in computer graphics when drawing or rendering using a so-called XOR mode.

The last group of statements demonstrates using a mask to select a single bit from a group of flag bits. The mask to select a particular bit must have that bit as 1 and all other bits as 0. To select a bit from `flags`, you just bitwise-AND the appropriate mask with the value of `flags`. To switch a bit off, you bitwise-AND `flags` with a mask containing 0 for the bit to be switched off and 1 everywhere else. You can easily produce this by applying the complement operator to a mask with the appropriate bit set, and `bit6mask` is just such a mask. Of course, if the bit to be switched off was already 0, it would remain as 0.

Enumerated Data Types

You'll sometimes need variables that have a limited set of possible values that can be usefully referred to by name—the days of the week, for example, or the months of the year. An *enumeration* provides this capability. When you define an enumeration, you're creating a new type, so it's also referred to as an *enumerated data type*. Let's create an example using one of the ideas we just mentioned—a type for variables that can assume values corresponding to days of the week. You can define this as follows:

```
enum class Day {Monday, Tuesday, Wednesday, Thursday, Friday, Saturday, Sunday};
```

This defines an enumerated data type called `Day`, and variables of this type can only have values from the set that appears between the braces, `Monday` through `Sunday`. If you try to set a variable of type `Day` to a value that isn't one of these values, the code won't compile. The symbolic names between the braces are called *enumerators*.

Each enumerator will be automatically defined to have a fixed integer value of type int by default. The first name in the list, Monday, will have the value 0, Tuesday will be 1, and so on, through to Sunday with the value 6. You can define today as a variable of the enumeration type Day with the following statement:

```
Day today {Day::Tuesday};
```

You use type Day just like any of the fundamental types. This definition for today initializes the variable with the value Day::Tuesday. When you reference an enumerator, it must be qualified by the type name.

To output the value of today, you must cast it to a numeric type because the standard output stream will not recognize the type Day:

```
std::cout << "Today is " << static_cast<int>(today) << std::endl;
```

This statement will output "Today is 1".

By default, the value of each enumerator is one greater than the previous one, and by default the values begin at 0. You can make the implicit values assigned to enumerators start at a different integer value, though. This definition of type Day has enumerator values 1 through 7:

```
enum class Day {Monday = 1, Tuesday, Wednesday, Thursday, Friday, Saturday, Sunday};
```

Monday is explicitly specified as 1, and subsequent enumerators will always be 1 greater than the preceding one. You can assign any integer values you like to the enumerators, and assigning these values is not limited to the first few enumerators either. The following definition, for instance, results in weekdays having values 3 through 7, Saturday having value 1, and Sunday having value 2:

```
enum class Day {Monday = 3, Tuesday, Wednesday, Thursday, Friday, Saturday = 1, Sunday};
```

The enumerators don't even need to have unique values. You could define Monday and Mon as both having the value 1, for example, like this:

```
enum class Day {Monday = 1, Mon = 1, Tuesday, Wednesday, Thursday, Friday, Saturday, Sunday };
```

You can now use either Mon or Monday as the first day of the week. A variable, yesterday, that you've defined as type Day could then be set with this statement:

```
yesterday = Day::Mon;
```

You can also define the value of an enumerator in terms of a previous enumerator. Throwing everything you've seen so far into a single example, you could define the type Day as follows:

```
enum class Day { Monday,                    Mon = Monday,
                 Tuesday   = Monday + 2,     Tues = Tuesday,
                 Wednesday = Tuesday + 2,    Wed = Wednesday,
                 Thursday = Wednesday  + 2,  Thurs = Thursday,
                 Friday    = Thursday + 2,   Fri = Friday,
                 Saturday = Friday  + 2,     Sat = Saturday,
                 Sunday    = Saturday + 2,   Sun = Sunday
               };
```

Now variables of type Day can have values from Monday to Sunday and from Mon to Sun, and the matching pairs of enumerators correspond to the integer values 0, 2, 4, 6, 8, 10, and 12. Values for enumerators must be *compile-time constants*, that is, constant expressions that the compiler can evaluate. Such expressions include literals, enumerators that have been defined previously, and variables that you've specified as const. You can't use non-const variables, even if you've initialized them using a literal.

The enumerators can be an integer type that you choose, rather than the default type int. You can also assign explicit values to all the enumerators. For example, you could define this enumeration:

```
enum class Punctuation : char {Comma = ',', Exclamation = '!', Question='?'};
```

The type specification for the enumerators goes after the enumeration type name and is separated from it by a colon. You can specify any integral data type for the enumerators. The possible values for variables of type Punctuation are defined as char literals and will correspond to the code values of the symbols. Thus, the values of the enumerators are 44, 33, and 63, respectively, in decimal, which also demonstrates (again) that the values don't have to be in ascending sequence.

Here's an example that demonstrates some of the things you can do with enumerations:

```
// Ex3_02.cpp
// Operations with enumerations
#include <iostream>
#include <iomanip>

int main()
{
  enum class Day { Monday, Tuesday, Wednesday, Thursday, Friday, Saturday, Sunday };
  Day yesterday{ Day::Monday }, today{ Day::Tuesday }, tomorrow{ Day::Wednesday };
  const Day poets_day{ Day::Friday };

  enum class Punctuation : char { Comma = ',', Exclamation = '!', Question = '?' };
  Punctuation ch{ Punctuation::Comma };

  std::cout << "yesterday's value is " << static_cast<int>(yesterday)
    << static_cast<char>(ch) << " but poets_day's is " << static_cast<int>(poets_day)
    << static_cast<char>(Punctuation::Exclamation) << std::endl;

  today = Day::Thursday;                    // Assign new ...
  ch = Punctuation::Question;               // ... enumerator values
  tomorrow = poets_day;                     // Copy enumerator value

  std::cout << "Is today's value(" << static_cast<int>(today)
            << ") the same as poets_day(" << static_cast<int>(poets_day)
            << ")' << static_cast<char>(ch) << std::endl;

//    ch = tomorrow;            // Uncomment ...
//    tomorrow = Friday;        // ... any of these ...
//    today = 6;                // ... for an error.
}
```

The output is as follows:

```
yesterday's value is 0, but poets_day's is 4!
Is today's value(3) the same as poets_day(4)?
```

We'll leave you to figure out why. Note the commented statements at the end of main(). They are all illegal operations. You should try them to see the compiler messages that result.

■ **Note**   The enumerations we have just described make obsolete the old syntax for enumerations. These are defined without using the `class` keyword. For example, the Day enumeration could be defined like this:

```
enum Day {Monday, Tuesday, Wednesday, Thursday, Friday, Saturday, Sunday};
```

Your code will be less error prone if you stick to `enum class` enumeration types, though. For one, old-style enumerators convert to values of integral or even floating-point types without a cast, which can easily lead to mistakes. The more strongly typed `enum classes` are always the better choice over old-style `enum` types.

Aliases for Data Types

You've seen how enumerations provide one way to define your own data types. The `using` keyword enables you to specify a *type alias*, which is your own data type *name* that serves as an alternative to an existing type name. Using `using`, you can define the type alias `BigOnes` as being equivalent to the standard type unsigned long long with the following statement:

```
using BigOnes = unsigned long long;     // Defines BigOnes as a type alias
```

It's important you realize this isn't defining a new type. This just defines `BigOnes` as an alternative name for type unsigned long long. You could use it to define a variable mynum with this statement:

```
BigOnes mynum {};                       // Define & initialize as type unsigned long long
```

There's no difference between this definition and using the standard type name. You can still use the standard type name as well as the alias, but it's hard to come up with a reason for using both.

There's an older syntax for defining an alias for a type name as well, which uses the `typedef` keyword. For example, you can define the type alias `BigOnes` like this:

```
typedef unsigned long long BigOnes;     // Defines BigOnes as a type alias
```

Among several other advantages,[1] however, the newer syntax is more intuitive, as it looks and feels like a regular assignment. With the old `typedef` syntax you always had to remember to invert the order of the existing type, unsigned long long, and the new name, BigOnes. Believe us, you would have struggled with this order each time you needed a type alias—we certainly have! Luckily, you'll never have to experience this, as long as you follow this simple guideline:

■ **Tip**   Always use the `using` keyword to define a type alias. In fact, if it weren't for legacy code, we'd be advising you to forget the keyword `typedef` even exists.

[1]The other advantages of the `using` syntax over the `typedef` syntax manifest themselves only when specifying aliases for more advanced types. Using `using`, for instance, it's much easier to specify aliases for function types. You'll see this in Chapter 18. The `using` keyword moreover allows you to specify so-called type *alias templates*, or parameterized type aliases, something that is not possible using the old `typedef` syntax. We'll show you an example of an alias template in Chapter 18 as well.

Because you are just creating a synonym for a type that already exists, this may appear to be a bit superfluous. This isn't the case. A major use for this is to simplify code that involves complex type names. For example, a program might involve a type name such as `std::map<std::shared_ptr<Contact>, std::string>`. You'll discover what the various components of this complex type mean later in this book, but for now it should already be clear that it can make for verbose and obscure code when such long types are repeated often. You can avoid cluttering the code by defining a type alias, like this:

```
using PhoneBook = std::map<std::shared_ptr<Contact>, std::string>;
```

Using PhoneBook in the code instead of the full type specification can make the code more readable. Another use for a type alias is to provide flexibility in the data types used by a program that may need to be run on a variety of computers. Defining a type alias and using it throughout the code allows the actual type to be modified by just changing the definition of the alias.

Still, type aliases, like most things in life, should be used with moderation. Type aliases can surely make your code more compact, yes. But compact code is never the goal. There are plenty of times where spelling out the concrete types makes the code easier to understand. Here's an example:

```
using StrPtr = std::shared_ptr<std::string>;
```

StrPtr, while compact, does not help at all in clarifying your code. On the contrary, such a cryptic and unnecessary alias just obfuscates your code. Some guidelines therefore go as far as forbidding type aliases altogether. We certainly wouldn't go that far; just use common sense when deciding whether an alias either helps or obfuscates, and you'll be fine.

The Lifetime of a Variable

All variables have a finite *lifetime*. They come into existence from the point at which you define them, and at some point they are destroyed—at the latest, when your program ends. How long a particular variable lasts is determined by its *storage duration*. There are four different kinds of storage duration:

- Variables defined within a block that are not defined to be `static` have *automatic storage duration*. They exist from the point at which they are defined until the end of the block, which is the closing curly brace, }. They are referred to as *automatic variables* or *local variables*. Automatic variables are said to have *local scope* or *block scope*. All the variables you have created so far have been automatic variables.

- Variables defined using the `static` keyword have *static storage duration*. They are called *static variables*. Static variables exist from the point at which they are defined and continue in existence until the program ends. You'll learn about static variables in Chapters 8 and 11.

- Variables for which you allocate memory at runtime have *dynamic storage duration*. They exist from the point at which you create them until you release their memory to destroy them. You'll learn how to create variables dynamically in Chapter 5.

- Variables declared with the `thread_local` keyword have *thread storage duration*. Thread local variables are an advanced topic, though, so we won't be covering them in this book.

Another property that variables have is *scope*. The scope of a variable is the part of a program in which the variable name is valid. Within a variable's scope, you can refer to it, set its value, or use it in an expression. Outside of its scope, you can't refer to its name. Any attempt to do so will result in a compiler error message. Note that a variable may still exist outside of its scope, even though you can't refer to it. You'll see examples of this situation later, when you learn about variables with static and dynamic storage duration.

▓ **Note**   Remember that the *lifetime* and *scope* of a variable are different things. Lifetime is the period of execution time over which a variable survives. Scope is the region of program code over which the variable name can be used. It's important not to get these two ideas confused.

Global Variables

You have great flexibility in where you define variables. The most important consideration is what scope the variables need to have. You should generally place a definition as close as possible to where the variable is first used. This makes your code easier for another programmer to understand. In this section, we'll introduce a first example where this is not the case: so-called global variables.

You can define variables outside all of the functions in a program. Variables defined outside of all blocks and classes are also called *globals* and have *global scope* (which is also called *global namespace scope*). This means they're accessible in all the functions in the source file following the point at which they're defined. If you define them at the beginning of a source file, they'll be accessible throughout the file. In Chapter 10, we'll show how to declare variables that can be used in multiple files.

Global variables have *static storage duration* by default, so they exist from the start of the program until execution of the program ends. Initialization of global variables takes place before the execution of main() begins, so they're always ready to be used within any code that's within the variable's scope. If you don't initialize a global variable, it will be zero-initialized by default. This is unlike automatic variables, which contain garbage values when uninitialized.

Figure 3-3 shows the contents of a source file, Example.cpp, and illustrates the extent of the scope of each variable in the file.

Program File Example.cpp

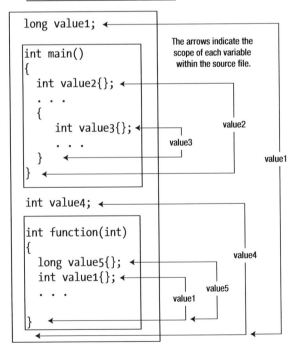

Figure 3-3. *Variable scope*

The variable value1 at the beginning of the file is defined at global scope, as is value4, which appears after the definition of main(). They will be initialized with zero by default. Remember, only global variables have default initial values, not automatic variables. The lifetime of global variables is from the beginning of program execution to when the program ends. Global variables have a scope that extends from the point at which they're defined to the end of the file. Even though value4 exists when execution starts, it can't be referred to in main() because main() isn't within its scope. For main() to use value4, you would need to move the definition of value4 to the beginning of the file.

The local variable called value1 in function() will hide the global variable of the same name. If you use the name value1 in the function, you are accessing the local automatic variable of that name. To access the global value1, you must qualify it with the scope resolution operator, ::. Here's how you could output the values of the local and global variables that have the name value1:

```
std::cout << "Global value1 = " << ::value1 << std::endl;
std::cout << "Local value1 = " << value1 << std::endl;
```

Because global variables continue to exist for as long as the program is running, you might be wondering, "Why not make all variables global and avoid messing around with local variables that disappear?" This sounds attractive at first, but there are serious disadvantages that completely outweigh any advantages. Real programs are composed of a huge number of statements, a significant number of functions, and a great many variables. Declaring all at global scope greatly magnifies the possibility of accidental, erroneous modification of a variable. It makes it hard to trace which part of the code is responsible for changes to global variables. It also makes the job of naming them sensibly quite intractable. Global variables, finally, occupy memory for the duration of program execution, so the program will require more memory than if you used local variables where the memory is reused.

By keeping variables local to a function or a block, you can be sure they have almost complete protection from external effects. They'll only exist and occupy memory from the point at which they're defined to the end of the enclosing block, and the whole development process becomes much easier to manage.

■ **Tip**   Common coding and design guidelines dictate that global variables are typically to be avoided, and with good reason. Global constants are a noble exception to this rule. That is, global variables that are declared with the const keyword. It is recommended to define all your constants only once, and global variables are perfectly suited for that.

Here's an example that shows aspects of global and automatic variables:

```
// Ex3_03.cpp
// Demonstrating scope, lifetime, and global variables
#include <iostream>
long count1{999L};          // Global count1
double count2{3.14};        // Global count2
int count3;                 // Global count3 - default initialization

int main()
{ /* Function scope starts here */
  int count1{10};           // Hides global count1
  int count3{50};           // Hides global count3
  std::cout << "Value of outer count1 = " << count1 << std::endl;
  std::cout << "Value of global count1 = " << ::count1 << std::endl;
  std::cout << "Value of global count2 = " << count2 << std::endl;
```

```
{ /* New block scope starts here... */
  int count1{20};        // This is a new variable that hides the outer count1
  int count2{30};        // This hides global count2
  std::cout << "\nValue of inner count1 = "<< count1 << std::endl;
  std::cout << "Value of global count1 = " << ::count1 << std::endl;
  std::cout << "Value of inner count2 = "  << count2 << std::endl;
  std::cout << "Value of global count2 = " << ::count2 << std::endl;

  count1 = ::count1 + 3;   // This sets inner count1 to global count1+3
  ++::count1;              // This changes global count1
  std::cout << "\nValue of inner count1 = " << count1 << std::endl;
  std::cout << "Value of global count1 = "  << ::count1 << std::endl;
  count3 += count2;        // Increments outer count3 by inner count2;

  int count4 {};
} /* ...and ends here. */

// std::cout << count4 << std::endl;    // count4 does not exist in this scope!

  std::cout << "\nValue of outer count1 = "<< count1 << std::endl
          << "Value of outer count3 = "  << count3 << std::endl;
  std::cout << "Value of global count3 = " << ::count3 << std::endl;

  std::cout << "Value of global count2 = " << count2 << std::endl;
} /* Function scope ends here */
```

The output from this example is as follows:

```
Value of outer count1 = 10
Value of global count1 = 999
Value of global count2 = 3.14

Value of inner count1 = 20
Value of global count1 = 999
Value of inner count2 = 30
Value of global count2 = 3.14

Value of inner count1 = 1002
Value of global count1 = 1000

Value of outer count1 = 10
Value of outer count3 = 80
Value of global count3 = 0
Value of global count2 = 3.14
```

We've duplicated names in this example to illustrate what happens—it's of course not a good approach to programming at all. Doing this kind of thing in a real program is confusing and totally unnecessary, and it results in code that is error prone.

There are three variables defined at global scope, count1, count2, and count3. These exist as long as the program continues to execute, but the names will be masked by local variables with the same name. The first two statements in main() define two integer variables, count1 and count3, with initial values of 10 and 50, respectively. Both variables exist from this point until the closing brace at the end of main(). The scope of these variables also extends to the closing brace at the end of main(). Because the local count1 hides the global count1, you must use the scope resolution operator to access the global count1 in the output statement in the first group of output lines. Global count2 is accessible just by using its name.

The second opening brace starts a new block. count1 and count2 are defined within this block with values 20 and 30, respectively. count1 here is different from count1 in the outer block, which still exists, but its name is masked by the second count1 and is not accessible here; global count1 is also masked but is accessible using the scope resolution operator. The global count2 is masked by the local variable with that name. Using the name count1 following the definition in the inner block refers to count1 defined in that block.

The first line of the second block of output is the value of the count1 defined in the inner scope—that is, inside the inner braces. If it was the outer count1, the value would be 10. The next line of output corresponds to the global count1. The following line of output contains the value of local count2 because you are using just its name. The last line in this block outputs global count2 by using the :: operator.

The statement assigning a new value to count1 applies to the variable in the inner scope because the outer count1 is hidden. The new value is the global count1 value plus 3. The next statement increments the global count1, and the following two output statements confirm this. The count3 that was defined in the outer scope is incremented in the inner block without any problem because it is not hidden by a variable with the same name. This shows that variables defined in an outer scope are still accessible in an inner scope as long as there is no variable with the same name defined in the inner scope.

After the brace ending the inner scope, count1 and count2 that are defined in the inner scope cease to exist. Their lifetime has ended. Local count1 and count3 still exist in the outer scope, and their values are displayed in the first two lines in the last group of output. This demonstrates that count3 was indeed incremented in the inner scope. The last lines of output correspond to the global count3 and count2 values.

Summary

These are the essentials of what you've learned in this chapter:

- You don't need to memorize the operator precedence and associativity for all operators, but you need to be conscious of it when writing code. Always use parentheses if you are unsure about precedence.

- The type-safe enumerations type are useful for representing fixed sets of values, especially those that have names, such as days of the week or suits in a pack of playing cards.

- The bitwise operators are necessary when you are working with flags—single bits that signify a state. These arise surprisingly often—when dealing with file input and output, for example. The bitwise operators are also essential when you are working with values packed into a single variable. One extremely common example thereof is RGB-like encodings, where three to four components of a given color are packed into one 32-bit integer value.

- The using keyword allows you to define aliases for other types. In legacy code, you might still encounter typedef being used for the same purpose.

- By default, a variable defined within a block is automatic, which means that it exists only from the point at which it is defined to the end of the block in which its definition appears, as indicated by the closing brace of the block that encloses its definition.

- Variables can be defined outside of all the blocks in a program, in which case they have global namespace scope and static storage duration by default. Variables with global scope are accessible from anywhere within the program file that contains them, following the point at which they're defined, except where a local variable exists with the same name as the global variable. Even then, they can still be reached by using the scope resolution operator (::).

EXERCISES

The following exercises enable you to try what you've learned in this chapter. If you get stuck, look back over the chapter for help. If you're still stuck, you can download the solutions from the Apress website (www.apress.com/source-code/), but that really should be a last resort.

Exercise 3-1. Create a program that prompts for input of an integer and store it as an int. Invert all the bits in the value and store the result. Output the original value, the value with the bits inverted, and the inverted value plus 1, each in hexadecimal representation and on one line. On the next line, output the same numbers in decimal representation. These two lines should be formatted such that they look like a table, where the values in the same column are right aligned in a suitable field width. All hexadecimal values should have leading zeros so eight hexadecimal digits always appear.

Note: Flipping all bits and adding one—ring any bells? Can you perhaps already deduce what the output will be before you run the program?

Exercise 3-2. Write a program to calculate how many square boxes can be contained in a single layer on a rectangular shelf, with no overhang. The dimensions of the shelf in feet and the dimension of a side of the box in inches are read from the keyboard. Use variables of type double for the length and depth of the shelf and type int for the length of the side of a box. Define and initialize an integer constant to convert from feet to inches (1 foot equals 12 inches). Calculate the number of boxes that the shelf can hold in a single layer of type long and output the result.

Exercise 3-3. Without running it, can you work out what the following code snippet will produce as output?

```
auto k {430u};
auto j {(k >> 4) & ~(~0u << 3)};
std::cout << j << std::endl;
```

Exercise 3-4. Write a program to read four characters from the keyboard and pack them into a single integer variable. Display the value of this variable as hexadecimal. Unpack the four bytes of the variable and output them in reverse order, with the low-order byte first.

Exercise 3-5. Write a program that defines an enumeration of type `Color` where the enumerators are Red, Green, Yellow, Purple, Blue, Black, and White. Define the type for enumerators as an unsigned integer type and arrange for the integer value of each enumerator to be the RGB combination for the color it represents (you can easily find the hexadecimal RGB encoding of any color online). Create variables of type `Color` initialized with enumerators for yellow, purple, and green. Access the enumerator value and extract and output the RGB components as separate values.

Exercise 3-6. We'll conclude with one more exercise for puzzle fans (and *exclusively* so). Write a program that prompts for two integer values to be entered and store them in integer variables, a and b, say. Swap the values of a and b *without* using a third variable. Output the values of a and b.

Hint: This is a particularly tough nut to crack. To solve this puzzle, you exclusively need one single compound assignment operator.

CHAPTER 4

■ ■ ■

Making Decisions

Decision-making is fundamental to any kind of computer programming. It's one of the things that differentiates a computer from a calculator. It means altering the sequence of execution depending on the result of a comparison. In this chapter, you'll explore how to make choices and decisions. This will allow you to validate program input and write programs that can adapt their actions depending on the input data. Your programs will be able to handle problems where logic is fundamental to the solution.

In this chapter, you'll learn:

- How to compare data values

- How to alter the sequence of program execution based on the result of a comparison

- What logical operators and expressions are and how you apply them

- How to deal with multiple-choice situations

Comparing Data Values

To make decisions, you need a mechanism for comparing things, and there are several kinds of comparisons. For instance, a decision such as "If the traffic signal is red, stop the car" involves a comparison for equality. You compare the color of the signal with a reference color, red, and if they are equal, you stop the car. On the other hand, a decision such as "If the speed of the car exceeds the limit, slow down" involves a different relationship. Here you check whether the speed of the car is greater than the current speed limit. Both of these comparisons are similar in that they result in one of two values: they are either *true* or *false*. This is precisely how comparisons work in C++.

You can compare data values using some new operators called *relational operators*. Table 4-1 lists the six operators for comparing two values.

Table 4-1. *Relational Operators*

Operator	Meaning
<	Less than
<=	Less than or equal to
>	Greater than
>=	Greater than or equal to
==	Equal to
!=	Not equal to

© Ivor Horton and Peter Van Weert 2018
I. Horton and P. Van Weert, *Beginning C++17*, https://doi.org/10.1007/978-1-4842-3366-5_4

■ **Caution**   The equal-to operator, ==, has two successive equal signs. It's a common mistake to use one equal sign instead of two to compare for equality. This will not necessarily result in a warning message from the compiler because the expression may be valid but just not what you intended, so you need to take particular care to avoid this error.

Each of these operators compares two values and results in a value of type bool. There are only two possible bool values, true and false. true and false are keywords and are literals of type bool. They are sometimes called *Boolean literals* (after George Boole, the father of Boolean algebra).

You create variables of type bool just like other fundamental types. Here's an example:

```
bool isValid {true};       // Define and initialize a logical variable
```

This defines the variable isValid as type bool with an initial value of true. If you initialize a bool variable using empty braces, {}, its initial value is false:

```
bool correct {};          // Define and initialize a logical variable to false
```

While explicitly using {false} here could arguably improve the readability of your code, it is good to remember that where numeric variables are initialized to zero, for instance, when using {}, Boolean variables will be initialized to false.

Applying the Comparison Operators

You can see how comparisons work by looking at a few examples. Suppose you have integer variables i and j, with values 10 and –5, respectively. Consider the following expressions:

```
i > j        i != j        j > -8        i <= j + 15
```

All of these expressions evaluate to true. Note that in the last expression, the addition, j + 15, executes first because + has a higher precedence than <=.

You could store the result of any of these expressions in a variable of type bool. Here's an example:

```
isValid = i > j;
```

If i is greater than j, true is stored in isValid; otherwise, false is stored. You can compare values stored in variables of character types, too. Assume that you define the following variables:

```
char first {'A'};
char last {'Z'};
```

You can write comparisons using these variables:

```
first < last        'E' <= first        first != last
```

Here you are comparing code values (recall from Chapter 1 that characters are mapped to integral codes using standard encoding schemes such as ASCII and Unicode). The first expression checks whether the value of first, which is 'A', is less than the value of last, which is 'Z'. This is always true. The result of the second expression is false because the code value for 'E' is greater than the value of first. The last expression is true, because 'A' is definitely not equal to 'Z'.

You can output bool values just as easily as any other type. Here's an example that shows how they look by default:

```
// Ex4_01.cpp
// Comparing data values
#include <iostream>

int main()
{
  char first {};                    // Stores the first character
  char second {};                   // Stores the second character

  std::cout << "Enter a character: ";
  std::cin >> first;

  std::cout << "Enter a second character: ";
  std::cin >> second;

  std::cout << "The value of the expression " << first << '<' << second
            << " is: " << (first < second) << std::endl;
  std::cout << "The value of the expression " << first << "==" << second
            << " is: " << (first == second) << std::endl;
}
```

Here's an example of output from this program:

```
Enter a character: ?
Enter a second character: H
The value of the expression ?<H is: 1
The value of the expression ?==H is: 0
```

The prompting for input and reading of characters from the keyboard is standard stuff that you have seen before. Note that the parentheses around the comparison expressions in the output statement *are* necessary here. If you omit them, the compiler outputs an error message (to understand why you should review the operator precedence rules from the beginning of the previous chapter). The expressions compare the first and second characters that the user entered. From the output you can see that the value true is displayed as 1, and the value false is displayed as 0. These are the default representations for true and false. You can make bool values output as true and false using the std::boolalpha manipulator. Just add this statement somewhere before the last four lines of the main() function:

```
std::cout << std::boolalpha;
```

If you compile and run the example again, you get bool values displayed as true or false. To return output of bool values to the default setting, insert the std::noboolalpha manipulator into the stream.

Comparing Floating-Point Values

Of course, you can also compare floating-point values. Let's consider some slightly more complicated numerical comparisons. First, define variables with the following statements:

```
int i {-10};
int j {20};
double x {1.5};
double y {-0.25E-10};
```

Now consider the following logical expressions:

```
-1 < y          j < (10 - i)          2.0*x >= (3 + y)
```

The comparison operators are all of lower precedence than the arithmetic operators, so none of the parentheses are strictly necessary, but they do help make the expressions clearer. The first comparison evaluates to true because y has a very small negative value (−0.000000000025), which is greater than −1. The second comparison results in false because the expression 10 - i has the value 20, which is the same as j. The third expression is true because 3 + y is slightly less than 3.

You can use relational operators to compare values of any of the fundamental types. When you learn about classes, you'll see how you can arrange for the comparison operators to work with types that you define, too. All you need now is a way to use the result of a comparison to modify the behavior of a program. Let's look into that immediately.

The if Statement

The basic if statement enables you to choose to execute a single statement, or a block of statements, when a given condition is true. Figure 4-1 illustrates how this works.

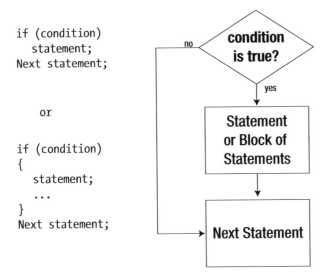

```
if (condition)
    statement;
Next statement;


    or


if (condition)
{
    statement;
    ...
}
Next statement;
```

The statement or block of statements that follows
the **if** is only executed if **condition** is **true**.

Figure 4-1. *Logic of the simple* if *statement*

Here is an example of an if statement that tests the value of a char variable, letter:

```
if (letter == 'A')
  std::cout << "The first capital, alphabetically speaking.\n"; // Only if letter equals 'A'

std::cout << "This statement always executes.\n";
```

If letter has the value 'A', the condition is true, and these statements produce the following output:

```
The first capital, alphabetically speaking.
This statement always executes.
```

If the value of letter is not equal to 'A', only the second line appears in the output. You put the condition to be tested between parentheses immediately following the keyword, if. We adopt the convention to add a space between the if and the parentheses (to differentiate visually from function calls), but this is not required. As usual, the compiler will ignore all whitespace, so the following are equally valid ways to write the test:

```
if(letter == 'A')       if( letter == 'A' )
```

The statement following the if is indented to indicate that it executes only as a result of the condition being true. The indentation is not necessary for the program to compile, but it does help you recognize the relationship between the if condition and the statement that depends on it. Sometimes, you will see simple if statements written on a single line, like this:

```
if (letter == 'A')  std::cout << "The first capital, alphabetically speaking\n.";
```

▓ **Caution**   Never put a semicolon (;) directly after the condition of the if statement. Unfortunately, doing so compiles without errors (at best, the compiler will issue a warning), but it does not mean at all what was intended:

```
if (letter == 'A');
  std::cout << "The first capital, alphabetically speaking.\n";
```

The semicolon on the first line results in a so-called empty statement or null statement. Superfluous semicolons, and therefore empty statements, are allowed to appear pretty much anywhere within a series of statements. The following, for instance, is legal C++:

```
int i = 0;; i += 5;; ; std::cout << i << std::endl  ;;
```

Usually, such empty statements have no effect at all. But when added immediately after the condition of an if, it binds the statement that is executed if the condition evaluates to true. In other words, writing a semicolon after the if (letter == 'A') test has the same effect as writing this:

```
if (letter == 'A') { /* Do nothing */ }
std::cout << "The first capital, alphabetically speaking.\n";   // Always executes!
```

So this states, if `letter` equals `'A'`, then do nothing. But what is worse is that the second line is always executed, unconditionally, even if `letter` is different from `'A'`—precisely what the `if` statement intended to prevent. Therefore, take care to never put a semicolon directly after a conditional test because it essentially nullifies the test!

You could extend the code fragment to change the value of `letter` if it contains the value `'A'`.

```
if (letter == 'A')
{
  std::cout << "The first capital, alphabetically speaking.\n";
  letter = 'a';
}

std::cout << "This statement always executes.\n";
```

All the statements in the block will be executed when the `if` condition is true. Without the braces, only the first statement would be the subject of the `if`, and the statement assigning the value `'a'` to `letter` would always be executed. Of course, each of the statements in the block is terminated by a semicolon. No semicolon is necessary, though, after the closing brace of the block. You can have as many statements as you like within the block; you can even have nested blocks. If and when `letter` has the value `'A'`, both statements within the block will be executed, so its value will be changed to `'a'` after the same message as before is displayed. Neither of these statements executes if the condition is `false`. The statement following the block always executes.

If you cast `true` to an integer type, the result will be 1; casting `false` to an integer results in 0. Conversely, you can also convert numerical values to type `bool`. Zero converts to `false`, and any nonzero value converts to `true`. When you have a numerical value where a `bool` value is expected, the compiler will insert an implicit conversion to convert the numerical value to type `bool`. This is useful in decision-making code.

Let's try an `if` statement for real. This program will range check the value of an integer entered from the keyboard:

```
// Ex4_02.cpp
// Using an if statement
#include <iostream>

int main()
{
  std::cout << "Enter an integer between 50 and 100: ";

  int value {};
  std::cin >> value;

  if (value)
    std::cout << "You have entered a value that is different from zero." << std::endl;

  if (value < 50)
    std::cout << "The value is invalid - it is less than 50." << std::endl;
```

```
    if (value > 100)
      std::cout << "The value is invalid - it is greater than 100." << std::endl;

    std::cout << "You entered " << value << std::endl;
}
```

The output depends on the value that you enter. For a value between 50 and 100, the output will be something like the following:

```
Enter an integer between 50 and 100: 77
You have entered a value that is different from zero.
You entered 77
```

Outside the range 50 to 100, a message indicating that the value is invalid will precede the output showing the value. If it is less than 50, for instance, the output will be as follows:

```
Enter an integer between 50 and 100: 27
You have entered a value that is different from zero.
The value is invalid - it is less than 50.
You entered 27
```

After prompting for and reading a value, the first if statement checks whether the value entered is different from zero:

```
if (value)
  std::cout << "You have entered a value that is different from zero." << std::endl;
```

Recall that any number is converted to true, except 0 (zero)—which is converted to false. So, value always converts to true, except if the number you entered is zero. You will often find such a test written like this, but if you prefer, you can easily make the test for zero more explicit as follows:

```
if (value != 0)
  std::cout << "You have entered a value that is different from zero." << std::endl;
```

The second if statement then checks if your input is less than 50:

```
if (value < 50)
  std::cout << "The value is invalid - it is less than 50."  << std::endl;
```

The output statement is executed only when the if condition is true, which is when value is less than 50. The next if statement checks the upper limit in essentially the same way and outputs a message when it is exceeded. Finally, the last output statement is always executed, and this outputs the value. Of course, checking for the upper limit being exceeded when the value is below the lower limit is superfluous. You could arrange for the program to end immediately if the value entered is below the lower limit, like this:

```
if (value < 50)
{
  std::cout << "The value is invalid - it is less than 50."  << std::endl;
  return 0;                            // Ends the program
}
```

You could do the same with the if statement that checks the upper limit. You can have as many return statements in a function as you need.

Of course, if you conditionally end the program like that, the code after both if statements is no longer executed anymore. That is, if the user enters an invalid number and one of these return statements is executed, then the last line of the program will no longer be reached. To refresh your memory, this line was as follows:

```
std::cout << "You entered " << value << std::endl;
```

Later this chapter, we will see other means to avoid the upper limit test if value was already found to be below the lower limit—means that do not involve ending the program.

Nested if Statements

The statement that executes when the condition in an if statement is true can itself be an if statement. This arrangement is called a nested if. The condition of the inner if is tested only if the condition for the outer if is true. An if that is nested inside another can also contain a nested if. You can nest ifs to whatever depth you require. We'll demonstrate the nested if with an example that tests whether a character entered is alphabetic:

```
// Ex4_03.cpp
// Using a nested if
#include <iostream>

int main()
{
  char letter {};              // Store input here
  std::cout << "Enter a letter: ";    // Prompt for the input
  std::cin >> letter;

  if (letter >= 'A')
  {                            // letter is 'A' or larger
    if (letter <= 'Z')
    {                          // letter is 'Z' or smaller
      std::cout << "You entered an uppercase letter." << std::endl;
      return 0;
    }
  }

  if (letter >= 'a')           // Test for 'a' or larger
    if (letter <= 'z')
    {                          // letter is >= 'a' and <= 'z'
      std::cout << "You entered a lowercase letter." << std::endl;
      return 0;
    }
  std::cout << "You did not enter a letter." << std::endl;
}
```

Here's some typical output:

```
Enter a letter: H
You entered an uppercase letter.
```

After creating the char variable letter with initial value zero, the program prompts you to enter a letter. The if statement that follows checks whether the character entered is 'A' or larger. If letter is greater than or equal to 'A', the nested if that checks for the input being 'Z' or less executes. If it *is* 'Z' or less, you conclude that it is an uppercase letter and display a message. You are done at this point, so you execute a return statement to end the program.

The next if, using essentially the same mechanism as the first, checks whether the character entered is lowercase, displays a message, and returns. You probably noticed that the test for a lowercase character contains only one pair of braces, whereas the uppercase test has two. The code block between the braces belongs to the inner if here. In fact, both sets of statements work as they should—remember that if (condition) {...} is effectively a single statement and does not need to be enclosed within more braces. However, the extra braces do make the code clearer, so it's a good idea to use them.

The output statement following the last if block executes only when the character entered is not a letter, and it displays a message to that effect. You can see that the relationship between the nested ifs and the output statement is much easier to follow because of the indentation. Indentation is generally used to provide visual cues to the logic of a program.

This program illustrates how a nested if works, but it is not a good way to test for characters. Using the Standard Library, you can write the program so that it works independently of the character coding. We'll explore how that works in the next subsection.

Character Classification and Conversion

The nested ifs of Ex4_03 rely on these three built-in assumptions about the codes that are used to represent alphabetic characters:

- The letters *A* to *Z* are represented by a set of codes where the code for 'A' is the minimum and the code for 'Z' is the maximum.

- The codes for the uppercase letters are contiguous, so no nonalphabetic characters lie between the codes for 'A' and 'Z'.

- All uppercase letters in the alphabet fall within the range *A* to *Z*.

While the first two assumptions will hold for any character encoding used in practice today, the third is definitely not true for many languages. The Greek alphabet, for instance, knows uppercase letters such as Δ, Θ, and Π; the Russian one contains Ж, Ф, and Щ; and even Latin-based languages such as French often use capital letters such as É and Ç whose encodings won't lie at all between 'A' and 'Z'. It is therefore not a good idea to build these kinds of assumptions into your code because it limits the portability of your program. Never assume that your program will be used only by fellow Anglophones!

To avoid making such assumptions in your code, the C and C++ Standard Libraries offer the concept of *locales*. A locale is a set of parameters that defines the user's language and regional preferences, including the national or cultural character set and the formatting rules for currency and dates. A complete coverage of this topic is far beyond the scope of this book, though. We only cover the character classification functions provided by the cctype header, listed in Table 4-2.

Table 4-2 lists the functions that the cctype header provides to classify characters. In each case, you pass the function a variable or literal that is the character to be tested.

Table 4-2. *Functions for Classifying Characters Provided by the cctype Header*

Function	Operation
isupper(c)	Tests whether c is an uppercase letter, by default 'A' to 'Z'.
islower(c)	Tests whether c is a lowercase letter, by default 'a' to 'z'.
isalpha(c)	Tests whether c is an uppercase or lowercase letter (or any alphabetic character that is neither uppercase nor lowercase, should the locale's alphabet contain such characters).
isdigit(c)	Tests whether c is a digit, '0' to '9'.
isxdigit(c)	Tests whether c is a hexadecimal digit, either '0' to '9', 'a' to 'f', or 'A' to 'F'.
isalnum(c)	Tests whether c is an alphanumeric character; same as isalpha(c) || isdigit(c).
isspace(c)	Tests whether c is whitespace, by default a space (' '), newline ('\n'), carriage return ('\r'), form feed ('\f'), or horizontal ('\t') or vertical tab ('\v').
isblank(c)	Tests whether c is a space character used to separate words within a line of text. By default either a space (' ') or a horizontal tab ('\t').
ispunct(c)	Tests whether c is a punctuation character. By default, this will be either a space or one of the following: _ { } [ ] # ( ) < > % : ; . ? * + - / ^ & | ~ ! = , \ " '
isprint(c)	Tests whether c is a printable character, which includes uppercase or lowercase letters, digits, punctuation characters, and spaces.
iscntrl(c)	Tests whether c is a control character, which is the opposite of a printable character.
isgraph(c)	Tests whether c has a graphical representation, which is true for any printable character other than a space.

Each of these functions returns a value of type int. The value will be nonzero (true) if the character is of the type being tested for, and 0 (false) if it isn't. You may be wondering why these functions don't return a bool value, which would make much more sense. The reason they don't return a bool value is that they originate from the C Standard Library and predate type bool in C++.

You could use cctype's character classification functions to implement Ex4_03 without any hard-coded assumptions about either the character set or its encoding. The character codes in different environments are always taken care of by the Standard Library functions. An additional advantage is that these functions also make the code simpler and easier to read:

```
if (std::isupper(letter))
{
  std::cout << "You entered an uppercase letter." << std::endl;
  return 0;
}

if (std::islower(letter))
{
  std::cout << "You entered a lowercase letter." << std::endl;
  return 0;
}
```

As cctype is part of the C++ Standard Library, it defines all its functions inside the std namespace. You therefore normally should prefix their names with std::. You'll find the adjusted program under the name Ex4_03A.cpp.

To conclude, the cctype header also provides the two functions shown in Table 4-3 for converting between uppercase and lowercase characters. The result will be returned as type int, so you need to explicitly cast it if you want to store it as type char, for instance.

Table 4-3. *Functions for Converting Characters Provided by the cctype Header*

Function	Operation
tolower(c)	If c is uppercase, the lowercase equivalent is returned; otherwise, c is returned.
toupper(c)	If c is lowercase, the uppercase equivalent is returned; otherwise, c is returned.

■ **Note** All standard character classification and conversion functions except for isdigit() and isxdigit() operate according to the rules of the current locale. All examples given in Table 4-2 are for the default, so-called "C" locale, which is a set of preferences similar to those used by English-speaking Americans. The C++ Standard Library offers an extensive library for working with other locales and character sets. You can use these to develop applications that work correctly irrespective of the user's language and regional conventions. This topic is a bit too advanced for this book, though. Consult a Standard Library reference for more details.

The if-else Statement

The if statement that you have been using executes a statement or block of statements if the condition specified is true. Program execution then continues with the next statement in sequence. Of course, you may want to execute one block of statements when the condition is true and another set when the condition is false. An extension of the if statement called an if-else statement allows this.

The if-else combination provides a choice between two options. Figure 4-2 shows its general logic.

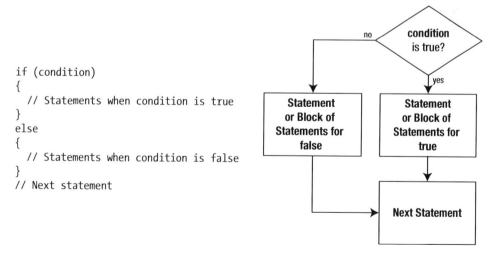

One of the two blocks in an if-else statement is always executed.

Figure 4-2. *The if-else statement logic*

99

The flowchart in Figure 4-2 shows the sequence in which statements execute, depending on whether the if condition is true or false. You can always use a block of statements wherever you can put a single statement. This allows any number of statements to be executed for each option in an if-else statement.

You could write an if-else statement that would report whether the character stored in the char variable letter was alphanumeric:

```
if (std::isalnum(letter))
{
  std::cout << "It is a letter or a digit." << std::endl;
}
else
{
  std::cout << "It is neither a letter nor a digit." << std::endl;
}
```

This uses the isalnum() function from the cctype header you saw earlier. If letter contains a letter or a digit, isalnum() returns a positive integer. This will be implicitly converted to a bool value, which will be true, so the first message is displayed. If letter contains other than a letter or a digit, isalnum() returns 0, which converts to false so the output statement after else executes. The braces are again not mandatory here because they contain single statements, but it's clearer if you put them in. The indentation in the blocks is a visible indicator of the relationship between various statements. You can clearly see which statement is executed for a true result and which is executed for false. You should always indent the statements in your programs to show their logical structure.

Here's an example of using if-else with a numerical value:

```
// Ex4_04.cpp
// Using the if-else statement
#include <iostream>

int main()
{
  long number {};                         // Stores input
  std::cout << "Enter an integer less than 2 billion: ";
  std::cin >> number;

  if (number % 2) // Test remainder after division by 2
  { // Here if remainder is 1
    std::cout << "Your number is odd." << std::endl;
  }
  else
  { // Here if remainder is 0
    std::cout << "Your number is even." << std::endl;
  }
}
```

Here's an example of output from this program:

```
Enter an integer less than 2 billion: 123456
Your number is even.
```

After reading the input into number, the program tests this value in the if condition. This is an expression that produces the remainder that results from dividing number by 2. The remainder will be 1 if number is odd, or 0 if it even, and these values convert to true and false, respectively. Thus, if the remainder is 1, the if condition is true, and the statement in the block immediately following the if executes. If the remainder is 0, the if condition is false, so the statement in the block following the else keyword executes.

You could specify the if condition as number % 2 == 0, in which case the sequence of blocks would need to be reversed because this expression evaluates to true when number is even.

Nested if-else Statements

You have already seen that you can nest if statements within if statements. You have no doubt anticipated that you can also nest if-else statements within ifs, ifs within if-else statements, and if-else statements within other if-else statements. This provides you with plenty of versatility (and considerable room for confusion), so let's look at a few examples. Taking the first case, an example of an if-else nested within an if might look like the following:

```
if (coffee == 'y')
  if (donuts == 'y')
    std::cout << "We have coffee and donuts." << std::endl;
  else
    std::cout << "We have coffee, but not donuts." << std::endl;
```

This would be better written with braces, but it's easier to make the point we want to make without. coffee and donuts are variables of type char that can have the value 'y' or 'n'. The test for donuts executes only if the result of the test for coffee is true, so the messages reflect the correct situation in each case. The else belongs to the if that tests for donuts. However, it is easy to get this confused.

If you write much the same thing but with incorrect indentation, you can be trapped into the wrong conclusion about what happens here:

```
if (coffee == 'y')
  if (donuts == 'y')
    std::cout << "We have coffee and donuts." << std::endl;
else                                            // This is indented incorrectly...
  std::cout << "We have no coffee..." << std::endl;  // ...Wrong!
```

The indentation now misleadingly suggests that this is an if nested within an if-else, which is not the case. The first message is correct, but the output as a consequence of the else executing is quite wrong. This statement executes only if the test for coffee is true, because the else belongs to the test for donuts, not the test for coffee. This mistake is easy to see here, but with larger and more complicated if structures, you need to keep in mind the following rule about which if owns which else:

▓ **Caution**   An else always belongs to the nearest preceding if that's not already spoken for by another else. The potential for confusion here is known as the *dangling else problem*.

Braces will always make the situation clearer:

```cpp
if (coffee == 'y')
{
  if (donuts == 'y')
  {
    std::cout << "We have coffee and donuts." << std::endl;
  }
  else
  {
    std::cout << "We have coffee, but not donuts." << std::endl;
  }
}
```

Now it's absolutely clear. The else definitely belongs to the if that is checking for donuts.

Understanding Nested ifs

Now that you know the rules, understanding an if nested within an if-else should be easy:

```cpp
if (coffee == 'y')
{
  if (donuts == 'y')
    std::cout << "We have coffee and donuts." << std::endl;
}
else if (tea == 'y')
{
  std::cout << "We have no coffee, but we have tea." << std::endl;
}
```

Notice the formatting of the code here. When an else block is another if, writing else if on one line is an accepted convention. The braces enclosing the test for donuts are essential. Without them the else would belong to the if that's looking out for donuts. In this kind of situation, it is easy to forget to include the braces and thus create an error that may be hard to find. A program with this kind of error compiles without a problem, as the code is correct. It may even produce the right results some of the time. If you removed the braces in this example, you'd get the right results only as long as coffee and donuts were both 'y' so that the check for tea wouldn't execute.

Nesting if-else statements in other if-else statements can get very messy, even with just one level of nesting. Let's beat the coffee and donuts analysis to death by using it again:

```cpp
if (coffee == 'y')
  if (donuts == 'y')
    std::cout << "We have coffee and donuts." << std::endl;
  else
    std::cout << "We have coffee, but not donuts." << std::endl;
else if (tea == 'y')
  std::cout << "We have no coffee, but we have tea, and maybe donuts..." << std::endl;
else
  std::cout << "No tea or coffee, but maybe donuts..." << std::endl;
```

The logic here doesn't look quite so obvious, even with the correct indentation. Braces aren't necessary, as the rule you saw earlier will verify, but it would look much clearer if you included them:

```
if (coffee == 'y')
{
  if (donuts == 'y')
  {
    std::cout << "We have coffee and donuts." << std::endl;
  }
  else
  {
    std::cout << "We have coffee, but not donuts." << std::endl;
  }
}
else
{
  if (tea == 'y')
  {
    std::cout << "We have no coffee, but we have tea, and maybe donuts..." << std::endl;
  }
  else
  {
    std::cout << "No tea or coffee, but maybe donuts..." << std::endl;
  }
}
```

There are much better ways of dealing with this kind of logic. If you put enough nested ifs together, you can almost guarantee a mistake somewhere. The next section will help to simplify things.

Logical Operators

As you have seen, using ifs where you have two or more related conditions can be cumbersome. You have tried your iffy talents on looking for coffee and donuts, but in practice, you may want to check much more complex conditions. For instance, you could be searching a personnel file for someone who is older than 21, younger than 35, is female, has a bachelor's or master's degree, is unmarried, and speaks Hindi or Urdu. Defining a test for this could involve the mother of all ifs.

The *logical operator*s provide a neat and simple solution. Using logical operators, you can combine a series of comparisons into a single expression so that you need just one if, almost regardless of the complexity of the set of conditions. What's more, you won't have trouble determining which one to use because there are just the three shown in Table 4-4.

Table 4-4. *Logical Operators*

Operator	Description
&&	Logical AND
||	Logical OR
!	Logical negation (NOT)

The first two, && and ||, are binary operators that combine two operands of type bool and produce a result of type bool. The third operator, !, is unary, so it applies to a single operand of type bool and produces a bool result. In the following pages we'll explain first how each of these is used; then we'll demonstrate them in an example. Finally, we'll compare these logical operators with the bitwise operators you learned about earlier.

Logical AND

You use the AND operator, &&, where you have two conditions that must both be true for a true result. For example, you want to be rich *and* healthy. Earlier, to determine whether a character was an uppercase letter, the value had to be both greater than or equal to 'A' *and* less than or equal to 'Z'. The && operator *only* produces a true result if both operands are true. If either or both operands are false, then the result is false. Here's how you could test a char variable, letter, for an uppercase letter using the && operator:

```
if (letter >= 'A' && letter <= 'Z')
{
  std::cout << "This is an uppercase letter." << std::endl;
}
```

The output statement executes only if both of the conditions combined by && are true. No parentheses are necessary in the expression because the precedence of the comparison operators is higher than that of &&. As usual, you're free to put parentheses in if you want. You could write the statement as follows:

```
if ((letter >= 'A') && (letter <= 'Z'))
{
  std::cout << "This is an uppercase letter." << std::endl;
}
```

Now there's no doubt that the comparisons will be evaluated first. Still, most experienced programmers probably wouldn't put these extra parentheses here.

Logical OR

The OR operator, ||, applies when you want a true result when either or both of the operands are true. The result is false only when both operands are false.

For example, you might be considered creditworthy enough for a bank loan if your income was at least $100,000 a year or if you had $1,000,000 in cash. This could be tested like this:

```
if (income >= 100'000.00 || capital >= 1'000'000.00)
{
  std::cout << "Of course, how much do you want to borrow?" << std::endl;
}
```

The response emerges when either or both of the conditions are true. (A better response might be "*Why* do you want to borrow?" It's strange how banks will only lend you money when you don't need it.)

Notice also that we've used digit separators to increase the readability of the integer literals: it is far more obvious that 1'000'000.00 equals one million than that 1000000.00 does. Would you even spot the difference between 100000.00 and 1000000.00 without the separators? (Should the bank ever make mistakes filling in either one of these numbers, you'd surely want it to be in your favor!)

Logical Negation

The third logical operator, !, applies to single bool operand and inverts its value. So, if the value of a bool variable, test, is true, then !test is false; if test is false, then !test results in the value true.

Like all logical operators, you can apply logical negation to any expressions that evaluate to true or false. Operands can be anything from a single bool variable to a complex combination of comparisons and bool variables. For example, suppose x has the value 10. Then the expression !(x > 5) evaluates to false because x > 5 is true. Of course, in that particular case, you may be better off simply writing x <= 5. The latter expression is equivalent, but because it does not contain the negation, it is probably easier to read.

■ **Caution**   Let foo, bar, and xyzzy be variables (or any expressions if you will) of type bool. Then beginning C++ programmers, such as yourself, often write statements like this:

```
if (foo == true) ...
if (bar == false) ...
if (xyzzy != true) ...
```

While technically correct, it is generally accepted that you should favor the following equivalent yet shorter if statements instead:

```
if (foo) ...
if (!bar) ...
if (!xyzzy) ...
```

Combining Logical Operators

You can combine conditional expressions and logical operators to any degree to which you feel comfortable. This example implements a questionnaire to decide whether a person is a good loan risk:

```
// Ex4_05.cpp
// Combining logical operators for loan approval
#include <iostream>

int main()
{
  int age {};             // Age of the prospective borrower
  int income {};          // Income of the prospective borrower
  int balance {};         // Current bank balance

  // Get the basic data for assessing the loan
  std::cout << "Please enter your age in years: ";
  std::cin  >> age;
  std::cout << "Please enter your annual income in dollars: ";
  std::cin  >> income;
  std::cout << "What is your current account balance in dollars: ";
  std::cin  >> balance;
```

```cpp
// We only lend to people who are over 21 years of age,
// who make over $25,000 per year,
// or have over $100,000 in their account, or both.
if (age >= 21 && (income > 25'000 || balance > 100'000))
{
  // OK, you are good for the loan - but how much?
  // This will be the lesser of twice income and half balance
  int loan {};                 // Stores maximum loan amount
  if (2*income < balance/2)
  {
    loan = 2*income;
  }
  else
  {
    loan = balance/2;
  }
  std::cout << "\nYou can borrow up to $" << loan << std::endl;
}
else      // No loan for you...
{
  std::cout << "\nUnfortunately, you don't qualify for a loan." << std::endl;
}
}
```

Here's some sample output:

```
Please enter your age in years: 25
Please enter your annual income in dollars: 28000
What is your current account balance in dollars: 185000

You can borrow up to $56000
```

The interesting bit is the if statement that determines whether a loan will be granted. The if condition is as follows:

```
age >= 21 && (income > 25'000 || balance > 100'000)
```

This condition requires that the applicant's age be at least 21 and that either their income is larger than $25,000 or their account balance is greater than $100,000. The parentheses around the expression (income > 25'000 || balance > 100'000) are necessary to ensure that the result of ORing the income and balance conditions together is ANDed with the result of the age test. Without the parentheses, the age test would be ANDed with the income test, and the result would be ORed with the balance test. This is because && has a higher precedence than ||, as you can see from the table in Chapter 3. Without the parentheses, the condition would have allowed an 8-year-old with a balance over $100,000 to get a loan. That's not what was intended. Banks never lend to minors or mynahs.

If the if condition is true, the block of statements that determine the loan amount executes. The loan variable is defined within this block and therefore ceases to exist at the end of the block. The if statement within the block determines whether twice the declared income is less than half the account balance. If it is, the loan is twice the income; otherwise, it is half the account balance. This ensures the loan corresponds to the least amount according to the rules.

■ **Tip**   When combining logical operators, it is recommended to always add parentheses to clarify the code. Suppose for argument's sake that the bank's condition for allowing a loan was as follows:

```
(age < 30 && income > 25'000) || (age >= 30 && balance > 100'000)
```

That is, for younger clients, the decision depends entirely on their yearly salary—yes, even toddlers get a loan, as long as they can submit proof of sufficient income, of course—whereas more mature clients must already have sufficient savings. Then you could also write this condition as follows:

```
age < 30 && income > 25'000 || age >= 30 && balance > 100'000
```

While both expressions are perfectly equivalent, you'll surely agree that the one with parentheses is much easier to read than the one without. When combining && and ||, it is therefore recommended to always clarify the meaning of the logical expression by adding parentheses, even when it strictly speaking is not necessary.

Logical Operators on Integer Operands

In a way, logical operators can be—and actually fairly often are—applied to integer operands instead of Boolean operands. For instance, earlier you saw that the following can be used to test whether an int variable value differs from zero:

```
if (value)
    std::cout << "You have entered a value that is different from zero." << std::endl;
```

Equally frequently, you will encounter a test of the following form:

```
if (!value)
    std::cout << "You have entered a value that equals zero." << std::endl;
```

Here, logical negation is applied to an integer operand—not to a Boolean operand as usual. Similarly, suppose you have defined two int variables, value1 and value2; then you could write the following:

```
if (value1 && value2)
    std::cout << "Both values are non-zero." << std::endl;
```

Because these expressions are so short, they are popular among C++ programmers. Typical use cases of such patterns occur if these integer values represent, for instance, the number of elements in a collection of objects. It is therefore important that you understand how they work: every numeric operand to a logical operator in expressions such as these is first converted to a bool using the familiar rule: zero converts to false, and every other number converts to true. Even if all operands are integers, the logical expression still evaluates to a bool, though.

Logical Operators vs. Bitwise Operators

It's important not to confuse the logical operators &&, ||, and ! that apply to operands that are convertible to bool with the bitwise operators &, |, and ~ that operate on the bits within integral operands.

From the previous subsection, you'll remember that logical operators always evaluate to a value of type bool, even if their operands are integers. The converse is true for bitwise operators: they always evaluate to an integer number, even if both operands are of type bool. Nevertheless, because the integer result of a bitwise operator always converts back to a bool, it may often seem that logical and bitwise operators can be used interchangeably. The central test in Ex4_05 to test whether a loan is admissible, for instance, could in principle be written like this:

```
if (age >= 21 & (income > 25'000 | balance > 100'000))
{
    ...
}
```

This will compile and have the same end result as before when && and || were still used. In short, what happens is that the bool values that result from the comparisons are converted to ints, which are then bitwise combined into a single int using the bitwise operators, after which this single int is again converted to a bool for the if statement. Confused? Don't worry, it's not really all that important. Such conversions back and forth between bool and integers are rarely a cause for concern.

What *is* important, though, is the second, more fundamental difference between the two sets of operators; namely, unlike bitwise operators, the binary logical operators are so-called short-circuit operators.

Short-Circuit Evaluation

Consider the following code snippet:

```
int x = 2;
if (x < 0 && (x*x + 632*x == 1268))
{
    std::cout << "Congrats: " << x << " is the correct solution!" << std::endl;
}
```

Quickly, is x = 2 the correct solution? Of course not, 2 is not less than 0! It does not even matter whether 2*2 + 632*2 equals 1268 or not (it does, actually…). Because the first operand of the AND operator is false already, the end result will be false as well. After all, false && true remains false; the only case where the AND operator evaluates to true is true && true.

Similarly, in the following snippet, it should be instantly clear that x = 2 is a correct solution:

```
int x = 2;
if (x == 2 || (x*x + 632*x == 1268))
{
    std::cout << "Congrats: " << x << " is a correct solution!" << std::endl;
}
```

Why? Because the first operand is true, you immediately know that the full OR expression will evaluate to true as well. There's no need to even compute the second operand.

Naturally, a C++ compiler knows this as well. Therefore, if the first operand to a binary logical expression already determines the outcome, the compiler will make sure no time is wasted evaluating the second operand. This property of the logical operators && and || is called *short-circuit evaluation*. The bitwise operators & and |, on the other hand, do not short-circuit. For these operators, both operands are always evaluated.

This short-circuiting semantics of logical operators is often exploited by C++ programmers:

- If you need to test for multiple conditions that are glued together with logical operators, then you should put the cheapest ones to compute first. Our two examples in this section already illustrate this to a point, but of course this technique only really pays off if one of the operands is truly expensive to calculate.

- Short-circuiting is more commonly utilized to prevent the evaluation of right-hand operands that would otherwise fail to evaluate—as in cause a fatal crash. This is done by putting other conditions first that short-circuit whenever the other operands would fail. As we will see later in this book, a popular application of this technique is to check that a pointer is not null before dereferencing it.

We will see several more examples of logical expressions that rely on short-circuit evaluation in later chapters. For now, just remember that the second operand of && is evaluated only after the first operand evaluates to true, and the second operand of || only after the first evaluates to false. For & and |, both operands are always evaluated.

And, oh yes, in case you were wondering, the correct solution for the equation earlier is x = -634.

Logical XOR

There is no counterpart of the bitwise XOR—short for eXclusive OR—operator, ^, among the logical operators. This is in part, no doubt, because short-circuiting this operator makes no sense (both operands must always be evaluated to know the correct outcome of this operator; perhaps take a second to think about this). Luckily, the XOR operator, like any of the bitwise operators, can simply be applied to Boolean operands as well. The following test, for instance, passes for most youngsters and millionaires. Adults with a normal bank balance will not pass the cut, though, and neither will teenage millionaires:

```
if ((age < 20) ^ (balance >= 1'000'000))
{
    ...
}
```

In other words, this test is equivalent to either one of the following combinations of logical operators:

```
if ((age < 20 || balance >= 1'000'000) && !(age < 20 && balance >= 1'000'000))
{
    ...
}

if ((age < 20 && balance < 1'000'000) || (age >= 20 && balance >= 1'000'000))
{
    ...
}
```

Convincing yourself that these three if statements are indeed equivalent makes for a nice little exercise in Boolean algebra.

The Conditional Operator

The *conditional operator* is sometimes called the *ternary operator* because it involves three operands—the only operator to do so. It parallels the if-else statement, in that instead of selecting one of two statement blocks to execute depending on a condition, it selects the value of one of two expressions. Thus, the conditional operator enables you to choose between two values. Let's consider an example.

Suppose you have two variables, a and b, and you want to assign the value of the greater of the two to a third variable, c. The following statement will do this:

```
c = a > b? a : b;          // Set c to the higher of a and b
```

The conditional operator has a logical expression as its first operand, in this case a > b. If this expression is true, the second operand—in this case a—is selected as the value resulting from the operation. If the first operand is false, the third operand—in this case b—is selected as the value. Thus, the result of the conditional expression is a if a is greater than b, and b otherwise. This value is stored in c. The assignment statement is equivalent to the if statement:

```
if (a > b)
{
  c = a;
}
else
{
  c = b;
}
```

Of course, you can use the conditional operator to select the lower of two values. In the previous program, you used an if-else to decide the value of the loan; you could use this statement instead:

```
loan = 2*income < balance/2? 2*income : balance/2;
```

This produces the same result. The condition is 2*income < balance/2. If this evaluates to true, then the expression 2*income evaluates and produces the result of the operation. If the condition is false, the expression balance/2 produces the result of the operation.

You don't need parentheses because the precedence of the conditional operator is lower than that of the other operators in this statement. Of course, if you think parentheses would make things clearer, you can include them:

```
loan = (2*income < balance/2)? (2*income) : (balance/2);
```

The general form of the conditional operator, which is often represented by ?:, is as follows:

```
condition ? expression1 : expression2
```

As usual, all whitespace before or after both the ? or the : is optional and ignored by the compiler. If condition evaluates to true, the result is the value of expression1; if it evaluates to false, the result is the value of expression2. If condition is an expression that results in a numerical value, then it is implicitly converted to type bool.

Note that only one of expression1 or expression2 will be evaluated. Similar to the short-circuiting evaluation of binary logical operands, this has significant implications for expressions such as the following:

```
divisor? (dividend / divisor) : 0;
```

110

Suppose both `divisor` and `dividend` are variables of type `int`. For integers, division by zero results in undefined behavior in C++. This means that, in the worst case, dividing an integer by zero may cause a fatal crash. If `divisor` equals zero in the previous expression, however, then (`dividend / divisor`) is not evaluated. If the condition to a conditional operator evaluates to `false`, the second operand is not evaluated at all. Instead, only the third operand is evaluated. In this case, this implies that the entire expression trivially evaluates to 0. That is a much better outcome indeed than a potential crash!

You can use the conditional operator to control output depending on the result of an expression or the value of a variable. You can vary a message by selecting one text string or another depending on a condition.

```
// Ex4_06.cpp
// Using the conditional operator to select output.
#include <iostream>

int main()
{
  int mice {};              // Count of all mice
  int brown {};             // Count of brown mice
  int white {};             // Count of white mice

  std::cout << "How many brown mice do you have? ";
  std::cin >> brown;
  std::cout << "How many white mice do you have? ";
  std::cin >> white;

  mice = brown + white;

  std::cout << "You have " << mice
            << (mice == 1? " mouse" : " mice")
            << " in total." << std::endl;
}
```

The output from this program might be as follows:

```
How many brown mice do you have? 2
How many white mice do you have? 3
You have 5 mice in total.
```

The only bit of interest is the output statement that is executed after the numbers of mice have been entered. The expression using the conditional operator evaluates to " mouse" if the value of mice is 1, or " mice" otherwise. This allows you to use the same output statement for any number of mice and select singular or plural as appropriate.

There are many other situations in which you can apply this sort of mechanism, such as when selecting between "is" and "are" or between "he" and "she" or indeed in any situation in which you have a binary choice. You can even combine two conditional operators to choose between three options. Here's an example:

```
std::cout << (a < b ? "a is less than b." :
                 (a == b ? "a is equal to b." : "a is greater than b."));
```

This statement outputs one of three messages, depending on the relative values of a and b. The second choice for the first conditional operator is the result of another conditional operator.

111

The switch Statement

You're often faced with a multiple-choice situation in which you need to execute a particular set of statements from a number of choices (that is, more than two), depending on the value of an integer variable or expression. The switch statement enables you to select from multiple choices. The choices are identified by a set of fixed integer or enumeration values, and the selection of a particular choice is determined by the value of a given integer or enumeration constant.

The choices in a switch statement are called *cases*. A lottery where you win a prize depending on your number coming up is an example of where it might apply. You buy a numbered ticket, and if you're lucky, you win a prize. For instance, if your ticket number is 147, you win first prize; if it's 387, you can claim a second prize; and ticket 29 gets you a third prize; any other ticket number wins nothing. The switch statement to handle this situation would have four cases: one for each of the winning numbers, plus a "default" case for all the losing numbers. Here's a switch statement that selects a message for a given ticket number:

```
switch (ticket_number)
{
case 147:
  std::cout << "You win first prize!";
  break;
case 387:
  std::cout << "You win second prize!";
  break;
case 29:
  std::cout << "You win third prize!";
  break;
default:
  std::cout << "Sorry, you lose.";
  break;
}
```

The switch statement is harder to describe than to use. The selection of a particular case is determined by the value of the integer expression between the parentheses that follow the keyword switch. In this example, it is simply the integer variable ticket_number.

■ **Note**   You can only switch on values of integral (int, long, unsigned short, etc.), character (char, etc.), and enumeration types (see Chapter 2). Technically, switching on Boolean values is allowed as well, but instead of a switch on Booleans, you should just use if/else statements. Unlike some other programming languages, however, C++ does not allow you to create switch() statements with conditions and labels that contain expressions of any other type. A switch that branches on different string values, for instance, is not allowed (we'll discuss strings in Chapter 7).

The possible choices in a switch statement appear in a block, and each choice is identified by a case value. A *case value* appears in a *case label*, which is of the following form:

```
case case_value:
```

It's called a case *label* because it labels the statements or block of statements that it precedes. The statements that follow a particular case label execute if the value of the selection expression is the same as that of the case value. Each case value must be unique, but case values don't need to be in any particular order, as the example demonstrates.

Each case value must be a *constant expression*, which is an expression that the compiler can evaluate at compile time. Case values are mostly either literals or const variables that are initialized with literals. Naturally, any case label must either be of the same type as the condition expression inside the preceding switch() or be convertible to that type.

The default label in the example identifies the *default case*, which is a catchall that is selected if none of the other cases is selected. If present, the default label does not have to be the last label. It often is, but it can in principle appear anywhere among the regular case labels. You also don't have to specify a default case. If you don't and none of the case values is selected, the switch does nothing.

The break statement that appears after each set of case statements is essential for the logic here. Executing a break statement breaks out of the switch and causes execution to continue with the statement following the closing brace. If you omit the break statement for a case, the statements for the following case will execute. Notice that we don't *need* a break after the final case (usually the default case) because execution leaves the switch at this point anyway. It's good programming style to include it, though, because it safeguards against accidentally falling through to another case that you might add to a switch later. switch, case, default, and break are all keywords.

This example demonstrates the switch statement:

```cpp
// Ex4_07.cpp
// Using the switch statement
#include <iostream>

int main()
{
  int choice {};              // Stores selection value

  std::cout << "Your electronic recipe book is at your service.\n"
            << "You can choose from the following delicious dishes:\n"
            << "1  Boiled eggs\n"
            << "2  Fried eggs\n"
            << "3  Scrambled eggs\n"
            << "4  Coddled eggs\n\n"
            << "Enter your selection number: ";
  std::cin >> choice;

  switch (choice)
  {
  case 1:
    std::cout << "Boil some eggs." << std::endl;
    break;
  case 2:
    std::cout << "Fry some eggs." << std::endl;
    break;
  case 3:
    std::cout << "Scramble some eggs." << std::endl;
    break;
```

```
  case 4:
    std::cout << "Coddle some eggs." << std::endl;
    break;
  default:
    std::cout << "You entered a wrong number - try raw eggs." << std::endl;
  }
}
```

After defining your options in the output statement and reading a selection number into the variable choice, the switch statement executes with the selection expression specified simply as choice in parentheses, immediately following the keyword switch. The possible choices in the switch are between braces and are each identified by a case label. If the value of choice corresponds with any of the case values, then the statements following that case label execute.

If the value of choice doesn't correspond with any of the case values, the statements following the default label execute. If you hadn't included a default case here and the value of choice was different from all the case values, then the switch would have done nothing, and the program would continue with the next statement after the switch—effectively executing return 0; because the end of main() has been reached.

You have only one statement plus a break statement for each case in this example, but in general you can have as many statements as you need following a case label, and you generally don't need to enclose them between braces. The cases where you do need to add braces are discussed in one of the next sections.

As we said earlier, each of the case values must be a compile-time constant and must be unique. The reason that no two case values can be the same is that if they are, the compiler has no way of knowing which statements should be executed when that particular value comes up. However, different case values don't need to have unique actions. Several case values can share the same action, as the following example shows:

```
// Ex4_08.cpp
// Multiple case actions
#include <iostream>
#include <cctype>

int main()
{
  char letter {};
  std::cout << "Enter a letter: ";
  std::cin >> letter;

  if (std::isalpha(letter))
  {
    switch (std::tolower(letter))
    {
    case 'a': case 'e': case 'i': case 'o': case 'u':
      std::cout << "You entered a vowel." << std::endl;
      break;
    default:
      std::cout << "You entered a consonant." << std::endl;
      break;
    }
  }
```

```
else
{
  std::cout << "You did not enter a letter." << std::endl;
}
}
```

Here is an example of some output:

```
Enter a letter: E
You entered a vowel.
```

The if condition first checks that you really do have a letter and not some other character using the
std::isalpha() classification function from the Standard Library. The integer returned will be nonzero
if the argument is alphabetic, and this will be implicitly converted to true, which causes the switch to
be executed. The switch condition converts the value to lowercase using the Standard Library character
conversion routine, tolower(),and uses the result to select a case. Converting to lowercase avoids the need
to have case labels for uppercase and lowercase letters. All of the cases that identify a vowel cause the same
statements to be executed. You can see that you can just write each of the cases in a series, followed by the
statements any of these cases is to select. If the input is not a vowel, it must be a consonant and the default
case deals with this.

If isalpha() returns 0, which converts to false, the switch doesn't execute because the else clause is
selected; this outputs a message indicating that the character entered was not a letter.

In Ex4_08.cpp, we put all case labels with vowel values on a single line. This is not required. You are
allowed to add line breaks (or any form of whitespace for that matter) in between the case labels as well.
Here's an example:

```
switch (std::tolower(letter))
{
  case 'a':
  case 'e':
  case 'i':
  case 'o':
  case 'u':
    std::cout << "You entered a vowel." << std::endl;
    break;
...
```

A break statement is not the only way to move control out of a switch statement. If the code following
a case label contains a return statement, control instantly exits not only the switch statement but the
surrounding function as well. So, in principle, you could rewrite the switch statement in Ex4_08 as follows:

```
switch (std::tolower(letter))
{
case 'a': case 'e': case 'i': case 'o': case 'u':
  std::cout << "You entered a vowel." << std::endl;
  return 0;                              // Ends the program
}

// We did not exit main() in the above switch, so letter is not a vowel:
std::cout << "You entered a consonant." << std::endl;
```

115

With this particular variant, we also again illustrate that a default case is optional. If you enter a vowel, the output will reflect this, and the return statement in the switch statement will terminate the program. Note that after a return statement you should never put a break statement anymore. If you enter a consonant, the switch statement does nothing. None of these cases apply, and there is no default case. Execution therefore continues after the statement and outputs that you have in fact entered a consonant—remember, if you would've entered a vowel, the program would've terminated already because of the return statement.

The code for this variant is available as Ex4_08A. We created it to show a few points, though, not because it necessarily reflects good programming style. The use of a default case is surely recommended over continuing after a switch statement after none of the cases executed a return.

Fallthrough

The break statement at the end of each group of case statements transfers execution to the statement after the switch. You could demonstrate the essential nature of the break statements by removing them from the switch statements of earlier example Ex4_07 or Ex4_08 and seeing what happens. You'll find that the code beneath the case label directly following the case without a break statement then gets executed as well. This phenomenon is called *fallthrough* because in a way we "fall through" into the next case.

More often than not, a missing break statement signals an oversight and therefore a bug. To illustrate this, let's return to an earlier example—the one with the lottery numbers:

```
switch (ticket_number)
{
case 147:
  std::cout << "You win first prize!" << std::endl;
case 387:
  std::cout << "You win second prize!" << std::endl;
  break;
case 29:
  std::cout << "You win third prize!" << std::endl;
  break;
default:
  std::cout << "Sorry, you lose." << std::endl;
  break;
}
```

You'll notice that this time, we have "accidentally" omitted the break statement after the first case. If you executed this switch statement now with ticket_number equal to 147, the output would be as follows:

```
You win first prize!
You win second prize!
```

Because ticket_number equals 147, the switch statement jumps to the corresponding case, and you win first prize. But because there is no break statement, execution simply goes on with the code underneath the next case label, and you win second prize as well—huzza! Clearly, this omission of break must be an accidental oversight. In fact, because more often than not fallthrough signals a bug, many compilers issue a warning if a nonempty switch case is not followed by either a break or a return statement. Empty switch cases, such as those used in Ex4_08 (to check for vowels), are common enough not to warrant a compiler warning.

Fallthrough does not always mean a mistake was made, though. It can at times be quite useful to purposely write a switch statement that employs fallthrough. Suppose that in our lottery multiple numbers win second and third prize (two and three numbers, respectively) and that one of the numbers winning third prize gets a special bonus prize. Then we could write this logic as follows:

```cpp
switch (ticket_number)
{
case 147:
  std::cout << "You win first prize!" << std::endl;
  break;
case 387:
case 123:
  std::cout << "You win second prize!" << std::endl;
  break;
case 929:
  std::cout << "You win a special bonus prize!" << std::endl;
case 29:
case 78:
  std::cout << "You win third prize!" << std::endl;
  break;
default:
  std::cout << "Sorry, you lose." << std::endl;
  break;
}
```

The idea is that if your ticket_number equals 929, the outcome should be the following:

```
You win a special bonus prize!
You win third prize!
```

If your number is either 29 or 78, however, you'd only win third prize. The slight annoyance with these atypical cases (pun intended) is that compilers may issue a fallthrough warning, even though you know for a fact that this time it is not a mistake. And of course, as a self-respecting programmer, you want to compile all your programs free of warnings. You could always rewrite the code and duplicate the statement to output that you won third prize. But in general, duplication is something you'd like to avoid as well. So, what to do?

Luckily, C++17 adds a new language feature to signal to both the compiler and the person reading your code that you are intentionally using fallthrough: you can add a [[fallthrough]] statement in the same place where you would otherwise add a break statement:

```cpp
switch (ticket_number)
{
...
case 929:
  std::cout << "You win a special bonus prize!" << std::endl;
  [[fallthrough]];
case 29:
case 78:
  std::cout << "You win third prize!" << std::endl;
  break;
...
}
```

For empty cases, such as the one for number 29, a [[fallthrough]] statement is allowed but not required. Compilers already do not issue warnings for this.

Statement Blocks and Variable Scope

A switch statement has its own block between braces that encloses the case statements. An if statement also often has braces enclosing the statements to be executed if the condition is true, and the else part may have such braces too. These statement blocks are no different from any other blocks when it comes to variable scope. Any variable declared within a block ceases to exist at the end of the block, so you cannot reference it outside the block.

For example, consider the following rather arbitrary calculation:

```
if (value > 0)
{
  int savit {value - 1};        // This only exists in this block
  value += 10;
}
else
{
  int savit {value + 1};        // This only exists in this block
  value -=  10;
}
std::cout << savit;             // This will not compile! savit does not exist
```

The output statement at the end causes a compiler error message because the savit variable is undefined at this point. Any variable defined within a block can be used only within that block, so if you want to access data that originates inside a block from outside it, you must define the variable storing that information in an outer block.

Variable definitions within a switch statement block must be reachable in the course of execution, and it must not be possible to bypass them by jumping to a case after the declaration and within the same scope; otherwise, the code will not compile. Most likely you don't understand at all yet what we mean. It'll be much easier to explain, though, by means of an example. The following code illustrates how illegal declarations can arise in a switch:

```
int test {3};
switch (test)
{
  int i {1};                 // ILLEGAL - cannot be reached

case 1:
  int j {2};                 // ILLEGAL - can be reached but can be bypassed
  std::cout << test + j << std::endl;
  break;

  int k {3};                 // ILLEGAL - cannot be reached

case 3:
{
  int m {4};                 // OK - can be reached and cannot be bypassed
  std::cout << test + m << std::endl;
  break;
}
```

```
default:
  int n {5};                    // OK - can be reached and cannot be bypassed
  std::cout << test + n << std::endl;
  break;
}
std::cout << j << std::endl;    // ILLEGAL - j doesn't exist here
std::cout << n << std::endl;    // ILLEGAL - n doesn't exist here
```

Only two of the variable definitions in this switch statement are legal: the ones for m and n. For a definition to be legal, it must first be possible for it to be reached and thus executed in the normal course of execution. Clearly, this is not the case for variables i and k. Second, it must not be possible during execution to enter the scope of a variable while bypassing its definition, which is the case for the variable j. If execution jumps to either the case with label 3 or the default case, it enters the scope in which the variable j was defined, while bypassing its actual definition. That's illegal. Variable m, however, is only "in scope" from its declaration to the end of the enclosing block, so this declaration cannot be bypassed. And the declaration of variable n cannot by bypassed because there are no cases after the default case. Note that it's not because it concerns the default case that the declaration of n is legal; if there were additional cases following the default one, the declaration of n would've been just as illegal.

Initialization Statements

Consider the following code snippet:

```
auto lower{ static_cast<char>(std::tolower(input)) };
if (lower >= 'a' && lower <= 'z') {
  std::cout << "You've entered the letter '" << lower << '\'' << std::endl;
}
// ... more code that does not use lower
```

We convert some input character to a lowercase character lower and use the outcome first to check whether the input was a letter and then, if so, to produce some output. For illustration's sake, ignore the fact that we could—*should* even—be using the portable std::isalpha() function here instead. You've learned all about that in this chapter already. The key point that we want to make with this example is that the lower variable is used only by the if statement and not anymore by any of the code that follows the snippet. In general, it is considered good coding style to limit the scope of variables to the region in which they are used, even if this means adding an extra scope as follows:

```
{
  auto lower{ static_cast<char>(std::tolower(input)) };
  if (lower >= 'a' && lower <= 'z') {
    std::cout << "You've entered the letter '" << lower << '\'' << std::endl;
  }
}
// ... more code (lower does not exist here)
```

The result is that, for the rest of the code, it is as if the lower variable never existed. Patterns such as this where an extra scope (and indentation) is introduced to bind local variables to if statements are relatively common. They are common enough for C++17 to introduce a new, specialized syntax for it. The general syntax is as follows:

```
if (initialization; condition) ...
```

119

The additional *initialization statement* is executed prior to evaluating the `condition` expression, the usual Boolean expression of the `if` statement. You will use such initialization statements mainly to declare variables local to the `if` statement. With this, our earlier example becomes the following:

```
if (auto lower{ static_cast<char>(std::tolower(input)) }; lower >= 'a' && lower <= 'z') {
  std::cout << "You've entered the letter '" << lower << '\'' << std::endl;
}
// ... more code (lower does not exist here)
```

Variables declared in the initialization statement can be used both in the `if` statement's condition expression and in the statement or block that immediately follows the `if`. For `if-else` statements, they can be used in the statement or block that follows the `else` as well. But for any code after the `if` or `if-else` statement, it is as if these variables never existed.

For completeness, C++17 adds a similar syntax for `switch` statements:

```
switch (initialization; condition) { ... }
```

■ **Caution**   At the time of writing, these extended `if` and `switch` statements are still new and not well known among C++ developers yet. And using unfamiliar syntax may hinder code readability. So if you're working in a team, it may be prudent to check with your colleagues whether you want to use it already in your code base. On the other hand, though, how is new syntax ever going to gain any traction if not for well-educated trendsetters such as yourself?

Summary

In this chapter, you added the capability for decision-making to your programs. You now know how *all* the decision-making statements in C++ work. The essential elements of decision-making that you have learned about in this chapter are as follows:

- You can compare two values using the comparison operators. This will result in a value of type `bool`, which can be either `true` or `false`.

- You can convert a `bool` value to an integer type—`true` will convert to `1`, and `false` will convert to `0`.

- Numerical values can be converted to type `bool`—a zero value converts to `false`, and any nonzero value converts to `true`. When a numerical value appears where a `bool` value is expected—such as in an `if` condition—the compiler will insert an implicit conversion of the numerical value to type `bool`.

- The `if` statement executes a statement or a block of statements depending on the value of a condition expression. If the condition is `true`, the statement or block executes. If the condition is `false`, it doesn't.

- The `if-else` statement executes a statement or block of statements when the condition is `true` and executes another statement or block when the condition is `false`.

- `if` and `if-else` statements can be nested.

- The logical operators &&, ||, and ! are used to string together more complex logical expressions. The arguments to these operators must either be Booleans or values that are convertible to Booleans (such as integral values).

- The conditional operator selects between two values depending on the value of an expression.

- The switch statement provides a way to select one from a fixed set of options, depending on the value of an expression of integral or enumeration type.

EXERCISES

The following exercises enable you to try what you've learned in this chapter. If you get stuck, look back over the chapter for help. If you're still stuck after that, you can download the solutions from the Apress website (www.apress.com/source-code/), but that really should be a last resort.

Exercise 4-1. Write a program that prompts for two integers to be entered and then uses an if-else statement to output a message that states whether the integers are the same.

Exercise 4-2. Write another program that prompts for two integers to be entered. This time, any negative number or zero is to be rejected. Next, check whether one of the (strictly positive) numbers is an exact multiple of the other. For example, 63 is a multiple of 1, 3, 7, 9, 21, or 63. Note that the user should be allowed to enter the numbers in any order. That is, it does not matter whether the user enters the largest number first or the smaller one; both should work correctly!

Exercise 4-3. Create a program that prompts for input of a number (nonintegral numbers are allowed) between 1 and 100. Use a nested if, first to verify that the number is within this range and then, if it is, to determine whether it is greater than, less than, or equal to 50. The program should output information about what was found.

Exercise 4-4. It's time to make good on a promise. Somewhere in this chapter we said we'd look for someone "who is older than 21, younger than 35, is female, has a bachelor's or master's degree, is unmarried, and speaks Hindi or Urdu." Write a program that prompts the user for these qualifications and then outputs whether they qualify for these very specific requirements. To this end, you should define an integer variable age, a character variable gender (to hold 'm' for male and 'f' for female), a variable degree of an enumeration type AcademicDegree (possible values: none, associate, bachelor, professional, master, doctor), and three Boolean variables: married, speaksHindi, and speaksUrdu. Emulate a trivial online job interview, and query your applicant for input on all these variables. People who enter invalid values do not qualify, of course, and should be ruled out as early as possible (that is, immediately after entering any invalid value; ruling them out precognitively prior to entering invalid values, sadly, is not possible yet in Standard C++).

Exercise 4-5. Add some code at the end of the main() function of Ex4_06.cpp to print an additional message. If you have exactly one mouse, output a message of the form "It is a brown/white mouse." Otherwise, if you have multiple mice, compose a grammatically correct message of the form "Of these mice, N is a/are brown mouse/mice." If you have no mice, no new message needs to be printed. Use an appropriate mixture of conditional operators and if/else statements.

Exercise 4-6. Write a program that determines, using only the conditional operator, if an integer that is entered has a value that is 20 or less, is greater than 20 but not greater than 30, is greater than 30 but not exceeding 100, or is greater than 100.

Exercise 4-7. Implement a program that prompts for input of a letter. Use a library function to determine whether the letter is a vowel and whether it is lowercase or not, and output the result. Finally, output the lowercase letter together with its character code as a binary value.

Hint: Even though starting with C++14, C++ supports binary integral literals (of form 0b11001010; see Chapter 2), C++ standard output functions and streams do not support outputting integral values in binary format. They mostly do support hexadecimal and octal formatting—for std::cout, for instance, you can use the std::hex and std::oct output manipulators defined in <ios>. But to output a character in binary format, you'll thus have to write some code yourself. It shouldn't be too hard, though: a char normally has only eight bits, remember? You can just stream these bits one by one. Perhaps these binary integer literals can be helpful as well—why else would we have mentioned them at the start of this hint?

Exercise 4-8. Create a program that prompts the user to enter an amount of money between $0 and $10 (decimal places allowed). Any other value is to be rejected politely. Determine how many quarters (25c), dimes (10c), nickels (5c), and pennies (1c) are needed to make up that amount. For our non-American readers, one dollar ($) equals 100 cents (c). Output this information to the screen and ensure that the output makes grammatical sense (for example, if you need only one dime, then the output should be "1 dime" and not "1 dimes").

CHAPTER 5

.oops

'a items of the same type using a single name, the array name.
' with a series of temperatures or the ages of a group of people,
\gramming facility. It provides a mechanism for repeating
\pplication requires. Loops are essential in the majority
\mpany payroll, for example, would not be practicable
_ach with their own particular area of application.

_ and how you create an array

., to use a for loop

- How the while loop works

- What the merits of the do-while loop are

- What the break and continue statements do in a loop

- What the continue statement does in a loop

- How to use nested loops

- How to create and use an array container

- How to create and use a vector container

Arrays

The variables you have created up to now can store only a single data item of the specified type—an integer, a floating-point value, a character, or a bool value. An array stores several data items of the same type. You can create an array of integers or an array of characters (or in fact an array of any type of data), and there can be as many as the available memory will allow.

Using an Array

An *array* is a variable that represents a sequence of memory locations, each storing an item of data of the same data type. Suppose, for instance, you've written a program to calculate the average temperature. You now want to extend the program to calculate how many samples are above that average and how many

© Ivor Horton and Peter Van Weert 2018
I. Horton and P. Van Weert, *Beginning C++17*, https://doi.org/10.1007/978-1-4842-3366-5_5

are below. You'll need to retain the original sample data to do this, but storing each data item in a separate variable would be tortuous to code and highly impractical. An array provides you with the means of doing this easily. You could store 366 temperature samples in an array defined as follows:

```
double temperatures[366];               // Define an array of 366 temperatures
```

This defines an array with the name `temperatures` to store 366 values of type `double`. The data values are called *elements*. The number of elements specified between the brackets is the *size* of the array. The array elements are not initialized in this statement, so they contain junk values.

The size of an array must always be specified using a *constant integer expression*. Any integer expression that the compiler can evaluate at compile time may be used, though mostly this will be either an integer literal or a `const` integer variable that itself was initialized using a literal.

You refer to an array element using an integer called an *index*. The index of a particular array element is its offset from the first element. The first element has an offset of 0 and therefore an index of 0; an index value of 3 refers to the fourth array element—three elements from the first. To reference an element, you put its index between square brackets after the array name, so to set the fourth element of the `temperatures` array to 99.0, you would write the following:

```
temperatures[3] = 99.0;                 // Set the fourth array element to 99
```

While an array of 366 elements nicely illustrates the need of arrays—just imagine having to define 366 distinct variables—creating figures with that many elements would be somewhat cumbersome. Let's therefore look at another array:

```
unsigned int height[6];                 // Define an array of six heights
```

The compiler will allocate six contiguous storage locations for storing values of type `unsigned int` as a result of this definition. Each element in the `height` array contains a different number. Because the definition of `height` doesn't specify any initial values for the array, the six elements will contain junk values (analogous to what happens if you define a single variable of type `unsigned int` without an initial value). You could define the array with proper initial values like this:

```
unsigned int height[6] {26, 37, 47, 55, 62, 75};  // Define & initialize array of 6 heights
```

The braced initializer contains six values separated by commas. These might be the heights of the members of a family, recorded to the nearest inch. Each array element will be assigned an initial value from the list in sequence, so the elements will have the values shown in Figure 5-1. Each box in the figure represents a memory location holding a single array element. As there are six elements, the index values run from 0 for the first element through to 5 for the last element. Each element can therefore be referenced using the expression above it.

height [0]	height [1]	height [2]	height [3]	height [4]	height [5]
26	37	47	55	62	75

Figure 5-1. *An array with six elements*

■ **Note**   The type of the array will determine the amount of memory required for each element. The elements of an array are stored in one contiguous block of memory. So if the `unsigned int` type is 4 bytes on your computer, the `height` array will occupy 24 bytes.

The initializer must not have more values than there are elements in the array; otherwise, the statement won't compile. There can be fewer values in the list, however, in which case the elements for which no initial value has been supplied will be initialized with zero (`false` for an array of `bool` elements). Here's an example:

```
unsigned int height[6] {26, 37, 47};        // Element values: 26 37 47 0 0 0
```

The first three elements will have the values that appear in the list. The last three will be zero. To initialize all the elements with zero, you can just use an empty initializer:

```
unsigned int height[6] {};                   // All elements 0
```

To define an array of values that cannot be modified, you simply add the keyword `const` to its type. The following defines an array of six `unsigned int` constants:

```
const unsigned int height[6] {26, 37, 47, 55, 62, 75};
```

Any modification to either one of these six array elements (be it an assignment, increment, or any other modification) will now be prevented by the compiler.

Array elements participate in arithmetic expressions like other variables. You could sum the first three elements of height like this:

```
unsigned int sum {};
sum = height[0] + height[1] + height[2];     // The sum of three elements
```

You use references to individual array elements such as ordinary integer variables in an expression. As you saw earlier, an array element can be on the left of an assignment to set a new value, so you can copy the value of one element to another in an assignment, like this:

```
height[3] = height[2];                       // Copy 3rd element value to 4th element
```

However, you can't copy *all* the element values from one array to the elements of another in an assignment. You can operate only on individual elements. To copy the values of one array to another, you must copy the values one at a time. What you need is a loop.

Understanding Loops

A *loop* is a mechanism that enables you to execute a statement or block of statements repeatedly until a particular condition is met. Two essential elements make up a loop: the statement or block of statements that is to be executed repeatedly forms the so-called *body* of the loop, and a *loop condition* of some kind that determines when to stop repeating the loop. A single execution of a loop's body is called an *iteration*.

A loop condition can take different forms to provide different ways of controlling the loop. For example, a loop condition can do the following:

- Execute a loop a given number of times

- Execute a loop until a given value exceeds another value

- Execute the loop until a particular character is entered from the keyboard

- Execute a loop for each element in a collection of elements

You choose the loop condition to suit the circumstances. You have the following varieties of loops:

- *The* for *loop* primarily provides for executing the loop a prescribed number of times, but there is considerable flexibility beyond that.

- *The range-based* for *loop* executes one iteration for each element in a collection of elements.

- *The* while *loop* continues executing as long as a specified condition is true. The condition is checked at the beginning of an iteration, so if the condition starts out as false, no loop iterations are executed.

- *The* do-while *loop* continues to execute as long as a given condition is true. This differs from the while loop in that the do-while loop checks the condition at the end of an iteration. This implies that at least one loop iteration always executes.

We'll start by explaining how the for loop works.

The for Loop

The for loop generally executes a statement or block of statements a predetermined number of times, but you can use it in other ways too. You specify how a for loop operates using three expressions separated by semicolons between parentheses following the for keyword. This is shown in Figure 5-2.

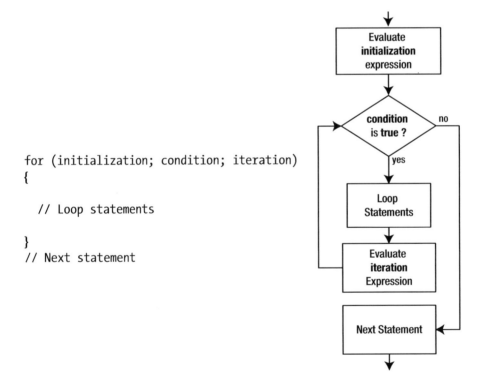

```
for (initialization; condition; iteration)
{

    // Loop statements

}
// Next statement
```

Figure 5-2. The logic of the for loop

You can omit any or all of the expressions controlling a for loop, but you must always include the semicolons. We'll explain later in this chapter why and when you might omit one or other of the control expressions. The initialization expression is evaluated only once, at the beginning of the loop. The loop condition is checked next, and if it is true, the loop statement or statement block executes. If the condition is false, the loop ends, and execution continues with the statement after the loop. After each execution of the loop statement or block, the iteration expression is evaluated, and the condition is checked to decide whether the loop should continue.

In the most typical usage of the for loop, the first expression initializes a counter, the second expression checks whether the counter has reached a given limit, and the third expression increments the counter. For example, you could copy the elements from one array to another like this:

```
double rainfall[12] {1.1, 2.8, 3.4, 3.7, 2.1, 2.3, 1.8, 0.0, 0.3, 0.9, 0.7, 0.5};
double copy[12] {};
for (size_t i {}; i < 12; ++i)    // i varies from 0 to 11
{
  copy[i] = rainfall[i];          // Copy ith element of rainfall to ith element of copy
}
```

The first expression defines i as type size_t with an initial value of 0. You might remember the size_t type from the values returned by the sizeof operator. It is an unsigned integer type that is generally used, for instance, for sizes and counts of things. As i will be used to index the arrays, using size_t makes sense. The second expression, the loop condition, is true as long as i is less than 12, so the loop continues while i is less than 12. When i reaches 12, the expression will be false, so the loop ends. The third expression increments i at the end of each loop iteration, so the loop block that copies the ith element from rainfall to copy will execute with values of i from 0 to 11.

▓ **Note**   size_t is not the name of a built-in fundamental type such as int, long, or double; it is a type alias defined by the Standard Library. More specifically, it is an alias for one of the unsigned integer types, sufficiently large to contain the size of any type the compiler supports (including any array). The alias is defined in the cstddef header, as well as in a number of other headers. In practice, however, you mostly do not need to include (with #include) any of these headers explicitly to use the size_t alias; the alias is often indirectly defined already by including other more high-level headers (such as the iostream header used by most of our examples).

▓ **Caution**   Array index values are not checked to verify that they are valid. It's up to you to make sure that you don't reference elements outside the bounds of the array. If you store data using an index value that's outside the valid range for an array, you'll either inadvertently overwrite something in memory or cause a so-called *segmentation fault* or *access violation* (both terms are synonymous and denote an error that is raised by the operating system if and when it detects unauthorized memory access). Either way, your program will almost certainly come to a sticky end.

As always, the compiler ignores all whitespace within the for statement. Also, if the loop's body consists of only a single statement, the curly braces are again optional. So, if you like, you could format the for loop from before like this:

```
for( size_t i {} ; i<12 ; ++i )     // i varies from 0 to 11
  copy[i] = rainfall[i];            // Copy ith element of rainfall to ith element of copy
```

In this book, we will follow the convention to put a single space after the for keyword (to differentiate loops from function calls), to put no spaces before the two semicolons (like with any other statement), and to generally use curly braces even for single-statement loop bodies (for better visual identification of loop bodies). You are free to follow any coding style you prefer, of course.

Not only is it *legal* to define variables such as i within a for loop initialization expression, it is common. This has some significant implications. A loop defines a scope. The loop statement or block, including any expressions that control the loop, falls within the scope of a loop. Any automatic variables declared within the scope of a loop do not exist outside it. Because i is defined in the first expression, it is local to the loop, so when the loop ends, i will no longer exist. When you need to be able to access the loop control variable after the loop ends, you just define it before the loop, like this:

```
size_t i {};
for (i = 0; i < 12; ++i)          // i varies from 0 to 11
{
  copy[i] = rainfall[i];          // Copy ith element of rainfall to ith element of copy
}
// i still exists here...
```

Now you can access i after the loop—its value will then be 12 in this case. i is initialized to 0 in its definition, so the first loop control expression is superfluous. You can omit any or all of the loop control expressions, so the loop can be written as follows:

```
size_t i {};
for ( ; i < 12; ++i)              // i varies from 0 to 11
{
  copy[i] = rainfall[i];          // Copy ith element of rainfall to ith element of copy
}
```

The loop works just as before. We'll discuss omitting other control expressions a little later in this chapter.

■ **Note**   At the end of the previous chapter we told you that C++17 has introduced new syntax for initialization statements for if and switch statements. These initialization statements are modeled after, and are therefore completely analogous to, those of for loops. The only difference is that with a for loop you cannot omit the first semicolon when forsaking the initialization statement.

Avoiding Magic Numbers

One minor problem with the code fragments in the preceding section is that they involve the "magic number" 12 for the array sizes. Suppose they invented a 13th month—Undecimber—and you had to add a rainfall value for that month. Then it wouldn't be unthinkable that after increasing the size of the rainfall array, you'd forget to update the 12 in the for loop. This is how bugs creep in!

A safer solution already is to define a const variable for the array size and use that instead of the explicit value:

```
const size_t size {12};
double rainfall[size] {1.1, 2.8, 3.4, 3.7, 2.1, 2.3, 1.8, 0.0, 0.3, 0.9, 0.7, 0.5};
double copy[size] {};
for (size_t i {}; i < size; ++i)  // i varies from 0 to size-1
{
  copy[i] = rainfall[i];          // Copy ith element of rainfall to ith element of copy
}
```

This is much less error prone, and it is clear that size is the number of elements in both arrays.

░ **Tip**   If the same constant is scattered around your code, it is easy to make a mistake by forgetting to update some of them. Therefore, define magic numbers, or any constant variable for that matter, only once. If you then have to change the constant, you have to do so in only one place.

Let's try a for loop in a complete example:

```
// Ex5_01.cpp
// Using a for loop with an array
#include <iostream>

int main()
{
  const unsigned size {6};                     // Array size
  unsigned height[size] {26, 37, 47, 55, 62, 75}; // An array of heights

  unsigned total {};                           // Sum of heights
  for (size_t i {}; i < size; ++i)
  {
    total += height[i];
  }

  const unsigned average {total/size};         // Calculate average height
  std::cout << "The average height is " << average << std::endl;

  unsigned count {};
  for (size_t i {}; i < size; ++i)
  {
    if (height[i] < average) ++count;
  }
  std::cout << count << " people are below average height." << std::endl;
}
```

The output is as follows:

```
The average height is 50
3 people are below average height.
```

The definition of the `height` array uses a `const` variable to specify the number of elements. The `size` variable is also used as the limit for the control variable in the two `for` loops. The first `for` loop iterates over each `height` element in turn, adding its value to `total`. The loop ends when the loop variable `i` is equal to `size`, and the statement following the loop is executed, which defines the `average` variable with the initial value as `total` divided by `size`.

After outputting the average height, the second `for` loop iterates over the elements in the array, comparing each value with `average`. The `count` variable is incremented each time an element is less than `average`, so when the loop ends, `count` will contain the number of elements less than `average`.

Incidentally, you could replace the `if` statement in the loop with this statement:

```
count += height[i] < average;
```

This works because the `bool` value that results from the comparison will be implicitly converted to an integer. The value `true` converts to `1`, and `false` converts to `0`, so `count` will be incremented only when the comparison results in `true`. However, while this new code is clever and fun, just the fact that it needs to be explained should be enough to stick with the original `if` statement instead. Always prefer code that reads (almost) like plain English over clever code![1]

Defining the Array Size with the Braced Initializer

You can omit the size of the array when you supply one or more initial values in its definition. The number of elements will be the number of initial values. Here's an example:

```
int values[] {2, 3, 4};
```

This defines an array with three elements of type `int` that will have the initial values 2, 3, and 4. It is equivalent to writing this:

```
int values[3] {2, 3, 4};
```

The advantage of omitting the size is that you can't get the array size wrong; the compiler determines it for you.

Determining the Size of an Array

You saw earlier how you can avoid magic numbers for the number of elements in an array by defining a constant initialized with the array size. You also don't want to be specifying a magic number for the array size when you let the compiler decide the number of elements from the braced initializer list. You need a fool-proof way of determining the size when necessary.

---

[1]Without going too much into the specifics, statements such as `count += height[i] < average;` are sometimes produced by "clever" C++ programmers because they assume they will run faster than the original conditional statement `if (height[i] < average) ++count;` (because the latter contains a so-called branching statement). The fact is that any self-respecting compiler will already rewrite this code for you in a similar manner. Our advice is that it's almost always best to leave the cleverness to the compiler; your job should be, in the first place, to produce code that is correct and clearly readable.

If your implementation supports it, the easiest and recommended way is to use the std::size() function provided by the array header of the Standard Library.[2] Suppose you've defined this array:

```
int values[] {2, 3, 5, 7, 11, 13, 17, 19, 23, 29};
```

Then you can use the expression std::size(values) to obtain the array's size, 10.

> **Note** The std::size() function works not only for arrays; you can also use it as an alternative means to obtain the size of just about any collection of elements defined by the Standard Library, including the std::vector<> and std::array<> containers we will introduce later in this chapter.

At the time of writing, the handy std::size() helper function is still quite new; it was added to the Standard Library in C++17. Before, people often used a different technique based on the sizeof operator. You know from Chapter 2 that the sizeof operator returns the number of bytes that a variable occupies. This works with an entire array as well as with a single array element. Thus, the sizeof operator provides a way to determine the number of elements in an array; you just divide the size of the array by the size of a single element. Let's try both:

```
// Ex5_02.cpp
// Obtaining the number of array elements
#include <iostream>
#include <array>          // for std::size()

int main()
{
  int values[] {2, 3, 5, 7, 11, 13, 17, 19, 23, 29};

  std::cout << "There are " << sizeof(values) / sizeof(values[0])
            << " elements in the array." << std::endl;

  int sum {};
  for (size_t i {}; i < std::size(values); ++i)
  {
    sum += values[i];
  }
  std::cout << "The sum of the array elements is " << sum << std::endl;
}
```

This example produces the following output:

```
There are 10 elements in the array.
The sum of the array elements is 129
```

---

[2]Technically, std::size() is primarily defined in the iterator header. But because it is such a commonly used utility, the Standard Library guarantees it to be available also when the array header is included (and with several other headers as well). Since you'll mostly use std::size() with arrays, we believe it is easier to remember to include the array header instead of the iterator header.

The number of elements in the `values` array is determined by the compiler from the number of initializing values in the definition. The first output statement uses the `sizeof` operator to calculate the number of array elements. The expression `sizeof(values)` evaluates to the number of bytes occupied by the entire array, and the expression `sizeof(values[0])` evaluates to the number of bytes occupied by a single element—any element will do, but usually one takes the first element. The expression `sizeof(values)` / `sizeof(values[0])` divides the number of bytes occupied by the whole array by the number of bytes for one element, so this evaluates to the number of elements in the array.

In the `for` loop, we use `std::size()` to control the number of iterations. Clearly, `std::size()` is much easier to use and understand than the old `sizeof`-based expression. So, if possible, you should always use `std::size()`.

The `for` loop itself determines the sum of the array elements. None of the control expressions has to be of a particular form. You have seen that you can omit the first control expression. In the `for` loop in the example, you could accumulate the sum of the elements within the third loop control expression. The loop would then become the following:

```
int sum {};
for (size_t i {}; i < std::size(values); sum += values[i++]);
```

The third loop control expression now does two things: it adds the value of the element at index i to sum, and then it increments the control variable, i. Note that earlier i was incremented using the prefix ++ operator, whereas now it is incremented using the postfix ++ operator. This is essential here to ensure the element selected by i is added to sum before i is incremented. If you use the prefix form, you get the wrong answer for the sum of the elements; you'll also use an invalid index value that accesses memory beyond the end of the array.

The single semicolon at the end of the line is an empty statement that constitutes the loop's body. In general, this is something to watch out for; you should never add a semicolon prior to a loop's body. In this case, however, it works because all calculations occur within the loop's control expressions already. An alternative, clearer way of writing a loop with an empty body is this:

```
int sum {};
for (size_t i {}; i < std::size(values); sum += values[i++]) {}
```

■ **Caution**   Performing actions beyond incrementing the loop index variable in the `for` loop's increment expression (the third and last components between the round parentheses) is unconventional, to say the least. In our example, it is far more common to simply update the `sum` variable in the loop's body, as in Ex5_02. We only showed you these alternatives here to give you a feeling of what is possible in principle. In general, however, you should always prefer conventional and clear code over code that is compact and clever!

Controlling a for Loop with Floating-Point Values

The `for` loop examples so far have used an integer variable to control the loop, but you can use anything you like. The following code fragment uses floating-point values to control the loop:

```
const double pi { 3.14159265358979323846 };
for (double radius {2.5}; radius <= 20.0; radius += 2.5)
{
  std:: cout << "radius = " << std::setw(12) << radius
```

```
              << "  area = " << std::setw(12)
              << pi * radius * radius << std::endl;
}
```

This loop is controlled by the radius variable, which is of type double. It has an initial value of 2.5 and is incremented at the end of each loop iteration until it exceeds 20.0, whereupon the loop ends. The loop statement calculates the area of a circle for the current value of radius, using the standard formula πr^2, where r is the radius of the circle. The manipulator setw() in the loop statement gives each output value the same field width; this ensures that the output values line up vertically. Of course, to use the manipulators in a program, you need to include the iomanip header.

You need to be careful when using a floating-point variable to control a for loop. Fractional values may not be representable exactly as a binary floating-point number. This can lead to some unwanted side effects, as this complete example demonstrates:

```
// Ex5_03.cpp
// Floating-point control in a for loop
#include <iostream>
#include <iomanip>

int main()
{
  const double pi { 3.14159265358979323846 }; // The famous pi
  const size_t perline {3};                    // Outputs per line
  size_t linecount {};                         // Count of output lines
  for (double radius {0.2}; radius <= 3.0; radius += 0.2)
  {
    std::cout << std::fixed << std::setprecision(2)
              << "  radius =" << std::setw(5) << radius
              << "  area =" << std::setw(6) << pi * radius * radius;
    if (perline == ++linecount)       // When perline outputs have been written...
    {
      std::cout << std::endl;         // ...start a new line...
      linecount = 0;                  // ...and reset the line counter
    }
  }
  std::cout << std::endl;
}
```

On our test system, this produces the following output:

```
radius = 0.20   area =   0.13   radius = 0.40   area =   0.50   radius = 0.60   area =   1.13
radius = 0.80   area =   2.01   radius = 1.00   area =   3.14   radius = 1.20   area =   4.52
radius = 1.40   area =   6.16   radius = 1.60   area =   8.04   radius = 1.80   area =  10.18
radius = 2.00   area =  12.57   radius = 2.20   area =  15.21   radius = 2.40   area =  18.10
radius = 2.60   area =  21.24   radius = 2.80   area =  24.63
```

The loop includes an if statement to output three sets of values per line. You would expect to see the area of a circle with radius 3.0 as the last output. After all, the loop should continue as long as radius is less than or equal to 3.0. But the last value displayed has the radius at 2.8; what's going wrong?

The loop ends earlier than expected because when 0.2 is added to 2.8, the result is greater than 3.0. This is an astounding piece of arithmetic at face value, but read on! The reason for this is a very small error in the representation of 0.2 as a binary floating-point number. 0.2 cannot be represented exactly in binary floating point. The error is in the last digit of precision, so if your compiler supports 15-digit precision for type double, the error is of the order of 10^{-15}. Usually, this is of no consequence, but here you depend on adding 0.2 successively to get *exactly* 3.0—which doesn't happen.

You can see what the difference is by changing the loop to output just one circle area per line and to display the difference between 3.0 and the next value of radius:

```
for (double radius {0.2}; radius <= 3.0; radius += .2)
{
  std::cout << std::fixed << std::setprecision(2)
          << "  radius =" << std::setw(5) << radius
          << "  area =" << std::setw(6) << pi * radius * radius
          << " delta to 3 = " << std::scientific << ((radius + 0.2) - 3.0) << std::endl;
}
```

On our machine, the last line of output is now this:

```
radius = 2.80  area = 24.63 delta to 3 = 4.44e-016
```

As you can see, radius + 0.2 is greater than 3.0 by around 4.44×10^{-16}. This causes the loop to terminate before the next iteration.

■ **Note** Any number that is a fraction with an odd denominator cannot be represented exactly as a binary floating-point value.

While this example may seem a tad academic, rounding errors do cause analogous bugs in practice. One of the authors remembers a real-life bug with a for loop similar to that of Ex5_03. It was a bug that very nearly resulted in the destruction of some high-tech piece of hardware worth well over $10,000—just because the loop occasionally ran for one iteration too many. Conclusion:

■ **Caution** Comparing floating-point numbers can be tricky. You should always be cautious when comparing the result of floating-point computations directly using operators such as ==, <=, or >=. Rounding errors almost always prevent the floating-point value from ever becoming exactly equal to the mathematical precise value.

For the for loop in Ex5_03, one option is to introduce an integral counter i specifically for controlling the loop. Another option is to replace the loop's condition with one that anticipates rounding errors. In this particular case, it suffices to use something like radius < 3.0 + 0.001. Instead of 0.001, you can use any number sufficiently greater than the expected rounding errors yet sufficiently less than the loop's .2 increment. A corrected version of the program can be found in Ex5_03A.cpp. Most math libraries and so-called unit test frameworks will offer utility functions to aid you with comparing floating-point numbers in a reliable manner.

More Complex for Loop Control Expressions

You can define and initialize more than one variable of a given type in the first for loop control expression. You just separate each variable from the next with a comma. Here's a working example that makes use of that:

```cpp
// Ex5_04.cpp
// Multiple initializations in a loop expression
#include <iostream>
#include <iomanip>

int main()
{
  unsigned int limit {};
  std::cout << "This program calculates n! and the sum of the integers"
            << " up to n for values 1 to limit.\n";
  std::cout << "What upper limit for n would you like? ";
  std::cin >> limit;

  // Output column headings
  std::cout << std::setw(8) << "integer" << std::setw(8) << " sum"
                           << std::setw(20) << " factorial" << std::endl;

  for (unsigned long long n {1}, sum {}, factorial {1}; n <= limit; ++n)
  {
    sum += n;                        // Accumulate sum to current n
    factorial *= n;                  // Calculate n! for current n
    std::cout << std::setw(8) << n << std::setw(8) << sum
              << std::setw(20) << factorial << std::endl;
  }
}
```

The program calculates the sum of the integers from 1 to n for each integer n from 1 to limit, where limit is an upper limit that you enter. It also calculates the factorial of each n. (The factorial of an integer *n*, written *n*!, is the product of all the integers from 1 to *n*; for example, $5! = 1 \times 2 \times 3 \times 4 \times 5 = 120$.) Don't enter large values for limit. Factorials grow rapidly and easily exceed the capacity of even a variable of type unsigned long long. Here's some typical output:

```
This program calculates n! and the sum of the integers up to n for values 1 to limit.
What upper limit for n would you like? 10
 integer     sum         factorial
       1       1                 1
       2       3                 2
       3       6                 6
       4      10                24
       5      15               120
       6      21               720
       7      28              5040
       8      36             40320
       9      45            362880
      10      55           3628800
```

First, you read the value for limit from the keyboard after displaying a prompt. The value entered for limit will not be large, so type unsigned int is more than adequate. Using setw() to specify the field width for the column headings for the output enables the values to be aligned vertically with the headings simply by specifying the same field widths. The for loop does all the work. The first control expression defines and initializes three variables of type unsigned long long. n is the loop counter, sum accumulates the sum of integers from 1 to the current n, and factorial will store n!. Type unsigned long long provides the maximum range of positive integers and so maximizes the range of factorials that can be calculated. Note that there will be no warning if a factorial value cannot be accommodated in the memory allocated; the result will just be incorrect.

■ **Note**   The optional initialization statement of if and switch statements is completely equivalent to that of for loops. So there too you can define multiple variables of the same type at once if you want.

The Comma Operator

Although the comma looks as if it's just a humble separator, it is actually a binary operator. It combines two expressions into a single expression, where the value of the operation is the value of its right operand. This means that anywhere you can put an expression, you can also put a series of expressions separated by commas. For example, consider the following statements:

```
int i {1};
int value1 {1};
int value2 {1};
int value3 {1};
std::cout << (value1 += ++i, value2 += ++i, value3 += ++i) << std::endl;
```

The first four statements define four variables with an initial value 1. The last statement outputs the result of three assignment expressions that are separated by the comma operator. The comma operator is left associative and has the lowest precedence of all the operators, so the expression evaluates like this:

```
(((value1 += ++i), (value2 += ++i)), (value3 += ++i));
```

The effect will be that value1 will be incremented by 2 to produce 3, value2 will be incremented by 3 to produce 4, and value3 will be incremented by 4 to produce 5. The value of the composite expression is the value of the rightmost expression in the series, so the value that is output is 5. You could use the comma operator to incorporate the calculations into the third loop control expression of the for loop in Ex5_04.cpp:

```
for (unsigned long long n {1}, sum {1}, factorial {1}; n <= limit;
                         ++n, sum += n, factorial *= n)
{
   std::cout << std::setw(8) << n << std::setw(8) << sum
           << std::setw(20) << factorial << std::endl;
}
```

The third control expression combines three expressions using the comma operator. The first expression increments n as before, the second adds the incremented n to sum, and the third multiplies factorial by that same value. It is important here that we *first* increment n and only *then* perform the other two calculations. Notice also that we initialize sum to 1 here, where before we initialized it to 0. The reason is that the third control expression is executed only for the first time *after* the first execution of the loop's body. Without this modification, the first iteration would start by printing out an incorrect sum of zero. If you replace the loop in Ex5_04.cpp by this new version and run the example again, you'll see that it works as before (see also Ex5_04A).

The Range-Based for Loop

The *range-based* for *loop* iterates over all the values in a range of values. This raises the immediate question: what is a range? An array is a range of elements, and a string is a range of characters. The *containers* provided by the Standard Library are all ranges as well. We'll introduce two Standard Library containers later in this chapter. This is the general form of the range-based for loop:

```
for (range_declaration : range_expression)
  loop statement or block;
```

The range_declaration identifies a variable that will be assigned each of the values in the range in turn, with a new value being assigned on each iteration. The range_expression identifies the range that is the source of the data. This will be clearer with an example. Consider these statements:

```
int values [] {2, 3, 5, 7, 11, 13, 17, 19, 23, 29};
int total {};
for (int x : values)
  total += x;
```

The variable x will be assigned a value from the values array on each iteration. It will be assigned values 2, 3, 5, and so on, in succession. Thus, the loop will accumulate the sum of all the elements in the values array in total. The variable x is local to the loop and does not exist outside it.

A braced initializer list itself is a valid range, so you could write the previous code even more compactly as follows:

```
int total {};
for (auto x : {2, 3, 5, 7, 11, 13, 17, 19, 23, 29})
  total += x;
```

Of course, the compiler knows the type of the elements in the values array, so you could also let the compiler determine the type for x by writing the former loop like this:

```
for (auto x : values)
  total += x;
```

Using the auto keyword causes the compiler to deduce the correct type for x. The auto keyword is used often with the range-based for loop. This is a nice way of iterating over all the elements in an array or other kind of range. You don't need to be aware of the number of elements. The loop mechanism takes care of that.

Note that the values from the range are *assigned* to the range variable, x. This means you cannot modify the elements of values by modifying the value of x. For example, this doesn't change the elements in the values array:

```
for (auto x : values)
  x += 2;
```

This just adds 2 to the local variable, x, not to the array element. The value stored in x is overwritten by the value of the next element from values on the next iteration. In the next chapter, you'll learn how you *can* change the values in a range using this loop.

The while Loop

The while loop uses a logical expression to control execution of the loop body. Figure 5-3 shows the general form of the while loop.

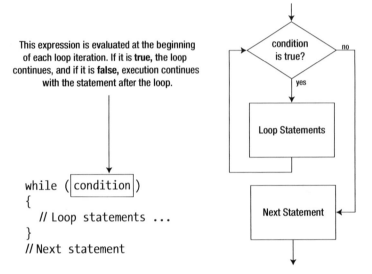

This expression is evaluated at the beginning of each loop iteration. If it is **true,** the loop continues, and if it is **false,** execution continues with the statement after the loop.

```
while (condition)
{
    // Loop statements ...
}
// Next statement
```

Figure 5-3. *How the while loop executes*

The flowchart in Figure 5-3 shows the logic of this loop. You can use any expression to control the loop, as long as it evaluates to a value of type bool or can be implicitly converted to type bool. If the loop condition expression evaluates to a numerical value, for example, the loop continues as long as the value is nonzero. A zero value ends the loop.

You could implement a version of Ex5_04.cpp using a while loop to see how it differs:

```
// Ex5_05.cpp
// Using a while loop to calculate the sum of integers from 1 to n and n!
#include <iostream>
#include <iomanip>

int main()
{
  unsigned int limit {};
  std::cout << "This program calculates n! and the sum of the integers"
            << " up to n for values 1 to limit.\n";
  std::cout << "What upper limit for n would you like? ";
  std::cin >> limit;

  // Output column headings
  std::cout << std::setw(8) << "integer" << std::setw(8) << " sum"
            << std::setw(20) << " factorial" << std::endl;
  unsigned int n {};
  unsigned int sum {};
  unsigned long long factorial {1ULL};
```

```
  while (++n <= limit)
  {
    sum += n;                     // Accumulate sum to current n
    factorial *= n;               // Calculate n! for current n
    std::cout << std::setw(8) << n << std::setw(8) << sum
              << std::setw(20) << factorial << std::endl;
  }
}
```

The output from this program is the same as Ex5_04.cpp if you entered it correctly. The variables n, sum, and factorial are defined before the loop. Here the types of the variables can be different, so n and sum are defined as unsigned int. The maximum value that can be stored in factorial limits the calculation, so this remains as type unsigned long long. Because of the way the calculation is implemented, the counter n is initialized to zero. The while loop condition increments n and then compares the new value with limit. The loop continues as long as the condition is true, so the loop executes with values of n from 1 up to limit. When n reaches limit+1, the loop ends. The statements within the loop body are the same as in Ex5_04.cpp.

▓ **Note**   Any for loop can be written as an equivalent while loop, and vice versa. For instance, a for loop has the following generic form:

for (*initialization*; *condition*; *iteration*)

 body

This can typically[3] be written using a while loop as follows:

{
 initialization;
 while (*condition*)
 {
  body
  iteration
 }
}

The while loop needs to be surrounded by an extra pair of curly braces to emulate the way the variables declared in the *initialization* code are scoped by the original for loop.

---

[3]If the for loop's *body* contains continue statements (covered later in this chapter), you'll need some additional work rewriting the loop to a while loop. Concretely, you'll have to ensure a copy of the *iteration* code is added prior to every continue statement.

The do-while Loop

The do-while loop is similar to the while loop in that the loop continues for as long as the specified loop condition remains true. The only difference is that the loop condition is checked at the *end* of the do-while loop, rather than at the beginning, so the loop statement is always executed at least once.

Figure 5-4 shows the logic and general form of the do-while loop. Note that the semicolon that comes after the condition between the parentheses is absolutely necessary. If you leave it out, the program won't compile.

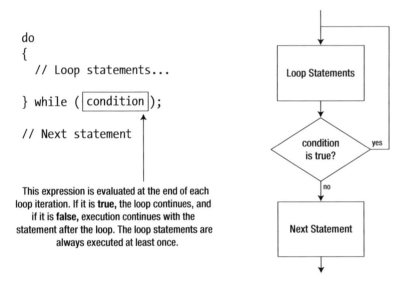

Figure 5-4. *How a do-while loop executes*

This kind of logic is ideal for situations where you have a block of code that you *always* want to execute once and may want to execute more than once. We can tell that you're not convinced that this is something that you'd ever need to do, so let's look at another example.

This program will calculate the average of an arbitrary number of input values—temperatures, for example—without storing them. You have no way of knowing in advance how many values will be entered, but it's safe to assume that you'll always have at least one, because if you didn't, there'd be no point to running the program. That makes it an ideal candidate for a do-while loop. Here's the code:

```
// Ex5_06.cpp
// Using a do-while loop to manage input
#include <iostream>
#include <cctype>                               // For tolower() function
```

```cpp
int main()
{
  char reply {};                          // Stores response to prompt for input
  int count {};                           // Counts the number of input values
  double temperature {};                  // Stores an input value
  double total {};                        // Stores the sum of all input values
  do
  {
    std::cout << "Enter a temperature reading: ";  // Prompt for input
    std::cin >> temperature;              // Read input value

    total += temperature;                 // Accumulate total of values
    ++count;                              // Increment count

    std::cout << "Do you want to enter another? (y/n): ";
    std::cin >> reply;                    // Get response
  } while (std::tolower(reply) == 'y');

  std::cout << "The average temperature is " << total/count << std::endl;
}
```

A sample session with this program produces the following output (for our non-American readers: the temperature readings we entered here are in degrees Fahrenheit, not Celsius, and are therefore not at all that extraordinary):

```
Enter a temperature reading: 53
Do you want to enter another? (y/n): y
Enter a temperature reading: 65.5
Do you want to enter another? (y/n): y
Enter a temperature reading: 74
Do you want to enter another? (y/n): Y
Enter a temperature reading: 69.5
Do you want to enter another? (y/n): n
The average temperature is 65.5
```

This program deals with any number of input values without prior knowledge of how many will be entered. After defining four variables that are required for the input and the calculation, the data values are read in a do-while loop. One input value is read on each loop iteration, and at least one value will always be read, which is not unreasonable. The response to the prompt that is stored in reply determines whether the loop ends. If the reply is y or Y, the loop continues; otherwise, the loop ends. Using the std::tolower() function that is declared in the cctype header ensures either uppercase or lowercase is accepted.

An alternative to using tolower() in the loop condition is to use a more complex expression for the condition. You could express the condition as reply == 'y' || reply == 'Y'. This ORs the two bool values that result from the comparisons so that either an uppercase or lowercase y entered will result in true.

■ **Caution**   While the semicolon after a do-while statement is required by the language, you should normally never add one after the while() of a regular while loop:

```
while (condition);        // You rarely want a semicolon here!!
  body
```

This creates a while loop with a body that equals an empty statement. In other words, it is equivalent to the following:

```
while (condition) {}  /* Do nothing until condition becomes false (if ever) */
body
```

Two things may happen if you accidentally add such a semicolon: either *body* becomes executed exactly once or never at all. The former would happen, for instance, if you add a semicolon to the while loop of Ex5_05. In general, however, it is more likely that a while loop's *body* is supposed to, after one or more iterations, make the evaluation of its *condition* flip from true to false. Adding an erroneous semicolon then causes the while loop to go on indefinitely.

Nested Loops

You can place a loop inside another loop. In fact, you can nest loops within loops to whatever depth you require to solve your problem. Furthermore, nested loops can be of any kind. You can nest a for loop inside a while loop inside a do-while loop inside a range-based for loop, if you have the need. They can be mixed in any way you want.

Nested loops are often applied in the context of arrays, but they have many other uses. We'll illustrate how nesting works with an example that provides lots of opportunity for nesting loops. Multiplication tables are the bane of many children's lives at school, but you can easily use a nested loop to generate one.

```cpp
// Ex5_07.cpp
// Generating multiplication tables using nested loops
#include <iostream>
#include <iomanip>
#include <cctype>

int main()
{
  size_t table {};             // Table size
  const size_t table_min {2};  // Minimum table size - at least up to the 2-times
  const size_t table_max {12}; // Maximum table size
  char reply {};               // Response to prompt

  do
  {
    std::cout << "What size table would you like ("
             << table_min << " to " << table_max << ")? ";
    std::cin >> table;         // Get the table size
    std::cout << std::endl;
```

```
    // Make sure table size is within the limits
    if (table < table_min || table > table_max)
    {
      std::cout << "Invalid table size entered. Program terminated." << std::endl;
      return 1;
    }

    // Create the top line of the table
    std::cout << std::setw(6) << " |";
    for (size_t i {1}; i <= table; ++i)
    {
      std::cout << " " << std::setw(3) << i << " |";
    }
    std::cout << std::endl;

    // Create the separator row
    for (size_t i {}; i <= table; ++i)
    {
      std::cout << "------";
    }
    std::cout << std::endl;

    for (size_t i {1}; i <= table; ++i)
    {     // Iterate over rows
      std::cout << " " << std::setw(3) << i << " |"; // Start the row

      // Output the values in a row
      for (size_t j {1}; j <= table; ++j)
      {
        std::cout << " " << std::setw(3) << i*j << " |";  // For each col.
      }
      std::cout << std::endl;                         // End the row
    }

    // Check if another table is required
    std::cout << "\nDo you want another table (y or n)? ";
    std::cin >> reply;

  } while (std::tolower(reply) == 'y');
}
```

Here's an example of the output:

```
What size table would you like (2 to 12)? 4
     |   1 |   2 |   3 |   4 |
------------------------------
   1 |   1 |   2 |   3 |   4 |
   2 |   2 |   4 |   6 |   8 |
   3 |   3 |   6 |   9 |  12 |
   4 |   4 |   8 |  12 |  16 |
```

```
Do you want another table (y or n)? y
What size table would you like (2 to 12)? 10

        |   1 |   2 |   3 |   4 |   5 |   6 |   7 |   8 |   9 |  10 |
--------------------------------------------------------------------
    1 |   1 |   2 |   3 |   4 |   5 |   6 |   7 |   8 |   9 |  10 |
    2 |   2 |   4 |   6 |   8 |  10 |  12 |  14 |  16 |  18 |  20 |
    3 |   3 |   6 |   9 |  12 |  15 |  18 |  21 |  24 |  27 |  30 |
    4 |   4 |   8 |  12 |  16 |  20 |  24 |  28 |  32 |  36 |  40 |
    5 |   5 |  10 |  15 |  20 |  25 |  30 |  35 |  40 |  45 |  50 |
    6 |   6 |  12 |  18 |  24 |  30 |  36 |  42 |  48 |  54 |  60 |
    7 |   7 |  14 |  21 |  28 |  35 |  42 |  49 |  56 |  63 |  70 |
    8 |   8 |  16 |  24 |  32 |  40 |  48 |  56 |  64 |  72 |  80 |
    9 |   9 |  18 |  27 |  36 |  45 |  54 |  63 |  72 |  81 |  90 |
   10 |  10 |  20 |  30 |  40 |  50 |  60 |  70 |  80 |  90 | 100 |

Do you want another table (y or n)? n
```

This example includes three standard headers, iostream, iomanip, and cctype. Just as a refresher, the first is for stream input/output, the second is for stream manipulators, and the third provides the tolower() and toupper() character conversion functions along with the various character classification functions.

The input value for the size of the table is stored in table. A table will be output presenting the results of all products from 1 × 1 up to table × table. The value entered is validated by comparing it with table_min and table_max. A table less than table_min doesn't make much sense, and table_max represents a size that is the maximum that is likely to look reasonable when it is output. If table is not within range, the program ends with a return code value of 1 to indicate it's not a normal end. (Granted, terminating the program after a bad user input is a tad drastic. Perhaps you could try to make it so that the program asks the user to try again instead?)

The multiplication table is presented in the form of a rectangular table—what else? The values along the left column and the top row are the operand values in a multiplication operation. The value at the intersection of a row and column is the product of the row and column values. The table variable is used as the iteration limit in the first for loop that creates the top line of the table. Vertical bars are used to separate columns, and the use of the setw() manipulator makes all the columns the same width.

The next for loop creates a line of dash characters to separate the top row of multipliers from the body of the table. Each iteration adds six dashes to the row. By starting the count at zero instead of one, you output table + 1 sets—one for the left column of multipliers and one for each of the columns of table entries.

The final for loop contains a nested for loop that outputs the left column of multipliers and the products that are the table entries. The nested loop outputs a complete table row, right after the multiplier for the row in the leftmost column is printed. The nested loop executes once for each iteration of the outer loop, so table rows are generated.

The code that creates a complete table is within a do-while loop. This provides for as many tables to be produced as required. If y or Y is entered in response to the prompt after a table has been output, another iteration of the do-while loop executes to allow another table to be created. This example demonstrates three levels of nesting: a for loop inside another for loop that is inside the do-while loop.

Skipping Loop Iterations

Situations arise where you want to skip one loop iteration and press on with the next. The continue statement does this:

```
continue;                    // Go to the next iteration
```

When this statement executes within a loop, execution transfers immediately to the end of the current iteration. As long as the loop control expression allows it, execution continues with the next iteration. This is best understood in an example. Let's suppose you want to output a table of characters with their character codes in hexadecimal and decimal formats. Of course, you don't want to output characters that don't have a graphical representation—some of these, such as tabs and newline, would mess up the output. So, the program should output just the printable characters. Here's the code:

```
// Ex5_08.cpp
// Using the continue statement to display ASCII character codes
#include <iostream>
#include <iomanip>
#include <cctype>
#include <limits>

int main()
{
  // Output the column headings
  std::cout << std::setw(11) << "Character " << std::setw(13) << "Hexadecimal "
            << std::setw(9)  << "Decimal "   << std::endl;
  std::cout << std::uppercase;                            // Uppercase hex digits

  // Output characters and corresponding codes
  unsigned char ch {};
  do
  {
    if (!std::isprint(ch))                                // If it's not printable...
      continue;                                           // ...skip this iteration
    std::cout << std::setw(6) << ch                       // Character
              << std::hex << std::setw(12) << static_cast<int>(ch)  // Hexadecimal
              << std::dec << std::setw(10) << static_cast<int>(ch)  // Decimal
              << std::endl;
  } while (ch++ < std::numeric_limits<unsigned char>::max());
}
```

This outputs all the printable characters with code values from 0 to the maximum unsigned char value so it displays a handy list of the codes for the printable ASCII characters. The do-while loop is the most interesting bit. The variable, ch, varies from zero up to the maximum value for its type, unsigned char. You saw the numeric_limits<>::max() function in Chapter 2, which returns the maximum value for the type you place between the angled brackets. Within the loop, you don't want to output details of any character that does not have a printable representation, and the isprint() function that is declared in the locale header only returns true for printable characters. Thus, the expression in the if statement will be true when ch contains the code for a character that is *not* printable. In this case, the continue statement executes, which skips the rest of the code in the current loop iteration.

The hex and dec manipulators in the output statements set the output mode for integers to what you require. You have to cast the value of ch to int in the output statement to display as a numeric value; otherwise, it would be output as a character. The judicious use of the setw() manipulator for the headings and the output in the loop ensures that everything lines up nicely.

We're sure you noticed when you run the example that the last character code in the output is 126. This is because the isprint() function is returning false for code values in excess of this. If you want to see character codes greater than 126 in the output, you could write the if statement in the loop as follows:

```
if (std::iscntrl(ch))
    continue;
```

This will execute the continue statement only for codes that represent control characters, which are code values from 0x00 to 0x1F. You'll now see some weird and wonderful characters in the last 128 characters; what these are depends on the language and regional settings of your platform.

Using unsigned char as the type for ch keeps the code simple. If you used char as the type for ch, you would need to provide for the possibility that it could be a signed or unsigned type. One complication of signed values is that you can no longer easily cover the range by counting up from 0. Overall, the loop's logic is far easier here if you simply stick with unsigned chars.

Note that, nevertheless, the straightforward for loop isn't suitable here, even with ch as type unsigned char. The condition in a for loop is checked before the loop block executes, so you might be tempted to write the loop as follows:

```
for (unsigned char ch {}; ch <= std::numeric_limits<unsigned char>::max(); ++ch)
{
    // Output character and code...
}
```

This loop never ends. After executing the loop block with ch at the maximum value, the next increment of ch gives it a value of 0, so the second loop control expression is never false. You could make it work by using type int for the control variable in a for loop and then casting the value to type unsigned char when you want to output it as a character.

Breaking Out of a Loop

Sometimes, you need to end a loop prematurely; something might arise within the loop statement that indicates there is no point in continuing. In this case, you can use the break statement. Its effect in a loop is much the same as it is in a switch statement; executing a break statement within a loop ends the loop immediately, and execution continues with the statement following the loop. The break statement is often used with an *indefinite loop*, so let's look next at what one of those looks like.

Indefinite Loops

An *indefinite loop* can potentially run forever. Omitting the second control expression in a for loop results in a loop that potentially executes an unlimited number of iterations. There has to be some way to end the loop within the loop block itself; otherwise, the loop repeats indefinitely.

Indefinite loops have many practical uses, such as programs that monitor some kind of alarm indicator, for instance, or that collect data from sensors in an industrial plant. An indefinite loop can be useful when you don't know in advance how many loop iterations will be required, such as when you are reading a variable quantity of input data. In these circumstances, you code the exit from the loop within the loop block, not within the loop control expression.

In the most common form of the indefinite for loop, all the control expressions are omitted, as shown here:

```
for (;;)
{
  // Statements that do something...
  // ... and include some way of ending the loop
}
```

You still need the semicolons (;), even though no loop control expressions exist. The only way this loop can end is if some code within the loop terminates it.

You can have an indefinite while loop, too:

```
while (true)
{
  // Statements that do something...
  // ... and include some way of ending the loop
}
```

The loop condition is always true, so you have an indefinite loop. This is equivalent to the for loop with no control expressions. Of course, you can also have a version of the do-while loop that is indefinite, but it is not normally used because it has no advantages over the other two types of loop.

The obvious way to end an indefinite loop is to use the break statement. You could have used an indefinite loop in Ex5_07.cpp to allow several tries at entering a valid table size, instead of ending the program immediately. This loop would do it:

```
const size_t max_tries {3};    // Max. number of times a user can try entering a table size
do
{
  for (size_t count {1}; ; ++count)  // Indefinite loop
  {
    std::cout << "What size table would you like ("
              << table_min << " to " << table_max << ")? ";
    std::cin >> table; // Get the table size

    // Make sure table size is within the limits
    if (table >= table_min && table <= table_max)
    {
      break;                                        // Exit the input loop
    }
    else if (count < max_tries)
    {
      std::cout << "Invalid input - try again.\n";
    }
    else
    {
      std::cout << "Invalid table size entered - yet again! \nSorry, only "
                << max_tries << " allowed - program terminated." << std::endl;
      return 1;
    }
  }
  ...
```

This indefinite for loop could replace the code at the beginning of the do-while loop in Ex5_07.cpp that handles input of the table size. This allows up to max_tries attempts to enter a valid table size. A valid entry executes the break statement, which terminates this loop and continues with the next statement in the do-while loop. You'll find the resulting program in Ex5_07A.cpp.

Here's an example that uses an indefinite while loop to sort the contents of an array in ascending sequence:

```cpp
// Ex5_09.cpp
// Sorting an array in ascending sequence - using an indefinite while loop
#include <iostream>
#include <iomanip>

int main()
{
  const size_t size {1000};            // Array size
  double x[size] {};                   // Stores data to be sorted
  size_t count {};                     // Number of values in array

  while (true)
  {
    double input {};                   // Temporary store for a value
    std::cout << "Enter a non-zero value, or 0 to end: ";
    std::cin >> input;
    if (input == 0)
      break;

    x[count] = input;

    if (++count == size)
    {
      std::cout << "Sorry, I can only store " << size << " values.\n";
      break;
    }
  }

  if (!count)
  {
    std::cout << "Nothing to sort..." << std::endl;
    return 0;
  }

  std::cout << "Starting sort." << std::endl;

  while (true)
  {
    bool swapped{ false };          // becomes true when not all values are in order
    for (size_t i {}; i < count - 1; ++i)
    {
      if (x[i] > x[i + 1])          // Out of order so swap them
      {
        const auto temp = x[i];
```

```
      x[i] = x[i+1];
      x[i + 1] = temp;
      swapped = true;
    }
  }

  if (!swapped)              // If there were no swaps
    break;                   // ...all values are in order...
}                            // ...otherwise, go round again.

  std::cout << "Your data in ascending sequence:\n"
            << std::fixed << std::setprecision(1);
  const size_t perline {10};          // Number output per line
  size_t n {};                        // Number on current line
  for (size_t i {}; i < count; ++i)
  {
    std::cout << std::setw(8) << x[i];
    if (++n == perline)               // When perline have been written...
    {
      std::cout << std::endl;         // Start a new line and...
      n = 0;                          // ...reset count on this line
    }
  }
  std::cout << std::endl;
}
```

Typical output looks like this:

```
Enter a non-zero value, or 0 to end: 44
Enter a non-zero value, or 0 to end: -7.8
Enter a non-zero value, or 0 to end: 56.3
Enter a non-zero value, or 0 to end: 75.2
Enter a non-zero value, or 0 to end: -3
Enter a non-zero value, or 0 to end: -2
Enter a non-zero value, or 0 to end: 66
Enter a non-zero value, or 0 to end: 6.7
Enter a non-zero value, or 0 to end: 8.2
Enter a non-zero value, or 0 to end: -5
Enter a non-zero value, or 0 to end: 0
Starting sort.
Your data in ascending sequence:
    -7.8    -5.0    -3.0    -2.0     6.7     8.2    44.0    56.3    66.0    75.2
```

The code limits the number of values that can be entered to size, which is set to 1000. Only users with amazing keyboard skill and persistence will find out this entire array. This is thus rather wasteful with memory, but you'll learn how you can avoid this in such circumstances later in this chapter.

Data entry is managed in the first while loop. This loop runs until either 0 is entered or the array, x, is full because size values have been entered. In the latter instance, the user will see a message, indicating the limit.

Each value is read into the variable input. This allows the value to be tested for zero before it is stored in the array. Each value is stored in the element of the array x at index count. In the if statement that follows, count is pre-incremented and thus incremented *before* it is compared to size. This ensures it represents the number of elements in the array by the time it is compared to size.

The elements are sorted in ascending sequence in the next indefinite while loop. Ordering the values of the array elements is carried out in the nested for loop that iterates over successive pairs of elements and checks whether they are in ascending sequence. If a pair of elements contains values that are not in ascending sequence, the values are swapped to order them correctly. The bool variable, swapped, records whether it was necessary to interchange any elements in any complete execution of the nested for loop. If it wasn't, then the elements are in ascending sequence, and the break statement is executed to exit the while loop. If any pair had to be interchanged, swapped will be true, so another iteration of the while loop will execute, and this causes the for loop to run through pairs of elements again.

This sorting method is called the *bubble sort* because elements gradually "bubble up" to their correct position in the array. It's not the most efficient sorting method, but it has the merit that it is very easy to understand, and it's a good demonstration of yet another use for an indefinite loop.

■ **Tip**   In general, indefinite loops, or even just break statements, should be used judiciously. They are sometimes considered bad coding style. You should, as much as possible, put the conditions that determine when a loop terminates between the round parentheses of the for or while statement. Doing so increases code readability because this is where every C++ programmer will be looking for such conditions. Any (additional) break statements inside the loop's body are much easier to miss and can therefore make code harder to understand.

Controlling a for Loop with Unsigned Integers

You probably didn't notice, but Ex5_09 actually contains a perfect example of a rather crucial caveat regarding controlling a for loop with unsigned integers, such as values of type size_t. Suppose we omit the following check from the program in Ex5_09.cpp:

```
if (!count)
{
  std::cout << "Nothing to sort..." << std::endl;
  return 0;
}
```

What would happen then, you think, if the user decides not to enter any values? That is, if count equals zero? Something bad, I'm sure you already guessed. And of course you guessed correctly! What'd happen is that execution would enter the following for loop with count equal to 0:

```
for (size_t i {}; i < count - 1; ++i)
{
  ...
}
```

Mathematically speaking, if count equals 0, count - 1 should become -1. But since count is an unsigned integer, it cannot actually represent a negative value such as -1. Instead, subtracting one from zero gives numeric_limits<size_t>::max() a very large unsigned value. On our test system this equals 18446744073709551615—a number well over 18 *quintillion*. This effectively turns the loop into the following:

```
for (size_t i {}; i < 18446744073709551615; ++i)
{
    ...
}
```

While technically not an indefinite loop, it would take even the fastest computer a fair amount of time to count to 18 quintillion (and a bit). In our case, though, the program will crash long before the counter i comes even close to that number. The reason is that the loop counter i is used in expressions such as x[i], which means that the loop will quickly start accessing and overwriting parts of memory it has no business touching.

■ **Caution**   Take care when subtracting from unsigned integers. Any value that mathematically speaking should be negative then wraps around to become a huge positive number. These types of errors can have catastrophic results in loop control expressions.

A first solution is to test that count does not equal zero prior to entering the loop, like we did in Ex5_09. Other options include casting to a signed integer or rewriting the loop such that it no longer uses subtraction:

```
// Cast to a signed integer prior to subtracting
for (int i {}; i < static_cast<int>(count) - 1; ++i)
    ...

// Rewrite to avoid subtracting from unsigned values
for (size_t i {}; i + 1 < count; ++i)
    ...
```

Similar caveats lurk when using a for loop to traverse an array in reverse order. Suppose we have an array my_array and we want to process it starting with the last element working our way back to the front of the array. Then an understandable first attempt could be a loop of the following form:

```
for (size_t i = std::size(my_array) - 1; i >= 0; --i)
    ... process my_array[i] ...
```

Let's assume we know that my_array is not an array of size zero. Let's ignore the truly awful things that would happen if that were the case. Even then we are in serious problems. Because the index variable i is of unsigned type, i is by definition always greater or equal to zero. That's what unsigned means. In other words, the loop's termination condition i >= 0, by definition, always evaluates to true, effectively turning this buggy reverse loop into an indefinite loop. We'll leave it to you to come up with a solution in the exercises at the end of the chapter.

Arrays of Characters

An array of elements of type char can have a dual personality. It can simply be an array of characters, in which each element stores one character, *or* it can represent a string. In the latter case, the characters in the string are stored in successive array elements, followed by a special string termination character called the *null character* that you write as '\0'. The null character marks the end of the string.

A character array that is terminated by '\0' is referred to as a *C-style string*. This contrasts with the string type from the Standard Library that we'll explain in detail in Chapter 7. Objects of type string are much more flexible and convenient for string manipulation than using arrays of type char. For the moment, we'll introduce C-style strings in the context of arrays in general and return to them and to type string in detail in Chapter 7.

You can define and initialize an array of elements of type char like this:

```
char vowels[5] {'a', 'e', 'i', 'o', 'u'};
```

This isn't a string—it's just an array of five characters. Each array element is initialized with the corresponding character from the initializer list. As with numeric arrays, if you provide fewer initializing values than there are array elements, the elements that don't have explicit initial values will be initialized with the equivalent of zero, which is the null character, '\0' in this case. This means that if there are insufficient initial values, the array will effectively contain a string. Here's an example:

```
char vowels[6] {'a', 'e', 'i', 'o', 'u'};
```

The last element will be initialized with '\0'. The presence of the null character means that this can be treated as a C-style string. Of course, you can still regard it as an array of characters.

You could leave it to the compiler to set the size of the array to the number of initializing values:

```
char vowels[] {'a', 'e', 'i', 'o', 'u'};    // An array with five elements
```

This also defines an array of five characters initialized with the vowels in the braced initializer.

You can also declare an array of type char and initialize it with a *string literal*, as follows:

```
char name[10] {"Mae West"};
```

This creates a C-style string. Because you're initializing the array with a string literal, the null character will be stored in the element following the last string character, so the contents of the array will be as shown in Figure 5-5:

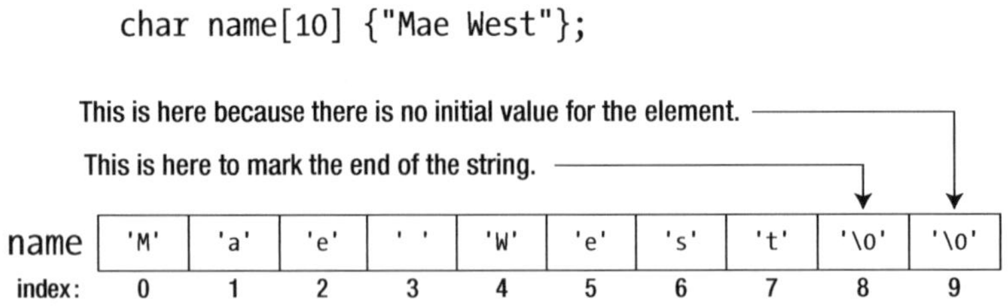

Figure 5-5. An array of elements of type char initialized with a string literal

You can leave the compiler to set the size of the array when you initialize it with a string literal:

```
char name[] {"Mae West"};
```

This time, the array will have nine elements: eight to store the characters in the string, plus an extra element to store the string termination character. Of course, you could have used this approach when you declared the vowels array:

```
char vowels[] {"aeiou"};                    // An array with six elements
```

There's a significant difference between this and the previous definition for vowels without an explicit array dimension. Here you're initializing the array with a string literal. This has '\0' appended to it implicitly to mark the end of the string, so the vowels array will contain six elements. The array created with the earlier definition will have only five elements and can't be used as a string.

You can output a string stored in an array just by using the array name. The string in the name array, for example, could be written to cout with this statement:

```
std::cout << name << std::endl;
```

This will display the entire string of characters, up to the '\0'. There *must* be a '\0' at the end. If there isn't, the standard output stream will continue to output characters from successive memory locations, which almost certainly contain garbage, until either a null character happens to turn up or an illegal memory access occurs.

■ **Caution**   You can't output the contents of an array of a numeric type by just using the array name. This works only for char arrays. And even a char array passed to an output stream must be terminated with a null character, or the program will likely crash.

This example analyzes an array of elements of type char to work out how many vowels and consonants are used in it:

```
// Ex5_10.cpp
// Classifying the letters in a C-style string
#include <iostream>
#include <cctype>

int main()
{
  const int max_length {100};            // Array size
  char text[max_length] {};              // Array to hold input string

  std::cout << "Enter a line of text:" << std::endl;

  // Read a line of characters including spaces
  std::cin.getline(text, max_length);
  std::cout << "You entered:\n" << text << std::endl;
```

```
size_t vowels {};                        // Count of vowels
size_t consonants {};                    // Count of consonants
for (int i {}; text[i] != '\0'; i++)
{
  if (std::isalpha(text[i]))             // If it is a letter...
  {
    switch (std::tolower(text[i]))
    {                                    // ...check lowercase...
      case 'a': case 'e': case 'i': case 'o': case 'u':
        ++vowels;                        // ...it is a vowel
        break;

      default:
        ++consonants;                    // ...it is a consonant
    }
  }
}
std::cout << "Your input contained " << vowels << " vowels and "
          << consonants << " consonants." << std::endl;
}
```

Here's an example of the output:

```
Enter a line of text:
A rich man is nothing but a poor man with money.
You entered:
A rich man is nothing but a poor man with money.
Your input contained 14 vowels and 23 consonants.
```

The text array of type char elements has the size defined by a const variable, max_length. This determines the maximum length of string that can be stored, including the terminating null character, so the longest string can contain max_length-1 characters.

You can't use the extraction operator to read the input because it won't read a string containing spaces; any whitespace character terminates the input operation with the >> operator. The getline() function for cin that is defined in the iostream header reads a sequence of characters, including spaces. By default, the input ends when a newline character, '\n', is read, which will be when you press the Enter key. The getline() function expects two arguments between the parentheses. The first argument specifies where the input is to be stored, which in this case is the text array. The second argument specifies the maximum number of characters that you want to store. This includes the string termination character, '\0', which will be automatically appended to the end of the input.

■ **Note**   The period between the name of the cin object and that of its so-called member function getline() is called the *direct member selection* operator. This operator is used to access members of a class object. You will learn all about defining classes and member functions from Chapter 11 onward.

Although you haven't done so here, you can optionally supply a *third* argument to the getline() function. This specifies an alternative to '\n' to indicate the end of the input. For example, if you want the end of the input string to be indicated by an asterisk, for example, you would use this statement to read the input:

```
std::cin.getline(text, maxlength, '*');
```

This would allow multiple lines of text to be entered because the '\n' that results from pressing Enter would no longer terminate the input operation. Of course, the total number of characters that you can enter in the read operation is still limited by maxlength.

Just to show that you can, the program outputs the string that was entered using just the array name, text. The text string is then analyzed in a straightforward manner in the for loop. The second control expression within the loop will be false when the character at the current index, i, is the null character, so the loop ends when the null character is reached.

Next, to work out the number of vowels and consonants, you only need to inspect alphabetic characters, and the if statement selects them; isalpha() only returns true for alphabetic characters. Thus, the switch statement executes only for letters. Converting the switch expression to lowercase avoids having to write cases for uppercase as well as lowercase letters. Any vowel will select the first case, and the default case is selected by anything that isn't a vowel, which must be a consonant, of course.

By the way, because the null character '\0' is the only character that converts to the Boolean false (analogous to 0 for integral values), you could write the for loop in Ex5_10 like this as well:

```
for (int i {}; text[i]; i++)
{
  ...
```

Multidimensional Arrays

All the arrays so far have required a single index value to select an element. Such an array is called a *one-dimensional array* because varying one index can reference all the elements. You can also define arrays that require two or more index values to access an element. These are referred to generically as *multidimensional arrays*. An array that requires two index values to reference an element is called a *two-dimensional array*. An array needing three index values is a *three-dimensional array*, and so on, for as many dimensions as you think you can handle.

Suppose, as an avid gardener, that you want to record the weights of the carrots you grow in your small vegetable garden. To store the weight of each carrot, which you planted in three rows of four, you could define a two-dimensional array:

```
double carrots[3][4] {};
```

This defines an array with three rows of four elements and initializes all elements to zero. To reference a particular element of the carrots array, you need two index values. The first index specifies the row, from 0 to 2, and the second index specifies a particular carrot in that row, from 0 to 3. To store the weight of the third carrot in the second row, you could write the following:

```
carrots[1][2] = 1.5;
```

Figure 5-6 shows the arrangement of this array in memory. The rows are stored contiguously in memory. As you can see, the two-dimensional array is effectively a *one*-dimensional array of three elements, each of which is a one-dimensional array with four elements. You have an array of three arrays that each has four elements of type double. Figure 5-6 also indicates that you can use the array name plus a *single* index value between square brackets to refer to an entire row.

```
double carrots[3][4] {};      // Array with 3 rows of 4 elements
```

You can refer to this row as carrots[0].

| carrots[0][0] | carrots[0][1] | carrots[0][2] | carrots[0][3] |

You can refer to this row as carrots[1].

| carrots[1][0] | carrots[1][1] | carrots[1][2] | carrots[1][3] |

You can refer to this row as carrots[2].

| carrots[2][0] | carrots[2][1] | carrots[2][2] | carrots[2][3] |

You can refer to the whole array as carrots

Figure 5-6. *Elements in a two-dimensional array*

You use two index values to refer to an element. The second index selects an element within the row specified by the first index; the second index varies most rapidly as you progress from one element to the next in memory. You can also envisage a two-dimensional array as a rectangular arrangement of elements in an array from left to right, where the first index specifies a row and the second index corresponds to a column. Figure 5-7 illustrates this. With arrays of more than two dimensions, the rightmost index value is always the one that varies most rapidly, and the leftmost index varies least rapidly.

```
double carrots [3][4] {};
```

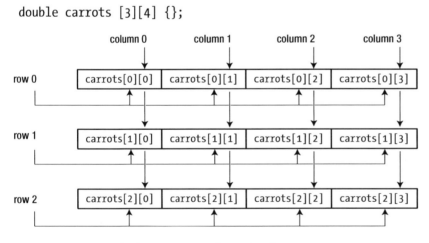

Figure 5-7. *Rows and columns in a two-dimensional array*

The array name by itself references the entire array. Note that with this array, you can't display the contents of either a row or the whole array using this notation. Here's an example:

```
std::cout << carrots << std::endl;    // Not what you may expect!
```

This statement will output a single hexadecimal value, which happens to be the address in memory of the first element of the array. You'll see why this is the case when we discuss pointers in the next chapter. Arrays of type char are a little different, as you saw earlier.

To display the entire array, one row to a line, you must write something like this:

```
for (size_t i {}; i < 3; ++i)      // Iterate over rows
{
  for (size_t j {}; j < 4; ++j)    // Iterate over elements within the row
  {
    std::cout << std::setw(12) << carrots[i][j];
  }
  std::cout << std::endl;          // A new line for a new row
}
```

This uses magic numbers, 3 and 4, which you can avoid by using std::size():

```
for (size_t i {}; i < std::size(carrots); ++i)
{
  for (size_t j {}; j < std::size(carrots[i]); ++j)
  {
    std::cout << std::setw(12) << carrots[i][j];
  }
  std::cout << std::endl;
}
```

■ **Note**   You can use range-based for loops here as well. However, to write the outer loop as a range-based for, you'll first need to learn about references. You'll do so in the next chapter.

It may also be better not to use magic numbers for the array dimension sizes in the first place, so you could define the array as follows:

```
const size_t nrows {3};            // Number of rows in the array
const size_t ncols {4};            // Number of columns, or number of elements per row
double carrots[nrows][ncols] {};
```

Defining an array of three dimensions just adds another set of square brackets. You might want to record three temperatures per day, seven days a week, for 52 weeks of the year. You could declare the following array to store such data as type int:

```
int temperatures[52][7][3] {};
```

The array stores three values in each row. There are seven such rows for a whole week's data and 52 sets of these for all the weeks in the year. This array will have a total of 1,092 elements of type long. They will all be initialized with zero. To display the middle temperature for day 3 of week 26, you could write this:

```
std::cout << temperatures[25][2][1] << std::endl;
```

Remember that all the index values start at 0, so the weeks run from 0 to 51, the days run from 0 to 6, and the samples in a day run from 0 to 2.

Initializing Multidimensional Arrays

You have seen that an empty braced initializer initializes an array with any number of dimensions to zero. It gets a little more complicated when you want initial values other than zero. The way in which you specify initial values for a multidimensional array derives from the notion that a two-dimensional array is an array of one-dimensional arrays. The initializing values for a one-dimensional array are written between braces and separated by commas. Following on from that, you could declare and initialize the two-dimensional carrots array, with this statement:

```
double carrots[3][4] {
                    {2.5, 3.2, 3.7, 4.1},   // First row
                    {4.1, 3.9, 1.6, 3.5},   // Second row
                    {2.8, 2.3, 0.9, 1.1}    // Third row
                  };
```

Each row is a one-dimensional array, so the initializing values for each row are contained within their own set of braces. These three lists are themselves contained within a set of braces because the two-dimensional array is a one-dimensional array of one-dimensional arrays. You can extend this principle to any number of dimensions—each extra dimension requires another level of nested braces enclosing the initial values.

A question that may immediately spring to mind is, "What happens when you omit some of the initializing values?" The answer is more or less what you might have expected from past experience. Each of the innermost pairs of braces contains the values for the elements in the rows. The first list corresponds to carrots[0], the second to carrots[1], and the third to carrots[2]. The values between each pair of braces are assigned to the elements of the corresponding row. If there aren't enough to initialize all the elements in the row, then the elements without values will be initialized to 0.

Let's look at an example:

```
double carrots[3][4] {
                    { 2.5, 3.2        },    // First row
                    { 4.1             },    // Second row
                    { 2.8, 2.3, 0.9 }       // Third row
                  };
```

The first two elements in the first row have initial values, whereas only one element in the second row has an initial value, and three elements in the third row have initial values. The elements without initial values in each row will therefore be initialized with zero, as shown in Figure 5-8.

carrots[0][0]	carrots[0][1]	carrots[0][2]	carrots[0][3]
2.5	3.2	0.0	0.0

carrots[1][0]	carrots[1][1]	carrots[1][2]	carrots[1][3]
4.1	0.0	0.0	0.0

carrots[2][0]	carrots[2][1]	carrots[2][2]	carrots[2][3]
2.8	2.3	0.9	0.0

Figure 5-8. *Omitting initial values for a two-dimensional array*

If you don't include sufficient sets of braces to initialize all of the rows in the array, the elements in the rows without braces enclosing initializing values will all be set to 0. If you include several initial values in the braced initializer but omit the nested braces enclosing values for the rows, values are assigned sequentially to the elements, as they're stored in memory—with the rightmost index varying most rapidly. For example, suppose you define the array like this:

```
double carrots[3][4] {1.1, 1.2, 1.3, 1.4, 1.5, 1.6, 1.7};
```

The first four values in the list will initialize elements in row 0. The last three values in the list will initialize the first three elements in row 1. The remaining elements will be initialized with zero.

Setting Dimensions by Default

You can let the compiler determine the size of the first (leftmost) dimension of an array with any number of dimensions from the set of initializing values. The compiler, however, can determine only *one* of the dimensions in a multidimensional array, and it has to be the first. You could define the two-dimensional carrots array with this statement:

```
double carrots[][4] {
                {2.5, 3.2      },    // First row
                {4.1           },    // Second row
                {2.8, 2.3,  0.9 }    // Third row
            };
```

The array will have three rows, as before, because there are three sets of braces within the outer pair. If there were only two sets, the array would have two rows. The number of inner pairs of braces determines the number of rows.

What you cannot do is have the compiler deduce any dimension other than the first one. Up to a point, this makes sense. If you were to supply 12 initial values for a two-dimensional array, for instance, there's no way for the compiler to know whether the array should be three rows of four elements, six rows of two elements, or indeed any combination that amounts to 12 elements. Still, this does mean that, rather unfortunately, array definitions such as the following should result in a compiler error as well:

```
double carrots[][] {              /* Does not compile! */
                {2.5, 3.2, 3.7, 4.1},    // First row
                {4.1, 3.9, 1.6, 3.5},    // Second row
                {2.8, 2.3, 0.9, 1.1}     // Third row
            };
```

You always have to explicitly specify all array dimensions except the first one. Here's an example of defining a three-dimensional array:

```
int numbers[][3][4] {
                    {
                      { 2,  4,  6,  8},
                      { 3,  5,  7,  9},
                      { 5,  8, 11, 14}
                    },
                    {
                      {12, 14, 16, 18},
                      {13, 15, 17, 19},
                      {15, 18, 21, 24}
                    }
                  };
```

This array has three dimensions of sizes 2, 3, and 4. The outer braces enclose two further sets of braces, and each of these in turn contains three sets, each of which contains the four initial values for the corresponding row. As this simple example demonstrates, initializing arrays of three dimensions or more gets increasingly complicated, and you need to take great care when placing the braces enclosing the initial values. The braces are nested to as many levels as there are dimensions in the array.

Multidimensional Character Arrays

You can define arrays of two or more dimensions to hold any type of data. A two-dimensional array of type char is interesting because it can be an array of C-style strings. When you initialize a two-dimensional array of char elements with string literals, you don't need the braces around the literal for a row—the double quotes delimiting the literal do the job of the braces in this case. Here's an example:

```
char stars[][80] {
                    "Robert Redford",
                    "Hopalong Cassidy",
                    "Lassie",
                    "Slim Pickens",
                    "Boris Karloff",
                    "Oliver Hardy"
                  };
```

This array will have six rows because there are six string literals as initial values. Each row stores a string containing the name of a movie star, and a terminating null character, '\0', will be appended to each string. Each row will accommodate up to 80 characters according to the row dimension you've specified. We can see this applied in the following example:

```
// Ex5_11.cpp
// Working with strings in an array
#include <iostream>
#include <array>              // for std::size()

int main()
{
  const size_t max_length{80};        // Maximum string length (including \0)
```

```
char stars[][max_length] {
                        "Fatty Arbuckle",  "Clara Bow",
                        "Lassie",          "Slim Pickens",
                        "Boris Karloff",   "Mae West",
                        "Oliver Hardy",    "Greta Garbo"
                      };
size_t choice {};

std::cout << "Pick a lucky star! Enter a number between 1 and "
          << std::size(stars) << ": ";
std::cin  >> choice;

if (choice >= 1 && choice <= std::size(stars))
{
  std::cout << "Your lucky star is " << stars[choice - 1] << std::endl;
}
else
{
  std::cout << "Sorry, you haven't got a lucky star." << std::endl;
}
}
```

This is some typical output from this program:

```
Pick a lucky star! Enter a number between 1 and 8: 6
Your lucky star is Mae West
```

Apart from its incredible inherent entertainment value, the main point of interest in the example is the definition of the array, stars. It's a two-dimensional array of char elements, which can hold multiple strings, each of which can contain up to max_length characters, including the terminating null that's automatically added by the compiler. The initializing strings for the array are enclosed between braces and separated by commas. Because the size of the first array dimension is omitted, the compiler creates the array with the number of rows necessary to accommodate all the initializing strings. As you saw earlier, you can omit the size of only the first dimension; you must specify the sizes of any other dimensions that are required.

The if statement arranges for the output to be displayed. Its condition checks that the integer that was entered is within range before attempting to display a name. When you need to reference a string for output, you only need to specify the first index value. A single index selects a particular 80-element subarray, and because this contains a string, the operation will output the contents of each element up to the terminating null character. The index is specified as choice-1 because the choice values start from 1, whereas the index values need to start from 0. This is quite a common idiom when you're programming with arrays.

Allocating an Array at Runtime

The C++17 standard does not permit an array dimension to be specified at runtime. That is, the array dimension must be a constant expression that can be evaluated by the compiler. However, some current C++ compilers do allow setting variable array dimensions at runtime because the current C standard, C11, permits this, and a C++ compiler will typically compile C code too.

These so-called variable-length arrays can be a useful feature, so in case your compiler supports this, we'll show how it works with an example. Keep in mind, though, that this is not strictly in conformance with the C++ language standard. Suppose you want to calculate the average height for a group of people, and you want to accommodate as many people as the user wants to enter heights for. As long as the user can input the number of heights to be processed, you can create an array that is an exact fit for the data that will be entered, like this:

```
size_t count {};
std::cout << "How many heights will you enter? ";
std::cin >> count;
unsigned int height[count];                     // Create the array of count elements
```

The height array is created when the code executes and will have count elements. Because the array size is not known at compile time, you cannot specify any initial values for the array.

Here's a working example using this:

```
// Ex5_12.cpp
// Allocating an array at runtime
#include <iostream>
#include <iomanip>        // for std::setprecision()

int main()
{
  size_t count {};
  std::cout << "How many heights will you enter? ";
  std::cin >> count;
  int height[count];                        // Create the array of count elements

  // Read the heights
  size_t entered {};
  while (entered < count)
  {
    std::cout <<"Enter a height: ";
    std::cin >> height[entered];
    if (height[entered] > 0)                 // Make sure value is positive
    {
      ++entered;
    }
    else
    {
      std::cout << "A height must be positive - try again.\n";
    }
  }

  // Calculate the sum of the heights
  unsigned int total {};
  for (size_t i {}; i < count; ++i)
  {
    total += height[i];
  }
```

```
    std::cout << std::fixed << std::setprecision(1);
    std::cout << "The average height is " << static_cast<float>(total) / count << std::endl;
}
```

Here's some sample output:

```
How many heights will you enter? 6
Enter a height: 47
Enter a height: 55
Enter a height: 0
A height must be positive - try again.
Enter a height: 60
Enter a height: 78
Enter a height: 68
Enter a height: 56
The average height is 60
```

The height array is allocated using the value entered for count. The height values are read into the array in the while loop. Within the loop, the if statement checks whether the value entered is zero. When it is nonzero, the entered variable that counts the number of values entered so far is incremented. When the value is zero, a message is output, and the next iteration executes without incrementing entered. Thus, the new attempt at entering a value will be read into the current element of height, which will overwrite the zero value that was read on the previous iteration. A straightforward for loop aggregates the total of all the heights, and this is used to output the average height. You could have used a range-based for loop here:

```
for (auto h : height)
{
  total += h;
}
```

Alternatively, you could accumulate the total of the heights in the while loop and dispense with the for loop altogether. This would shorten the program significantly. The while loop would then look like this (this variant can also be found in Ex5_12A):

```
  unsigned int total {};
  size_t entered {};
  while (entered < count)
  {
    std::cout <<"Enter a height: ";
    std::cin >> height[entered];
    if (height[entered])                        // Make sure value is positive
    {
      total += height[entered++];
    }
    else
    {
      std::cout << "A height must be positive - try again.\n";
    }
  }
```

Using the postfix increment operator in the expression for the index to the `height` array when adding the most recent element value to `total` ensures the current value of `entered` is used to access the array element before it is incremented for the next loop iteration.

■ **Note**   If your compiler does not allow variable-length arrays, you can achieve the same result—and much more—using a `vector`, which we'll discuss shortly.

Alternatives to Using an Array

The Standard Library defines a rich collection of data structures called *containers* that offer a variety of ways to organize and access your data. You'll learn more about these different containers in Chapter 19. In this section, however, we briefly introduce you to the two most elemental containers: `std::array<>` and `std::vector<>`. These form a direct alternative to the plain arrays built in to the C++ language, but they are much easier to work with, are much safer to use, and provide significantly more flexibility than the more low-level, built-in arrays. Our discussion here won't be exhaustive, though; it's just enough for you to use them like the built-in arrays you've seen thus far. More information will follow in Chapter 19.

Like all containers, `std::array<>` and `std::vector<>` are defined as *class templates*—two C++ concepts you're not yet familiar with. You'll learn all about classes from Chapter 11 onward and all about templates in Chapters 9 and 16. Still, we prefer to introduce these containers here because they're so important and because then we can use them in the examples and exercises of upcoming chapters. Also, given a clear initial explanation and some examples, we're certain that you'll be able to successfully use these containers already. After all, these containers are specifically designed to behave analogously to built-in arrays and can thus act as near drop-in replacements for them.

The compiler uses the `std::array<T,N>` and `std::vector<T>` templates to create a concrete type based on what you specify for the template parameters, T and N. For example, if you define a variable of type `std::vector<int>`, the compiler will generate a `vector<>` container class that is specifically tailored to hold and manipulate an array of `int` values. The power of templates lies in the fact that any type T can be used. We'll mostly omit both the namespace `std` and the type parameters T and N when referring to them generically in text, as in `array<>` and `vector<>`.

Using array<T,N> Containers

The `array<T,N>` template is defined in the `array` header, so you must include this in a source file to use the container type. An `array<T,N>` container is a fixed sequence of N elements of type T, so it's just like a regular array except that you specify the type and size a little differently. Here's how you create an `array<>` of 100 elements of type `double`:

```
std::array<double, 100> values;
```

This creates an object that has 100 elements of type `double`. The specification for the parameter N must be a constant expression—just like in declarations of regular arrays. In fact, for most intents and purposes, a variable of type `std::array<double, 100>` behaves in *exactly* the same manner as a regular array variable declared like this:

```
double values[100];
```

If you create an `array<>` container without specifying initial values, it will contain garbage values as well—just like with a plain array. Most Standard Library types, including `vector<>` and all other containers, always initialize their elements, typically to the value zero. But array<> is special in the sense that it is specifically designed to mimic built-in arrays as closely as possible. Naturally, you can initialize an array<>'s elements in the definition as well, just like a normal array:

```
std::array<double, 100> values {0.5, 1.0, 1.5, 2.0};    // 5th and subsequent elements are 0.0
```

The four values in the initializer list are used to initialize the first four elements; subsequent elements will be zero. If you want all values to be initialized to zero, you can use empty braces:

```
std::array<double, 100> values {};      // Zero-initialize all 100 elements
```

You can easily set all the elements to any other given value as well using the fill() function for the array<> object. Here's an example:

```
values.fill(3.14159265358979323846);     // Set all elements to pi
```

The fill() function belongs to the array<> object. The function is a so-called member of the class type, array<double, 100>. All array<> objects will therefore have a fill() member, as well as several other members. Executing this statement causes all elements to be set to the value you pass as the argument to the fill() function. Obviously, this must be of a type that can be stored in the container. You'll understand the relationship between the fill() function and an array<> object better after Chapter 11.

The size() function for an array<> object returns the number of elements as type size_t. With the same values variable from before, the following statement therefore outputs 100:

```
std::cout << values.size() << std::endl;
```

In a way, the size() function provides the first real advantage over a standard array because it means that an array<> object always knows how many elements there are. You'll only be able to fully appreciate this, though, after Chapter 8, where you learn all about passing arguments to functions. You'll learn that passing a regular array to a function in such a way that it preserves knowledge over its size requires some advanced, hard-to-remember syntax. Even programmers with years of experience—yours truly included—mostly don't know this syntax by heart. Many, we're sure, won't even know that it exists. Passing an array<> object to a function, on the other hand, will turn out to be straightforward, and the object always knows its size by means of the size() function.

Accessing Individual Elements

You can access and use elements using an index in the same way as for a standard array. Here's an example:

```
values[4] = values[3] + 2.0*values[1];
```

The fifth element is set to the value of the expression that is the right operand of the assignment. As another example, this is how you could compute the sum of all elements in the values object:

```
double total {};
for (size_t i {}; i < values.size(); ++i)
{
  total += values[i];
}
```

Because an `array<>` object is a range, you can use the range-based `for` loop to sum the elements more simply:

```
double total {};
for (auto value : values)
{
  total += value;
}
```

Accessing the elements in an `array<>` object using an index between square brackets doesn't check for invalid index values. The `at()` function for an `array<>` object does and therefore will detect attempts to use an index value outside the legitimate range. The argument to the `at()` function is an index, the same as when you use square brackets, so you could write the `for` loop that totals the elements like this:

```
double total {};
for (size_t i {}; i < values.size(); ++i)
{
  total += values.at(i);
}
```

The expression `values.at(i)` is equivalent to `values[i]` but with the added security that the value of i will be checked. For example, this code will fail:

```
double total {};
for (size_t i {}; i <= values.size(); ++i)
{
  total += values.at(i);
}
```

The second loop condition now using the `<=` operator allows `i` to reference beyond the last element. This will result in the program terminating at runtime with a message relating to an exception of type `std::out_of_range` being thrown. Throwing an exception is a mechanism for signaling exceptional error conditions. You'll learn more about exceptions in Chapter 15. If you code this using `values[i]`, the program will silently access the element beyond the end of the array and add whatever it contains to total. The `at()` function provides a further advantage over standard arrays.

The `array<>` template also offers convenience functions to access the first and last elements. Given an `array<>` variable values, the expression `values.front()` is equivalent to `values[0]`, and `values.back()` is equivalent to `values[values.size() - 1]`.

Operations on array<>s As a Whole

You can compare entire `array<>` containers using any of the comparison operators as long as the containers are of the same size and they store elements of the same type. Here's an example:

```
std::array<double,4> these {1.0, 2.0, 3.0, 4.0};
std::array<double,4> those {1.0, 2.0, 3.0, 4.0};
std::array<double,4> them  {1.0, 1.0, 5.0, 5.0};

if (these == those) std::cout << "these and those are equal."    << std::endl;
if (those != them)  std::cout << "those and them are not equal." << std::endl;
if (those > them)   std::cout << "those are greater than them."  << std::endl;
if (them < those)   std::cout << "them are less than those."     << std::endl;
```

Containers are compared element by element. For a true result for ==, all pairs of corresponding elements must be equal. For inequality, at least one pair of corresponding elements must be different for a true result. For all the other comparisons, the first pair of elements that differ produces the result. This is essentially the way in which words in a dictionary are ordered, where the first pair of corresponding letters that differ in two words determines their order. All the comparisons in the code fragment are true, so all four messages will be output when this executes.

To convince you of how truly convenient this is, let's try exactly the same thing with plain arrays:

```
double these[4] {1.0, 2.0, 3.0, 4.0};
double those[4] {1.0, 2.0, 3.0, 4.0};
double them[4]  {1.0, 1.0, 5.0, 5.0};

if (these == those) std::cout << "these and those are equal."     << std::endl;
if (those != them)  std::cout << "those and them are not equal."  << std::endl;
if (those > them)   std::cout << "those are greater than them."   << std::endl;
if (them < those)   std::cout << "them are less than those."      << std::endl;
```

This code still compiles. That looks promising. However, running this on our test system now produces the following disappointing result:

```
those and them are not equal.
```

You can try it for yourself by running Ex5_13.cpp. The results differ depending on which compiler you use, but it's unlikely that you'll see all four messages appear again like before. But what exactly is going on here? Why does comparing regular arrays not work as expected? You'll find out in the next chapter. (You see, it's not just comics and television shows that know how to employ a cliffhanger.) For now just remember that applying comparison operators to plain array names is not at all that useful because it clearly does not result in their elements being compared.

Unlike standard arrays, you can also assign one array<> container to another, as long as they both store the same number of elements of the same type. Here's an example:

```
them = those;      // Copy all elements of those to them
```

Moreover, array<> objects can be stored inside other containers. Regular arrays cannot. The following, for instance, creates a vector<> container that can hold array<> objects as elements, each in turn containing three int values:

```
std::vector<std::array<int, 3>> triplets;
```

The vector<> container is discussed in the next section.

Conclusion and Example

We've given you plenty of reasons—at least seven by our count—to use an array<> container in your code in preference to a standard array. And what's more, there's absolutely no disadvantage to using array<> either. Using an array<> container carries no performance overhead at all compared to a standard array (that is, unless you use the at() function instead of the [] operator of array<>—bounds checking, of course, may come at a small runtime cost).

▓ **Note**   Even if in your code you use `std::array<>` containers, it still remains perfectly possible to call legacy functions that expect plain arrays as input. You can always access the built-in array that is encapsulated within the `array<>` object using its `data()` member.

Here's an example that demonstrates array<> containers in action:

```cpp
// Ex5_14.cpp
// Using array<T,N> to create Body Mass Index (BMI) table
// BMI = weight/(height*height)
// weight in kilograms, height in meters

#include <iostream>
#include <iomanip>
#include <array>                         // For array<T,N>

int main()
{
  const unsigned min_wt {100};          // Minimum weight in table (in pounds)
  const unsigned max_wt {250};          // Maximum weight in table
  const unsigned wt_step {10};
  const size_t wt_count {1 + (max_wt - min_wt) / wt_step};

  const unsigned min_ht {48};           // Minimum height in table (inches)
  const unsigned max_ht {84};           // Maximum height in table
  const unsigned ht_step {2};
  const size_t ht_count { 1 + (max_ht - min_ht) / ht_step };

  const double lbs_per_kg {2.2};        // Pounds per kilogram
  const double ins_per_m {39.37};       // Inches per meter
  std::array<unsigned, wt_count> weight_lbs {};
  std::array<unsigned, ht_count> height_ins {};

  // Create weights from 100lbs in steps of 10lbs
  for (size_t i{}, w{ min_wt }; i < wt_count; w += wt_step, ++i)
  {
    weight_lbs[i] = w;
  }
  // Create heights from 48 inches in steps of 2 inches
  for (size_t i{}, h{ min_ht }; h <= max_ht; h += ht_step)
  {
    height_ins.at(i++) = h;
  }
  // Output table headings
  std::cout << std::setw(7) << " |";
  for (auto w : weight_lbs)
    std::cout << std::setw(5) << w << "  |";
  std::cout << std::endl;
```

```
  // Output line below headings
  for (size_t i{1}; i < wt_count; ++i)
    std::cout << "---------";
  std::cout << std::endl;

  double bmi {};                              // Stores BMI
  unsigned int feet {};                       // Whole feet for output
  unsigned int inches {};                     // Whole inches for output
  const unsigned int inches_per_foot {12U};
  for (auto h : height_ins)
  {
    feet = h / inches_per_foot;
    inches = h % inches_per_foot;
    std::cout <<  std::setw(2) << feet << "'" << std::setw(2) << inches << '"' << '|';
    std::cout << std::fixed << std::setprecision(1);
    for (auto w : weight_lbs)
    {
      bmi = h / ins_per_m;
      bmi = (w / lbs_per_kg) / (bmi*bmi);
        std::cout << std::setw(2) << " " << bmi << " |";
    }
    std::cout << std::endl;
  }
  // Output line below table
  for (size_t i {1}; i < wt_count; ++i)
    std::cout << "---------";
  std::cout << "\nBMI from 18.5 to 24.9 is normal" << std::endl;
}
```

We leave you to run the program to see the output because it takes quite a lot of space. There are two sets of four const variables defined that relate to the range of weights and heights for the BMI table. The weights and heights are stored in array<> containers with elements of type unsigned (short for unsigned int) because all the weights and heights are integral. The containers are initialized with the appropriate values in for loops. The second loop that initializes height_ins uses a different approach to setting the values just to demonstrate the at() function. This is appropriate in this loop because the loop is not controlled by the index limits for the container, so it's possible that a mistake could be made that would use an index outside the legal range for the container. The program would be terminated if this occurred, which would not be the case using square brackets to reference an element.

The next two for loops output the table column headings and a line to separate the headings from the rest of the table. The table is created using nested range-based for loops. The outer loop iterates over the heights and outputs the height in the leftmost column in feet and inches. The inner loop iterates over the weights and outputs a row of BMI values for the current height.

Using std::vector<T> Containers

The vector<T> container is a sequence container that may seem much like the array<T,N> container, but that is in fact far more powerful. There's no need to know the number of elements a vector<> will store in advance, at compile time. In fact, there is even no need to know the number of elements it will store in advance, at runtime. That is, the size of a vector<> can grow automatically to accommodate any number of elements. You can add some now and then some more later. A vector<> will grow as you add more and more elements; additional space is allocated automatically whenever required. There is no real maximum number of elements either—other than the one imposed by the amount of memory available to your process, of course—which is the reason you need only the type parameter T. There's no need for the N with a vector<>. Using the vector<> container needs the vector header to be included in your source file.

Here's an example of creating a vector<> container to store values of type double:

```
std::vector<double> values;
```

This typically has no space for elements allocated yet, so memory will need to be allocated dynamically when you add the first data item. You can add an element using the push_back() function for the container object. Here's an example:

```
values.push_back(3.1415);          // Add an element to the end of the vector
```

The push_back() function adds the value you pass as the argument—3.1415 in this case—as a new element at the end of the existing elements. Since there are no existing elements here, this will be the first, which probably will cause memory to be allocated for the first time.

You can initialize a vector<> with a predefined number of elements, like this:

```
std::vector<double> values(20);       // Vector contains 20 double values - all zero
```

Unlike a built-in array or an array<> object, a vector<> container *always* initializes its elements. In this case, our container starts out with 20 elements that are initialized with zero. If you don't like zero as the default value for your elements, you can specify another value explicitly:

```
std::vector<long> numbers(20, 99L); // Vector contains 20 long values - all 99
```

The second argument between the parentheses specifies the initial value for all elements, so all 20 elements will be 99L. Unlike most other array types you've seen so far, the first argument that specifies the number of elements—20 in our example—does *not* need to be a constant expression. It could be the result of an expression executed at runtime or read in from the keyboard. Of course, you can add new elements to the end of this or any other vector using the push_back() function.

A further option for creating a vector<> is to use a braced list to specify initial values:

```
std::vector<unsigned int> primes { 2, 3, 5, 7, 11, 13, 17, 19 };
```

The primes vector container will be created with eight elements with the given initial values.

▮ **Caution**   You may have noticed before that we didn't initialize the values and numbers vector<> objects using the usual braced initializer syntax but instead using round parentheses:

```
std::vector<double> values(20);       // Vector contains 20 double values - all zero
std::vector<long> numbers(20, 99L);   // Vector contains 20 long values - all 99
```

This is because using braced initializers here has a significantly different effect, as the comments next to the statements explain:

```
std::vector<double> values{20};       // Vector contains 1 single double value: 20
std::vector<long> numbers{20, 99L};   // Vector contains 2 long values: 20 and 99
```

When you use curly braces to initialize a vector<>, the compiler always interprets it as a sequence of initial values. This is to accommodate for initializing vectors in the same manner as you did with regular arrays or array<> containers before:

```
std::vector<int> six_initial_values{ 7, 9, 7, 2, 0, 4 };
```

This is one of only few occasions where the so-called uniform initialization syntax is not quite so uniform. To initialize a vector<> with a given number of identical values—without repeating that same value over and over, that is—you cannot use curly braces. If you do, it is interpreted by the compiler as a list of one or two initial values.

You can use an index between square brackets to set a value for an existing element or just to use its current value in an expression. Here's an example:

```
values[0] = 3.14159265358979323846;     // Pi
values[1] = 5.0;                         // Radius of a circle
values[2] = 2.0*values[0]*values[1];     // Circumference of a circle
```

Index values for a vector<> start from 0, just like a standard array. You can always reference existing elements using an index between square brackets, but you cannot create new elements this way. For that, you need to use, for instance, the push_back() function. The index values are not checked when you index a vector like this. So, you can accidentally access memory outside the extent of the vector and store values in such locations using an index between square brackets. The vector<> object again provides the at() function as well, just like an array<> container object, so you could consider using the at() function to refer to elements whenever there is the potential for the index to be outside the legal range.

Besides the at() function, nearly all other advantages of array<> containers directly transfer to vector<> as well:

- Each vector<> knows its size and has a size() member to query it.

- Passing a vector<> to a function is straightforward (see Chapter 8).

- Each vector<> has the convenience functions front() and back() to facilitate accessing the first and last elements of the vector<>.

- Two vector<> containers can be compared using <, >, <=, >=, ==, and != operators. Unlike with array<>, this even works for vectors that do not contain the same number of elements. The semantics then is the same as when you alphabetically compare words of different length. We all know that *aardvark* precedes *zombie* in the dictionary, even though the former has more letters. Also, *love* comes before *lovesickness*—both in life and in the dictionary. The comparison of vector<> containers is analogous. The only difference is that the elements are not always letters but can be any values the compiler knows how to compare using <, >, <=, >=, ==, and !=. In technical speak, this principle is called a *lexicographical comparison*.

- Assigning a vector<> to another vector<> variable copies all elements of the former into the latter, overwriting any elements that may have been there before, even if the new vector<> is shorter. If need be, additional memory will be allocated to accommodate more elements as well.

- A vector<> can be stored inside other containers, so you can, for instance, create a vector of vectors of integers.

A vector<> does not have a fill() member, though. Instead, it offers assign() functions that can be used to reinitialize the contents of a vector<>, much like you would when initializing it for the first time:

```
std::vector<long> numbers(20, 99L);    // Vector contains 20 long values - all 99
numbers.assign(99, 20L);               // Vector contains 99 long values - all 20
numbers.assign({99L, 20L});            // Vector contains 2 long values - 99 and 20
```

Deleting Elements

You can remove all the elements from a vector<> by calling the clear() function for the vector object. Here's an example:

```
std::vector<int> data(100, 99);        // Contains 100 elements initialized to 99
data.clear();                          // Remove all elements
```

▓ **Caution**   Both vector<> and array<> also provide an empty() function, which is sometimes wrongfully called in an attempt to clear a vector<>. But empty() does not empty a vector<>; clear() does. Instead, the empty() member checks whether a given container is empty. That is, it evaluates to the Boolean value true if and only if the container contains no elements and does not modify the container at all in the process.

You can remove the last element from a vector object by calling its pop_back() function. Here's an example:

```
std::vector<int> data(100, 99);        // Contains 100 elements initialized to 99
data.pop_back();                       // Remove the last element
```

The second statement removes the last element, so the size of data will be 99.

This is by no means all there is to using vector<> containers. For instance, we showed you only how to add or remove elements from the end of a vector<>, while it's perfectly possible to insert or remove elements at arbitrary positions. You'll learn more about working with vector<> containers in Chapter 19.

Example and Conclusion

You are now in a position to create a new version of Ex5_09.cpp that uses only the memory required for the current input data:

```
// Ex5_15.cpp
// Sorting an array in ascending sequence - using a vector<T> container
#include <iostream>
#include <iomanip>
#include <vector>

int main()
{
  std::vector<double> x;                 // Stores data to be sorted
```

```cpp
  while (true)
  {
    double input {};                    // Temporary store for a value
    std::cout << "Enter a non-zero value, or 0 to end: ";
    std::cin >> input;
    if (input == 0)
      break;

    x.push_back(input);
  }

  if (x.empty())
  {
    std::cout << "Nothing to sort..." << std::endl;
    return 0;
  }

  std::cout << "Starting sort." << std::endl;

  while (true)
  {
    bool swapped{ false };          // becomes true when not all values are in order
    for (size_t i {}; i < x.size() - 1; ++i)
    {
      if (x[i] > x[i + 1])          // Out of order so swap them
      {
        const auto temp = x[i];
        x[i] = x[i+1];
        x[i + 1] = temp;
        swapped = true;
      }
    }

    if (!swapped)                   // If there were no swaps
      break;                        // ...all values are in order...
  }                                 // ...otherwise, go round again.

  std::cout << "Your data in ascending sequence:\n"
            << std::fixed << std::setprecision(1);
  const size_t perline {10};        // Number output per line
  size_t n {};                      // Number on current line
  for (size_t i {}; i < x.size(); ++i)
  {
    std::cout << std::setw(8) << x[i];
    if (++n == perline)             // When perline have been written...
    {
      std::cout << std::endl;       // Start a new line and...
      n = 0;                        // ...reset count on this line
    }
  }
  std::cout << std::endl;
}
```

The output will be the same as Ex5_09.cpp. Because the data is now stored in a container of type vector<double>, there is no longer a maximum of 1,000 elements imposed onto our more diligent users. Memory is allocated incrementally to accommodate whatever input data is entered. We also no longer need to track a count of the values the user enters; the vector<> already takes care of that for us.

Other than these simplifications, all other code inside the function remains the same as before. This shows that you can use a std::vector<> in the same manner as you would a regular array. But it gives you the added bonus that you do not need to specify its size using a compile-time constant. This bonus comes at a small cost, though, as we're sure you'll understand. Luckily, this small performance overhead is rarely a cause for concern, and you'll soon find that std::vector<> will be the container you use most frequently. We'll return to this in more detail later, but for now just follow this simple guideline:

■ **Tip**   If you know the exact number of elements at compile time, use std::array<>. Otherwise, use std::vector<>.

Summary

You will see further applications of containers and loops in the next chapter. Almost any program of consequence involves a loop of some kind. Because they are so fundamental to programming, you need to be sure you have a good grasp of the ideas covered in this chapter. These are the essential points you learned in this chapter:

- An array stores a fixed number of values of a given type.

- You access elements in a one-dimensional array using an index value between square brackets. Index values start at 0, so in a one-dimensional array, an index is the offset from the first element.

- An array can have more than one dimension. Each dimension requires a separate index value to reference an element. Accessing elements in an array with two or more dimensions requires an index between square brackets for each array dimension.

- A loop is a mechanism for repeating a block of statements.

- There are four kinds of loop that you can use: the while loop, the do-while loop, the for loop, and the range-based for loop.

- The while loop repeats for as long as a specified condition is true.

- The do-while loop always performs at least one iteration and continues for as long as a specified condition is true.

- The for loop is typically used to repeat a given number of times and has three control expressions. The first is an initialization expression, executed once at the beginning of the loop. The second is a loop condition, executed before each iteration, which must evaluate to true for the loop to continue. The third is executed at the end of each iteration and is usually used to increment a loop counter.

- The range-based for loop iterates over all elements within a range. An array is a range of elements, and a string is a range of characters. The array and vector containers define a range so you can use the range-based for loop to iterate over the elements they contain.

- Any kind of loop may be nested within any other kind of loop to any depth.

- Executing a `continue` statement within a loop skips the remainder of the current iteration and goes straight to the next iteration, as long as the loop control condition allows it.

- Executing a `break` statement within a loop causes an immediate exit from the loop.

- A loop defines a scope so that variables declared within a loop are not accessible outside the loop. In particular, variables declared in the initialization expression of a `for` loop are not accessible outside the loop.

- The `array<T,N>` container stores a sequence of N elements of type T. An `array<>` container provides an excellent alternative to using the arrays that are built in to the C++ language.

- The `vector<T>` container stores a sequence of elements of type T that increases dynamically in size as required when you add elements. You use a `vector<>` container instead of a standard array when the number of elements cannot be determined in advance.

EXERCISES

The following exercises enable you to try what you've learned in this chapter. If you get stuck, look back over the chapter for help. If you're still stuck after that, you can download the solutions from the Apress website (`www.apress.com/source-code`), but that really should be a last resort.

Exercise 5-1. Write a program that outputs the squares of the odd integers from 1 up to a limit that is entered by the user.

Exercise 5-2. Write a program that uses a `while` loop to accumulate the sum of an arbitrary number of integers entered by the user. After every iteration, ask the user whether he or she is done entering numbers. The program should output the total of all the values and the overall average as a floating-point value.

Exercise 5-3. Create a program that uses a `do-while` loop to count the number of nonwhitespace characters entered on a line. The count should end when the first # character is found.

Exercise 5-4. Use `std::cin.getline(…)` to obtain a C-style string of maximum 1,000 characters from the user. Count the number of characters the user entered using an appropriate loop. Next, write a second loop that prints out all characters, one by one, but in a reverse order.

Exercise 5-5. Write a program equivalent to that of Exercise 5-4, except for the following:

If before you used a `for` loop to count the characters, you now use `while`, or vice versa.

This time you should first reverse the characters in the array, before printing them out left to right (for the sake of the exercise you could still use a loop to print out the characters one by one).

Exercise 5-6. Create a `vector<>` container with elements containing the integers from 1 to an arbitrary upper bound entered by the user. Output the elements from the vector that contain values that are not multiples of 7 or 13. Output them 10 on a line, aligned in columns.

Exercise 5-7. Write a program that will read and store an arbitrary sequence of records relating to products. Each record includes three items of data—an integer product number, a quantity, and a unit price. For product number 1001, the quantity is 25, and the unit price is $9.95. Because you do not know yet how to create compound types, simply use three different array-like sequences to represent these records. The program should output each product on a separate line and include the total cost. The last line should output the total cost for all products. Columns should align, so the output should be something like this:

Product	Quantity	Unit Price	Cost
1001	25	$9.95	$248.75
1003	10	$15.50	$155.00
			$403.75

Exercise 5-8. The famous Fibonacci series is a sequence of integers with the first two values as 1 and the subsequent values as the sum of the two preceding values. So, it begins 1, 1, 2, 3, 5, 8, 13, and so on. This is not just a mathematical curiosity. The sequence also regularly appears in biological settings, for instance. It relates to the way shells grow in a spiral, and the number of petals on many flowers is a number from this sequence. Create an `array<>` container with 93 elements. Store the first 93 numbers in the Fibonacci series in the array and then output them one per line. Any idea why we'd be asking you to generate 93 Fibonacci numbers and not, say, 100?

CHAPTER 6

■ ■ ■

Pointers and References

The concepts of pointers and references have similarities, which is why we have put them together in a single chapter. Pointers are important because they provide the foundation for allocating memory dynamically. Pointers can also make your programs more effective and efficient in other ways. Both references and pointers are fundamental to object-oriented programming.

In this chapter, you'll learn

- What pointers are and how they are defined

- How to obtain the address of a variable

- How to create memory for new variables while your program is executing

- How to release memory that you've allocated dynamically

- The many hazards of raw dynamic memory allocation and what the much safer alternatives are that you have at your disposal

- The difference between raw pointers and smart pointers

- How to create and use smart pointers

- What a reference is and how it differs from a pointer

- How you can use a reference in a range-based for loop

What Is a Pointer?

Every variable in your program is located somewhere in memory, so they all have a unique *address* that identifies where they are stored. These addresses depend on where your program is loaded into memory when you run it, so they may vary from one execution to the next. A *pointer* is a variable that can store an address of another variable, of some piece of data elsewhere in memory. Figure 6-1 shows how a pointer gets its name: it "points to" a location in memory where some other value is stored.

© Ivor Horton and Peter Van Weert 2018
I. Horton and P. Van Weert, *Beginning C++17*, https://doi.org/10.1007/978-1-4842-3366-5_6

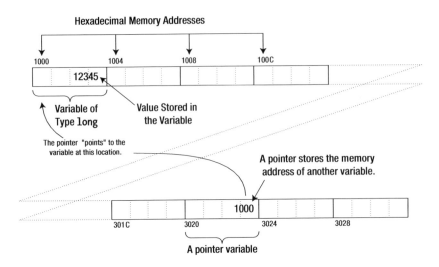

Figure 6-1. *What a pointer is*

As you know, an integer has a different representation from a floating-point value, and the number of bytes occupied by an item of data depends on what it is. So, to use a data item stored at the address contained in a pointer, you need to know the type of the data. If a pointer were nothing more than the address of some arbitrary data, it would not be all that interesting. Without knowing the type of data, a pointer is not of much use. Each pointer therefore points *to a particular type of data item at that address.* This will become clearer when we get down to specifics, so let's look at how to define a pointer. The definition of a pointer is similar to that of an ordinary variable except that the type name has an asterisk following it to indicate that it's a pointer and not a variable of that type. Here's how you define a pointer called pnumber that can store the address of a variable of type long:

```
long* pnumber {};             // A pointer to type long
```

The type of pnumber is "pointer to long," which is written as long*. This pointer can only store an address of a variable of type long. An attempt to store the address of a variable that is other than type long will not compile. Because the initializer is empty, the statement initializes pnumber with the pointer equivalent of zero, which is a special address that doesn't point to anything. This special pointer value is written as nullptr, and you could specify this explicitly as the initial value:

```
long* pnumber {nullptr};
```

You are not obliged to initialize a pointer when you define it, but it's reckless not to. Uninitialized pointers are more dangerous than ordinary variables that aren't initialized. Therefore:

■ **Tip**   As a rule, you should always initialize a pointer when you define it. If you cannot give it its intended value yet, initialize the pointer to nullptr.

It's relatively common to use variable names beginning with p for pointers, although this convention has fallen out of favor lately. Those adhering to what is called Hungarian notation—a somewhat dated naming scheme for variables—argue that it makes it easier to see which variables in a program are pointers, which in turn can make the code easier to follow. We will occasionally use this notation in this book, especially in more artificial examples where we mix pointers with regular variables. But in general, to be honest, we do not believe that adding type-specific prefixes such as p to variable names adds much value at all. In real code, it is almost always clear from the context whether something is a pointer or not.

In the examples earlier, we wrote the pointer type with the asterisk next to the type name, but this isn't the only way to write it. You can position the asterisk adjacent to the variable name, like this:

```
long *pnumber {};
```

This defines precisely the same variable as before. The compiler accepts either notation. The former is perhaps more common because it expresses the type, "pointer to long," more clearly.

However, there *is* potential for confusion if you mix definitions of ordinary variables and pointers in the same statement. Try to guess what this statement does:

```
long* pnumber {}, number {};
```

This defines two variables: one called pnumber of type "pointer to long," which is initialized with nullptr, and one called number of type long—not pointer to long!—which is initialized with 0L. The fact that number isn't simply a second variable of type long* no doubt surprises you. The fact that you're surprised is no surprise at all; the notation that juxtaposes the asterisk and the type name makes it less than clear what the type of the second variable will be to say the least. It's a little clearer already if you define the two variables in this form:

```
long *pnumber {}, number {};
```

This is a bit less confusing because the asterisk is now more clearly associated with the variable pnumber. Still, the only good solution really is to avoid the problem in the first place. It's much better to always define pointers and ordinary variables in separate statements:

```
long number {};            // Variable of type long
long* pnumber {};          // Variable of type 'pointer to long'
```

Now there's no possibility of confusion, and there's the added advantage that you can append comments to explain how the variables are used.

Note that if you did want number to be a second pointer, you could write the following:

```
long *pnumber {}, *number {};  // Define two variables of type 'pointer to long'
```

You can define pointers to any type, including types that you define. Here are definitions for pointer variables of a couple of other types:

```
double* pvalue {};          // Pointer to a double value
char32_t* char_pointer {};  // Pointer to a 32-bit character
```

No matter the type or size of the data a pointer refers to, though, the size of the pointer variable itself will always be the same. To be precise, all pointer variables *for a given platform* will have the same size. The size of pointer variables depends only on the amount of addressable memory of your target platform. To find out what that size is for you, you can run this little program:

```cpp
// Ex6_01.cpp
// The size of pointers
#include <iostream>

int main()
{
  // Print out the size (in number of bytes) of some data types
  // and the corresponding pointer types:
  std::cout << sizeof(double)  << " > "  << sizeof(char)  << std::endl;
  std::cout << sizeof(double*) << " == " << sizeof(char*) << std::endl;
}
```

On our test system, the result is as follows:

```
8 > 1
8 == 8
```

For nearly all platforms today, the size of pointer variables will be either 4 or 8 bytes (for 32- and 64-bit computer architectures, respectively—terms you've no doubt heard about before). In principle, you may encounter other values as well, such as if you target more specialized embedded systems.

The Address-Of Operator

The *address-of* operator, &, is a unary operator that obtains the address of a variable. You could define a variable, number, and a pointer, pnumber, initialized with the address of number with these statements:

```cpp
long number {12345L};
long* pnumber {&number};
```

&number produces the address of number, so pnumber has this address as its initial value. pnumber can store the address of any variable of type long, so you can write the following assignment:

```cpp
long height {1454L};        // Stores the height of a building
pnumber = &height;          // Store the address of height in pnumber
```

The result of the statement is that pnumber contains the address of height. The effect is illustrated in Figure 6-2.

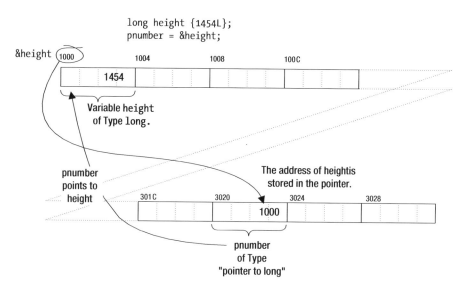

```
long height {1454L};
pnumber = &height;
```

Figure 6-2. *Storing an address in a pointer*

The & operator can be applied to a variable of any type, but you can only store the address in a pointer of the appropriate type. If you want to store the address of a double variable, for example, the pointer must have been declared as type double*, which is "pointer to double."

Naturally, you could have the compiler deduce the type for you as well by using the auto keyword:

```
auto pmynumber {&height};        // deduced type: long* (pointer to long)
```

We recommend you use auto* here instead to make it clear from the declaration that it concerns a pointer. Using auto*, you define a variable of a compiler-deduced pointer type:

```
auto* mynumber {&height};
```

A variable declared with auto* can be initialized only with a pointer value. Initializing it with a value of any other type will result in a compiler error.

Taking the address of a variable and storing it in a pointer is all very well, but the really interesting thing is how you can use it. Accessing the data in the memory location to which the pointer points is fundamental, and you do this using the *indirection operator*.

The Indirection Operator

Applying the *indirection operator*, *, to a pointer accesses the contents of the memory location to which it points. The name *indirection operator* stems from the fact that the data is accessed "indirectly." The indirection operator is often called the *dereference operator* as well, and the process of accessing the data in the memory location pointed to by a pointer is termed *dereferencing* the pointer. To access the data at the address contained in the pointer pnumber, you use the expression *pnumber. Let's see how dereferencing works in practice with an example. The example is designed to show various ways of using pointers. The way it works will be fairly pointless but far from pointerless:

```cpp
// Ex6_02.cpp
// Dereferencing pointers
// Calculates the purchase price for a given quantity of items
#include <iostream>
#include <iomanip>

int main()
{
  int unit_price {295};              // Item unit price in cents
  int count {};                      // Number of items ordered
  int discount_threshold {25};       // Quantity threshold for discount
  double discount {0.07};            // Discount for quantities over discount_threshold

  int* pcount {&count};              // Pointer to count
  std::cout << "Enter the number of items you want: ";
  std::cin >> *pcount;
  std::cout << "The unit price is " << std::fixed << std::setprecision(2)
            << "$" << unit_price/100.0 << std::endl;

  // Calculate gross price
  int* punit_price{ &unit_price };       // Pointer to unit_price
  int price{ *pcount * *punit_price };   // Gross price via pointers
  auto* pprice {&price};                 // Pointer to gross price

  // Calculate net price in US$
  double net_price{};
  double* pnet_price {nullptr};
  pnet_price = &net_price;
  if (*pcount > discount_threshold)
  {
    std::cout << "You qualify for a discount of "
              << static_cast<int>(discount*100.0) << " percent.\n";
    *pnet_price = price*(1.0 - discount) / 100.0;
  }
  else
  {
    net_price = *pprice / 100.0;
  }
  std::cout << "The net price for " << *pcount
            << " items is $" << net_price << std::endl;
}
```

Here's some sample output:

```
Enter the number of items you want: 50
The unit price is $2.95
You qualify for a discount of 7 percent.
The net price for 50 items is $137.17
```

We're sure you realize that this arbitrary interchange between using a pointer and using the original variable is not the right way to code this calculation. However, the example does demonstrate that using a dereferenced pointer is the same as using the variable to which it points. You can use a dereferenced pointer in an expression in the same way as the original variable, as the expression for the initial value of price shows.

It may seem confusing that you have several different uses for the same symbol, *. It's the multiplication operator and the indirection operator, and it's also used in the declaration of a pointer. The compiler is able to distinguish the meaning of * by the context. The expression *pcount * *punit_price may look slightly confusing, but the compiler has no problem determining that it's the product of two dereferenced pointers. There's no other meaningful interpretation of this expression. If there was, it wouldn't compile. You could always add parentheses to make the code easier to read, though: (*pcount) * (*punit_price).

Why Use Pointers?

A question that usually springs to mind at this point is "Why use pointers at all?" After all, taking the address of a variable you already know about and sticking it in a pointer so that you can dereference it later seems like an overhead you can do without. There are several reasons pointers are important:

- Later in this chapter you'll learn how to allocate memory for new variables dynamically—that is, during program execution. This allows a program to adjust its use of memory depending on the input. You can create new variables while your program is executing, as and when you need them. When you allocate new memory, the memory is identified by its address, so you need a pointer to record it.

- You can also use pointer notation to operate on data stored in an *array*. This is completely equivalent to the regular array notation, so you can pick the notation that is best suited for the occasion. Mostly, as the name suggests, array notation is more convenient when it comes to manipulating arrays, but pointer notation has its merits as well.

- When you define your own functions in Chapter 8, you'll see that pointers are used extensively to enable a function to access large blocks of data that are defined outside the function.

- Pointers are fundamental to enabling *polymorphism* to work. Polymorphism is perhaps the most important capability provided by the object-oriented approach to programming. You'll learn about polymorphism in Chapter 14.

■ **Note** The last two items in this list apply equally well to references—a language construct of C++ that is similar to pointers in many ways. References are discussed near the end of this chapter.

Pointers to Type char

A variable of type "pointer to char" has the interesting property that it can be initialized with a string literal. For example, you can declare and initialize such a pointer with this statement:

```
char* pproverb {"A miss is as good as a mile."};        // Don't do this!
```

This looks similar to initializing a char array with a string literal, and indeed it is. The statement creates a null-terminated string literal (actually, an array of elements of type const char) from the character string between the quotes and stores the address of the first character in pproverb. This is shown in Figure 6-3.

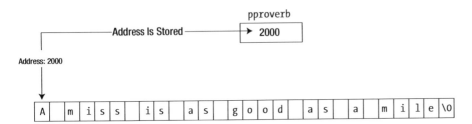

Figure 6-3. Initializing a pointer of type char*

Unfortunately, all is not quite as it seems. A string literal is a C-style char array that you're not supposed to change. You'll recall from earlier that the const specifier is used for the type of variables that cannot or must not be changed. So, in other words, the type of the characters in a string literal is const. But this is not reflected in the type of our pointer! The statement nevertheless doesn't create a modifiable copy of the string literal; it merely stores the address of the first character. This means that if you attempt to modify the string, there will be trouble. Look at this statement, which tries to change the first character of the string to 'X':

```
*pproverb = 'X';
```

Some compilers won't complain because they see nothing wrong. The pointer, pproverb, wasn't declared as const, so the compiler is happy. With other compilers, you get a warning that there is a deprecated conversion from type const char* to type char*. In some environments, you'll get an error when you run the program, resulting in a program crash. In other environments, the statement does nothing, which presumably is not what was required or expected either. The reason for this is that the string literal is still a constant, and you're not allowed to change it.

You might wonder, with good reason, why the compiler allowed you to assign a pointer-to-const value to a pointer-to-non-const type in the first place, particularly when it causes these problems. The reason is that string literals only became constants with the release of the first C++ standard, and there's a great deal of legacy code that relies on the "incorrect" assignment. Its use is deprecated, and the correct approach is to declare the pointer like this:

```
const char* pproverb {"A miss is as good as a mile."};   // Do this instead!
```

This defines pproverb to be of type const char*. Because it is a pointer-to-const type, the type is now consistent with that of the string literal. Any assignment to the literal's characters through this pointer will now be stopped by the compiler as well. There's plenty more to say about using const with pointers, so we'll come back to this later in this chapter. For now, let's see how using variables of type const char* operates in an example. This is a version of the "lucky stars" example, Ex5_11.cpp, using pointers instead of an array:

```
// Ex6_03.cpp
// Initializing pointers with strings
#include <iostream>
```

```
int main()
{
  const char* pstar1 {"Fatty Arbuckle"};
  const char* pstar2 {"Clara Bow"};
  const char* pstar3 {"Lassie"};
  const char* pstar4 {"Slim Pickens"};
  const char* pstar5 {"Boris Karloff"};
  const char* pstar6 {"Mae West"};
  const char* pstar7 {"Oliver Hardy"};
  const char* pstar8 {"Greta Garbo"};
  const char* pstr {"Your lucky star is "};

  std::cout << "Pick a lucky star! Enter a number between 1 and 8: ";
  size_t choice {};
  std::cin >> choice;

  switch (choice)
  {
  case 1: std::cout << pstr << pstar1 << std::endl; break;
  case 2: std::cout << pstr << pstar2 << std::endl; break;
  case 3: std::cout << pstr << pstar3 << std::endl; break;
  case 4: std::cout << pstr << pstar4 << std::endl; break;
  case 5: std::cout << pstr << pstar5 << std::endl; break;
  case 6: std::cout << pstr << pstar6 << std::endl; break;
  case 7: std::cout << pstr << pstar7 << std::endl; break;
  case 8: std::cout << pstr << pstar8 << std::endl; break;
  default: std::cout << "Sorry, you haven't got a lucky star." << std::endl;
  }
}
```

The output will be the same as Ex5_11.cpp.

Obviously the original array version is far more elegant, but let's look past that. In this reworked version, the array has been replaced by eight pointers, pstar1 to pstar8, each initialized with a string literal. There's an additional pointer, pstr, initialized with the phrase to use at the start of a normal output line. Because these pointers contain addresses of string literals, they are specified as const.

A switch statement is easier to use than an if statement to select the appropriate output message. Incorrect values entered are taken care of by the default option of the switch.

Outputting a string pointed to by a pointer couldn't be easier. You just use the pointer name. Clearly, the insertion operator << for cout treats pointers differently, depending on their type. In Ex6_02.cpp, you had this statement:

```
std::cout << "The net price for " << *pcount
          << " items is $" << net_price << std::endl;
```

If pcount wasn't dereferenced here, the address contained in pcount would be output. Thus, a pointer to a numeric type must be dereferenced to output the value to which it points, whereas applying the insertion operator to a pointer to type char that is not dereferenced presumes that the pointer contains the address of a null-terminated string. If you output a dereferenced pointer to type char, the single character at that address will be written to cout. Here's an example:

```
std::cout << *pstar5 << std::endl;    // Outputs 'B'
```

Arrays of Pointers

So, what have you gained in Ex6_03.cpp? Well, using pointers has eliminated the waste of memory that occurred with the array in Ex5_11.cpp because each string now occupies just the number of bytes necessary. However, the program is a little long-winded now. If you were thinking "Surely, there must be a better way," then you'd be right; you could use an array of pointers:

```
// Ex6_04.cpp
// Using an array of pointers
#include <iostream>
#include <array>                  // for std::size()

int main()
{
  const char* pstars[] {
                       "Fatty Arbuckle", "Clara Bow",
                       "Lassie", "Slim Pickens",
                       "Boris Karloff", "Mae West",
                       "Oliver Hardy", "Greta Garbo"
                      };

  std::cout << "Pick a lucky star! Enter a number between 1 and "
            << std::size(pstars) << ": ";
  size_t choice {};
  std::cin >> choice;

  if (choice >= 1 && choice <= std::size(pstars))
  {
    std::cout << "Your lucky star is " << pstars[choice - 1] << std::endl;
  }
  else
  {
    std::cout << "Sorry, you haven't got a lucky star." << std::endl;
  }
}
```

Now you're *nearly* getting the best of all possible worlds. You have a one-dimensional array of pointers defined such that the compiler works out the array size from the number of initializing strings. The memory usage that results from this statement is illustrated in Figure 6-4.

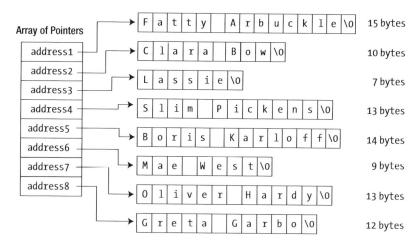

Array of Pointers

| address1 |
| address2 |
| address3 |
| address4 |
| address5 |
| address6 |
| address7 |
| address8 |

F	a	t	t	y		A	r	b	u	c	k	l	e	\0	15 bytes
C	l	a	r	a		B	o	w	\0						10 bytes
L	a	s	s	i	e	\0									7 bytes
S	l	i	m		P	i	c	k	e	n	s	\0			13 bytes
B	o	r	i	s		K	a	r	l	o	f	f	\0		14 bytes
M	a	e		W	e	s	t	\0							9 bytes
O	l	i	v	e	r		H	a	r	d	y	\0			13 bytes
G	r	e	t	a		G	a	r	b	o	\0				12 bytes

Figure 6-4. *An array of pointers*

With the char array of Ex5_11, each row had to have at least the length of the longest string, which resulted in quite some wasted bytes. Figure 6-4 clearly shows that by allocating all strings separately in the free store this is no longer an issue in Ex6_04. Granted, you do need some extra memory to store the addresses of the strings, typically 4 or 8 bytes per string pointer. And since in our example the difference in string lengths is not that great yet, we might not actually have gained much yet (on the contrary even). In general, however, the cost of an extra pointer is often negligible compared to the memory required for the strings themselves. And even for our test program this is not entirely unthinkable. Suppose, for instance, that we'd ask you to add the following name as a ninth option: "Rodolfo Alfonso Raffaello Pierre Filibert Guglielmi di Valentina d'Antonguolla" (an iconic star of the silent movie era)!

Saving space isn't the only advantage that you get by using pointers. In many circumstances, you can save time too. For example, think of what happens if you want to swap "Greta Garbo" with "Mae West" in the array. You'd need to do this to sort the strings into alphabetical order, for example. With the pointer array, you just reorder the pointers—the strings can stay right where they are. With a char array, a great deal of copying would be necessary. Interchanging the string would require the string "Greta Garbo" to be copied to a temporary location, after which you would copy "Mae West" in its place. Then you would need to copy "Greta Garbo" to its new position. All of this would require significantly more execution time than interchanging two pointers. The code using an array of pointers is similar to that using a char array. The number of array elements that is used to check that the selection entered is valid is calculated in the same way.

▓ **Note**   In our pursuit of highlighting some of the advantages of pointer arrays, we may have been somewhat overly positive about the use of const char*[] arrays. This approach works nicely as long as you know the exact number of strings at compile time and provided all of them are defined by literals. In real applications, however, you're much more likely to gather a variable number of strings, either from user input or from files. Working with plain character arrays then rapidly becomes cumbersome and very unsafe. In the next chapter, you'll learn about a more high-level string type, std::string, which is much safer to use than plain char* arrays and certainly much better suited for more advanced applications. For one, std::string objects are designed to be fully compatible with standard containers, allowing among other things for fully dynamic and perfectly safe std::vector<std::string> containers!

Constant Pointers and Pointers to Constants

In your latest "lucky stars" program, Ex6_04.cpp, you made sure that the compiler would pick up any attempts to modify the strings pointed to by elements of the pstars array by declaring the array using the const keyword:

```
const char* pstars[] {
                    "Fatty Arbuckle", "Clara Bow",
                    "Lassie", "Slim Pickens",
                    "Boris Karloff", "Mae West",
                    "Oliver Hardy", "Greta Garbo"
                };
```

Here you are specifying that the char elements pointed to by the elements of the pstar array are constant. The compiler inhibits any direct attempt to change these, so an assignment statement such as this would be flagged as an error by the compiler, thus preventing a nasty problem at runtime:

```
*pstars[0] = 'X';                    // Will not compile...
```

However, you could still legally write the next statement, which would copy the *address* stored in the element on the right of the assignment operator to the element on the left:

```
pstars[5] = pstars[6];               // OK
```

Those lucky individuals due to be awarded Ms. West would now get Mr. Hardy, because both pointers now point to the same name. Of course, this *hasn't* changed the object pointed to by the sixth array element—it has only changed the address stored in it, so the const specification hasn't been contravened.

You really ought to be able to inhibit this kind of change as well, because some people may reckon that good old Ollie may not have quite the same sex appeal as Mae, and of course you can. Look at this statement:

```
const char* const pstars[] {
                        "Fatty Arbuckle", "Clara Bow",
                        "Lassie", "Slim Pickens",
                        "Boris Karloff", "Mae West",
                        "Oliver Hardy", "Greta Garbo"
                    };
```

The extra const keyword following the element type specification defines the elements as constant, so now the pointers *and* the strings they point to are defined as constant. Nothing about this array can be changed.

Perhaps we made it a bit too complicated starting you out with an array of pointers. Because it's important that you understand the different options, let's go over things once more using a basic nonarray variable, pointing to just one celebrity. We'll consider this definition:

```
const char* my_favorite_star{ "Lassie" };
```

This defines an array that contains const char elements. This means the compiler will, for instance, not let you rename Lassie to Lossie:

```
my_favorite_star[1] = 'o';           // Error: my_favorite_star[1] is const!
```

The definition of my_favorite_star, however, does not prevent you from changing your mind about which star you prefer. This is because the my_favorite_star variable itself is not const. In other words, you're free to overwrite the pointer value stored in my_favorite_star, as long as you overwrite it with a pointer that refers to const char elements:

```
my_favorite_star = "Mae West";      // my_favorite_star now points to "Mae West"
my_favorite_star = pstars[1];       // my_favorite_star now points to "Clara Bow"
```

If you want to disallow such assignments, you have to add a second const to protect the content of the my_favorite_star variable:

```
const char* const forever_my_favorite{ "Oliver Hardy" };
```

To summarize, you can distinguish three situations that arise using const when applied to pointers and the things to which they point:

- *A pointer to a constant*: You can't modify what's pointed to, but you can set the pointer to point to something else:

  ```
  const char* pstring {"Some text that cannot be changed"};
  ```

  Of course, this also applies to pointers to other types. Here's an example:

  ```
  const int value {20};
  const int* pvalue {&value};
  ```

  Here value is a constant and can't be changed, and pvalue is a pointer to a constant, so you can use it to store the address of value. You couldn't store the address of value in a pointer to non-const int (because that would imply that you can modify a constant through a pointer), but you *could* assign the address of a non-const variable to pvalue. In the latter case, you would be making it illegal to modify the variable through the pointer. In general, it's always possible to strengthen const-ness, but weakening it isn't permitted.

- *A constant pointer*: The address stored in the pointer can't be changed. A constant pointer can only ever point to the address that it's initialized with. However, the *contents* of that address aren't constant and can be changed. Suppose you define an integer variable data and a constant pointer pdata:

  ```
  int data {20};
  int* const pdata {&data};
  ```

  pdata is const, so it can only ever point to data. Any attempt to make it point to another variable will result in an error message from the compiler. The value stored in data isn't const, though, so you can change it:

  ```
  *pdata = 25;              // Allowed, as pdata points to a non-const int
  ```

  Again, if data was declared as const, you could not initialize pdata with &data. pdata can only point to a non-const variable of type int.

- *A constant pointer to a constant*: Here, both the address stored in the pointer and the item pointed to are constant, so neither can be changed. Taking a numerical example, you can define a variable value like this:

```
const float value {3.1415f};
```

value is a constant, so you can't change it. You can still initialize a pointer with the address of value, though:

```
const float* const pvalue {&value};
```

pvalue is a constant pointer to a constant. You can't change what it points to, and you can't change what is stored at that address.

■ **Tip**   In some rare cases, the need for even more complex types arises, such as pointers to pointers. A practical tip then is that you can read all type names right to left. While doing so, you read every asterisk as "pointer to." Consider this variant—an equally legal one, by the way—of our latest variable declaration:

```
float const * const pvalue {&value};
```

Reading right to left then reveals that pvalue is indeed a const pointer to const floats. This trick always works (even when references enter the arena later in this chapter). You can give it a try with the other definitions in this section. The only additional complication is that the first const is typically written prior to the element type.

```
const float* const pvalue {&value};
```

So when reading types right to left, you often still have to swap around this const with the element type. It shouldn't be hard to remember, though. After all, "const pointer to float const" just doesn't have the same ring to it!

Pointers and Arrays

There is a close connection between pointers and array names. Indeed, there are many situations in which you can use an array name as though it were a pointer. An array name by itself mostly behaves like a pointer when it's used in an output statement, for instance. That is, if you try to output an array by just using its name, you'll just get the hexadecimal address of the array—unless it's a char array, of course, for which all standard output streams assume it concerns a C-style string. Because an array name can be interpreted as an address, you can use one to initialize a pointer as well:

```
double values[10];
double* pvalue {values};
```

This will store the address of the values array in the pointer pvalue. Although an array name represents an address, it is not a pointer. You can modify the address stored in a pointer, whereas the address that an array name represents is fixed.

190

Pointer Arithmetic

You can perform arithmetic operations on a pointer to alter the address it contains. You're limited to addition and subtraction for modifying the address contained in a pointer, but you can also compare pointers to produce a logical result. You can add an integer (or an expression that evaluates to an integer) to a pointer, and the result is an address. You can subtract an integer from a pointer, and that also results in an address. You can subtract one pointer from another, and the result is an integer, not an address. No other arithmetic operations on pointers are legal.

Arithmetic with pointers works in a special way. Suppose you add 1 to a pointer with a statement such as this:

```
++pvalue;
```

This apparently increments the pointer by 1. Exactly *how* you increment the pointer by 1 doesn't matter. You could use an assignment or the += operator to obtain the same effect so that the result would be exactly the same with this statement:

```
pvalue += 1;
```

The address stored in the pointer *won't* be incremented by 1 in the normal arithmetic sense, however. Pointer arithmetic implicitly assumes that the pointer points to an array. Incrementing a pointer by 1 means incrementing it by one *element* of the type to which it points. The compiler knows the number of bytes required to store the data item to which the pointer points. Adding 1 to the pointer increments the address by that number of bytes. In other words, adding 1 to a pointer increments the pointer so that it points to the next element in the array. For example, if pvalue is "pointer to double" and type double is 8 bytes, then the address in pvalue will be incremented by 8. This is illustrated in Figure 6-5.

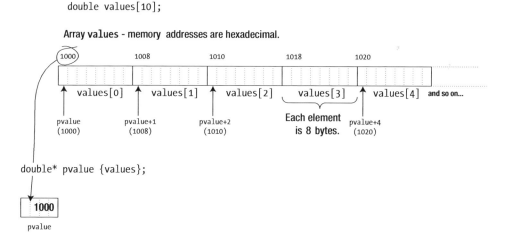

Figure 6-5. *Incrementing a pointer*

As Figure 6-5 shows, pvalue starts out with the address of the first array element. Adding 1 to pvalue increments the address it contains by 8, so the result is the address of the next array element. It follows that incrementing the pointer by 2 moves the pointer two elements along. Of course, pvalue need not necessarily point to the beginning of the values array. You could store the address of the third element of the array in the pointer with this statement:

```
pvalue = &values[2];
```

Now the expression pvalue + 1 would evaluate to the address of values[3], the fourth element of the values array, so you could make the pointer point to this element with this statement:

```
pvalue += 1;
```

In general, the expression pvalues + n, in which n can be any expression resulting in an integer, will add n * sizeof(double) to the address in pvalue because pvalue is of type "pointer to double."

The same logic applies to subtracting an integer from a pointer. If pvalue contains the address of values[2], the expression pvalue - 2 evaluates to the address of the first array element, values[0]. In other words, incrementing or decrementing a pointer works in terms of the type of the object pointed to. Incrementing a pointer to long by 1 changes its contents to the next long address and so increments the address by sizeof(long) bytes. Decrementing it by 1 decrements the address by sizeof(long).

Of course, you can dereference a pointer on which you have performed arithmetic. (There wouldn't be much point to it, otherwise!) For example, consider this statement:

```
*(pvalue + 1) = *(pvalue + 2);
```

Assuming pvalue is still pointing to values[3], this statement is equivalent to the following:

```
values[4] = values[5];
```

Remember that an expression such as pvalue + 1 doesn't change the address in pvalue. It's just an expression that evaluates to a result that is of the same type as pvalue. On the other hand, the expressions ++pvalue and pvalue += n *do* change pvalue.

When you dereference the address resulting from an expression that increments or decrements a pointer, parentheses around the expression are essential because the precedence of the indirection operator is higher than that of the arithmetic operators, + and -. The expression *pvalue + 1 adds 1 to the value stored at the address contained in pvalue, so it's equivalent to executing values[3] + 1. The result of *pvalue + 1 is a numerical value, not an address; its use in the previous assignment statement would cause the compiler to generate an error message.

Of course, when you store a value using a pointer that contains an invalid address, such as an address outside the limits of the array to which it relates, you'll attempt to overwrite the memory located at that address. This generally leads to disaster, with your program failing one way or another. It may not be obvious that the cause of the problem is the misuse of a pointer.

The Difference Between Pointers

Subtracting one pointer from another is meaningful only when they are of the same type and point to elements in the same array. Suppose you have a one-dimensional array, numbers, of type long defined as follows:

```
long numbers[] {10, 20, 30, 40, 50, 60, 70, 80};
```

Suppose you define and initialize two pointers like this:

```
long *pnum1 {&numbers[6]};          // Points to 7th array element
long *pnum2 {&numbers[1]};          // Points to 2nd array element
```

You can calculate the difference between these two pointers like so:

```
auto difference {pnum1 - pnum2};        // Result is 5
```

The difference variable will be set to the integer value 5 because the difference between two pointers is again measured in terms of elements, not in terms of bytes. Only one question remains, though: what will the type of difference be? Clearly, it should be a signed integer type to accommodate for statements such as the following:

```
auto difference2 {pnum2 - pnum1};       // Result is -5
```

As you know, the size of pointer variables such as pnum1 and pnum2 is platform specific—it's typically either 4 or 8 bytes. This, of course, implies that the number of bytes required to store pointer offsets cannot possibly be the same on all platforms either. The C++ language therefore prescribes that subtracting two pointers results in a value of type std::ptrdiff_t, a platform-specific type alias for one of the signed integer types defined by the cstddef header. So:

```
std::ptrdiff_t difference2 {pnum2 - pnum1};        // Result is -5
```

Depending on your target platform, std::ptrdiff_t is typically an alias for either int, long, or long long.

Comparing Pointers

You can safely compare pointers of the same type using the familiar ==, !=, <, >, <=, and >= operators. The outcome of these comparisons will of course be compatible with your intuitions about pointer and integer arithmetic. Using the same variables as before, the expression pnum2 < pnum1 will thus evaluate to true, as pnum2 - pnum1 < 0 as well (pnum2 - pnum1 equals -5). In other words, the further the pointer points in the array or the higher the index of the element it points to, the larger the pointer is.

Using Pointer Notation with an Array Name

You can use an array name as though it was a pointer for addressing the array elements. Suppose you define this array:

```
long data[5] {};
```

You can refer to the element data[3] using pointer notation as *(data + 3). This notation can be applied generally so that corresponding to the elements data[0], data[1], data[2], ..., you can write *data, *(data + 1), *(data + 2), and so on. The array name by itself refers to the address of the beginning of the array, so an expression such as data+2 produces the address of the element two elements along from the first.

You can use pointer notation with an array name in the same way as you use an index between square brackets—in expressions or on the left of an assignment. You could set the values of the data array to even integers with this loop:

```
for (size_t i {}; i < std::size(data); ++i)
{
  *(data + i) = 2 * (i + 1);
}
```

The expression *(data + i) refers to successive elements of the array: *(data + 0), which is the same as *data, corresponds to data[0], *(data + 1) refers to data[1], and so on. The loop will set the values of the array elements to 2, 4, 6, 8, and 10. You could sum the elements of the array like this:

```
long sum {};
for (size_t i {}; i < std::size(data); ++i)
{
  sum += *(data + i);
}
```

Let's try some of this in a practical context that has a little more meat. This example calculates prime numbers (a prime number is an integer that is divisible only by 1 and itself). Here's the code:

```
// Ex6_05.cpp
// Calculating primes using pointer notation
#include <iostream>
#include <iomanip>

int main()
{
  const size_t max {100};          // Number of primes required
  long primes[max] {2L};           // First prime defined
  size_t count {1};                // Count of primes found so far
  long trial {3L};                 // Candidate prime

  while (count < max)
  {
    bool isprime {true};           // Indicates when a prime is found

    // Try dividing the candidate by all the primes we have
    for (size_t i {}; i < count && isprime; ++i)
    {
      isprime = trial % *(primes + i) > 0;   // False for exact division
    }

    if (isprime)
    {                              // We got one...
      *(primes + count++) = trial; // ...so save it in primes array
    }

    trial += 2;                    // Next value for checking
  }
```

```
  // Output primes 10 to a line
  std::cout << "The first " << max << " primes are:" << std::endl;
  for (size_t i{}; i < max; ++i)
  {
    std::cout << std::setw(7) << *(primes + i);
    if ((i+1) % 10 == 0)                 // Newline after every 10th prime
      std::cout << std::endl;
  }
  std::cout << std::endl;
}
```

The output is as follows:

The first 100 primes are:									
2	3	5	7	11	13	17	19	23	29
31	37	41	43	47	53	59	61	67	71
73	79	83	89	97	101	103	107	109	113
127	131	137	139	149	151	157	163	167	173
179	181	191	193	197	199	211	223	227	229
233	239	241	251	257	263	269	271	277	281
283	293	307	311	313	317	331	337	347	349
353	359	367	373	379	383	389	397	401	409
419	421	431	433	439	443	449	457	461	463
467	479	487	491	499	503	509	521	523	541

The constant max defines the number of primes to be produced. The primes array that stores the results has a first prime defined to start off the process. The variable count records how many primes have been found, so it's initialized to 1.

The trial variable holds the next candidate to be tested. It starts out at 3 because it's incremented in the loop that follows. The bool variable isprime is a flag that indicates when the current value in trial is prime.

All the work is done in two loops: the outer while loop picks the next candidate to be checked and adds the candidate to the primes array if it's prime, and the inner loop checks the current candidate to see whether it's prime. The outer loop continues until the primes array is full.

The algorithm in the loop that checks for a prime is simple. It's based on the fact that any number that isn't a prime must be divisible by a smaller number that *is* a prime. You find the primes in ascending order, so at any point primes contains all the prime numbers lower than the current candidate. If none of the values in primes is a divisor of the candidate, then the candidate must be prime. Once you realize this, writing the inner loop that checks whether trial is prime should be straightforward:

```
  // Try dividing the candidate by all the primes we have
  for (size_t i {}; i < count && isprime; ++i)
  {
    isprime = trial % *(primes + i) > 0;    // False for exact division
  }
```

In each iteration, isprime is set to the value of the expression trial % *(primes + i) > 0. This finds the remainder after dividing trial by the number stored at the address primes + i. If the remainder is positive, the expression is true. The loop ends if i reaches count or whenever isprime is false. If any of the primes in the primes array divides into trial exactly, trial isn't prime, so this ends the loop. If none of the primes divides into trial exactly, isprime will always be true, and the loop will be ended by i reaching count.

After the inner loop ends, either because isprime was set to false or because the set of divisors in the primes array has been exhausted, whether or not the value in trial was prime is indicated by the value in isprime. This is tested in an if statement:

```
if (isprime)
{                                  // We got one...
  *(primes + count++) = trial;     // ...so save it in primes array
}
```

If isprime contains false, then one of the divisions was exact, so trial isn't prime. If isprime is true, the assignment statement stores the value from trial in primes[count] and then increments count with the postfix increment operator. When max primes have been found, the outer while loop ends, and the primes are output 10 to a line with a field width of 10 characters as a result of these statements in a for loop.

Dynamic Memory Allocation

Most code you've written up to now allocates space for data at compile time. The most notable exceptions are the times when you used a std::vector<> container, which dynamically allocates all and any memory it needs to hold its elements. Apart from that, you've mostly specified all variables and arrays that you needed in the code up front, and that's what will be allocated when the program starts, whether you needed the entire array or not. Working with a fixed set of variables in a program can be very restrictive, and it's often wasteful.

Dynamic memory allocation is allocating the memory you need to store the data you're working with at runtime, rather than having the amount of memory predefined when the program is compiled. You can change the amount of memory your program has dedicated to it as execution progresses. By definition, dynamically allocated variables can't be defined at compile time, so they can't be named in your source program. When you allocate memory dynamically, the space that is made available is identified by its address. The obvious and only place to store this address is in a pointer. With the power of pointers and the dynamic memory management tools in C++, writing this kind of flexibility into your programs is quick and easy. You can add memory to your application when it's needed and then release the memory you have acquired when you are done with it. Thus, the amount of memory dedicated to an application can increase and decrease as execution progresses.

In Chapter 3, we introduced the three kinds of storage duration that variables can have—automatic, static, and dynamic—and we discussed how variables of the first two varieties are created. Variables for which memory is allocated at runtime always have *dynamic* storage duration.

The Stack and the Free Store

You know that an automatic variable is created when its definition is executed. The space for an automatic variable is allocated in a memory area called the *stack*. The stack has a fixed size that is determined by your compiler. There's usually a compiler option that enables you to change the stack size, although this is rarely necessary. At the end of the block in which an automatic variable is defined, the memory allocated for the variable on the stack is released and is thus free to be reused. When you call a function, the arguments you pass to the function will be stored on the stack along with the address of the location to return to when execution of the function ends.

Memory that is not occupied by the operating system or other programs that are currently loaded is called the *free store*.[1] You can request that space be allocated within the free store at runtime for a new variable of any type. You do this using the new operator, which returns the address of the space allocated, and you store the address in a pointer. The new operator is complemented by the delete operator, which releases memory that you previously allocated with new. Both new and delete are keywords, so you must not use them for other purposes.

You can allocate space in the free store for variables in one part of a program and then release the space and return it to the free store in another part of the program when you no longer need it. The memory then becomes available for reuse by other dynamically allocated variables later in the same program or possibly other programs that are executing concurrently. This uses memory very efficiently and allows programs to handle much larger problems involving considerably more data than might otherwise be possible.

When you allocate space for a variable using new, you create the variable in the free store. The variable remains reserved for you until the memory it occupies is released by the delete operator. Until the moment you release it using delete, the block of memory allocated for your variable can no longer be used by subsequent calls of new. Note that the memory continues to be reserved regardless of whether you still record its address. If you don't use delete to release the memory, it will be released automatically when program execution ends.

Using the new and delete Operators

Suppose you need space for a variable of type double. You can define a pointer of type double* and then request that the memory is allocated at execution time. Here's one way to do this:

```
double* pvalue {};              // Pointer initialized with nullptr
pvalue = new double;            // Request memory for a double variable
```

This is a good moment to recall that *all pointers should be initialized*. Using memory dynamically typically involves having a lot of pointers floating around, and it's important that they do not contain spurious values. You should always ensure that a pointer contains nullptr if it doesn't contain a legal address.

The new operator in the second line of the code returns the address of the memory in the free store allocated to a double variable, and this is stored in pvalue. You can use this pointer to reference the variable in the free store using the indirection operator, as you've seen. Here's an example:

```
*pvalue = 3.14;
```

Of course, under extreme circumstances it may not be possible to allocate the memory. The free store could be completely allocated at the time of the request. More aptly, it could be that no area of the free store is available that is large enough to accommodate the space you have requested. This isn't likely with the space required to hold a single double value, but it might just happen when you're dealing with large entities such as arrays or complicated class objects. This is something that you may need to consider later, but for now you'll assume that you always get the memory you request. When it does happen, the new operator throws something called an *exception*, which by default will end the program. We'll come back to this topic in Chapter 17 when we discuss exceptions.

---

[1] A term that is often used as a synonym for the free store is the *heap*. In fact, it is probably more common to hear the term *heap* than *free store*. Nevertheless, some would argue that the heap and the free store are different memory pools. From their point of view, C++'s new and delete operators operate on the free store, whereas C's memory management functions such as malloc and free operate on the heap. While we take no stance in this technical, terminological debate, in this book we consistently use the term *free store* because this is what the C++ standard uses as well.

You can initialize a variable that you create in the free store. Let's reconsider the previous example: the double variable allocated by new, with its address stored in pvalue. The memory slot for the double variable itself (typically 8 bytes large) still holds whatever bits were there before. As always, an uninitialized variable contains garbage. You could have initialized its value to, for instance, 3.14, though, as it was created by using this statement:

```
pvalue = new double {3.14};        // Allocate a double and initialize it
```

You can also create and initialize the variable in the free store and use its address to initialize the pointer when you create it:

```
double* pvalue {new double {3.14}};  // Pointer initialized with address in the free store
```

This creates the pointer pvalue, allocates space for a double variable in the free store, initializes the variable in the free store with 3.14, and initializes pvalue with the address of the variable.

It should come as no surprise anymore by now that the following initializes the double variable pointed to by pvalue to zero (0.0):

```
double* pvalue {new double {}};    // Pointer initialized with address in the free store
                                   // pvalue points to a double variable initialized with 0.0
```

Note the difference with this, though:

```
double* pvalue {};                 // Pointer initialized with nullptr
```

When you no longer need a dynamically allocated variable, you free the memory that it occupies using the delete operator:

```
delete pvalue;                     // Release memory pointed to by pvalue
```

This ensures that the memory can be used subsequently by another variable. If you don't use delete and you store a different address in pvalue, it will be impossible to free up the original memory because access to the address will have been lost. The memory will be retained for use by your program until the program ends. Of course, you can't use it because you no longer have the address. Note that the delete operator frees the memory but does *not* change the pointer. After the previous statement has executed, pvalue still contains the address of the memory that was allocated, but the memory is now free and may be allocated immediately to something else. A pointer that contains such a spurious address is sometimes called a *dangling pointer*. Dereferencing a dangling pointer is a sweet recipe for disaster, so you should get in the habit of always resetting a pointer when you release the memory to which it points, like this:

```
delete pvalue;                     // Release memory pointed to by pvalue
pvalue = nullptr;                  // Reset the pointer
```

Now pvalue doesn't point to anything. The pointer cannot be used to access the memory that was released. Using a pointer that contains nullptr to store or retrieve data will terminate the program immediately, which is better than the program staggering on in an unpredictable manner with data that is invalid.

> **■ Tip** It is perfectly safe to apply `delete` on a pointer variable that holds the value `nullptr`. The statement then has no effect at all. Using `if` tests such as the following is therefore not necessary:

```
if (pvalue)          // No need for this test: 'delete nullptr' is harmless!
{
  delete pvalue;
  pvalue = nullptr;
}
```

Dynamic Allocation of Arrays

Allocating memory for an array at runtime is equally straightforward. This, for instance, allocates space for an array of 100 values of type double and stores its address in data.

```
double* data {new double[100]};          // Allocate 100 double values
```

As always, the memory of this array contains uninitialized garbage values. Naturally, you can initialize the dynamic array's elements just like you would with a regular array:

```
double* data {new double[100] {}};        // All 100 values are initialized to 0.0
int* one_two_three {new int[3] {1, 2, 3}}; // 3 integers with a given initial value
float* fdata{ new float[20] { .1f, .2f }}; // All but the first 2 floats are initialized to 0.0f
```

Unlike with regular arrays, however, you cannot have the compiler deduce the array's dimensions. The following definition is therefore not valid in C++:

```
int* one_two_three {new int[] {1, 2, 3}};  // Does not compile!
```

To remove the array from the free store when you are done with it, you use an operator similar to the delete operator, yet this time the delete has to be followed with []:

```
delete[] data;        // Release array pointed to by data
```

The square brackets are important because they indicate that you're deleting an array. When removing arrays from the free store, you must include the square brackets, or the results will be unpredictable. Note that you don't specify any dimensions, simply []. In principle you can add whitespace between delete and [] as well, should you prefer to do so:

```
delete [] fdata;      // Release array pointed to by data
```

Of course, it's again good practice to reset the pointer now that it no longer points to memory that you own:

```
data = nullptr;       // Reset the pointer
```

Let's see how dynamic memory allocation works in practice. Like Ex6_05, this program calculates primes. The key difference is that this time the number of primes is not hard-coded into the program. Instead, the number of primes to compute, and hence the number of elements to allocate, is entered by the user at runtime.

```cpp
// Ex6_06.cpp
// Calculating primes using dynamic memory allocation
#include <iostream>
#include <iomanip>
#include <cmath>                                   // For square root function

int main()
{
  size_t max {};                                   // Number of primes required

  std::cout << "How many primes would you like? ";
  std::cin >> max;                                 // Read number required

  if (max == 0) return 0;                          // Zero primes: do nothing

  auto* primes {new unsigned[max]};                // Allocate memory for max primes

  size_t count {1};                                // Count of primes found
  primes[0] = 2;                                   // Insert first seed prime

  unsigned trial {3};                              // Initial candidate prime

  while (count < max)
  {
    bool isprime {true};                           // Indicates when a prime is found

    const auto limit = static_cast<unsigned>(std::sqrt(trial));
    for (size_t i {}; primes[i] <= limit && isprime; ++i)
    {
      isprime = trial % primes[i] > 0;             // False for exact division
    }

    if (isprime)                                   // We got one...
      primes[count++] = trial;                     // ...so save it in primes array

    trial += 2;                                    // Next value for checking
  }

  // Output primes 10 to a line
  for (size_t i{}; i < max; ++i)
  {
    std::cout << std::setw(10) << primes[i];
    if ((i + 1) % 10 == 0)                         // After every 10th prime...
      std::cout << std::endl;                      // ...start a new line
  }
  std::cout << std::endl;

  delete[] primes;                                 // Free up memory...
  primes = nullptr;                                // ... and reset the pointer
}
```

The output is essentially the same as the previous program, so we won't reproduce it here. Overall, the program is similar but not the same as the previous version. After reading the number of primes required from the keyboard and storing it in max, you allocate an array of that size in the free store using the new operator. The address that's returned by new is stored in the pointer, primes. This will be the address of the first element of an array of max elements of type unsigned (int).

Unlike Ex06_05, all statements and expressions involving the primes array in this program use the array notation. But only because this is easier; you could equally well use and write them using pointer notation: *primes = 2, *(primes + i), *(primes + count++) = trial, and so on.

Before allocating the primes array and inserting the first prime, 2, we verify that the user did not enter the number zero. Without this safety measure, the program would otherwise write the value 2 into a memory location beyond the bounds of the allocated array, which would have undefined and potentially catastrophic results.

Notice also that the determination of whether a candidate is prime is improved compared to Ex6_05.cpp. Dividing the candidate in trial by existing primes ceases when primes up to the square root of the candidate have been tried, so finding a prime will be faster. The sqrt() function from the cmath header does this.

When the required number of primes has been output, you remove the array from the free store using the delete[] operator, not forgetting to include the square brackets to indicate that it's an array you're deleting. The next statement resets the pointer. It's not essential here, but it's good to get into the habit of always resetting a pointer after freeing the memory to which it points; it could be that you add code to the program at a later date.

Of course, if you use a vector<> container that you learned about in Chapter 5 to store the primes, you can forget about memory allocation for elements and deleting it when you are done; it's all taken care of by the container. In practice, you should therefore nearly always use std::vector<> to manage dynamic memory for you. In fact, the examples and exercises on dynamic memory allocation in this book should probably be one of the last occasions at which you should still manage dynamic memory directly. But we're getting ahead of ourselves: we'll return to the risks, downsides, and alternatives to low-level dynamic memory allocation at length later in this chapter!

Multidimensional Arrays

In the previous chapter, you learned how to create arrays of multiple static dimensions. The example we used was this 3 × 4 multidimensional array to hold the weights of the carrots you grow in your garden:

```
double carrots[3][4] {};
```

Of course, as an avid gardener in heart and soul, you plant carrots each year but not always in the same quantity or the same configuration of three rows and four columns. As recompiling from source for each new sowing season is such a drag, let's see how we can allocate a multidimensional array in a dynamic manner. A natural attempt then would be to write this:

```
size_t rows {}, columns {};
std::cout << "How many rows and columns of carrots this year?" << std::endl;
std::cin >> rows >> columns;
auto carrots{ new double[rows][columns] {} };            // Won't work!
...
delete[] carrots;      // Or delete[][]? No such operator exists though!
```

Alas! Multidimensional arrays with multiple dynamic dimensions are not supported by standard C++, at least not as a built-in language feature. The furthest you can get with built-in C++ types are arrays where the value of the first dimension is dynamic. If you are happy always planting your carrots in columns of four, C++ does allow you to write this:

```
size_t rows {};
std::cout << "How many rows, each of four carrots, this year?" << std::endl;
std::cin >> rows;
double (*carrots)[4]{ new double[rows][4] {} };
...
delete[] carrots;
```

The required syntax is plain dreadful, though—the parentheses around *carrots are mandatory—so much so that most programmers won't be familiar with this. But at least it's possible. The good news also is that ever since C++11, you can of course avoid this syntax altogether using the auto keyword as well:

```
auto carrots{ new double[rows][4] {} };
```

With a bit of effort, it's actually not too hard to emulate a fully dynamic two-dimensional array using regular one-dimensional dynamic arrays either. After all, what is a two-dimensional array if not an array of rows? For our gardening example, one way would be to write this as follows:

```
double** carrots{ new double*[rows] {} };
for (size_t i = 0; i < rows; ++i)
   carrots[i] = new double[columns] {};
...
for (size_t i = 0; i < rows; ++i)
   delete[] carrots[i];
delete[] carrots;
```

The carrots array is a dynamic array of double* pointers, each in turn containing the address of an array of double values. The latter arrays, representing the rows of the multidimensional array, are allocated in the free store as well, one by one, by the first for loop. Once you're done with the array, you must deallocate its rows again, one by one, using a second loop, before disposing of the carrots array itself.

Given the amount of boilerplate code required to set up such a multidimensional array and again to tear it down, it's highly recommended to encapsulate such functionality in a reusable class. We'll leave that to you as an exercise, after learning all about creating your own class types in upcoming chapters.

■ **Tip** The naïve technique we presented here to represent dynamic multidimensional arrays is not the most efficient one. It allocates all rows separately in the free store, meaning they are likely not contiguous in memory anymore. Programs tend to run much, much faster when operating on contiguous memory. That's why classes that encapsulate multidimensional arrays generally allocate only a single array of rows * columns elements and then map array accesses at row i and column j to a single index using the formula i * columns + j.

Member Selection Through a Pointer

A pointer can store the address of an object of a class type, such as a vector<T> container. Objects usually have member functions that operate on the object—you saw that the vector<T> container has an at() function for accessing elements and a push_back() function for adding an element, for example. Suppose pdata is a pointer to a vector<> container. This container could be allocated in the free store with a statement such as this:

```
auto* pdata {new std::vector<int>{}};
```

But it might just as well be the address of a local object, obtained using the address-of operator.

```
std::vector<int> data;
auto* pdata = &data;
```

In both cases, the compiler deduces the type of pdata to be vector<int>*, which is a "pointer to a vector of int elements." For what follows, it does not matter whether the vector<> is created in the free store or on the stack as a local object. To add an element, you call the push_back() function for the vector<int> object, and you have seen how you use a period between the variable representing the vector and the member function name. To access the vector object using the pointer, you could use the dereference operator, so the statement to add an element looks like this:

```
(*pdata).push_back(66);        // Add an element containing 66
```

The parentheses around *pdata are essential for the statement to compile because the . operator is of higher precedence than the * operator. This clumsy-looking expression would occur very frequently when you are working with objects, which is why C++ provides an operator that combines dereferencing a pointer to an object and then selecting a member of the object. You can write the previous statement like this:

```
pdata->push_back(66);          // Add an element containing 66
```

The -> operator is formed by a minus sign and a greater-than character and is referred to as the *arrow operator* or *indirect member selection operator*. The arrow is much more expressive of what is happening here. You'll be using this operator extensively later in the book.

Hazards of Dynamic Memory Allocation

There are many kinds of serious problems that you can run into when you allocate memory dynamically using new. In this section, we name the most common ones. Unfortunately, these hazards are all too real, as any developer who has worked with new and delete will corroborate. As a C++ developer, a significant portion of the more serious bugs you deal with often boil down to mismanagement of dynamic memory.

In this section, we will thus paint you a seemingly very bleak picture, filled with all kinds of hazards of dynamic memory. But don't despair. We will show you the way out of this treacherous minefield soon enough! Right after this section we will list the proven idioms and utilities that actually make it easy for you to avoid most if not all of these problems. In fact, you already know about one such utility: the std::vector<> container. This container is almost always the better choice over allocating dynamic memory directly using new[]. Other facilities of the Standard Library to better manage dynamic memory are discussed in upcoming sections. But first let's dwell on all these lovely risks, hazards, pitfalls, and other perils alike associated with dynamic memory.

Dangling Pointers and Multiple Deallocations

A *dangling pointer*, as you know, is a pointer variable that still contains the address to free store memory that has already been deallocated by either delete or delete[]. Dereferencing a dangling pointer makes you read from or, often worse, write to memory that might already be allocated to and used by other parts of your program, resulting in all kinds of unpredictable and unexpected results. *Multiple deallocations*, which occur when you deallocate an already deallocated (and hence dangling) pointer for a second time using either delete or delete[], is another recipe for disaster.

We taught you one basic strategy already to guard yourself against dangling pointers, that is, to always reset a pointer to nullptr after the memory it points to is released. In more complex programs, however, different parts of the code often collaborate by accessing the same memory—an object or an array of objects—all through distinct copies of the same pointer. In such cases our simple strategy rapidly falls short. Which part of the code is going to call delete/delete[]? And when? That is, how do you be sure no other part of the code is still using the same dynamically allocated memory?

Allocation/Deallocation Mismatch

A dynamically allocated array, allocated using new[], is captured in a regular pointer variable. But so is a single allocated value that is allocated using new:

```
int* single_int{ new int{123} };      // Pointer to a single integer, initialized with 123
int* array_of_ints{ new int[123] };  // Pointer to an array of 123 uninitialized integers
```

After this, the compiler has no way to distinguish between the two, especially once such a pointer gets passed around different parts of the program. This means that the following two statements will compile without error (and in many cases even without a warning):

```
delete[] single_int;      // Wrong!
delete array_of_ints;      // Wrong!
```

What'll happen if you mismatch your allocation and deallocation operators depends entirely on the implementation associated with your compiler. But it won't be anything good.

■ **Caution**   Every new must be paired with a single delete; every new[] must be paired with a single delete[]. Any other sequence of events leads to either undefined behavior or memory leaks (discussed next).

Memory Leaks

A memory leak occurs when you allocate memory using new or new[] and fail to release it. If you lose the address of free store memory you have allocated, by overwriting the address in the pointer you were using to access it, for instance, you have a memory leak. This often occurs in a loop, and it's easier to create this kind of problem than you might think. The effect is that your program gradually consumes more and more of the free store, with the program potentially slowing more and more down, or even failing at the point when all of the free store has been allocated.

When it comes to scope, pointers are just like any other variable. The lifetime of a pointer extends from the point at which you define it in a block to the closing brace of the block. After that it no longer exists, so the address it contained is no longer accessible. If a pointer containing the address of a block of memory in the free store goes out of scope, then it's no longer possible to delete the memory.

It's still relatively easy to see where you've simply forgotten to use `delete` to free memory when use of the memory ceases at a point close to where you allocated it, but you'd be surprised how often programmers make mistakes like this, especially if, for instance, `return` statements creep in between the allocation and deallocation of your variable. And, naturally, memory leaks are even more difficult to spot in complex programs, where memory may be allocated in one part of a program and should be released in a completely separate part.

One basic strategy for avoiding memory leaks is to immediately add the `delete` operation at an appropriate place each time you use the `new` operator. But this strategy is by no means fail-safe. We cannot stress this enough: humans, even C++ programmers, are fallible creatures. So, whenever you manipulate dynamic memory directly, you *will*, sooner or later, introduce memory leaks. Even if it works at the time of writing, all too often bugs find their way into the program as it evolves further. `return` statements are added, conditional tests change, exceptions are thrown (see Chapter 15), and so on. And all of a sudden there are scenarios where your memory is no longer freed correctly!

Fragmentation of the Free Store

Memory fragmentation can arise in programs that frequently allocate and release memory blocks. Each time the `new` operator is used, it allocates a contiguous block of bytes. If you create and destroy many memory blocks of different sizes, it's possible to arrive at a situation in which the allocated memory is interspersed with small blocks of free memory, none of which is large enough to accommodate a new memory allocation request by your program. The aggregate of the free memory can be quite large, but if all the individual blocks are small (smaller than a current allocation request), the allocation request will fail. Figure 6-6 illustrates the effect of memory fragmentation.

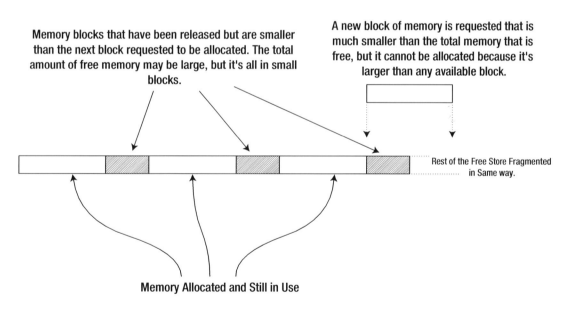

Figure 6-6. Fragmentation of the free store

We mention this problem here mostly for completeness because it arises relatively infrequently these days. Virtual memory provides a large memory address space even on quite modest computers. And the algorithms behind new/delete are clever and designed to counteract such phenomena as much as possible. It's only in rare cases that you need to worry about fragmentation anymore. For instance, for the most performance-critical parts of your code, operating on fragmented memory may seriously degrade performance. The way to avoid fragmentation of the free store then is not to allocate many small blocks of memory. Allocate larger blocks and manage the use of the memory yourself. But this is an advanced topic, well outside the scope of this book.

Golden Rule of Dynamic Memory Allocation

After spending more than half a dozen pages learning how to use the new and delete operators, our golden rule of dynamic memory allocation may come as a bit of a surprise. It's nevertheless one of the single most valuable pieces of advice we give you in this book:

■ **Tip**　Never use the operators new, new[], delete, and delete[] directly in day-to-day coding. These operators have no place in modern C++ code. Always use either the std::vector<> container (to replace dynamic arrays) or a smart pointer (to dynamically allocate objects and manage their lifetimes). These high-level alternatives are much, much safer than the low-level memory management primitives and will help you tremendously by instantly eradicating all dangling pointers, multiple deallocations, allocation/ deallocation mismatches, and memory leaks from your programs.

The std::vector<> container you already know from the previous chapter, and smart pointers are explained in the next section. The main reason we still teach you about the low-level dynamic memory allocation primitives is not because we'd invite you to use them (often or at all) but because you will surely still encounter them in existing code. This also, unfortunately, implies that you will be tasked with fixing bugs caused by their use (bonus tip: a good first step then would be to rewrite this code using better, more modern memory management utilities; more often than not, the underlying problem then reveals itself). In your own code, you should normally avoid manipulating dynamic memory directly.

Raw Pointers and Smart Pointers

All the pointer types we have discussed up to now are part of the C++ language. These are referred to as *raw pointers* because variables of these types contain nothing more than an address. A raw pointer can store the address of an automatic variable or a variable allocated in the free store. A *smart pointer* is an object that mimics a raw pointer in that it contains an address, and you can use it in the same way in many respects. Smart pointers are normally used only to store the address of memory allocated in the free store. A smart pointer does much more than a raw pointer, though. By far the most notable feature of a smart pointer is that you don't have to worry about using the delete or delete[] operator to free the memory. It will be released automatically when it is no longer needed. This means that multiple deallocations, allocation/deallocation mismatches, and memory leaks will no longer be possible. If you consistently use smart pointers, dangling pointers will be a thing of the past as well.

Smart pointers are particularly useful for managing class objects that you create dynamically, so smart pointers will be of greater relevance from Chapter 11 on. You can also store them in an array<T,N> or vector<T> container, which is again very useful when you are working with objects of a class type.

Smart pointer types are defined by templates inside the `memory` header of the Standard Library, so you must include this in your source file to use them. There are three types of smart pointers, all defined in the `std` namespace:

- A `unique_ptr<T>` object behaves as a pointer to type `T` and is "unique" in the sense that there can be only one single `unique_ptr<>` object containing the same address. In other words, there can never be two or more `unique_ptr<T>` objects pointing to the same memory address at the same time. A `unique_ptr<>` object is said to *own* what it points to *exclusively*. This uniqueness is enforced by the fact that the compiler will never allow you to copy a `unique_ptr<>`.[2]

- A `shared_ptr<T>` object also behaves as a pointer to type `T`, but in contrast with `unique_ptr<T>` there can be any number of `shared_ptr<T>` objects that contain—or, share—the same address. Thus, `shared_ptr<>` objects allow *shared ownership* of an object in the free store. At any given moment, the number of `shared_ptr<>` objects that contain a given address in time is known by the runtime. This is called *reference counting*. The reference count for a `shared_ptr<>` containing a given free store address is incremented each time a new `shared_ptr<>` object is created containing that address, and it's decremented when a `shared_ptr<>` containing the address is destroyed or assigned to point to a different address. When there are no `shared_ptr<>` objects containing a given address, the reference count will have dropped to zero, and the memory for the object at that address will be released automatically. All `shared_ptr<>` objects that point to the same address have access to the count of how many there are. You'll understand how this is possible when you learn about classes in Chapter 11.

- A `weak_ptr<T>` is linked to a `shared_ptr<T>` and contains the same address. Creating a `weak_ptr<>` does not increment the reference count associated to the linked `shared_ptr<>` object, though, so a `weak_ptr<>` does not prevent the object pointed to from being destroyed. Its memory will still be released when the last `shared_ptr<>` referencing it is destroyed or reassigned to point to a different address, even when associated `weak_ptr<>` objects still exist. If this happens, the `weak_ptr<>` will nevertheless not contain a dangling pointer, at least not one that you could inadvertently access. The reason is that you cannot access the address encapsulated by a `weak_ptr<T>` directly. Instead, the compiler will force you to first create a `shared_ptr<T>` out of it that refers to the same address. If the memory address for the `weak_ptr<>` is still valid, forcing to create a `shared_ptr<>` first makes sure that the reference count is again incremented and that the pointer can be used safely again. If the memory is released already, however, this operation will result in a `shared_ptr<>` containing `nullptr`.

One use for having `weak_ptr<>` objects is to avoid so-called reference cycles with `shared_ptr<>` objects. Conceptually, a reference cycle is where a `shared_ptr<>` inside an object x points to some other object y that contains a `shared_ptr<>`, which points back to x. With this situation, neither x nor y can be destroyed. In practice, this may occur in ways that are more complicated. `weak_ptr<>` smart pointers allow you to break such reference cycles. Another use for weak pointers is the implementation of object caches.

However, as you no doubt already started to sense, weak pointers are used only in more advanced use cases. As they are used only sporadically, we'll not discuss them any further here. The other two smart pointer types, however, you should use literally all the time, so let's dig a bit deeper into them.

---

[2]In Chapter 17, you'll learn that while copying a `unique_ptr<>` is not possible, you *can* "move" the address stored by one `unique_ptr<>` object to another by using the `std::move()` function. After this move operation the original smart pointer will be empty again.

Using unique_ptr<T> Pointers

A unique_ptr<T> object stores an address uniquely, so the value to which it points is owned exclusively by the unique_ptr<T> smart pointer. When the unique_ptr<T> is destroyed, so is the value to which it points. Like all smart pointers, a unique_ptr<> is most useful when working with dynamically allocated objects. Objects then should not be shared by multiple parts of the program or where the lifetime of the dynamic object is naturally tied to that of a single other object in your program. One common use for a unique_ptr<> is to hold something called a *polymorphic pointer*, which in essence is a pointer to a dynamically allocated object that can be of any number of related class types. To cut a long story short, you'll only fully appreciate this smart pointer type after learning all about class objects and polymorphism in Chapters 11 through 15.

For now, our examples will simply use dynamically allocated values of fundamental types, which do not really excel in usefulness. What should become obvious already, though, is why these smart pointers are that much safer to use than the low-level allocation and deallocation primitives; that is, they make it impossible for you to forget or mismatch deallocation!

In the (not so) old days, you had to create and initialize a unique_ptr<T> object like this:

```
std::unique_ptr<double> pdata {new double{999.0}};
```

This creates pdata containing the address of a double variable in the free store that is initialized with 999.0. While this syntax remains valid, the recommended way to create a unique_ptr<> today is by means of the std::make_unique<>() function template (introduced by C++14). To define pdata, you should therefore normally use the following:

```
std::unique_ptr<double> pdata { std::make_unique<double>(999.0) };
```

The arguments to std::make_unique<T>(…) are exactly those values that would otherwise appear in the braced initializer of a dynamic allocation of the form new T{…}. In our example, that's the single double literal 999.0. To save you some typing, you'll probably want to combine this syntax with the use of the auto keyword:

```
auto pdata{ std::make_unique<double>(999.0) };
```

That way, you only have to type the type of the dynamic variable, double, once.

▓ **Tip**   To create a std::unique_ptr<T> object that points to a newly allocated T value, always use the std::make_unique<T>() function. Not only is this shorter (provided you use the auto keyword in the variable definition), this function is safer as well against some more subtle memory leaks.

You can dereference pdata just like an ordinary pointer, and you can use the result in the same way:

```
*pdata = 8888.0;
std::cout << *pdata << std::endl;     // Outputs 8888
```

The big difference is that you no longer have to worry about deleting the double variable from the free store.

You can access the address that a smart pointer contains by calling its get() function. Here's an example:

```
std::cout << std::hex << std::showbase << pdata.get() << std::endl;
```

This outputs the value of the address contained in pdata as a hexadecimal value. All smart pointers have a get() function that will return the address that the pointer contains. You should only ever access the raw pointer inside a smart pointer to pass it to functions that use this pointer only briefly, never to functions or objects that would make and hang on to a copy of this pointer. It's not recommended to store raw pointers that point to the same object as a smart pointer because this may lead to dangling pointers again, as well as all kinds of related problems.

You can create a unique pointer that points to an array as well. The older syntax to do this looks as follows:

```
const size_t n {100};                        // Array size
std::unique_ptr<double[]> pvalues {new double[n]};  // Dynamically create array of n elements
```

As before, we recommend you always use std::make_unique<T[]>() instead:

```
auto pvalues{ std::make_unique<double[]>(n) };    // Dynamically create array of n elements
```

Either way, pvalues points to the array of n elements of type double in the free store. Like a raw pointer, you can use array notation with the smart pointer to access the elements of the array it points to:

```
for (size_t i {}; i < n; ++i)
  pvalues[i] = i + 1;
```

This sets the array elements to values from 1 to n. The compiler will insert an implicit conversion to type double for the result of the expression on the right of the assignment. You can output the values of the elements in a similar way:

```
for (size_t i {}; i < n; ++i)
{
  std::cout << pvalues[i] << ' ';
  if ((i + 1) % 10 == 0)
    std::cout << std::endl;
}
```

This just outputs the values ten on each line. Thus, you can use a unique_ptr<T[]> variable that contains the address of an array just like an array name.

■ **Tip**   It is mostly recommended to use a vector<T> container instead of a unique_ptr<T[]> because this container type is far more powerful and flexible than the smart pointer. We refer to the end of the previous chapter for a discussion of the various advantages of using vectors.

You can reset the pointer contained in a unique_ptr<>, or any type of smart pointer for that matter, by calling its reset() function:

```
pvalues.reset();                      // Address is nullptr
```

pvalues still exists, but it no longer points to anything. This is a unique_ptr<double> object, so because there can be no other unique pointer containing the address of the array, the memory for the array will be released as a result. Naturally, you can check whether a smart pointer contains nullptr by explicitly comparing it to nullptr, but a smart pointer also conveniently converts to a Boolean value in the same manner as a raw pointer (that is, it converts to false if and only if it contains nullptr):

```
if (pvalues)                    // Short for:   if (pvalues != nullptr)
  std::cout << "The first value is " << pvalues[0] << std::endl;
```

You create a smart pointer that contains `nullptr` either by using empty braces, {}, or simply by omitting the braces:

```
std::unique_ptr<int> my_number;     // Or:   ... my_number{};
                                    // Or:   ... my_number{ nullptr };
if (!my_number)
  std::cout << "my_number points to nothing yet" << std::endl;
```

Creating empty smart pointers would be of little use, were it not that you can always change the value a smart pointer points to. You can do this again using `reset()`:

```
my_number.reset(new int{ 123 });    // my_number points to an integer value 123
my_number.reset(new int{ 42 });     // my_number points to an integer 42
```

Calling `reset()` without arguments is thus equivalent to calling `reset(nullptr)`. When calling `reset()` on a `unique_ptr<T>` object, either with or without arguments, any memory that was previously owned by that smart pointer will be deallocated. So, with the second statement in the previous snippet, the memory containing the integer value 123 gets deallocated, after which the smart pointer takes ownership of the memory slot holding the number 42.

Next to `get()` and `reset()`, a `unique_ptr<>` object also has a member function called `release()`. This function is essentially used to turn the smart pointer back into a dumb raw pointer.

```
int* raw_number = my_number.release();  // my_number points to nullptr after this
...
delete raw_number;                      // The smart pointer now no longer does this for
you!
```

Take care, though; when calling `release()`, it becomes your responsibility again to apply `delete` or `delete[]`. You should therefore use this function only when absolutely necessary, typically when handing over dynamically allocated memory to legacy code. If you do this, always make absolutely sure that this legacy code effectively releases the memory—if not, `get()` is what you should be calling instead!

■ **Caution** Never call `release()` without capturing the raw pointer that comes out. That is, never write a statement of the following form:

```
pvalues.release();
```

Why? Because this introduces a whopping memory leak, of course! You release (with `release()`) the smart pointer from the responsibility of deallocating the memory, but since you neglect to capture the raw pointer, there's no way you or anyone else can still apply `delete` or `delete[]` to it anymore. While this may seem obvious now, you'd be surprised how often `release()` is mistakenly called when instead a `reset()` statement of the following form was intended:

```
pvalues.reset();          // Not the same as release(); !!!
```

The confusion no doubt stems from the facts that the `release()` and `reset()` functions have alliterative names and both functions put the pointer's address to `nullptr`. These similarities notwithstanding, there's of course one rather critical difference: `reset()` deallocates any memory previously owned by the `unique_ptr<>`, whereas `release()` does not. In general, `release()` is a function you should use only sporadically and with great care not to introduce leaks.

Using shared_ptr<T> Pointers

You can define a `shared_ptr<T>` object in a similar way to a `unique_ptr<T>` object:

```
std::shared_ptr<double> pdata {new double{999.0}};
```

You can also dereference it to access what it points to or to change the value stored at the address:

```
*pdata = 8888.0;
std::cout << *pdata << std::endl;        // Outputs 8888
*pdata = 8889.0;
std::cout << *pdata << std::endl;        // Outputs 8889
```

Creating a `shared_ptr<T>` object involves a more complicated process than creating a `unique_ptr<T>`, not least because of the need to maintain a reference count. The definition of pdata involves one memory allocation for the `double` variable and another allocation relating to the smart pointer object. Allocating memory in the free store is expensive on time. You can make the process more efficient by using the make_shared<T>() function that is defined in the memory header to create a smart pointer of type `shared_ptr<T>`:

```
auto pdata{ std::make_shared<double>(999.0) };  // Points to a double variable
```

The type of variable to be created in the free store is specified between the angled brackets. This statement allocates memory for the `double` variable and allocates memory for the smart pointer in a single step, so it's faster. The argument between the parentheses following the function name is used to initialize the `double` variable it creates. In general, there can be any number of arguments to the make_shared() function, with the actual number depending on the type of object being created. When you are using make_shared() to create objects in the free store, there will often be two or more arguments separated by commas. The `auto` keyword causes the type for pdata to be deduced automatically from the object returned by make_shared<T>(), so it will be `shared_ptr<double>`.

You can initialize a `shared_ptr<T>` with another when you define it:

```
std::shared_ptr<double> pdata2 {pdata};
```

pdata2 points to the same variable as pdata. You can also assign one `shared_ptr<T>` to another:

```
std::shared_ptr<double> pdata{new double {999.0}};
std::shared_ptr<double> pdata2;           // Pointer contains nullptr
pdata2 = pdata;                           // Copy pointer - both point to the same variable
std::cout << *pdata2 << std::endl;        // Outputs 999
```

Of course, copying pdata increases the reference count. Both pointers have to be reset or destroyed for the memory occupied by the `double` variable to be released.

While we may not have explicitly mentioned it in the previous subsection, neither of these operations would be possible with unique_ptr<> objects. The compiler would never allow you to create two unique_ptr<> objects pointing to the same memory location.[3] With good reason, if it were allowed, both would end up deallocating the same memory, with potentially catastrophic results.

Another option, of course, is to store the address of an array<T> or vector<T> container object that you create in the free store. Here's a working example:

```cpp
// Ex6_07.cpp
// Using smart pointers
#include <iostream>
#include <iomanip>
#include <memory>                                  // For smart pointers
#include <vector>                                  // For vector container
#include <cctype>                                  // For toupper()

int main()
{
  std::vector<std::shared_ptr<std::vector<double>>> records;  // Temperature records by days
  size_t day{ 1 };                                 // Day number

  while (true)                                     // Collect temperatures by day
  {
    // Vector to store current day's temperatures created in the free store
    auto day_records{ std::make_shared<std::vector<double>>() };
    records.push_back(day_records);                // Save pointer in records vector

    std::cout << "Enter the temperatures for day " << day++
              << " separated by spaces. Enter 1000 to end:\n";

    while (true)
    { // Get temperatures for current day
      double t{};                                  // A temperature
      std::cin >> t;
      if (t == 1000.0) break;

      day_records->push_back(t);
    }

    std::cout << "Enter another day's temperatures (Y or N)? ";
    char answer{};
    std::cin >> answer;
    if (std::toupper(answer) != 'Y') break;
  }

  day = 1;
```

---

[3]Not unless you bypass the compiler's safety checks by using raw pointers, that is, for instance by calling get(). Mixing raw pointers and smart pointers is generally a bad idea.

```
std::cout << std::fixed << std::setprecision(2) << std::endl;
for (auto record : records)
{
  double total{};
  size_t count{};

  std::cout << "\nTemperatures for day " << day++ << ":\n";
  for (auto temp : *record)
  {
    total += temp;
    std::cout << std::setw(6) << temp;
    if (++count % 5 == 0) std::cout << std::endl;
  }

  std::cout << "\nAverage temperature: " << total / count << std::endl;
}
}
```

Here's how the output looks with arbitrary input values:

```
23 34 29 36 1000
Enter another day's temperatures (Y or N)? y
Enter the temperatures for day 2 separated by spaces. Enter 1000 to end:
34 35 45 43 44 40 37 35 1000
Enter another day's temperatures (Y or N)? y
Enter the temperatures for day 3 separated by spaces. Enter 1000 to end:
44 56 57 45 44 32 28 1000
Enter another day's temperatures (Y or N)? n

Temperatures for day 1:
 23.00 34.00 29.00 36.00
Average temperature: 30.50

Temperatures for day 2:
 34.00 35.00 45.00 43.00 44.00
 40.00 37.00 35.00
Average temperature: 39.13

Temperatures for day 3:
 44.00 56.00 57.00 45.00 44.00
 32.00 28.00
Average temperature: 43.71
```

This program reads an arbitrary number of temperature values recorded during a day, for an arbitrary number of days. The accumulation of temperature records is stored in the records vector, which has elements of type shared_ptr<vector<double>>. Thus, each element is a smart pointer to a vector of type vector<double>.

The containers for the temperatures for any number of days are created in the outer while loop. The temperature records for a day are stored in a vector container that is created in the free store by this statement:

```
auto day_records{ std::make_shared<std::vector<double>>() };
```

The day_records pointer type is determined by the pointer type returned by the make_shared<>() function. The function allocates memory for the vector<double> object in the free store along with the shared_ptr<vector<double>> smart pointer that is initialized with its address and returned. Thus, day_records is type shared_ptr<vector<double>>, which is a smart pointer to a vector<double> object. This pointer is added to the records container.

The vector pointed to by day_records is populated with data that is read in the inner while loop. Each value is stored using the push_back() function for the current vector pointed to by day_records. The function is called using the indirect member selection operator. This loop continues until 1000 is entered, which is an unlikely value for a temperature during the day, so there can be no mistaking it for a real value. When all the data for the current day has been entered, the inner while loop ends, and there's a prompt asking whether another day's temperatures are to be entered. If the answer is affirmative, the outer loop continues and creates another vector in the free store. When the outer loop ends, the records vector will contain smart pointers to vectors containing each day's temperatures.

The next loop is a range-based for loop that iterates over the elements in the records vector. The inner range-based for loop iterates over the temperature values in the vector that the current records' element points to. This inner loop outputs the data for the day and accumulates the total of the temperatures values. This allows the average temperature for the current day to be calculated when the inner loop ends. In spite of having a fairly complicated data organization with a vector of smart pointers to vectors in the free store, accessing the data and processing the data are easy tasks using range-based for loops.

The example illustrates how using containers and smart pointers can be a powerful and flexible combination. This program deals with any number of sets of input, with each set containing any number of values. Free store memory is managed by the smart pointers, so there is no need to worry about using the delete operator or the possibility of memory leaks. The records vector could also have been created in the free store too, but we'll leave that as an exercise for you to try.

▓ **Note** We've used shared pointers in Ex6_07 mainly for the sake of creating a first example. Normally, you'd simply use a vector of type std::vector<std::vector<double>> instead. The need for shared pointers only really arises when multiple parts of the same program truly share the same object. Realistic uses of shared pointers hence generally involve objects, as well as more lines of code than is feasible to show in a book.

Understanding References

A reference is similar to a pointer in many respects, which is why we're introducing it here. You'll only get a real appreciation of the value of references, though, once you learn how to define functions in Chapter 8. References become even more important in the context of object-oriented programming later.

A reference is a name that you can use as an alias for another variable. Obviously, it must be like a pointer insofar as it refers to something else in memory, but there are a few crucial differences. Unlike a pointer, you cannot declare a reference and not initialize it. Because a reference is an alias, the variable for which it is an alias must be provided when the reference is initialized. Also, a reference cannot be modified to be an alias for something else. Once a reference is initialized as an alias for some variable, it keeps referring to that same variable for the remainder of its lifetime.

Defining References

Suppose you defined this variable:

```
double data {3.5};
```

You can define a reference as an alias for data like this variable:

```
double& rdata {data};          // Defines a reference to the variable data
```

The ampersand following the type name indicates that the variable being defined, rdata, is a reference to a variable of type double. The variable that it represents is specified in the braced initializer. Thus, rdata is of type "reference to double." You can use the reference as an alternative to the original variable name. Here's an example:

```
rdata += 2.5;
```

This increments data by 2.5. None of the dereferencing that you need with a pointer is necessary—you just use the name of the reference as though it is a variable. A reference always acts as a true alias, otherwise indistinguishable from the original variable. If you take the address of a reference, for instance, the result will even be a pointer to the original variable. In the following snippet, the addresses stored in pdata1 and pdata2 will thus be identical:

```
double* pdata1 {&rdata};       // pdata1 == pdata2
double* pdata2 {&data};
```

Let's ram home the difference between a reference and a pointer by contrasting the reference rdata in the previous code with the pointer pdata defined in this statement:

```
double* pdata {&data};         // A pointer containing the address of data
```

This defines a pointer, pdata, and initializes it with the address of data. This allows you to increment data like this:

```
*pdata += 2.5;                 // Increment data through a pointer
```

You must dereference the pointer to access the variable to which it points. With a reference, there is no need for dereferencing; it just doesn't apply. In some ways, a reference is like a pointer that has already been dereferenced, although it also can't be changed to reference something else. Make no mistake, though; given our rdata reference variable from before, the following snippet *does* compile:

```
double other_data = 5.0;       // Create a second double variable called other_data
rdata = other_data;            // Assign other_data's current value to data (through rdata)
```

Key is that this last statement does not make rdata refer to the other_data variable. The rdata reference variable is defined to be an alias for data and will forever be an alias for data. A reference is and always remains the complete equivalent of the variable to which it refers. In other words, the second statement acts exactly as if you wrote this:

```
data = other_data;            // Assign the value of other_data to data (directly)
```

A pointer is different. With our pointer pdata, for instance, we can do the following:

```
pdata = &other_data;          // Make pdata point to the other_data variable
```

A reference variable is thus much like a const pointer variable:

```
double* const pdata {&data};  // A const pointer containing the address of data
```

215

Take care: we didn't say a pointer-to-const variable but a const pointer variable. That is, the const needs to come after the asterisk. Reference-to-const variables exist as well. You define such a reference variable by using the const keyword:

```
const double& const_ref{ data };
```

Such a reference is similar to a pointer-to-const variable—a const pointer-to-const variable to be exact—in the sense that it is an alias through which one cannot modify the original variable. The following statement, for instance, will therefore not compile:

```
const_ref *= 2;                    // Illegal attempt to modify data through a reference-to-const
```

In Chapter 8 you'll see that reference-to-const variables play a particularly important role when defining functions that operate on arguments of nonfundamental object types.

Using a Reference Variable in a Range-Based for Loop

You know that you can use a range-based for loop to iterate over all the elements in an array:

```
double sum {};
unsigned count {};
double temperatures[] {45.5, 50.0, 48.2, 57.0, 63.8};
for (auto t : temperatures)
{
  sum += t;
  ++count;
}
```

The variable t is initialized to the value of the current array element on each iteration, starting with the first. The t variable does not access that element itself. It is just a local copy with the same value as the element. You therefore also cannot use t to modify the value of an element. However, you can change the array elements if you use a reference:

```
const double F2C {5.0/9.0};        // Fahrenheit to Celsius conversion constant
for (auto& t : temperatures)       // Reference loop variable
  t = (t - 32.0) * F2C;
```

The loop variable, t, is now of type double&, so it is an alias for each array element. The loop variable is redefined on each iteration and initialized with the current element, so the reference is never changed after being initialized. This loop changes the values in the temperatures array from Fahrenheit to Celsius. You can use the alias t in any context in which you'd be able to use the original variable or array element. Another way to write the previous loop, for instance, is this:

```
const double F2C {5.0/9.0};        // Fahrenheit to Celsius conversion constant
for (auto& t : temperatures) {     // Reference loop variable
  t -= 32.0;
  t *= F2C;
}
```

Using a reference in a range-based for loop is efficient when you are working with collections of objects. Copying objects can be expensive on time, so avoiding copying by using a reference type makes your code more efficient.

When you use a reference type for the variable in a range-based for loop and you don't need to modify the values, you can use a reference-to-const type for the loop variable:

```
for (const auto& t : temperatures)
  std::cout << std::setw(6) << t;
std::cout << std::endl;
```

You still get the benefits of using a reference type to make the loop as efficient as possible (no copies of the elements are being made!), and at the same time you prevent the array elements from being inadvertently changed by this loop.

Summary

You explored some important concepts in this chapter. You will undoubtedly make extensive use of pointers and particularly smart pointers in real-world C++ programs, and you'll see a lot more of them throughout the rest of the book:

These are the vital points this chapter covered:

- A pointer is a variable that contains an address. A basic pointer is referred to as a raw pointer.

- You obtain the address of a variable using the address-of operator, &.

- To refer to the value pointed to by a pointer, you use the indirection operator, *. This is also called the dereference operator.

- You access a member of an object through a pointer or smart pointer using the indirect member selection operator, ->.

- You can add integer values to or subtract integer values from the address stored in a raw pointer. The effect is as though the pointer refers to an array, and the pointer is altered by the number of array elements specified by the integer value. You cannot perform arithmetic with a smart pointer.

- The new and new[] operators allocate a block of memory in the free store—holding a single variable and an array, respectively—and return the address of the memory allocated.

- You use the delete or delete[] operator to release a block of memory that you've allocated previously using either the new or, respectively, the new[] operator. You don't need to use these operators when the address of free store memory is stored in a smart pointer.

- Low-level dynamic memory manipulation is synonymous for a wide range of serious hazards such as dangling pointers, multiple deallocations, deallocation mismatches, memory leaks, and so on. Our golden rule is therefore this: never use the low-level new/new[] and delete/delete[] operators directly. Containers (and std::vector<> in particular) and smart pointers are nearly always the smarter choice!

- A smart pointer is an object that can be used like a raw pointer. A smart pointer, by default, is used only to store free store memory addresses.

- There are two commonly used varieties of smart pointers. There can only ever be one type unique_ptr<T> pointer in existence that points to a given object of type T, but there can be multiple shared_ptr<T> objects containing the address of a given object of type T. The object will then be destroyed when there are no shared_ptr<T> objects containing its address.

- A reference is an alias for a variable that represents a permanent storage location.

- You can use a reference type for the loop variable in a range-based for loop to allow the values of the elements in the range to be modified.

EXERCISES

The following exercises enable you to try what you've learned in this chapter. If you get stuck, look back over the chapter for help. If you're still stuck after that, you can download the solutions from the Apress website (www.apress.com/source-code), but that really should be a last resort.

Exercise 6-1. Write a program that declares and initializes an array with the first 50 odd (as in not even) numbers. Output the numbers from the array ten to a line using pointer notation and then output them in reverse order, also using pointer notation.

Exercise 6-2. Revisit the previous exercise, but instead of accessing the array values using the loop counter, this time you should employ pointer increments (using the ++ operator) to traverse the array when outputting it for the first time. After that, use pointer decrements (using --) to traverse the array again in the reverse direction.

Exercise 6-3. Write a program that reads an array size from the keyboard and dynamically allocates an array of that size to hold floating-point values. Using pointer notation, initialize all the elements of the array so that the value of the element at index position n is $1 / (n + 1)^2$. Calculate the sum of the elements using array notation, multiply the sum by 6, and output the square root of that result.

Exercise 6-4. Repeat the calculation in Exercise 6-3 but using a vector<> container allocated in the free store. Test the program with more than 100,000 elements. Do you notice anything interesting about the result?

Exercise 6-5. Revisit Exercise 6-3, but this time use a smart pointer to store the array, that is, if you haven't already done so from the start. A good student should've known not to use the low-level memory allocation primitives....

Exercise 6-6. Revisit Exercise 6-4 and replace any raw pointers with smart pointers there as well.

CHAPTER 7

■■ ■

Working with Strings

This chapter is about handling textual data much more effectively and safely than the mechanism provided by a C-style string stored in an array of char elements:

In this chapter, you'll learn

- How to create variables of type string

- What operations are available with objects of type string and how you use them

- How to chain together various bits and pieces to form one single string

- How you can search a string for a specific character or a substring

- How you can modify an existing string

- How to convert a string such as "3.1415" into the corresponding number

- How to use streams and stream manipulators for advanced string formatting

- How you can work with strings containing Unicode characters

- What a raw string literal is

A Better Class of String

You've seen how you can use an array of elements of type char to store a null-terminated (C-style) string. The cstring header provides a wide range of functions for working with C-style strings including capabilities for joining strings, searching a string, and comparing strings. All these operations depend on the null character being present to mark the end of a string. If it is missing or gets overwritten, many of these functions will march happily through memory beyond the end of a string until a null character is found at some point or some catastrophe stops the process. Even if your process survives, it often results in memory being arbitrarily overwritten. And once that happens, all bets are off! Using C-style strings is therefore inherently unsafe and represents a serious security risk. Fortunately, there's a better alternative.

The string header of the C++ Standard Library defines the std::string type, which is much easier to use than a null-terminated string. The string type is defined by a class (or to be more precise, a class template), so it isn't one of the fundamental types. Type string is a *compound type*, which is a type that's a composite of several data items that are ultimately defined in terms of fundamental types of data. Next to the characters that make up the string it represents, a string object contains other data as well, such as number of characters in the string. Because the string type is defined in the string header, you must include this header when you're using string objects. The string type name is defined within the std namespace, so you'd need a using declaration to use the type name in its unqualified form. We'll start by explaining how you create string objects.

© Ivor Horton and Peter Van Weert 2018
I. Horton and P. Van Weert, *Beginning C++17*, https://doi.org/10.1007/978-1-4842-3366-5_7

Defining string Objects

An object of type `string` contains a sequence of characters of type `char`, which can be empty. This statement defines a variable of type `string` that contains an empty string:

```
std::string empty;              // An empty string
```

This statement defines a `string` object that you refer to using the name `empty`. In this case, `empty` contains a string that has no characters and so it has zero length.

You can initialize a `string` object with a string literal when you define it:

```
std::string proverb {"Many a mickle makes a muckle."};
```

`proverb` is a `string` object that contains a copy of the string literal shown in the initializer. Internally, the character array encapsulated by a `string` object is always terminated by a null character as well. This is done to assure compatibility with the numerous existing functions that expect C-style strings.

■ **Note**   You can convert a `std::string` object to a C-style string using two similar methods. The first is by calling its `c_str()` member function (short for *C-string*):

```
const char* proverb_c_str = proverb.c_str();
```

This conversion results in a C-string of type `const char*`. Because it's `const`, this pointer cannot be used to modify the characters of the `string`, only to access them. Your second option is the `string`'s `data()` function, which starting from C++17 evaluates to a non-`const char*` pointer[1] (prior to C++17, `data()` resulted in a `const char*` pointer as well):

```
char* proberb_data = proverb.data();
```

You should convert to C-style strings only when calling legacy C-style functions. In your own code, we of course recommend you consistently use `std::string` objects because these are far safer and more convenient than plain `char` arrays.

All `std::string` functions, though, are defined in such a way that you normally never need to worry about the terminating null character anymore. For instance, you can obtain the length of the string for a `string` object using its `length()` function, which takes no arguments. This length never includes the string termination character:

```
std::cout << proverb.length();          // Outputs 29
```

This statement calls the `length()` function for the `proverb` object and outputs the value it returns to `cout`. The record of the string length is guaranteed to be maintained by the object itself. That is, to find out the length of the encapsulated string, the `string` object does not have to traverse the entire string looking

---

[1]Unless `proverb` itself is of type `const std::string`; if that's the case, `data()` results in a `const char*` pointer as well. Refer to Chapter 11 for more details on the relation between `const` objects and member functions.

for the terminating null character. When you append one or more characters, the length is increased automatically by the appropriate amount and decreased if you remove characters.

There are some other possibilities for initializing a string object. You can use an initial sequence from a string literal, for instance:

```
std::string part_literal { "Least said soonest mended.", 5 };  // "Least"
```

The second initializer in the list specifies the length of the sequence from the first initializer to be used to initialize the part_literal object.

You can't initialize a string object with a single character between single quotes—you must use a string literal between double quotes, even when it's just one character. However, you *can* initialize a string with any number of instances of a given character. You can define and initialize a sleepy time string object like this:

```
std::string sleeping(6, 'z');
```

The string object, sleeping, will contain "zzzzzz". The string length will be 6. If you want to define a string object that's more suited to a light sleeper, you could write this:

```
std::string light_sleeper(1, 'z');
```

This initializes light_sleeper with the string literal "z".

▓ **Caution**   To initialize a string with repeated character values, you must not use curly braces like this:

```
std::string sleeping{6, 'z'};
```

This curly braces syntax does compile but for sure won't do what you expect. In our example, the literal 6 would be interpreted as the code for a letter character, meaning sleeping would be initialized to some obscure two-letter word instead of the intended "zzzzzz". If you recall, you encountered an analogous quirk of C++'s near-uniform initialization syntax already before with std::vector<> in the previous chapter.

A further option is to use an existing string object to provide the initial value. Given that you've defined proverb previously, you can define another object based on that:

```
std::string sentence {proverb};
```

The sentence object will be initialized with the string literal that proverb contains, so it too will contain "Many a mickle makes a muckle." and have a length of 29.

You can reference characters within a string object using an index value starting from 0, just like an array. You can use a pair of index values to identify part of an existing string and use that to initialize a new string object. Here's an example:

```
std::string phrase {proverb, 0, 13};  // Initialize with 13 characters starting at index 0
```

Figure 7-1 illustrates this process.

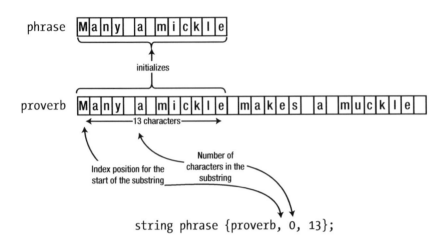

Figure 7-1. *Creating a new string from part of an existing string*

The first element in the braced initializer is the source of the initializing string. The second is the index of the character in proverb that begins the initializing substring, and the third initializer in the list is the number of characters in the substring. Thus, phrase will contain "Many a mickle".

■ **Caution** The third entry in the {proverb, 0, 13} initializer, 13, is the *length* of the substring, *not an index*, indicating the last (or one past the last) character of the substring. So, to extract, for instance, the substring "mickle", you should use the initializer {proverb, 7, 6} and not {proverb, 7, 13}. This is a common source of confusion and bugs, especially for beginning C++ developers who have past experience in languages such as JavaScript or Java where substrings are commonly designated using start and end indices.

To show which substring is created, you can insert the phrase object in the output stream, cout:

```
std::cout << phrase << std::endl;
```

Thus, you can output string objects just like C-style strings. Extraction from cin is also supported for string objects:

```
std::string name;
std::cout << "enter your name: ";
std::cin >> name;                        // Pressing Enter ends input
```

This reads characters up to the first whitespace character, which ends the input process. Whatever was read is stored in the string object, name. You cannot enter text with embedded spaces with this process. Of course, reading entire phrases complete with spaces is possible as well, just not with >>. We'll explain how you do this later.

To summarize, we have described six options for defining and initializing a string object; the following comments identify the initializing string in each case:

- No initializer (or empty braces, {}):

```
std::string empty;                          // The string ""
```

- An initializer containing a string literal:

```
std::string proverb{ "Many a mickle makes a muckle." };   // The given literal
```

- An initializer containing an existing string object:

```
std::string sentence{ proverb };          // Duplicates proverb
```

- An initializer containing a string literal followed by the length of the sequence in the literal to be used to initialize the string object:

```
std::string part_literal{ "Least said soonest mended.", 5 };  // "Least"
```

- An initializer containing a repeat count followed by the character literal that is to be repeated in the string that initializes the string object (mind the round parentheses!):

```
std::string open_wide(5, 'a');            // "aaaaa"
```

- An initializer containing an existing string object, an index specifying the start of the substring, and the length of the substring:

```
std::string phrase{proverb, 5, 8};        // "a mickle"
```

Operations with String Objects

Many operations with string objects are supported. Perhaps the simplest is assignment. You can assign a string literal or another string object to a string object. Here's an example:

```
std::string adjective {"hornswoggling"};    // Defines adjective
std::string word {"rubbish"};               // Defines word
word = adjective;                           // Modifies word
adjective = "twotiming";                    // Modifies adjective
```

The third statement assigns the value of adjective, which is "hornswoggling", to word, so "rubbish" is replaced. The last statement assigns the literal "twotiming" to adjective, so the original value "hornswoggling" is replaced. Thus, after executing these statements, word will contain "hornswoggling", and adjective will contain "twotiming".

Concatenating Strings

You can join strings using the addition operator; the technical term for this is *concatenation*. You can concatenate the objects defined earlier like this:

```
std::string description {adjective + " " + word + " whippersnapper"};
```

After executing this statement, the `description` object will contain the string `"twotiming hornswoggling whippersnapper"`. You can see that you can concatenate string literals with `string` objects using the + operator. This is because the + operator has been redefined to have a special meaning with `string` objects. When one operand is a `string` object and the other operand is either another `string` object or a string literal, the result of the + operation is a new `string` object containing the two strings joined together.

Note that you *can't* concatenate two string literals using the + operator. One of the two operands of the + operator must always be an object of type `string`. The following statement, for example, won't compile:

```
std::string description {" whippersnapper" + " " + word};    // Wrong!!
```

The problem is that the compiler will try to evaluate the initializer value as follows:

```
std::string description {(" whippersnapper" + " ") + word};    // Wrong!!
```

In other words, the first expression that it evaluates is (`" whippersnapper"` + `" "`), and the + operator doesn't work with both operands as two string literals. The good news is that you have at least five ways around this:

- Naturally, you can write the first two string literals as a single string literal: `{" whippersnapper " + word}`.

- You can omit the + between the two literals: `{" whippersnapper" " " + word}`. Two or more string literals in sequence will be concatenated into a single literal by the compiler.

- You can introduce parentheses: `{"whippersnapper" + (" " + word)}`. The expression between parentheses that joins `" "` with `word` is then evaluated first to produce a `string` object, which can subsequently be joined to the first literal using the + operator.

- You can turn one or both of the literals into a `std::string` object using the familiar initialization syntax: `{std::string{" whippersnapper"} + " " + word}`.

- You can turn one or both of the literals into a `std::string` object by adding the suffix s to the literal, such as in `{" whippersnapper"s + " " + word}`. For this to work, you first have to add a `using namespace std::string_literals;` directive. You can add this directive either at the beginning of your source file or locally inside your function. Once this directive is in scope, appending the letter s to a string literal turns it into a `std::string` object, much like, for instance, adding u to an integer literal creates an `unsigned` integer.

That's enough theory for the moment. It's time for a bit of practice. This program reads your first and second names from the keyboard:

```cpp
// Ex7_01.cpp
// Concatenating strings
#include <iostream>
#include <string>

int main()
{
  std::string first;                    // Stores the first name
  std::string second;                   // Stores the second name

  std::cout << "Enter your first name: ";
  std::cin >> first;                    // Read first name

  std::cout << "Enter your second name: ";
  std::cin >> second;                   // Read second name

  std::string sentence {"Your full name is "};  // Create basic sentence
  sentence += first + " " + second + ".";       // Augment with names

  std::cout << sentence << std::endl;           // Output the sentence
  std::cout << "The string contains "           // Output its length
            << sentence.length() << " characters." << std::endl;
}
```

Here's some sample output:

```
Enter your first name: Phil
Enter your second name: McCavity
Your full name is Phil McCavity.
The string contains 32 characters.
```

After defining two empty string objects, first and second, the program prompts for input of a first name and then a second name. The input operations will read anything up to the first whitespace character. So, if your name consists of multiple parts, say Van Weert, this program won't let you enter it. If you do enter, for instance, Van Weert for the second name, the >> operator will only extract the Van part from the stream. You'll learn how you can read a string that includes whitespace later in this chapter.

After getting the names, you create another string object that is initialized with a string literal. The sentence object is concatenated with the string object that results from the right operand of the += assignment operator:

```cpp
sentence += first + " " + second + ".";         // Augment with names
```

The right operand concatenates first with the literal " ", then second is appended to that result, and finally the literal "." is appended to that to produce the final result that is concatenated with the left operand of the += operator. This statement demonstrates that the += operator also works with objects of type string in a similar way to the basic types. The statement is equivalent to this statement:

```cpp
sentence = sentence + (first + " " + second + ".");  // Augment with names
```

Finally, the program uses the stream insertion operator to output the contents of sentence and the length of the string it contains.

■ **Tip**   The append() function of a std::string object is an alternative for the += operator. Using this, you could write the previous example as follows:

```
sentence.append(first).append(" ").append(second).append(".");
```

In its basic form, append() is not all that interesting—unless you enjoy typing, that is, or if the + key on your keyboard is broken. But of course there's more to it than that. The append() function is more flexible than += because it allows, for instance, the concatenation of substrings, or repeated characters:

```
std::string compliment("~~~ What a beautiful name... ~~~");
sentence.append(compliment, 3, 22);      // Appends " What a beautiful name"
sentence.append(3, '!');                 // Appends "!!!"
```

Concatenating Strings and Characters

Next to two string objects, or a string object and a string literal, you can also concatenate a string object and a single character. The string concatenation in Ex7_01, for example, could also be expressed as follows (see also Ex7_01A.cpp):

```
sentence += first + ' ' + second + '.';
```

Another option, just to illustrate the possibilities, is to use the following two statements:

```
sentence += first + ' ' + second;
sentence += '.';
```

What you cannot do, though, as before, is concatenate two individual characters. One of the operands to the + operand should always be a string object.

To observe an additional pitfall of adding characters together, you could replace the concatenation in Ex7_01 with this variant:

```
sentence += second;
sentence += ',' + ' ';
sentence += first;
```

Surprisingly, perhaps, this code does compile. But a possible session might then go as follows:

```
Enter your first name: Phil
Enter your second name: McCavity
Your full name is McCavityLPhil.
The string contains 32 characters.
```

Of particular interest is the third line in this session; notice the comma and space characters between McCavity and Phil have somehow mysteriously fused into a single capital letter *L*. The reason this happens is that the compiler does not concatenate two characters; instead, it adds the character codes for the two characters together. Nearly all compilers use ASCII codes for the basic Latin characters (ASCII encoding was explained in Chapter 1). The ASCII code for ',' is 44, and that of the ' ' character is 32. Their sum, 32 + 44, therefore equals 76, which happens to be the ASCII code for the capital letter 'L'.

Notice that this example would've worked fine if you had written it as follows:

```
sentence += second + ',' + ' ' + first;
```

The reason, analogous to before, is that the compiler would evaluate this statement from left to right, as if the following parentheses were present:

```
sentence += ((second + ',') + ' ') + first;
```

With this statement, one of the two concatenation operands is thus always a std::string. Confusing? Perhaps a bit. The general rule with std::string concatenation is easy enough, though: concatenation is evaluated left to right and will work correctly only as long as one of the operands of the concatenation operator, +, is a std::string object.

■ **Note** Up to this point, we have always used literals to initialize or concatenate with string objects—either string literals or character literals. Everywhere we used string literals, you can of course also use any other form of C-style string: char[] arrays, char* variables, or any expression that evaluates to either of these types. Similarly, all expressions involving character literals will work just as well with any expression that results in a value of type char.

Concatenating Strings and Numbers

An important limitation in C++ is that you can only concatenate std::string objects with either strings or characters. Concatenation with most other types, such as a double, will generally fail to compile:

```
const std::string result_string{ "The result equals: " };
double result = 3.1415;
std::cout << (result_string + result) << std::endl;      // Compiler error!
```

Worse, such concatenations might even compile, even though they'll of course never produce the desired result. Any given number will again be treated as a character code, like in the following example (the ASCII code for the letter 'E' is 69):

```
std::string song_title { "Summer of '" };
song_title += 69;
std::cout << song_title << std::endl;      // Summer of 'E
```

This limitation might frustrate you at first, especially if you're used to working with strings in, for instance, Java or C#. In those languages, the compiler implicitly converts values of any type to strings. Not so in C++: in C++, you have to explicitly convert these values to strings yourself. There are several ways you might accomplish this. For values of fundamental numeric types, the easiest by far is to use the std::to_string() family of functions, defined in the string header:

```
const std::string result_string{ "The result equals: " };
double result = 3.1415;
std::cout << (result_string + std::to_string(result)) << std::endl;
```

```
std::string song_title { "Summer of '" };
song_title += std::to_string(69);
std::cout << song_title << std::endl;     // Summer of '69
```

Accessing Characters in a String

You refer to a particular character in a string by using an index value between square brackets, just as you do with a character array. The first character in a string object has the index value 0. You could refer to the third character in sentence, for example, as sentence[2]. You can use such an expression on the left of the assignment operator, so you can *replace* individual characters as well as access them. The following loop changes all the characters in sentence to uppercase:

```
for (size_t i {}; i < sentence.length(); ++i)
  sentence[i] = std::toupper(sentence[i]);
```

This loop applies the toupper() function to each character in the string in turn and stores the result in the same position in the string. The index value for the first character is 0, and the index value for the last character is one less than the length of the string, so the loop continues as long as i < sentence.length() is true.

A string object is a range, so you could also do this with a range-based for loop:

```
for (auto& ch : sentence)
  ch = std::toupper(ch);
```

Specifying ch as a reference type allows the character in the string to be modified within the loop. This loop and the previous loop require the cctype header to be included to compile.

You can exercise this array-style access method in a version of Ex5_11.cpp that determined the number of vowels and consonants in a string. The new version will use a string object. It will also demonstrate that you can use the getline() function to read a line of text that includes spaces:

```
// Ex7_02.cpp
// Accessing characters in a string
#include <iostream>
#include <string>
#include <cctype>

int main()
{
  std::string text;                         // Stores the input
  std::cout << "Enter a line of text:\n";
  std::getline(std::cin, text);             // Read a line including spaces

  unsigned vowels {};                       // Count of vowels
  unsigned consonants {};                   // Count of consonants
  for (size_t i {}; i < text.length(); ++i)
  {
    if (std::isalpha(text[i]))              // Check for a letter
    {
```

```
    switch (std::tolower(text[i]))              // Convert to lowercase
    {
      case 'a': case 'e': case 'i': case 'o': case 'u':
        ++vowels;
        break;

      default:
        ++consonants;
        break;
    }
  }
}

std::cout << "Your input contained " << vowels << " vowels and "
          << consonants << " consonants." << std::endl;
}
```

Here's an example of the output:

```
Enter a line of text:
A nod is as good as a wink to a blind horse.
Your input contained 14 vowels and 18 consonants.
```

The text object contains an empty string initially. You read a line from the keyboard into text using the getline() function. This version of getline() is declared in the string header; the versions of getline() that you have used previously were declared in the iostream header. This version reads characters from the stream specified by the first argument, cin in this case, until a newline character is read, and the result is stored in the string object specified by the second argument, which is text in this case. This time you don't need to worry about how many characters are in the input. The string object will automatically accommodate however many characters are entered, and the length will be recorded in the object.

You can change the delimiter that signals the end of the input by a using a version of getline() with a third argument that specifies the new delimiter for the end of the input:

```
std::getline(std::cin, text, '#');
```

This reads characters until a '#' character is read. Because newline doesn't signal the end of input in this case, you can enter as many lines of input as you like, and they'll all be combined into a single string. Any newline characters that were entered will be present in the string.

You count the vowels and consonants in much the same way as in Ex5_11.cpp, using a for loop. Naturally, you could also use a range-based for loop instead:

```
for (const auto ch : text)
{
  if (std::isalpha(ch))                    // Check for a letter
  {
    switch (std::tolower(ch))              // Convert to lowercase
    {
      ...
```

This code, available in Ex7_02A.cpp, is simpler and easier to understand than the original. The major advantage of using a string object in this example compared to Ex5_11.cpp, though, remains the fact that you don't need to worry about the length of the string that is entered.

Accessing Substrings

You can extract a substring from a string object using its substr() function. The function requires two arguments. The first is the index position where the substring starts, and the second is the number of characters in the substring. The function returns the substring as a string object. Here's an example:

```
std::string phrase {"The higher the fewer."};
std::string word1 {phrase.substr(4, 6)};        // "higher"
```

This extracts the six-character substring from phrase that starts at index position 4, so word1 will contain "higher" after the second statement executes. If the length you specify for the substring overruns the end of the string object, then the substr() function just returns an object containing the characters up to the end of the string. The following statement demonstrates this behavior:

```
std::string word2 {phrase.substr(4, 100)};       // "higher the fewer."
```

Of course, there aren't 100 characters in phrase, let alone in a substring. In this case, the result will be that word2 will contain the substring from index position 4 to the end, which is "higher the fewer.". You could obtain the same result by omitting the length argument and just supplying the first argument that specifies the index of the first character of the substring:

```
std::string word {phrase.substr(4)};            // "higher the fewer."
```

This version of substr() also returns the substring from index position 4 to the end. If you omit both arguments to substr(), the whole of phrase will be selected as the substring.

If you specify a starting index for a substring that is outside the valid range for the string object, an *exception* of type std::out_of_range will be thrown, and your program will terminate abnormally—unless you've implemented some code to handle the exception. You don't know how to do that yet, but we'll discuss exceptions and how to handle them in Chapter 15.

▓ **Caution**   As before, substrings are always specified using their begin index and length, not using their begin and end indexes. Keep this in mind, especially when migrating from languages such as JavaScript or Java!

Comparing Strings

In example Ex7_02 you used an index to access individual characters in a string object for comparison purposes. When you access a character using an index, the result is of type char, so you can use the comparison operators to compare individual characters. You can also compare entire string objects using any of the comparison operators. These are the comparison operators you can use:

```
>        >=        <        <=        ==        !=
```

You can use these to compare two objects of type `string` or to compare a `string` object with a string literal or C-style string. The operands are compared character by character until either a pair of corresponding characters contains different characters or the end of either or both operands is reached. When a pair of characters differs, numerical comparison of the character codes determines which of the strings has the lesser value. If no differing character pairs are found and the strings are of different lengths, the shorter string is "less than" the longer string. Two strings are equal if they contain the same number of characters and all corresponding character codes are equal. Because you're comparing character codes, the comparisons are obviously going to be case sensitive.

The technical term for this string comparison algorithm is *lexicographical comparison*, which is just a fancy way of saying that strings are ordered in the same manner as they are in a dictionary.

You could compare two `string` objects using this `if` statement:

```
std::string word1 {"age"};
std::string word2 {"beauty"};
if (word1 < word2)
  std::cout << word1 << " comes before " << word2 << '.' << std::endl;
else
  std::cout << word2 << " comes before " << word1 << '.' << std::endl;
```

Executing these statements will result in the following output:

```
age comes before beauty.
```

This shows that the old saying must be true. The preceding code looks like a good candidate for using the conditional operator. You can produce a similar result with the following statement:

```
std::cout << word1 << (word1 < word2? " comes " : " does not come ")
          << "before " << word2 << '.' << std::endl;
```

Let's compare strings in a working example. This program reads any number of names and sorts them into ascending sequence:

```
// Ex7_03.cpp
// Comparing strings
#include <iostream>                     // For stream I/O
#include <iomanip>                      // For stream manipulators
#include <string>                       // For the string type
#include <cctype>                       // For character conversion
#include <vector>                       // For the vector container

int main()
{
  std::vector<std::string> names;       // Vector of names
  std::string input_name;               // Stores a name
  char answer {};                       // Response to a prompt

  do
  {
    std::cout << "Enter a name: ";
    std::cin >> input_name;             // Read a name and...
    names.push_back(input_name);        // ...add it to the vector
```

```
    std::cout << "Do you want to enter another name? (y/n): ";
    std::cin >> answer;
  } while (std::tolower(answer) == 'y');

  // Sort the names in ascending sequence
  bool sorted {};
  do
  {
    sorted = true;                        // remains true when names are sorted
    for (size_t i {1}; i < names.size(); ++i)
    {
      if (names[i-1] > names[i])
      { // Out of order - so swap names
        names[i].swap(names[i-1]);
        sorted = false;
      }
    }
  } while (!sorted);

  // Find the length of the longest name
  size_t max_length{};
  for (const auto& name : names)
    if (max_length < name.length())
      max_length = name.length();

  // Output the sorted names 5 to a line
  const size_t field_width = max_length + 2;
  size_t count {};

  std::cout <<"In ascending sequence the names you entered are:\n";
  for (const auto& name : names)
  {
    std::cout << std::setw(field_width) << name;
    if (!(++count % 5)) std::cout << std::endl;
  }

  std::cout << std::endl;
}
```

Here's some sample output:

```
Enter a name: Zebediah
Do you want to enter another name? (y/n): y
Enter a name: Meshak
Do you want to enter another name? (y/n): y
Enter a name: Eshak
Do you want to enter another name? (y/n): y
Enter a name: Abegnego
Do you want to enter another name? (y/n): y
Enter a name: Moses
Do you want to enter another name? (y/n): y
```

232

```
Enter a name: Job
Do you want to enter another name? (y/n): n
In ascending sequence the names you entered are:
  Abegnego     Eshak      Job    Meshak     Moses
  Zebediah
```

The names are stored in a vector of `string` elements. As you know, using a `vector<>` container means that an unlimited number of names can be accommodated. The container also acquires memory as necessary to store the string objects and deletes it when the vector is destroyed. The container will also keep track of how many there are, so there's no need to count them independently.

▓ **Note**   The fact that `std::strings` can be stored in containers is yet another major advantage `string` objects offer over regular C-style strings; plain `char` arrays cannot be stored into containers.

Sorting is implemented using the same bubble sort algorithm that you have seen applied to numerical values before, in `Ex5_09`. Because you need to compare successive elements in the vector and swap them when necessary, the `for` loop iterates over the index values for vector elements; a range-based `for` loop is not suitable here. The `names[i].swap(names[i-1])` statement in the `for` loop swaps the contents of two `string` objects; it has, in other words, the same effect as the following sequence of assignments:

```
auto temp = names[i];              // Out of order - so swap names
names[i] = names[i-1];
names[i-1] = temp;
```

At the end of the program, the sorted names are output in a range-based `for` loop. You can do this because a `vector<>` container represents a range. To align the names vertically using the `setw()` manipulator, you need to know the maximum name length, which is found by the range-based `for` loop that precedes the output loop.

▓ **Tip**   Most Standard Library types offer a `swap()` function. Besides `std::string`, this includes all container types (such as `std::vector<>` and `std::array<>`), `std::optional<>`, all smart pointer types, and many more. The `std` namespace also defines a nonmember function template that can be used to the same effect:

```
std::swap(names[i], names[i-1]);
```

The advantage of this nonmember template function is that it works for fundamental types such as `int` or `double` as well. You could try this in `Ex5_09` (you may have to include the `utility` header first, though, as this is where the basic `std::swap()` function template is defined).

The compare() Function

The `compare()` function for a `string` object can compare the object, as always, with either another `string` object, a string literal, or a C-style string. Here's an example of an expression that calls `compare()` for a `string` object, `word`, to compare it with a string literal:

```
word.compare("and")
```

233

word is compared with the argument to compare(). The function returns the result of the comparison as a value of type int. This will be a positive integer if word is greater than "and", zero if word is equal to "and", and a negative integer if word is less than "and".

▓ **Caution**   A common mistake is to write an if statement of the form if (word.compare("and")), assuming this condition will evaluate to true if word and "and" equal. But the result, of course, is precisely the opposite. For equal operands, compare() returns zero. And zero, as always, converts to the Boolean value false. To compare for equality, you should use the == operator instead.

In the previous example, you could have used the compare() function in place of using the comparison operator:

```
for (size_t i {1}; i < names.size(); ++i)
{
  if (names[i-1].compare(names[i]) > 0)
  { // Out of order - so swap names
    names[i].swap(names[i-1]);
    sorted = false;
  }
}
```

This is less clear than the original code, but you get an idea of how the compare() function can be used. The > operator is better in this instance, but there are circumstances where compare() has the advantage. The function tells you in a single step the relationship between two objects. If > results in false, you still don't know whether the operands are equal, whereas with compare() you do.

The function has another advantage. You can compare a substring of a string object with the argument:

```
std::string word1 {"A jackhammer"};
std::string word2 {"jack"};
int result{ word1.compare(2, word2.length(), word2) };
if (result == 0)
  std::cout << "word1 contains " << word2 << " starting at index 2" << std::endl;
```

The expression that initializes result compares the four-character substring of word1 that starts at index position 2 with word2. This is illustrated in Figure 7-2.

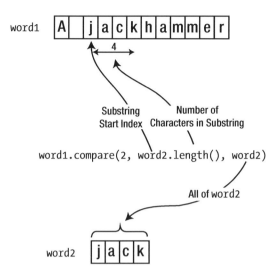

Figure 7-2. *Using compare() with a substring*

The first argument to compare() is the index position of the first character in a substring of word1 that is to be compared with word2. The second argument is the number of characters in the substring, which is sensibly specified as the length of the third argument, word2. Obviously, if the substring length you specify is not the same as the length of the third argument, the substring and the third argument are unequal by definition.

You could use the compare function to search for a substring. Here's an example:

```
std::string text {"Peter Piper picked a peck of pickled pepper."};
std::string word {"pick"};
for (size_t i{}; i < text.length() - word.length() + 1; ++i)
  if (text.compare(i, word.length(), word) == 0)
    std::cout << "text contains " << word << " starting at index " << i << std::endl;
```

This loop finds word at index positions 12 and 29 in text. The upper limit for the loop variable allows the last word.length() characters in text to be compared with word. This is not the most efficient implementation of the search. When word is found, it would be more efficient to arrange that the next substring of text that is checked is word.length() characters further along, but only if there is still word.length() characters before the end of text. However, there are easier ways to search a string object, as you'll see very soon.

You can compare a substring of one string with a substring of another using the compare() function. This involves passing *five* arguments to compare()! Here's an example:

```
std::string text {"Peter Piper picked a peck of pickled pepper."};
std::string phrase {"Got to pick a pocket or two."};
for (size_t i{}; i < text.length() - 3; ++i)
  if (text.compare(i, 4, phrase, 7, 4) == 0)
    std::cout << "text contains " << phrase.substr(7, 4)
              << " starting at index " << i << std::endl;
```

The two additional arguments are the index position of the substring in phrase and its length. The substring of text is compared with the substring of text.

And we're not done yet! The compare() function can also compare a substring of a string object with a null-terminated string.

```
std::string text{ "Peter Piper picked a peck of pickled pepper." };
for (size_t i{}; i < text.length() - 3; ++i)
  if (text.compare(i, 4, "pick") == 0)
    std::cout << "text contains \"pick\" starting at index " << i << std::endl;
```

The output from this will be the same as the previous code; "pick" is found at index positions 12 and 29.

Still another option is to select the first n characters from a null-terminated string by specifying the number of characters. The if statement in the loop could be as follows:

```
  if (text.compare(i, 4, "picket", 4) == 0)
    std::cout << "text contains \"pick\" starting at index " << i << std::endl;
```

The fourth argument to compare() specifies the number of characters from "picket" that are to be used in the comparison.

■ **Note** You have seen that the compare() function works quite happily with different numbers of arguments of various types. The same was true for the append() function we briefly mentioned earlier. What you have here are several different functions with the same name. These are called *overloaded functions*, and you'll learn how and why you create them in the next chapter.

Comparisons Using substr()

Of course, if you have trouble remembering the sequence of arguments to the more complicated versions of the compare() function, you can use the substr() function to extract the substring of a string object. You can then use the result with the comparison operators in many cases. For instance, to check whether two substrings are equal, you could write a test as follows:

```
std::string text {"Peter Piper picked a peck of pickled pepper."};
std::string phrase {"Got to pick a pocket or two."};
for (size_t i{}; i < text.length() - 3; ++i)
  if (text.substr(i, 4) == phrase.substr(7, 4))
    std::cout << "text contains " << phrase.substr(7, 4)
              << " starting at index " << i << std::endl;
```

Unlike the equivalent operation using the compare() function from earlier, this new code is readily understood. Sure, it will be slightly less efficient (because of the creation of the temporary substring objects), but code clarity and readability are far more important here than marginal performance improvements. In fact, this is an important guideline to live by. You should always prefer correct and maintainable code over error-prone, obfuscated code, even if the latter may be a few percent faster. You should only ever complicate matters if benchmarking shows a significant performance increase is feasible.

Searching Strings

Beyond compare(), you have many other alternatives for searching within a string object. They all involve functions that return an index. We'll start with the simplest sort of search. A string object has a find() function that finds the index of a substring within it. You can also use it to find the index of a given character. The substring you are searching for can be another string object or a string literal. Here's a small example showing these options:

```cpp
// Ex7_04.cpp
// Searching within strings
#include <iostream>
#include <string>

int main()
{
  std::string sentence {"Manners maketh man"};
  std::string word {"man"};
  std::cout << sentence.find(word) << std::endl;        // Outputs 15
  std::cout << sentence.find("Ma") << std::endl;        // Outputs 0
  std::cout << sentence.find('k') << std::endl;         // Outputs 10
  std::cout << sentence.find('x') << std::endl;         // Outputs std::string::npos
}
```

In each output statement, sentence is searched from the beginning by calling its find() function. The function returns the index of the first character of the first occurrence of whatever is being sought. In the last statement, 'x' is not found in the string, so the value std::string::npos is returned. This is a constant that is defined in the string header. It represents an illegal character position in a string and is used to signal a failure in a search.

On our computer, our little program thus produces these four numbers:

```
15
0
10
18446744073709551615
```

As you can tell from this output, std::string::npos is defined to be a very large number. More specifically, it is the largest value that can be represented by the type size_t. For 64-bit platforms, this value equals $2^{64}-1$, a number in the order of 10^{19}—a one followed by *19* zeros. It is therefore fairly unlikely that you'll be working with strings that are long enough for npos to represent a valid index. To give you an idea, last we counted, you could fit all characters of the English edition of Wikipedia in a string of a mere 27 billion characters—still about 680 *million* times less than npos.

Of course, you can use npos to check for a search failure with a statement such as this:

```cpp
if (sentence.find('x') == std::string::npos)
  std::cout << "Character not found" << std::endl;
```

■ **Caution**   The std::string::npos constant does not evaluate to false—it evaluates to true. The only numeric value that evaluates to false is zero, and zero is a perfectly valid index value. As a consequence, you should take care not to write code such as this:

```
if (!sentence.find('x'))   std::cout << "Character not found" << std::endl;
```

While it may read like something sensible, what this if statement actually does makes little sense at all. It prints "Character not found" when the character 'x' is found at index 0, that is, for all sentences starting with 'x'.

Searching Within Substrings

Another variation on the find() function allows you to search part of a string starting from a specified position. For example, with sentence defined as before, you could write this:

```
std::cout << sentence.find("an", 1) << std::endl;       // Outputs 1
std::cout << sentence.find("an", 3) << std::endl;       // Outputs 16
```

Each statement searches sentence from the index specified by the second argument, to the end of the string. The first statement finds the first occurrence of "an" in the string. The second statement finds the second occurrence because the search starts from index position 3.

You could search for a string object by specifying it as the first argument to find(). Here's an example:

```
std::string sentence {"Manners maketh man"};
std::string word {"an"};
int count {};                                       // Count of occurrences
for (size_t i {}; i <= sentence.length() - word.length(); )
{
  size_t position = sentence.find(word, i);
  if (position == std::string::npos)
    break;
  ++count;
  i = position + 1;
}
std::cout << '"' << word << "\" occurs in \"" << sentence
          << "\" " << count << " times." << std::endl;    // Two times...
```

A string index is of type size_t, so position that stores values returned by find() is of that type. The loop index, i, defines the starting position for a find() operation, so this is also of type size_t. The last occurrence of word in sentence has to start at least word.length() positions back from the end of sentence, so the maximum value of i in the loop is sentence.length() - word.length(). There's no loop expression for incrementing i because this is done in the loop body.

If find() returns npos, then word wasn't found, so the loop ends by executing the break statement. Otherwise, count is incremented, and i is set to one position beyond where word was found, ready for the next iteration. You might think you should set i to be i + word.length(), but this wouldn't allow overlapping occurrences to be found, such as if you were searching for "ana" in the string "ananas".

You can also search a `string` object for a substring of a C-style string or a string literal. In this case, the first argument to `find()` is the null-terminated string, the second is the index position at which you want to start searching, and the third is the number of characters of the null-terminated string that you want to take as the string you're looking for. Here's an example:

```
std::cout << sentence.find("akat", 1, 2) << std::endl;  // Outputs 9
```

This searches for the first two characters of "akat" (that is, "ak") in sentence, starting from position 1. The following searches would both fail and return npos:

```
std::cout << sentence.find("akat", 1, 3) << std::endl;  // Outputs std::string::npos
std::cout << sentence.find("akat", 10, 2) << std::endl; // Outputs std::string::npos
```

The first search fails because "aka" isn't in sentence. The second is looking for "ak", which *is* in sentence, but it fails because it doesn't occur after position 10.

Here is a program that searches a `string` object for a given substring and determines how many times the substring occurs:

```cpp
// Ex7_05.cpp
// Searching within substrings
#include <iostream>
#include <string>

int main()
{
  std::string text;                     // The string to be searched
  std::string word;                     // Substring to be found
  std::cout << "Enter the string to be searched and press Enter:\n";
  std::getline(std::cin, text);

  std::cout << "Enter the string to be found and press Enter:\n";
  std::getline(std::cin, word);

  size_t count{};                       // Count of substring occurrences
  size_t index{};                       // String index
  while ((index = text.find(word, index)) != std::string::npos)
  {
    ++count;
    index += word.length();
  }

  std::cout << "Your text contained " << count << " occurrences of \""
            << word << "\"." << std::endl;
}
```

Here's some sample output:

```
Enter the string to be searched and press Enter:
Smith, where Jones had had "had had", had had "had". "Had had" had had the examiners' approval.
Enter the string to be found and press Enter:
had
Your text contained 10 occurrences of "had".
```

There are only ten occurrences of "had". "Had" doesn't count because it starts with an uppercase letter. The program searches text for the string in word, both of which are read from the standard input stream using getline(). Input is terminated by a newline, which occurs when you press Enter. The search is conducted in the while loop, which continues as long as the find() function for text does not return npos. A return value of npos indicates that the search target is not found in text from the specified index to the end of the string, so the search is finished. On each iteration when a value other than npos is returned, the string in word has been found in text, so count is incremented, and index is incremented by the length of the string; this assumes that we are not searching for overlapping occurrences. There is quite a lot happening in this loop, so to help you follow the action, the process is shown in Figure 7-3.

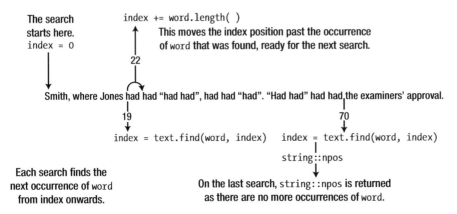

Figure 7-3. *Searching a string*

Searching for Any of a Set of Characters

Suppose you have a string—a paragraph of prose, perhaps—that you want to break up into individual words. You need to find where the separators are, and those could be any of a number of different characters such as spaces, commas, periods, colons, and so on. A function that can find any of a given set of characters in a string would help. This is exactly what the find_first_of() function for a string object does:

```
std::string text {"Smith, where Jones had had \"had had\", had had \"had\"."
                   " \"Had had\" had had the examiners' approval."};
std::string separators {" ,.\""};
std::cout << text.find_first_of(separators) << std::endl;        // Outputs 5
```

The set of characters sought are defined by a string object that you pass as the argument to the find_first_of() function. The first character in text that's in separators is a comma, so the last statement will output 5. You can also specify the set of separators as a null-terminated string. If you want to find the first vowel in text, for example, you could write this:

```
std::cout << text.find_first_of("AaEeIiOoUu") << std::endl;      // Outputs 2
```

The first vowel in text is 'i', at index position 2.

You can search backwards from the end of a string object to find the *last* occurrence of a character from a given set by using the find_last_of() function. For example, to find the last vowel in text, you could write this:

```
std::cout << text.find_last_of("AaEeIiOoUu") << std::endl;       // Outputs 92
```

The last vowel in text is the second 'a' in approval, at index 92.

You can specify an extra argument to find_first_of() and find_last_of() that specifies the index where the search process is to begin. If the first argument is a null-terminated string, there's an optional third argument that specifies how many characters from the set are to be included.

A further option is to find a character that's *not* in a given set. The find_first_not_of() and find_last_not_of() functions do this. To find the position of the first character in text that isn't a vowel, you could write this:

```
std::cout << text.find_first_not_of("AaEeIiOoUu") << std::endl; // Outputs 0
```

The first character that isn't a vowel is clearly the first, at index 0.

Let's try some of these functions in a working example. This program extracts the words from a string. This combines the use of find_first_of() and find_first_not_of(). Here's the code:

```cpp
// Ex7_06.cpp
// Searching a string for characters from a set
#include <iostream>
#include <iomanip>
#include <string>
#include <vector>

int main()
{
  std::string text;                                       // The string to be searched
  std::cout << "Enter some text terminated by *:\n";
  std::getline(std::cin, text, '*');

  const std::string separators{ " ,;:.\"!?'\n" };         // Word delimiters
  std::vector<std::string> words;                         // Words found
  size_t start { text.find_first_not_of(separators) };   // First word start index

  while (start != std::string::npos)                      // Find the words
  {
    size_t end = text.find_first_of(separators, start + 1);  // Find end of word
    if (end == std::string::npos)                        // Found a separator?
      end = text.length();                               // No, so set to end of text
    words.push_back(text.substr(start, end - start));    // Store the word
    start = text.find_first_not_of(separators, end + 1); // Find first character of next word
  }

  std::cout << "Your string contains the following " << words.size() << " words:\n";
  size_t count{};                                        // Number output
  for (const auto& word : words)
  {
    std::cout << std::setw(15) << word;
    if (!(++count % 5))
      std::cout << std::endl;
  }
  std::cout << std::endl;
}
```

Here's some sample output:

```
Enter some text terminated by *:
To be, or not to be, that is the question.
Whether tis nobler in the mind to suffer the slings and
arrows of outrageous fortune, or by opposing, end them.*
Your string contains the following 30 words:
            To          be          or        not          to
            be        that          is        the    question
       Whether         tis      nobler         in         the
          mind          to      suffer        the       slings
           and      arrows          of  outrageous     fortune
            or          by    opposing        end        them
```

The string variable, text, will contain a string read from the keyboard. The string is read from cin by the getline() function with an asterisk specified as the termination character, which allows multiple lines to be entered. The separators variable defines the set of word delimiters. It's defined as const because these should not be modified. The interesting part of this example is the analysis of the string.

You record the index of the first character of the first word in start. As long as this is a valid index, which is a value other than npos, you know that start will contain the index of the first character of the first word. The while loop finds the end of the current word, extracts the word as a substring, and stores it in the words vector. It also records the result of searching for the index of the first character of the next word in start. The loop continues until a first character is not found, in which case start will contain npos to terminate the loop.

It's possible that the last search in the while loop will fail, leaving end with the value npos. This can occur if text ends with a letter or anything other than one of the specified separators. To deal with this, you check the value of end in the if statement, and if the search did fail, you set end to the length of text. This will be one character beyond the end of the string (because indexes start at 0, not 1) because end should correspond to the position *after* the last character in a word.

Searching a String Backward

The find() function searches forward through a string, either from the beginning or from a given index. The rfind() function, named from reverse find, searches a string in reverse. rfind() comes in the same range of varieties as find(). You can search a whole string object for a substring that you can define as another string object or as a null-terminated string. You can also search for a character. Here's an example:

```cpp
std::string sentence {"Manners maketh man"};
std::string word {"an"};
std::cout << sentence.rfind(word) << std::endl;    // Outputs 16
std::cout << sentence.rfind("man") << std::endl;   // Outputs 15
std::cout << sentence.rfind('e')   << std::endl;   // Outputs 11
```

Each search finds the last occurrence of the argument to rfind() and returns the index of the first character where it was found. Figure 7-4 illustrates the use of rfind().

Using `rfind()` with one argument

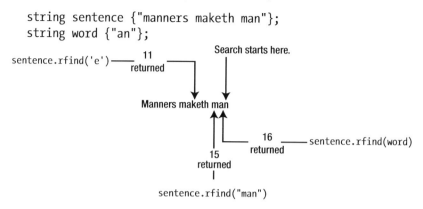

```
string sentence {"manners maketh man"};
string word {"an"};
```

sentence.rfind('e') — 11 returned

Search starts here.

Manners maketh man

16 returned — sentence.rfind(word)

15 returned

sentence.rfind("man")

As with `find()`, if the argument is not found,
then the value `string::npos` is returned.

Figure 7-4. *Searching backward through a string*

Searching with word as the argument finds the last occurrence of "an" in the string. The rfind()
function returns the index position of the first character in the substring sought.

If the substring isn't present, npos will again be returned. For example, the following statement will
result in this:

```
std::cout << sentence.rfind("miners") << std::endl; // Outputs std::string::npos
```

sentence doesn't contain the substring "miners", so npos will be returned and displayed by this
statement. The other two searches illustrated in Figure 7-4 are similar to the first. They both search backward
from the end of the string looking for the first occurrence of the argument.

Just as with find(), you can supply an extra argument to rfind() to specify the starting index for the
backward search, and you can add a third argument when the first argument is a C-style string. The third
argument specifies the number of characters from the C-style string that are to be taken as the substring for
which you're searching.

Modifying a String

When you've searched a string and found what you're looking for, you may well want to change the string
in some way. You've already seen how you can use an index between square brackets to select a single
character in a string object. You can also insert a string into a string object at a given index or replace a
substring. Unsurprisingly, to insert a string, you use a function called insert(), and to replace a substring in
a string, you use a function called replace(). We'll explain inserting a string first.

Inserting a String

Perhaps the simplest sort of insertion involves inserting a `string` object before a given position in another `string` object. Here's an example of how you do this:

```
std::string phrase {"We can insert a string."};
std::string words {"a string into "};
phrase.insert(14, words);
```

Figure 7-5 illustrates what happens. The `words` string is inserted immediately *before* the character at index 14 in `phrase`. After the operation, `phrase` will contain the string `"We can insert a string into a string."`.

You can also insert a null-terminated string into a `string` object. For example, you could achieve the same result as the previous operation with this statement:

```
phrase.insert(14, "a string into ");
```

Of course, the `'\0'` character is discarded from a null-terminated string before insertion.

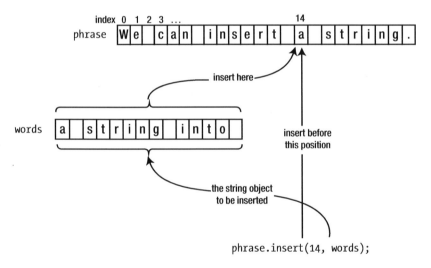

Figure 7-5. *Inserting a string into another string*

The next level of sophistication is the insertion of a substring of a `string` object into another `string` object. You need to supply two extra arguments to `insert()`: one specifies the index of the first character in the substring to be inserted, and the other specifies the number of characters in the substring. Here's an example:

```
phrase.insert(13, words, 8, 5);
```

This inserts the five-character substring that starts at position 8 in `words`, into `phrase`, preceding index position 13. Given that `phrase` and `words` contain the strings as earlier, this inserts `" into"` into `"We can insert a string."` so that `phrase` becomes `"We can insert into a string."`.

There is a similar facility for inserting a number of characters from a null-terminated string into a string object. The following statement produces the same result as the previous one:

```
phrase.insert(13, " into something", 5);
```

This inserts the first five characters of " into something" into phrase preceding the character at index 13.

There's even a version of insert() that inserts a sequence of identical characters:

```
phrase.insert(16, 7, '*');
```

This inserts seven asterisks in phrase immediately before the character at index 16. phrase will then contain the uninformative sentence "We can insert a *******string.".

Replacing a Substring

You can replace any substring of a string object with a different string—even if the inserted string and the substring to be replaced have different lengths. We'll return to an old favorite and define text like this:

```
std::string text {"Smith, where Jones had had \"had had\", had had \"had\"."};
```

You can replace "Jones" with a less common name with this statement:

```
text.replace(13, 5, "Gruntfuttock");
```

The first argument is the index in text of the first character of the substring to be replaced, and the second is the length of the substring. Thus, this replaces the five characters of text that start at index 13 with "Gruntfuttock". If you now output text, it would be as follows:

```
Smith, where Gruntfuttock had had "had had", had had "had".
```

A more realistic application of this is to search for the substring to be replaced first. Here's an example:

```
const std::string separators {" ,;:.\"!'\n"};              // Word delimiters
size_t start {text.find("Jones")};                         // Find the substring
size_t end {text.find_first_of(separators, start + 1)};    // Find the end
text.replace(start, end - start, "Gruntfuttock");
```

This finds the position of the first character of "Jones" in text and uses it to initialize start. The character following the last character of "Jones" is found next by searching for a delimiter from separators using the find_first_of() function. These index positions are used in the replace() operation.

The replacement string can be a string object or a null-terminated string. In the former case, you can specify a start index and a length to select a substring as the replacement string. For example, the previous replace operation could have been this:

```
std::string name {"Amos Gruntfuttock"};
text.replace(start, end - start, name, 5, 12);
```

These statements have the same effect as the previous use of replace() because the replacement string starts at position 5 of name (which is the 'G') and contains 12 characters.

If the first argument is a null-terminated string, you can specify the number of characters that are the replacement string. Here's an example:

```
text.replace(start, end - start, "Gruntfuttock, Amos", 12);
```

This time, the string to be substituted consists of the first 12 characters of "Gruntfuttock, Amos", so the effect is the same as the previous replace operation.

A further possibility is to specify the replacement string as multiples of a given character. For example, you could replace "Jones" by three asterisks with this statement:

```
text.replace(start, end - start, 3, '*');
```

This assumes that start and end are determined as before. The result is that text will contain the following:

```
Smith, where *** had had "had had", had had "had".
```

Let's try the replace operation in an example. This program replaces all occurrences of a given word in a string with another word:

```cpp
// Ex7_07.cpp
// Replacing words in a string
#include <iostream>
#include <string>

int main()
{
  std::string text;                              // The string to be modified
  std::cout << "Enter a string terminated by *:\n";
  std::getline(std::cin, text, '*');

  std::string word;                              // The word to be replaced
  std::cout << "Enter the word to be replaced: ";
  std::cin >> word;

  std::string replacement;                       // The word to be substituted
  std::cout << "Enter the string to be substituted for " << word << ": ";
  std::cin >> replacement;

  if (word == replacement)                       // Verify there's something to do
  {
    std::cout << "The word and its replacement are the same.\n"
              << "Operation aborted." << std::endl;
    return 1;
  }

  size_t start {text.find(word)};                // Index of 1st occurrence of word
  while (start != std::string::npos)             // Find and replace all occurrences
  {
```

```
        text.replace(start, word.length(), replacement);    // Replace word
        start = text.find(word, start + replacement.length());
    }

    std::cout << "\nThe string you entered is now:\n" << text << std::endl;
}
```

Here's a sample of the output:

```
Enter a string terminated by *:
A rose is a rose is a rose.*
Enter the word to be replaced: rose
Enter the string to be substituted for rose: dandelion

The string you entered is now:
A dandelion is a dandelion is a dandelion.
```

The string that is to have words replaced is read into text by getline(). Any number of lines can be entered and terminated by an asterisk. The word to be replaced and its replacement are read using the extraction operator and therefore cannot contain whitespace. The program ends immediately if the word to be replaced and its replacement are the same.

The index position of the first occurrence of word is used to initialize start. This is used in the while loop that finds and replaces successive occurrences of word. After each replacement, the index for the next occurrence of word in text is stored in start, ready for the next iteration. When there are no further occurrences of word in text, start will contain npos, which ends the loop. The modified string in text is then output.

Removing Characters from a String

You could always remove a substring from a string object using the replace() function: you just specify the replacement as an empty string. But there's also a specific function for this purpose, erase(). You specify the substring to be erased by the index position of the first character and the length. For example, you could erase the first six characters from text like this:

```
text.erase(0, 6);          // Remove the first 6 characters
```

You would more typically use erase() to remove a specific substring that you had previously searched for, so a more usual example might be as follows:

```
std::string word {"rose"};
size_t index {text.find(word)};
if (index != std::string::npos)
    text.erase(index, word.length());
```

This searches for word in text and, after confirming that it exists, removes it using erase(). The number of characters in the substring to be removed is obtained by calling the length() function for word.

The erase() function can also be used with either one or no arguments; here's an example:

```
text.erase(5);             // Removes all but the first 5 characters
text.erase();              // Removes all characters
```

After this last statement executes, text will be an empty string. Another function that removes all characters from a string object is clear():

```
text.clear();
```

■ **Caution**   Yet another common mistake is to call erase(i) with a single argument i in an attempt to remove a single character at the given index i. The effect of this call, however, is quite different. It removes *all* characters starting from the one at index i all the way until the end of the string! To remove a single character at index i, you should use erase(i,1) instead.

---

std::string vs. std::vector<char>

You may have already noticed that std::string is similar to std::vector<char>. Both are dynamic arrays of char elements, complete with a [] operator to emulate plain char[] arrays. But the similarity goes well beyond that. A std::string object supports nearly all member functions a std::vector<char> does. Evidently, this includes vector<> functions you already know from Chapter 5:

- A string has a push_back() function to insert a new character at the end of the string (right before the termination character). It's not used that often, though, as std::string objects support the more convenient += syntax to append characters.

- A string has an at() function that, unlike the [] operator, performs bounds checking for the given index.

- A string has a size() function, which is an alias for length(). The latter was added because it's more common to talk about the "length of a string" than the "size of a string."

- A string offers front() and back() convenience functions to access its first and last characters (not counting the null termination character).

- A string supports a range of assign() functions to reinitialize it. These functions accept argument combinations similar to those you can use between the braced initializers when first initializing a string. So, s.assign(3, 'X'), for instance, reinitializes s to "XXX", and s.assign("Reinitialize", 2, 4) overwrites the contents of the string object s with "init".

If this chapter has made one thing clear, though, then it's that a std::string is so much more than a simple std::vector<char>. On top of the functions provided by a vector<char>, it offers a wide range of additional, useful functions for common string manipulations such as concatenation, substring access, string searches and replacements, and so on. And of course, a std::string is aware of the null character that terminates its char array and knows to take this into account in members such as size(), back(), and push_back().

Converting Strings into Numbers

Earlier this chapter you learned that you can use std::to_string() to convert numbers into strings. But what about the other direction: how do you convert strings such as "123" and "3.1415" into the numbers? There are several ways to accomplish this in C++, but it's again the string header itself that provides you with the easiest option. Its std::stoi() function, short for "string to int," converts a given string to an int:

```
std::string s{ "123" };
int i{ std::stoi(s) };        // i == 123
```

The string header similarly offers stol(), stoll(), stoul(), stoull(), stof(), stod(), and stold(), all within the std namespace, to convert a string into a value of, respectively, type long, long long, unsigned long, unsigned long long, float, double, and long double.

String Streams

Suppose that you're handed an array of floating-point values and that you're tasked with composing a single string that contains the textual representation of all these numbers with a precision of four digits, five per line, and right-aligned in columns that are seven characters wide. Sure, this is possible with std::string using an intricate series of concatenations, interleaved with some calls to std::to_string() and substr(). But that approach would be particularly tedious and error-prone. If only you had been asked to stream these numbers to std::cout—now *that* would have been a walk in the park! All that you'd need then is a couple of stream manipulators from the iomanip header.

The good news is that the Standard Library offers a different type of streams that, rather than outputting characters directly to the computer screen, gathers them all into a string object. At any time, you can then retrieve this string for further processing. This stream type is aptly named std::stringstream and is defined by the sstream header. You use it in the same manner as std::cout, as this example shows:

```cpp
// Ex7_08.cpp
// Formatting using string streams
#include <iostream>
#include <iomanip>
#include <sstream>
#include <string>
#include <vector>

int main()
{
  std::vector<double> values;

  std::cout << "How many numbers do you want to enter? ";
  size_t num {};
  std::cin >> num;
  for (size_t i {}; i < num; ++i)     // Stream in all 'num' user inputs
  {
    double d {};
    std::cin >> d;
    values.push_back(d);
  }

  std::stringstream ss;               // Create a new string stream
  for (size_t i {}; i < num; ++i)     // Use it to compose the requested string
  {
    ss << std::setprecision(4) << std::setw(7) << std::right << values[i];
    if ((i+1) % 5 == 0) ss << std::endl;
  }
```

```
    std::string s{ ss.str() };          // Extract the resulting string using the str() function
    std::cout << s << std::endl;
}
```

A possible session might go as follows:

```
How many numbers do you want to enter? 7
1.23456
3.1415
1.4142
-5
17.0183
-25.1283
1000.456
   1.235  3.142  1.414      -5  17.02
  -25.13   1000
```

The program gathers a series of floating-point numbers from the user and pushes them into a vector. Next, it streams all these values into a `stringstream` object ss through its << operator. Working with string streams is exactly like working with `std::cout`. You simply replace `std::cout` with a variable of type `std::stringstream`, ss in Ex7_08. Beyond that, all you need to know is the stream's `str()` function. Using that function you obtain a `std::string` object containing all the characters the stream has accumulated up to that point.

Note that not only can you use a `std::stringstream` object to write numbers *to* a string, you can use it to read values *from* a given input string as well. Naturally, you do so using its >> operator, and of course this works in the same manner as the corresponding operator of `std::cin`. You'll get to try this in one of the exercises for this chapter.

Streams are a testament to the power of *abstraction*. Given a stream, it does not matter whether this stream interacts with a computer screen, a `string` object, or even a file or network socket. You can interact with all these stream targets and sources using the same interface. In Chapters 11 and beyond, we'll show you that abstraction is one of the hallmarks of object-oriented programming.

Strings of International Characters

You'll remember from Chapter 1 that, internationally, many more characters are in use than the 128 that are defined by the standard ASCII character set. French and Spanish, for instance, often use accented letters such as ê, á, or ñ. Languages such as Russian, Arabic, Malaysian, or Japanese of course use characters that are even completely different from those defined by the ASCII standard. The 256 different characters you could potentially represent with a single 8-bit char are not nearly enough to represent all these possible characters. The Chinese script alone consists of many tens of thousands of characters!

Supporting multiple national character sets is an advanced topic, so we'll only introduce the basic facilities that C++ offers, without going into detail of how you apply any them. Thus, this section is just a pointer to where you should look when you have to work with different national character sets. Potentially, you have three options for working with strings that may contain extended character sets:

- You can define `std::wstring` objects that contain strings of characters of type `wchar_t`—the *wide-character type* that is built into your C++ implementation.

- You can define `std::u16string` objects that store strings of 16-bit Unicode characters, which are of type `char16_t`.

- You can define `std::u32string` objects that contain strings of 32-bit Unicode characters, which are of type `char32_t`.

The `string` header defines all these types.

■ **Note**　All four string types defined by the `string` header are actually just type aliases for particular instantiations of the same class template, namely, `std::basic_string<CharType>`. `std::string`, for instance, is an alias for `std::basic_string<char>`, and `std::wstring` is shorthand for `std::basic_string<wchar_t>`. This explains why all string types offer the exact same set of functions. You'll understand better how exactly this works after learning all about creating your own class templates in Chapter 16.

Strings of wchar_t Characters

The `std::wstring` type that is defined in the `string` header stores strings of characters of type `wchar_t`. You use objects of type `wstring` in essentially the same way as objects of type `string`. You could define a *wide string* object with this statement:

```
std::wstring quote;
```

You write string literals containing characters of type `wchar_t` between double quotes, but with `L` prefixed to distinguish them from string literals containing `char` characters. Thus, you can define and initialize a `wstring` variable like this:

```
std::wstring saying {L"The tigers of wrath are wiser than the horses of instruction."};
```

The `L` preceding the opening double quote specifies that the literal consists of characters of type `wchar_t`. Without it, you would have a `char` string literal, and the statement would not compile.

To output wide strings, you use the `wcout` stream. Here's an example:

```
std::wcout << saying << std::endl;
```

Nearly all functions we've discussed in the context of `string` objects apply equally well for `wstring` objects, so we won't wade through them again. Other functionalities—such as the `to_wstring()` function and the `wstringstream` class—just take an extra `w` in their name but are otherwise entirely equivalent. Just remember to specify the `L` prefix with string and character literals when you are working with `wstring` objects and you'll be fine!

One problem with type `wstring` is that the character encoding that applies with type `wchar_t` is implementation defined, so it can vary from one compiler to another. Native APIs of the Windows operating system generally expect strings encoded using UTF-16, so when compiling for Windows, `wchar_t` strings will normally consist of 2-byte UTF-16 encoded characters as well. Most other implementations, however, use 4-byte UTF-32 encoded `wchar_t` characters. If you need to support portable multinational character sets, you may therefore be better off using either types `u16string` or `u32string` that are described in the next section.

Objects That Contain Unicode Strings

The `string` header defines two further types that store strings of Unicode characters. Objects of type `std::u16string` store strings of characters of type `char16_t`, and objects of type `std::u32string` store strings of characters of type `char32_t`. They are intended to contain character sequences that are encoded using UTF-16 and UTF-32, respectively. Like `wstring` objects, you must use a literal of the appropriate type to initialize a `u16string` or `u32string` object. Here's an example:

```
std::u16string question {u"Whither atrophy?"};                    // char16_t characters
std::u32string sentence {U"This sentence contains three errars."};  // char32_t characters
```

These statements demonstrate that you prefix a string literal containing `char16_t` characters with u and a literal containing `char32_t` characters with U. Objects of the `u16string` and `u32string` types have the same set of functions as the `string` type.

In theory, you can use the `std::string` type you have explored in detail in this chapter to store strings of UTF-8 characters. You define a UTF-8 string by prefixing a regular string literal with u8, such as u8 `"This is a UTF-8 string."`. However, the `string` type stores characters as type `char` and knows nothing about Unicode encodings. The UTF-8 encoding uses from 1 to 4 bytes to encode each character, and the functions that operate on string objects will not recognize this. This means, for instance, that the `length()` function will return the wrong length if the string includes any characters that require two or three bytes to represent them, as this code snippet illustrates:

```
std::string s(u8"字符串"); // UTF-8 encoding of the Chinese word for "string"
std::cout << s.length();   // Length: 9 code units!
```

■ **Tip**   At the time of writing, in our experience, support for manipulating Unicode strings in the Standard Library is limited and even more so in some of its implementations. For one, there is no `std::u16cout` or `std::u32stringstream`, nor does the Standard regular expression library support `u16strings` or `u32strings`. In C++17, moreover, most functionality that the Standard Library offers to convert between the various Unicode encodings has been deprecated. If producing and manipulating portable Unicode-encoded text is important for your application, you would therefore be much better off using a third-party library (viable candidates include the powerful ICU library or the Boost.Locale library, which is built on top of ICU).

Raw String Literals

Regular string literals, as you know, must not contain line breaks or tab characters. To include such special characters, they have to be escaped—line breaks and tab then become \n and \t, respectively. The double quote character must also be escaped to \", for obvious reasons. Because of these escape sequences, the backslash character itself needs to be escaped to \\ as well.

At times, however, you'll find yourself having to define string literals that contain some or even many of these special characters. Having to continuously escape these characters then is not only tedious but also renders these literals unreadable. Here are some examples:

```
auto escape{ "The \"\\\\\" escape sequence is a backslash character, \\." };
auto path{ "C:\\ProgramData\\MyCompany\\MySoftware\\MyFile.ext" };
auto text{ L"First line.\nSecond line.\nThird line.\nThe end." };
std::regex reg{ "\\*" };                 // Regular expression that matches a single * character
```

The latter is an example of a *regular expression*—a string that defines a process for searching and transforming text. Essentially a regular expression defines patterns that are to be matched in a string, and patterns that are found can be replaced or reordered. C++ supports regular expressions via the regex header, though a discussion of this falls outside the scope of this book. The main point here is that regular expression strings often contain backslash characters. Having to use the escape sequence for each backslash character can make a regular expression particularly difficult to specify correctly and very hard to read.

The *raw string literal* was introduced to solve these problems. A raw string literal can include any character, including backslashes, tabs, double quotes, and newlines, so no escape sequences are necessary. A raw string literal includes an R in the prefix, and on top of that the character sequence of the literal is surrounded by round parentheses. The basic form of a raw string literal is thus R"(...)". The parentheses themselves are not part of the literal. Any of the types of literal you have seen can be specified as raw literals by adding the same prefix as before—L, u, U, or u8—prior to the R. Using raw string literals, our earlier examples thus become as follows:

```
auto escape{ R"(The "\\" escape sequence is a backslash character, \.)" };
auto path{ R"(C:\ProgramData\MyCompany\MySoftware\MyFile.ext)" };
auto text
{ LR"(First line.
Second line.
Third line.
The end.)" };
std::regex reg{ R"(\*)" };           // Regular expression that matches a single * character
```

Within a raw string literal, no escaping is required. This means you can simply copy and paste, for instance, a Windows path sequence into them or even an entire play of Shakespeare complete with quote characters and line breaks. In the latter case, you should take care about leading whitespace and all line breaks, as these will be included into the string literal as well, together with all other characters between the surrounding "( )" delimiters.

Notice that not even double quotes need or even can be escaped, which begs the question: what if your string literal itself somewhere contains the sequence)"? That is, what if it contains a) character followed by a "? Here's such a problematic literal:

```
R"(The answer is "(a - b)" not "(c - d)")"        // Error!
```

The compiler will object to this string literal because the raw literal appears to be terminated somewhere halfway already, right after (a - b. But if escaping is not an option—any backslash characters would simply be copied into the raw literal as is—how else can you make it clear to the compiler that the string literal should include this first)" sequence, as well as the next one after (c - d? The answer is that the delimiters that mark the start and end of a raw string literal are flexible. You can use any delimiter of the form "char_sequence(to mark the beginning of the literal, as long as you mark the end with a matching sequence,)char_sequence". Here's an example:

```
R"*(The answer is "(a - b)" not "(c - d)")*"
```

This is now a valid raw string literal that contains char32_t characters. You can basically choose any char_sequence you want, as long as you use the same sequence at both ends:

```
R"Fa-la-la-la-la(The answer is "(a - b)" not "(c - d)")Fa-la-la-la-la"
```

The only other limitations are that char_sequence must not be longer than 16 characters and may not contain any parentheses, spaces, control characters, or backslash characters.

Summary

In this chapter, you learned how you can use the `string` type that's defined in the Standard Library. The `string` type is much easier and safer to use than C-style strings, so it should be your first choice when you need to process character strings.

The following are the important points from this chapter:

- The `std::string` type stores a character string.

- Like `std::vector<char>`, it is a dynamic array—meaning it will allocate more memory when necessary.

- Internally, the terminating null character is still present in the array managed by a `std::string` object, but only for compatibility with legacy and/or C functions. As a user of `std::string`, you normally do not need to know that it even exists. All `string` functionality transparently deals with this legacy character for you.

- You can store `string` objects in an array or, better still, in a sequence container such as a vector.

- You can access and modify individual characters in a `string` object using an index between square brackets. Index values for characters in a `string` object start at 0.

- You can use the + operator to concatenate a `string` object with a string literal, a character, or another `string` object.

- If you want to concatenate a value of one of the fundamental numeric types, such as for instance an `int` or a `double`, you must first convert these numbers into a string. Your easiest—though least flexible—option for this is the `std::to_string()` function template defined in the `string` header.

- Objects of type `string` have functions to search, modify, and extract substrings.

- The `string` header offers functions such as `std::stoi()` and `std::stod()` to convert strings to values of numeric types such as `int` and `double`.

- A more powerful option to write numbers to a `string`, or conversely to read them from a `string`, is `std::stringstream`. You can use string streams in exactly the same manner as you would `std::cout` and `std::cin`.

- Objects of type `wstring` contain strings of characters of type `wchar_t`.

- Objects of type `u16string` contain strings of characters of type `char16_t`.

- Objects of type `u32string` contain strings of characters of type `char32_t`.

EXERCISES

The following exercises enable you to try what you've learned in this chapter. If you get stuck, look back over the chapter for help. If you're still stuck after that, you can download the solutions from the Apress website (`www.apress.com/source-code`), but that really should be a last resort.

Exercise 7-1. Write a program that reads and stores the first names of any number of students, along with their grades. Calculate and output the average grade and output the names and grades of all the students in a table with the name and grade for three students on each line.

Exercise 7-2. Write a program that reads text entered over an arbitrary number of lines. Find and record each unique word that appears in the text and record the number of occurrences of each word. Output the words and their occurrence counts. Words and counts should align in columns. The words should align to the left; the counts to the right. There should be three words per row in your table.

Exercise 7-3. Write a program that reads a text string of arbitrary length from the keyboard and prompts for entry of a word that is to be found in the string. The program should find and replace all occurrences of this word, regardless of case, by as many asterisks as there are characters in the word. It should then output the new string. Only whole words are to be replaced. For example, if the string is "Our house is at your disposal." and the word that is to be found is "our", then the resultant string should be as follows: "*** house is at your disposal." and not "*** house is at y*** disposal.".

Exercise 7-4. Write a program that prompts for the input of two words and determines whether one is an anagram of the other. An anagram of a word is formed by rearranging its letters, using each of the original letters precisely once. For instance, *listen* and *silent* are anagrams of one another, but *listens* and *silent* are not.

Exercise 7-5. Generalize the program of Exercise 7-4 such that it ignores spaces when deciding whether two strings are anagrams. With this generalized definition, *funeral* and *real fun* are considered anagrams, as are *eleven plus two* and *twelve plus one*, along with *desperation* and *a rope ends it*.

Exercise 7-6. Write a program that reads a text string of arbitrary length from the keyboard followed by a string containing one or more letters. Output a list of all the whole words in the text that begin with any of the letters, uppercase or lowercase.

Exercise 7-7. Create a program that reads an arbitrarily long sequence of integer numbers typed by the user into a single string object. The numbers of this sequence are to be separated by spaces and terminated by a # character. In other words, the user does not have to press Enter between two consecutive numbers. Next, use a string stream to extract all numbers from the string one by one, add these numbers together, and output their sum.

Before you get started, you'll need a bit more information on how to use string streams for input. First, you construct a std::stringstream object that contains the same character sequence as a given std::string object my_string as follows:

```
std::stringstream ss{ my_string };
```

Alternatively, you can assign the contents of a given string to an existing string stream:

```
ss.str(my_string);
```

Second, unlike `std::cin`, there's a limit to the number of values you can extract from a string stream. For this exercise, you can check whether there are more numbers left to extract by converting the stream to a Boolean. As long as a stream is capable of producing more values, it will convert to `true`. Once the stream is depleted, it will convert to `false`. In other words, you should simply use your string input stream variable `ss` in a loop of the following form:

```
while (ss) { /* Extract next number from the stream */ }
```

Exercise 7-8. Repeat Exercise 7-7, only this time the user inputs the numbers one by one, each time followed by an enter. The input should be gathered as a sequence of distinct strings—for the sake of the exercise still not directly as integers—which are then concatenated to a single string. The input is still terminated by a # character. Also, this time, you're not allowed to use a string stream anymore to extract the numbers from the resulting string.

CHAPTER 8

■ ■ ■

Defining Functions

Segmenting a program into manageable chunks of code is fundamental to programming in every language. A *function* is a basic building block in C++ programs. So far, every example has had one function, `main()`, and has typically used functions from the Standard Library. This chapter is all about defining your own functions with names that you choose.

In this chapter, you will learn:

- What a function is and why you should segment your programs into functions

- How to declare and define functions

- How data is passed to a function and how a function can return a value

- What the difference is between "pass-by-value" and "pass-by-reference" and how to choose between both mechanisms

- What the best way is to pass strings to a function

- How to specify default values for function parameters

- What the preferred way is to return a function's output in modern C++

- How to handle optional input parameters and optional return values

- How using `const` as a qualifier for a parameter type affects the operation of a function

- The effect of defining a variable as `static` within a function

- What an inline function is

- How to create multiple functions that have the same name but different parameters—a mechanism you'll come to know as *function overloading*

- What recursion is and how to apply it to implement elegant algorithms

Segmenting Your Programs

All the programs you have written so far have consisted of just one function, `main()`. A real-world C++ application consists of many functions, each of which provides a distinct well-defined capability. Execution starts in `main()`, which must be defined in the global namespace. `main()` calls other functions, each of which may call other functions, and so on. The functions other than `main()` can be defined in a namespace that you create.

© Ivor Horton and Peter Van Weert 2018
I. Horton and P. Van Weert, *Beginning C++17*, https://doi.org/10.1007/978-1-4842-3366-5_8

When one function calls another that calls another that calls another, you have a situation where several functions are in action concurrently. Each that has called another that has not yet returned will be waiting for the function that was called to end. Obviously something must keep track of from where in memory each function call was made and where execution should continue when a function returns. This information is recorded and maintained automatically in the *stack*. We introduced the stack when we explained free store memory, and the stack is often referred to as the *call stack* in this context. The call stack records all the outstanding function calls and details of the data that was passed to each function. The debugging facilities that come with most C++ development systems usually provide ways for you to view the call stack while your program executes.

Functions in Classes

A class defines a new type, and each class definition will usually contain functions that represent the operations that can be carried out with objects of the class type. You have already used functions that belong to a class extensively. In the previous chapter, you used functions that belong to the `string` class, such as the `length()` function, which returns the number of characters in the `string` object, and the `find()` function for searching a string. The standard input and output streams `cin` and `cout` are objects, and using the stream insertion and extraction operators calls functions for those objects. Functions that belong to classes are fundamental in object-oriented programming, which you'll learn about from Chapter 11 onward.

Characteristics of a Function

A function should perform a single, well-defined action and should be relatively short. Most functions do not involve many lines of code, certainly not hundreds of lines. This applies to all functions, including those that are defined within a class. Several of the working examples you saw earlier could easily be divided into functions. If you look again at `Ex7_05.cpp`, for instance, you can see that what the program does falls naturally into three distinct actions. First the text is read from the input stream, then the words are extracted from the text, and finally the words that were extracted are output. Thus, the program could be defined as three functions that perform these actions, plus the `main()` function that calls them.

Defining Functions

A *function* is a self-contained block of code with a specific purpose. Function definitions in general have the same basic structure as `main()`. A function definition consists of a *function header* followed by a block that contains the code for the function. The function header specifies three things:

- The return type, which is the type of value, if any, that the function returns when it finishes execution. A function can return data of any type, including fundamental types, class types, pointer types, or reference types. It can also return nothing, in which case you specify the return type as `void`.

- The name of the function. Functions are named according to the same rules as variables.

- The number and types of data items that can be passed to the function when it is called. This is called the *parameter list*, and it appears as a comma-separated list between parentheses following the function name.

A general representation of a function looks like this:

```
return_type function_name(parameter_list)
{
  // Code for the function...
}
```

Figure 8-1 shows an example of a function definition. It implements the well-known fundamental mathematical power or exponentiation operation, which for any integral number $n > 0$ is defined as follows:

$$\mathrm{power}(x,0) = 1$$

$$\mathrm{power}(x,n) = x^n = \underbrace{x * x * \cdots * x}_{n \text{ times}} \quad \mathrm{power}(x,-n) = x^{-n} = \frac{1}{\underbrace{x * x * \cdots * x}_{n \text{ times}}}$$

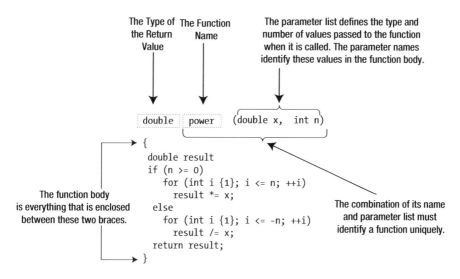

Figure 8-1. *An example of a function definition*

If nothing is to be passed to a function when it is called, then nothing appears between the parentheses. If there is more than one item in the parameter list, they are separated by commas. The power() function in Figure 8-1 has two *parameters*, x and n. The parameter names are used in the body of the function to access the corresponding values that were passed to the function. Our power function could be called from elsewhere in the program as follows:

```
double number {3.0};
const double result { power(number, 2) };
```

When this call to power() is evaluated, the code in the function body gets executed with the parameters x and n initialized to 3.0 and 2, respectively, with 3.0 being the value of the number variable. The term *argument* is used for the values that are passed to a function when called. So in our example, number and 2 are arguments, and x and n are the corresponding parameters. The sequence of arguments in a function call must correspond to the sequence of the parameters in the parameter list of the function definition.

CHAPTER 8 ▓ DEFINING FUNCTIONS

More specifically, their types should match. If they do not match exactly, the compiler will apply implicit conversions whenever possible. Here's an example:

```
float number {3.0f};
const double result { power(number, 2) };
```

Even though the type of the first argument passed here is `float`, this code snippet will still compile; the compiler implicitly converts the argument to the type of its corresponding parameter. If no implicit conversion is possible, compilation will, of course, fail.

The conversion from `float` to `double` is lossless since a `double` generally has twice as many bits available to represent the number—and hence the name `double`. So, this conversion is always safe. The compiler will happily perform the opposite conversion for you as well, though. That is, it will implicitly convert a `double` argument when assigned to a `float` parameter. This is a so-called narrowing conversion; because a `double` can represent numbers with much greater precision than a `float`, information may be lost during this conversion. Most compilers will issue a warning when it performs such narrowing conversions.

The combination of the function name and the parameter list is called the *signature* of a function. The compiler uses the signature to decide which function is to be called in any particular instance. Thus, functions that have the same name must have parameter lists that differ in some way to allow them to be distinguished. As we will discuss in detail later, such functions are called *overloaded* functions.

▓ **Tip**   While it made for compact code that fitted nicely in Figure 8-1, from a coding style point of view the parameter names x and n used by our definition of `power()` do not particularly excel in clarity. One could perhaps argue that x and n are still acceptable in this specific case because `power()` is a well-known mathematical function and x and n are commonplace in mathematical formulae. That notwithstanding, in general we highly recommend you use more descriptive parameter names. Instead of x and n, for instance, you should probably use base and exponent, respectively. In fact, you should always choose descriptive names for just about everything: function names, variable names, class names, and so on. Doing so consistently will go a long way toward keeping your code easy to read and understand.

Our `power()` function returned a value of type `double`. Not every function, though, has to return a value—it might just write something to a file or a database or modify some global state. The `void` keyword is used to specify that a function does not return a value as follows:

```
void printDouble(double value) { std::cout << value << std::endl; }
```

▓ **Note**   A function with a return type specified as `void` doesn't return a value, so it can't be used in most expressions. Attempting to use such a function in this way will cause a compiler error message.

The Function Body

Calling a function executes the statements in the function body with the parameters having the values you pass as arguments. Returning to our definition of `power()` in Figure 8-1, the first line of the function body defines the double variable, `result`, initialized with `1.0`. `result` is an automatic variable so only exists within the body of the function. This means that `result` ceases to exist after the function finishes executing.

The calculation is performed in one of two `for` loops, depending on the value of n. If n is greater than or equal to zero, the first `for` loop executes. If n is zero, the body of the loop doesn't execute at all because the loop condition is immediately `false`. In this case, `result` is left at `1.0`. Otherwise, the loop variable i assumes successive values from 1 to n, and `result` is multiplied by x on each iteration. If n is negative, the second `for` loop executes, which divides `result` by x on each loop iteration.

The variables that you define within the body of a function and all the parameters are local to the function. You can use the same names in other functions for quite different purposes. The scope of each variable you define within a function is from the point at which it is defined until the end of the block that contains it. The only exceptions to this rule are variables that you define as `static`, and we'll discuss these later in the chapter.

Let's give the `power()` function a whirl in a complete program.

```cpp
// Ex8_01.cpp
// Calculating powers
#include <iostream>
#include <iomanip>

// Function to calculate x to the power n
double power(double x, int n)
{
  double result {1.0};
  if (n >= 0)
  {
    for (int i {1}; i <= n; ++i)
      result *= x;
  }
  else // n < 0
  {
    for (int i {1}; i <= -n; ++i)
      result /= x;
  }
  return result;
}

int main()
{
  // Calculate powers of 8 from -3 to +3
  for (int i {-3}; i <= 3; ++i)
    std::cout << std::setw(10) << power(8.0, i);

  std::cout << std::endl;
}
```

This program produces the following output:

```
0.00195313    0.015625     0.125        1        8       64       512
```

All the action occurs in the `for` loop in `main()`. The `power()` function is called seven times. The first argument is 8.0 on each occasion, but the second argument has successive values of i, from –3 to +3. Thus, seven values are outputs that correspond to 8^{-3}, 8^{-2}, 8^{-1}, 8^0, 8^1, 8^2, and 8^3.

> ▓ **Tip** While it is instructive to write your own `power()` function, there is of course already one provided by the Standard Library. The `cmath` header offers a variety of `std::pow(base, exponent)` functions similar to our version, except that they are designed to work optimally with all numeric parameter types—that is, not just with `double` and `int` but also, for instance, with `float` and `long`, with `long double` and `unsigned short`, or even with noninteger exponents. You should always prefer the predefined mathematical functions of the `cmath` header; they will almost certainly be far more efficient and accurate than anything you could write yourself.

Return Values

A function with a return type other than `void` *must* return a value of the type specified in the function header. The only exception to this rule is the `main()` function, where, as you know, reaching the closing brace is equivalent to returning 0. Normally, though, the return value is calculated within the body of the function and is returned by a `return` statement, which ends the function, and execution continues from the calling point. There can be several `return` statements in the body of a function with each potentially returning a different value. The fact that a function can return only a single value might appear to be a limitation, but this isn't the case. The single value that is returned can be anything you like: an array, a container such as `std::vector<>`, or even a container with elements that are containers.

How the return Statement Works

The `return` statement in the previous program returns the value of `result` to the point where the function was called. The `result` variable is local to the function and ceases to exist when the function finishes executing, so how is it returned? The answer is that a *copy* of the `double` being returned is made automatically, and this copy is made available to the calling function. The general form of the return statement is as follows:

```
return expression;
```

`expression` must evaluate to a value of the type that is specified for the return value in the function header or must be convertible to that type. The expression can be anything, as long as it produces a value of an appropriate type. It can include function calls and can even include a call of the function in which it appears, as you'll see later in this chapter.

If the return type is specified as `void`, no expression can appear in a `return` statement. It must be written simply as follows:

```
return;
```

If the last statement in a function body executes so that the closing brace is reached, this is equivalent to executing a `return` statement with no expression. In a function with a return type other than `void`, this is an error, and the function will not compile—except for `main()`, of course.

Function Declarations

Ex8_01.cpp works perfectly well as written, but let's try rearranging the code so that the definition of main() *precedes* the definition of the power() function in the source file. The code in the program file will look like this:

```
// Ex8_02.cpp
// Calculating powers - rearranged
#include <iostream>
#include <iomanip>

int main()
{
  // Calculate powers of 8 from -3 to +3
  for (int i {-3}; i <= 3; ++i)
    std::cout << std::setw(10) << power(8.0, i);

  std::cout << std::endl;
}

// Function to calculate x to the power n
double power(double x, int n)
{
  double result {1.0};
  if (n >= 0)
  {
    for (int i {1}; i <= n; ++i)
      result *= x;
  }
  else // n < 0
  {
    for (int i {1}; i <= -n; ++i)
      result /= x;
  }
  return result;
}
```

If you attempt to compile this, you won't succeed. The compiler has a problem because the power() function that is called in main() is not defined yet when it is processing main(). The reason is that the compiler processes a source file from top to bottom. Of course, you could revert to the original version, but in some situations this won't solve the problem. There are two important issues to consider:

- As you'll see later, a program can consist of several source files. The definition of a function that is called in one source file may be contained in a separate source file.

- Suppose you have a function A() that calls a function B(), which in turn calls A(). If you put the definition of A() first, it won't compile because it calls B(); the same problem arises if you define B() first because it calls A().

Naturally, there is a solution to these difficulties. You can *declare* a function before you use or define it by means of a *function prototype*.

■ **Note** Functions that are defined in terms of each other, such as the A() and B() functions we described just now, are called *mutually recursive functions*. We'll talk more about recursion near the end of this chapter.

Function Prototypes

A *function prototype* is a statement that describes a function sufficiently for the compiler to be able to compile calls to it. It defines the function name, its return type, and its parameter list. A function prototype is sometimes referred to as a *function declaration*. A function can be compiled only if the call is preceded by a function declaration in the source file. The definition of a function also doubles as a declaration, which is why you didn't need a function prototype for power() in Ex8_01.cpp.

You could write the function prototype for the power() function as follows:

```
double power(double x, int n);
```

If you place function prototypes at the beginning of a source file, the compiler is able to compile the code regardless of where the function definitions are. Ex8_02.cpp will compile if you insert the prototype for the power() function before the definition of main().

The function prototype shown earlier is identical to the function header with a semicolon appended. A function prototype is always terminated by a semicolon, but in general, it doesn't have to be *identical* to the function header. You can use different names for the parameters from those used in the function definition (but not different types, of course). Here's an example:

```
double power(double value, int exponent);
```

This works just as well. The compiler only needs to know the *type* each parameter is, so you can omit the parameter names from the prototype, like this:

```
double power(double, int);
```

There is no particular merit in writing function prototypes like this. It is much less informative than the version with parameter names. If both function parameters were of the same type, then a prototype like this would not give any clue as to which parameter was which. We recommend that you always include descriptive parameter names in function prototypes.

It could be a good idea to always write prototypes for each function that is defined in a source file—with the exception of main(), of course, which never requires a prototype. Specifying prototypes near the start of the file removes the possibility of compiler errors arising from functions not being sequenced appropriately. It also allows other programmers to get an overview of the functionality of your code.

Most of the examples in the book use functions from the Standard Library, so where are the prototypes for them? The standard headers contain them. A primary use of header files is to collect the function prototypes for a related group of functions.

Passing Arguments to a Function

It is important to understand precisely how arguments are passed to a function. This affects how you write functions and ultimately how they operate. There are also a number of pitfalls to be avoided. In general, the function arguments should correspond in type and sequence to the list of parameters in the function definition. You have no latitude so far as the sequence is concerned, but you do have some flexibility in the argument types. If you specify a function argument of a type that doesn't correspond to the parameter type, then the compiler inserts an implicit conversion of the argument to the type of the parameter where possible. The rules for automatic conversions of this kind are the same as those for automatic conversions in an assignment statement. If an automatic conversion is not possible, you'll get an error message from the compiler. If such implicit conversions result in potential loss of precision, compilers generally issue a warning. Examples of such narrowing conversions are conversions from long to int, double to float, or int to float (see also Chapter 2).

There are two mechanisms by which arguments are passed to functions, *pass-by-value* and *pass-by-reference*. We'll explain the pass-by-value mechanism first.

Pass-by-Value

With the pass-by-value mechanism, the values of variables or constants you specify as arguments are not passed to a function at all. Instead, copies of the arguments are created, and these copies are transferred to the function. This is illustrated in Figure 8-2, using the power() function again.

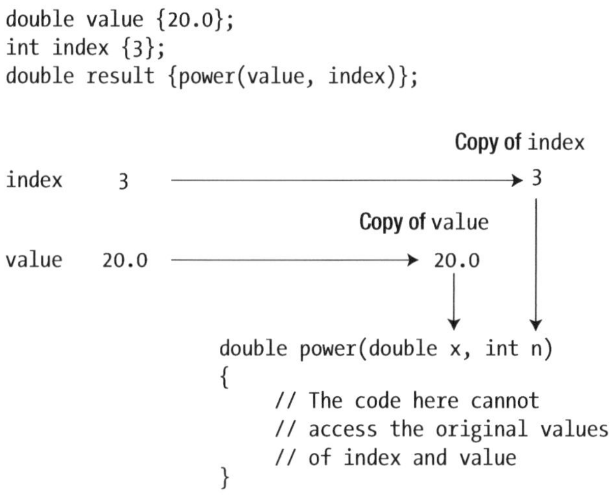

```
double value {20.0};
int index {3};
double result {power(value, index)};
```

Figure 8-2. The pass-by-value mechanism for arguments to a function

Each time you call the power() function, the compiler arranges for copies of the arguments to be stored in a temporary location in the call stack. During execution, all references to the function parameters in the code are mapped to these temporary copies of the arguments. When execution of the function ends, the copies of the arguments are discarded.

We can demonstrate the effects of this with a simple example. The following calls a function that attempts to modify one of its arguments, and of course, it fails miserably:

```cpp
// Ex8_03.cpp
// Failing to modify the original value of a function argument
#include <iostream>

double changeIt(double value_to_be_changed);    // Function prototype

int main()
{
```

```
  double it {5.0};
  double result {changeIt(it)};

  std::cout << "After function execution, it = " << it
          << "\nResult returned is " << result << std::endl;
}

// Function that attempts to modify an argument and return it
double changeIt(double it)
{
  it += 10.0;                               // This modifies the copy
  std::cout << "Within function, it = " << it << std::endl;
  return it;
}
```

This example produces the following output:

```
Within function, it = 15
After function execution, it = 5
Result returned is 15
```

The output shows that adding 10 to it in the changeIt() function has no effect on the variable it in main(). The it variable in changeIt() is local to the function, and it refers to a copy of whatever argument value is passed when the function is called. Of course, when the value of it that is local to changeIt() is returned, a copy of its current value is made, and it's this copy that's returned to the calling program.

Pass-by-value is the default mechanism by which arguments are passed to a function. It provides a lot of security to the calling function by preventing the function from modifying variables that are owned by the calling function. However, sometimes you do want to modify values in the calling function. Is there a way to do it when you need to? Sure there is; one way is to use a pointer.

Passing a Pointer to a Function

When a function parameter is a pointer type, the pass-by-value mechanism operates just as before. However, a pointer contains the address of another variable; a copy of the pointer contains the same address and therefore points to the same variable.

If you modify the definition of the first changeIt() function to accept an argument of type double*, you can pass the address of it as the argument. Of course, you must also change the code in the body of changeIt() to dereference the pointer parameter. The code is now like this:

```
// Ex8_04.cpp
// Modifying the value of a caller variable
#include <iostream>

double changeIt(double* pointer_to_it);          // Function prototype

int main()
{
  double it {5.0};
  double result {changeIt(&it)};                  // Now we pass the address
```

```
    std::cout << "After function execution, it = " << it
              << "\nResult returned is " << result << std::endl;
}

// Function to modify an argument and return it
double changeIt(double* pit)
{
    *pit += 10.0;                                   // This modifies the original double
    std::cout << "Within function, *pit = " << *pit << std::endl;
    return *pit;
}
```

This version of the program produces the following output:

```
Within function, *pit = 15
After function execution, it = 15
Result returned is 15
```

Figure 8-3 illustrates the way this works.

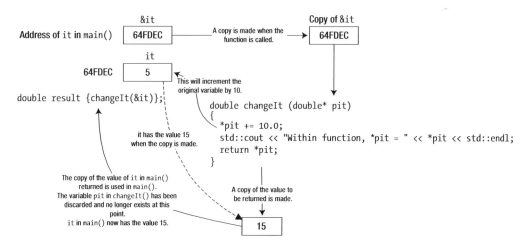

Figure 8-3. *Passing a pointer to a function*

This version of changeIt() serves only to illustrate how a pointer parameter can allow a variable in the calling function to be modified—it is not a model of how a function should be written. Because you are modifying the value of it directly, returning its value is somewhat superfluous.

Passing an Array to a Function

An array name is essentially an address, so you can pass the address of an array to a function just by using its name. The address of the array is copied and passed to the function. This provides several advantages:

First, passing the address of an array is an efficient way of passing an array to a function. Passing all the array elements by value would be time-consuming because every element would be copied. In fact, you can't pass all the elements in an array by value as a single argument because each parameter represents a single item of data.

Second, and more significantly, because the function does not deal with the original array variable but with a copy, the code in the body of the function can treat a parameter that represents an array as a pointer in the fullest sense, including modifying the address that it contains. This means you can use the power of pointer notation in the body of a function for parameters that are arrays. Before we get to that, let's try the most straightforward case first—handling an array parameter using array notation.

This example includes a function to compute the average of the elements in an array:

```cpp
// Ex8_05.cpp
// Passing an array to a function
#include <iostream>
#include <array>            // For std::size()

double average(double array[], size_t count);      // Function prototype

int main()
{
  double values[] {1.0, 2.0, 3.0, 4.0, 5.0, 6.0, 7.0, 8.0, 9.0, 10.0};
  std::cout << "Average = " << average(values, std::size(values)) << std::endl;
}

// Function to compute an average
double average(double array[], size_t count)
{
  double sum {};                            // Accumulate total in here
  for (size_t i {}; i < count; ++i)
    sum += array[i];                        // Sum array elements
  return sum / count;                       // Return average
}
```

This produces the following brief output:

Average = 5.5

The average() function works with an array containing any number of double elements. As you can see from the prototype, it accepts two arguments: the array address and a count of the number of elements. The type of the first parameter is specified as an array of any number of values of type double. You can pass any one-dimensional array of elements of type double as an argument to this function, so the second parameter that specifies the number of elements is essential. The function will rely on the correct value for the count parameter being supplied by the caller. There's no way to verify that it is correct, so the function will quite happily access memory locations outside the array if the value of count is greater than the array length. With this definition, it is up to the caller to ensure that this doesn't happen.

And in case you were wondering, no, you cannot circumvent the need for the count parameter by using either the sizeof operator or std::size() inside the average() function. Remember, an array parameter such as array simply stores the address of the array, not the array itself. So, the expression sizeof(array) would return the size of the memory location that contains the *address* of the array and not the size of

CHAPTER 8 ▨ DEFINING FUNCTIONS

the entire array. A call of `std::size()` with an array parameter name will simply not compile because `std::size()` has no way of determining the array's size either. Without the definition of the array, the compiler has no way to determine its size. It cannot do so from only the array's address.

Within the body of `average()`, the computation is expressed in the way you would expect. There's no difference between this and the way you would write the same computation directly in `main()`. The `average()` function is called in `main()` in the output statement. The first argument is the array name, `values`, and the second argument is an expression that evaluates to the number of array elements.

The elements of the array that is passed to `average()` are accessed using normal array notation. We've said that you can also treat an array passed to a function as a pointer and use pointer notation to access the elements. Here's how `average()` would look in that case:

```
double average(double* array, size_t count)
{
  double sum {};                        // Accumulate total in here
  for (size_t i {}; i < count; ++i)
    sum += *array++;                     // Sum array elements
  return sum/count;                      // Return average
}
```

For all intents and purposes, both notations are completely equivalent. In fact, as you saw in Chapter 5, you can freely mix both notations. You can, for instance, use array notation with a pointer parameter:

```
double average(double* array, size_t count)
{
  double sum {};                        // Accumulate total in here
  for (size_t i {}; i < count; ++i)
    sum += array[i];                     // Sum array elements
  return sum/count;                      // Return average
}
```

There really is no difference at all in the way any of these function definitions are evaluated. In fact, the following two function prototypes are considered identical by the compiler:

```
double average(double array[], size_t count);
double average(double* array, size_t count);
```

We will revisit this later in the section on function overloading.

▨ **Caution**   There exists a common and potentially dangerous misconception about passing fixed-size arrays to functions. Consider the following variant of the `average()` function:

```
double average10(double array[10])    /* The [10] does not mean what you might expect! */
{
  double sum {};                        // Accumulate total in here
  for (size_t i {}; i < 10; ++i)
    sum += array[i];                     // Sum array elements
  return sum / 10;                       // Return average
}
```

Clearly, the author of this function wrote it to average exactly ten values; no more, no less. We invite you to replace average() in Ex8_05.cpp with the previous average10() function and update the function call in main() accordingly. The resulting program should compile and run just fine. So, what's the problem? The problem is that the signature of this function—which unfortunately is perfectly legal C++ syntax—creates the false expectation that the compiler would enforce that only arrays of size exactly 10 can be passed as arguments to this function. To verify, let's see what happens if we change the body of the main() function of our example program to pass only three values (you can find the resulting program in Ex8_05A.cpp):

```
double values[] { 1.0, 2.0, 3.0 };          // Only three values!!!
std::cout << "Average = " << average10(values) << std::endl;
```

Even though we now called average10() with an array that is considerably shorter than the required ten values, the resulting program should still compile. If you run it, the average10() function will blindly read well beyond the bounds of the values array. Obviously, no good can come of this. Either the program will crash or it will produce garbage output. The root of the problem is that, unfortunately, the C++ language dictates that a compiler is supposed to treat a function signature of the form

```
double average10(double array[10])
```

yet again as synonymous with either one of the following:

```
double average10(double array[])
double average10(double* array)
```

Because of this, you should never use a dimension specification when passing an array by value; it only creates false expectations. An array that is passed by value is *always* passed as a pointer, and its dimensions are not checked by the compiler. We will see later that you can safely pass given-size arrays to a function using pass-by-reference instead of pass-by-value.

const Pointer Parameters

The average() function only needs to access values of the array elements; it doesn't need to change them. It would be a good idea to make sure that the code in the function does not inadvertently modify elements of the array. Specifying the parameter type as const will do that:

```
double average(const double* array, size_t count)
{
  double sum {};                           // Accumulate total in here
  for (size_t i {}; i < count; ++i)
    sum += *array++;                       // Sum array elements
  return sum/count;                        // Return average
}
```

Now the compiler will verify that the elements of the array are not modified in the body of the function. So if you now, for instance, accidentally type (*array)++ instead of *array++, compilation will fail. Of course, you must modify the function prototype to reflect the new type for the first parameter; remember that pointer-to-const types are quite different from pointer-to-non-const types.

Specifying a pointer parameter as const has two consequences: the compiler checks the code in the body of the function to ensure that you don't try to change the value pointed to, and it allows the function to be called with an argument that points to a constant.

▓ **Note** In our latest definition of average(), we didn't declare the function's count parameter const as well. If a parameter of a fundamental type such as int or size_t is passed by value, it does not need to be declared const, at least not for the same reason. The pass-by-value mechanism makes a *copy* of the argument when the function is called, so you are already protected from modifying the original value from within the function.

Nonetheless, it does remain good practice to mark variables as const if they will or should not change during a function's execution. This general guideline applies to *any* variable—including those declared in the parameter list. For that reason, and for that reason only, you might still consider declaring count as const. This would, for instance, prevent you from accidentally writing ++count somewhere in the function's body, which could have disastrous results indeed. But know that you would then be marking *a local copy* as a constant and that it is by no means required to add const to prevent changes to the original value.

Passing a Multidimensional Array to a Function

Passing a multidimensional array to a function is quite straightforward. Suppose you have a two-dimensional array defined as follows:

```
double beans[3][4] {};
```

The prototype of a hypothetical yield() function would look like this:

```
double yield(double beans[][4], size_t count);
```

In theory, you could specify the first array dimension in the type specification for the first parameter as well, but it is best not to. The compiler would again simply ignore this, analogous to what happened for the average10() function we discussed earlier. The size of the second array dimension does have the desired effect, though—C++ is fickle that way. Any two-dimensional array with 4 as a second dimension can be passed to this function, but arrays with 3 or 5 as a second dimension cannot.

Let's try passing a two-dimensional array to a function in a concrete example:

```
// Ex8_06.cpp
// Passing a two-dimensional array to a function
#include <iostream>
#include <array>          // For std::size()

double yield(const double values[][4], size_t n);

int main()
{
```

```
  double beans[3][4] { { 1.0,    2.0,    3.0,    4.0},
                       { 5.0,    6.0,    7.0,    8.0},
                       { 9.0,   10.0,   11.0,   12.0}  };

  std::cout << "Yield = " << yield(beans, std::size(beans))
           << std::endl;
}

// Function to compute total yield
double yield(const double array[][4], size_t size)
{
  double sum  {};
  for (size_t i {}; i < size; ++i)            // Loop through rows
  {
    for (size_t j {}; j < 4; ++j)             // Loop through elements in a row
    {
      sum += array[i][j];
    }
  }
  return sum;
}
```

This produces the following output:

```
Yield = 78
```

The first parameter to the yield() function is defined as a const array of an arbitrary number of rows of four elements of type double. When you call the function, the first argument is the beans array, and the second argument is the total length of the array in bytes divided by the length of the first row. This evaluates to the number of rows in the array.

Pointer notation doesn't apply particularly well with a multidimensional array. In pointer notation, the statement in the nested for loop would be as follows:

```
sum += *(*(array+i)+j);
```

Surely, you'll agree that the computation is clearer in array notation!

▓ **Note**   The definition of yield in Ex8_06 contains a "magic number" 4 in the inner for loop. In Chapter 5 we warned you that such numbers are mostly a bad idea. After all, if at some point the row length in the function signature is changed, it would be easy to also forget to update the number 4 in the for loop. A first solution would to replace the hard-coded number 4 with std::size(array[i]); another is to replace the inner loop with a range-based for loop:

```
    for (double val : array[i])             // Loop through elements in a row
    {
      sum += val;
    }
```

Note that you cannot replace the outer loop with a range-based loop as well, and you cannot use `std::size()` there. Remember, there is no way for the compiler to know the first dimension of the `double[][4]` array; only the second dimension or higher of an array can be fixed when passing it by value.

Pass-by-Reference

As you may recall, a *reference* is an alias for another variable. You can specify a function parameter as a reference as well, in which case the function uses the *pass-by-reference* mechanism with the argument. When the function is called, an argument corresponding to a reference parameter is not copied. Instead, the reference parameter is initialized with the argument. Thus, it becomes an alias for the argument in the calling function. Wherever the parameter name is used in the body of the function, it is as if it accesses the argument value in the calling function directly.

You specify a reference type by adding & after the type name. To specify a parameter type as "reference to string," for example, you write the type as `string&`. Calling a function that has a reference parameter is no different from calling a function where the argument is passed by value. Using references, however, improves performance with objects such as type `string`. The pass-by-value mechanism copies the object, which would be time-consuming with a long string and memory-consuming as well for that matter. With a reference parameter, there is no copying.

References vs. Pointers

In many regards, references are similar to pointers. To see the similarity, let's use a variation of Ex8_04 with two functions: one that accepts a pointer as an argument and one that accepts a reference instead:

```cpp
// Ex8_07.cpp
// Modifying the value of a caller variable - references vs pointers
#include <iostream>

void change_it_by_pointer(double* reference_to_it);    // Pass pointer (by value)
void change_it_by_reference(double& reference_to_it);  // Pass by reference

int main()
{
  double it {5.0};

  change_it_by_pointer(&it);                    // Now we pass the address
  std::cout << "After first function execution, it = " << it << std::endl;

  change_it_by_reference(it);                   // Now we pass a reference, not the value!
  std::cout << "After second function execution, it = " << it << std::endl;
}

void change_it_by_pointer(double* pit)
{
  *pit += 10.0;            // This modifies the original double
}
void change_it_by_reference(double& pit)
{
  pit += 10.0;            // This modifies the original double as well!
}
```

The result is that the original it value in main() is updated twice, once per function call:

```
After first function execution, it = 15
After second function execution, it = 25
```

The most obvious difference is that to pass a pointer, you need to take the address of a value first using the address-of operator. Inside the function you then, of course, have to dereference that pointer again to access the value. For a function that accepts its arguments by reference, you have to do neither. But note that this difference is purely syntactical; in the end, both have the same effect. In fact, compilers will mostly compile references in the same way as pointers.

So, which mechanism should you use, as they appear to be functionally equivalent? That's a fair question. Let's therefore consider some of the facets that play a role in this decision.

The single most distinctive feature of a pointer is that it can be nullptr, whereas a reference must always refer to something. So if you want to allow the possibility of a null argument, you cannot use a reference. Of course, precisely because a pointer parameter can be null, you're almost forced to always test for nullptr before using it. References have the advantage that you do not need to worry about nullptrs.

As Ex8_07 shows, the syntax for calling a function with a reference parameter is indeed no different from calling a function where the argument is passed by value. On the one hand, because you do not need the address-of and dereferencing operators, reference parameters allow for a more elegant syntax. On the other hand, however, precisely the fact that there is no syntactical difference means that references can sometimes cause surprises. And code that surprises is bad code because surprises lead to bugs. Consider, for instance, the following function call:

```
do_it(it);
```

Without a prototype or the definition of do_it(), you have no way of knowing whether the argument to this function is passed either by reference or by value. So, you also have no way of knowing whether the previous statement will modify the it value—provided it itself is not const, of course. This property of pass-by-reference can sometimes make code harder to follow, which may lead to surprises if values passed as arguments are changed when you did not expect them to be. Therefore:

▪ **Tip** Always declare variables as const whenever their values are not supposed to change anymore after initialization. This will make your code more predictable and hence easier to read and less prone to subtle bugs. Moreover, and perhaps even more importantly, in your function signatures, *always* declare pointer or reference parameters with const as well if the function does not modify the corresponding arguments. First, this makes it easier for programmers to use your functions because they can easily understand what will or will not be modified by a function just by looking at its signature. Second, reference-to-const parameters allow your functions to be called with const values. As we will show in the next section, const values—which as you now know should be used as much as possible—cannot be assigned to a reference-to-non-const parameter.

To summarize, because they are so similar, the choice between pointer or reference arguments is not always clear-cut. In fact, it often is a matter of personal preference which one to use. Here are some guidelines:

- If you want to allow nullptr arguments, you cannot use references. Conversely, pass-by-reference can be seen as a contract that a value is not allowed to be null. Note already that instead of representing optional values as a nullable pointer, you may also want to consider the use of std::optional<>. We'll discuss this option later in this chapter.

- Using reference parameters allows for a more elegant syntax but may mask that a function is changing a value. Never change an argument value if it is not clear from the context—from the function name, for instance—that this will happen.

- Because of the potential risks, some coding guidelines advise to never use reference-to-non-const parameters and advocate to instead always use pointer-to-non-const parameters. Personally, we would not go that far. There is nothing inherently wrong with a reference-to-non-const, as long as it is predictable for the caller which arguments may become modified. Choosing descriptive function and parameter names is always a good start to make a function's behavior more predictable.

- Passing arguments by reference-to-const is generally preferred over passing a pointer-to-const value. Because this is such a common case, we'll present you with a bigger example in the next subsection.

Input vs. Output Parameters

In the previous section, you saw that a reference parameter enables the function to modify the argument within the calling function. However, calling a function that has a reference parameter is syntactically indistinguishable from calling a function where the argument is passed by value. This makes it particularly important to use a reference-to-const parameter in a function that does not change the argument. Because the function won't change a reference-to-const parameter, the compiler will allow both const and non-const arguments. But only non-const arguments can be supplied for a reference-to-non-const parameter.

Let's investigate the effect of using reference parameters in a new version of Ex7_06.cpp that extracts words from text:

```cpp
// Ex8_08.cpp
// Using a reference parameter
#include <iostream>
#include <iomanip>
#include <string>
#include <vector>

using std::string;
using std::vector;

void find_words(vector<string>& words, const string& str, const string& separators);
void list_words(const vector<string>& words);

int main()
{
  string text;                                        // The string to be searched
  std::cout << "Enter some text terminated by *:\n";
  std::getline(std::cin, text, '*');

  const string separators {" ,;:.\"!?'\n"};           // Word delimiters
  vector<string> words;                               // Words found

  find_words(words, text, separators);
  list_words(words);
}
```

```
void find_words(vector<string>& words, const string& str, const string& separators)
{
  size_t start {str.find_first_not_of(separators)};        // First word start index
  size_t end {};                                           // Index for end of a word

  while (start != string::npos)                            // Find the words
  {
    end = str.find_first_of(separators, start + 1);        // Find end of word
    if (end == string::npos)                               // Found a separator?
      end = str.length();                                  // No, so set to last + 1

    words.push_back(str.substr(start, end - start));       // Store the word
    start = str.find_first_not_of(separators, end + 1);    // Find 1st character of next word
  }
}

void list_words(const vector<string>& words)
{
  std::cout << "Your string contains the following" << words.size() << "words:\n";
  size_t count {};                                         // Number output
  for (const auto& word : words)
  {
    std::cout << std::setw(15) << word;
    if (!(++count % 5))
      std::cout << std::endl;
  }
  std::cout << std::endl;
}
```

The output is the same as Ex7_06.cpp. Here's a sample:

```
Enter some text terminated by *:
Never judge a man until you have walked a mile in his shoes.
Then, who cares? He is a mile away and you have his shoes!*
Your string contains the following 26 words:
          Never           judge               a             man           until
            you            have          walked               a            mile
             in             his           shoes            Then             who
          cares              He              is               a            mile
           away             and             you            have             his
          shoes
```

There are now two functions in addition to main(): find_words() and list_words(). Note how the code in both functions is the same as the code that was in main() in Ex7_05.cpp. Dividing the program into three functions makes it easier to understand and does not increase the number of lines of code significantly.

The find_words() function finds all the words in the string identified by the second argument and stores them in the vector specified by the first argument. The third parameter is a string object containing the word separator characters.

The first parameter of find_words() is a reference, which avoids copying the vector<string> object. More important, though, it is a reference to a *non-const* vector<>, which allows us to add values to the vector from inside the function. Such a parameter is therefore sometimes called an *output parameter* because it is used to collect a function's output. Parameters whose values are purely used as input are then called *input parameters*.

▨ **Tip**   In principle, a parameter can act as both an input and an output parameter. Such a parameter is called an *input-output parameter*. A function with such a parameter, in one way or another, first reads from this parameter, uses this input to produce some output, and then stores the result into the same parameter. It is generally better to avoid input-output parameters, though, even if that means adding an extra parameter to your function. Code tends to be much easier to follow if each parameter serves a single purpose—a parameter should be either input or output, not both.

The find_words() function does not modify the values passed to the second and third parameters. Both are, in other words, input parameters and should therefore never be passed by reference-to-non-const. Reference-to-non-const parameters should be reserved for those cases where you need to modify the original value—in other words, for output parameters. For input parameters, only two main contenders remain: pass-by-reference-to-const or pass-by-value. And because string objects would otherwise be copied, the only logical conclusion is to declare both input parameters as const string&.

In fact, if you'd declare the third parameter to find_words() as a reference to a non-const string, the code wouldn't even compile. Give it a try if you will. The reason is that the third argument in the function call in main(), separators, is a const string object. You cannot pass a const object as the argument for a reference-to-non-const parameter. That is, you can pass a non-const argument to a reference-to-const parameter but never the other way around. In short, a T value can be passed to both T& and const T& references, whereas a const T value can be passed only to a const T& reference. And this is only logical. If you have a value that you're allowed to modify, there's no harm in passing it to a function that will not modify it—not modifying something that you're allowed to modify is fine. The converse is not true: if you have a const value, you'd better not be allowed to pass it to a function that might modify it!

The parameter for list_words(), finally, is reference-to-const because it too is an input parameter. The function only accesses the argument; it doesn't change it.

▨ **Tip**   Input parameters should usually be references-to-const. Only smaller values, most notably those of fundamental types, are to be passed by value. Use reference-to-non-const only for output parameters, and even then you should often consider returning a value instead. We'll study how to return values from functions soon.

Passing Arrays by Reference

At first sight, it may seem that for arrays there would be little benefit from passing them by reference. After all, if you pass an array by value, the array elements themselves already do not get copied. Instead, a copy is made of the pointer to the first element of the array. Passing an array also already allows you to modify the values of the original array—unless you add const, of course. So surely this already covers both advantages typically attributed to passing by reference: no copying and the possibility to modify the original value?

While this is most certainly true, you did already discover the main limitation with passing an array by value earlier, namely, that there is no way to specify the array's first dimension in a function signature, at least not in such a way that the compiler enforces that only arrays of exactly that size are passed to the function. A lesser-known fact, though, is that you *can* accomplish this by passing arrays by reference.

To illustrate, we invite you to again replace the average() function in Ex8_05.cpp with an average10() function, but this time with the following variant:

```
double average10(const double (&array)[10])   /* Only arrays of length 10 can be passed! */
{
  double sum {};                       // Accumulate total in here
  for (size_t i {}; i < 10; ++i)
    sum += array[i];                   // Sum array elements
  return sum / 10;                     // Return average
}
```

As you can see, the syntax for passing an array by reference is somewhat more complex. The const could in principle be omitted from the parameter type, but it is preferred here because you do not modify the values of the array in the function's body. The extra parentheses surrounding &array are required, though. Without them, the compiler would no longer interpret the parameter type as a reference to an array of doubles but as an array of references to double. Because arrays of references are not allowed in C++, this would then result in a compiler error:

```
double average10(const double& array[10])     // error: array of double& is not allowed
```

With our new and improved version of average10() in place, the compiler does live up to expectations. Attempting to pass any array of a different length should now result, as desired, in a compiler error:

```
double values[] { 1.0, 2.0, 3.0 };               // Only three values!!!
std::cout << "Average = " << average10(values) << std::endl;     // Error...
```

Note, moreover, that if you pass a fixed-size array by reference, it *can* be used as input to operations such as sizeof(), std::size(), and range-based for loops. This was not possible with arrays that are passed by value. You can use this to eliminate the two occurrences of 10 from the body of average10():

```
double average10(const double (&array)[10])
{
  double sum {};                       // Accumulate total in here
  for (double val : array)
    sum += val;                        // Sum array elements
  return sum / std::size(array);       // Return average
}
```

▨ **Tip**   You have already seen a more modern alternative to working with arrays of fixed length in Chapter 5: std::array<>. Using values of this type, you can just as safely pass fixed-size arrays by reference and without having to remember the tricky syntax for passing plain fixed-size arrays by reference:

```
double average10(const std::array<double,10>& values)
```

We made three variants of this program available to you: Ex8_09A, which uses pass-by-reference; Ex8_09B, which eliminates the magic numbers; and Ex8_09C, to show the use of std::array<>.

References and Implicit Conversions

A program often uses many different types, and as you know, the compiler is usually quite happy to assist you by implicitly converting between them. Whether or not you should always be happy about such conversions is another matter, though. That aside, most of the time it is convenient that code such as the following snippet will compile just fine, even though it assigns an int value to a differently typed double variable:

```
int i{};         // Declare some differently typed variables
double d{};
...
d = i;           // Implicit conversion from int to double
```

For function arguments that employ pass-by-value, it is only natural that such conversions occur as well. For instance, given the same two variables i and d, a function with signature f(double) can hence be called not only with f(d) or f(1.23) but also with differently typed arguments such as f(i), f(123), or f(1.23f).

Implicit conversions thus remain quite straightforward for pass-by-value. Let's take a look now how they fare with reference arguments:

```
// Ex8_10.cpp
// Implicit conversions of reference parameters
#include <iostream>

void double_it(double& it)       { it *= 2; }
void print_it(const double& it) { std::cout << it << std::endl; }

int main()
{
  double d{123};
  double_it(d);
  print_it(d);

  int i{456};
  // double_it(i);          /* error, does not compile! */
  print_it(i);
}
```

We first define two trivial functions: one that doubles doubles and one that streams them to std::cout. The first part of main() then shows that these, of course, work for a double variable—obviously, you should thus see the number 246 appear in the output. The interesting parts of this example are its final two statements, of which the first is commented out because it would not compile.

Let's consider the print_it(i) statement first and explain why it is in fact already a minor miracle that this even works at all. The function print_it() operates on a reference to a const double, a reference that as you know is supposed to act as an alias for a double that is defined elsewhere. On a typical system, print_it() will ultimately read the 8 bytes found in the memory location behind this reference and print out the 64 bits it finds there in some human-readable format to std::cout. But the value that we passed to the function as an argument is no double; it is an int! This int is generally only 4 bytes big, and its 32 bits are laid out completely differently than those of a double. So, how can this function be reading from an alias for a double if there is no such double defined anywhere in the program? The answer is that the compiler, before it calls print_it(), implicitly creates a temporary double value somewhere in memory, assigns it the converted int value, and then passes a reference to this temporary memory location to print_it().

Such implicit conversions are only supported for reference-to-const parameters, not for reference-to-non-const parameters. Suppose for argument's sake that the double_it(i) statement on the second-to-last line will compile without error. Surely, the compiler will then similarly convert the int value 456 to a double value 456.0, store this temporary double somewhere in memory, and apply the function body of double_it() to it. Then you'd have a temporary double somewhere, now with value 912.0, and an int value i that is still equal to 456. Now, while in theory the compiler could convert the resulting temporary value back to an int, the designers of the C++ programming language decided that that would be a bridge too far. The reason is that generally such inverse conversions would inevitably mean loss of information. In our case, this would involve a conversion from double to int, which would result in the loss of at least the fractional part of the number. The creation of temporaries is therefore never allowed for reference-to-non-const parameters. This is also why the statement double_it(i) is invalid in standard C++ and should fail to compile.

String Views: The New Reference-to-const-string

As we explained earlier, the main motivation for passing input arguments by reference-to-const instead of by value is to avoid unnecessary copies. Copying bigger strings too often, for instance, can become quite expensive, in terms of both time and memory. This is why for functions that do not modify the std::strings they operate on, your natural instinct by now should be to declare the corresponding input parameters as const string&. We did this, for example, in Ex8_08 for find_words().

```
void find_words(vector<string>& words, const string& str, const string& separators);
```

Unfortunately, const string& parameters are not perfect. While they do avoid copies of std::string objects, they have some shortcomings. To illustrate why, suppose that we alter the main() function of Ex8_08 a bit as follows:

```
int main()
{
  string text;                                    // The string to be searched
  std::cout << "Enter some text terminated by *:\n";
  std::getline(std::cin, text,'*');

 // const string separators {",;:.\"!?'\n"}; /* no more 'separators' constant this time! */
  vector<string> words;                           // Words found

  find_words(words, text,",;:.\"!?'\n");
  list_words(words);
}
```

The difference is that we no longer first store the separators in a separate separators constant of type const std::string. Instead, the corresponding string literal is passed directly as the third argument to the call of find_words(). You can easily verify that this still compiles and works correctly.

The first question then is, why does this compile and work? After all, the third parameter of find_words() expects a reference to a std::string object, but the argument that we've passed is a string literal. And a string literal is, as you may recall, of type const char[]—array of characters—and therefore definitely not a std::string object. Naturally, you already know the answer from the previous section: the compiler must be applying some form of implicit conversion. That is, the function's reference will not actually refer to the literal but instead to some *temporary* std::string *object* the compiler has implicitly created somewhere in memory. We will explain in later chapters exactly how such conversions work for nonfundamental types, but for now believe us when we say that in this case the temporary string object will be initialized with *a full copy* of all characters in the string literal.

Being the careful reader that you are, you have now realized why passing strings by reference-to-const is still somewhat flawed. Our motivation for using references was to avoid copies, but, alas, string literals still become copied when passed to reference-to-const-std::string parameters. They become copied into temporary std::string objects that emanate from implicit conversions.

This brings us to the second and real question of this section: how to create functions that never copy input string arguments, not even string literals or other character arrays? And we do not want to use const char* for this because you'd have to pass the string's length along separately as well, and then you'd miss out on the many nice helper functions offered by std::string.

The answer is provided by std::string_view, a type defined in the string_view header, added to the Standard Library with C++17. Values of this type will act analogously to values of type const std::string—mind the const!—only with one major difference: the strings they encapsulate can *never* be modified through their public interface. That is, string_views are in a way inherently const. To paraphrase *The Boss*, you can look (view) but not touch a string_view's characters. Interestingly, this limitation implies that these objects, unlike std::strings, do not need their own copy of the character array they operate on. Instead, it suffices they simply point to any character sequence stored inside either an actual std::string object, a string literal, or any other character array for that matter. Because it does not involve copying an entire character array, initializing and copying a string_view is very cheap.

So, std::strings copy characters when created, implicitly or explicitly, and string_views don't. All this might get you wondering how object creation works exactly and how your Standard Library implementation makes this behave differently for string_views and strings. And not to worry: we explain it in depth in upcoming chapters. For now, though, remember the following best-practice guideline:

▓ **Tip** Always use the type std::string_view instead of const std::string& for input string parameters. While there is nothing wrong with using const std::string_view&, you might as well pass std::string_view by value because copying these objects is cheap.

Using String View Function Parameters

For our new version of Ex8_08 (see earlier), the find_words() function is thus probably better declared as follows:

```
void find_words(vector<string>& words, std::string_view str, std::string_view separators);
```

In many cases, nothing more would have to change about the program. The std::string_view type can mostly be used as a drop-in replacement for either const std::string& or const std::string. But not in our example, which is fortunate because it allows us to explain when it might go wrong and why. To make the find_words() function definition compile with its new and improved signature, you have to slightly alter it, like so (also available in Ex8_08A.cpp):

```
void find_words(vector<string>& words, std::string_view str, std::string_view separators)
{
  size_t start{ str.find_first_not_of(separators) };      // First word start index
  size_t end{};                                           // Index for end of a word

  while (start != string::npos)                           // Find the words
  {
    end = str.find_first_of(separators, start + 1);       // Find end of word
    if (end == string::npos)                              // Found a separator?
```

```
        end = str.length();                          // No, so set to last + 1

    words.push_back(std::string{str.substr(start, end - start)});    // Store the word
    start = str.find_first_not_of(separators, end+1);    // Find 1st character of next word
  }
}
```

The modification we had to make is in the second-to-last statement, which originally did not include the explicit `std::string{ ... }` initialization:

```
    words.push_back(str.substr(start, end - start));
```

The compiler, however, will refuse any and all implicit conversions of `std::string_view` objects to values of type `std::string` (give it a try!). The rationale behind this deliberate restriction is that you normally use `string_view` to avoid more expensive string copy operations, and converting a `string_view` back to a `std::string` always involves copying the underlying character array. To protect you from accidentally doing so, the compiler is not allowed to ever implicitly make this conversion. You always have to explicitly add the conversion in this direction yourself.

■ **Note**   There exist two other cases where a `string_view` is not exactly equivalent to `const string`. First, `string_view` does not provide a `c_str()` function to convert it to a `const char*` array. Luckily, it does share with `std::string` its `data()` function, though, which for most intents and purposes is equivalent. Second, `string_view`s cannot be concatenated using the addition operator (+). To use a `string_view` value view in a concatenation expression, you have to convert it to a `std::string` first, for instance using `string{view}`.

String literals are generally not that big, so you may wonder whether it is really such a big deal if they are copied. Perhaps not. But a `std::string_view` can be created from any C-style character array, which can be as big as you want. So, while for `find_words()` you likely did not gain much from making `seperators` a `string_view`, for the other argument, `str`, it could indeed make a big difference, as illustrated by this snippet:

```
char* text = ReadHugeTextFromFile();        // last character in text array is null ('\0')
find_words(words, text, " ,;:.\"!?'\n");
delete[] text;
```

In this case, the char array is assumed to be terminated by a null character element, a convention common in C and C++ programming. If this is not the case, you'll have to use something more of this form:

```
char* text = ...;                   // again a huge amount of characters...
size_t numCharacters = ...;         // the huge amount
find_words(words, std::string_view{text, numCharacters}, " ,;:.\"!?'\n");
delete[] text;
```

The bottom line in either case is that if you use `std::string_view`, the huge text array is not copied when passing it to `find_words()`, whereas it would be if you'd use `const std::string&`.

Default Argument Values

There are many situations in which it would be useful to have default argument values for one or more function parameters. This would allow you to specify an argument value only when you want something different from the default. A simple example is a function that outputs a standard error message. Most of the time, a default message will suffice, but occasionally an alternative is needed. You can do this by specifying a default parameter value in the function prototype. You could define a function to output a message like this:

```
void show_error(string_view message)
{
  std::cout << message << std::endl;
}
```

You specify the default argument value like this:

```
void show_error(string_view message = "Program Error");
```

If both are separate, you need to specify default values in the function prototype and not in the function definition. The reason is that when resolving the function calls, the compiler needs to know whether a given number of arguments is acceptable.

To output the default message, you call such functions without the corresponding argument:

```
show_error();                              // Outputs "Program Error"
```

To output a particular message, you specify the argument:

```
show_error("Nothing works!");
```

In the previous example, the parameter happens to be passed by value. You specify default values for nonreference and reference parameters in the same manner:

```
void show_error(const string& message = "Program Error");
```

From what you learned in previous sections, it also should come as no surprise that default values for which the implicit conversion requires the creation of a temporary object—as is in the previous example—are illegal for reference-to-non-const parameters. Hence, the following should not compile:

```
// void show_error(string& message = "Program Error");    /* Error: does not compile */
```

Specifying default parameter values can make functions simpler to use. Naturally, you aren't limited to just one parameter with a default value.

Multiple Default Parameter Values

All function parameters that have default values must be placed together at the end of the parameter list. When an argument is omitted in a function call, all subsequent arguments in the list must also be omitted. Thus, parameters with default values should be sequenced from the least likely to be omitted to the most likely at the end. These rules are necessary for the compiler to be able to process function calls.

Let's contrive an example of a function with several default parameter values. Suppose that you wrote a function to display one or more data values, several to a line, as follows:

```
void show_data(const int data[], size_t count, std::string_view title,
                                          size_t width, size_t perLine)
{
  std::cout << title << std::endl;              // Display the title

  // Output the data values
  for (size_t i {}; i < count; ++i)
  {
    std::cout << std::setw(width) << data[i];   // Display a data item
    if ((i+1) % perLine == 0)                   // Newline after perLine values
      std::cout << '\n';
  }
  std::cout << std::endl;
}
```

The data parameter is an array of values to be displayed, and count indicates how many there are. The third parameter of type string_view specifies a title that is to head the output. The fourth parameter determines the field width for each item, and the last parameter is the number of data items per line. This function has a lot of parameters. It's clearly a job for default parameter values! Here's an example:

```
// Ex8_11.cpp
// Using multiple default parameter values
#include <iostream>
#include <iomanip>
#include <string_view>

// The function prototype including defaults for parameters
void show_data(const int data[], size_t count = 1, std::string_view title = "Data Values",
                                          size_t width = 10, size_t perLine = 5);
int main()
{
  int samples[] {1, 2, 3, 4, 5, 6, 7, 8, 9, 10, 11, 12};

  int dataItem {-99};
  show_data(&dataItem);

  dataItem = 13;
  show_data(&dataItem, 1, "Unlucky for some!");

  show_data(samples, std::size(samples));
  show_data(samples, std::size(samples), "Samples");
  show_data(samples, std::size(samples), "Samples", 6);
  show_data(samples, std::size(samples), "Samples", 8, 4);
}
```

The definition of show_data() in Ex8_11.cpp can be taken from earlier in this section. Here's the output:

```
Data Values
      -99
Unlucky for some!
       13
Data Values
       1        2        3        4        5
       6        7        8        9       10
      11       12
Samples
       1        2        3        4        5
       6        7        8        9       10
      11       12
Samples
       1        2        3        4        5
       6        7        8        9       10
      11       12
Samples
       1        2        3        4
       5        6        7        8
       9       10       11       12
```

The prototype for show_data() specifies default values for all parameters except the first. You have five ways to call this function: you can specify all five arguments, or you can omit the last one, the last two, the last three, or the last four. You can supply just the first to output a single data item, as long as you are happy with the default values for the remaining parameters.

Remember that you can omit arguments only at the end of the list; you are not allowed to omit the second and the fifth. Here's an example:

```
show_data(samples, , "Samples", 15);                    // Wrong!
```

Arguments to main()

You can define main() so that it accepts arguments that are entered on the command line when the program executes. The parameters you can specify for main() are standardized; either you can define main() with no parameters or you can define main() in the following form:

```
int main(int argc, char* argv[])
{
  // Code for main()...
}
```

The first parameter, argc, is a count of the number of string arguments that were found on the command line. It is type int for historical reasons, not size_t as you might expect from a parameter that cannot be negative. The second parameter, argv, is an array of pointers to the command-line arguments, including the program name. The array type implies that all command-line arguments are received as C-style strings. The program name used to invoke the program is normally recorded in the first element of argv, argv[0].[1] The last element in argv (argv[argc]) is always nullptr, so the number of elements in argv will be argc+1. We'll give you a couple of examples to make this clear. Suppose that to run the program, you enter just the program name on the command line:

```
Myprog
```

In this case, argc will be 1, and argv[] contains two elements. The first is the address of the string "Myprog", and the second will be nullptr.

Suppose you enter this:

```
Myprog  2 3.5  "Rip Van Winkle"
```

Now argc will be 4, and argv will have five elements. The first four elements will be pointers to the strings "Myprog", "2", "3.5", and "Rip Van Winkle". The fifth element, argv[4], will be nullptr.

What you do with the command-line arguments is entirely up to you. The following program shows how you access the command-line arguments:

```cpp
// Ex8_12.cpp
// Program that lists its command line arguments
#include <iostream>

int main(int argc, char* argv[])
{
  for (int i {}; i < argc; ++i)
    std::cout << argv[i] << std::endl;
}
```

This lists the command-line arguments, including the program name. Command-line arguments can be anything at all—file names to a file copy program, for example, or the name of a person to search for in a contact file. They can be anything that is useful to have entered when program execution is initiated.

Returning Values from a Function

As you know, you can return a value of any type from a function. This is quite straightforward when you're returning a value of one of the basic types, but there are some pitfalls when you are returning a pointer or a reference.

Returning a Pointer

When you return a pointer from a function, it must contain either nullptr or an address that is still valid in the calling function. In other words, the variable pointed to must still be in scope after the return to the calling function. This implies the following absolute rule:

■ **Caution**   *Never* return the address of an automatic, stack-allocated local variable from a function.

---

[1]If, for whatever reason, the operating system cannot determine the name that was used to invoke the program, argv[0] will be an empty string. This does not happen in normal use.

Suppose you define a function that returns the address of the larger of two argument values. This could be used on the left of an assignment so that you could change the variable that contains the larger value, perhaps in a statement such as this:

```
*larger(value1, value2) = 100;            // Set the larger variable to 100
```

You can easily be led astray when implementing this. Here's an implementation that doesn't work:

```
int* larger(int a, int b)
{
   if (a > b)
      return &a;                           // Wrong!
   else
      return &b;                           // Wrong!
 }
```

It's relatively easy to see what's wrong with this: a and b are local to the function. The argument values are copied to the local variables a and b. When you return &a or &b, the variables at these addresses no longer exist back in the calling function. You usually get a warning from your compiler when you compile this code.

You can specify the parameters as pointers:

```
int* larger(int* a, int* b)
{
  if (*a > *b)
     return a;                            // OK
  else
     return b;                            // OK
}
```

If you do, do not forget to also dereference the pointers. The previous condition (a > b) would still compile, but then you'd not be comparing the values themselves. You'd instead be comparing the *addresses* of the memory locations holding these values. You could call the function with this statement:

```
*larger(&value1, &value2) = 100;          // Set the larger variable to 100
```

A function to return the address of the larger of two values is not particularly useful, but let's consider something more practical. Suppose we need a program to normalize a set of values of type double so that they all lie between 0.0 and 1.0 inclusive. To normalize the values, we can first subtract the minimum sample value from them to make them all non-negative. Two functions will help with that, one to find the minimum and another to adjust the values by any given amount. Here's a definition for the first function:

```
const double* smallest(const double data[], size_t count)
{
  if (!count) return nullptr;        // There is no smallest in an empty array

  size_t index_min {};
  for (size_t i {1}; i < count; ++i)
    if (data[index_min] > data[i])
      index_min = i;

  return &data[index_min];
}
```

CHAPTER 8 ■ DEFINING FUNCTIONS

You shouldn't have any trouble seeing what's going on here. The index of the minimum value is stored in index_min, which is initialized arbitrarily to refer to the first array element. The loop compares the value of the element at index_min with each of the others, and when one is less, its index is recorded in index_min. The function returns the address of the minimum value in the array. It probably would be more sensible to return the index, but we're demonstrating pointer return values among other things. The first parameter is const because the function doesn't change the array. With this parameter const you must specify the return type as const. The compiler will not allow you to return a non-const pointer to an element of a const array.

A function to adjust the values of array elements by a given amount looks like this:

```
double* shift_range(double data[], size_t count, double delta)
{
  for (size_t i {}; i < count; ++i)
    data[i] += delta;
  return data;
}
```

This function adds the value of the third argument to each array element. The return type could be void so it returns nothing, but returning the address of data allows the function to be used as an argument to another function that accepts an array. Of course, the function can still be called without storing or otherwise using the return value.

You could combine using this with the previous function to adjust the values in an array, samples, so that all the elements are non-negative:

```
const size_t count {std::size(samples)};  // Element count
shift_range(samples, count, -(*smallest(samples, count))); // Subtract min from elements
```

The third argument to shift_range() calls smallest(), which returns a pointer to the minimum element. The expression negates the value, so shift_range() will subtract the minimum from each element to achieve what we want. The elements in data are now from zero to some positive upper limit. To map these into the range from 0 to 1, we need to divide each element by the maximum element. We first need a function to find the maximum:

```
const double* largest(const double data[], size_t count)
{
  if (!count) return nullptr;     // There is no largest in an empty array

  size_t index_max {};
  for (size_t i {1}; i < count; ++i)
    if (data[index_max] < data[i])
      index_max = i;

  return &data[index_max];
}
```

This works in essentially the same way as smallest(). We could use a function that scales the array elements by dividing by a given value:

```
double* scale_range(double data[], size_t count, double divisor)
{
  if (!divisor) return data;                  // Do nothing for a zero divisor
```

```
    for (size_t i {}; i < count; ++i)
      data[i] /= divisor;
    return data;
}
```

Dividing by zero would be a disaster, so when the third argument is zero, the function just returns the original array. We can use this function in combination with largest() to scale the elements that are now from 0 to some maximum to the range 0 to 1:

```
scale_range(samples, count, *largest(samples, count));
```

Of course, what the user would probably prefer is a function that will normalize an array of values, thus avoiding the need to get into the gory details:

```
double* normalize_range(double data[], size_t count)
{
  return scale_range(shift_range(data, count, -(*smallest(data, count))),
                                  count, *largest(data, count));
}
```

Remarkably this function requires only one statement. Let's see if it all works in practice:

```
// Ex8_13.cpp
// Returning a pointer
#include <iostream>
#include <iomanip>
#include <string_view>
#include <array>                    // for std::size()

void show_data(const double data[], size_t count = 1, std::string_view title = "Data Values",
                                      size_t width = 10, size_t perLine = 5);
const double* largest(const double data[], size_t count);
const double* smallest(const double data[], size_t count);
double* shift_range(double data[], size_t count, double delta);
double* scale_range(double data[], size_t count, double divisor);
double* normalize_range(double data[], size_t count);

int main()
{
  double samples[] {
                    11.0,   23.0,   13.0,   4.0,
                    57.0,   36.0,  317.0,  88.0,
                     9.0,  100.0,  121.0,  12.0
                   };

  const size_t count{std::size(samples)};         // Number of samples
  show_data(samples, count, "Original Values");    // Output original values
  normalize_range(samples, count);                 // Normalize the values
  show_data(samples, count, "Normalized Values", 12);  // Output normalized values
}
```

```
// Outputs an array of double values
void show_data(const double data[], size_t count, std::string_view title,
                                                    size_t width, size_t perLine)
{
  std::cout << title << std::endl;                  // Display the title

  // Output the data values
  for (size_t i {}; i < count; ++i)
  {
    std::cout << std::setw(width) << data[i];       // Display a data item
    if ((i + 1) % perLine == 0)                     // Newline after perLine values
      std::cout << '\n';
  }
  std::cout << std::endl;
}
```

If you compile and run this example complete with the definitions of largest(), smallest(), shift_range(), scale_range(), and normalize_range() shown earlier, you should get the following output:

Original Values				
11	23	13	4	57
36	317	88	9	100
121	12			
Normalized Values				
0.0223642	0.0607029	0.028754	0	0.169329
0.102236	1	0.268371	0.0159744	0.306709
0.373802	0.0255591			

The output demonstrates that the results are what was required. The last two statements in main() could be condensed into one by passing the address returned by normalize_range() as the first argument to show_data():

```
show_data(normalize_range(samples, count), count, "Normalized Values", 12);
```

This is more concise but clearly not necessarily clearer.

Returning a Reference

Returning a pointer from a function is useful, but it can be problematic. Pointers can be null, and dereferencing nullptr generally results in the failure of your program. The solution, as you will surely have guessed from the title of this section, is to return a *reference*. A reference is an alias for another variable, so we can state the following golden rule for references:

■ **Caution**   *Never* return a reference to an automatic local variable in a function.

By returning a reference, you allow a function call to the function to be used on the left of an assignment. In fact, returning a reference from a function is the only way you can enable a function to be used (without dereferencing) on the left of an assignment operation.

Suppose you code a larger() function like this:

```
string& larger(string& s1, string& s2)
{
  return s1 > s2? s1 : s2;              // Return a reference to the larger string
}
```

The return type is "reference to string," and the parameters are references to non-const values. Because you want to return a reference-to-non-const referring to one or other of the arguments, you must not specify the parameters as const.

You could use the function to change the larger of the two arguments, like this:

```
string str1 {"abcx"};
string str2 {"adcf"};
larger(str1, str2) = "defg";
```

Because the parameters are not const, you can't use string literals as arguments; the compiler won't allow it. A reference parameter permits the value to be changed, and changing a constant is not something the compiler will knowingly go along with. If you make the parameters const, you can't use a reference-to-non-const as the return type.

You're not going to examine an extended example of using reference return types at this moment, but you can be sure that you'll meet them again before long. As you'll discover, reference return types become essential when you are creating your own data types using classes.

Returning vs. Output Parameters

You now know two ways a function can pass the outcome it produces back to its caller: it can either return a value or put values into output parameters. In Ex8_08, you encountered the following example of the latter:

```
void find_words(vector<string>& words, const string& str, const string& separators);
```

Another way of declaring this function, however, is as follows:

```
vector<string> find_words(const string& str, const string& separators);
```

When your function outputs an object, you of course do not want this object to be copied, especially if this object is as expensive to copy as, for instance, a vector of strings. Prior to C++11, the recommended approach then was mostly to use output parameters. This was the only way you could make absolutely sure that all strings in the vector<> did not get copied when returning the vector<> from the function. This advice has changed drastically with C++11, however:

▒ **Tip**   In modern C++, you should generally prefer returning values over output parameters. This makes function signatures and calls much easier to read. Arguments are for input, and all output is returned. The mechanism that makes this possible is called *move semantics* and is discussed in detail in Chapter 17. In a nutshell, move semantics ensures that returning objects that manage dynamically allocated memory—such as vectors and strings—no longer involves copying that memory and is therefore very cheap. Notable exceptions are arrays or objects that contain an array, such as std::array<>. For these it is still better to use output parameters.

Return Type Deduction

Just like you can let the compiler deduce the type of a variable from its initialization, you can have the compiler deduce the return type of a function from its definition. You can write the following, for instance:

```
auto getAnswer() { return 42; }
```

From this definition, the compiler will deduce that the return type of getAnswer() is int. Naturally, for a type name as short as int, there is little point in using auto. In fact, it even results in one extra letter to type. But later you'll encounter type names that are much more verbose (iterators are a classical example). For these, type deduction can save you time. Or you may want your function to return the same type as some other function, and for whatever reason you do not feel the need to look up what type that is or to type it out. In general, the same considerations apply here as for using auto for declaring variables. If it is clear enough from the context what the type will be or if the exact type name matters less for the clarity of your code, return type deduction can be practical.

■ **Note**   Another context where return type deduction can be practical is to specify the return type of a function template. You'll learn about this in the next chapter.

The compiler can even deduce the return type of a function with multiple return statements, provided their expressions evaluate to a value of exactly the same type. That is, no implicit conversions will be performed because the compiler has no way to decide which of the different types to deduce. For instance, consider the following function to obtain a string's first letter in the form of another string:

```
auto getFirstLetter(string_view text)   // function to get first letter,
{                                        // not as a char but as another string
   if (text.empty())
      return " ";                        // deduced type: const char*
   else
      return text.substr(0, 1);          // deduced type: std::string_view
}
```

This will fail to compile. The compiler finds one return statement that returns a value of type const char* and a second that returns a value of type std::string_view. The fact that a substring of a string_view is again a string_view is something you can find in your Standard Library documentation. Don't let that distract you, though. The main point here is that the compiler has no way to decide which of these two types to pick for the return type. To make this definition compile, your options include the following:

- Replace auto in the function with std::string_view. This will allow the compiler to perform the necessary type conversions for you.

- Replace the first return statement with return std::string_view{" "}. The compiler will then deduce std::string_view as the return type.

- Replace the second return statement with return text.substr(0, 1).data(). Because the data() function—as your Standard Library documentation will confirm—returns a const char* pointer, the return type of getFirstLetter() then deduces to const char* as well.

Return Type Deduction and References

You need to take extra care with return type deduction if you want the return type to be a reference. Suppose you write the larger() function shown earlier using an auto-deduced return type instead:

```
auto larger(string& s1, string& s2)
{
  return s1 > s2? s1 : s2;              // Return a reference to the larger string
}
```

In this case, the compiler will deduce std::string as a return type, not std::string&. That is, a copy will be returned rather than a reference. If you want to return a reference for larger(), your options include the following:

- Explicitly specify the std::string& return type as before.

- Specify auto& instead of auto. Then the return type will always be a reference.

While discussing all details and intricacies of C++ type deduction is well outside our scope, the good news is that one simple rule covers most cases:

▓ **Caution**   auto never deduces to a reference type, always to a value type. This implies that even when you assign a reference to auto, the value still gets copied. This copy will moreover not be const, unless you explicitly use const auto. To have the compiler deduce a reference type, you can use auto& or const auto&.

Naturally, this rule is not specific to return type deduction. The same holds if you use auto for local variables as well:

```
string test = "Your powers of deduction never cease to amaze me";
const string& ref_to_test = test;
auto auto_test = ref_to_test;
```

In the previous code snippet, auto_test has type std::string and therefore contains a copy of test. Unlike ref_to_test, this new copy isn't const anymore either.

Working with Optional Values

When writing your own functions, you will often encounter input arguments that are optional or functions that can return a value only if nothing went wrong. Consider the following function prototype:

```
int find_last_in_string(string_view string, char char_to_find, int start_index);
```

From this declaration, you can imagine that this function searches a given string for a given character, back to front, starting from a given starting index. Once found, it will then return the index of the last occurrence of that character. But what happens if the character doesn't occur in the string? And what do you do if you want the algorithm to consider the entire string? Of course, passing string.length()-1 as a start index will work, but that's somewhat tedious. Would it perhaps work as well if you pass, say, -1 to the third argument? Without interface documentation or a peek at the implementation code, there is no way of knowing how this function will behave exactly.

The traditional solution is to pick some specific value or values to use when the caller wants the function to use its default settings or to return when no actual value could be computed. A typical choice for indices is -1. A possible specification for find_last_in_string() would thus be that it returns -1 if char_to_find does not occur in the given string and that the entire string is searched if -1 or any negative value is passed as a start_index. In fact, std::string and std::string_view define their own find() functions, and they use the special size_t constants std::string::npos and std::string_view::npos for these purposes.

The problem is that, in general, it can be hard to remember how every function encodes "not provided" or "not computed." Conventions tend to differ between different libraries or even within the same library. Some may return 0 upon failure, and others may return a negative value. Some may accept nullptr for a const char* parameter, and others won't. And so on.

To aid the users of a function, optional parameters are typically given a valid default value. Here's an example:

```
int find_last_in_string(string_view string, char char_to_find, int start_index = -1);
```

However, this technique, of course, does not extend to return values. Another problem with the traditional approaches is that, in general, there may not even be an obvious way of encoding an optional value. One reason for this may be the type of the optional value. Think about it, how would you encode an optional bool, for instance? Another reason would be the specific situation. Suppose, for instance, that you need to define a function that reads a configuration override from a given configuration file. Then you'd probably prefer to give that function the following form:

```
int read_configuration_override(string_view fileName, string_view overrideName);
```

But what should happen if the configuration file does not contain a value with the given name? Because this is intended to be a generic function, you cannot a priori assume that an int value such as 0, -1, or any other value isn't a valid configuration override as well. Traditional workarounds include the following:

```
// Returns the 'default' value provided by the caller if the override is not found
int read_configuration_override(string_view file, string_view overrideName, int default);

// Puts the override in the output parameter if found and return true; or return false otherwise
bool read_configuration_override(string_view file, string_view overrideName, int& value);
```

While these work, the C++17 Standard Library now offers std::optional<>, a utility we believe can help make your function declarations much cleaner and easier to read.

std::optional

As of C++17, the Standard Library provides std::optional<>, which constitutes an interesting alternative to all the implicit encodings of optional values we discussed earlier. Using this auxiliary type, any optional int can be explicitly declared with optional<int> as follows:

```
optional<int> find_last_in_string(string_view string, char to_find, optional<int> start_index);
optional<int> read_configuration_override(string_view fileName, string_view overrideName);
```

The fact that these parameters or return values are optional is now stated explicitly, making these prototypes self-documenting. Your code therefore becomes much easier to use and read than code that uses traditional approaches. Let's take a look at the basic use of std::optional<> in some real code:

```
// Ex8_14.cpp
// Working with std::opional
```

```cpp
#include <iostream>
#include <optional>
#include <string_view>
using std::optional;
using std::string_view;

optional<size_t> find_last(string_view string, char to_find,
                                           optional<size_t> start_index = std::nullopt);
int main()
{
  const auto string = "Growing old is mandatory; growing up is optional.";

  const optional<size_t> found_a{ find_last(string, 'a') };
  if (found_a)
    std::cout << "Found the last a at index " << *found_a << std::endl;

  const auto found_b{ find_last(string, 'b') };
  if (found_b.has_value())
    std::cout << "Found the last b at index " << found_b.value() << std::endl;

  // const size_t found_c{ find_last(string, 'c') };     /* error: cannot convert to size_t */

  const auto found_early_i{ find_last(string, 'i', 10) };
  if (found_early_i != std::nullopt)
    std::cout << "Found an early i at index " << *found_early_i << std::endl;
}

optional<size_t> find_last(string_view string, char to_find, optional<size_t> start_index)
{
  // code below will not work for empty strings
  if (string.empty())
    return std::nullopt;        // or: 'return optional<size_t>{};'
                                // or: 'return {};'

  // determine the starting index for the loop that follows:
  size_t index = start_index.value_or(string.size() - 1);

  while (true)                  // never use while (index >= 0) here, as size_t is always >= 0!
  {
    if (string[index] == to_find) return index;
    if (index == 0) return std::nullopt;
    --index;
  }
}
```

The output produced by this program is as follows:

```
Found the last a at index 46
Found an early i at index 4
```

To showcase `std::optional<>`, we define `find_last()`, a variation of the `find_last_in_string()` function we used as an example earlier. Notice that because `find_last()` uses unsigned `size_t` indexes instead of `int` indexes, using -1 as a default value would already be less obvious here. A second, more interesting difference, though, is the default value for the function's third argument. This value, `std::nullopt`, is the special constant defined by the Standard Library to initialize `optional<T>` values that do not (yet) have a T value assigned. We will see shortly why using this as a default parameter value can be interesting.

After the function's prototype, you see the program's `main()` function. In `main()`, we call `find_last()` three times to search for the letters `'a'`, `'b'`, and `'i'` in some sample string. And there is really nothing surprising about the calls themselves. If you want a nondefault start index, you simply pass a number to `find_last()`, like we did for our third call. The compiler then implicitly converts this number to a `std::optional<>` object, exactly like you'd expect. If you're OK with the default starting index, though, you could always pass `std::nullopt` explicitly. We opted to have the default parameter value take care of that for us, though.

These are the most interesting lessons to learn from the `main()` function:

- How you can check whether an `optional<>` value returned by `find_last()` was assigned an actual value

- How you subsequently extract this value from the `optional<>` to use it

For the former, `main()` shows three alternatives, in this order: either you have the compiler convert the `optional<>` to a Boolean for you or you call the `has_value()` function or you compare the `optional<>` to `nullopt`. For the latter, `main()` presents two options: you can either use the `*` operator or call the `value()` function. Assigning the `optional<size_t>` return value directly to a `size_t`, however, would not be possible. The compiler cannot convert values of type `optional<size_t>` to values of type `size_t`.

From the body of `find_last()`, aside from some interesting challenges with empty strings and unsigned index types, we'd mostly like you to pay attention to two more aspects related to `optional<>`. First, notice that returning a value is straightforward. Either you return `std::nullopt` or you return an actual value. Both will then be converted to a suitable `optional<>` by the compiler. Second, we've used `value_or()` there. If the `optional<>` `start_index` contains a value, this function will return the same as `value()`; if it does not contain a value, `value_or()` simply evaluates to the value you pass it as an argument. The `value_or()` function is therefore a welcome alternative to equivalent `if-else` statements or conditional operator expressions that would first call `has_value()` and then `value()`.

■ **Note**   Ex8_14 covers most there is to know about `std::optional<>`. As always, if you need to know more, please consult your favorite Standard Library reference. One thing to note already, though, is that next to the `*` operator, `std::optional<>` also supports the `->` operator. That is, in the following example the last two statements are equivalent:

```
std::optional<std::string> os{ "Falling in life is inevitable--staying down is optional." };
if (os) std::cout << (*os).size() << std::endl;
if (os) std::cout << os->size() << std::endl;
```

Note that while this syntax makes optional <> objects look and feel like pointers, they most certainly aren't pointers. Each `optional<>` object contains a copy of any value assigned to it, and this copy is not kept in the free store. That is, while copying a pointer doesn't copy the value it points to, copying an `optional<>` always involves copying the entire value that is stored inside it.

Static Variables

In the functions you have seen so far, nothing is retained within the body of the function from one execution to the next. Suppose you want to count how many times a function has been called. How can you do that? One way is to define a variable at file scope and increment it from within the function. A potential problem with this is that *any* function in the file can modify the variable, so you can't be sure that it's being incremented only when it should be.

A better solution is to define a variable in the function body as static. A static variable that you define within a function is created the first time its definition is executed. It then continues to exist until the program terminates. This means you can carry over a value from one call of a function to the next. To specify a variable as static, you prefix the type name in the definition with the static keyword. Let's consider this simple example:

```
unsigned int nextInteger()
{
  static unsigned int count {0};
  return ++count;
}
```

The first time the statement starting with static executes, count is created and initialized to 0. Subsequent executions of the statement have no further effect. This function then increments the static variable count and returns the incremented value. The first time the function is called, it therefore returns 1. The second time, it returns 2. Each time the function is called, it returns an integer that is one larger than the previous value. count is created and initialized only once, the first time the function is called. Subsequent calls simply increment count and return the resulting value. count survives for as long as the program is executing.

You can specify any type of variable as static, and you can use a static variable for anything that you want to remember from one function call to the next. You might want to hold on to the number of the previous file record that was read, for example, or the highest value of previous arguments.

If you don't initialize a static variable, it will be zero-initialized by default. In the previous example, you could therefore omit the {0} initialization and still get the same result. Take care, though, because such zero-initialization does *not* occur for regular local variables. If you do not initialize these, they will contain junk values.

Inline Functions

With functions that are short, the overhead of the code the compiler generates to deal with passing arguments and returning a result is significant compared to the code involved in doing the actual calculation. The execution times of the two types of code may be similarly related. In extreme cases, the code for calling the function may occupy more memory than the code in the body of the function. In such circumstances, you can suggest to the compiler that it replaces a function call with the code from the body of the function, suitably adjusted to deal with local names. This could make the program shorter, faster, or possibly both.

You do this using the inline keyword in the function definition. Here's an example:

```
inline int larger(int m, int n)
{
  return m > n ? m  : n;
}
```

This definition indicates that the compiler can replace calls with inline code. However, it is only a suggestion, and it's down to the compiler as to whether your suggestion is taken up. When a function is specified as inline, the definition must be available in every source file that calls the function. For this reason, the definition of an inline function usually appears in a header file rather than in a source file, and the header is included in each source file that uses the function. Most if not all modern compilers will make short functions inline, even when you don't use the inline keyword in the definition. If a function you specify as inline is used in more than one source file, you should place the definition in a header file that you include in each source file that uses the function. If you don't, you'll get "unresolved external" messages when the code is linked.

Function Overloading

You'll often find that you need two or more functions that do essentially the same thing, but with parameters of different types. The largest() and smallest() functions in Ex8_13.cpp are likely candidates. You would want these operations to work with arrays of different types such as int[], double[], float[], or even string[]. Ideally, all such functions would have the same name, smallest() or largest(). Function overloading makes that possible.

Function overloading allows several functions in a program with the same name as long as they all have a parameter list that is different from each other. You learned earlier in this chapter that the compiler identifies a function by its *signature*, which is a combination of the function name and the parameter list. Overloaded functions have the same name, so the signature of each overloaded function must be differentiated by the parameter list alone. That allows the compiler to select the correct function for each function call based on the argument list. Two functions with the same name are different if at least one of the following is true:

- The functions have different numbers of parameters.

- At least one pair of corresponding parameters is of different types.

▓ **Note** The return type of a function is not part of the function's signature. To decide which function overload to use, the compiler looks only at the number and types of the function parameters and arguments. If you declare two functions with the same name and parameter list but with a different return type, your program will fail to compile.

Here's an example that uses overloaded versions of the largest() function:

```
// Ex8_15.cpp
// Overloading a function
#include <iostream>
#include <string>
#include <vector>
using std::string;
using std::vector;

// Function prototypes
double largest(const double data[], size_t count);
double largest(const vector<double>& data);
int largest(const vector<int>& data);
string largest(const vector<string>& words);
// int largest(const vector<string>& words); /* would not compile: overloaded functions must
//                                              differ in more than just their return type! */
```

```
int main()
{
  double values[] {1.5, 44.6, 13.7, 21.2, 6.7};
  vector<int> numbers {15, 44, 13, 21, 6, 8, 5, 2};
  vector<double> data{3.5, 5, 6, -1.2, 8.7, 6.4};
  vector<string> names {"Charles Dickens", "Emily Bronte", "Jane Austen",
                        "Henry James", "Arthur Miller"};
  std::cout << "The largest of values is " << largest(values, std::size(values))<< std::endl;
  std::cout << "The largest of numbers is " << largest(numbers)<< std::endl;
  std::cout << "The largest of data is " << largest(data)<< std::endl;
  std::cout << "The largest of names is " << largest(names)<< std::endl;
}

// Finds the largest of an array of double values
double largest(const double data[], size_t count)
{
  double max{ data[0] };
  for (size_t i{ 1 }; i < count; ++i)
    if (max < data[i]) max = data[i];
  return max;
}

// Finds the largest of a vector of double values
double largest(const vector<double>& data)
{
  double max {data[0]};
  for (auto value : data)
    if (max < value) max = value;
  return max;
}

// Finds the largest of a vector of int values
int largest(const vector<int>& data)
{
  int max {data[0]};
  for (auto value : data)
    if (max < value) max = value;
  return max;
}

// Finds the largest of a vector of string objects
string largest(const vector<string>& words)
{
  string max_word {words[0]};
  for (const auto& word : words)
    if (max_word < word) max_word = word;
  return max_word;
}
```

This produces the following output:

```
The largest of values is 44.6
The largest of numbers is 44
The largest of data is 8.7
The largest of names is Jane Austen
```

The compiler selects the version of largest() to be called in main() based on the argument list. Each version of the function has a unique signature because the parameter lists are different. It's important to note that the parameters that accept vector<T> arguments are references. If they are not specified as references, the vector object will be passed by value and thus copied. This could be expensive for a vector with a lot of elements. Parameters of array types are different. Only the address of an array is passed in this case, so they do not need to be reference types.

■ **Note**   Did it bother you that several of the largest() functions in Ex8_15.cpp had the exact same implementation, only for a different type? If so, good. A good programmer should always be wary of repeating the same code multiple times—and not just because programmers are a lazy bunch. Later, we'll call this *code duplication* and explain to you some other downsides of doing this beyond having to type a lot. To avoid this particular type of duplication—where multiple functions perform the same task but for different parameter types—you need function templates. You will learn about function templates in the next chapter.

Overloading and Pointer Parameters

Pointers to different types are different, so the following prototypes declare different overloaded functions:

```
int largest(int* pValues, size_t count);        // Prototype 1
int largest(float* pValues, size_t count);       // Prototype 2
```

Note that a parameter of type int* is treated in the same way as a parameter type of int[]. Hence, the following prototype declares the same function as Prototype 1 earlier:

```
int largest(int values[], size_t count);        // Identical signature to prototype 1
```

With either parameter type, the argument is an address and therefore not differentiated. In fact, you might recall from earlier that even the following prototype declares the same function:

```
int largest(int values[100], size_t count);     // Identical signature to prototype 1
```

Because such array dimension specifications are completely ignored by the compiler, we argued earlier that they are thus dangerously misleading and advised you to never use this form. If a dimension specification is what you want, the recommended approach instead is either to use std::array<> or to pass arrays by reference.

Overloading and Reference Parameters

You need to be careful when you are overloading functions with reference parameters. You can't overload a function with a parameter type data_type with a function that has a parameter type data_type&. The compiler cannot determine which function you want from the argument. These prototypes illustrate the problem:

```
void do_it(std::string number);        // These are not distinguishable...
void do_it(std::string& number);       // ...from the argument type
```

Suppose you write the following statements:

```
std::string word {"egg"};
do_it(word);                           // Calls which???
```

The second statement could call either function. The compiler cannot determine which version of do_it() should be called. Thus, you can't distinguish overloaded functions based on a parameter for one version being of a given type and the other being a reference to that type.

You should also be wary when you have overloaded a function where one version has a parameter of type type1 and another has a parameter *reference to* type2—even if type1 and type2 are different. Which function is called depends on the sort of arguments you use, but you may get some surprising results. Let's explore this a little with an example:

```cpp
// Ex8_16.cpp
// Overloading a function with reference parameters
#include <iostream>

double larger(double a, double b);      // Non-reference parameters
long& larger(long& a, long& b);         // Reference parameters

int main()
{
  double a_double {1.5}, b_double {2.5};
  std::cout << "The larger of double values "
            << a_double << " and " << b_double << " is "
            << larger(a_double, b_double) << std::endl;

  int a_int {15}, b_int {25};
  std::cout << "The larger of int values "
            << a_int << " and " << b_int << " is "
            << larger(static_cast<long>(a_int), static_cast<long>(b_int))
            << std::endl;
}

// Returns the larger of two floating point values
double larger(double a, double b)
{
  std::cout << "double larger() called." << std::endl;
  return a > b ? a : b;
}
```

```
// Returns the larger of two long references
long& larger(long& a, long& b)
{
  std::cout << "long ref larger() called" << std::endl;
  return a > b ? a : b;
}
```

This produces the following output:

```
double larger() called.
The larger of double values 1.5 and 2.5 is 2.5
double larger() called.
The larger of int values 15 and 25 is 25
```

The third line of output may not be what you were anticipating. You might expect the second output statement in main() to call the version of larger() with long& parameters. This statement has called the version with double parameters—but why? After all, you *did* cast both arguments to long.

That is exactly where the problem lies. The arguments are not a_int and b_int but temporary locations that contain the same values after conversion to type long. As we explained earlier, the compiler will not use a temporary address to initialize a reference-to-non-const.

So, what *can* you do about this? You have a couple of choices. If a_int and b_int were type long, the compiler will call the version of larger() with parameters of type long&. If the variables can't be type long, you could specify the parameters as references-to-const like this:

```
long larger(const long& a, const long& b);
```

Clearly, you must change the function prototype too. The function works with either const or non-const arguments. The compiler knows that the function won't modify the arguments, so it will call this version for arguments that are temporary values instead of the version with double parameters. Note that you return type long now. If you insist on returning a reference, the return type must be const because the compiler cannot convert from a reference-to-const to a reference-to-non-const.

Overloading and const Parameters

A const parameter is only distinguished from a non-const parameter for references and pointers. For a fundamental type such as int, for example, const int is identical to int. Hence, the following prototypes are not distinguishable:

```
long larger(long a, long b);
long larger(const long a, const long b);
```

The compiler ignores the const attribute of the parameters in the second declaration. This is because the arguments are passed *by value*, meaning that a *copy* of each argument is passed into the function, and thus the original is protected from modification by the function. There is no point to specifying parameters as const in a function prototype when the arguments are passed by value.

Naturally, while it is pointless in a function *prototype*, in a function *definition* it can certainly make sense to declare parameter variables const. You can do this to prevent the function-local *copies* from the arguments from being modified, and you can even do this if some earlier function prototype did not contain the const specifiers. The following is therefore perfectly valid—and even quite sensible:

```
// Function prototype
long larger(long a, long b);                    // const specifiers would be pointless here

/* ... */

// Function definition for the same function we declared earlier as a prototype
long larger(const long a, const long b)      // local a and b variables are contants
{
  return a > b ? a : b;
}
```

Overloading with const Pointer Parameters

Overloaded functions are different if one has a parameter of type type* and the other has a parameter of const type*. The parameters are pointers to different things—so they are different types. For example, these prototypes have different function signatures:

```
long* larger(long* a, long* b);                       // Prototype 1: pointer-to-long parameters
const long* larger(const long* a, const long* b); // Prototype 2: pointer-to-const-long
                                                      // parameters
```

Applying the const modifier to a pointer prevents the value at the address from being modified. Without the const modifier, the value can be modified through the pointer; the pass-by-value mechanism does not inhibit this in any way. In this example, the first function shown earlier is called with these statements:

```
long num1 {1L};
long num2 {2L};
long num3 {*larger(&num1, &num2)};      // Calls larger() that has non-const parameters
```

The latter version of larger() with const parameters is called by the following code:

```
const long num4 {1L};
const long num5 {2L};
const long num6 {*larger(&num4, &num5)};  // Calls larger() that has const parameters
```

The compiler won't pass a pointer-to-const value to a function in which the parameter is a pointer-to-non-const. Allowing a pointer-to-const value to be passed through a pointer-to-non-const pointer would violate the const-ness of the variable. The compiler hence selects the version of larger() with const pointer parameters to compute num6.

Two overloaded functions are *the same*, however, if one of them has a parameter of type "*pointer to type*" and the other has a parameter "const *pointer to* type." Here's an example:

```
long* larger(long* const a, long* const b);                       // Identical to Prototype 1
const long* larger(const long* const a, const long* const b); // Identical to Prototype 2
```

The reason is clear when you consider that the const specifiers after the asterisk (*) of a pointer type make the pointer variables themselves constants. That is, they cannot be reassigned another value. Since a function prototype does not define any code that could be doing such reassignments, it is again pointless to add these const specifiers after the asterisk in a prototype; doing so should again only be considered in a function definition.

Overloading and Reference-to-const Parameters

Reference parameters are more straightforward when it comes to const. Adding const after the ampersand (&), for one, is not allowed. References are already constant by nature, in the sense that they will always keep referring to the same value. And type T& and type const T& are always differentiated, so type const int& is always different from type int&. This means you can overload functions in the manner implied by these prototypes:

```
long& larger(long& a, long& b);
long larger(const long& a, const long& b);
```

Each function will have the same function body, which returns the larger of the two arguments, but the functions behave differently. The first prototype declares a function that doesn't accept constants as arguments, but you can use the function on the left of an assignment to modify one or the other of the reference parameters. The second prototype declares a function that accepts constants and nonconstants as arguments, but the return type is not a reference, so you can't use the function on the left of an assignment.

Overloading and Default Argument Values

You know that you can specify default parameter values for a function. However, default parameter values for overloaded functions can sometimes affect the compiler's ability to distinguish one call from another. For example, suppose you have two versions of a show_error() function that outputs an error message. Here's a version that has a C-style string parameter:

```
void show_error(const char* message)
{
  std::cout << message << std::endl;
}
```

This version accepts a string_view argument:

```
void show_error(string_view message)
{
  std::cout << message << std::endl;
}
```

You should not specify a default argument for both functions because it would create an ambiguity. The statement to output the default message in either case would be as follows:

```
show_error();
```

The compiler has no way of knowing which function is required. Of course, this is a silly example: you have no reason to specify defaults for both functions. A default for just one does everything that you need. However, circumstances can arise where it is not so silly, and overall, you must ensure that all function calls uniquely identify the function that should be called.

Recursion

A function can call itself, and a function that contains a call to itself is referred to as a *recursive function*. Recursion may seem to be a recipe for a loop that executes indefinitely, and if you are not careful, it certainly can be. A prerequisite for avoiding a loop of unlimited duration is that the function must contain some means of stopping the process.

A recursive function call can be indirect. For example, a function fun1() calls another function fun2(), which in turn calls fun1(). In this case, fun1() and fun2() are also called *mutually recursive functions*. We will not see any real examples of mutually recursive functions, though, and restrict ourselves to the easier and far more common case where a single function fun() recursively calls itself.

Recursion can be used in the solution of many different problems. Compilers are sometimes implemented using recursion because language syntax is usually defined in a way that lends itself to recursive analysis. Data that is organized in a tree structure is another example. Figure 8-4 illustrates a tree structure. This shows a tree that contains structures that can be regarded as subtrees. Data that describes a mechanical assembly such as a car is often organized as a tree. A car consists of subassemblies such as the body, the engine, the transmission, and the suspension. Each of these consists of further subassemblies and components until, ultimately, the leaves of the tree are reached, which are all components with no further internal structure.

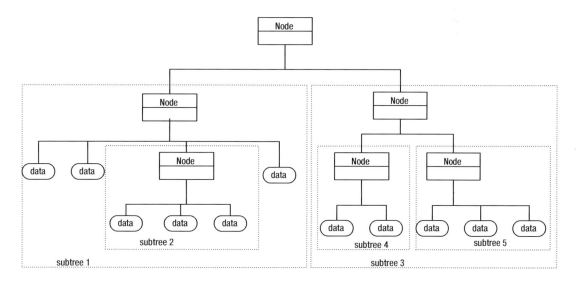

Figure 8-4. *An example of a tree structure*

Data that is organized as a tree can be traversed effectively using recursion. Each branch of a tree can be regarded as a subtree, so a function for accessing the items in a tree can simply call itself when a branch node is encountered. When a data item is encountered, the function does what is required with the item and returns to the calling point. Thus, finding the leaf nodes of the tree—the data items—provides the means by which the function stops the recursive calls of itself.

Basic Examples

There are many things in physics and mathematics that you can think of as involving recursion. A simple example is the factorial of a positive integer n (written as $n!$), which is the number of different ways in which n things can be arranged. For a given positive integer, n, the factorial of n is the product $1 \times 2 \times 3 \times \ldots \times n$. The following recursive function calculates this:

```cpp
long long factorial(int n)
{
  if (n == 1) return 1LL;

  return n * factorial(n - 1);
}
```

If this function is called with an argument value of 4, the return statement that calls the function with a value of 3 in the expression executes. This will execute the return to call the function with an argument of 2, which will call factorial() with an argument of 1. The if expression will be true in this case, so 1 will be returned, which will be multiplied by 2 in the next level up, and so on, until the first call returns the value $4 \times 3 \times 2 \times 1$. This is often the example given to show recursion, but it is an inefficient process. It would certainly be much faster to use a loop.

■ **Caution** Consider for a second what would happen if our factorial() function is called with zero. The first recursive call would be factorial(-1), the next factorial(-2), and so on. That is, n just becomes more and more negative. This will go on for a very long time, most likely up to the point that the program fails. The lesson here is that you must always ensure that recursion eventually reaches the stopping conditions or you risk running into what is called *infinite recursion*, which generally results in a program crash. A correct definition of factorial(), for instance, would therefore be the following:

```cpp
unsigned long long factorial(unsigned int n)    // n < 0 impossible due to unsigned type!
{
  if (n <= 1) return 1;         // 0! is normally defined as 1 as well
  return n * factorial(n - 1);
}
```

Here's another recursive function in a working example—it's a recursive version of the power() function you encountered at the beginning of this chapter:

```cpp
// Ex8_17.cpp
// Recursive version of function for x to the power n, n positive or negative
#include <iostream>
#include <iomanip>

double power(double x, int n);
```

```
int main()
{
  for (int i {-3}; i <= 3; ++i)              // Calculate powers of 8 from -3 to +3
    std::cout << std::setw(10) << power(8.0, i);

  std::cout << std::endl;
}

// Recursive function to calculate x to the power n
double power(double x, int n)
{
  if (n == 0)        return 1.0;
  else if (n > 0)  return x * power(x, n - 1);
  else /* n < 0 */ return 1.0 / power(x, -n);
}
```

The output is as follows:

0.00195313	0.015625	0.125	1	8	64	512

The first line in power() returns 1.0 if n is 0. For positive n, the next line returns the result of the expression x * power(x, n-1). This causes a further call of power() with the index value reduced by 1. If, in this recursive function execution, n is still positive, then power() is called again with n reduced by 1. Each recursive call is recorded in the call stack, along with the arguments and return location. This repeats until n eventually is 0, whereupon 1 is returned and the successive outstanding calls unwind, multiplying by x after each return. For a given value of n greater than 0, the function calls itself n times. For negative powers of x, the reciprocal of xn is calculated using the same process.

With this example, the recursive call process is inefficient compared to a loop. Every function call involves a lot of housekeeping. Implementing the power() function using loops like we did earlier in this chapter makes it execute a lot faster. Essentially, you need to make sure that the depth of recursion necessary to solve a problem is not itself a problem. For instance, if a function calls itself a million times, a large amount of stack memory will be needed to store copies of argument values and the return address for each call. Even up to the point where your runtime runs out of stack memory, the amount of memory allocated for the call stack is generally fixed and limited; surpassing this limit generally causes a fatal crash. In such cases, it is therefore generally better to use a different approach, such as a loop. However, in spite of the overhead, using recursion can often simplify the coding considerably. Sometimes this gain in simplicity can be well worth the loss in efficiency that you get with recursion.

Recursive Algorithms

Recursion is often favored in sorting and merging operations. Sorting data can be a recursive process in which the same algorithm is applied to smaller and smaller subsets of the original data. We can develop an example that uses recursion with a well-known sorting algorithm called *quicksort*. The example will sort a sequence of words. We have chosen this because it demonstrates a lot of different coding techniques and it's sufficiently complicated to tax a few brain cells more than the examples you've seen up to now. The example involves more than 100 lines of code, so we'll show and discuss each of the functions in the book separately and leave you to assemble them into a complete working program. The complete program is available in the code download as Ex8_18.cpp.

The Quicksort Algorithm

Applying the quicksort algorithm to a sequence of words involves choosing an arbitrary word in the sequence and arranging the other words so that all those "less than" the chosen word precede it and all those "greater than" the chosen word follow it. Of course, the words on either side of the chosen word in the sequence will not necessarily be in sequence themselves. Figure 8-5 illustrates this process.

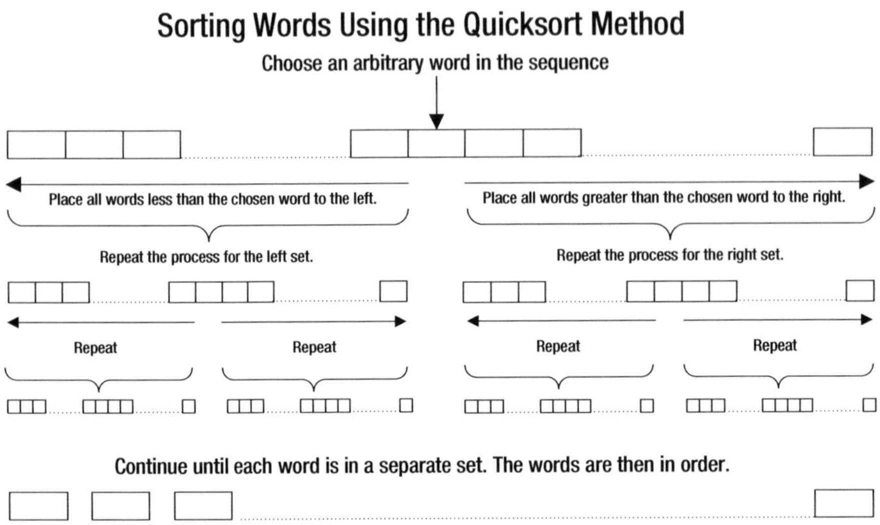

Figure 8-5. *How the quicksort algorithm works*

The same process is repeated for smaller and smaller sets of words until each word is in a separate set. When that is the case, the process ends, and the words are in ascending sequence. Of course, you'll rearrange addresses in the code, not move words around. The address of each word can be stored as a smart pointer to a string object, and the pointers can be stored in a vector container.

The type of a vector of smart pointers to string objects is going to look a bit messy, so it won't help the readability of the code. The following type alias will help to make the code easier to read:

```
using Words = std::vector<std::shared_ptr<std::string>>;
```

The main() Function

The definition of main() will be simple because all the work will be done by other functions. There will be several #include directives and prototypes for the other functions in the application preceding the definition of main():

```
#include <iostream>
#include <iomanip>
#include <memory>
#include <string>
#include <string_view>
#include <vector>
```

```
using Words = std::vector<std::shared_ptr<std::string>>;

void swap(Words& words, size_t first, size_t second);
void sort(Words& words);
void sort(Words& words, size_t start, size_t end);
void extract_words(Words& words, std::string_view text, std::string_view separators);
void show_words(const Words& words);
size_t max_word_length(const Words& words);
```

We think by now you know why all these Standard Library headers are needed. memory is for smart pointer template definitions, and vector contains the templates for vector containers. The type alias will make the code less cluttered.

There are five function prototypes:

- swap() is a helper function that interchanges the elements at indexes first and second in the words vector.

- The overload of sort() with three function parameters will use the quicksort algorithm to sort a contiguous sequence of elements in words from index start to index end inclusive. Indexes specifying a range are needed because the quicksort algorithm involves sorting subsets of a sequence, as you saw earlier.

- The overload of sort() with one single parameter simply calls the one with three parameters (see later); it is there only for your convenience—to allow you to call sort() with a single vector<> argument.

- extract_words() extracts words from text and stores smart pointers to the words in the words vector.

- show_words() outputs the words in words.

- max_word_length() determines the length of the longest word in words and is just to help make the output pretty.

The last two functions have reference-to-const parameters for the words vector because they don't need to change it. The others have regular reference parameters because they do. Here's the code for main():

```
int main()
{
  Words words;
  std::string text;                        // The string to be sorted
  const auto separators{" ,.!?\"\n"};      // Word delimiters

  // Read the string to be searched from the keyboard
  std::cout << "Enter a string terminated by *:" << std::endl;
  getline(std::cin, text, '*');

  extract_words(words, text, separators);
  if (words.empty())
  {
    std::cout << "No words in text." << std::endl;
    return 0;
  }
```

```
  sort(words);                    // Sort the words
  show_words(words);              // Output the words
}
```

The vector of smart pointers is defined using the type alias, Words. The vector will be passed by reference to each function to avoid copying the vector and to allow it to be updated when necessary. Forgetting the & in the type parameter can lead to a mystifying error. If the parameter to a function that changes words is not a reference, then words is passed by value, and the changes will be applied to the copy of words that is created when the function is called. The copy is discarded when the function returns, and the original vector will be unchanged.

The process in main() is straightforward. After reading some text into the string object text, the text is passed to the extract_words() function that stores pointers to the words in words. After a check to verify that words is not empty, sort() is called to sort the contents of words, and show_words() is called to output the words.

The extract_words() Function

You have seen a function similar to this. Here's the code:

```
void extract_words(Words& words, std::string_view text, std::string_view separators)
{
  size_t start {text.find_first_not_of(separators)};    // Start 1st word
  size_t end {};                                         // Index for the end of a word

  while (start != std::string_view::npos)
  {
    end = text.find_first_of(separators, start + 1);     // Find end separator
    if (end == std::string_view::npos)                   // End of text?
      end = text.length();                               // Yes, so set to last+1
    words.push_back(std::make_shared<std::string>(text.substr(start, end - start)));
    start = text.find_first_not_of(separators, end + 1); // Find next word
  }
}
```

The last two parameters are string_views because the function won't change the arguments corresponding to them. The separators object could conceivably be defined as a static variable within the function, but passing it as an argument makes the function more flexible. The process is essentially the same as you have seen previously. Each substring that represents a word is passed to the make_shared() function that is defined in the memory header. The substring is used by make_shared() to create a string object in the free store along with a smart pointer to it. The smart pointer that make_shared() returns is passed to the push_back() function for the words vector to append it as a new element in the sequence.

The swap() Function

There'll be a need to swap pairs of addresses in the vector in several places, so it's a good idea to define a helper function to do this:

```
void swap(Words& words, size_t first, size_t second)
{
  auto temp{words[first]};
```

```
    words[first] = words[second];
    words[second] = temp;
}
```

This just swaps the addresses in words at indexes first and second.

The sort() Functions

You can use swap() in the implementation of the quicksort method because it involves rearranging the elements in the vector. The code for the sorting algorithm looks like this:

```
void sort(Words& words, size_t start, size_t end)
{
  // start index must be less than end index for 2 or more elements
  if (!(start < end))
    return;

  // Choose middle address to partition set
  swap(words, start, (start + end) / 2);          // Swap middle address with start

  // Check words against chosen word
  size_t current {start};
  for (size_t i {start + 1}; i <= end; i++)
  {
    if (*words[i] < *words[start])                // Is word less than chosen word?
      swap(words, ++current, i);                  // Yes, so swap to the left
  }

  swap(words, start, current);                    // Swap chosen and last swapped words

  if (current > start) sort(words, start, current - 1);  // Sort left subset if exists
  if (end > current + 1) sort(words, current + 1, end);  // Sort right subset if exists
}
```

The parameters are the vector of addresses and the index positions of the first and last addresses in the subset to be sorted. The first time the function is called, start will be 0, and end will be the index of the last element. In subsequent recursive calls, a subsequence of the vector elements is to be sorted, so start and/or end will be interior index positions in many cases.

The steps in the sort() function code are as follows:

1. The check for start not being less than end stops the recursive function calls. If there's one element in a set, the function returns. In each execution of sort(), the current sequence is partitioned into two smaller sequences in the last two statements that call sort() recursively, so eventually you must end up with a sequence that has only one element.

2. After the initial check, an address in the middle of the sequence is chosen arbitrarily as the pivot element for the sort. This is swapped with the address at index start, just to get it out of the way. You could also put it at the end of the sequence.

3. The for loop compares the chosen word with the words pointed to by elements following start. If a word is *less* than the chosen word, its address is swapped into a position following start: the first into start+1, the second into start+2, and so on. The effect of this process is to position all the words less than the chosen word before all the words that are greater than or equal to it. When the loop ends, current contains the index of the address of the last word found to be less than the chosen word. The address of the chosen word at start is swapped with the address at current, so the addresses of words less than the chosen word are now to the left of current, and the addresses of words that are greater or equal are to the right.

4. The last step sorts the subsets on either side of current by calling sort() for each subset. The indexes of words less than the chosen word run from start to current-1, and the indexes of those greater run from current+1 to end.

With recursion, the code for the sort is relatively easy to follow. And that's not all; if you'd try to implement quicksort without recursion, meaning using just loops, you'd notice that this is not only much harder but also that you need to keep track of a stack of sorts of your own. Consequently, it is quite challenging to be faster with a loop than with recursion for quicksort. So, recursion not only makes for very natural, elegant algorithms, but their performance can be close enough to optimal for many uses as well.

A slight downside of this recursive sort() function is that it requires three arguments; it's slightly unfortunate that sorting a vector requires you to decipher what to pass as second and third arguments. We therefore provide a more convenient single-parameter sort() function you can call instead:

```
// Sort strings in ascending sequence
void sort(Words& words)
{
  if (!words.empty())
    sort(words, 0, words.size() - 1);
}
```

This is actually a fairly common pattern. To get the recursion going, you provide a nonrecursive helper function. Often the recursive function is then not even exposed to the user (you'll learn later to encapsulate or locally define functions).

Mind also the check for empty inputs. Any idea what would happen for empty inputs should you omit it? Precisely. Subtracting one from an unsigned size_t value equal to zero would result in a huge number (see, for instance, Chapter 5 for a complete explanation), which in this case would result in the recursive sort() function accessing the vector<> with indices that are massively out of bounds. And the latter, in turn, would of course almost certainly result in a crash!

The max_word_length() Function

This is a helper function that is used by the show_words() function:

```
size_t max_word_length(const Words& words)
{
  size_t max {};
  for (auto& pword : words)
    if (max < pword->length()) max = pword->length();
  return max;
}
```

This steps through the words that the vector elements point to and finds and returns the length of the longest word. You could put the code in the body of this function directly in the show_words() function. However, code is easier to follow if you break it into small, well-defined chunks. The operation that this function performs is self-contained and makes a sensible unit for a separate function.

The show_words() Function

This function outputs the words pointed to by the vector elements. It's quite long because it lists all words beginning with the same letter on the same line, with up to ten words per line. Here's the code:

```
void show_words(const Words& words)
{
  const size_t field_width {max_word_length(words) + 1};
  const size_t words_per_line {8};
  std::cout << std::left << std::setw(field_width) << *words[0]; // Output the first word

  size_t words_in_line {};                                  // Words in current line
  for (size_t i {1}; i < words.size(); ++i)
  { // Output newline when initial letter changes or after 8 per line
    if ((*words[i])[0] != (*words[i - 1])[0] || ++words_in_line == words_per_line)
    {
      words_in_line = 0;
      std::cout << std::endl;
    }
    std::cout << std::setw(field_width) << *words[i];        // Output a word
  }
  std::cout << std::endl;
}
```

The field_width variable is initialized to two more than the number of characters in the longest word. The variable is used for the field width for each word, so they will be aligned neatly in columns. There's also words_per_line, which is the maximum number of words on a line. The first word is output before the for loop. This is because the loop compares the initial character in the current word with that of the previous word to decide whether it should be on a new line. Outputting the first word separately ensures we have a previous word at the start. The std::left manipulator that is defined in the iostream header causes data to be left aligned in the output field. There's a complementary std::right manipulator. The rest of the words are output within the for loop. This outputs a newline character when eight words have been written on a line or when a word with an initial letter that is different from the preceding word is encountered.

If you assemble the functions into a complete program, you'll have a good-sized example of a program split into several functions. Here's an example of the output:

```
Enter a string terminated by *:
It was the best of times, it was the worst of times, it was the age of wisdom, it was the
age of foolishness, it was the epoch of belief, it was the epoch of incredulity, it was the
season of Light, it was the season of Darkness, it was the spring of hope, it was the winter
of despair, we had everything before us, we had nothing before us, we were all going direct
to Heaven, we were all going direct the other way—in short, the period was so far like the
present period, that some of its noisiest authorities insisted on its being received, for
good or for evil, in the superlative degree of comparison only.*
Darkness
Heaven
```

313

It							
Light							
age	age	all	all	authorities			
before	before	being	belief	best			
comparison							
degree	despair	direct	direct				
epoch	epoch	everything	evil				
far	foolishness	for	for				
going	going	good					
had	had	hope					
in	incredulity	insisted	it	it	it	it	it
it	it	it	it	its	its		
like							
noisiest	nothing						
of	of	of	of	of	of	of	of
of	of	of	of	on	only	or	other
period	period	present					
received							
season	season	short	so	some	spring	superlative	
that	the	the	the	the	the	the	the
the	the	the	the	the	the	the	times
times	to						
us	us						
was	was	was	was	was	was	was	was
was	was	was	way-in	we	we	we	we
were	were	winter	wisdom	worst			

Of course, words beginning with an uppercase letter precede all words beginning with lowercase letters.

Summary

This marathon chapter introduced you to writing and using functions. This isn't everything relating to functions, though. The next chapter covers function templates, and you'll see even more about functions in the context of user-defined types starting in Chapter 11. The following are the important bits that you should take away from this chapter:

- Functions are self-contained compact units of code with a well-defined purpose. A well-written program consists of a large number of small functions, not a small number of large functions.

- A function definition consists of the function header that specifies the function name, the parameters, and the return type, followed by the function body containing the executable code for the function.

- A function prototype enables the compiler to process calls to a function even though the function definition has not been processed.

- The pass-by-value mechanism for arguments to a function passes copies of the original argument values, so the original argument values are not accessible from within the function.

- Passing a pointer to a function allows the function to change the value that is pointed to, even though the pointer itself is passed by value.

- Declaring a pointer parameter as `const` prevents modification of the original value.

- You can pass the address of an array to a function as a pointer. If you do, you should generally pass the array's length along as well.

- Specifying a function parameter as a reference avoids the copying that is implicit in the pass-by-value mechanism. A reference parameter that is not modified within a function should be specified as `const`.

- Input parameters should be reference-to-`const`, except for smaller values such as those of fundamental types. Returning values is preferred over output parameters, except for very large values such as `std::array<>`.

- Specifying default values for function parameters allows arguments to be optionally omitted.

- Default values can be combined with `std::optional<>` to make signatures more self-documenting. `std::optional<>` can be used for optional return values as well.

- Returning a reference from a function allows the function to be used on the left of an assignment operator. Specifying the return type as a reference-to-`const` prevents this.

- The signature of a function is defined by the function name together with the number and types of its parameters.

- Overloaded functions are functions with the same name but with different signatures and therefore different parameter lists. Overloaded functions cannot be differentiated by the return type.

- A recursive function is a function that calls itself. Implementing an algorithm recursively can result in elegant and concise code. Sometimes, but certainly not always, this is at the expense of execution time when compared to other methods of implementing the same algorithm.

EXERCISES

These exercises enable you to try some of what you've learned in this chapter. If you get stuck, look back over the chapter for help. If you're still stuck, you can download the solutions from the Apress website (`www.apress.com/source-code`), but that really should be a last resort.

Exercise 8-1. Write a function, `validate_input()`, that accepts two integer arguments that represent the upper and lower limits for an integer that is to be entered. It should accept a third argument that is a string describing the input, with the string being used in the prompt for input to be entered. The function should prompt for input of the value within the range specified by the first two arguments and include the string identifying the type of value to be entered. The function should check the input and continue to prompt for input until the value entered by the user is valid. Use the `validate_input()` function in a program that obtains a user's date of birth and outputs it in the form of this example:

```
November 21, 2012
```

The program should be implemented so that separate functions, month(), year(), and day(), manage the input of the corresponding numerical values. Don't forget leap years—February 29, 2017, is not allowed!

Exercise 8-2. Write a function that reads a string or array of characters as input and reverses it. Justify your choice of parameter type? Provide a main() function to test your function that prompts for a string of characters, reverses them, and outputs the reversed string.

Exercise 8-3. Write a program that accepts from two to four command-line arguments. If it is called with less than two or more than four arguments, output a message telling the user what they should do and then exit. If the number of arguments is correct, output them, each on a separate line.

Exercise 8-4. Create a function, plus(), that adds two values and returns their sum. Provide overloaded versions to work with int, double, and strings, and test that they work with the following calls:

```
const int n {plus(3, 4)};
const double d {plus(3.2, 4.2)};
const string s {plus("he", "llo")};
const string s1 {"aaa"};
const string s2 {"bbb"};
const string s3 {plus(s1, s2)};
```

Can you explain why the following doesn't work?

```
const auto d {plus(3, 4.2)};
```

Exercise 8-5. Define a function that checks whether a given number is prime. Your primal check does not have to be efficient; any algorithm you can think of will do. In case you have forgotten, a prime number is a natural number strictly greater than 1 and with no positive divisors other than 1 and itself. Write another function that generates a vector<> with all natural numbers less or equal to a first number and starting from another. By default it should start from 1. Create a third function that given a vector<> of numbers outputs another vector<> containing all the prime numbers it found in its input. Use these three functions to create a program that prints out all prime numbers less or equal to a number chosen by the user (print, for instance, 15 primes per line). Note: In principle, you do not need any vectors to print these prime numbers; obviously, these extra functions have been added for the sake of the exercise.

Exercise 8-6. Implement a program that queries the user for a number of grades. A grade is an integer number between 0 and 100 (both inclusive). The user can stop at any time by entering a negative number. Once all grades have been collected, your program is to output the following statistics: the five highest grades, the five lowest grades, the average grade, the median grade, and the standard deviation and variance of the grades. Of course, you're to write a separate function to compute each of these statistics. Also, you must write the code to print five values only once. To practice, use arrays to store any five extremes and not, for instance, vectors.

Hint: As a preprocessing step, you should first sort the grades the user enters; you'll see that this will make writing the functions to compute the statistics much easier. You can adapt the quicksort algorithm from `Ex8_18` to work with grade numbers.

Caution: Make sure to do something sensible if the user enters less than five or even zero grades. Anything is fine, as long as it does not crash. Perhaps you can practice `std::optional<>` to deal with inputs such as an empty series of grades?

Note: The median is the value that appears in the middle position of a sorted list. If there is an even number of grades, there obviously is no single middle value—the median is then defined as the mean of the two middle values. The formulas to compute mean (μ) and standard deviation (σ) of a series of n grades xi are as follows:

$$\mu = \frac{1}{n}\sum_{i=0}^{n-1} x_i \qquad \sigma = \sqrt{\frac{1}{n}\sum_{i=0}^{n-1}\left(x_i - \mu\right)^2}$$

The variance is then defined as σ^2. The `cmath` header of the Standard Library defines `std::sqrt()` to compute square roots.

Exercise 8-7. The so-called Fibonacci function is popular among lecturers in computer science and mathematics for introducing recursion. This function has to compute the nth number from the famous Fibonacci sequence, named after Italian mathematician Leonardo of Pisa, known also as Fibonacci. This sequence of positive integer numbers is characterized by the fact that every number after the first two is the sum of the two preceding ones. For n ≥ 1, the sequence is defined as follows:

1, 1, 2, 3, 5, 8, 13, 21, 34, 55, 89, 144, 233, 377, 610, 987, 1597, 2584, 4181...

For convenience, computer scientists mostly define an additional zeroth Fibonacci number as zero. Write a function to compute the nth Fibonacci number recursively. Test it with a simple program that prompts the user for how many numbers should be computed and then prints them out one by one, each on a different line.

Extra: While the naive recursive version of the Fibonacci function is very elegant—the code matches nearly verbatim with common mathematical definitions—it is notorious for being very slow. If you ask the computer to compute, say, 100 Fibonacci numbers, you'll notice that it becomes noticeably slower and slower as n becomes larger. Do you think you can rewrite the function to use a loop instead of recursion? How many numbers can you correctly compute now?

Hint: In each iteration of the loop, you'll naturally want to compute a next number. To do this, all you need are the previous two numbers. So, there should be no need to keep track of the full sequence in, for instance, a `vector<>`.

Exercise 8-8. If written using a more mathematical notation, the `power()` functions we wrote in `Ex8_01` and especially `Ex8_17` both essentially compute a `power(x,n)` for n > 0, as follows:

```
power(x,n) = x * power(x,n-1)
           = x * (x * power(x,n-2))
           = ...
           = x * (x * (x * ... (x * x)...)))
```

Clearly, this method requires exactly n-1 multiplications. It may surprise you, but there is another, much more effective way. Suppose n is even; then you know the following:

```
power(x,n) = power(x,n/2) * power(x,n/2)
```

As both operands of this multiplication are identical, you need to compute this value only once. That is, you have just reduced the computation of power(x,n) to that of power(x,n/2), which obviously at most requires half as many multiplications. Moreover, because you can now apply this formula recursively, you'll need even far fewer multiplications than that—only something in the order of $\log_2(n)$ to be exact. To give you an idea, this means that for n in the order of 1000, you only need in the order of 10 multiplications! Can you apply this idea to create a more efficient recursive version of power()? You can start from the program in Ex8_17.cpp.

Note: This principle is something you'll often see in recursive algorithms. In each recursive call, you reduce a problem to a problem of half the size. If you think back, you'll realize that we applied the same principle in the quicksort algorithm as well, for instance. Because this solution strategy is that common, it also has a name; it's called *divide and conquer*, after the famous phrase of Julius Caesar.

Exercise 8-9. Modify the solution of Exercise 8-8 such that it counts the number of times the call power(1.5,1000) performs a multiplication. Do so by replacing each multiplication with a helper function mult() that takes two arguments, prints a message of how many multiplications have been performed thus far, and then simply returns the product of both arguments. Use at least one static variable.

CHAPTER 9

▨ ▨ ▨

Function Templates

In the section on overloading in the previous chapter, you may have noticed that some of the overloaded functions consisted of exactly the same code. The only difference is the types that appear in the parameter list. It seems an unnecessary overhead to have to write the same code over and over, and indeed it is. In such situations, you can write the code just once, as a *function template*. The Standard Library, for instance, makes heavy use of this feature to ensure that its functions work optimally with any type, including your own custom types, which of course it cannot know about in advance. This chapter introduces the basics of defining your own function templates that work with any type you desire.

In this chapter, you will learn:

- How to define parameterized function templates that generate a family of related functions

- That parameters to function templates are mostly, but not always, types

- That template arguments are mostly deduced by the compiler and how to specify them explicitly when necessary

- How to specialize and overload function templates if the generic function definition provided by the template isn't suited for certain types

- Why return type deduction is really powerful in combination with templates

- What the decltype keyword does

Function Templates

A *function template* itself it is not a definition of a function; it is a blueprint or a recipe for defining an entire family of functions. A function template is a parametric function definition, where a particular function instance is created by one or more parameter values. The compiler uses a function template to generate a function definition when necessary. If it is never necessary, no code results from the template. A function definition that is generated from a template is an *instance* or an instantiation of the template. The parameters of a function template are usually data types, where an instance can be generated for a parameter value of type int, for example, and another with a parameter value of type string. But parameters are not necessarily types. They can be other things such as a dimension, for example. Let's consider a specific example.

In the previous chapter, we defined various overloads of larger(), often for different parameter types. It makes for a good candidate for a template. Figure 9-1 shows a template for this function.

© Ivor Horton and Peter Van Weert 2018
I. Horton and P. Van Weert, *Beginning C++17*, https://doi.org/10.1007/978-1-4842-3366-5_9

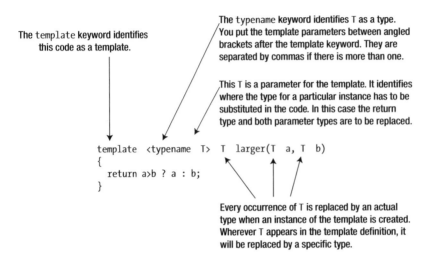

Figure 9-1. A simple function template

The function template starts with the template keyword to identify it as such. This is followed by a pair of angled brackets that contains a list of one or more *template parameters*. In this case, there's only one, the parameter T. T is commonly used as a name for a parameter because most parameters are types, but you can use whatever name you like for a parameter; names such as my_type or Comparable are equally valid. Especially if there are multiple parameters, using more descriptive names may be recommended.

The typename keyword identifies that T is a type. T is hence called a *template type parameter*. You can also use the keyword class here, but we prefer typename because the type argument can be a fundamental type as well, not just a class type.

The rest of the definition is similar to a normal function except that the parameter name T is sprinkled around. The compiler creates an instance of the template by replacing T throughout the definition with a specific type. The type assigned to a type parameter T during instantiation is called a *template type argument*.

You can position the template in a source file in the same way as a normal function definition; you can also specify a prototype for a function template. In this case, it would be as follows:

```
template<typename T> T larger(T a, T b);     // Prototype for function template
```

Either the prototype or the definition of the template must appear in the source file before any statement that results in an instance of the template.

Creating Instances of a Function Template

The compiler creates instances of the template from any statement that uses the larger() function. Here's an example:

```
std::cout << "Larger of 1.5 and 2.5 is " << larger(1.5, 2.5) << std::endl;
```

You just use the function in the normal way. You don't need to specify a value for the template parameter T. The compiler deduces the type that is to replace T from the arguments in the larger() function call. This mechanism is referred to as *template argument deduction*. The arguments to larger() are literals of type double, so this call causes the compiler to search for an existing definition of larger() with double parameters. If it doesn't find one, the compiler creates this version of larger() from the template by substituting double for T in the template definition.

The resulting function definition accepts arguments of type double and returns a double value. With double plugged into the template in place of T, the template instance will effectively be as follows:

```
double larger(double a, double b)
{
  return a > b ? a : b;
}
```

The compiler makes sure to generate each template instance only once. If a subsequent function call requires the same instance, then it calls the instance that exists. Your program only ever includes a single copy of the definition of each instance, even if the same instance is generated in different source files. Now that you are familiar with the concepts, let's road test a function template:

```
// Ex9_01.cpp
// Using a function template
#include <iostream>
#include <string>

template<typename T> T larger(T a, T b);     // Function template prototype

int main()
{
  std::cout << "Larger of 1.5 and 2.5 is " << larger(1.5, 2.5) << std::endl;
  std::cout << "Larger of 3.5 and 4.5 is " << larger(3.5, 4.5) << std::endl;

  int big_int {17011983}, small_int {10};
  std::cout << "Larger of " << big_int << " and " << small_int << " is "
            << larger(big_int, small_int) << std::endl;

  std::string a_string {"A"}, z_string {"Z"};
  std::cout << "Larger of \"" << a_string << "\" and \"" << z_string << "\" is "
            << '"' << larger(a_string, z_string) << '"' << std::endl;
}

// Template for functions to return the larger of two values
template <typename T>
T larger(T a, T b)
{
    return a > b ? a : b;
}
```

This produces the following output:

```
Larger of 1.5 and 2.5 is 2.5
Larger of 3.5 and 4.5 is 4.5
Larger of 17011983 and 10 is 17011983
Larger of "A" and "Z" is "Z"
```

The compiler creates a definition of larger() that accepts arguments of type double as a result of the first statement in main(). The same instance will be called in the next statement. The third statement requires a version of larger() that accepts an argument of type int, so a new template instance is created. The last statement results in yet another template instance being created that has parameters of type std::string and returns a value of type std::string.

Template Type Parameters

The name of a template type parameter can be used anywhere in the template's function signature, return type, and body. It is a placeholder for a type and can thus be put in any context you would normally put the concrete type. That is, suppose T is a template parameter name; then you can use T to construct derived types such as T&, const T&, T*, and T[][3]. Or you can use T as an argument to a class template, as for instance in std::vector<T>.

Our larger() function template, for instance, currently instantiates functions that accept their arguments by value:

```
template <typename T>
T larger(T a, T b)
{
    return a > b ? a : b;
}
```

As witnessed by Ex9_01, this template can be instantiated with class types such as std::string as well. In the previous chapter, you learned that passing objects by value results in gratuitous copies of these objects, which is something you should avoid if possible. The standard mechanism for this, of course, is to pass the arguments by reference instead. We would therefore be better off redefining our template as follows:

```
template <typename T>
const T& larger(const T& a, const T& b)
{
    return a > b ? a : b;
}
```

■ **Note**   The algorithm header of the Standard Library defines a std::max() function template that is completely analogous. It takes two arguments by reference-to-const and returns a reference-to-const that refers to the largest of the two function arguments. The same header also defines the std::min() template, which of course instantiates functions that determine the smallest of two values.

While our latest definition of the larger() template is definitely superior, in the remainder of this chapter we'll mostly keep using the version that passes the arguments by value. This makes it easier to explain a few additional aspects of function templates.

Explicit Template Arguments

If you add the following statement to `main()` in `Ex9_01.cpp`, it will not compile:

```
std::cout << "Larger of " << small_int << " and 19.6 is "
          << larger(small_int, 19.6) << std::endl;
```

The arguments to `larger()` are of different types, whereas the parameters for `larger()` in the template are of the same type. The compiler cannot create a template instance that has different parameter types. Obviously, one argument could be converted to the type of the other, but you have to code this explicitly; the compiler won't do it. You could define the template to allow the parameters for `larger()` to be different types, but this adds a complication that we'll discuss later in this chapter: which of the two do you use for the return type? For now, let's focus on how you can specify the argument for a template parameter explicitly when you call the function. This allows you to control which version of the function is used. The compiler no longer deduces the type to replace T; it accepts what you specify.

You can resolve the problem of using different arguments types with `larger()` with an explicit instantiation of the template:

```
std::cout << "Larger of " << small_int << " and 19.6 is "
          << larger<double>(small_int, 19.6) << std::endl;    // Outputs 19.6
```

You put the explicit type argument for the function template between angled brackets after the function name. This generates an instance with T as type `double`. When you use explicit template arguments, the compiler has complete faith that you know what you are doing. It will insert an implicit type conversion for the first argument to type `double`. It will provide implicit conversions, even when this may not be what you want. Here's an example:

```
std::cout << "Larger of " << small_int << " and 19.6 is "
          << larger<int>(small_int, 19.6) << std::endl;    // Outputs 19
```

You are telling the compiler to use a template instance with T as type `int`. This necessitates an implicit conversion of the second argument to `int`. The result of this conversion is the value 19, which may not be what you really want in this case. If you're lucky, your compiler will warn you about such dangerous conversions, though not all compilers will.

Function Template Specialization

Suppose that you extended `Ex9_01.cpp` to call `larger()` with arguments that are pointers:

```
std::cout << "Larger of " << big_int << " and " << small_int << " is "
          << *larger(&big_int, &small_int) << std::endl;        // Output may be 10!
```

The compiler instantiates the template with the parameter as type `int*`. The prototype of this instance is as follows:

```
int* larger(int*, int*);
```

The return value is an address, and you have to dereference it to output the value. However, the result may very well be 10, which is incorrect. This is because the comparison is between addresses passed as arguments, not the values at those addresses. The compiler is free to rearrange the memory locations of local variables, so the actual outcome may vary across compilers, but given that the small_int variable comes second, it is certainly not unthinkable that its address would be larger. This illustrates how easy it is to create hidden errors using templates. You need to be particularly careful when using pointer types as template arguments.

▓ **Note** If for your compiler the output of the previous snippet is not 10, you can try to rearrange the order in which big_int and small_int are declared. Surely the comparison of two integer values should not depend on their declaration order?

You can define a *specialization* of the template to accommodate a template argument that is a pointer type. For a specific parameter value or set of values in the case of a template with multiple parameters, a template specialization defines a behavior that is different from the standard template. The definition of a template specialization must come after a declaration or definition of the original template. If you put a specialization first, then the program won't compile. The specialization must also appear before its first use.

The definition of a specialization starts with the template keyword, but the parameter is omitted, so the angled brackets following the keyword are empty. You must still define the type of argument for the specialization, and you place this between angled brackets immediately following the template function name. The definition for a specialization of larger() for type int* is as follows:

```
template <>
int* larger<int*>(int* a, int* b)
{
  return *a > *b ? a : b;
}
```

The only change to the body of the function is to dereference the arguments a and b so that you compare values rather than addresses. To use this in Ex9_01.cpp, the specialization would need to be placed after the prototype for the template and before main().

Function Templates and Overloading

You can overload a function template by defining other functions with the same name. Thus, you can define "overrides" for specific cases, which will always be used by the compiler in preference to a template instance. As always, each overloaded function must have a unique signature.

Let's reconsider the previous situation in which you need to overload the larger() function to take pointer arguments. Instead of using a template specialization for larger(), you could define an overloaded function. The following overloaded function prototype would do it:

```
int* larger(int* a, int* b);          // Function overloading the larger template
```

In place of the specialization definition, you'd use this function definition:

```
int* larger(int* a, int* b)
{
  return *a > *b ? a : b;
}
```

It's also possible to overload an existing template with another template. For example, you could define a template that overloads the `larger()` template in Ex9_01.cpp to find the largest value contained in an array:

```
template <typename T>
T larger(const T data[], size_t count)
{
  T result {data[0]};
  for (size_t i {1}; i < count; ++i)
    if (data[i] > result) result = data[i];

  return result;
}
```

The parameter list differentiates functions produced from this template from instances of the original template. You could define another template overload for vectors:

```
template <typename T>
T larger(const std::vector<T>& data)
{
  T result {data[0]};
  for (auto& value : data)
    if (value > result) result = value;

  return result;
}
```

▓ **Note**   Our latest two overloads of `larger<>()` work correctly only if there is at least one element in the input data. Bad things are bound to happen if they are called with an empty array or `vector<>`—do you see why? As an optional exercise, can you perhaps come up with a way to reformulate these functions such that they can cope with empty inputs as well? We do stress, though, that this is an *optional* exercise.

In fact, and this is a bit more subtle, you could even overload the original template with another template specifically for pointer types:

```
template<typename T>
T* larger(T* a, T* b)
{
  return *a > *b ? a : b;
}
```

Note that this is *not* a specialization of the original template but instead a second, distinct template that will be instantiated only for pointer types. You do not need to know the details of exactly why and how this works. It suffices to know that if the compiler encounters a call `larger(x,y)` where x and y are pointers to values of the same type, it will instantiate an instance of this second function template; otherwise, it will still use an appropriate instance from our previous template.

You could extend Ex9_01.cpp to demonstrate this. Add the previous templates to the end of the source file and these prototypes at the beginning:

```
template <typename T> T larger(const T data[], size_t count);
template <typename T> T larger(const std::vector<T>& data);
template <typename T> T* larger(T*, T*);
```

Naturally, you'll also need an #include directive for the vector header. The code in main() can be changed to the following:

```
int big_int {17011983}, small_int {10};
std::cout << "Larger of " << big_int << " and " << small_int << " is "
          << larger(big_int, small_int) << std::endl;
std::cout << "Larger of " << big_int << " and " << small_int << " is "
          << *larger(&big_int, &small_int) << std::endl;

const char text[] {"A nod is as good as a wink to a blind horse."};
std::cout << "Largest character in \"" << text << "\" is '"
          << larger(text, std::size(text)) << "'" << std::endl;

std::vector<std::string> words {"The", "higher", "the", "fewer"};
std::cout << "The largest word in words is \"" << larger(words)
          << '"' << std::endl;

std::vector<double> data {-1.4, 7.3, -100.0, 54.1, 16.3};
std::cout << "The largest value in data is " << larger(data) << std::endl;
```

The complete example is in the code download as Ex9_02.cpp. This generates instances of all three overloaded templates. If you compile and execute it, the output will be as follows:

```
Larger of 17011983 and 10 is 17011983
Larger of 17011983 and 10 is 17011983
Largest character in "A nod is as good as a wink to a blind horse." is 'w'
The largest word in words is "the"
The largest value in data is 54.1
```

Function Templates with Multiple Parameters

You've been using function templates with a single parameter, but there can be several parameters. Recall from earlier that we had some trouble compiling the following:

```
std::cout << "Larger of " << small_int << " and 9.6 is "
          << larger(small_int, 9.6) << std::endl;
```

The compiler failed to deduce the template type argument because the two function arguments have a different type: int and double, respectively. We solved this before by explicitly specifying the type. But perhaps you were wondering why we could not simply create a larger() template for which the function arguments are allowed to be different? This could then look something like this:

```
template <typename T1, typename T2>
??? larger(T1 a, T2 b)
{
  return a > b ? a : b;
}
```

Allowing different types for each function argument is easy enough and can often be a good idea to keep your templates as generic as possible. However, in cases such as this, you run into trouble when specifying the return type. That is, in the previous pseudocode, what should we put instead of the three question marks? T1? T2? Neither is correct in general because both could lead to undesired conversions.

A first possible solution is to add an extra template type argument to provide a way of controlling the return type. Here's an example:

```
template <typename TReturn, typename TArg1, typename TArg2>
TReturn larger(TArg1 a, TArg2 b)
{
  return a > b ? a : b;
}
```

The compiler, however, cannot deduce this return type, TReturn. Template argument deduction works on the basis of the arguments passed in the function's argument list alone. You must therefore always specify the TReturn template argument yourself. The compiler can deduce the type for the arguments, though, so you can get away with specifying just the return type. In general, if you specify fewer template arguments than the number of template parameters, the compiler will deduce the others. The following three lines are therefore equivalent:

```
std::cout << "Larger of 1.5 and 2 is " << larger<size_t>(1.5, 2) << std::endl;
std::cout << "Larger of 1.5 and 2 is " << larger<size_t, double>(1.5, 2) << std::endl;
std::cout << "Larger of 1.5 and 2 is " << larger<size_t, double, int>(1.5, 2) << std::endl;
```

Clearly, the sequence of parameters in the template definition is important here. If you had the return type as the second parameter, you'd always have to specify both parameters in a call. If you specify only one parameter, it would be interpreted as the argument type, leaving the return type undefined. Because we specified the return type as size_t, in all three cases, the results of these function calls will all be 2. The compiler creates a function that accepts arguments of type double and int and then converts its result to a value of type size_t.

While we did illustrate how multiple parameters can be defined and what that means for template argument deduction, you may have noticed that we still haven't found a satisfactory solution that would allow us to write the following:

```
std::cout << "Larger of " << small_int << " and 9.6 is "
          << larger(small_int, 9.6) << std::endl;
```

We'll resolve this once and for all in the next section.

Return Type Deduction for Templates

In the previous chapter, you learned about automatic return type deduction for functions. For regular functions, the use of return type deduction was somewhat limited. While it may save you some typing, it does come with the risk of making your code less obvious to read. After all, the reader needs to make the same deduction as the compiler.

In the context of function templates, however, return type deduction can be a godsend. The return type of a template function with one or more type parameters may depend on the types used to instantiate the template. We have seen this already with the following example:

```
template <typename T1, typename T2>
??? larger(T1 a, T2 b)
{
  return a > b ? a : b;
}
```

There is no easy way you can specify which type should be returned here. But there is an easy way to have the compiler deduce it for you after instantiating the template:

```
template <typename T1, typename T2>
auto larger(T1 a, T2 b)
{
  return a > b ? a : b;
}
```

With this definition, the following statements will compile just fine, without the need to explicitly specify any type argument:

```
int small_int {10};
std::cout << "Larger of " << small_int << " and 9.6 is "
        << larger(small_int, 9.6) << std::endl;         // deduced return type: double

std::string a_string {"A"};
std::cout << "Larger of \"" << a_string << "\" and \"Z\" is \""
        << larger(a_string, "Z") << '"' << std::endl;    // deduced return type:
std::string
```

With our original definition of larger() in Ex9_01, which had only one type parameter, both of these instantiations would've been ambiguous and thus would've failed to compile. A working program using the two-parameter version is found in Ex9_03.cpp.

decltype() and Trailing Return Types

Function return type deduction was only introduced recently—in C++14 to be exact. Before, template writers had to resort to other means when a function template's return type is that of an expression that depends on one or more template type arguments. In our running example, the larger() template, this expression is the expression a > b ? a : b. So, without return type deduction, how could you derive a type from an expression, and how could you use this in a function template specification?

The `decltype` keyword provides the solution, at least in part. `decltype(expression)` produces the type of the result of evaluating `expression`. You could use this to rewrite the `larger()` template as follows:

```
template <typename T1, typename T2>
decltype(a > b ? a : b) larger(T1 a, T2 b)    // Won't compile yet!
{
  return a > b ? a : b;
}
```

The return type is now specified to be the type of the value produced by the expression in the function body. This template definition expresses what you want, but it won't compile. The compiler processes the template from left to right. So, when the return type specification is processed, the compiler does not know the types of a and b. To overcome this, the *trailing return type* syntax was introduced that permits the return type specification to appear after the parameter list, like this:

```
template <typename T1, typename T2>
auto larger(T1 a, T2 b) -> decltype(a > b ? a : b)
{
  return a > b ? a : b;
}
```

As you can see, putting the `auto` keyword before the function name does not always say to the compiler that the return type needs to be deduced. Instead, it may also indicate that the return type specification will come at the end of the function header. You write this trailing return type following the arrow, `->`, after the parameter list.

In the context of templates, the `decltype()` specifier is not only useful in trailing return types, where its use has mostly been superseded by return type deduction. Suppose you need a template function to generate the sum of the products of corresponding elements in two vectors of the same size. Then you can define the template like this (using the `std::min()` template defined in `<algorithm>`):

```
template<typename T1, typename T2>
auto vector_product(const std::vector<T1>& data1, const std::vector<T2>&  data2)
{
  // safeguard against vectors of different sizes
  const auto count = std::min(data1.size(), data2.size());

  decltype(data1[0]*data2[0]) sum {};
  for (size_t i {}; i < count; ++i)
    sum += data1[i] * data2[i];

  return sum;
}
```

Without `decltype()`, you would have a hard time specifying a proper type for the `sum` variable, especially if you also want to support empty vectors. Note that `decltype()` never actually evaluates the expression it is applied to. The expression is only a hypothetical, used by the compiler to obtain a type at compile time. It is therefore safe to use the previous template also with empty vectors.

You can take this function for a spin with the test program we wrote in `Ex9_04.cpp`.

decltype(auto) and decltype() vs. auto

In the previous section, you encountered the following example of the trailing return type syntax:

```
template <typename T1, typename T2>
auto larger(T1 a, T2 b) -> decltype(a > b ? a : b)
{
  return a > b ? a : b;
}
```

Partially because repeating expressions from the function body like that inside a trailing decltype() is rather tedious, C++14 introduced the decltype(auto) syntax:

```
template <typename T1, typename T2>
decltype(auto) larger(T1 a, T2 b)
{
  return a > b ? a : b;
}
```

Using this syntax, the compiler will again deduce the type from the return statements in the function body. The previous declaration is thus completely equivalent to the one with the trailing return type earlier.

Return type deduction using either a trailing decltype() or decltype(auto), however, is not equivalent to return type deduction using auto. In essence, the difference is that unlike auto, decltype() and decltype(auto) *will* deduce to reference types and preserve const specifiers. You may recall from the previous chapter that auto always deduces to a value type. This means that auto return type deduction may at times introduce unwanted copies of values when returning from a template function. The exact differences are a bit too advanced, though, for this book to warrant a more extensive discussion.

Default Values for Template Parameters

You can specify default values for function template parameters. For example, you could specify double as the default return type in the prototype for the template introduced earlier like this:

```
template <typename TReturn=double, typename TArg1, typename TArg2>
TReturn larger(const TArg1&, const TArg2&);
```

If you don't specify any template parameter values, the return type will be double. Note that we only use this example to introduce default values for template parameters, not because it is necessarily a good idea to define larger() like this! The reason this is not such a great idea is that this default, double, is not always what you want. The larger() function resulting from the following statement, for instance, accepts arguments of type int and returns the result as type double:

```
std::cout << larger(123, 543) << std::endl;
```

The main point we want to convey with this example, though, is that you can specify default values for template arguments at the beginning of the template argument list. You'll recall that for function parameters it was only possible to define default values at the end of the list. You have quite some more flexibility when specifying default values for template parameters. In our first example, TReturn is the first in the list. But you can also specify default values for parameters in the middle of the list or at the end. Here is yet another larger() template to illustrate the latter:

```
template <typename TArg, typename TReturn=TArg>
TReturn larger(const TArg&, const TArg&);
```

In this example, we use the TArg as the default value for the TReturn template parameter. Using a template parameter name in the default value of other parameters is possible only if that name, TArg in our example, appears earlier in the parameter list. This example again mostly serves to illustrate what is possible and less as something that is necessarily a good idea. If the default value for TReturn does not suit you and you have to specify another type explicitly, you would have to specify all other arguments as well. Nevertheless, it is common practice to specify default values for template parameters at the end of the list. The Standard Library uses this extensively, often also for nontype template parameters. Nontype template parameters are discussed next.

Nontype Template Parameters

All the template parameters you have seen so far have been types. Function templates can also have *nontype* parameters that require nontype arguments.

You include any nontype template parameters in the parameter list along with any other type parameters when you define the template. You'll see an example in a moment. The type of a nontype template parameter can be one of the following:

- An integral type, such as int or long

- An enumeration type

- A pointer or reference to an object type

- A pointer or a reference to a function

- A pointer to a class member

You haven't met these last two. The former is introduced in Chapter 18; the latter is a more advanced feature we won't discuss in this book. The application of nontype template parameters to all these types is beyond the scope of this book as well. We'll only consider a few elementary examples with integral type parameters, just to show how it works.

The compiler needs to be able to evaluate the arguments corresponding to nontype parameters at compile time. For integral type parameters, for instance, this mostly means they will be either integral literals or integral compile-time constants.

Suppose you need a function to perform range checking on a value. You could define a template to handle a variety of types:

```
template <typename T, int lower, int upper>
bool is_in_range(const T& value)
{
  return (value <= upper) && (value >= lower);
}
```

This template has a type parameter, T, and two nontype parameters, lower and upper, that are both of type int. The compiler can't deduce all of the template parameters from the use of the function. The following function call won't compile:

```
double value {100.0};
std::cout << is_in_range(value);              // Won't compile - incorrect usage
```

Compilation fails because upper and lower are unspecified. To use this template, you must specify the template parameter values. The correct way to use this is as follows:

```
std::cout << is_in_range<double, 0, 500>(value);  // OK - checks 0 to 500
```

It would be better to put the nontype template parameters before the template type parameter as follows:

```
template <int lower, int upper, typename T>
bool is_in_range(const T& value)
{
  return (value <= upper) && (value >= lower);
}
```

If you define your template like that, the compiler is capable of deducing the type argument:

```
std::cout << is_in_range<0, 500>(value);          // OK - checks 0 to 500
```

Even better, however, would be to use function parameters for the limits in this case. Function parameters give you the flexibility of being able to pass values that are calculated at runtime, whereas here you must supply the limits at compile time.

Templates for Functions with Fixed-Size Array Arguments

In the previous chapter, in the section on passing arrays by reference, we defined the following function:

```
double average10(const double (&array)[10])  // Only arrays of length 10 can be passed!
{
  double sum {};                    // Accumulate total in here
  for (size_t i {}; i < 10; ++i)
    sum += array[i];                // Sum array elements
  return sum / 10;                  // Return average
}
```

Clearly, it would be great if you could create a function that would work for any array size, not just for arrays of exactly 10 values. A template with nontype template arguments allows you to do this as shown next. For good measure, we'll generalize it even further such that it works for arrays of any numerical type as well, so not just for arrays of double:

```
template <typename T, size_t N>
T average(const T (&array)[N])
{
  T sum {};                         // Accumulate total in here
  for (size_t i {}; i < N; ++i)
```

```
    sum += array[i];                    // Sum array elements
  return sum / N;                       // Return average
}
```

Template argument deduction is even powerful enough to deduce the nontype template argument N from the type of the arguments passed to such a template. We can confirm this using a little test program:

```
// Ex9_05.cpp
// Defining templates for functions that accept fixed-size arrays
#include <iostream>

template <typename T, size_t N>
T average(const T (&array)[N]);

int main()
{
    double doubles[2] { 1.0, 2.0 };
    std::cout << average(doubles) << std::endl;

    double moreDoubles[] { 1.0, 2.0, 3.0, 4.0 };
    std::cout << average(moreDoubles) << std::endl;

    // double* pointer = doubles;
    // std::cout << average(pointer) << std::endl;       /* will not compile */

    std::cout << average( { 1.0, 2.0, 3.0, 4.0 } ) << std::endl;

    int ints[] = { 1, 2, 3, 4 };
    std::cout << average(ints) << std::endl;
}
```

This example outputs the following:

```
1.5
2.5
2.5
2
```

There are five calls to average() inside main(), one of which is commented out. The first is the most basic case and proves that the compiler can correctly deduce that T needs to be substituted in the template instance with double, and N with 2. The second shows that this even works if you did not explicitly specify the dimension of the array in the type. The compiler still knows that the size of moreDoubles is 4. The third call is commented out because it would not compile. Even though arrays and pointers are mostly equivalent, the compiler has no way of deducing the array size from a pointer. The fourth call shows that you can even call average() by directly passing the brace-enclosed list as an argument. For the fourth call, the compiler does not have to create another template instance. It will reuse the one generated for the second call. The fifth and final call illustrates that if T is deduced to be int, the result will be of type int as well—and hence the outcome of an integer division.

While, at least in theory, such templates could lead to quite some code bloat if used with arrays of many different sizes, it is still relatively common to define overloads of functions based on such templates. The Standard Library, for instance, regularly uses this technique.

Summary

In this chapter, you learned how to define your own parameterized templates for functions and how to instantiate them to create functions. This allows you to create functions that work correctly and efficiently for any number of related types. The important bits that you should take away from this chapter are as follows:

- A function template is a parameterized recipe used by the compiler to generate overloaded functions.

- The parameters in a function template can be type parameters or nontype parameters. The compiler creates an instance of a function template for each function call that corresponds to a unique set of template parameter arguments.

- A function template can be overloaded with other functions or function templates.

- Both auto and decltype(auto) can be used to let the compiler deduce the return type of a function. This is particularly powerful in the context of templates because their return type may depend on the value of one or more template type arguments.

EXERCISES

These exercises enable you to try some of what you've learned in this chapter. If you get stuck, look back over the chapter for help. If you're still stuck, you can download the solutions from the Apress website (www.apress.com/source-code), but that really should be a last resort.

Exercise 9-1. In C++17, the Standard Library algorithm header gained the handy std::clamp() function template. The expression clamp(a,b,c) is used to clamp the value a to a given closed interval [b,c]. That is, if a is less than b, the result of the expression will be b; and if a is greater than c, the result will be c; otherwise, if a lies within the interval [b,c], clamp() simply returns a. Write your own my_clamp() function template and try it with a little test program.

Exercise 9-2. Alter the last lines of Ex9_01's main() function as follows:

```
const auto a_string = "A", z_string = "Z";
std::cout << "Larger of " << a_string << " and " << z_string
         << " is " << larger(a_string, z_string) << std::endl;
```

If you now run the program, you may very well get the following output (if not, try rearranging the order in which a_string and z_string are declared):

```
Larger of 1.5 and 2.5 is 2.5
Larger of 3.5 and 4.5 is 4.5
Larger of 17011983 and 10 is 17011983
Larger of A and Z is A
```

What's that? "A" is larger than "Z"? Can you explain exactly what went wrong? Can you fix it?

Hint: To compare two character arrays, you could perhaps first convert them to another string representation.

Exercise 9-3. Write a function template `plus()` that takes two arguments of potentially different types and returns a value equal to the sum of both arguments. Next, make sure that `plus()` can be used as well to add the values pointed to by two given pointers.

Extra: Can you now make it so that you can also concatenate two string literals using `plus()`? Warning: This may not be as easy as you think!

Exercise 9-4. Write your own version of the `std::size()` family of functions called `my_size()` that work not only for fixed-size arrays but also for `std::vector<>` and `std::array<>` objects. You are not allowed to use the `sizeof()` operator.

Exercise 9-5. Can you think of a way to verify that the compiler generates only one instance of a function template for any given argument type? Do so for the `larger()` function in `Ex9_01.cpp`.

Exercise 9-6. In the previous chapter, you studied a quicksort algorithm that worked for pointers-to-`strings`. Generalize the implementation of `Ex8_18.cpp` so that it works for `vectors` of any type (any type for which the < operator exists, that is). Write a `main()` function that uses this to sort some `vectors` with different element types and outputs both the unsorted and unsorted element lists. Naturally, you should do this by also creating a function template that streams `vectors` with arbitrary element types to `std::cout`.

CHAPTER 10

■ ■ ■

Program Files and Preprocessing Directives

This chapter is more about managing code than writing code. We'll discuss how multiple program files and header files interact and how you manage and control their contents. The material in this chapter has implications for how you define your data types, which you'll learn about starting in the next chapter.

In this chapter, you will learn:

- How header files and source files interrelate

- What a translation unit is

- What linkage is and why it is important

- More about how you use namespaces

- What preprocessing is and how to use the preprocessing directives to manage code

- The basic ideas in debugging and the debugging help you can get from preprocessing and the Standard Library

- How you use the `static_assert` keyword

Understanding Translation Units

You know that header files primarily contain declarations that are used by the source files that contain the executable code. Sure, headers can contain definitions with executable code, and source files will often declare new functionality that appears in no header as well. But for the most part, the basic idea is that header files contain function declarations and type definitions, which are used by source files to create additional function definitions. The contents of a header file are made available in a source file by using an `#include` preprocessing directive.

So far you have used only preexisting header files that provide the information necessary for using Standard Library capabilities. The program examples have been short and simple; consequently, they have not warranted the use of separate header files containing your own definitions. In the next chapter, when you learn how to define your own data types, the need for header files will become even more apparent. A typical practical C++ program involves many header files that are included in many source files.

Each source file, along with the contents of *all* the header files that you include in it, is called a *translation unit*. The term is a somewhat abstract term because this isn't necessarily a file in general, although it will be with the majority of C++ implementations. The compiler processes each translation unit in a program independently to generate an object file. The object file contains machine code and

© Ivor Horton and Peter Van Weert 2018
I. Horton and P. Van Weert, *Beginning C++17*, https://doi.org/10.1007/978-1-4842-3366-5_10

information about references to entities such as functions that were not defined in the translation unit—external entities in other words. The set of object files for a complete program is processed by the *linker*, which establishes all necessary connections between the object files to produce the executable program module. If an object file contains references to an external entity that is not found in any of the other object files, no executable module will result, and there will be one or more error messages from the linker. The combined process of compiling and linking translation units is referred to as *translation*.

The One Definition Rule

The *one definition rule* (ODR) is an important concept in C++. Despite its name, ODR is not really one single rule; it's more like a set of rules—one rule per type of entity you might define in a program. Our exposition of these rules won't be exhaustive, nor will it use the formal jargon you'd need for it to be 100 percent accurate. Our main intent is to familiarize you with the general ideas behind the ODR restrictions. This will help you later to better understand how to organize the code of your program in multiple files and to decipher and resolve the compiler and linker errors you'll encounter when you violate an ODR rule.

In a given translation unit, no variable, function, class type, enumeration type, or template must ever be *defined* more than once. You can have more than one *declaration* for a variable or function, for example, but there must never be more than one *definition* that determines what it is and causes it to be created. If there's more than one definition within the same translation unit, the code will not compile.

▦ **Note**   A declaration introduces a name into a scope. A definition not only introduces the name but also defines what it is. In other words, all definitions are declarations, but not all declarations are definitions.

You have seen that you can define variables in different blocks to have the same name, but this does not violate the one definition rule; the variables may have the same name, but they are distinct.

Most functions and variables must be defined *once and only once* within an entire program. No two definitions are allowed, even if they're identical and appear defined in different translation units. Exceptions to this rule are inline functions and variables (the latter have existed only since C++17). For `inline` functions and variables, a definition must appear *once in every* translation unit that uses them. All these definitions of a given inline function or variable have to be identical, though. For this reason, you should always define inline functions and variables in a header file that you include in a source file whenever one is required.

If you define a class or enumeration type, you usually want to use it in more than one translation unit. Several translation units in a program can thus each include a definition for the type, again provided all these definitions are identical. In practice, you achieve this by placing the definition for a type in a header file and use an `#include` directive to add the header file to any source file that requires the type definition. However, duplicate definitions for a given type remain illegal within a single translation unit, so you need to be careful how you define the contents of header files. You must make sure that duplicate type definitions within a translation unit cannot occur. You'll see how you do this later in this chapter.

▦ **Note**   In the next chapter, we'll disclose how a class definition declares the various member functions and variables for that class. For the class type itself, one definition is required within every translation unit that uses it. Its members, however, follow ODR rules analogous to those of regular functions and variables. In other words, noninline class members must have only one single definition within the entire program. That's why, unlike class type definitions, class member definitions will mostly appear in source files rather than in header files.

The one definition rule applies differently to function templates (or class member function templates, covered in Chapter 16). Because the compiler needs to know how to instantiate the template, each translation unit in which you instantiate a template using a previously unseen set of template arguments needs to contain a definition of that template. In a way, the compiler does preserve an ODR-like behavior by instantiating each template only once for a given combination of arguments.

Program Files and Linkage

Entities defined in one translation unit often need to be accessed from code in another translation unit. Functions are obvious examples of where this is the case, but you can have others—variables defined at global scope that are shared across several translation units, for instance, or the definitions of nonfundamental types. Because the compiler processes one translation unit at a time, such references can't be resolved by the compiler. Only the linker can do this when all the object files from the translation units in the program are available.

The way that names in a translation unit are handled in the compile/link process is determined by a property that a name can have called *linkage*. Linkage expresses where in the program code the entity that is represented by a name can be. Every name that you use in a program either has linkage or doesn't. A name has linkage when you can use it to access something in your program that is *outside* the scope in which the name is declared. If this isn't the case, it has no linkage. If a name has linkage, then it can have *internal linkage* or *external linkage*. Therefore, every name in a translation unit has internal linkage, external linkage, or no linkage.

Determining Linkage for a Name

The linkage that applies to a name is not affected by whether its declaration appears in a header file or a source file. The linkage for each name in a translation unit is determined *after* the contents of any header files have been inserted into the `.cpp` file that is the basis for the translation unit. The linkage possibilities have the following meanings:

> *Internal linkage*: The entity that the name represents can be accessed from anywhere within the same translation unit. For example, the names of non-`inline` variables defined at global scope that are specified as `const` have internal linkage by default.

> *External linkage*: A name with external linkage can be accessed from another translation unit in addition to the one in which it is defined. In other words, the entity that the name represents can be shared and accessed throughout the entire program. All the functions that we have written so far have external linkage and so do both non-`const` and `inline` variables defined at global scope.

> *No linkage*: When a name has no linkage, the entity it refers to can be accessed only from within the scope that applies to the name. All names that are defined within a block—local names, in other words—have no linkage.

External Functions

In a program made up of several files, the linker establishes (or *resolves*) the connection between a function call in one source file and the function definition in another. When the compiler compiles a *call* to the function, it only needs the information contained in a function prototype to create the call. This prototype is contained within each *declaration* of the function. The compiler doesn't mind whether the function's *definition* occurs in the same file or elsewhere. This is because function names have external linkage by default. If a function is not defined within the translation unit in which it is called, the compiler flags the call as external and leaves it for the linker to sort out.

It's high time to clarify this with a first example. For this, we'll adapt Ex8_17.cpp and move the definition of its power() function to a different translation unit:

```
// Ex10_01.cpp
// Calling external functions
#include <iostream>
#include <iomanip>

double power(double x, int n);        // Declaration of an external power() function

int main()
{
  for (int i {-3}; i <= 3; ++i)       // Calculate powers of 8 from -3 to +3
    std::cout << std::setw(10) << power(8.0, i);

  std::cout << std::endl;
}
```

All the files for examples with more than one file will be in a separate folder in the code download, so the files for this example will be in the Ex10_01 folder.

The Ex10_01 translation unit consists of the code in Ex10_01.cpp, combined with all declarations brought in by including the iostream and iomanip headers. Note that, indirectly, these headers in turn surely #include many more Standard Library headers. That way, a lot of code may get pulled into a translation unit, even by the #include of only a single header.

Even though power() is called by main(), no definition of this function is present in the Ex10_01 translation unit. But that's OK. All the compiler needs to carry out a call to power() is its prototype. The compiler then simply makes note of a call to an externally defined power() function inside the object file for the Ex10_01 translation unit, making it the linker's job to hook up—or *link*—the call with its definition. If the linker doesn't find the appropriate definition in one of the other translation units of the program, it will signal this as a translation failure.

To make the Ex10_01 program translate correctly, you'll therefore need a second translation unit with the definition of power():

```
// Power.cpp
// The power function called from Ex10_01.cpp is defined in a different translation unit

double power(double x, int n)
{
  if (n == 0)        return 1.0;
  else if (n > 0)    return x * power(x, n - 1);
  else /* n < 0 */   return 1.0 / power(x, -n);
}
```

By linking the object files of the Ex10_01 and Power translation units, you obtain a program that is otherwise completely equivalent to that of Ex8_17.

Note that in order to use the power() function in Ex10_01.cpp, we still had to supply the compiler with a prototype in the beginning of the source file. It would not be very practical if you had to do this explicitly for every externally defined function. This is why function prototypes are typically gathered in header files, which you can then conveniently #include into your translation units. Later in this chapter we explain how you can create your own header files.

External Variables

Suppose that in Ex10_01.cpp, you wanted to replace the magic constants -3 and 3 using an externally defined variable power_range, like so:

```
for (int i {-power_range}; i <= power_range; ++i)      // Calculate powers of 8
  std::cout << std::setw(10) << power(8.0, i);
```

The first step is to create an extra source file, Range.cpp, containing the variable's definition:

```
// Range.cpp

int power_range{ 3 };              // A global variable with external linkage
```

Non-const variables have external linkage by default, just like functions do. So other translation units will have no problem accessing this variable. The interesting question, though, is this: how do you declare a variable in the Ex10_02 translation unit without it becoming a second definition? A reasonable first attempt would be this:

```
// Ex10_02.cpp
// Using an externally defined variable
#include <iostream>
#include <iomanip>

double power(double x, int n);      // Declaration of an external power() function
int power_range;                    // Not an unreasonable first attempt, right?

int main()
{
  for (int i {-power_range}; i <= power_range; ++i)      // Calculate powers of 8
    std::cout << std::setw(10) << power(8.0, i);

  std::cout << std::endl;
}
```

The compiler will have no problem with this declaration of power_range. The linker, however, will signal an error! We recommend you give this a try as well to familiarize yourself with this error message. In principle (linker error messages do not always excel in clarity), you should then be able to deduce that we have supplied two distinct definitions for power_range: one in Range.cpp and one in Ex10_02.cpp. This, of course, violates the one definition rule!

The underlying problem is that our declaration of the power_range variable in Ex10_02.cpp is not just any old variable declaration; it's a variable *definition*:

```
int power_range;
```

In fact, you might've already known this would happen. Surely, you'll remember that variables generally contain garbage if you neglect to initialize them. Near the end of Chapter 3, however, we've also covered *global* variables. And global variables, as we told you, will be initialized with zero, even if you omit the braced initializer from their definition. In other words, our declaration of the global power_range variable in Ex10_02.cpp is equivalent to the following definition:

```
int power_range {};
```

ODR does not allow for two definitions of the same variable. The compiler therefore needs to be told that the definition for the global variable power_range will be external to the current translation unit, Ex10_02. If you want to access a variable that is defined *outside* the current translation unit, then you must declare the variable name using the extern keyword:

```
extern int power_range;          // Declaration of an externally defined variable
```

This statement is a declaration that power_range is a name that is defined elsewhere. The type must correspond exactly to the type that appears in the definition. You can't specify an initial value in an extern declaration because it's a declaration of the name, not a definition of a variable. Declaring a variable as extern implies that it is defined in another translation unit. This causes the compiler to mark the use of the externally defined variable. It is the linker that makes the connection between the name and the variable to which it refers.

■ **Note**   You're allowed to add extern specifiers in front of function declarations as well. For example, in Ex10_02.cpp you could've declared the power() function with an explicit extern specifier to call attention to the fact that the function's definition will be part of a different translation unit:

```
extern double power(double x, int n);
```

While arguably nicer for consistency and code clarity, adding extern here is optional.

---

const Variables with External Linkage

Given its nature, you'd of course want to define the power_range variable from Range.cpp of Ex10_02 as a global constant, rather than a modifiable global variable:

```
// Range.cpp
const int power_range {3};
```

A const variable, however, has internal linkage by default, which makes it unavailable in other translation units. You can override this by using the extern keyword in the definition:

```
// Range.cpp
extern const int power_range {3};     // Definition of a global constant with external
linkage
```

The extern keyword tells the compiler that the name should have external linkage, even though it is const. When you want to access power_range in another source file, you must declare it as const and external:

```
extern const int power_range;         // Declaration of an external global constant
```

You can find this in a fully functioning example in Ex10_02A. Within any block in which this declaration appears, the name power_range refers to the constant defined in another file. The declaration can appear in any translation unit that needs access to power_range. You can place the declaration either at global scope in a translation unit so that it's available throughout the code in the source file or within a block in which case it is available only within that local scope.

Global variables can be useful for constant values that you want to share because they are accessible in any translation unit. By sharing constant values across all of the program files that need access to them, you can ensure that the same values are being used for the constants throughout your program. However, although up to now we have shown constants defined in source files, the best place for them is in a header file. You'll see an example of this later in this chapter.

Internal Names

If there's a way to specify that names should have external linkage, surely there must be one as well to specify that they should have internal linkage, right? There is, but it's not what you'd expect.

Let's first illustrate when and why you'd need this possibility. Perhaps you noticed that upon every recursive call of power() of Ex10_01 the function checks whether its argument n is positive or negative. This is somewhat wasteful because the sign of n, of course, never changes. One option is to rewrite power() in the following manner:

```
// Power.cpp

double compute(double x, unsigned n)
{
  return n == 0? 1.0 : x * compute(x, n - 1);
}

double power(double x, int n)
{
  return n >= 0 ? compute(x, static_cast<unsigned>(n))
               : 1.0 / compute(x, static_cast<unsigned>(-n));
}
```

The power() function itself is now no longer recursive. Instead, it calls the recursive helper function compute(), which is defined to work only for positive (unsigned) arguments n. Using this helper, it's easy to rewrite power() in such a way that it checks whether the given n is positive only once.

In this case, compute() could in principle be a useful function in its own right—best renamed then to become a second overload of power(), that is, one specific for unsigned exponents. For argument's sake, however, suppose we want compute() to be nothing more than a local helper function, one that is only to be called by power(). You'll find that the need for this occurs quite often; you need a function to make your local code clearer or to reuse within one specific translation unit, but that function is too specific for it to be exported to the rest of the program for reuse.

Our compute() function currently has external linkage as well, just like power(), and can therefore be called from within any translation unit. Worse, the one definition rule implies that no other translation unit may define a compute() function with the same signature anymore either! If all local helper functions always had external linkage, they'd all need unique names as well, which would soon make it even harder to avoid name conflicts in larger programs.

What we need is a way to tell the compiler that a function such as compute() should have internal linkage rather than external linkage. An obvious attempt would be to add an intern specifier. That might've worked, if not for the little detail that there's no such keyword in C++. Instead, in the old days, the way to mark a name (function or variable name) for internal linkage was by adding the static keyword. Here's an example:

```
static double compute(double x, unsigned n)      // compute() now has internal linkage
{
  return n == 0 ? 1.0 : x * compute(x, n - 1);
}
```

While this notation will still work—you can try it for yourself in Ex10_03—this use of the keyword static is no longer recommended. The only reason that this syntax is not deprecated or removed from the C++ Standard yet (or anymore, for those who know their history) is that you'll still find it a lot in legacy code. Nevertheless, the recommended way to define names with internal linkage today is through unnamed namespaces, as we'll explain later in this chapter.

■ **Caution**   Never use static anymore to mark names that should have internal linkage; always use unnamed namespaces instead.

Preprocessing Your Source Code

Preprocessing is a process executed by the compiler before a source file is compiled into machine instructions. Preprocessing prepares and modifies the source code for the compile phase according to instructions that you specify by *preprocessing directives*. All preprocessing directives begin with the symbol #, so they are easy to distinguish from C++ language statements. Table 10-1 shows the complete set.

Table 10-1. *Preprocessing Directives*

Directive	Description
#include	Supports header file inclusion.
#if	Enables conditional compilation.
#else	else for #if.
#elif	Equivalent to #else #if.
#endif	Marks the end of an #if directive.
#define	Defines an identifier.
#undef	Deletes an identifier previously defined using #define.
#ifdef (or #if defined)	Does something if an identifier is defined.
#ifndef (or #if !defined)	Does something if an identifier is not defined.
#line	Redefines the current line number. Optionally changes the filename as well.
#error	Outputs a compile-time error message and stops the compilation. This is typically part of a conditional preprocessing directive sequence.
#pragma	Offers vendor-specific features while retaining overall C++ compatibility.

The preprocessing phase analyzes, executes, and then removes all preprocessing directives from a source file. This generates the translation unit that consists purely of C++ statements that is then compiled. The linker must then process the object file that results along with any other object files that are part of the program to produce the executable module.

You may wonder why you would want to use the #line directive to change the line number. The need for this is rare, but one example is a program that maps some other language into C or C++. An original language statement may generate several C++ statements, and by using the #line directive, you can ensure that C++ compiler error messages identify the line number in the original code, rather than the C++ that results. This makes it easier to identify the statement in the original code that is the source of the error.

Several of these directives are primarily applicable in C and are not so relevant with current C++. The language capabilities of C++ provide much more effective and safer ways of achieving the same result as some of the preprocessing directives. We'll mostly focus on the preprocessing directives that are important in C++. You are already familiar with the #include directive. There are other directives that can provide considerable flexibility in the way in which you specify your programs. Keep in mind that preprocessing operations occur before your program is compiled. Preprocessing modifies the statements that constitute your program, and the preprocessing directives no longer exist in the source file that is compiled.

Defining Preprocessor Macros

A #define directive specifies a so-called *macro*. A macro is a rewrite rule that instructs the preprocessor which text replacements to apply to the source code prior to handing it over to the compiler. The simplest form of the #define preprocessing directive is the following:

```
#define IDENTIFIER sequence of characters
```

This macro effectively defines IDENTIFIER as an alias for sequence of characters. IDENTIFIER must conform to the usual definition of an identifier in C++, that is, any sequence of letters and digits, the first of which is a letter, and where the underline character counts as a letter. A macro identifier does not have to be in all caps, though this is certainly a widely accepted convention. sequence of characters can be any sequence of characters, including an empty sequence or a sequence that contains whitespace.

One use for #define is to define an identifier that is to be replaced in the source code by a substitute string during preprocessing. Here's how you could define PI to be an alias for a sequence of characters that represents a numerical value:

```
#define PI 3.14159265
```

PI *looks* like a variable, but this has nothing to do with variables. PI is a symbol, or *token*, that is exchanged for the specified sequence of characters by the preprocessor before the code is compiled. 3.14159265 is not a numerical value in the sense that no validation is taking place; it is merely a string of characters. The string PI will be replaced during preprocessing by its definition, the sequence of characters 3.14159265, wherever the preprocessing operation deems that the substitution makes sense. If you wrote 3,!4!5 as the replacement character sequence, the substitution would still occur.

The #define directive is often used to define symbolic constants in C, but don't do this in C++. It is much better to define a constant variable, like this:

```
inline const double pi {3.14159265358979323846};
```

pi is a constant value of a particular type. The compiler ensures that the value for pi is consistent with its type. You could place this definition in a header file for inclusion in any source file where the value is required or define it with external linkage:

```
extern const double pi {3.14159265358979323846};
```

Now you may access pi from any translation unit just by adding an extern declaration for it wherever it is required.

■ **Note** To date, the C++ Standard Library does not define any mathematical constants, not even one as fundamental as π. Nevertheless, most compiler libraries will offer nonstandard definitions of π, so it may therefore be worth checking your documentation first. Otherwise, the easiest portable solution is to define a simple macro for it or otherwise one constant per floating-point type.[1] When doing so, however, it is critical you use sufficient digits after the comma. Never define π, for instance, as simply 3.1415—using such an approximation would result in particularly inaccurate results! The macro we defined earlier this section has sufficient digits to be safe for use in float, double, or long double computations on most platforms.

■ **Caution** Using a #define directive to define an identifier that you use to specify a value in C++ code has three major disadvantages: there's no type checking support, it doesn't respect scope, and the identifier name cannot be bound within a namespace. In C++, you should always use const variables instead.

Here's another example:

```
#define BLACK WHITE
```

Any occurrence of BLACK in the file will be replaced by WHITE. The identifier will be replaced only when it is a token. It will not be replaced if it forms part of an identifier or appears in a string literal or a comment. There's no restriction on the sequence of characters that is to replace the identifier. It can even be absent in which case the identifier exists but with no predefined substitution string—the substitution string is empty. If you don't specify a substitution string for an identifier, then occurrences of the identifier in the code will be replaced by an empty string; in other words, the identifier will be removed. Here's an example:

```
#define VALUE
```

The effect is that all occurrences of VALUE that follow the directive will be removed. The directive also defines VALUE as an identifier, and its existence can be tested by other directives, as you'll see.

Note that the preprocessor is completely agnostic about C or C++. It will blindly perform any replacement you ask it to do, even if the result is no longer valid C or C++ code. You could even use it to replace C++ keywords as follows (we'll leave it up to you to decide whether you *should...*):

```
#define true false
#define break
```

The major use for the #define directive with C++ is in the management of header files, as you'll see later in this chapter.

Defining Function-Like Macros

The #define directives you've seen so far have been similar to variable definitions in C++. You can define function-like text replacement macros as well. Here's an example:

```
#define MAX(A, B) A >= B ? A : B
```

---

[1] C++ language purists often insist you do not use macros, as these are considered more reminiscent of C. Starting with C++14, the recommended way for defining variables such as π in standard C++ is using *variable templates*. This is a more advanced feature, though, which we do not cover in this book.

While this looks an awful lot like one, this most certainly isn't a function. There are no argument types, nor is there a return value. A macro is not something that is called, nor does its right side necessarily specify statements to be executed at runtime. Our sample macro simply instructs the preprocessor to replace all occurrences of MAX(*anything1*, *anything2*) in the source code with the character sequence that appears in the second half of the #define directive. During this replacement process, all occurrences of A in A >= B? A : B are of course replaced by *anything1*, and all occurrences of B are replaced with *anything2*. The preprocessor makes no attempt at interpreting the *anything1* and *anything2* character sequences; all it does is blind text replacement. Suppose, for instance, your code contains this statement:

```
std::cout << MAX(expensive_computation(), 0) << std::endl;
```

Then the preprocessor expands it to the following source code before handing it over to the compiler:

```
std::cout << expensive_computation() >= 0 ? expensive_computation() : 0 << std::endl;
```

This example exposes two problems:

- The resulting code will not compile. If you use the ternary operator together with the streaming operator <<, the operator precedence rules tell us that the expression with the ternary operator should be between parentheses. A better definition of our MAX() macro would therefore be the following:

    ```
    #define MAX(A, B) (A >= B ? A : B)
    ```

    Even better would be to add parentheses around all occurrences of A and B to avoid similar operator precedence problems there as well:

    ```
    #define MAX(A, B) ((A) >= (B) ? (A) : (B))
    ```

- The expensive_computation() function is called up to two times. If a macro parameter such as A appears more than once in the replacement, the preprocessor will blindly copy the macro arguments more than once. This undesired behavior with macros is harder to avoid.

These are just two of the common pitfalls with macro definitions. We therefore recommend you never create function-like macros, unless you have a good reason for doing so. While some advanced scenarios do call for such macros, C++ mostly offers alternatives that are far superior. Macros are popular among C programmers because they allow the creation of function-like constructs that work for any parameter type. But of course you already know that C++ offers a much better solution for this: function templates. After Chapter 9, it should be a breeze for you to define a C++ function template that replaces the C-style MAX() macro. And this template inherently avoids both the shortcomings of macro definitions we listed earlier.

■ **Caution**   Never use preprocessor macros to define operations such as min(), max(), or abs(). Instead, you should always use either regular C++ functions or function templates. Function templates are far superior to preprocessor macros for defining blueprints of functions that work for any argument type. In fact, the cmath header of the Standard Library already offers precisely such function templates—including std::min(), std::max(), and std::abs()—so there's often no need for you to define them yourself.

Preprocessor Operators

For completeness, Table 10-2 lists the two operators you can apply to the parameters of a function-like text replacement macro.

Table 10-2. Preprocessor Operators

#	The so-called stringification operator. Turns the argument in a string literal containing its value (by surrounding it with double quotes and adding the necessary character escape sequences).
##	The concatenation operator. Concatenates (pastes together, similar to what the + operator does for the values of two std::strings) the values of two identifiers.

The following toy program illustrates how you might use these operators:

```
// Ex10_04.cpp
// Working with preprocessor operators
#include <iostream>

#define DEFINE_PRINT_FUNCTION(NAME, COUNT, VALUE) \
  void NAME##COUNT() { std::cout << #VALUE << std::endl; }

DEFINE_PRINT_FUNCTION(fun, 123, Test 1 "2" 3)

int main()
{
  fun123();
}
```

Before we get to the use of both preprocessor operators, Ex10_04.cpp shows one additional thing: macro definitions are not really allowed to span multiple lines. By default, the preprocessor simply replaces any occurrences of the macro's identifier (possibly taking a number of arguments) with all the characters it finds on the same line to the right of the identifier. However, it is not always practical to fit the entire definition on one single line. The preprocessor therefore allows you to add line breaks, as long as they are immediately preceded with a backslash character. All such escaped line breaks are discarded from the substitution. That is, the preprocessor first concatenates the entire macro definition back into one single line (in fact, it does so even outside of a macro definition).

■ **Note** In Ex10_04.cpp we added the line break before the right side of the macro definition, which is probably the most natural thing to do. But since the preprocessor always just stitches any sliced lines back together, without interpreting the characters, such escaped line breaks can really appear anywhere you want. Not that this is in any way recommended, but this means you could in extremis even write the following:

```
#define DEFINE_PRINT_FUNCT\
ION(NAME, COUNT, VALUE) vo\
id NAME##COUNT() { std::co\
ut << #VALUE << std::endl; }
```

Mind you, if you do splice identifiers like this, for whatever crazy reason, take care not to add whitespace characters at the beginning of the next line, as these are not discarded by the preprocessor when it puts the pieces back together.

Enough about line breaks; let's get back to the topic at hand: preprocessor operators. The macro definition in Ex10_04 uses both ## and #:

```
#define DEFINE_PRINT_FUNCTION(NAME, COUNT, VALUE) \
  void NAME##COUNT() { std::cout << #VALUE << std::endl; }
```

With this definition, the line DEFINE_PRINT_FUNCTION(fun, 123, Test 1 "2" 3) in Ex10_04.cpp expands to the following:

```
  void fun123() { std::cout << "Test 1 \"2\" 3" << std::endl; }
```

Without the ## operator, you'd have the choice between either NAMECOUNT or NAME COUNT. In the former, the preprocessor would not recognize NAME or COUNT, whereas the latter in our example would expand to fun 123, which is not a valid function name (C++ identifiers must not contain spaces). And, clearly, without the # operator you'd have a hard time turning a given character sequence into a valid C++ string literal.

Because the preprocessor runs first, the fun123() function definition will thus be present by the time the C++ compiler gets to see the source code. This is why you can call fun123() in the program's main() function, where it produces the following result:

```
Test 1 "2" 3
```

Undefining Macros

You may want to have the identifier resulting from a #define directive exist in only *part* of a program file. You can nullify a definition for an identifier using the #undef directive. You can negate a previously defined VALUE macro with this directive:

```
#undef VALUE
```

VALUE is no longer defined following this directive, so no substitutions for VALUE can occur. The following code fragment illustrates this:

```
#define PI 3.14159265358979323846264343383279502884
// All occurrences of PI in code from this point will be replaced
// by 3.14159265358979323846264343383279502884
// ...
#undef PI
// PI is no longer defined from here on so no substitutions occur.
// Any references to PI will be left in the code.
```

Between the #define and #undef directives, preprocessing replaces appropriate occurrences of PI in the code with 3.14159265358979323846264343383279502884. Elsewhere, occurrences of PI are left as they are. The #undef directive also works for function-like macros. Here's an example:

```
#undef MAX
```

Including Header Files

A header file is an external file whose contents are included in a source file using the `#include` preprocessing directive. Header files contain primarily type definitions, template definitions, function prototypes, and constants. You are already completely familiar with statements such as this:

```
#include <iostream>
```

The contents of the `iostream` Standard Library header replaces the `#include` directive. This will be the definitions required to support input and output with the standard streams. Any Standard Library header name can appear between the angled brackets. If you `#include` a header that you don't need, the primary effect is to extend the compilation time, and the executable may occupy more memory than necessary. It may also be confusing for anyone who reads the program.

You include your own header files into a source file with a slightly different syntax where you enclose the header file name between double quotes. Here's an example:

```
#include "myheader.h"
```

The contents of the file named `myheader.h` are introduced into the program in place of the `#include` directive. The contents of any file can be included into your program in this way. You simply specify the file name of the file between quotes as in the example. With the majority of compilers, the file name can use uppercase and lowercase characters. In theory, you can assign any name and extension you like to your header files; you don't have to use the extension `.h`. However, it is a convention adhered to by most C++ programmers, and we recommend that you follow it too.

■ **Note**   Some libraries use the `.hpp` extension for C++ header files and reserve the use of the `.h` extension for header files that contain either pure C functions or functions that are compatible with both C and C++. Mixing C and C++ code is an advanced topic, which we do not cover in this book.

The process used to find a header file depends on whether you specify the file name between double quotes or between angled brackets. The precise operation is implementation-dependent and should be described in your compiler documentation. Usually, the compiler only searches the default directories that contain the Standard Library headers for the file when the name is between angled brackets. This implies that your header files will not be found if you put the name between angled brackets. If the header name is between *double quotes*, the compiler searches the current directory (typically the directory containing the source file that is being compiled) followed by the directories containing the standard headers. If the header file is in some other directory, you may need to put the complete path for the header file or the path relative to the directory containing the source file between the double quotes.

Preventing Duplication of Header File Contents

A header file that you include into a source file can contain `#include` directives of its own, and this process can go on many levels deep. This feature is used extensively in large programs and in the Standard Library headers. With a complex program involving many header files, there's a good chance that a header file may potentially be `#included` more than once in a source file. In some situations this may even be unavoidable. The one definition rule, however, prohibits the same definition from appearing more than once in the same translation unit. We therefore need a way to prevent this from occurring.

▧ **Note** Occasionally, a header that is included into some header A.h may even, directly or indirectly, include header A.h again. Without a mechanism to prevent the same header from being included into itself, this would introduce an infinite recursion of #includes, causing the compiler to implode into itself.

You have already seen that you don't have to specify a value when you define an identifier:

```
#define MY_IDENTIFIER
```

This creates MY_IDENTIFIER, so it exists from here on and represents an empty character sequence. You can use the #if defined directive to test whether a given identifier has been defined and include code or not in the file depending on the result:

```
#if defined MY_IDENTIFIER
   // The code here will be placed in the source file if MY_IDENTIFIER has been defined.
   // Otherwise it will be omitted.
#endif
```

All the lines following #if defined up to the #endif directive will be kept in the file if the identifier, MY_IDENTIFIER, has been defined previously and omitted if it has not. The #endif directive marks the end of the text that is controlled by the #if defined directive. You can use the abbreviated form, #ifdef, if you prefer:

```
#ifdef MY_IDENTIFIER
   // The code here will be placed in the source file if MY_IDENTIFIER has been defined.
   // Otherwise it will be omitted.
#endif
```

You can use the #if !defined or its equivalent, #ifndef, to test for an identifier not having been defined:

```
#if !defined MY_IDENTIFIER
   // The code down to #endif will be placed in the source file
   // if MY_IDENTIFIER has NOT been defined. Otherwise, the code will be omitted.
#endif
```

Here, the lines following #if !defined down to the #endif are included in the file to be compiled provided the identifier has not been defined previously. This pattern is the basis for the mechanism that is used to ensure that the contents of a header file are not duplicated in a translation unit:

```
// Header file myheader.h
#ifndef MYHEADER_H
#define MYHEADER_H
   // The entire code for myheader.h is placed here.
   // This code will be placed in the source file,
   // but only if MYHEADER_H has NOT been defined previously.
#endif
```

If a header file, myheader.h, that has contents like this is included into a source file more than once, the first #include directive will include the code because MYHEADER_H has not been defined. In the process it will define MYHEADER_H. Any subsequent #include directives for myheader.h in the source file or in other header files that are included into the source file will not include the code because MYHEADER_H will have been defined previously.

351

Naturally, you should choose a unique identifier to use instead of MYHEADER_H for each header. Different naming conventions are used, although most base these names on that of the header file itself. In this book we'll use identifiers of the form HEADERNAME_H.

The previous #ifndef - #define - #endif pattern is common enough to have its own name; this particular combination of preprocessor directives is called an #include *guard*. All header files should be surrounded with an #include guard to eliminate the potential for violations of the one definition rule.

■ **Tip** Most compilers offer a #pragma directive to achieve the same effect as the pattern we have described. With nearly all compilers, placing a line containing #pragma once at the beginning of a header file is all that is necessary to prevent duplication of the contents. While nearly all compilers support this #pragma, it is not standard C++, so for this book we'll continue to use #include guards.

Your First Header File

For your first header file, we start again from Ex10_01 and this time put the prototype declaration of the power function into its own header file. Power.cpp remains the same as before. The only difference is the way the function prototype of power() makes it into the main translation unit:

```
// Ex10_05.cpp
// Creating and including your own header file
#include <iostream>
#include <iomanip>
#include "Power.h"        // Contains the prototype for the power() function

int main()
{
  for (int i {-3}; i <= 3; ++i)     // Calculate powers of 8 from -3 to +3
    std::cout << std::setw(10) << power(8.0, i);

  std::cout << std::endl;
}
```

This source file is completely identical to Ex10_01.cpp, except that this time the declaration of power() is pulled in by including this Power.h header:

```
// Power.h
#ifndef POWER_H
#define POWER_H

// Function to calculate x to the power n
double power(double x, int n);

#endif
```

Usually, you will not create a header for each individual function. The Power.h header could be the start of a larger Math.h header that groups any number of useful, reusable mathematical functions.

> ▓ **Tip**   Naturally the Standard Library already offers a header with mathematical functions. It's called `cmath`,
> and it defines more than 75 different functions and function templates for common (and some far less common)
> mathematical functions. One of these functions, of course, is `std::pow()`.

Namespaces

We introduced *namespaces* in Chapter 1, but there's a bit more to it than we explained then. With large
programs, choosing unique names for all the entities that have external linkage can become difficult.
When an application is developed by several programmers working in parallel and/or when it incorporates
headers and source code from various third-party C++ libraries, using namespaces to prevent name clashes
becomes essential. Name clashes are perhaps most likely in the context of user-defined types, or classes,
which you will meet in the next few chapters.

A namespace is a block that attaches an extra name—the namespace name—to every entity name that
is declared or defined within it. The full name of each entity is the namespace name followed by the scope
resolution operator, ::, followed by the basic entity name. Different namespaces can contain entities with
the same name, but the entities are differentiated because they are qualified by different namespace names.

You typically use a separate namespace within a single program for each collection of code that
encompasses a common purpose. Each namespace would represent some logical grouping of functions,
together with any related global variables and declarations. A namespace would also be used to contain a
unit of release, such as a library.

You are already aware that Standard Library names are declared within the `std` namespace. You also
know that you can reference any name from a namespace without qualifying it with the namespace name by
using a blanket `using` directive:

```
using namespace std;
```

However, this risks defeating the purpose of using namespaces in the first place and increases the
likelihood of errors because of the accidental use of a name in the `std` namespace. It is thus often better to use
qualified names or add `using` declarations for the names from another namespace that you are referencing.

> ▓ **Tip**   Especially in header files, both `using` directives and `using` declarations are considered "not done" because
> they force anyone who wants to use the header's types and functionality to `#include` these `using` directives and
> declarations as well. Inside source files, however, opinions differ. Personally we believe that `using` should be used
> only sporadically, for longer or nested namespaces, and as locally as possibly. So, you should definitely not use
> it for for the three-letter `std` namespace. But, like we said, opinions are divided on the subject, as with most
> matters of coding style. It is therefore always best to check what the conventions are within your team or company.

The Global Namespace

All the programs that you've written so far have used names that you defined in the *global namespace*.
The global namespace applies by default if a namespace hasn't been defined. All names within the global
namespace are just as you declare them, without a namespace name being attached. In a program with
multiple source files, all the names with linkages are within the global namespace.

To explicitly access names defined in the global namespace, you use the scope resolution operator without a left operand, for example, ::power(2.0, 3). This is only really required, though, if there is a more local declaration with the same name that hides that global name.

With small programs, you can define your names within the global namespace without running into any problems. With larger applications, the potential for name clashes increases, so you should use namespaces to partition your code into logical groupings. That way, each code segment is self-contained from a naming perspective, and name clashes are prevented.

Defining a Namespace

You can define a namespace with these statements:

```
namespace myRegion
{
  // Code you want to have in the namespace,
  // including function definitions and declarations,
  // global variables, enum types, templates, etc.
}
```

Note that no semicolon is required after the closing brace in a namespace definition. The namespace name here is myRegion. The braces enclose the scope for the namespace myRegion, and every name declared within the namespace scope has the name myRegion attached to it.

■ **Caution**   You must not include the main() function within a namespace. The runtime environment expects main() to be defined in the global namespace.

You can extend a namespace scope by adding a second namespace block with the same name. For example, a program file might contain the following:

```
namespace calc
{
  // This defines namespace calc
  // The initial code in the namespace goes here
}
namespace sort
{
  // Code in a new namespace, sort
}
namespace calc
{
  /* This extends the calc namespace
     Code in here can refer to names in the previous
     calc namespace block without qualification */
}
```

There are two blocks defined as namespace calc, separated by a namespace sort. The second calc block is treated as a continuation of the first, so functions declared within each of the calc blocks belong to the same namespace. The second block is called an *extension namespace* definition because it extends the original namespace definition. You can have several extension namespace definitions in a translation unit.

Of course, you wouldn't choose to organize a source file so that it contains multiple namespace blocks in this way, but it can occur anyway. If you include several header files into a source file, then you may effectively end up with the sort of situation we just described. An example of this is when you include several Standard Library headers (each of which contributes to the namespace std), interspersed with your own header files:

```
#include <iostream>         // In namespace std
#include "mystuff.h"        // In namespace calc
#include <string>           // In namespace std - extension namespace
#include "morestuff.h"      // In namespace calc - extension namespace
```

Note that references to names from inside the same namespace do not need to be qualified. For example, names that are defined in the namespace calc can be referenced from within calc without qualifying them with the namespace name.

Let's look at an example that illustrates the mechanics of declaring and using a namespace. Of course, now that you can create your own header files, you should organize the code nicely in multiple files from now on. The program will therefore consist of two files: one header file and one source file. The header file defines a few common mathematical constants in the namespace with name constants:

```
// Constants.h
// Using a namespace
#ifndef CONSTANTS_H
#define CONSTANTS_H

namespace constants
{
  inline const double pi { 3.14159265358979323846 };    // the famous pi constant
  inline const double e  { 2.71828182845904523536 };    // base of the natural logarithm
  inline const double sqrt_2 { 1.41421356237309504880 }; // square root of 2
}

#endif
```

The #include guard makes sure that these definitions will never appear more than once in the same translation unit. That does not prevent them from being #included into two or more distinct translation units, though. All three constants are therefore defined to be inline variables as well. This allows their definitions to appear in multiple translation units without violating ODR. If your compiler does not support inline variables yet (this language feature was introduced with C++17), you have to move the variable definitions to a source file instead. The header might then look as follows:

```
// Constants.h
// Declares three constants that are defined externally
#ifndef CONSTANTS_H
#define CONSTANTS_H

namespace constants
{
  extern const double pi;       // the famous pi constant
  extern const double e;        // base of the natural logarithm
  extern const double sqrt_2;   // square root of 2
}

#endif
```

You can find the corresponding source file in the Ex10_06A directory of the online downloads. It is similar to our original Constants.h, except that there's no #include guard, and all occurrences of the inline keyword have been replaced with extern.

Either way, the main source file can use these constants as follows:

```
// Ex10_06.cpp
// Using a namespace
#include <iostream>
#include "Constants.h"

int main()
{
  std::cout << "pi has the value " << constants::pi << std::endl;
  std::cout << "This should be 2: " << constants::sqrt_2 * constants::sqrt_2 << std::endl;
}
```

This example produces the following output:

```
pi has the value 3.14159
This should be 2: 2
```

Applying using Declarations

Just to formalize what we have been doing in previous examples, we'll remind you of the using declaration for a single name from a namespace:

```
using namespace_name::identifier;
```

using is a keyword, namespace_name is the name of the namespace, and identifier is the name that you want to use unqualified. This declaration introduces a single name from the namespace, which could represent anything that has a name. For instance, a set of overloaded functions defined within a namespace can be introduced with a single using declaration.

Although we've placed using declarations and directives at global scope in the examples, you can also place them within a namespace, within a function, or even within a statement block. In each case, the declaration or directive applies until the end of the block that contains it.

▓ **Note**   When you use an unqualified name, the compiler first tries to find the definition in the current scope, prior to the point at which it is used. If the definition is not found, the compiler looks in the immediately enclosing scope. This continues until the global scope is reached. If a definition for the name is not found at global scope (which could be an extern declaration), the compiler concludes that the name is not defined.

Functions and Namespaces

For a function to exist within a namespace, it is sufficient for the function prototype to appear in the namespace. You can define the function elsewhere using the qualified name for the function; in other words, the function definition doesn't have to be enclosed in a namespace block (it can, but it doesn't have to be). Let's explore an example. Suppose you write two functions, max() and min(), that return the maximum and minimum of a vector of values. You can put the declarations for the functions in a namespace as follows:

```
// compare.h
// For Ex10_07.cpp
#ifndef COMPARE_H
#define COMPARE_H
#include <vector>

namespace compare
{
  double max(const std::vector<double>& data);
  double min(const std::vector<double>& data);
}
#endif
```

This code would be in a header file, compare.h, which can be included by any source file that uses the functions. The definitions for the functions can now appear in a .cpp file. You can write the definitions without enclosing them in a namespace block, as long as the name of each function is qualified with the namespace name. The contents of the file would be as follows:

```
// compare.cpp
// For Ex10_07.cpp
#include "compare.h"
#include <limits>                // For std::numeric_limits<>::infinity()

// Function to find the maximum
double compare::max(const std::vector<double>& data)
{
  double result { -std::numeric_limits<double>::infinity() };
  for (const auto value : data)
    if (value > result) result = value;
  return result;
}

// Function to find the minimum
double compare::min(const std::vector<double>& data)
{
  double result { std::numeric_limits<double>::infinity() };
  for (const auto value : data)
    if (value < result) result = value;
  return result;
}
```

You need the `compare.h` header file to be included so that the `compare` namespace is identified. This tells the compiler to deduce that the `min()` and `max()` functions are *declared* within the namespace. Next, there's an #include directive for `limits`. This Standard Library header provides facilities to query for properties and special values of numeric data types. In this particular case, we use it to obtain the special value that the fundamental double type normally has for infinity. Positive infinity (mathematical notation $+\infty$) is a special double value greater than any other double value, and negative infinity ($-\infty$) is one that is less than any other double. The standard syntax to obtain these special values in C++ is `std::numeric_limits<double>::infinity()`. They readily allow us to write `min()` and `max()` functions that do something sensible for empty vectors as well.

Note that there's an #include directive for the `vector` header that is also included in `compare.h`. The contents of the `vector` header will appear only once in this file because all the Standard Library headers have preprocessing directives to prevent duplication. In general, it can sometimes be a good idea to have #include directives for every header that a file uses, even when one header may include another header that you use. This makes the file independent of potential changes to the header files.

You could place the code for the function definitions within the `compare` namespace directly as well. In that case, the contents of `compare.cpp` would be as follows:

```cpp
#include <vector>
#include <limits>                 // For std::numeric_limits<>::infinity()

namespace compare
{
  double max(const std::vector<double>& data)
  {
    // Code for max() as above...
  }

  double min(const std::vector<double>& data)
  {
    // Code for min() as above...
  }
}
```

If you write the function definitions in this way, then you don't need to #include `compare.h` into this file. This is because the definitions are within the namespace. Doing it this way, however, is really unconventional. You'd normally #include a header `MyFunctionality.h` in a source file with the same base name, `MyFunctionality.cpp`, and define all functions there by explicitly qualifying them with their namespace using `::`.

Using the `min()` and `max()` functions is the same, however you have defined them. To confirm how easy it is, let's try it with the functions you've just defined. Create the `compare.h` header file with the contents we discussed earlier. Create the first version of `compare.cpp` where the definitions are not defined in a namespace block. All you need now is a `.cpp` file containing the definition of `main()` to try the functions:

```cpp
// Ex10_07.cpp
// Using functions in a namespace
#include <iostream>
#include <vector>
#include "compare.h"

using compare::max;                      // Using declaration for max
```

```
int main()
{
  using compare::min;                    // Using declaration for min

  std::vector<double> data {1.5, 4.6, 3.1, 1.1, 3.8, 2.1};
  std::cout << "Minimum double is " << min(data) << std::endl;
  std::cout << "Maximum double is " << max(data) << std::endl;
}
```

If you compile the two .cpp files and link them, executing the program produces the following output:

```
Minimum double is 1.1
Maximum double is 4.6
```

There is a using declaration for both functions in compare.h, so you can use the names without having to add the namespace name. Just to show you that it's possible, we've added the declaration for compare::max() in the global scope and that for compare::min() at function scope. The result is that max() can be used unqualified in the entire source file, but min() only within the main() function. Of course, this distinction would've made much more sense had there been multiple functions in your source file.

In this case, you could equally well have used a using directive for the compare namespace in this case:

```
using namespace compare;
```

The namespace only contains the functions max() and min(), so this would have been just as good and one less line of code. You can again insert this using namespace directive either at the global or function scope. Either way, the semantics are as you'd expect.

Without the using declarations for the function names (or a using directive for the compare namespace), you would have to qualify the functions like this:

```
std::cout << "Minimum double is " << compare::min(data) << std::endl;
std::cout << "Maximum double is " << compare::max(data) << std::endl;
```

Unnamed Namespaces

You don't have to assign a name to a namespace, but this doesn't mean it doesn't have a name. You can declare an unnamed namespace with the following code:

```
namespace
{
   // Code in the namespace, functions, etc.
}
```

This creates a namespace that has a unique internal name that is generated by the compiler. Only one "unnamed" namespace exists within each translation unit, so additional namespace declarations without a name will be extensions of the first. However, unnamed namespaces within distinct translation units always are distinct unnamed namespaces.

Note that an unnamed namespace is not within the global namespace. This fact, combined with the fact that an unnamed namespace is unique to a translation unit, has significant consequences. It means that functions, variables, and anything else declared within an unnamed namespace are local to the translation unit in which they are defined. They can't be accessed from another translation unit. It should come therefore as no surprise that the compiler assigns internal linkage to all names declared in an unnamed namespace.

In other words, placement of function definitions within an unnamed namespace has the same effect as declaring the functions as static in the global namespace. Declaring functions and variables as static at global scope used to be how one ensured they weren't accessible outside their translation unit. However, as noted already before, this practice is de facto deprecated. An unnamed namespace is a much better way of restricting accessibility where necessary.

▓ **Tip**   All names declared inside an unnamed namespace have internal linkage (even names defined with an extern specifier). If a function is not supposed to be accessible from outside a particular translation unit, you should always define it in an unnamed namespace. Using a static specifier for this purpose is no longer recommended.

Nested Namespaces

You can define one namespace inside another. The mechanics of this are easiest to understand if we look at a specific context. For instance, suppose you have the following nested namespaces:

```
//outin.h
#ifndef OUTIN_H
#define OUTIN_H
#include <vector>

namespace outer
{
  double max(const std::vector<double>& data)
  {
    // body code...
  }

  double min(const std::vector<double>& data)
  {
   // body code...
  }

  namespace inner
  {
    void normalize(std::vector<double>& data)
    {
      // ...
      double minValue{ min(data) };   // Calls min() in outer namespace
      // ...
    }
  }
}
#endif // OUTIN_H
```

From within the inner namespace, the normalize() function can call the function min() in the namespace outer without qualifying the name. This is because the declaration of normalize() in the inner namespace is also within the outer namespace.

To call `min()` from the global namespace, you qualify the function name in the usual way:

```
double result{ outer::min(data) };
```

Of course, you could use a `using` declaration for the function name or specify a `using` directive for the namespace. To call `normalize()` from the global namespace, you must qualify the function name with both namespace names:

```
outer::inner::normalize(data);
```

The same applies if you include the function prototype within the namespace and supply the definition separately. You could write just the prototype of `normalize()` within the `inner` namespace and place the definition of `normalize()` in the file `outin.cpp`:

```
// outin.cpp
#include "outin.h"
void outer::inner::normalize(std::vector<double>& data)
{
  // ...
  double minValue{ min(data) };          // Calls min() in outer
  // ...
}
```

To compile this successfully, the compiler needs to know about the namespaces. Therefore, `outin.h`, which we `#include` here prior to the function definition, needs to contain the namespace declarations.

To declare or define something in the nested `inner` namespace, you must always nest the block for the `inner` namespace inside a block for the `outer` namespace. Here's an example:

```
namespace outer
{
  namespace inner
  {
    double average(const std::vector<double>& data) { /* body code... */ }
  }
}
```

If you would have defined the `average()` function without the surrounding `namespace outer` block, you'd have defined a new namespace called `inner` next to—instead of nested into—`outer`:

```
namespace inner
{
    double average(const std::vector<double>& data) { /* body code... */ }
}
```

In other words, the `average()` function would then have to be qualified as `inner::average(data)`, instead of `outer::inner::average(data)`.

Because defining inside nested namespaces that way can become cumbersome quite fast—especially as the number of levels grows to, say, three or more—the latest C++17 version of the language has introduced a new, more convenient syntax for this. In C++17, you can write our earlier example like this:

```
namespace outer::inner
{
  double average(const std::vector<double>& data) { /* body code... */ }
}
```

Namespace Aliases

In a large program with multiple development groups, long namespace names or more deeply nested namespaces may become necessary to ensure that you don't have accidental name clashes (although we'd probably advise you to avoid this if at all possible). Such long names may be unduly cumbersome to use; having to attach names such as Group5_Process3_Subsection2 or Group5::Process3::Subsection2 to every function call would be more than a nuisance. To get over this, you can define an alias for a namespace name on a local basis. The general form of the statement you'd use to define an alias for a namespace name is as follows:

```
namespace alias_name = original_namespace_name;
```

You can then use alias_name in place of original_namespace_name to access names within the namespace. For example, to define an alias for the namespace name in the previous paragraph, you could write this:

```
namespace G5P3S2 = Group5::Process3::Subsection2;
```

Now you can call a function within the original namespace with a statement such as this:

```
int maxValue {G5P3S2::max(data)};
```

Logical Preprocessing Directives

The logical #if works in essentially the same way as an if statement in C++. Among other things this allows conditional inclusion of code and/or further preprocessing directives in a file, depending on whether preprocessing identifiers have been defined or based on identifiers having specific values. This is particularly useful when you want to maintain one set of code for an application that may be compiled and linked to run in different hardware or operating system environments. You can define preprocessing identifiers that specify the environment for which the code is to be compiled and select code or #include directives accordingly.

The Logical #if Directive

You have seen in the context of managing the contents of a header file that a logical #if directive can test whether a symbol has been previously defined. Suppose you put the following code in your program file:

```
// Code that sets up the array data[]...

#ifdef CALC_AVERAGE
  double average {};
  for (size_t i {}; i < std::size(data); ++i)
    average += data[i];
  average /= std::size(data);
  std::cout << "Average of data array is " << average << std::endl;
#endif

// rest of the program...
```

If the identifier CALC_AVERAGE has been defined by a previous preprocessing directive, the code between the #if and #endif directives is compiled as part of the program. If CALC_AVERAGE has not been defined, the code won't be included. You used a similar technique before to create #include guards that protect the contents of a header file from multiple inclusions into source files.

You can also use the #if directive, though, to test whether a constant expression is true. Let's explore that a bit further.

Testing for Specific Identifier Values

The general form of the #if directive is as follows:

```
#if constant_expression
```

The constant_expression must be an integral constant expression that does not contain casts. All arithmetic operations are executed with the values treated as type long or unsigned long, though Boolean operators (| |, &&, and !) are definitely supported as well. If the value of constant_expression evaluates to nonzero, then lines following the #if down to the #endif will be included in the code to be compiled. The most common application of this uses simple comparisons to check for a particular identifier value. For example, you might have the following sequence of statements:

```
#if ADDR == 64
   // Code taking advantage of 64-bit addressing...
#endif
```

The statements between the #if directive and #endif are included in the program here only if the identifier ADDR has been defined as 64 in a previous #define directive.

■ **Tip**   There is no cross-platform macro identifier to detect whether the current target platform uses 64-bit addressing. Most compilers, however, do offer some platform-specific macro that it will define for you whenever it's targeting a 64-bit platform. A concrete test that should work for the Visual C++, GCC, and Clang compilers, for instance, would look something like this:

```
#if _WIN64 || __x86_64__ || __ppc64__
   // Code taking advantage of 64-bit addressing...
#endif
```

Consult your compiler documentation for these and other predefined macro identifiers.

Multiple-Choice Code Selection

The #else directive works in the same way as the C++ else statement, in that it identifies a sequence of lines to be included in the file if the #if condition fails. This provides a choice of two blocks, one of which will be incorporated into the final source. Here's an example:

```
#if ADDR == 64
   std::cout << "64-bit addressing version." << std::endl;
   // Code taking advantage of 64-bit addressing...
```

```
#else
  std::cout << "Standard 32-bit addressing version." << std::endl;
  // Code for older 32-bit processors...
#endif
```

One or the other of these sequences of statements will be included in the file, depending on whether or not ADDR has been defined as 64.

There is a special form of #if for multiple-choice selections. This is the #elif directive, which has the following general form:

```
#elif constant_expression
```

Here is an example of how you might use this:

```
#if LANGUAGE == ENGLISH
  #define Greeting "Good Morning."
#elif LANGUAGE == GERMAN
  #define Greeting "Guten Tag."
#elif LANGUAGE == FRENCH
  #define Greeting "Bonjour."
#else
  #define Greeting "Ola."
#endif
  std::cout << Greeting << std::endl;
```

With this sequence of directives, the output statement will display one of a number of different greetings, depending on the value assigned to LANGUAGE in a previous #define directive.

▓ **Caution**   Any undefined identifiers that appear after the conditional directives #if and #elif are replaced with the number 0. This implies that, should LANGUAGE for instance not be defined in the earlier example, it may still compare equal to ENGLISH should that be either undefined or explicitly defined to be zero.

Another possible use is to include different code depending on an identifier that represents a version number:

```
#if VERSION == 3
  // Code for version 3 here...
#elif VERSION == 2
  // Code for version 2 here...
#else
  // Code for original version 1 here...
#endif
```

This allows you to maintain a single source file that compiles to produce different versions of the program depending on how VERSION has been set in a #define directive.

■ **Tip**   Your compiler likely allows you to specify the value of preprocessing identifiers by passing a command-line argument to the compiler (if you're using a graphical IDE, there should be a corresponding properties dialog somewhere). That way you can compile different versions or configurations of the same program without changing any code.

Standard Preprocessing Macros

There are several standard predefined preprocessing macros, and the most useful are listed in Table 10-3.

Table 10-3. *Predefined Preprocessing Macros*

Macro	Description
__LINE__	The line number of the current source line as a decimal integer literal.
__FILE__	The name of the source file as a character string literal.
__DATE__	The date when the source file was preprocessed as a character string literal in the form Mmm dd yyyy. Here, Mmm is the month in characters, (Jan, Feb, etc.); dd is the day in the form of a pair of characters 1 to 31, where single-digit days are preceded by a blank; and yyyy is the year as four digits (such as 2014).
__TIME__	The time at which the source file was compiled, as a character string literal in the form hh:mm:ss, which is a string containing the pairs of digits for hours, minutes, and seconds separated by colons.
__cplusplus	A number of type long that corresponds to the highest version of the C++ standard that your compiler supports. This number is of the form yyyymm, where yyyy and mm represent the year and month in which that version of the standard was approved. At the time of writing, possible values are 199711 for nonmodern C++, 201103 for C++11, 201402 for C++14, and 201703 for C++17. Compilers may use intermediate numbers to signal support for earlier drafts of the standard as well.

Note that each of the macro names in Table 10-3 start, and most end, with two underscore characters. The __LINE__ and __FILE__ macros expand to reference information relating to the source file. You can modify the current line number using the #line directive, and subsequent line numbers will increment from that. For example, to start line numbering at 1000, you would add this directive:

```
#line 1000
```

You can use the #line directive to change the string returned by the __FILE__ macro. It usually produces the fully qualified file name, but you can change it to whatever you like. Here's an example:

```
#line 1000 "The program file"
```

This directive changes the line number of the next line to 1000 and alters the string returned by the __FILE__ macro to "The program file". This doesn't alter the file name, just the string returned by the macro. Of course, if you just wanted to alter the apparent file name and leave the line numbers unaltered, the best you can do is to use the __LINE__ macro in the #line directive:

```
#line __LINE__ "The program file"
```

It depends on the implementation what exactly happens after this directive. There are two possibly outcomes: either the line numbers remain unaltered or they are all decremented by one (it depends on whether the value returned by __LINE__ takes the line upon which the #line directive appears into account).

You can use the date and time macros to record when your program was last compiled with a statement such as this:

```
std::cout << "Program last compiled at " << __TIME__ << " on "<< __DATE__ << std::endl;
```

When this statement is compiled, the values displayed by the statement are fixed until you compile it again. Thus, the program outputs the time and date of its last compilation. These macros can be useful for use in either about screens or log files.

Testing for Available Headers

Each version of the Standard Library provides a multitude of new header files defining new features. These new features and functionalities allow you to write code that would've taken a lot more effort before or that would've been less performant or less robust. On the one hand, you therefore normally always want to use the best and latest that C++ has to offer. On the other hand, however, your code is sometimes supposed to compile and run correctly with multiple compilers—either multiple versions of the same compiler or different compilers for different target platforms. This sometimes requires a way for you to test, at compile time, what features the current compiler supports to enable or disable different versions of your code.

The __has_include() macro, recently introduced by C++17, can be used to check for the availability of any header file. Here's an example:

```
#if __has_include(<SomeStandardLibaryHeader>)
  #include <SomeStandardLibaryHeader>

  // ... Definitions that use functionality of some Standard Library header ...

#elif __has_include("SomeHeader.h")
  #include "SomeHeader.h"

  // ... Alternative definitions that use functionality of SomeHeader.h ...

#else
  #error("Need at least SomeStandardLibaryHeader or SomeHeader.h")
#endif
```

We're sure that you can figure out how this works from this example alone.

■ **Tip**   The __has_include() macro itself is still very new. You can check whether it is supported using the #ifdef directive, as in #ifdef __has_include.

Debugging Methods

Most of your programs will contain errors, or *bugs*, when you first complete them. There are many ways in which bugs can arise. Most simple typos will be caught by the compiler, so you'll find these immediately. Logical errors or failing to consider all possible variations in input data will take longer to find. Debugging is the process of eliminating these errors. Debugging a program represents a substantial proportion of the total time required to develop it. The larger and more complex the program, the more bugs it's likely to contain and the more time and effort you'll need to make it run properly. Very large programs—operating systems, for example, or complex applications such as word processing systems or even the C++ program development system that you may be using at this moment—can be so complex that the system will never be completely bug free. You will already have some experience with this through the regular patches and updates to the operating system and some of the applications on your computer. Most bugs in this context are relatively minor and don't limit the usability of the product greatly. The most serious bugs in commercial products tend to be security issues.

Your approach to writing a program can significantly affect how difficult it will be to test and debug. A well-structured program that consists of compact functions, each with a well-defined purpose, is much easier to test than one without these attributes. Finding bugs will also be easier with a program that has well-chosen variable and function names and comments that document the operation and purpose of its component functions. Good use of indentation and statement layout can also make testing and fault-finding simpler.

It is beyond the scope of this book to deal with debugging comprehensively. The book concentrates on the standard C++ language and library, independent of any particular C++ development system, and it's more than likely you'll be debugging your programs using tools that are specific to the development system you have. Nevertheless, we'll explain some basic ideas that are common to most debugging systems. We'll also introduce the rather elementary debugging aids within the Standard Library.

Integrated Debuggers

Many C++ compilers come with a program development environment that has extensive debugging tools built in. These potentially powerful facilities can dramatically reduce the time needed to get a program working, and if you have such a development environment, familiarizing yourself with how you use it for debugging will pay substantial dividends. Common tools include the following:

- *Tracing program flow*: This allows you to execute a program by stepping through the source code one statement at a time. It continues with the next statement when you press a designated key. A program may have to be compiled in what is commonly called *debug mode* to make this possible. Other provisions of the debug environment usually allow you to display information about all relevant variables at each pause.

- *Setting breakpoints*: Stepping through a large program one statement at a time can be tedious. It may even be impossible to step through the program in a reasonable period of time. Stepping through a loop that executes 10,000 times is an unrealistic proposition. Breakpoints identify specific statements in a program at which execution pauses to allow you to check the program state. Execution continues to the next breakpoint when you press a specified key.

- *Setting watches*: A watch identifies a specific variable whose value you want to track as execution progresses. The values of variables identified by watches you have set are displayed at each pause point. If you step through your program statement by statement, you can see the exact point at which values are changed and sometimes when they unexpectedly don't change.

- *Inspecting program elements*: You can usually examine a variety of program components when execution is paused. For example, at breakpoints you can examine details of a function, such as its return type and its arguments, or information relating to a pointer, such as its location, the address it contains, and the data at that address. It is sometimes possible to access the values of expressions and to modify variables. Modifying variables can often allow problem areas to be bypassed, allowing subsequent code to be executed with correct data.

Preprocessing Directives in Debugging

Although many C++ development systems provide powerful debug facilities, adding your own tracing code can still be useful. You can use conditional preprocessing directives to include blocks of code to assist during testing and omit the code when testing is complete. You can control the formatting of data that will be displayed for debugging purposes, and you can arrange for the output to vary according to conditions or relationships within the program.

We'll illustrate how you can use preprocessing directive to help with debugging through a somewhat contrived program. This example also gives you a chance to review a few of the techniques that you should be familiar with by now. Just for this exercise you'll declare three functions that you'll use in the example within a namespace, fun. First, you'll put the namespace declaration in a header file:

```
// functions.h
#ifndef FUNCTIONS_H
#define FUNCTIONS_H
namespace fun
{
  // Function prototypes
  int sum(int, int);              // Sum arguments
  int product(int, int);          // Product of arguments
  int difference(int, int);       // Difference between arguments
}
#endif
```

Enclosing the contents of the header file between an #include guard prevents the contents from being #included into a translation unit more than once. The prototypes are defined within the namespace, fun, so the function names are qualified with fun, and the function definitions must appear in the same namespace.

You can put the functions definitions in the file functions.cpp:

```
// functions.cpp

//#define TESTFUNCTION             // Uncomment to get trace output

#ifdef TESTFUNCTION
#include <iostream>                // Only required for trace output...
#endif

#include "functions.h"

// Definition of the function sum
int fun::sum(int x, int y)
{
  #ifdef TESTFUNCTION
```

```
  std::cout << "Function sum called." << std::endl;
  #endif

  return x+y;
}

/* The definitions of the functions product() and difference() are analogous... */
```

You only need the iostream header because you use stream output statements to provide trace information in each function. The iostream header will be included and the output statements compiled only if the identifier TESTFUNCTION is defined in the file. TESTFUNCTION isn't defined at present because the directive is commented out.

The main() function is in a separate .cpp file:

```
// Ex10_08.cpp
// Debugging using preprocessing directives
#include <iostream>
#include <cstdlib>                    // For random number generator
#include <ctime>                      // For time function
#include "functions.h"

#define TESTRANDOM

// Function to generate a random integer 0 to count-1
size_t random(size_t count)
{
  return static_cast<size_t>(std::rand() / (RAND_MAX / count + 1));
}

int main()
{
  const int a{10}, b{5};             // Some arbitrary values
  int result{};                      // Storage for results

  const size_t num_functions {3};
  std::srand(static_cast<unsigned>(std::time(nullptr))); // Seed random generator

  // Select function at random
  for (size_t i{}; i < 5; i++)
  {
    size_t select = random(num_functions); // Generate random number (0 to num_functions-1)

#ifdef TESTRANDOM
    std::cout << "Random number = " << select << ' ';
    if (select >= num_functions)
    {
      std::cout << "Invalid random number generated!" << std::endl;
      return 1;
    }
#endif
```

```
  switch (select)
  {
    case 0: result = fun::sum(a, b); break;
    case 1: result = fun::product(a, b); break;
    case 2: result = fun::difference(a, b); break;
  }
  std::cout << "result = " << result << std::endl;
}
}
```

Here's an example of the output:

```
Random number = 2 result = 5
Random number = 2 result = 5
Random number = 1 result = 50
Random number = 0 result = 15
Random number = 1 result = 50
```

In general, you should get something different. If you want to get the trace output for the functions in the namespace fun as well, you must uncomment the #define directive at the beginning of functions.cpp.

The #include directive for functions.h adds the prototypes for sum(), product(), and difference(). The functions are defined within the namespace fun. These functions are called in main() using a random number and a switch statement. The number is produced by random(). The Standard Library function rand() from cstdlib that is called in random() generates a sequence of pseudorandom numbers of type int in the range 0 to RAND_MAX, where RAND_MAX is a symbol defined as an integer in the cstdlib header. Somehow the range of values returned by rand() therefore needs to be scaled to the range of values you need. You need to take care, however, what expression you use to do this. The expression rand() % count, for instance, would work but is known to produce numbers that are distressingly nonrandom. The expression we used in Ex10_08 has been proven to fare much better (trust us, it works!), provided count is sufficiently small compared to RAND_MAX.

▓ **Caution**   The rand() function in the stdlib header does not generate random numbers that have satisfactory properties for applications that require truly random numbers (such as cryptography). It is acceptable (just) for the simplest of applications, but for any more serious use of random numbers, we recommend that you investigate the functionality provided by the random header of the Standard Library. The details of this extensive and relatively complex random number generation library are outside the scope of this book, though.

You must initialize the sequence that rand() produces before the first rand() call by passing an unsigned integer seed value to srand(). Each different seed value will typically result in a different integer sequence from successive rand() calls. The time() function that is declared in the ctime header returns the number of seconds since January 1, 1970, as an integer, so using this as the argument to srand() ensures that you get a different random sequence each time the program executes.

Defining the identifier TESTRANDOM in Ex10_08.cpp switches on diagnostic output in main(). With TESTRANDOM defined, the code to output diagnostic information in main() will be included in the source that is compiled. If you remove the #define directive, the trace code will not be included. The trace code checks to make sure you use a valid number for the switch statement. Because you don't expect to generate invalid random values, you shouldn't get this output!

▓ **Tip** It's easy to generate invalid values and verify the diagnostic code works. To do this, the `random()` function must generate a number other than 0, 1, or 2. If you add 1 to the value produced in the `return` statement, you should get an illegal value roughly 33 percent of the time.

If you define the TESTFUNCTION identifier in `functions.cpp`, you'll get trace output from each function. This is a convenient way of controlling whether the trace statements are compiled into the program. You can see how this works by looking at one of the functions that may be called, `product()`:

```
int fun::product(int x, int y)
{
#ifdef TESTFUNCTION
  std::cout << "Function product called." << std::endl;
#endif

  return x * y;
}
```

The output statement simply displays a message, each time the function is called, but the output statement will be compiled only if TESTFUNCTION has been defined. A #define directive for a preprocessing symbol such as TESTFUNCTION is local to the source file in which it appears, so each source file that requires TESTFUNCTION to be defined needs to have its own #define directive. One way to manage this is to put all your directives that control trace and other debug output into a separate header file. You can then include this into all your .cpp files. In this way, you can alter the kind of debug output you get by making adjustments to this one header file.

Of course, diagnostic code is included only while you are testing the program. Once you think the program works, you quite sensibly leave it out. Therefore, you need to be clear that this sort of code is no substitute for error detection and recovery code that deals with unfortunate situations arising in your fully tested program (as they most certainly will).

▓ **Tip** Some compilers define a specific macro if and only if the code is being compiled in debug mode. For Visual C++, for instance, that macro is _DEBUG. At times, it's interesting to use such macro identifiers to control the inclusion of debugging statements.

Using the assert() Macro

The `assert()` preprocessor macro is defined in the Standard Library header `cassert`. This enables you to test logical expressions in your program. Including a line of the form `assert(expression)` results in code that causes the program to be terminated with a diagnostic message if `expression` evaluates to `false`. We can demonstrate this with this simple example:

```
// Ex10_09.cpp
// Demonstrating assertions
#include <iostream>
#include <cassert>
int main()
```

```
{
  int y {5};

  for (int x {}; x < 20; ++x)
  {
    std::cout << "x = " << x << " y = " << y << std::endl;
    assert(x < y);
  }
}
```

You should see an assertion message in the output when the value of x reaches 5. The program is terminated by the assert() macro by calling std::abort() when x < y evaluates to false. The abort() function is from the Standard Library, and its effect is to terminate the program immediately. As you can see from the output, this happens when x reaches the value 5. The macro displays the output on the standard error stream, cerr, which is always the command line. The message contains the condition that failed and also the file name and line number in which the failure occurred. This is particularly useful with multifile programs, where the source of the error is pinpointed exactly.

Assertions are often used for critical conditions in a program where if certain conditions are not met, disaster will surely ensue. You would want to be sure that the program wouldn't continue if such errors arise. You can use any logical expression as the argument to the assert() macro, so you have a lot of flexibility.

Using assert() is simple and effective, and when things go wrong, it provides sufficient information to pin down where the program has terminated.

■ **Tip**   Some debuggers, in particular those integrated into graphical IDEs, allow you to pause each time an assertion is triggered, right before the application terminates. This greatly increases the value of assertions during debugging sessions.

Switching Off assert() Macros

You can switch off the preprocessor assertion mechanism when you recompile the program by defining NDEBUG at the beginning of the program file:

```
#define NDEBUG
```

This causes all assertions in the translation unit to be ignored. If you add this #define at the beginning of Ex10_09.cpp, you'll get output for all values of x from 0 to 19 and no diagnostic message. Note that this directive is effective only if it's placed before the #include statement for cassert.

■ **Tip**   Most compilers also allow you to define macros such as NDEBUG globally for all source and header files at once (for instance by passing a command-line argument or by filling in some field in your IDE's configuration windows). Often NDEBUG is defined that way for fully optimizing so-called "release" configurations but not for the configurations that are used during debugging. Consult your compiler's documentation for more details.

▓ **Caution**   assert() is for detecting programming errors, not for handling errors at runtime. Evaluation of the logical expression shouldn't cause side effects or be based on something beyond the programmer's control (such as whether opening a file succeeds). Your program should include code to handle all error conditions that might be expected to occur occasionally.

Static Assertions

Static assertions, unlike the assert() macro, are part of the C++ language itself. That is, they are no Standard Library addition but built into the language. The assert() macro is for checking conditions *dynamically, at runtime*, whereas static assertions are for checking conditions *statically, at compile time*.

A static assertion is a statement of either of the following forms:

```
static_assert(constant_expression);
static_assert(constant_expression, error_message);
```

static_assert is a keyword, constant_expression must produce a result at compile time that can be converted to type bool, and error_message is an optional string literal. If constant_expression evaluates to false, then the compilation of your program should fail. The compiler will abort the compilation and output a diagnostics message that contains error_message if you provided it. If you did not specify an error_message, the compiler will generate one for you (usually based on constant_expression). When constant_expression is true, a static assertion does nothing.

▓ **Note**   The fact that you can omit the error_message string literal in static assertions is new in C++17.

The compiler needs to be able to evaluate constant_expression during compilation. This limits the range of expressions you can use. Typical static_assert() expressions consist of literals, const variables that are initialized by literals, macros, the sizeof() operator, template arguments, and so on. A static assertion cannot, for instance, check the size() of a std::string or use the value of a function argument or any other non-const variable—such expressions can be evaluated only at runtime.

As a first example, suppose that your program does not support 32-bit compilation, for instance, because it needs to address more than 2GB of memory. Then you could put the following static assertion anywhere in your source file:

```
static_assert(sizeof(int*) > 4, "32-bit compilation is not supported.");
```

As you know, the sizeof operator evaluates to the number of bytes that is used to represent a type or variable. For a 32-bit program, any pointer occupies 32 bits, or 4 bytes. Note that we picked int*, but any pointer type would do. Obviously the compiler knows the size of an int* pointer at compile time. Adding this static assertion will thus ensure that you cannot inadvertently compile as a 32-bit program.

> ▦ **Note**   With every new edition of the C++ standard, and C++14 in particular, the range of expressions and
> functions that compilers should be able to evaluate at compile time is increasing. You can define all kinds of
> functions, variables, and even lambda expressions (C++17) that it should be able to evaluate statically simply by
> adding the `constexpr` keyword to their declaration. Naturally, such functions remain bound by certain restrictions;
> not everything is possible at compile time. The use of `constexpr`, however, is beyond the scope of this book.

A common use for static assertions is in template definitions to verify the characteristics of a template
parameter. Suppose that you define a function template for computing the average of elements of type T.
Clearly, this is an arithmetic operation, so you want to be sure the template cannot be used with collections
of non-numeric types. A static assertion can do that:

```
// average.h
#ifndef AVERAGE_H
#define AVERAGE_H

#include <type_traits>
#include <vector>
#include <cassert>

template<typename T>
T average(const std::vector<T>& values)
{
  static_assert(std::is_arithmetic_v<T>,
                "Type parameter for average() must be arithmetic.");
  assert(!values.empty());    // Not possible using static_assert()!

  T sum {};
  for (auto& value : values)
    sum += value;
  return sum / values.size();
}
#endif
```

A static assertion inside a function template gets evaluated each time the compiler instantiates the
template with a given list of arguments—again always at compile time. At that time, the compiler knows the
properties of the types assigned to type template parameters such as T, as well as the values assigned to any
non-type template parameters. Static assertions pertaining to properties of types typically employ templates
defined in the type_traits Standard Library header. One example of such a so-called *type trait* is is_
arithmetic<T>. This type trait has a value member, which you can access as is_arithmetic<T>::value and
which will be true if T is an arithmetic type and false otherwise. An arithmetic type is any floating-point or
integral type. Since C++17, you can also write is_arithmetic_v<T> instead of is_arithmetic<T>::value.

> ▦ **Note**   The type_traits header contains a large number of type testing templates including is_integral_
> v<T>, is_signed_v<T>, is_unsigned_v<T>, is_floating_point_v<T>, and is_enum_v<T>. There are many
> other useful templates in the type_traits header, and it is well worth exploring the contents further, especially
> once you have learned about class templates in Chapter 16.

You cannot *statically* assert, however, that the given `values` vector must be nonempty. After all, the same instance of this function template may be called many times, each time with `vectors` of different size. In general, the compiler has no way of knowing whether this vector will be empty or not—the only way to know this is to check the size during the execution of your program. In other words, asserting this condition is clearly a job for the `assert()` macro!

You can use the following program to see static assertions in action:

```
// Ex10_10.cpp
// Using a static assertion
#include <vector>
#include <iostream>
#include <string>
#include "average.h"

int main()
{
   std::vector<double> vectorData {1.5, 2.5, 3.5, 4.5};
   std::cout << "The average of vectorData is " << average(vectorData) << std::endl;

// Uncomment the next lines for compiler errors...
//   std::vector<std::string> words {"this", "that", "them", "those"};
//   std::cout << "The average of words values is " << average(words) << std::endl;

   std::vector<float> emptyVector;
   average(emptyVector);                  // Will trigger a runtime assertion!
}
```

In case you were wondering, yes, even if we had not added the `static_assert()` statement, the `average()` template would still fail to instantiate for nonarithmetic types such as `std::string`. After all, you cannot divide a `string` by its size. Depending on your compiler, the error message you will then get may be rather cryptic. To see the difference, we invite you to remove the static assertion from the `average()` template, uncomment the two lines of the test program, and then recompile. Static assertions like this are thus added sometimes not so much to make the compilation fail but rather to provide more helpful diagnostic messages.

Summary

This chapter discussed capabilities that operate between, within, and across program files. C++ programs typically consist of many files, and the larger the program, the more files you have to contend with. It's vital that you really understand namespaces, preprocessing, and debugging techniques if you are to develop real-world C++ programs.

The important points from this chapter include the following:

- Each entity in a translation unit must have only one definition. If multiple definitions are allowed throughout a program, they must still all be identical.

- A name can have internal linkage, meaning that the name is accessible throughout a translation unit; external linkage, meaning that the name is accessible from any translation unit; or it can have no linkage, meaning that the name is accessible only in the block in which it is defined.

- You use header files to contain definitions and declarations required by your source files. A header file can contain template and type definitions, enumerations, constants, function declarations, `inline` function and variable definitions, and named namespaces. By convention, header file names use the extension `.h`.

- Your source files will typically contain the definitions for all non-`inline` functions and variables declared in the corresponding header. A C++ source file usually has the file name extension `.cpp`.

- You insert the contents of a header file into a `.cpp` file by using an `#include` directive.

- A `.cpp` file is the basis for a translation unit that is processed by the compiler to generate an object file.

- A namespace defines a scope; all names declared within this scope have the namespace name attached to them. All declarations of names that are not in an explicit namespace scope are in the global namespace.

- A single namespace can be made up of several separate namespace declarations with the same name.

- Identical names that are declared within different namespaces are distinct.

- To refer to an identifier that is declared within a namespace from outside the namespace, you need to specify the namespace name and the identifier, separated by the scope resolution operator, `::`.

- Names declared within a namespace can be used without qualification from inside the namespace.

- The preprocessing phase executes directives to transform the source code in a translation unit prior to compilation. When all directives have been processed, the translation unit will only contain C++ code, with no preprocessing directives remaining.

- You can use conditional preprocessing directives to ensure that the contents of a header file are never duplicated within a translation unit.

- You can use conditional preprocessing directives to control whether trace or other diagnostic debug code is included in your program.

- The `assert()` macro enables you to test logical conditions during execution and issue a message and abort the program if the logical condition is `false`.

- You can use `static_assert` to check type arguments for template parameters in a template instance to ensure that a type argument is consistent with the template definition.

EXERCISES

The following exercises enable you to try what you've learned in this chapter. If you get stuck, look back over the chapter for help. If you're still stuck after that, you can download the solutions from the Apress website (www.apress.com/source-code), but that really should be a last resort.

Exercise 10-1. Write a program that calls two functions, print_this(std::string_view) and print_that(std::string_view), each of which calls a third function, print(std::string_view), to print the string that is passed to it. Define each function and main() in separate source files, and create three header files to contain the prototypes for print_this(), print_that(), and print().

Exercise 10-2. Modify the program from Exercise 10-1 so that print() uses a global integer variable to count the number of times it has been called. Output the value of this variable in main() after calls to print_this() and print_that().

Exercise 10-3. In the print.h header file from Exercise 10-1, delete the existing prototype for print(), and instead create two namespaces, print1 and print2, each of which contains a print(string_view) function. Implement both functions in the print.cpp file so that they print the namespace name and the string. Change print_this() so that it calls print() defined in the print1 namespace, and change print_that() to call the version in the print2 namespace. Run the program, and verify that the correct functions are called.

Exercise 10-4. Modify the main() function from the previous exercise so that print_this() is called only if a DO_THIS preprocessing identifier is defined. When this is not the case, print_that() should be called.

CHAPTER 11

■ ■ ■

Defining Your Own Data Types

In this chapter, we'll introduce one of the most fundamental tools in the C++ programmer's toolbox: classes. We'll also present some ideas that are implicit in object-oriented programming and show how they are applied.

In this chapter, you'll learn:

- What the basic principles in objected-oriented programming are

- How you define a new data type as a class and how you can create and use objects of a class type

- What the different building blocks of a class are—member variables, member functions, class constructors, and destructors—and how to define them

- What a default constructor is and how you can supply your own version

- What a copy constructor is and how to create a custom implementation

- The difference between private and public members

- What the pointer this is and how and when you use it

- What a friend function is and what privileges a friend class has

- What const functions in a class are and how they are used

- What a class destructor is and when you should define it

- What a nested class is and how to use it

Classes and Object-Oriented Programming

You define a new data type by defining a *class*, but before we get into the language, syntax, and programming techniques of classes, we'll explain how your existing knowledge relates to the concept of object-oriented programming. The essence of *object-oriented programming* (commonly abbreviated to *OOP*) is that you write programs in terms of objects in the domain of the problem you are trying to solve, so part of the program development process involves designing a set of types to suit the problem context. If you're writing a program to keep track of your bank account, you'll probably need to have data types such as Account and Transaction. For a program to analyze baseball scores, you may have types such as Player and Team.

Almost everything you have seen up to now has been *procedural programming*, which involves programming a solution in terms of fundamental data types. The variables of the fundamental types don't allow you to model real-world objects (or even imaginary objects) very well, though. It's not possible to model a baseball player realistically in terms of just an int or double value, or any other fundamental data type. You need several values of a variety of types for any meaningful representation of a baseball player.

© Ivor Horton and Peter Van Weert 2018
I. Horton and P. Van Weert, *Beginning C++17*, https://doi.org/10.1007/978-1-4842-3366-5_11

Classes provide a solution. A class type can be a composite of variables of other types—of fundamental types or of other class types. A class can also have functions as an integral part of its definition. You could define a class type called Box that contains three variables of type double that store a length, a width, and a height to represent boxes. You could then define variables of type Box, just as you define variables of fundamental types. Similarly, you could define arrays of Box elements, just as you would with fundamental types. Each of these variables or array elements would be called an *object* or *instance* of the same Box class. You could create and manipulate as many Box objects as you need in a program, and each of them would contain their own length, width, and height dimensions.

This goes quite a long way toward making programming in terms of real-world objects possible. Obviously, you can apply this idea of a class to represent a baseball player or a bank account or anything else. You can use classes to model whatever kinds of objects you want and write your programs around them. So, that's object-oriented programming all wrapped up then, right?

Well, not quite. A class as we've defined it up to now is a big step forward, but there's more to it than that. As well as the notion of user-defined types, object-oriented programming incorporates some additional important ideas (famously *encapsulation* and *data hiding*, *inheritance*, and *polymorphism*). We'll give you a rough, intuitive idea of what these additional OOP concepts mean right now. This will provide a reference frame for the detailed programming you'll be getting into in this and the next three chapters.

Encapsulation

In general, the definition of an object of a given type requires a combination of a specific number of different properties—the properties that make the object what it is. An object contains a precise set of data values that describe the object in sufficient detail for your needs. For a box, it could be just the three dimensions of length, width, and height. For an aircraft carrier, it is likely to be much more. An object can also contain a set of functions that operate on it—functions that use or change the properties, for example, or provide further characteristics of an object such as the volume of a box. The functions in a class define the set of operations that can be applied to an object of the class type, in other words, what you can do with it or to it. Every object of a given class incorporates the same combination of things, specifically, the set of data values as *member variables* of the class that characterize an object and the set of operations as *member functions* of the class. This packaging of data values and functions within an object is referred to as *encapsulation*.[1]

Figure 11-1 illustrates this with the example of an object that represents a loan account with a bank. Every LoanAccount object has its properties defined by the same set of member variables; in this case, one holds the outstanding balance, and the other holds the interest rate. Each object also contains a set of member functions that define operations on the object. The object shown in Figure 11-1 has three member functions: one to calculate interest and add it to the balance and two for managing credit and debit accounting entries. The properties and operations are all encapsulated in every object of the type LoanAccount. Of course, this choice of what makes up a LoanAccount object is arbitrary. You might define it quite differently for your purposes, but however you define the LoanAccount type, all the properties and operations that you specify are encapsulated within every object of the type.

Note that we said earlier that the data values defining an object needed to be "sufficient for your needs," not "sufficient to define the object in general." A person could be defined simply, perhaps just by the name, address, and phone number if you were writing an address book application. A person as a company employee or as a medical patient is likely to be defined by many more properties, and many more operations would be required. You just decide what you need in the contexts in which you intend to use the object.

---

[1] In the context of object-oriented programming, you'll find that the term *encapsulation* may actually refer to two related yet distinct notions. Some authors define encapsulation like we do, namely, as the bundling of data with the functions that operate on that data, while others define it as a language mechanism for restricting direct access to an object's members. The latter is what we refer to as *data hiding* in the next subsection. Enough ink has been spilled discussing which definition is right, so we will not go there—though obviously it's ours. When reading other texts or when discussing with your peers, just keep in mind that encapsulation is often used as a synonym for data hiding.

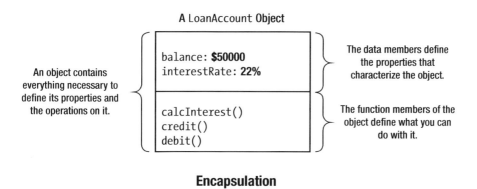

Encapsulation

Figure 11-1. *An example of encapsulation*

Data Hiding

Of course, the bank wouldn't want the balance for a loan account (or the interest rate for that matter) changed arbitrarily from outside an object. Permitting this would be a recipe for chaos. Ideally, the member variables of a LoanAccount object are protected from direct outside interference and are only modifiable in a controlled way. The ability to make the data values for an object generally inaccessible is called *data hiding* or *information hiding.*

Figure 11-2 shows data hiding applied to a LoanAccount object. With a LoanAccount object, the member functions of the object can provide a mechanism that ensures any changes to the member variables follow a particular policy and that the values set are appropriate. Interest shouldn't be negative, for instance, and generally, the balance should reflect the fact that money is owed to the bank, not the reverse.

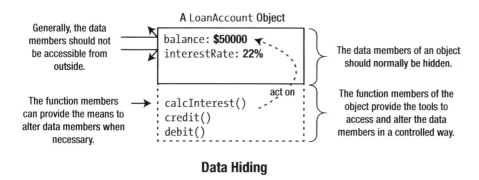

Data Hiding

Figure 11-2. *An example of data hiding*

Data hiding is important because it is necessary if you are to maintain the integrity of an object. If an object is supposed to represent a duck, it should not have four legs; the way to enforce this is to make the leg count inaccessible, in other words, to "hide" the data. Of course, an object may have data values that can legitimately vary, but even then you often want to control the range; after all, a duck doesn't usually weigh 300 pounds, and its weight is definitely rarely zero or negative. Hiding the data belonging to an object prevents it from being accessed directly, but you can provide access through functions that are members of the object, either to alter a data value in a controlled way or simply to obtain its value. Such functions can check that the change they're being asked to make is legal and within prescribed limits where necessary.

You can think of the member variables as representing the *state* of the object, and the member functions that manipulate them as representing the object's *interface* to the outside world. Using the class then involves programming using the functions declared as the interface. A program using the class interface is dependent only on the function names, parameter types, and return types specified for the interface. The internal mechanics of these functions don't affect the rest of the program that is creating and using objects of the class. That means it's important to get the class interface right at the design stage. You can subsequently change the implementation to your heart's content without necessitating any changes to programs that use the class.

For instance, as a program evolves over time, you may need to change the member variables that constitute an object's state. Instead of storing an interest rate in each individual LoanAccount object, for example, you may want to change it so that every LoanAccount object refers to an object of a new class AccountType and store the interest rate in there instead. Figure 11-3 illustrates this redesigned representation of LoanAccount objects.

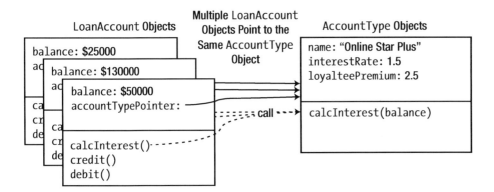

Figure 11-3. *Reworking the representation of the internal state of objects while preserving their interface*

LoanAccount objects now no longer store their interest rate themselves but instead point to an AccountType, which stores all necessary member variables for calculating an account's interest. The calcInterest() member function of LoanAccount therefore calls upon the associated AccountType to do the actual calculation; for this, all the latter needs from an account is its current balance. This more object-oriented design allows you to easily modify the interest rates of all LoanAccounts pointing to the same AccountType all at once or to change the type of an account without re-creating it.

The main point we want to make with this example is that even though both the internal representation (the interestRate member) and the workings (the calcInterest() member) of a LoanAccount have changed drastically, its interface to the outside world remained constant. As far as the rest of the program is concerned, it therefore appears as if nothing has changed at all. Such an overhaul of a LoanAccount's representation and logic would've been much harder if code from outside of its class definition would've been accessing the old, now-removed interestRate member variable of LoanAccounts directly. We would then have had to rework all code using LoanAccount objects as well. Thanks to data hiding, external code can only access member variables through well-defined interface functions. So, all we had to do is to redefine these member functions; we didn't have to worry about the rest of the program.

Notice moreover that because external code could obtain the annual interest only through the calcInterest() interface function, it was trivial for us to introduce an extra "loyalty premium" and use this during interest calculations. This again would've been near impossible if external code would've been reading the old interestRate member directly to calculate interests themselves.

Hiding the data within an object is not mandatory, but it's generally a good idea. In a way, direct access to the values that define an object undermines the whole idea of object-oriented programming. Object-oriented programming is supposed to be programming in terms of *objects*, not in terms of the bits that make up an object. While this may sound rather abstract, we have already seen at least two very good, concrete reasons to consistently hide an object's data and to only access or manipulate it through the functions in its interface:

- Data hiding facilitates maintaining the integrity of an object. It allows you to make sure that an object's internal state—the combination of all its member variables— remains valid at all times.

- Data hiding, combined with a well-thought-out interface, allows you to rework both an object's internal representation (that is, its *state*) and the implementation of its member functions (that is, its *behavior*) without having to rework the rest of the program as well. In object-oriented speak we say that data hiding reduces the *coupling* between a class and the code that uses it. Interface stability is, of course, even more critical if you are developing a software library that is used by external customers.

A third motivation for accessing member variables only through interface functions is that it allows you to inject some extra code into these functions. Such code could add an entry to a log file marking the access or change, could make sure the data can be accessed safely by multiple callers at the same time (we'll briefly discuss C++'s concurrency facilities near the end of the book), or could notify other objects that some state has been modified (these other objects could then, for instance, update the user interface of your application, say to reflect updates to a LoanAccount's balance), and so on. None of this would be possible if you allow external code to access member variables directly.

A fourth and final motivation for not allowing direct access to data variables is that it complicates debugging. Most development environments support the concept of breakpoints. Breakpoints are user-specified points during debugging runs of the code where the execution becomes paused, allowing you to inspect the state of your objects. While some environments have more advanced functionality to put breakpoints if a particular member variable changes, putting breakpoints on function calls or specific lines of code inside functions is much easier.

In this section, we created an extra AccountType class to facilitate working with different types of accounts. This is by no means the only way to model these real-world concepts into classes and objects. In the next section we'll present a powerful alternative called *inheritance*. Which design you should use will depend on the exact needs of your concrete application.

Inheritance

Inheritance is the ability to define one type in terms of another. For example, suppose you have defined a BankAccount type that contains members that deal with the broad issues of bank accounts. Inheritance allows you to create the LoanAccount type as a specialized kind of BankAccount. You could define a LoanAccount as being like a BankAccount, but with a few extra properties and functions of its own. The LoanAccount type *inherits* all the members of BankAccount, which is referred to as its *base class*. In this case, you'd say that LoanAccount is *derived* from BankAccount.

Each LoanAccount object contains all the members that a BankAccount object does, but it has the option of defining new members of its own or of *redefining* the functions it inherits so that they are more meaningful in its context. Redefining a base class's function in a derived class is called *overriding*; the latter function is said to *override* the former. This last ability is very powerful, as you'll see.

Extending the current example, you might also want to create a new CheckingAccount type by adding different characteristics to BankAccount. This situation is illustrated in Figure 11-4.

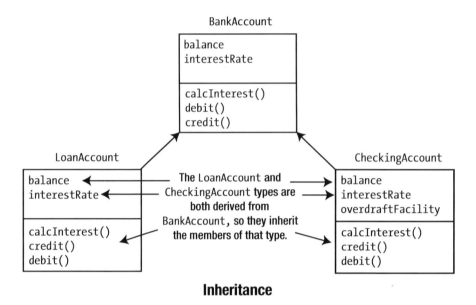

Figure 11-4. *An example of inheritance*

Both of the LoanAccount and CheckingAccount types are defined so that they are derived from the type BankAccount. They inherit the member variables and member functions of BankAccount, but they are free to define new characteristics that are specific to their own type.

In this example, CheckingAccount has added a member variable called overdraftFacility that is unique to itself, and both the derived classes can override any of the member functions that they inherit from the base class. It's likely they would override calcInterest(), for example, because calculating and dealing with the interest for a checking account involves something rather different than doing it for a loan account.

Polymorphism

Polymorphism means the ability to assume different forms at different times. Polymorphism in C++ always involves calling a member function of an object using either a pointer or a reference. Such function calls can have different effects at different times—sort of Jekyll and Hyde function calls. The mechanism works only for objects of types that are derived from a common base type, such as the BankAccount type. Polymorphism means that objects belonging to a "family" of inheritance-related classes can be passed around and operated on using base class pointers and references.

The LoanAccount and CheckingAccount objects can both be passed around using a pointer or reference to BankAccount. The pointer or reference can be used to call the inherited member functions of whatever object it refers to. The idea and implications of this will be easier to appreciate if we look at a specific case.

Suppose you have the LoanAccount and CheckingAccount types defined as before, based on the BankAccount type. Suppose further that you have defined objects of these types, debt and cash, respectively, as illustrated in Figure 11-5. Because both types are based on the BankAccount type, a variable of type *pointer to* BankAccount, such as pAcc in Figure 11-5, can store the address of either of these objects.

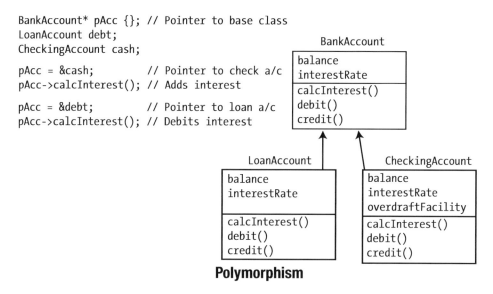

```
BankAccount* pAcc {}; // Pointer to base class
LoanAccount debt;
CheckingAccount cash;

pAcc = &cash;           // Pointer to check a/c
pAcc->calcInterest(); // Adds interest

pAcc = &debt;           // Pointer to loan a/c
pAcc->calcInterest(); // Debits interest
```

Figure 11-5. *An example of polymorphism*

The beauty of polymorphism is that the function called by pAcc->calcInterest() varies depending on what pAcc points to. If it points to a LoanAccount object, then the calcInterest() function for that object is called, and interest is debited from the account. If it points to a CheckingAccount object, the result is different because the calcInterest() function for that object is called, and interest is credited to the account. The particular function that is called through the pointer is decided at runtime. That is, it is decided not when the program is compiled but when it executes. Thus, the same function call can do different things depending on what kind of object the pointer points to. Figure 11-5 shows just two different types, but in general, you can get polymorphic behavior with as many different types derived from a common base class as your application requires. You need quite a bit of C++ language know-how to accomplish what we've described, and that's exactly what you'll be exploring in the rest of this chapter and throughout the next three chapters.

Terminology

Here's a summary of the terminology that is used when discussing classes. It includes some terms that you've come across already:

- A *class* is a user-defined data type.

- The variables and functions defined within a class are *members* of the class. The variables are *member variables*, and the functions are *member functions*. Member functions are also often referred to as *methods*; member variables are called either *data members* or *fields*.

- Variables of a class type store *objects*. Objects are sometimes called *instances* of the class. Defining an instance of a class is referred to as *instantiation*.

- *Object-oriented programming* is a programming style based on the idea of defining your own data types as classes. It involves the ideas of *encapsulation, data hiding,* class *inheritance,* and *polymorphism.*

When you get into the detail of object-oriented programming, it may seem a little complicated in places. Getting back to the basics can often help make things clearer, so use this list to always keep in mind what objects are really about. Object-oriented programming is about writing programs in terms of the objects that are specific to the domain of your problem. All the facilities around classes are there to make this as comprehensive and flexible as possible.

Defining a Class

A *class* is a user-defined type. The definition of a type uses the `class` keyword. The basic organization of a class definition looks like this:

```
class ClassName
{
  // Code that defines the members of the class...
};
```

The name of this class type is `ClassName`. It's a common convention to use the uppercase name for user-defined classes to distinguish class types from variable names. We'll adopt this convention in the examples. The members of the class are all specified between the braces. For now we will include the definitions of all member functions inside the class definition, but later in this chapter we'll see that they can be defined outside the class definition as well. Note that the semicolon after the closing brace for the class definition must be present.

All the members of a class are `private` by default, which means they cannot be accessed from outside the class. This is obviously not acceptable for the member functions that form the interface. You use the `public` keyword followed by a colon to make all subsequent members accessible from outside the class. Members specified after the `private` keyword are not accessible from outside the class. `public` and `private` are *access specifiers* for the class members. There's another access specifier, `protected`, that you'll meet later. Here's how an outline class looks with access specifiers:

```
class ClassName
{
private:
  // Code that specifies members that are not accessible from outside the class...

public:
  // Code that specifies members that are accessible from outside the class...
};
```

`public` and `private` precede a sequence of members that are or are not accessible outside the class. The specification of `public` or `private` applies to all members that follow until there is a different specification. You could omit the first `private` specification here and get the default status of `private`, but it's better to make it explicit. Members in a `private` section of a class can be accessed only from functions that are members of the same class. Member variables or functions that need to be accessed by a function that is not a member of the class must be specified as `public`. A member function can reference any other member of the same class, regardless of the access specification, by just using its name. To make all this generality clearer, let's start with an example of defining a class to represent a box:

```
class Box
{
private:
  double length {1.0};
  double width {1.0};
  double height {1.0};

public:
  // Function to calculate the volume of a box
  double volume()
  {
    return length * width * height;
  }
};
```

length, width, and height are member variables of the Box class and are all of type double. They are also private and therefore cannot be accessed from outside the class. Only the public volume() member function can refer to these private members. In general, you can repeat any of the access specifiers in a class definition as many times as you want. This enables you to place member variables and member functions in separate groups within the class definition, each with their own access specifier. It can be easier to see the internal structure of a class definition if you arrange to group the member variables and the member functions separately, according to their access specifiers.

Each of the member variables is initialized to 1.0 because a zero dimension for a box would not make much sense. You don't have to initialize member variables in this way—there are other ways of setting their values, as you'll see in the next section. If their values are not set by some mechanism, though, they will contain junk values.

Every Box object will have its own set of member variables. This is obvious really; if they didn't have their own member variables, all objects would be identical. You can create a variable of type Box like this:

```
Box myBox;                              // A Box object with all dimensions 1
```

The myBox variable refers to a Box object with the default member variable values. You could call the volume() member for the object to calculate the volume:

```
std::cout << "Volume of myBox is " << myBox.volume() << std::endl;  // Volume is 1.0
```

Of course, the volume will be 1 because the initial values for the three dimensions are 1.0. The fact that the member variables of the Box class are private means that we have no way to set these members. You could specify the member variables as public, in which case you can set them explicitly from outside the class, like this:

```
myBox.length = 1.5;
myBox.width = 2.0;
myBox.height = 4.0;
std::cout << "Volume of myBox is " << myBox.volume() << std::endl;  // Volume is 12.0
```

We said earlier that it's bad practice to make member variables public. To set the values of private member variables when an object is created, you must add a public member function of a special kind to the class, called a *constructor*. Objects of a class type can only be created using a constructor.

▪ **Note**   C++ also includes the ability to define a *structure* to define a type. The structure originated in C. Structures and classes are nearly completely equivalent. You define a structure in the same way as a class, only using the `struct` keyword instead of the `class` keyword. The main difference between the two is that in contrast to members of a class, the members of a structure are `public` by default. If you always state your access specifiers explicitly like we recommended, however, this difference becomes moot. Structures are still used frequently in C++ programs to define types that represent simple aggregates of several variables of different types—the margin sizes and dimensions of a printed page, for example. Such structures then typically don't have many member functions; they're mostly used to aggregate some publically accessible member variables. We won't discuss structures as a separate topic because aside from the default access specification and the use of the `struct` keyword, you define and use a structure in the same way as a class.

Constructors

A class *constructor* is a special kind of function in a class that differs in a few significant respects from an ordinary member function. A constructor is called whenever a new instance of the class is defined. It provides the opportunity to initialize the new object as it is created and to ensure that member variables contain valid values. A class constructor always has the same name as the class. Box(), for example, is a constructor for the Box class. A constructor does not return a value and therefore has no return type. It is an error to specify a return type for a constructor.

Default Constructors

Hang on a moment! We created a Box object in the previous section and calculated its volume. How could that have happened? There was no constructor defined. Well, there's no such thing as a class without constructors. If you don't define a constructor for a class, the compiler will supply a *default default constructor*. And no, the two "defaults" is no typo. We'll get back to this shortly. Thanks to this default default constructor, the Box class effectively behaves as if defined as follows:

```
class Box
{
private:
  double length {1};
  double width {1};
  double height {1};

public:
  // The default constructor that was supplied by the compiler...
  Box()
  {
    // Empty body so it does nothing...
  }
```

```
  // Function to calculate the volume of a box
  double volume()
  {
    return length * width * height;
  }
};
```

A *default constructor* is a constructor that can be called without arguments. If you do not define *any* constructor for a class—so no default constructor or any other constructor—the compiler generates a default constructor for you. That's why it's called a default default constructor; it is a default constructor that is generated by default. A compiler-generated default constructor has no parameters, and its sole purpose is to allow an object to be created. It does nothing else, so the member variables will have their default values. If no initial value is specified for a member variable of either a pointer (int*, const Box* ...) or fundamental type (double, int, bool ...), it will contain an arbitrary junk value. Note that as soon as you do define any constructor, even a nondefault one with parameters, the default default constructor is no longer supplied. There are circumstances in which you need a constructor with no parameters in addition to a constructor that you define that has parameters. In this case, *you* must ensure that there is a definition for the no-arg constructor in the class.

Defining a Class Constructor

Let's extend the Box class from the previous example to incorporate a constructor and then check that it works:

```
// Ex11_01.cpp
// Defining a class constructor
#include <iostream>

// Class to represent a box
class Box
{
private:
  double length {1.0};
  double width {1.0};
  double height {1.0};

public:
  // Constructor
  Box(double lengthValue, double widthValue, double heightValue)
  {
    std::cout << "Box constructor called."  << std::endl;
    length = lengthValue;
    width = widthValue;
    height = heightValue;
  }
```

```
  // Function to calculate the volume of a box
  double volume()
  {
    return length * width * height;
  }
};

int main()
{
  Box firstBox {80.0, 50.0, 40.0};                // Create a box
  double firstBoxVolume {firstBox.volume()};      // Calculate the box volume
  std::cout << "Volume of Box object is " << firstBoxVolume << std::endl;

  // Box secondBox;                               // Causes a compiler error message
}
```

This produces the following output:

```
Box constructor called.
Volume of Box object is 160000
```

The constructor for the Box class has three parameters of type double, corresponding to the initial values for the length, width, and height members of an object. No return type is allowed, and the name of the constructor must be the same as the class name, Box. The first statement in the constructor body outputs a message to show when it's called. You wouldn't do this in production programs, but it's helpful when you're testing a program and to understand what's happening and when. We'll use it regularly to trace what is happening in the examples. The rest of the code in the body of the constructor assigns the arguments to the corresponding member variables. You could include checks that look for valid, non-negative arguments that are the dimensions of a box. In the context of a real application, you'd probably want to do this, but here you only need to learn how a constructor works, so we'll keep it simple for now.

The firstBox object is created with this statement:

```
Box firstBox {80.0, 50.0, 40.0};
```

The initial values for the member variables, length, width, and height, appear in the braced initializer and are passed as arguments to the constructor. Because there are three values in the list, the compiler looks for a Box constructor with three parameters. When the constructor is called, it displays the message that appears as the first line of output, so you know that the constructor that you have added to the class is called.

We said earlier that once you define a constructor, the compiler won't supply a default constructor anymore, at least not by default. That means this statement will no longer compile:

```
Box secondBox;            // Causes a compiler error message
```

This object would have the default dimensions. If you want to allow Box objects to be defined like this, you must add a definition for a constructor without arguments. We will do so in the next section.

Using the default Keyword

As soon as you add a constructor, *any* constructor, the compiler no longer implicitly defines a default default constructor. If you then still want your objects to be default-constructible, it is up to you to ensure that the class has a default constructor. Your first option, of course, is to define one yourself. For the Box class of Ex11_01.cpp, for instance, all you'd have to do is add the following constructor definition somewhere in the public section of the class:

```
Box() {}                      // Default constructor
```

Because the member variables of a Box are already given a valid value, 1.0, during their initialization, there is nothing left for you to do in the body of the default constructor.

Instead of defining a default constructor with an empty function body, you can also use the default keyword. This keyword can be used to instruct the compiler to generate a default default constructor, even if there are other user-defined constructors present. For Box, this looks as follows:

```
Box() = default;              // Default constructor
```

Both the equals sign and the semicolon are required. A modified version of Ex11_01 with a defaulted constructor is available online in Ex11_01A.cpp.

While an explicit empty body definition and a defaulted constructor declaration are nearly equivalent, the use of the default keyword is preferred in modern C++ code:

■ **Tip**   If there is nothing to do in a default constructor's body (or initializer list, as we'll encounter this later), always prefer = default; over {}. Not only does this make it more apparent that it concerns a default default constructor, there are also a few subtle technical reasons outside the scope of this discussion that make the compiler-generated version the better choice.

Defining Functions and Constructors Outside the Class

We said earlier that the definition of a member function can be placed outside the class definition. This is also true for class constructors. This can all be done in a single file if you want, but it is far more common to put the class definition in a header file and the definitions of the member functions and constructors in a corresponding source file. We can define the Box class in a header file like this:

```
// Box.h
#ifndef BOX_H
#define BOX_H

class Box
{
private:
  double length {1.0};
  double width {1.0};
  double height {1.0};
```

```
public:
  // Constructors
  Box(double lengthValue, double widthValue,  double heightValue);
  Box() = default;

  double volume();              // Function to calculate the volume of a box
};
```

```
#endif
```

The definitions for the volume() member and the constructor then go in a .cpp file. The name of each member function and constructor in the source must be qualified with the class name so the compiler knows to which class they belong:

```
// Box.cpp
#include "Box.h"
#include <iostream>

// Constructor definition
Box::Box(double lengthValue, double widthValue, double heightValue)
{
  std::cout << "Box constructor called." << std::endl;
  length = lengthValue;
  width = widthValue;
  height = heightValue;
}

// Function to calculate the volume of a box
double Box::volume()
{
  return length * width * height;
}
```

If Box.h was not included into Box.cpp, the compiler would not know that Box is a class, so the code would not compile. Notice that a constructor that is defaulted using the default keyword in the class definition must not have a definition in the source file.

Separating the definitions of classes from the definitions of their members makes the code easier to manage. For a large class with lots of member functions and constructors, it would be very cumbersome if all the function definitions appeared within the class. More important, any source file that creates objects of type Box just needs to include the header file Box.h. A programmer using this class doesn't need access to the source code definitions of the member functions, only to the class definition in the header file. As long as the *class* definition remains fixed, you're free to change the implementations of the member functions without affecting the operation of programs that use the class.

The previous example would look like this with the Box class split into .h and .cpp files:

```
// Ex11_01B.cpp
// Defining functions and constructors outside the class definition
#include <iostream>
#include "Box.h"
```

```
int main()
{
  Box firstBox{80.0, 50.0, 40.0};            // Create a box
  double firstBoxVolume{firstBox.volume()};    // Calculate the box volume
  std::cout << "Volume of the first Box object is " << firstBoxVolume << std::endl;

  Box secondBox;                              // Uses compiler-generated default constructor
  double secondBoxVolume{secondBox.volume()};  // Calculate the box volume
  std::cout << "Volume of the second Box object is " << secondBoxVolume << std::endl;
}
```

This is the same version of main() as in the previous example. The only difference is the #include directive for the Box.h header file that contains the definition of the Box class.

■ **Note** Defining a member function outside a class is actually not quite the same as placing the definition inside the class. One subtle difference is that function definitions *within* a class definition are implicitly `inline`. (This doesn't necessarily mean they will be *implemented* as inline functions, though—the compiler still decides that, as we discussed in Chapter 8.)

Default Constructor Parameter Values

When we discussed "ordinary" functions, you saw that you can specify *default values* for the parameters in the function prototype. You can do this for class member functions, including constructors. Default parameter values for constructors and member functions always go inside the class, not in an external constructor or function definition. We can change the class definition in the previous example to the following:

```
class Box
{
private:
  double length, width, height;

public:
  // Constructors
  Box(double lv = 1.0, double wv = 1.0, double hv = 1.0);
  Box() = default;

  double volume();          // Function to calculate the volume of a box
};
```

If you make this change to the previous example, what happens? You get an error message from the compiler, of course! The message basically says that you have multiple default constructors defined. The reason for the confusion is the constructor with three parameters allows all three arguments to be omitted, which is indistinguishable from a call to the no-arg constructor. A constructor for which all parameters have a default value still counts as a default constructor. The obvious solution is to get rid of the defaulted constructor that accepts no parameters in this instance. If you do so, everything compiles and executes OK.

Using a Member Initializer List

So far, you've set values for member variables in the body of a constructor using explicit assignment. You can use an alternative and more efficient technique that uses a *member initializer list*. We'll illustrate this with an alternative version of the Box class constructor:

```
// Constructor definition using a member initializer list
Box::Box(double lv, double wv, double hv) : length {lv}, width {wv}, height {hv}
{
  std::cout << "Box constructor called." << std::endl;
}
```

The values of the member variables are specified as initializing values in the initialization list that is part of the constructor header. length is initialized with lv, for example. The initialization list is separated from the parameter list by a colon (:), and each initializer is separated from the next by a comma (,). If you substitute this version of the constructor in the previous example, you'll see that it works just as well.

This is more than just a different notation, though. When you initialize a member variable using an assignment statement in the body of the constructor, the member variable is first created (using a constructor call if it is an instance of a class) after which the assignment is carried out as a separate operation. When you use an initialization list, the initial value is used to initialize the member variable *as it is created*. This can be a much more efficient process, particularly if the member variable is a class instance. This technique for initializing parameters in a constructor is important for another reason. As you'll see, it is the *only* way of setting values for certain types of member variables.

There is one small caveat to watch out for. The order in which the member variables are initialized is determined by the order in which they are declared in the class definition—so *not* as you may expect by the order in which they appear in the member initializer list. This only matters, of course, if the member variables are initialized using expressions for which the order of evaluation matters. Plausible examples would be where a member variable is initialized either by using the value of another one or by calling a member function that relies on other member variables being initialized already. Relying on this evaluation order in production code can be dangerous. Even if everything is working correctly today, next year someone may change the declaration order and inadvertently break the correctness of one of the class's constructors!

▪ **Tip** As a rule, prefer to initialize all member variables in the constructor's member initializer list. This is generally more efficient. To avoid any confusion, you ideally put the member variables in the initializer list in the same order as they are declared in the class definition. You should initialize member variables in the body of the constructor only if either more complex logic is required or the order in which they are initialized is important.

Using the explicit Keyword

A problem with class constructors with a *single* parameter is that the compiler can use such a constructor as an implicit conversion from the type of the parameter to the class type. This can produce undesirable results in some circumstances. Let's consider a particular situation. Suppose that you define a class that defines boxes that are cubes for which all three sides have the same length:

```
// Cube.h
#ifndef CUBE_H
#define CUBE_H
class Cube
{
private:
  double side;

public:
  Cube(double aSide);                     // Constructor
  double volume();                        // Calculate volume of a cube
  bool hasLargerVolumeThan(Cube aCube);   // Compare volume of a cube with another
};
#endif
```

You can define the constructor in Cube.cpp as follows:

```
Cube::Cube(double aSide) : side{aSide}
{
  std::cout << "Cube constructor called." << std::endl;
}
```

The definition of the function that calculates the volume will be as follows:

```
double Cube::volume() { return side * side * side; }
```

One Cube object is greater than another if its volume is the greater of the two. The hasLargerVolumeThan() member can thus be defined as follows:

```
bool Cube::hasLargerVolumeThan(Cube aCube) { return volume() > aCube.volume(); }
```

The constructor requires only one argument of type double. Clearly, the compiler could use the constructor to convert a double value to a Cube object, but under what circumstances is that likely to happen? The class defines a volume() function and a function to compare the current object with another Cube object passed as an argument, which returns true if the current object has the greater volume. You might use the Cube class in the following way:

```
// Ex11_02.cpp
// Problems of implicit object conversions
#include <iostream>
#include "Cube.h"

int main()
{
  Cube box1 {7.0};
  Cube box2 {3.0};
  if (box1.hasLargerVolumeThan(box2))
    std::cout << "box1 is larger than box2." << std::endl;
  else
    std::cout << "Volume of box1 is less than or equal to that of box2." << std::endl;
```

```
  std::cout << "volume of box1 is " << box1.volume() << std::endl;
  if (box1.hasLargerVolumeThan(50.0))
    std::cout << "Volume of box1 is greater than 50"<< std::endl;
  else
    std::cout << "Volume of box1 is less than or equal to 50"<< std::endl;
}
```

Here's the output:

```
Cube constructor called.
Cube constructor called.
box1 is larger than box2.
volume of box1 is 343
Cube constructor called.
Volume of box1 is less than or equal to 50
```

The output shows that the volume of box1 is definitely not less than 50, but the last line of output indicates the opposite. The code presumes that hasLargerVolumeThan() compares the volume of the current object with 50.0. In reality, the function compares two Cube objects. The compiler knows that the argument to the hasLargerVolumeThan() function should be a Cube object, but it compiles this quite happily because a constructor is available that converts the argument 50.0 to a Cube object. The code the compiler produces is equivalent to the following:

```
  if (box1.hasLargerVolumeThan(Cube{50.0}))
    std::cout << "Volume of box1 is greater than 50"<< std::endl;
  else
    std::cout << "Volume of box1 is less than or equal to 50"<< std::endl;
```

The function is not comparing the volume of the box1 object with 50.0, but with 125000.0, which is the volume of a Cube object with a side of length 50.0! The result is very different from what was expected.

Happily, you can prevent this nightmare from happening by declaring the constructor as explicit:

```
class Cube
{
public:
  double side;

  explicit Cube(double aSide);              // Constructor
  double volume();                          // Calculate volume of a cube
  bool hasLargerVolumeThan(Cube aCube);     // Compare volume of a cube with another
};
```

With this definition for Cube, Ex11_02.cpp will not compile. The compiler never uses a constructor declared as explicit for an implicit conversion; it can be used only explicitly in the program. By using the explicit keyword with constructors that have a single parameter, you prevent implicit conversions from the parameter type to the class type. The hasLargerVolumeThan() member only accepts a Cube object as an argument, so calling it with an argument of type double does not compile.

■ **Tip** Implicit conversions may lead to confusing code; most of the time it becomes far more obvious why code compiles and what it does if you use explicit conversions. By default, you should therefore declare all single-argument constructors as `explicit` (note that this includes constructors with multiple parameters where at least all but the first have default values); omit `explicit` only if implicit type conversions are truly desirable.

Delegating Constructors

A class can have several constructors that provide different ways of creating an object. The code for one constructor can call another of the same class in the initialization list. This can avoid repeating the same code in several constructors. Here's a simple illustration of this using the Box class:

```
class Box
{
private:
  double length {1.0};
  double width {1.0};
  double height {1.0};

public:
  // Constructors
  Box(double lv, double wv, double hv);
  explicit Box(double side);                 // Constructor for a cube
  Box() = default;                           // No-arg constructor

  double volume();                           // Function to calculate the volume of a box
};
```

Notice that we have restored the initial values for the member variables and removed the default values for the constructor parameters. This is because the compiler would not be able to distinguish between a call of the constructor with a single parameter and a call of the constructor with three parameters with the last two arguments omitted. This removes the capability for creating an object with no arguments, and the compiler will not supply the default, so we have added the definition of the no-arg constructor to the class.

The implementation of the first constructor can be as follows:

```
Box::Box(double lv, double wv, double hv) : length {lv}, width {wv}, height {hv}
{
  std::cout << "Box constructor 1 called." << std::endl;
}
```

The second constructor creates a Box object with all sides equal, and we can implement it like this:

```
Box::Box(double side) : Box{side, side, side}
{
  std::cout << "Box constructor 2 called." << std::endl;
}
```

This constructor just calls the previous constructor in the initialization list. The side argument is used as all three values in the argument list for the previous constructor. This is called a *delegating constructor* because it delegates the construction work to the other constructor. Delegating constructors help to shorten and simplify constructor code and can make the class definition easier to understand. Here's an example that exercises this:

```
// Ex11_03.cpp
// Using a delegating constructor
#include <iostream>
#include "Box.h"

int main()
{
  Box box1 {2.0, 3.0, 4.0};            // An arbitrary box
  Box box2 {5.0};                      // A box that is a cube
  std::cout << "box1 volume = " << box1.volume() << std::endl;
  std::cout << "box2 volume = " << box2.volume() << std::endl;
}
```

The complete code is in the download. The output is as follows:

```
Box constructor 1 called.
Box constructor 1 called.
Box constructor 2 called.
box1 volume = 24
box2 volume = 125
```

You can see from the output that creating the first object just calls constructor 1. Creating the second object calls constructor 1 followed by constructor 2. This also shows that execution of the initialization list for a constructor occurs before the code in the body of the constructor. The volumes are as you would expect.

You should only call a constructor for the same class in the initialization list for a constructor. Calling a constructor of the same class in the body of a delegating constructor is not the same. Further, you must not initialize member variables in the initialization list of a delegating constructor. The code will not compile if you do. You can set values for member variables in the body of a delegating constructor, but in that case you should consider whether the constructor should really be implemented as a delegating constructor.

The Copy Constructor

Suppose you add the following statement to main() in Ex11_03.cpp:

```
  Box box3 {box2};
  std::cout << "box3 volume = " << box3.volume() << std::endl;    // Volume = 125
```

The output shows that box3 does indeed have the dimensions of box2, but there's no constructor defined with a parameter of type Box, so how was box3 created? The answer is that the compiler supplied a default *copy constructor*, which is a constructor that creates an object by copying an existing object. The default copy constructor copies the values of the member variables of the object that is the argument to the new object.

The default behavior is fine in the case of Box objects, but it can cause problems when one or more member variables are pointers. Just copying a pointer does not duplicate what it points to, which means that when an object is created by the copy constructor, it is interlinked with the original object. Both objects will contain a member pointing to the same thing. A simple example is if an object contains a pointer to a string. A duplicate object will have a member pointing to the same string, so if the string is changed for one object, it will be changed for the other. This is not usually what you want. In this case, *you* must define a copy constructor. We return to the questions of whether, when, and why to define a copy constructor in Chapter 17. For now, we'll just focus on the how.

Implementing the Copy Constructor

The copy constructor must accept an argument of the same class type and create a duplicate in an appropriate manner. This poses an immediate problem that you must overcome; you can see it clearly if you try to define the copy constructor for the Box class like this:

```
Box::Box(Box box) : length {box.length}, width {box.width}, height {box.height} // Wrong!!
{}
```

Each member variable of the new object is initialized with the value of the object that is the argument. No code is needed in the body of the copy constructor in this instance. This looks OK, but consider what happens when the constructor is called. The argument is passed *by value*, but because the argument is a Box object, the compiler arranges to call the copy constructor for the Box class to make a copy of the argument. Of course, the argument to this call of the copy constructor is passed by value, so another call to the copy constructor is required, and so on. In short, you've created a situation where an unlimited number of recursive calls to the copy constructor will occur. Your compiler won't allow this code to compile.

To avoid the problem the parameter for the copy constructor must be a *reference*. More specifically, it should be a reference-to-const parameter. For the Box class, this looks like this:

```
Box::Box(const Box& box) : length {box.length}, width {box.width}, height {box.height}
{}
```

Now that the argument is no longer passed by value, recursive calls of the copy constructor are avoided. The compiler initializes the parameter box with the object that is passed to it. The parameter should be reference-to-const because a copy constructor is only in the business of creating duplicates; it should not modify the original. A reference-to-const parameter allows const and non-const objects to be copied. If the parameter was a reference-to-non-const, the constructor would not accept a const object as the argument, thus disallowing copying of const objects. You can conclude from this that the parameter type for a copy constructor is *always* a reference to a const object of the same class type. In other words, the form of the copy constructor is the same for any class:

```
Type::Type(const Type& object)
{
  // Code to duplicate the object...
}
```

Of course, the copy constructor may also have an initialization list and may even delegate to other, non-copy constructors as well. Here's an example:

```
Box::Box(const Box& box) : Box{box.length, box.width, box.height}
{}
```

Accessing Private Class Members

Inhibiting all external access to the values of `private` member variables of a class is rather extreme. It's a good idea to protect them from unauthorized modification, but if you don't know what the dimensions of a particular Box object are, you have no way to find out. Surely it doesn't need to be that secret, right?

It doesn't, and you don't need to expose the member variables by using the `public` keyword. You can provide access to the values of `private` member variables by adding member functions to return their values. To provide access to the dimensions of a Box object from outside the class, you just need to add these three functions to the class definition:

```cpp
class Box
{
private:
  double length {1.0};
  double width {1.0};
  double height {1.0};

public:
  // Constructors
  Box() = default;
  Box(double length, double width, double height);

  double volume();                  // Function to calculate the volume of a box

  // Functions to provide access to the values of member variables
  double getLength() { return length; }
  double getWidth()  { return width;  }
  double getHeight() { return height; }
};
```

The values of the member variables are fully accessible, but they can't be changed from outside the class, so the integrity of the class is preserved without the secrecy. Functions of this kind often have their definitions within the class because they are short, and this makes them `inline` by default. Consequently, the overhead involved in accessing the value of a member variable is minimal. Functions that retrieve the values of member variables are often referred to as *accessor* functions.

Using these accessor functions is simple:

```cpp
Box myBox {3.0, 4.0, 5.0};
std::cout << "myBox dimensions are " << myBox.getLength()
          << " by " << myBox.getWidth()
          << " by " << myBox.getHeight() << std::endl;
```

You can use this approach for any class. You just write an accessor function for each member variable that you want to make available to the outside world.

There will be situations in which you *do* want to allow member variables to be changed from outside the class. If you supply a member function to do this rather than exposing the member variable directly, you have the opportunity to perform integrity checks on the value. For example, you could add functions to allow the dimensions of a Box object to be changed as well:

```
class Box
{
private:
  double length {1.0};
  double width {1.0};
  double height {1.0};

public:
  // Constructors
  Box() = default;
  Box(double length, double width, double height);

  double volume();                    // Function to calculate the volume of a box

  // Functions to provide access to the values of member variables
  double getLength() { return length; }
  double getWidth()  { return width; }
  double getHeight() { return height; }

  // Functions to set member variable values
  void setLength(double lv) { if (lv > 0) length = lv;}
  void setWidth(double wv)  { if (wv > 0) width = wv; }
  void setHeight(double hv) { if (hv > 0) height = hv; }
};
```

The if statement in each set function ensures that you only accept new values that are positive. If a new value is supplied for a member variable that is zero or negative, it will be ignored. Member functions that allow member variables to be modified are sometimes called *mutators*. Using these simple mutators is equally straightforward:

```
myBox.setLength(-20.0);                     // ignored!
myBox.setWidth(40.0);
myBox.setHeight(10.0);
std::cout << "myBox dimensions are now " << myBox.getLength()     // 3 (unchanged)
          << " by " << myBox.getWidth()                          // by 40
          << " by " << myBox.getHeight() << std::endl;           // by 10
```

You can find a complete test program that puts everything together inside Ex11_04.

▓ **Note** By popular convention, the member function to access a member variable called myMember is mostly called getMyMember(), and the function to update a variable setMyMember(). Because of this, such member functions are commonly referred to simply as *getters* and *setters*, respectively. One popular exception to this naming convention is that accessors for members of type bool are often named isMyMember(). That is, the getter for a Boolean member variable valid is usually called isValid() instead of getValid(). And no, this does not mean we're now calling them *issers*; these Boolean accessors are still just called *getters*.

The this Pointer

The volume() function in the Box class was implemented in terms of the unqualified class member names. *Every* object of type Box contains these members, so there must be a way for the function to refer to the members of the particular object for which it has been called. In other words, when the code in volume() accesses the length member, there has to be a way for length to refer to the member of the object for which the function is called, and not some other object.

When a class member function executes, it automatically contains a hidden pointer with the name this, which contains the address of the object for which the function was called. For example, suppose you write this statement:

```
std::cout << myBox.volume() << std::endl;
```

The this pointer in the volume() function contains the address of myBox. When you call the function for a different Box object, this will contain the address of that object. This means that when the member variable length is accessed in the volume() function during execution, it is actually referring to this->length, which is the fully specified reference to the object member that is being used. The compiler takes care of adding the this pointer name to the member names in the function. In other words, the compiler implements the function as follows:

```
double Box::volume()
{
  return this->length * this->width * this->height;
}
```

You could write the function explicitly using the pointer this if you wanted, but it isn't necessary. However, there are situations where you *do* need to use this explicitly, such as when you need to return the address of the current object.

■ **Note**   You'll learn about static member functions of a class later in this chapter. These do not contain a this pointer.

Returning this from a Function

If the return type for a member function is a pointer to the class type, you can return this. You can then use the pointer returned by one member function to call another. Let's consider an example of where this would be useful.

Suppose you alter the mutator functions of the Box class from Ex11_04 to, after setting the length, width, and height of a box, return a copy of the this pointer:

```
class Box
{
private:
  double length {1.0};
  double width {1.0};
  double height {1.0};
```

```
public:
  // ... rest of the class definition as before in Ex11_04

  // Mutator functions
  Box* setLength(double lv);
  Box* setWidth(double wv);
  Box* setHeight(double hv);
};
```

You can implement these in Box.cpp as follows:

```
Box* Box::setLength(double lv)
{
  if (lv > 0) length = lv;
  return this;
}
Box* Box::setWidth(double wv)
{
  if (wv > 0) width = wv;
  return this;
}
Box* Box::setHeight(double hv)
{
  if (hv > 0) height = hv;
  return this;
}
```

Now you can modify all the dimensions of a Box object in a single statement:

```
Box myBox{3.0, 4.0, 5.0};                                 // Create a box
myBox.setLength(-20.0)->setWidth(40.0)->setHeight(10.0);  // Set all dimensions of myBox
```

Because the mutator functions return the this pointer, you can use the value returned by one function to call the next. Thus, the pointer returned by setLength() is used to call setWidth(), which returns a pointer you can use to call setHeight(). Isn't that nice?

Instead of a pointer, you can of course return a reference as well. The setLength() function, for instance, would then become defined as follows:

```
Box& Box::setLength(double lv)
{
  if (lv > 0) length = lv;
  return *this;
}
```

If you do the same for setWidth() and setHeight(), you obtain the Box class of Ex11_05. The sample program in Ex11_05.cpp then shows that returning references to *this allows you to chain member function calls together as follows:

```
myBox.setLength(-20.0).setWidth(40.0).setHeight(10.0);    // Set all dimensions of myBox
```

This pattern is called *method chaining*. If the goal is to facilitate statements that employ method chaining, it is commonly done using references. You will encounter several conventional examples of this pattern in the next chapter when we discuss operator overloading.

const Objects and const Member Functions

A const variable is a variable whose value cannot be altered. You know this already. Naturally, you can also define const variables of class types. These variables are then called *const objects*. None of the member variables that constitute the state of a const object can be altered. In other words, any member variable of a const object is itself a const variable and thus immutable.

Suppose for a moment that the length, width, and height member variables of our favorite Box class are public. Then the following would still not compile:

```
const Box myBox {3.0, 4.0, 5.0};
std::cout << "The length of myBox is " << myBox.length << std::endl;      // ok
myBox.length = 2.0;          // Error! Assignment to a member variable of a const object...
myBox.width *= 3.0;          // Error! Assignment to a member variable of a const object...
```

Reading a member variable from the const object myBox is allowed, but any attempt to assign a value to one or to otherwise modify such a member variable will result in a compiler error.

From Chapter 8, you'll recall that this principle extends to pointer-to-const and reference-to-const variables as well:

```
Box myBox {3.0, 4.0, 5.0};        // A non-const, mutable Box

const Box* boxPointer = &myBox;  // A pointer-to-const-Box variable
boxPointer->length = 2;            // Error!
boxPointer->width *= 3;            // Error!
```

In the previous snippet, myBox object itself is a non-const, mutable Box object. Nevertheless, if you store its address in a variable of type pointer-to-const-Box, you can no longer modify the state of myBox using that pointer. The same would hold if you replace the pointer with a reference-to-const.

You'll also recall that this plays a critical role when objects are either passed to, or returned from, a function, either by reference or using a pointer. Let printBox() be a function with the following signature:

```
void printBox(const Box& box);
```

Then printBox() cannot modify the state of the Box object it is passed as an argument, even if that original Box object will be non-const.

In the examples in the remainder of this section, we'll mostly be using const objects. Always remember, though, that the same restrictions apply when accessing an object through a pointer-to-const or a reference-to-const as when accessing a const object directly.

const Member Functions

To see how member functions behave for const objects, let's go back to the Box class of Ex11_04. In this version of the class, the member variables of a Box object are properly hidden and can be manipulated only through public getter and setter member functions. Suppose now that you change the code in the main() function of Ex11_04 so that myBox is const:

```
const Box myBox {3.0, 4.0, 5.0};
std::cout << "myBox dimensions are " << myBox.getLength()
          << " by " << myBox.getWidth()
          << " by " << myBox.getHeight() << std::endl;

myBox.setLength(-20.0);
myBox.setWidth(40.0);
myBox.setHeight(10.0);
```

Now the example will no longer compile! Of course, the fact that the compiler refuses to compile the last three lines in the previous code fragment is exactly what you want. After all, you should not be able to alter the state of a const object. We said earlier already the compiler prevents direct assignments to member variables—supposing you have access—so why should it allow indirect assignments inside member functions? The Box object would not be much of an immutable constant if you were allowed to call these setters, now would it?

Unfortunately, however, the getter functions cannot be called on a const object either simply because there's the risk that they could change the object. In our example, this means that the compiler will not only refuse to compile the last three lines but also the statement before that. Similarly, any attempt to call the volume() member function on a const myBox would result in a compilation error:

```
std::cout << "myBox's volume is " << myBox.volume() << std::endl;   // will not compile!
```

Even though *you* know that volume() doesn't alter the object, the compiler does not. All it has available when compiling this volume() expression is the function's prototype in the Box.h header file. And even if it does know the function's definition from inside the class definition—as with our three getters earlier—the compiler makes no attempt to deduce whether a function modifies the object's state. All the compiler uses in this setting is the function's signature.

So, with our current definition of the Box class, const Box objects are rather useless. You cannot call any of its member functions, not even the ones that clearly do not modify any state! To solve this, you'll have to improve the definition of the Box class. You need a way to tell the compiler which member functions are allowed to be called on const objects. The solutions are so-called *const member functions*.

First, you need to specify all functions that don't modify an object as const in the class definition:

```
class Box
{
  // Rest of the class as before...

  double volume() const;            // Function to calculate the volume of a box

  // Functions to provide access to the values of member variables
  double getLength() const { return length; }
  double getWidth() const  { return width; }
  double getHeight() const { return height; }

  // Functions to set member variable values
  void setLength(double lv) { if (lv > 0) length = lv;}
  void setWidth(double wv)  { if (wv > 0) width = wv; }
  void setHeight(double hv) { if (hv > 0) height = hv; }
};
```

405

Next, you must change the function definition in Box.cpp accordingly:

```
double Box::volume() const
{
  return length * width * height;
}
```

With these changes, all the calls we expect to work for a const myBox object will effectively work. Of course, calling a setter on it remains impossible. A complete example can be downloaded as Ex11_06.

■ **Tip**   For const objects you can only call const member functions. You should therefore specify all member functions that don't change the object for which they are called as const.

---

const Correctness

For const objects you can only call const member functions. The idea is that const objects must be totally immutable, so the compiler will only allow you to call member functions that do not, and never will, modify them. Of course, this only truly makes sense if const member functions effectively cannot modify an object's state. Suppose you were allowed to write the following:

```
void setLength(double lv) const { if (lv > 0) length = lv; }      // Will not compile!
void setWidth(double wv) const  { if (wv > 0) width = wv; }
void setHeight(double hv) const { if (hv > 0) height = hv; }
```

These three functions clearly modify the state of a Box. So if they were allowed to be declared const like this, you'd again be able to call these setters on const Box objects. This means you would again be able to modify the value of supposedly immutable objects. This would defeat the purpose of const objects. Luckily, the compiler enforces that you can never (inadvertently) modify a const object from inside a const member function. Any attempt to modify an object's member variable from within a const member functions will result in a compiler error.

Specifying a member function as const effectively makes the this pointer const for that function. The type of the this pointer inside our three setters from before, for instance, would be const Box*, which is pointer to a const Box. And you cannot assign to member variables through a pointer-to-const. Similarly, this implies you cannot call any non-const member functions from within a const member function (because you cannot call non-const member functions on either a pointer-to-const or a reference-to-const). Calling setLength() from within a const volume() member would therefore not be allowed:

```
double Box::volume() const
{
  setLength(32);                        // Not const (may modify the object): will not compile!
  return length * width * height;
}
```

Calling const member functions, on the other hand, is allowed:

```
double Box::volume() const
{
  return getLength() * getWidth() * getHeight();
}
```

Since these three getter function are const as well, calling them from within the volume() function is no problem. The compiler knows they will not modify the object either.

The combination of these compiler-enforced restrictions is called *const correctness*—it prevents const objects from being mutated. We'll see one final aspect of this at the end of the next subsection.

Overloading on const

Declaring whether a member function is const is part of the function's signature. This implies that you can overload a non-const member function with a const version. This can be useful and is often done for functions that return a pointer or a reference to (part of) the internal data that is encapsulated by an object. Suppose that instead of the traditional getters and setters for a Box's member variables, we create functions of this form:

```
class Box
{
private:
  double _length{1.0};
  double _width{1.0};
  double _height{1.0};

public:
  // Rest of the class definition...

  double& length() { return _length; };        // Return references to dimension variable
  double& width()  { return _width; };
  double& height() { return _height; };
}
```

Note that we added underscores to the names of the member variable to avoid them clashing with the names of the member functions. These member functions could now be used as follows:

```
Box box;
box.length() = 2;   // References can be used to the right of an assignment
std::cout << box.length() << std::endl;  // Prints 2
```

In a way, these functions are an attempt at a hybrid between a getter and a setter. It's a failed attempt thus far, because you can currently no longer access the dimensions of a const Box:

```
const Box constBox;
// constBox.length() = 2;                            // Does not compile: good!
// std::cout << constBox.length() << std::endl;      // Does not compile either: bad!
```

You could solve this by overloading the member functions with versions specific for const objects. In general, these extra overloads would have the following form:

```
  const double& length() const { return _length; };  // Return references to const variables
  const double& width()  const { return _width; };
  const double& height() const { return _height; };
```

Because double is a fundamental type, however, one will often return them by value in these overloads rather than by reference:

```
double length() const { return _length; };    // Return copies of dimension variables
double width()  const { return _width; };
double height() const { return _height; };
```

Either way, this enables the overloaded length(), width(), and height() functions to be called on const objects as well. Which of the two overloads of each function get used depends on the const-ness of the object upon which the member is called. You could confirm this by adding output statements to both overloads. You can find a little program that does exactly this under Ex11_07.

Note that while it is certainly done at times, in this particular case we do not really recommend using functions of this form to replace the more conventional getter and setters shown earlier. One reason is that statements of the following form are unconventional and hence harder to read or write:

```
box.length() = 2;           // Less clear than 'box.setLength(2);'
```

Also, and more important, by adding public member functions that return references to private member variables, you basically forsake most of the advantages of data hiding mentioned earlier in this chapter. You can no longer perform integrity checks on the values assigned to the member variables (such as checking whether all Box dimensions remain positive), change the internal representation of an object, and so on. In other words, it's almost as bad as simply making the variables public!

There are certainly other circumstances, though, where overloading on const is recommended. You will encounter several examples later, such as when overloading the array access operator in the next chapter.

▨ **Note**   To preserve const correctness, the following variation of a Box's getters does not compile:

```
// Attempt to return non-const references to member variables from const functions
double& length() const { return _length; };    // This must not be allowed to compile!
double& width()  const { return _width; };
double& height() const { return _height; };
```

Because these are const member functions, their implicit this pointers are of type const-pointer-to-Box (const Box*), which in turn makes the Box member variable names references-to-const within the scope of these member function definitions. From a const member function, you can thus never return a reference or a pointer to non-const parts of an object's states. And this is a good thing. Otherwise, such members would provide a backdoor to modify a const object—an object that in other words should be immutable.

Casting Away const

Very rarely circumstances can arise where a function is dealing with a const object, either passed as an argument or as the object pointed to by this, and it is necessary to make it non-const. The const_cast<>() operator enables you to do this. The const_cast<>() operator is mostly used in one of the following two forms:

```
const_cast<Type*>(expression)
const_cast<Type&>(expression)
```

For the first form, the type of expression must be either const Type*; or Type*; for the second, it can be either const Type*, const Type&, Type, or Type&.

▓ **Caution**   The use of const_cast is nearly always frowned upon because it can be used to misuse objects. You should never use this operator to undermine the const-ness of an object. If an object is const, it normally means that you are not expected to modify it. And making unexpected changes is a perfect recipe for bugs. The only situations in which you should use const_cast are those where you are sure the const nature of the object won't be violated as a result, such as because someone else forgot to add a const in a function declaration, even though you are positive the function doesn't modify the object. Another example is when you implement the idiom we branded const-and-back-again, which you'll learn about in Chapter 16.

Using the mutable Keyword

Ordinarily the member variables of a const object cannot be modified. Sometimes you want to allow particular class members to be modifiable even for a const object. You can do this by specifying such members as mutable. In Ex11_08, for example, we started again from Ex11_06 and added an extra, mutable member variable to the declaration of Box in Box.h as follows:

```
class Box
{
private:
  double length{1.0};
  double width{1.0};
  double height{1.0};
  mutable unsigned count{};    // Counts the amount of time printVolume() is called

public:
  // Constructors
  Box() = default;
  Box(double length, double width, double height);

  double volume() const;      // Function to calculate the volume of a box
  void printVolume() const;   // Function to print out the volume of a box

  // Getters and setters like before...
};
```

The mutable keyword indicates that the count member can be changed, even when the object is const. In Box.cpp, we can thus modify the count member in some debugging/logging code inside the newly created printVolume() member function, even though it is declared to be const:

```
void Box::printVolume() const
{
  // Count how many times printVolume() is called using a mutable member in a const function
  std::cout << "The volume of this box is " << volume() << std::endl;
  std::cout << "printVolume() has been called " << ++count << " time(s)" << std::endl;
}
```

If count would not have been explicitly declared to be mutable, modifying it from within the const printVolume() function would've been disallowed by the compiler. Any member function, both const and non-const, can always make changes to member variables specified as mutable.

Note that you should only need mutable member variables in rare cases. Usually, if you need to modify an object from within a const function, it probably shouldn't have been const. Typical uses of mutable member variables include debugging or logging, caching, and thread synchronization members. The latter two are more advanced, so we won't be giving any examples of these here.

Friends

Under normal circumstances, you'll hide the member variables of your classes by declaring them as private. You may well have private member functions of the class too. In spite of this, it is sometimes useful to treat selected functions that are not members of the class as "honorary members" and allow them to access non-public members of a class object. That is, you do not want the world to access the internal state of your objects, just a select few related functions. Such functions are called *friends* of the class. A friend can access any of the members of a class object, however, regardless of their access specification. Therefore:

■ **Caution**   Friend declarations risk undermining one of the cornerstones of object-oriented programming: data hiding. They should therefore be used only when absolutely necessary, and this need does not arise that often. You'll meet one circumstance where it is needed in the next chapter when you learn about operator overloading. Nevertheless, only most classes should not need any friends at all. While that may sound somewhat sad and lonely, the following humorous definition of the C++ programming language should forever remind you why, in C++, one should choose his friends very wisely indeed: "C++: where your friends can access your private parts."

That being said, we will consider two ways a class can declare what its friends are; either an individual function can be specified as a friend of a class or a whole class can be specified as a friend of another class. In the latter case, all the member functions of the friend class have the same access privileges as a normal member of the class. We'll consider individual functions as friends first.

The Friend Functions of a Class

To make a function a friend of a class, you must declare it as such within the class definition using the `friend` keyword. It's the class that determines its friends; there's no way to make a function a friend of a class from outside the class definition. A friend function can be a global function, or it can be a member of another class. By definition a function can't be a friend of the class of which it is a member, so access specifiers don't apply to the friends of a class.

The need for friend functions in practice is limited. They are useful in situations where a function needs access to the internals of two different kinds of objects; making the function a friend of both classes makes that possible. We will demonstrate how they work in simpler contexts that don't necessarily reflect a situation where they are required. Suppose that you want to implement a friend function in the Box class to compute the surface area of a Box object. To make the function a friend, you must declare it as such within the Box class definition. Here's a version that does that:

```cpp
class Box
{
private:
  double length;
  double width;
  double height;

public:
  // Constructor
  Box(double lv = 1.0, double wv = 1.0, double hv = 1.0);

  double volume() const;                      // Function to calculate the volume of a box

  friend double surfaceArea(const Box& aBox);  // Friend function for the surface area
};
```

`Box.cpp` will contain the definition of the constructor and `volume()` member. There is nothing in this source file that you haven't already seen several times before. Here is the code to try the friend function:

```cpp
// Ex11_09.cpp
// Using a friend function of a class
#include <iostream>
#include <memory>
#include "Box.h"

int main()
{
  Box box1 {2.2, 1.1, 0.5};          // An arbitrary box
  Box box2;                          // A default box
  auto box3 = std::make_unique<Box>(15.0, 20.0, 8.0); // Dynamically allocated Box

  std::cout << "Volume of box1 = " << box1.volume() << std::endl;
  std::cout << "Surface area of box1 = " << surfaceArea(box1) << std::endl;

  std::cout << "Volume of box2 = "<< box2.volume() << std::endl;
  std::cout << "Surface area of box2 = " << surfaceArea(box2) << std::endl;
```

```
    std::cout << "Volume of box3 = " << box3->volume() << std::endl;
    std::cout << "Surface area of box3 = " << surfaceArea(*pBox3) << std::endl;
}

// friend function to calculate the surface area of a Box object
double surfaceArea(const Box& aBox)
{
    return 2.0*(aBox.length*aBox.width + aBox.length*aBox.height +aBox.height*aBox.width);
}
```

Here's the expected output:

```
Box constructor called.
Box constructor called.
Box constructor called.
Volume of box1 = 1.21
Surface area of box1 = 8.14
Volume of box2 = 1
Surface area of box2 = 6
Volume of box3 = 2400
Surface area of box3 = 1160
```

You declare the surfaceArea() function as a friend of the Box class by writing the function prototype within the Box class definition preceded by the friend keyword. The function doesn't alter the Box object that is passed as the argument, so it's sensible to use a const reference parameter specification. It's also a good idea to be consistent when placing the friend declaration within the definition of the class. You can see that we've chosen to position this declaration at the end of all the public members of the class. The rationale for this is that the function is part of the class interface because it has full access to all class members.

surfaceArea() is a global function, and its definition follows that of main(). You could put it in Box.cpp because it is related to the Box class, but placing it in the main file helps indicate that it's a global function.

Notice that you access the member variables of the object within the definition of surfaceArea() by using the Box object that is passed to the function as a parameter. A friend function is *not* a class member, so the member variables can't be referenced by their names alone. They each have to be qualified by an object name in the same way as they would be in an ordinary function that accesses public members of a class. A friend function is the same as an ordinary function, except that it can access all the members of a class without restriction.

The main() function creates one Box object by specifying its dimensions; one object with no dimensions specified (so the defaults will apply), and one dynamically allocated Box object. The latter shows that you can create a smart pointer to a Box object allocated in the free store in the way that you have seen with std::string objects. From the output you can see that everything works as expected with all three objects.

Although this example demonstrates how you write a friend function, it is not very realistic. You could have used accessor member functions to return the values of the member variables. Then surfaceArea() wouldn't need to be a friend function. Perhaps the best option would have been to make surfaceArea() a public member function of the class so that the capability for computing the surface area of a box becomes part of the class interface. A friend function should always be a last resort.

Friend Classes

You can declare a whole class to be a friend of another class. All the member functions of a friend class have unrestricted access to all the members of the class of which it has been declared a friend.

For example, suppose you have defined a Carton class and want to allow the member functions of the Carton class to have access to the members of the Box class. Including a statement in the Box class definition that declares Carton to be a friend will enable this:

```
class Box
{
  // Public members of the class...

  friend class Carton;

  // Private members of the class...
};
```

Friendship is not a reciprocal arrangement. Functions in the Carton class can access all the members of the Box class, but functions in the Box class have no access to the private members of the Carton class. Friendship among classes is not transitive either; just because class A is a friend of class B and class B is a friend of class C, it doesn't follow that class A is a friend of class C.

A typical use for a friend class is where the functioning of one class is highly intertwined with that of another. A linked list basically involves two class types: a List class that maintains a list of objects (usually called *nodes*) and a Node class that defines what a node is. The List class needs to stitch the Node objects together by setting a pointer in each Node object so that it points to the next Node object. Making the List class a friend of the class that defines a node would enable members of the List class to access the members of the Node class directly. Later in this chapter we'll discuss nested classes, a viable alternative for friend classes in such cases.

Arrays of Class Objects

You can create an array of objects of a class type in the same way as you create an array of elements of any other type. Each array element has to be created by a constructor, and for each element that does not have an initial value specified, the compiler arranges for the no-arg constructor to be called. You can see this happening with an example. The Box class definition in Box.h is as follows:

```
// Box.h
#ifndef BOX_H
#define BOX_H
#include <iostream>

class Box
{
private:
  double length {1.0};
  double width {1.0};
  double height {1.0};
```

```
public:
  /* Constructors */
  Box(double lv, double wv, double hv);
  Box(double side);        // Constructor for a cube
  Box();                   // Default constructor
  Box(const Box& box);     // Copy constructor

  double volume() const;                      // Function to calculate the volume of a box
};
#endif
```

The contents of Box.cpp are as follows:

```
#include <iostream>
#include "Box.h"

Box::Box(double lv, double wv, double hv)        // Constructor definition
  : length {lv}, width {wv}, height {hv}
{
  std::cout << "Box constructor 1 called." << std::endl;
}

Box::Box(double side) : Box {side, side, side}  // Constructor for a cube
{
  std::cout << "Box constructor 2 called." << std::endl;
}

Box::Box()                                       // Default constructor
{
  std::cout << "Default Box constructor called." << std::endl;
}

Box::Box(const Box& box)                         // Copy constructor
  : length {box.length}, width {box.width}, height {box.height}
{
  std::cout << "Box copy constructor called." << std::endl;
}

// Function to calculate the volume of a box
double Box::volume() const { return length * width * height; }
```

Finally, the Fx11_10.cpp source file that defines the program's main() function will contain the following:

```
// Ex11_10.cpp
// Creating an array of objects
#include <iostream>
#include "Box.h"
```

414

```
int main()
{
  const Box box1 {2.0, 3.0, 4.0};            // An arbitrary box
  Box box2 {5.0};                            // A box that is a cube
  std::cout << "box1 volume = " << box1.volume() << std::endl;
  std::cout << "box2 volume = " << box2.volume() << std::endl;
  Box box3 {box2};
  std::cout << "box3 volume = " << box3.volume() << std::endl;    // Volume = 125

  std::cout << std::endl;

  Box boxes[6] {box1, box2, box3, Box {2.0}};
}
```

The output is as follows:

```
Box constructor 1 called.
Box constructor 1 called.
Box constructor 2 called.
box1 volume = 24
box2 volume = 125
Box copy constructor called.
box3 volume = 125

Box copy constructor called.
Box copy constructor called.
Box copy constructor called.
Box constructor 1 called.
Box constructor 2 called.
Default Box constructor called.
Default Box constructor called.
```

The interesting bit is the last seven lines, which results from the creation of the array of Box objects. The initial values for the first three array elements are existing objects, so the compiler calls the copy constructor to duplicate box1, box2, and box3. The fourth element is initialized with an object that is created in the braced initializer for the array by the constructor 2, which calls constructor 1 in its initialization list. The last two array elements have no initial values specified, so the compiler calls the default constructor to create them.

The Size of a Class Object

You obtain the size of a class object by using the sizeof operator in the same way you have previously with fundamental data types. You can apply the operator to a particular object or to the class type. The size of a class object is generally the sum of the sizes of the member variables of the class, although it may turn out to be greater than this. This isn't something that should bother you, but it's nice to know why.

On most computers, for performance reasons, two-byte variables must be placed at an address that is a multiple of two, four-byte variables must be placed at an address that is a multiple of four, and so on. This is called *boundary alignment*. A consequence of this is that sometimes the compiler must leave gaps between the memory for one value and the next. If, on such a machine, you have three variables that occupy two bytes, followed by a variable that requires four bytes, a gap of two bytes may be left in order to place the fourth variable on the correct boundary. In this case, the total space required by all four is greater than the sum of the individual sizes.

Static Members of a Class

You can declare members of a class as `static`. *Static member variables* of a class are used to provide class-wide storage of data that is independent of any particular object of the class type but is accessible by any of them. They record properties of the class as a whole, rather than of individual objects. You can use static member variables to store constants that are specific to a class, or you could store information about the objects of a class in general, such as how many there are in existence.

A *static member function* is independent of any individual class object but can be invoked by any class object if necessary. It can also be invoked from outside the class if it is a public member. A common use of static member functions is to operate on static member variables, regardless of whether any objects of the class have been defined. In general:

■ **Tip** If a member function does not access any nonstatic member variables, it may be a good candidate for being declared as a `static` member function.

Static Member Variables

Static member variables of a class are associated with the class as a whole, not with any particular object of the class. When you declare a member variable of a class as `static`, the static member variable is defined only once and will exist even if no class objects have been created. Each static member variable is accessible in any object of the class and is shared among however many objects there are. An object gets its own independent copies of the ordinary member variables, but only one instance of each static member variable exists, regardless of how many class objects have been defined.

One use for a static member variable is to count how many objects of a class exist. You could add a static member variable to the Box class by adding the following statement to your class definition:

```
static inline size_t objectCount {};    // Count of objects in existence
```

Figure 11-6 shows how this member exists outside of any objects but is available to all of them.

```
class Box
{
  private:
    static inline size_t objectCount {};
    double length;
    double width;
    double height;
    ...
};
```

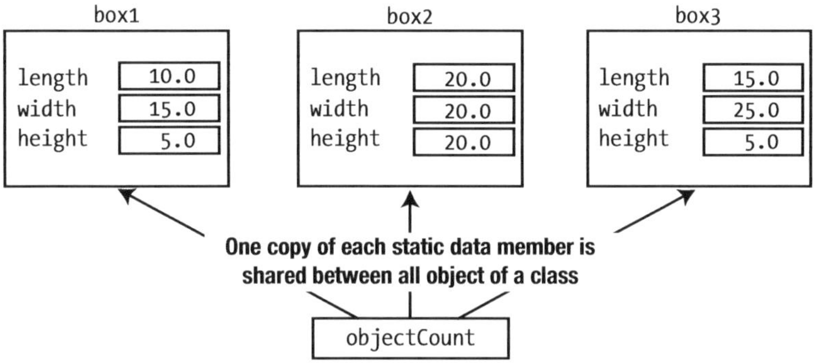

Figure 11-6. *Static class members are shared between objects.*

The static objectCount member is private, so you can't access objectCount from outside the Box class. Naturally, static members can be either public or protected as well.

The objectCount variable is furthermore specified to be inline to allow its variable definition to be #included in multiple translation units without violating the one definition rule (ODR). This is analogous to what we explained in the previous chapter for variables at namespace or global scope.

▨ **Note**   Inline variables have been supported only since C++17. Before C++17, your only option was to declare objectCount as follows (this syntax, of course, remains valid today as well):

```
class Box
{
private:
  static size_t objectCount;
  ...
};
```

Doing so, however, creates somewhat of a problem. How do you initialize a noninline static member variable? You don't want to initialize it in a constructor because you want to initialize it only once, not each time a constructor is called; and anyway, it exists even if no objects exist (and therefore no constructors have been

417

called). And without inline variables, you cannot initialize the variable in the header either, as that would lead to violations of the ODR. The answer is to initialize each noninline `static` member outside the class with a statement such as this:

```
size_t Box::objectCount {};       // Initialize static member of Box class to 0
```

This *defines* objectCount; the line in the class definition only *declares* that it is a noninline `static` member of the class—a member that is to be *defined* elsewhere. Note that the `static` keyword must not be included in such an out-of-class definition. You do have to qualify the member name with the class name, `Box`, though, so that the compiler understands that you are referring to a `static` member of the class. Otherwise, you'd simply be creating a global variable that has nothing to do with the class. Because such a statement *defines* the class `static` member, it must not occur more than once in a program; otherwise you'd again be breaking the ODR. The logical place to put it would thus be the `Box.cpp` file. Even though the `static` member objectCount variable is specified as `private`, you could still initialize it in this fashion.

Clearly, inline variables are far more convenient, as they can be initialized in the header file without a separate definition in the source file.

Let's add the `static inline` objectCount member variable and the object counting capability to Ex11_10. You need two extra statements in the class definition: one to define the new static member variable and another to declare a function that will retrieve its value.

```
class Box
{
private:
  double length {1.0};
  double width {1.0};
  double height {1.0};
  static inline size_t objectCount {};   // Count of objects in existence

public:
  // Constructors
  Box(double lv, double wv, double hv);
  Box(double side);                       // Constructor for a cube
  Box();                                  // Default constructor
  Box(const Box& box);                    // Copy constructor

  double volume() const;                  // Function to calculate the volume of a box

  size_t getObjectCount() const { return objectCount; }
};
```

The getObjectCount() function has been declared as const because it doesn't modify any of the member variables of the class, and you might want to call it for const or non-const objects.

The constructors in the Box.cpp file need to increment objectCount (except for the constructor that delegates to another Box constructor, of course; otherwise, the count would be incremented twice):

```
#include <iostream>
#include "Box.h"

// Constructor definition
Box::Box(double lv, double wv, double hv) : length {lv}, width {wv}, height {hv}
{
  ++objectCount;
  std::cout << "Box constructor 1 called." << std::endl;
}

Box::Box(double side) : Box {side, side, side}  // Constructor for a cube
{
  std::cout << "Box constructor 2 called." << std::endl;
}

Box::Box()                                       // Default constructor
{
  ++objectCount;
  std::cout << "Default Box constructor called." << std::endl;
}

Box::Box(const Box& box)                         // Copy constructor
  : length {box.length}, width {box.width}, height {box.height}
{
  ++objectCount;
  std::cout << "Box copy constructor called." << std::endl;
}

// Function to calculate the volume of a box
double Box::volume() const
{
  return length * width * height;
}
```

These constructor definitions now update the count when an object is created. You can modify the version of main() from Ex11_10 to output the object count:

```
// Ex11_11.cpp
// Using a static member variable
#include <iostream>
#include "Box.h"

int main()
{
  const Box box1 {2.0, 3.0, 4.0};                // An arbitrary box
  Box box2 {5.0};                                // A box that is a cube
  std::cout << "box1 volume = " << box1.volume() << std::endl;
  std::cout << "box2 volume = " << box2.volume() << std::endl;
```

```
  Box box3 {box2};
  std::cout << "box3 volume = " << box3.volume() << std::endl;    // Volume = 125

  std::cout << std::endl;

  Box boxes[6] {box1, box2, box3, Box {2.0}};

  std::cout << "\nThere are now " << box1.getObjectCount() << " Box objects." << std::endl;
}
```

This program will produce the same output as before, only this time it will be terminated by the following line:

```
...

There are now 9 Box objects.
```

This code shows that, indeed, only one copy of the static member objectCount exists, and all the constructors are updating it. The getObjectCount() function is called for the box1 object, but you could use any object including any of the array elements to get the same result. Of course, you're only counting the number of objects that get created. The count that is output corresponds to the number of objects created here. In general, you have no way to know when objects are destroyed yet, so the count won't necessarily reflect the number of objects that are around at any point. You'll find out later in this chapter how to account for objects that get destroyed.

Note that the size of a Box object will be unchanged by the addition of objectCount to the class definition. This is because static member variables are not part of any object; they belong to the class. Furthermore, because static member variables are not part of a class object, a const member function can modify non-const static member variables without violating the const nature of the function.

Accessing Static Member Variables

Suppose that in a reckless moment, you declared objectCount as a public class member. You then no longer need the getObjectCount() function to access it. To output the number of objects in main(), just write this:

```
std::cout << "Object count is " << box1.objectCount << std::endl;
```

There's more. We claimed that a static member variable exists even if no objects have been created. This means that you should be able to get the count *before* you create the first Box object, but how do you refer to the member variable? The answer is that you use the class name, Box, as a qualifier:

```
std::cout << "Object count is " << Box::objectCount << std::endl;
```

Try it out by modifying the previous example; you'll see that it works as described. You can always use the class name to access a public static member of a class. It doesn't matter whether any objects exist. In fact, it is recommended to always use the latter syntax to access static members precisely because this makes it instantly clear when reading the code that it concerns a static member.

Static Constants

Static member variables are often used to define constants. This makes sense. Clearly there's no point in defining constants as non-`static` member variables because then an exact copy of this constant would be made for every single object. If you define constants as static members, there is only one single instance of that constant that is shared between all objects.

Prior to C++17, the rules that governed when you could or could not initialize a constant static member variable directly inside a class definition were somewhat complicated (it depended on the type of the variable). Some static constants could be defined in-class, whereas others needed a definition in the corresponding source file. The introduction of inline variables in C++17, however, has made life considerably easier:

■ **Tip** You typically define all member variables that are both `static` and `const` as `inline` as well. This allows you to initialize them directly inside the class definition, irrespective of their type.

If you, for whatever reason, do prefer to define them in the source file instead, though (using the syntax we showed you earlier), you have to omit the `inline` keyword.

Some examples are shown in this definition of a class of cylindrical boxes, which is the latest novelty in the boxing world:

```
class CylindricalBox
{
public:
  static inline const float maxRadius { 35.0f };
  static inline const float maxHeight { 60.0f };
  static inline const std::string defaultMaterial { "paperboard" };

  CylindricalBox(double radius, double height, std::string_view material = defaultMaterial);

  float volume() const;

private:
  // The value of PI used by CylindricalBox's volume() function
  static inline const float PI { 3.141592f };

  float radius;
  float height;
  std::string material;
};
```

This class defines four inline static constants: `maxRadius`, `maxHeight`, `defaultMaterial`, and `PI`. Note that, unlike regular member variables, there is no harm in making constants `public`. In fact, it is quite common to define public constants containing, for instance, boundary values of function parameters (such as maxRadius and maxHeight) or suggested default values (defaultMaterial). Using these, code outside the class can create a narrow, very high CylindricalBox out of its default material as follows:

```
CylindricalBox bigBox{ 1.23f, CylindricalBox::maxHeight, CylindricalBox::defaultMaterial };
```

Inside the body of a member function of the CylindricalBox class, there is no need to qualify the class's static constant members with the class name:

```
float CylindricalBox::volume() const
{
  return PI * radius * radius * height;
}
```

This function definition uses PI without prepending CylindricalBox::. You'll find a small test program that exercises this CylindricalBox class in Ex11_12.

■ **Note** The three keywords static, inline, and const may appear in any order you like. For the definition of CylindricalBox we used the same sequence static inline const four times (consistency is always a good idea!), but all five other permutations would've been valid as well. All three keywords must appear before the variable's type name, though.

Static Member Variables of the Class Type

A static member variable is not part of a class object, so it can be of the same type as the class. The Box class can contain a static member variable of type Box, for example. This might seem a little strange at first, but it can be useful. We'll use the Box class to illustrate just how. Suppose you need a standard "reference" box for some purpose; you might want to relate Box objects in various ways to a standard box, for example. Of course, you could define a standard Box object outside the class, but if you are going to use it within member functions of the class, it creates an external dependency that it would be better to lose. Suppose we only need it for internal use; then you'd declare this constant as follows:

```
class Box
{
private:
  const static Box refBox;                  // Standard reference box

  // Rest of the class as before...
};
```

refBox is const because it is a standard Box object that should not be changed. However, you must still define and initialize it outside the class. You could put a statement in Box.cpp to define refBox:

```
const Box Box::refBox {10.0, 10.0, 10.0};
```

This calls the Box class constructor to create refBox. Because static member variables of a class are created before any objects are created, at least one Box object will always exist. Any of the static or nonstatic member functions can access refBox. It isn't accessible from outside the class because it is a private member. A class constant is one situation where you might want to make the member variable public if it has a useful role outside the class. As long as it is declared as const, it can't be modified.

■ **Note**   The `constexpr` keyword cannot be used to declare a `Box` static constant inside the definition of the `Box` class itself, simply because at that moment the compiler has not yet seen the complete definition of `Box`. Furthermore, even inside other class declarations `static constexpr Box` members would not yet work, at least not until you declare the constructors of `Box` as `constexpr` as well. Discussing this further, however, is outside the scope of this book.

Static Member Functions

A static member function is independent of any class object. A `public` static member function can be called even if no class objects have been created. Declaring a static function in a class is easy. You simply use the `static` keyword as you did with `objectCount`. You could have declared the `getObjectCount()` function as static in the previous example. You call a static member function using the class name as a qualifier. Here's how you could call the static `getObjectCount()` function:

```
std::cout << "Object count is " << Box::getObjectCount() << std::endl;
```

Of course, if you have created class objects, you can call a static member function through an object of the class in the same way as you call any other member function. Here's an example:

```
std::cout << "Object count is " << box1.getObjectCount() << std::endl;
```

While the latter is certainly valid syntax, it is not recommended. The reason is that it needlessly obfuscates the fact that it concerns a static member function.

A static member function has no access to the object for which it is called. For a static member function to access an object of the class, it would need to be passed as an argument to the function. Referencing members of a class object from within a static function must then be done using qualified names (as you would with an ordinary global function accessing a public member variable).

A static member function is a full member of the class in terms of access privileges, though. If an object of the same class is passed as an argument to a static member function, it can access `private` as well as `public` members of the object. It wouldn't make sense to do so, but just to illustrate the point, you could include a definition of a static function in the Box class, as shown here:

```
static double edgeLength(const Box& aBox)
{
  return 4.0 * (aBox.length + aBox.width + aBox.height);
}
```

Even though you are passing the Box object as an argument, the `private` member variables can be accessed. Of course, it would make more sense to do this with an ordinary member function.

■ **Caution**   Static member functions can't be `const`. Because a static member function isn't associated with any class object, it has no `this` pointer, so `const`-ness doesn't apply.

Destructors

If the delete operator is applied to it or at the end of a block in which a class object is created, the object is destroyed, just like a variable of a fundamental type. When an object is destroyed, a special member of the class called a *destructor* is executed to deal with any cleanup that may be necessary. A class can have only one destructor. If you don't define one, the compiler provides a default version of the destructor that does nothing. The definition of the default constructor looks like this:

```
~ClassName() {}
```

The name of the destructor for a class is always the class name prefixed with a tilde, ~. The destructor cannot have parameters or a return type. The default destructor in the Box class is as follows:

```
~Box() {}
```

Of course, if the definition is placed outside the class, the name of the destructor would be prefixed with the class name:

```
Box::~Box() {}
```

If the body of your destructor is to be empty, however, you are again better off using the default keyword:

```
Box::~Box() = default;        // Have the compiler generate a default destructor
```

The destructor for a class is always called automatically when an object is destroyed. The circumstances where you need to call a destructor explicitly are so rare you can ignore the possibility. Calling a destructor when it is not necessary can cause problems.

You only need to define a class destructor when something needs to be done when an object is destroyed. A class that deals with physical resources such as a file or a network connection that needs to be closed is one example, and of course, if memory is allocated by a constructor using new, the destructor is the place to release the memory. In Chapter 17 we'll argue that defining a destructor should in fact be reserved for only a small minority of your classes—those specifically designated to manage a given resource. This notwithstanding, the Box class in Ex11_11 would surely definitely benefit from a destructor implementation as well, namely, one that decrements objectCount:

```
class Box
{
private:
  double length {1.0};
  double width {1.0};
  double height {1.0};
  static inline size_t objectCount {};    // Count of objects in existence

public:
  // Constructors
  Box(double lv, double wv, double hv);
  Box(double side);       // Constructor for a cube
  Box();                  // Default constructor
  Box(const Box& box);    // Copy constructor
```

```
  double volume() const;                          // Function to calculate the volume of a box

  static size_t getObjectCount() { return objectCount; }

  ~Box();                                         // Destructor
};
```

The destructor has been added to decrement objectCount, and getObjectCount() is now a static member function. The implementation of the Box destructor can be added to the Box.cpp file from Ex11_11 as follows. It outputs a message when it is called so you can see when this occurs:

```
Box::~Box()                                       // Destructor
{
  std::cout << "Box destructor called." << std::endl;
  --objectCount;
}
```

The following code will check the destructor operation out:

```
// Ex11_13.cpp
// Implementing a destructor
#include <iostream>
#include <memory>
#include "Box.h"

int main()
{
  std::cout << "There are now " << Box::getObjectCount() << " Box objects." << std::endl;

  const Box box1 {2.0, 3.0, 4.0};       // An arbitrary box
  Box box2 {5.0};                        // A box that is a cube

  std::cout << "There are now " << Box::getObjectCount() << " Box objects." << std::endl;

  for (double d {} ; d < 3.0 ; ++d)
  {
    Box box {d, d + 1.0, d + 2.0};
    std::cout << "Box volume is " << box.volume() << std::endl;
  }

  std::cout << "There are now " << Box::getObjectCount() << " Box objects." << std::endl;

  auto pBox = std::make_unique<Box>(1.5, 2.5, 3.5);
  std::cout << "Box volume is " << pBox->volume() << std::endl;
  std::cout << "There are now " << pBox->getObjectCount() << " Box objects." << std::endl;
}
```

The output from this example is as follows:

```
There are now 0 Box objects.
Box constructor 1 called.
Box constructor 1 called.
Box constructor 2 called.
There are now 2 Box objects.
Box constructor 1 called.
Box volume is 0
Box destructor called.
Box constructor 1 called.
Box volume is 6
Box destructor called.
Box constructor 1 called.
Box volume is 24
Box destructor called.
There are now 2 Box objects.
Box constructor 1 called.
Box volume is 13.125
There are now 3 Box objects.
Box destructor called.
Box destructor called.
Box destructor called.
```

This example shows when constructors and the destructor are called and how many objects exist at various points during execution. The first line of output shows there are no Box objects at the outset. objectCount clearly exists without any objects because we retrieve its value using the static getObjectCount() member. box1 and box2 are created in the way you saw in the previous example, and the output shows that there are indeed two objects in existence. The for loop created a new object on each iteration, and the output shows that the new object is destroyed at the end of the current iteration, after its volume has been output. After the loop ends, there are just the original two objects in existence. The last object is created by calling the make_unique<Box>() function template, which is defined in the memory header. This calls the Box constructor that has three parameters to create the object in the free store. Just to show that you can, getObjectCount() is called using the smart pointer, pBox. You can see the output from the three destructor calls that occur when main() ends and that destroy the remaining three Box objects.

You now know that the compiler will add a default constructor, a default copy constructor, and a destructor to each class when you don't define these. There are other members that the compiler can add to a class, and you'll learn about them in Chapters 12 and 17.

Using Pointers as Class Members

Real-life programs generally consist of large collections of collaborating objects, linked together using pointers, smart pointers, and references. All these networks of objects need to be created, linked together, and in the end destroyed again. For the latter, making sure all objects are deleted in a timely manner, smart pointers help tremendously:

- A std::unique_ptr<> makes sure that you can never accidentally forget to delete an object allocated from the free store.

- A std::shared_ptr<> is invaluable if multiple objects point to and use the same object—either intermittently or even concurrently—and it is not a priori clear when they will all be done using it. In other words, it is not a priori clear which object should be responsible to delete the shared object because there may always be other objects around that still need it.

░ **Tip** In modern C++ you should normally never need the delete keyword anymore. A dynamically allocated object should always be managed by a smart pointer instead. This principle is called Resource Acquisition Is Initialization—RAII for short. Memory is a resource, and to acquire it you should initialize a smart pointer. We'll return to the RAII principle in Chapter 15 where we'll have even more compelling reasons to use it!

Note that you should use std::make_unique<>() and std::make_shared<>() as much as possible as well instead of the new and new[] operators.

Detailing the object-oriented design principles and techniques required to set up and manage larger programs consisting of many classes and objects would lead us too far here. In this section, we'll walk you through a first somewhat larger example and while doing so point out some of the basic considerations you need to make—for instance when choosing between the different pointer types or the impact of const correctness on the design of your classes. Concretely, we'll define a class with a member variable that is a pointer and use instances of the class to create a *linked list* of objects.

The Truckload Example

We'll define a class that represents a collection of any number of Box objects. The contents of the header file for the Box class definition will be as follows:

```
// Box.h
#ifndef BOX_H
#define BOX_H
#include <iostream>
#include <iomanip>

class Box
{
private:
  double length {1.0};
  double width {1.0};
  double height {1.0};
```

```
public:
  // Constructors
  Box(double lv, double wv, double hv) : length {lv}, width {wv}, height {hv} {};

  Box() = default;                              // Default constructor

  double volume() const                         // Volume of a box
  {
    return length * width * height;
  }

  int compare(const Box& box) const
  {
    if (volume() < box.volume()) return -1;
    if (volume() == box.volume()) return 0;
    return +1;
  }

  void listBox() const
  {
    std::cout << " Box(" << std::setw(2) << length << ','
                         << std::setw(2) << width  << ','
                         << std::setw(2) << height << ')';
  }
};
#endif
```

We have omitted the accessor member functions because they are not required here, but we have added a listBox() member to output a Box object. In this case, a Box object represents a unit of a product to be delivered, and a collection of Box objects represents a truckload of boxes, so we'll call the class Truckload; the collection of Box objects will be a linked list. A linked list can be as long or as short as you need it to be, and you can add objects anywhere in the list. The class will allow a Truckload object to be created from a single Box object or from a vector of Box objects. It will provide for adding and deleting a Box object and for listing all the Box objects in the Truckload.

A Box object has no built-in facility for linking it with another Box object. Changing the definition of the Box class to incorporate this capability would be inconsistent with the idea of a box—boxes aren't like that. One way to collect Box objects into a list is to define another type of object, which we'll call Package. A Package object will have two members: a pointer to a Box object and a pointer to another Package object. The latter will allow us to create a chain of Package objects.

Figure 11-7 shows how each Package object points to a Box object—SharedBox will be a type alias for std::shared_ptr<Box>—and also forms a link in a chain of Package objects that are connected by pointers. This chain of Package objects forms a data structure that is known as a *linked list*. The list can be of unlimited length. As long as you can access the first Package object, you can access the next Package through the pNext pointer it contains, which allows you to reach the next through the pNext pointer that it contains, and so on, through all objects in the list. Each Package object can provide access to the Box object through its pBox member. This arrangement is superior to the Package class having a member that is of type Box, which would require a new Box object to be created for each Package object. The Package class is just a means of tying Box objects together in a linked list, and each Box object should exist independently from the Package objects.

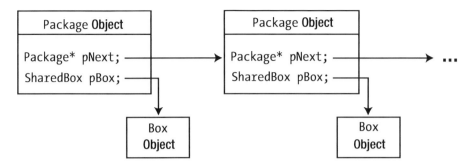

Figure 11-7. *Linked Package objects*

A Truckload object will create and manage a list of Package objects. A Truckload object represents an instance of a truckload of boxes. There can be any number of boxes in a truckload, and each box will be referenced from within a package. A Package object provides the mechanism for the Truckload object to access the pointer to the Box object it contains. Figure 11-8 illustrates the relationship between these objects.

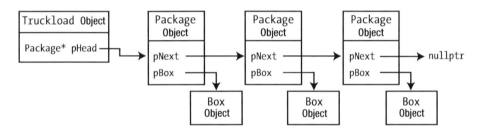

Figure 11-8. *A Truckload object managing a linked list of three Package objects*

Figure 11-8 shows a Truckload object that manages a list of Package objects; each Package object contains a Box object and a pointer to the next Package object. The Truckload object only needs to keep track of the first Package object in the list; the pHead member contains its address. By following the pNext pointer links, you can find any of the objects in the list. In this elementary implementation, the list can only be traversed from the start. A more sophisticated implementation could provide each Package object with a pointer to the previous object in the list, which would allow the list to be traversed backward as well as forward. Let's put the ideas into code.

▦ **Note**   You don't need to create your own classes for linked lists. Very flexible versions are already defined in the list and forward_list standard library headers. Moreover, as we'll discuss in Chapter 19, in most cases you are better off using a std::vector<> instead. Defining your own class for a linked list is very educational, though.

Defining the Package Class

Based on the preceding discussion, the Package class can be defined in Package.h like this:

```cpp
// Package.h
#ifndef PACKAGE_H
#define PACKAGE_H
#include <memory>
#include "Box.h"

using SharedBox = std::shared_ptr<Box>;

class Package
{
private:
  SharedBox pBox;          // Pointer to the Box object contained in this Package
  Package* pNext;          // Pointer to the next Package in the list

public:
  Package(SharedBox pb) : pBox{pb}, pNext{nullptr} {}      // Constructor
  ~Package() { delete pNext; }                             // Destructor

  // Retrieve the Box pointer
  SharedBox getBox() const { return pBox; }

  // Retrieve or update the pointer to the next Package
  Package* getNext() { return pNext; }
  void setNext(Package* pPackage) { pNext = pPackage; }
};
#endif
```

To make the rest of the code a bit less cluttered, we first define the type alias SharedBox as shorthand for std::shared_ptr<Box>. The SharedBox member of the Package class will store the address of a Box object. Every Package object refers to exactly one Box object.

By using shared_ptr<> pointers for all Box objects, we made sure that, at least in theory, we can share these same Boxes with the rest of the program without having to worry about their lifetime—that is, without having to worry which class should delete the Box objects and when. As a consequence, the same Box object could, hypothetically, be shared between a Truckload, a truck's destination manifest, the online shipment tracking system for customers, and so on. If these Boxes are only referred to by the Truckload class, a shared_ptr<> wouldn't be the most appropriate smart pointer. A std::unique_ptr<> would then be more appropriate. But let's say that in this case our Truckload classes are to become part of a larger program entirely built around these Boxes and that this justifies the use of std::shared_ptr<>.

The pNext member variable of a Package will point to the next Package object in the list. The pNext member for the last Package object in a list will contain nullptr. The constructor allows a Package object to be created that contains the address of the Box argument. The pNext member will be nullptr by default, but it can be set to point to a Package object by calling the setNext() member. The setNext() function updates pNext to the next Package in the list. To add a new Package object to the end of the list, you pass its address to the setNext() function for the last Package object in a list.

Packages themselves are not intended to be shared with the rest of the program. Their sole purpose is to form a chain in one Truckload's linked list. A shared_ptr<> is therefore not a good match for the pNext member variable. Normally, you should consider using a unique_ptr<> pointer for this member. The reason is that, in essence, every Package is always pointed to by exactly one object, either by the previous Package in the list or, for the head of the list, by the Truckload itself. And if the Truckload is destroyed, so should all its Packages be. However, in the spirit of the current chapter, and in particular its previous section, we decided to use a raw pointer here instead and thus to grab this opportunity to show you some examples of nondefault destructors.

If a Package object is deleted, its destructor deletes the next Package in the list as well. This in turn will delete the next one, and so on. So, to delete its linked list of Packages, all a Truckload has to do is delete the first Package object in the list, which is the head; the rest of the Packages in the list will then be deleted, one by one, by the destructors of the Packages.

■ **Note**   For the last Package in the list, pNext will be nullptr. Nevertheless, you don't need to test for nullptr in the destructor before applying delete. That is, you don't need to write the destructor like this:

```
~Package() { if (pNext) delete pNext; }
```

You'll often encounter such overly cautious tests in production code. But they are completely redundant. The delete operator is defined to simply do nothing when passed a nullptr. Also noteworthy is that, in this destructor, there is little value in setting pNext to nullptr after the deletion. We told you earlier that, in general, it is considered good practice to reset a pointer to null after deleting the value it points to. This is done to avoid any further use or secondary deletes. But since the pNext member can no longer be accessed once the destructor is done executing—the corresponding Package object no longer exists!—there is little point in doing it here.

Defining the Truckload Class

A Truckload object will encapsulate a list of Package objects. The class must provide everything necessary to create a new list and to extend the list and delete from it, as well as the means by which Box objects can be retrieved. A pointer to the first Package object in the list as a member variable will allow you to get to any Package object in the list by stepping through the chain of pNext pointers, using the getNext() function from the Package class. The getNext() function will be called repeatedly to step through the list one Package object at a time, so the Truckload object will need to track the object that was retrieved most recently. It's also useful to store the address of the last Package object because this makes it easy to add a new object to the end of the list. Figure 11-9 shows this.

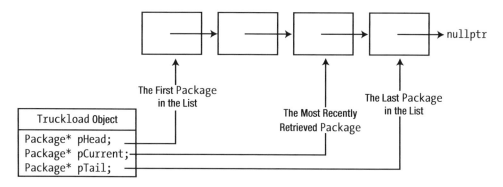

Figure 11-9. Information needed in a Truckload object to manage the list

Consider how retrieving Box objects from a Truckload object could work. This inevitably involves stepping through the list so the starting point is the first object in the list. You could define a getFirstBox() member function in the Truckload class to retrieve the pointer to the first Box object and record the address of the Package object that contained it in pCurrent. You can then implement a getNextBox() member function that will retrieve the pointer to the Box object from the *next* Package object in the list and then update pCurrent to reflect that. Another essential capability is the ability to add a Box to the list and remove a Box from the list, so you'll need member functions to do that; addBox() and removeBox() would be suitable names for these. A member function to list all the Box objects in the list will also be handy.

Here's a definition for the Truckload class based on these ideas:

```
class Truckload
{
private:
  Package* pHead {};                          // First in the list
  Package* pTail {};                          // Last in the list
  Package* pCurrent {};                       // Last retrieved from the list

public:
  Truckload() = default;                      // Default constructor - empty truckload

  Truckload(SharedBox pBox)                   // Constructor - one Box
  {  pHead = pTail = new Package{pBox}; }

  Truckload(const std::vector<SharedBox>& boxes);  // Constructor - vector of Boxes

  Truckload(const Truckload& src);            // Copy constructor

  ~Truckload() { delete pHead; }              // Destructor: clean up the list

  SharedBox getFirstBox();                    // Get the first Box
  SharedBox getNextBox();                     // Get the next Box
  void addBox(SharedBox pBox);                // Add a new Box
  bool removeBox(SharedBox pBox);             // Remove a Box from the Truckload
  void listBoxes() const;                     // Output the Boxes
};
```

The member variables are private because they don't need to be accessible outside the class. The getFirstBox() and getNextBox() members provide the mechanism for retrieving Box objects. Each of these needs to modify the pCurrent pointer, so they cannot be const. The addBox() and removeBox() functions also change the list so they cannot be const either.

There are four constructors. The default constructor defines an object containing an empty list. You can also create an object from a single pointer to a Box object, from a vector of pointers, or as a copy of another Truckload. The destructor of the class makes sure the linked list it encapsulates is properly cleaned up. As described earlier, deleting the first Package will trigger all other Packages in the list to be deleted as well.

The constructor that accepts a vector of pointers to Box objects, the copy constructor, and the other member functions of the class require external definitions, which we'll put in a Truckload.cpp file so they will not be inline. You could define them as inline and include the definitions in Truckload.h.

Traversing the Boxes Contained in a Truckload

Before we look at how the linked list is constructed, we'll look at the member functions that traverse the list. We start with the const member function listBoxes() that outputs the contents of the Truckload object, which could be implemented like this:

```
void Truckload::listBoxes() const
{
  const size_t boxesPerLine = 5;
  size_t count {};
  Package* currentPackage{pHead};
  while (currentPackage)
  {
    currentPackage->getBox()->listBox();
    if (! (++count % boxesPerLine)) std::cout << std::endl;
    currentPackage = currentPackage->getNext();
  }
  if (count % boxesPerLine) std::cout << std::endl;
}
```

The loop steps through the Package objects in the linked list, starting from pHead, until a nullptr is reached. For each Package, it outputs the Box object that it contains by calling listBox() on the corresponding SharedBox. Box objects are output five on a line. The last statement of the function outputs a newline when the last line contains output for less than five Box objects.

If you want, you could also write this while loop as an equivalent for loop:

```
void Truckload::listBoxes() const
{
  const size_t boxesPerLine = 5;
  size_t count {};
  for (Package* package{pHead}; package; package = package->getNext())
  {
    package->getBox()->listBox();
    if (! (++count % boxesPerLine)) std::cout << std::endl;
  }
  if (count % boxesPerLine) std::cout << std::endl;
}
```

Both loops are completely equivalent, so you're free to use either pattern to traverse linked lists. Arguably, the for loop is somewhat nicer because there is a clearer distinction between the initialization and advancement code of the package pointer (nicely grouped in front of the body, between the round brackets of the for (...) statement) and the core logic of the listing algorithm (the loop's body, which now is no longer cluttered by any list traversal code).

To allow code outside the Truckload class to traverse the SharedBoxes stored in a Truckload in a similar fashion, the class offers the getFirstBox() and getNextBox() member functions. Before we discuss their implementation, it's better to give you an idea already how these functions are intended to be used. The pattern used to traverse the Boxes in a Truckload by external code will look similar to that of the listBoxes() member function (of course, an equivalent while loop could be used as well):

```
Truckload truckload{ ... };
...
for (SharedBox box{truckload.getFirstBox()}; box; box = truckload.getNextBox())
{
  ...
}
```

The getFirstBox() and getNextBox() functions operate using the pCurrent member variable of Truckload, a pointer that must at all times point to the Package whose Box was last returned by either function. Such an assertion is known as a *class invariant*—a property of the member variables of a class that must hold at all times. Before returning, all member functions should therefore make sure that all class invariants hold again. Conversely, they can trust that the invariants hold at the start of their execution. Other invariants for the Truckload class include that pHead points to the first Package in the list and pTail to the last one (see also Figure 11-9). With these invariants in mind, implementing getFirstBox() and getNextBox() is actually not that hard:

```
SharedBox Truckload::getFirstBox()
{
  // Return pHead's box (or nullptr if the list is empty)
  pCurrent = pHead;
  return pCurrent? pCurrent->getBox() : nullptr;
}

SharedBox Truckload::getNextBox()
{
  if (!pCurrent)                        // If there's no current...
    return getFirstBox();               // ...return the 1st Box

  pCurrent = pCurrent->getNext();       // Move to the next package

  return pCurrent? pCurrent->getBox() : nullptr;   // Return its box (or nullptr...).
}
```

The getFirstBox() function is a piece of cake—just two statements. We know that the address of the first Package object in the list is stored in pHead. Calling the getBox() function for this Package object obtains the address of its Box object, which is the desired result for getFirstBox(). Only if the list is empty will pHead be nullptr. For an empty Truckload, getFirstBox() should return a nulled SharedBox as well. Before returning, getFirstBox() also stores the address of the first Package object in pCurrent. This is done because the class invariants state that pCurrent must always refer to the last Package whose Box was retrieved.

If at the start of getNextBox() the pCurrent pointer is nullptr, then the first in the list (if any) is obtained and returned by calling getFirstBox(). Otherwise, the getNextBox() function accesses the Package object that follows the one whose Box was returned last by calling pCurrent->getNext(). If this Package* is nullptr, the end of the list has been reached, and nullptr is returned. Otherwise, the Box of the current Package is returned. Of course, getNextBox() also correctly updates pCurrent to respect its class invariant.

Adding and Removing Boxes

We'll start with the easiest of the remaining members: the vector<>-based constructor definition. This creates a list of Package objects from a vector of smart pointers to Box objects:

```
Truckload::Truckload(const std::vector<SharedBox>& boxes)
{
  for (const auto& pBox : boxes)
  {
    addBox(pBox);
  }
}
```

The parameter is a reference to avoid copying the argument. The vector elements are of type SharedBox, which is an alias for std::shared_ptr<Box>. The loop iterates through the vector elements passing each one to the addBox() member of the Truckload class, which will create and add a Package object on each call.

The copy constructor simply iterates over all packages in the source Truckload and calls addBox() for each box to add it to the newly constructed Truckload:

```
Truckload::Truckload(const Truckload& src)
{
  for (Package* package{src.pHead}; package; package = package->getNext())
  {
    addBox(package->getBox());
  }
}
```

Both of these constructors are made easy because all the heavy lifting is delegated to addBox(). The definition of this member will be as follows:

```
void Truckload::addBox(SharedBox pBox)
{
  auto pPackage = new Package{pBox};        // Create a new Package

  if (pTail)                                // Check list is not empty
    pTail->setNext(pPackage);               // Append the new object to the tail
  else                                      // List is empty
    pHead = pPackage;                       // so new object is the head

  pTail = pPackage;                         // Either way: the latest object is the (new)
tail
}
```

The function creates a new Package object from the pBox pointer in the free store and stores its address in a local pointer, pPackage. For an empty list, both pHead and pTail will be null. If pTail is non-null, then the list is not empty, and the new object is added to the end of the list by storing its address in the pNext member of the last Package that is pointed to by pTail. If the list is empty, the new Package is the head of the list. In either case, the new Package object is at the end of the list, so pTail is updated to reflect this.

The most complicated of all Truckload member functions is removeBox(). This function also has to traverse the list, looking for the Box to remove. The initial outline of the function is therefore as follows:

```
bool Truckload::removeBox(SharedBox boxToRemove)
{
  Package* current{pHead};
  while (current)
  {
    if (current->getBox() == boxToRemove)        // We found the Box!
    {
      // remove the *current Package from the linked list...

      return true;                               // Return true: we found and removed the box
    }
    current = current->getNext();                // move along to the next Package
  }

  return false;                                  // boxToRemove was not found: return false
}
```

You know this pattern already from the previous section. Once current points to the Package that needs to be removed, the only challenge remaining is how to correctly remove this Package from the linked list. Figure 11-10 illustrates what needs to be done:

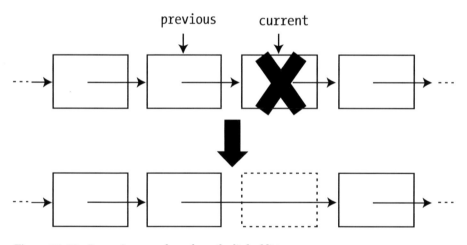

Figure 11-10. *Removing a package from the linked list*

The figure clearly shows that in order to remove a Package somewhere in the middle of the linked list, we need to update the pNext pointer of the *previous* Package in the list. In Figure 11-10 this is the Package pointed to by previous. This is not yet possible with our initial outline of the function. The current pointer has moved past the Package that needs to be updated, and there is no way to go back.

The standard solution is to keep track of both a previous and a current pointer while traversing the linked list, with previous at all times pointing to the Package that precedes the one pointed to by current. The previous pointer is sometimes called a *trailing pointer* because it always trails one Package behind the traversal pointer, current. The full function definition looks as follows:

```
bool Truckload::removeBox(SharedBox boxToRemove)
{
  Package* previous {nullptr};       // no previous yet
  Package* current {pHead};          // initialize current to the head of the list
  while (current)
  {
    if (current->getBox() == boxToRemove)    // We found the Box!
    {
      if (previous)                          // If there is a previous Package...
      {
        previous->setNext(current->getNext()); // ...make it point to the next Package
      }
      else
      {                                      // If there is no previous, we are removing the
        pHead = current->getNext();          // first Package in the list, so update pHead
      }

      current->setNext(nullptr);             // Disconnect the current Package from the list
      delete current;                        // and delete it

      return true;                           // Return true: we found and removed the box
    }
                                             // Move both pointers along (mind the order!)
    previous = current;                      //  - first current becomes the new previous
    current = current->getNext();            //  - then move current along to the next Package
  }

  return false;                              // Return false: boxToRemove was not found
}
```

Once you know about the trailing pointer technique, putting it all together is not that hard anymore. As always, you have to provide a special case for removing the head of the list, but that's not too hard. One more thing to watch out for is that the Package that you take out has to be deleted. Before doing that, though, it is important to set its pNext pointer to null first. Otherwise, the destructor of the Package would start deleting the entire list of Packages that used to follow the deleted Package, starting with its pNext.

Putting It All Together

You should put the class definition in Truckload.h and collect all function definitions in Truckload.cpp. With these in place, you can try the Truckload class using the following code:

```
// Ex11_14.cpp
// Using a linked list
#include <cstdlib>        // For random number generation
#include <ctime>          // For the std::time() function
#include "Truckload.h"
```

```
// Function to generate a random integer between 1 and count
inline unsigned random(size_t count)
{
  return 1 + static_cast<unsigned>(std::rand() / (RAND_MAX / count + 1));
}
// Function to generate a Box with random dimensions
inline SharedBox randomBox()
{
  const size_t dimLimit {99};            // Upper limit on Box dimensions
  return std::make_shared<Box>(random(dimLimit), random(dimLimit), random(dimLimit));
}

int main()
{
  // Initialize the random number generator
  std::srand(static_cast<unsigned>(std::time(nullptr)));

  Truckload load1;                       // Create an empty list

  // Add 12 random Box objects to the list
  const size_t boxCount {12};
  for (size_t i {} ; i < boxCount ; ++i)
    load1.addBox(randomBox());

  std::cout << "The first list:\n";
  load1.listBoxes();

  // Copy the truckload
  Truckload copy{load1};
  std::cout << "The copied truckload:\n";
  copy.listBoxes();

  // Find the largest Box in the list
  SharedBox largestBox{load1.getFirstBox()};

  SharedBox nextBox{load1.getNextBox()};
  while (nextBox)
  {
    if (nextBox->compare(*largestBox) > 0)
      largestBox = nextBox;
    nextBox = load1.getNextBox();
  }

  std::cout << "\nThe largest box in the first list is ";
  largestBox->listBox();
  std::cout << std::endl;
  load1.removeBox(largestBox);
  std::cout << "\nAfter deleting the largest box, the list contains:\n";
  load1.listBoxes();
```

```
  const size_t nBoxes {20};              // Number of vector elements
  std::vector<SharedBox> boxes;          // Array of Box objects

  for (size_t i {} ; i < nBoxes ; ++i)
    boxes.push_back(randomBox());

  Truckload load2{boxes};
  std::cout << "\nThe second list:\n";
  load2.listBoxes();

  auto smallestBox = load2.getFirstBox();
  for (auto nextBox = load2.getNextBox(); nextBox; nextBox = load2.getNextBox())
    if (nextBox->compare(*smallestBox) < 0)
      smallestBox = nextBox;

  std::cout << "\nThe smallest box in the second list is ";
  smallestBox->listBox();
  std::cout << std::endl;
}
```

Here's some sample output from this program:

```
The first list:
 Box(69,78,42) Box(42,85,57) Box(91,16,41) Box(20,91,78) Box(89,66,17)
 Box(19,72,90) Box(82,68,98) Box(88,11,79) Box(21,93,75) Box(49,65,93)
 Box(92,90,39) Box(99,21, 3)
The copied truckload:
 Box(69,78,42) Box(42,85,57) Box(91,16,41) Box(20,91,78) Box(89,66,17)
 Box(19,72,90) Box(82,68,98) Box(88,11,79) Box(21,93,75) Box(49,65,93)
 Box(92,90,39) Box(99,21, 3)

The largest box in the first list is: Box(82,68,98)

After deleting the largest box, the list contains:
 Box(69,78,42) Box(42,85,57) Box(91,16,41) Box(20,91,78) Box(89,66,17)
 Box(19,72,90) Box(88,11,79) Box(21,93,75) Box(49,65,93) Box(92,90,39)
 Box(99,21, 3)

The second list:
 Box( 6,66,81) Box(98, 2, 7) Box(67,67,72) Box(68,69,64) Box(50,89,69)
 Box( 8,87,92) Box(57,99,64) Box(74,31, 2) Box(56,37,52) Box( 9,50,35)
 Box(46,74, 9) Box(13,18,78) Box(20,27,88) Box(17,74,37) Box(21,21, 5)
 Box(70,85,64) Box(57,32,13) Box(38,62,15) Box(79,86,59) Box(88, 6,91)

The smallest box in the second list is Box(21,21, 5)
```

The main() function first creates an empty Truckload object, then adds Box objects in the for loop, and makes a copy of this Truckload object. It then finds the largest Box object in the list and deletes it. The output demonstrates that all these operations are working correctly. Just to show it works, main() creates a Truckload object from a vector of pointers to Box objects. It then finds the smallest Box object and outputs it. Clearly, the capability to list the contents of a Truckload object is also working well. Note that the SharedBox type alias can be used in main() because it is defined in Package.h and therefore available in this source file.

Nested Classes

It's sometimes desirable to limit the accessibility of a class. The Package class was designed to be used specifically within the TruckLoad class. It would make sense to ensure that Package objects can only be created by member functions of the TruckLoad class. What you need is a mechanism where Package objects are private to Truckload class members and not available to the rest of the world. You can do this by using a *nested class*.

A *nested class* is a class that has its definition inside another class definition. The name of the nested class is within the scope of the enclosing class and is subject to the member access specification in the enclosing class. We could put the definition of the Package class inside the definition of the TruckLoad class, like this:

```
#include "Box.h"
#include <memory>
#include <vector>

using SharedBox = std::shared_ptr<Box>;

class Truckload
{
private:
  class Package
  {
  public:
    SharedBox pBox;            // Pointer to the Box object contained in this Package
    Package* pNext;            // Pointer to the next Package in the list

    Package(SharedBox pb) : pBox{pb}, pNext{nullptr} {}    // Constructor
    ~Package() { delete pNext; }                           // Destructor
  };

  Package* pHead {};                         // First in the list
  Package* pTail {};                         // Last in the list
  Package* pCurrent {};                      // Last retrieved from the list

public:
  // Exact same public member functions as before...
};
```

The Package type is now local to the scope of the TruckLoad class definition. Because the definition of the Package class is in the private section of the TruckLoad class, Package objects cannot be created or used from outside the TruckLoad class. Because the Package class is entirely private to the TruckLoad class, there's also no harm in making all its members public. Hence, they're directly accessible to member functions of a TruckLoad object. The getBox() and getNext() members of the original Package class are no longer needed. All of the Package members are directly accessible from Truckload objects but inaccessible outside the class.

The definitions of the member functions of the TruckLoad class need to be changed to access the member variables of the Package class directly. This is trivial. Just replace all occurrences of getBox(), getNext(), and setNext() in Truckload.cpp with code that directly accesses the corresponding member variable. The resulting Truckload class definition with Package as a nested class will work with the Ex11_14.cpp source file. A working example is available in the code download as Ex11_15.

▓ **Note**   Nesting the Package class inside the TruckLoad class simply defines the Package type in the context of the TruckLoad class. Objects of type TruckLoad aren't affected in any way—they'll have the same members as before.

Member functions of a nested class can directly reference static members of the enclosing class, as well as any other types or enumerators defined in the enclosing class. Other members of the enclosing class can be accessed from the nested class in the normal ways: via a class object or a pointer or a reference to a class object. When accessing members of the outer class, the member functions of a nested class have the same access privileges as member functions of the outer class; that is, member functions of a nested class are allowed to access the private members of objects of the outer class.

Nested Classes with Public Access

Of course, you could put the Package class definition in the public section of the TruckLoad class. This would mean that the Package class definition was part of the public interface so it *would* be possible to create Package objects externally. Because the Package class name is within the scope of the TruckLoad class, you can't use it by itself. You must qualify the Package class name with the name of the class in which it is nested. Here's an example:

```
TruckLoad::Package aPackage(aBox);            // Define a Package object
```

Of course, making the Package type public in the example would defeat the rationale for making it a nested class in the first place! Of course, there can be other circumstances where a public nested class makes sense. We'll see one such example in the next subsection.

A Better Mechanism for Traversing a Truckload: Iterators

The getFirstBox() and getNextBox() members allowed you to traverse all Boxes stored in a Truckload. It is not unheard of to add analogous members to a class—we have encountered it on at least two occasions in real code—but this pattern has some serious flaws. Perhaps you can already think of one?

Suppose you find—rightfully so—that the main() function of Ex11_14 is too long and crowded and you decide to split off some of its functionality in reusable functions. A good first candidate would then be a helper function to find the largest Box in a Truckload. A natural way to write this is as follows:

```
SharedBox findLargestBox(const Truckload& truckload)
{
  SharedBox largestBox{ truckload.getFirstBox() };

  SharedBox nextBox{ truckload.getNextBox() };
  while (nextBox)
  {
    if (nextBox->compare(*largestBox) > 0)
      largestBox = nextBox;
    nextBox = truckload.getNextBox();
  }

  return largestBox;
}
```

Unfortunately, however, this function does not compile! Can you see why not? The root cause of the problem is that both getFirstBox() and getNextBox() have to update the pCurrent member inside truckload. This implies that they both must be non-const member functions, which in turn implies that neither of these functions can be called on truckload, which is a reference-to-const argument. Nevertheless, using a reference-to-const parameter is the normal thing to do here. Nobody would or should expect that searching for the largest Box requires a Truckload to be modified. As it stands, however, it is impossible to traverse the content of a const Truckload, which renders const Truckload objects nearly useless. Proper const Truckload& references would be extremely useful, though. In principle, they should allow you to pass a Truckload to code that you'd like to traverse the Boxes contained in it but that at the same time should not be allowed to call either AddBox() or RemoveBox().

■ **Note** You could try to work around the problem by making the pCurrent member variable of the Truckload class mutable. That would then allow you to turn both getFirstBox() and getNextBox() into const members. While this may be interesting for you as a bonus exercise, this solution still suffers some drawbacks in general. First, you'd run into problems with nested loops over the same collection. Second, even though concurrency is out of the scope of this discussion, you can probably imagine that using the mutable approach would never allow for concurrent traversals by multiple threads of execution either. In both cases, one pCurrent pointer would be required per traversal—not one per Truckload object.

The correct solution to this problem is the so-called *iterator pattern*. The principle is easy enough. Instead of storing the pCurrent pointer inside the Truckload object itself, you move it to another object specifically designed and created to aid with traversing the Truckload. Such an object is then called an *iterator*.

■ **Note** Later in this book, you'll learn that the containers and algorithms of the Standard Library make extensive use of iterators. While Standard Library iterators have a slightly different interface than the Iterator class we are about to define for Truckload, the underlying principle is the same: iterators allow external code to traverse the content of a container without having to know about the data structure's internals.

Let's see what that could look like for us. We'll start from the Truckload class of Ex11_15—the version where Package is already a nested class—and add a second nested class called Iterator:

```
#include "Box.h"
#include <memory>
#include <vector>

using SharedBox = std::shared_ptr<Box>;

class Truckload
{
private:
  class Package
  {
  public:
    SharedBox pBox;                 // Pointer to the Box object contained in this Package
    Package* pNext;                 // Pointer to the next Package in the list

    Package(SharedBox pb) : pBox{pb}, pNext{nullptr} {}     // Constructor
    ~Package() { delete pNext; }                            // Destructor
  };

  Package* pHead {};                                        // First in the list
  Package* pTail {};                                        // Last in the list

public:
  class Iterator
  {
  private:
    Package* pHead;                 // The head of the linked list (needed for getFirstBox())
    Package* pCurrent;              // The package whose Box was last retrieved

    friend class Truckload;         // Only a Truckload can create an Iterator
    explicit Iterator(Package* head) : pHead{head}, pCurrent{nullptr} {}

  public:
    SharedBox getFirstBox();        // Get the first Box
    SharedBox getNextBox();         // Get the next Box
  };

  Iterator getIterator() const { return Iterator{pHead}; }

  // Exact same public member functions as before,
  // only without getFirstBox() and getNextBox()...
};
```

The pCurrent, getFirstBox(), and getNextBox() members have been moved from the Truckload into its nested Iterator class. Both functions are implemented in the same manner as before, except that now they no longer update a pCurrent member variable of the Truckload itself. Instead, they operate using the pCurrent member of an Iterator object specifically created to traverse this Truckload by getIterator(). As multiple Iterators can exist at the same time for a single Truckload, each with their own pCurrent pointer, both nested and concurrent traversals of the same Truckload become possible. Moreover, and more importantly, creating an iterator does not modify the Truckload, so getIterator() can be a const member function. This allows us to properly implement the findLargestBox() function from earlier with a reference-to-const-Truckload parameter:

```
SharedBox findLargestBox(const Truckload& truckload)
{
  auto iterator = truckload.getIterator();         // type of iterator is Truckload::Iterator
  SharedBox largestBox{ iterator.getFirstBox() };

  SharedBox nextBox{ iterator.getNextBox() };
  while (nextBox)
  {
    if (nextBox->compare(*largestBox) > 0)
      largestBox = nextBox;
    nextBox = iterator.getNextBox();
  }

  return largestBox;
}
```

We'll leave the completion of this example to you as an exercise (see Exercise 11-6). Before we conclude the chapter, though, let's first take a closer look at the access rights within the definition of Truckload and its nested classes. Iterator is a nested class of Truckload, so it has the same access privileges as Truckload member functions. This is fortunate because otherwise it couldn't have used the nested Package class, which is declared to be for private use only within the Truckload class. Naturally, Iterator itself must be a public nested class; otherwise, code outside of the class would not be able to use it. Notice that we did decide to make the primary constructor of the Iterator class private, however, because external code cannot (it never has access to any Package objects) and should not create Iterators that way. Only the getIterator() function will be creating Iterators with this constructor. For it to access this private constructor, however, we need a friend declaration. Even though you can access private members of the outer class from within a nested class, the same does not hold in the other direction. That is, an outer class has no special privileges when it comes to accessing the members of an inner class. It is treated like any other external code. Without the friend declaration, the getIterator() function would therefore not have been allowed to access the private constructor of the nested Iterator class.

■ **Note**   Even though external code cannot create a new Iterator using our private constructor, it does remain possible to create a new Iterator object as a copy of an existing one. The default copy constructor generated by the compiler remains public.

Summary

In this chapter, you learned the basic ideas involved with defining and using class types. However, although you covered a lot of ground, this is just the start. There's a great deal more to implementing the operations applicable to class objects, and there are subtleties in this too. In subsequent chapters, you'll be building on what you learned here, and you'll see more about how you can extend the capabilities of your classes. In addition, you'll explore more sophisticated ways to use classes in practice. The key points to keep in mind from this chapter are as follows:

- A *class* provides a way to define your own data types. Classes can represent whatever types of *objects* your particular problem requires.

- A class can contain *member variables* and *member functions*. The member functions of a class always have free access to the member variables of the same class.

- Objects of a class are created and initialized using member functions called *constructors*. A constructor is called automatically when an object declaration is encountered. Constructors can be overloaded to provide different ways of initializing an object.

- A copy constructor is a constructor for an object that is initialized with an existing object of the same class. The compiler generates a default copy constructor for a class if you don't define one.

- Members of a class can be specified as public, in which case they are freely accessible from any function in a program. Alternatively, they can be specified as private, in which case they may be accessed only by member functions, friend functions of the class, or members of nested classes.

- Member variables of a class can be static. Only one instance of each static member variable of a class exists, no matter how many objects of the class are created.

- Although static member variables of a class are accessible in a member function of an object, they aren't part of the object and don't contribute to its size.

- Every non-static member function contains the pointer this, which points to the current object for which the function is called.

- static member functions can be called even if no objects of the class have been created. A static member function of a class doesn't contain the pointer this.

- const member functions can't modify the member variables of a class object unless the member variables have been declared as mutable.

- Using references to class objects as arguments to function calls can avoid substantial overheads in passing complex objects to a function.

- A destructor is a member function that is called for a class object when it is destroyed. If you don't define a class destructor, the compiler supplies a default destructor.

- A nested class is a class that is defined inside another class definition.

EXERCISES

The following exercises enable you to try what you've learned in this chapter.

If you get stuck, look back over the chapter for help. If you're still stuck after that, you can download the solutions from the Apress website (www.apress.com/source-code), but that really should be a last resort.

Exercise 11-1. Create a class called `Integer` that has a single, `private` member variable of type `int`. Provide a class constructor that outputs a message when an object is created. Define member functions to *get* and *set* the member variable and to output its value. Write a test program to create and manipulate at least three `Integer` objects and verify that you can't assign a value directly to the member variable. Exercise all the class member functions by getting, setting, and outputting the value of the member variable of each object. Make sure to create at least one `const Integer` object and verify which operations you can and cannot apply on it.

Exercise 11-2. Modify the `Integer` class in the previous exercise so that an `Integer` object can be created without an argument. The member value should then be initialized to zero. Can you think of two ways to do this? Also, implement a copy constructor that prints a message when called.

Next, add a member function that compares the current object with an `Integer` object passed as an argument. The function should return −1 if the current object is less than the argument, 0 if the objects are equal, and +1 if the current object is greater than the argument. Try two versions of the `Integer` class, one where the `compare()` function argument is passed by value and the other where it is passed by reference. What do you see output from the constructors when the function is called? Make sure you understand why this is so. You can't have both functions present in the class as overloaded functions. Why not?

Exercise 11-3. Implement member functions `add()`, `subtract()`, and `multiply()` for the `Integer` class that will add, subtract, and multiply the current object by the value represented by the argument of type `Integer`. Demonstrate the operation of these functions in your class with a version of `main()` that creates several `Integer` objects encapsulating integer values and then uses these to calculate the value of $4\times5^3+6\times5^2+7\times5+8$. Implement the functions so that the calculation and the output of the result can be performed in a single statement.

Exercise 11-4. Change your solution for Exercise 11-2 so that it implements the `compare()` function as a `friend` of the `Integer` class. Afterward, ask yourself whether it was really necessary for this function to be a friend.

Exercise 11-5. Implement a `static` function `printCount()` for the `Integer` class that you created earlier in Exercise 11-2 that outputs the number of `Integer`s in existence. Modify the `main()` function such that it tests that this number correctly goes up and down when needed.

Exercise 11-6. Finish the nested `Truckload::Iterator` class that we started at the end of the chapter. Starting from `Ex11_15`, add the `Iterator` class to its definition as listed earlier, and implement its member functions. Use the `Iterator` class to implement the `findLargestBox()` function as outlined earlier (perhaps you can do it without looking at the solution?), and rework the `main()` function of Ex11_15 to make use of this. Do the same with an analogous `findSmallestBox()` function.

Exercise 11-7. Modify the `Package` class in the solution of Exercise 11-6 so that it contains an additional pointer to the previous object in the list. This makes it a so-called doubly linked list—naturally, the data structure we were using before is called a *singly linked list*. Modify the `Package`, `Truckload`, and `Iterator` classes to make use of this, including providing the ability to iterate through `Box` objects in the list in reverse order and to list the objects in a `Truckload` object in reverse sequence. Devise a `main()` program to demonstrate the new capabilities.

Exercise 11-8. A scrutinous analysis of the `main()` function of Ex11_14 (and thus also that of Ex11_15 and the solutions of the previous two exercises) reveals the following performance flaw: to remove the largest `Box`, we perform two linear traversals of the linked list. First we look for the largest `Box`, and then we look inside `removeBox()` to look for the `Package` to unlink. Devise a solution based on the `Iterator` class of Exercise 11-7 to avoid this second search.

Hint: The solution hinges on a member function with the following signature:

```
bool removeBox(Iterator iterator);
```

CHAPTER 12

Operator Overloading

In this chapter, you'll learn how to add support for operators such as add and subtract to your classes so that they can be applied to objects. This will make the types that you define behave more like fundamental data types and offer a more natural way to express some of the operations between objects. You've already seen how classes can have member functions that operate on the member variables of an object. Operator overloading enables you to write member functions that enable the basic operators to be applied to class objects.

In this chapter, you will learn:

- What operator overloading is

- Which operators you can implement for your own data types

- How to implement member functions that overload operators

- How and when to implement operator functions as ordinary functions

- How to implement comparison and arithmetic operators for a class

- How overloading the << operator allows objects of your own type to be streamed out to, for instance, std::cout

- How to overload unary operators, including the increment and decrement operators

- How to overload the array subscript operator (informally known as the square brackets operator, [ ]) if your class represents a collection of values

- How to define type conversions as operator functions

- What copy assignment is and how to implement your own assignment operator

Implementing Operators for a Class

The Box class in the previous chapter could be applied in an application that is primarily concerned with the volume of a box. For such an application, you obviously need the ability to compare box volumes so that you can determine the relative sizes of the boxes. In Ex11_14, there was this code:

```
if (nextBox->compare(*largestBox) > 0)
    largestBox = nextBox;
```

Wouldn't it be nice if you could write the following instead?

```
if (*nextBox > *largestBox)
  largestBox = nextBox;
```

Using the greater-than operator is much clearer and easier to understand than the original. You might also like to add the volumes of two Box objects with an expression such as Box1 + Box2 or multiply Box as 10*box1 to obtain a new Box object that has the capacity to hold ten box1 boxes. We'll explain how you can do all this and more by implementing functions that overload the basic operators for objects of a class type.

Operator Overloading

Operator overloading enables you to apply standard operators such as +, -, *, <, and many more, to objects of your own class types. In fact, you have used several such overloaded operators already with objects of Standard Library types, probably without realizing that these were implemented as overloaded functions. For instance, you have compared std::string objects using operators such as < and ==, concatenated strings using +, and sent them to the std::cout output stream using the overloaded << operator. This underlines the beauty of operator overloading. If applied properly, it leads to very natural, elegant code—the kind of code that you intuitively would want to write and can read without a moment's thought.

To define an operator for objects of your own type, all you need to do is write a function that implements the desired behavior. For the most part, operator function definitions are the same as any other function definition you have written so far. The main difference lies in the function name. The name of a function that overloads a given operator is composed of the operator keyword followed by the operator that you are overloading. The best way to understand how operator overloading works is to step through an example. In the next section, we'll start by explaining how you implement the less-than operator, <, for the Box class.

Implementing an Overloaded Operator

A binary operator that is implemented as a class member has *one* parameter. We'll explain in a moment why there is only one. Here's the member function to overload the < operator in the Box class definition:

```
class Box
{
private:
  // Members as before...

public:
  bool operator<(const Box& aBox) const;          // Overloaded 'less-than' operator

  // The rest of the Box class as before...
};
```

Because you're implementing a comparison, the return type is bool. The operator<() function will be called as a result of comparing two Box objects using <. The function will be called as a member of the object that is the left operand, and the argument will be the right operand, so this will point to the left operand. Because the function doesn't change either operand, the parameter and the function are specified as const. To see how this works, consider the following statement:

```
if (box1 < box2)
  std::cout << "box1 is less than box2" << std::endl;
```

The `if` expression will result in the operator function being called. The expression is equivalent to the function call `box1.operator<(box2)`. If you were so inclined, you could write it like this in the `if` statement:

```
if (box1.operator<(box2))
  std::cout << "box1 is less than box2" << std::endl;
```

This shows you that an overloaded binary operator is indeed, for the most part, just a function with two special properties: it has a special name, and the function may be called by writing the operator in between its two operands.

Knowing how the operands in the expression box1 < box2 map to the function call makes implementing the overloaded operator easy. Figure 12-1 shows the definition.

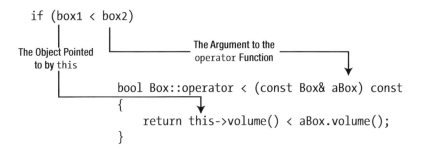

Figure 12-1. *Overloading the less-than operator*

The reference function parameter avoids unnecessary copying of the argument. The `return` expression calls the `volume()` member to calculate the volume of the object pointed to by `this` and compares that with the volume of aBox using the basic < operator. Thus, `true` is returned if the object pointed to by `this` has a smaller volume than the object passed as the argument—and `false` otherwise.

▓ **Note**   We used the `this` pointer in Figure 12-1 just to show the association with the first operand. It isn't necessary to use `this` explicitly here.

Let's see if this works in an example. Here's how Box.h looks:

```
// Box.h
#ifndef BOX_H
#define BOX_H
#include <iostream>

class Box
{
private:
  double length {1.0};
  double width {1.0};
  double height {1.0};
```

```
public:
  // Constructors
  Box(double lv, double wv, double hv) : length{lv}, width{wv}, height{hv} {}

  Box() = default;                    // No-arg constructor

  double volume() const               // Function to calculate the volume
  { return length * width * height;}

  // Accessors
  double getLength() const { return length; }
  double getWidth() const { return width; }
  double getHeight() const { return height; }

  bool operator<(const Box& aBox) const          // Less-than operator
  { return volume() < aBox.volume(); }
};
#endif
```

All member functions are defined inside the class, so Box.cpp is not needed. Defining trivial operator functions inside their class definition can be a good idea. It ensures they are inline, which should maximize efficiency. Still, you could implement the function in a separate Box.cpp file. In that case, the function definition would have to look like the one shown in Figure 12-1. That is, the Box:: qualifier must immediately precede the operator keyword.

Here is a little program to exercise the less-than operator for Boxes:

```
// Ex12_01.cpp
// Implementing a less-than operator
#include <iostream>
#include <vector>
#include "Box.h"

int main()
{
  std::vector<Box> boxes {Box {2.0, 2.0, 3.0}, Box {1.0, 3.0, 2.0},
                          Box {1.0, 2.0, 1.0}, Box {2.0, 3.0, 3.0}};
  Box smallBox {boxes[0]};
  for (const auto& box : boxes)
  {
    if (box < smallBox) smallBox = box;
  }

  std::cout << "The smallest box has dimensions: "
    << smallBox.getLength() << 'x'
    << smallBox.getWidth()  << 'x'
    << smallBox.getHeight() << std::endl;
}
```

This produces the following output:

```
The smallest box has dimensions: 1x2x1
```

The main() function first creates a vector initialized with four Box objects. You arbitrarily assume that the first array element is the smallest and use it to initialize smallBox, which will involve the copy constructor, of course. The range-based for loop compares each element of boxes with smallBox, and a smaller element is stored in smallBox in an assignment statement. When the loop ends, smallBox contains the Box object with the smallest volume. If you want to track calls of the operator<() function, add an output statement to it.

Notice that the smallBox = box; statement shows that the assignment operator works with Box objects. This is because the compiler supplies a default version of operator=() in the class that copies the values of the members of the right operand to the members of the left operand, just like it did for the copy constructor. This is not always satisfactory, and you'll see later in this chapter how you can define your own version of the assignment operator.

Nonmember Operator Functions

In the previous section, you learned that an operator overload can be defined as a member function. Most operators can be implemented as a regular, nonmember function as well. For instance, because the volume() function is a public member of the Box class, you could easily implement operator<() as an ordinary function as well. The definition would then be as follows:

```
inline bool operator<(const Box& box1, const Box& box2)
{
  return box1.volume() < box2.volume();
}
```

The operator<() function is specified as inline because you want it to be compiled as such if possible. With the operator defined in this way, the previous example would work in the same way. Of course, you must not declare this version of the operator function as const; const only applies to functions that are members of a class. Because this is specified as inline, you would put the definition in Box.h. This ensures that it's available to any source file that uses the Box class.

Even if an operator function needs access to private members of the class, it's still possible to implement it as an ordinary function by declaring it as a friend of the class. Generally, though, if a function must access private members of a class, it is best to define it as a class member whenever possible.

■ **Tip**   Always define nonmember operators in the same namespace as the class of the objects they operate on. Because our Box class is part of the global namespace, the previous operator<() should be as well.

Implementing Full Support for an Operator

Implementing an operator such as < for a class creates expectations. You can write expressions like box1 < box2, but what about box1 < 25.0 or 10.0 < box2? The current operator<() won't handle either of these. When you implement overloaded operators for a class, you need to consider the likely range of circumstances in which the operator might be used.

▨ **Caution**   In Chapter 8 we advised you to add the keyword `explicit` to most single-parameter constructors, remember? We explained that without this keyword the compiler uses such constructors for implicit conversions, which may lead to surprising results—and thus bugs. Suppose, for instance, that you did again define a nonexplicit single-parameter constructor for Box like so:

```
Box(double side) : Box{side, side, side} {}        // Constructor for cube-shaped Boxes
```

Then expressions such as box1 < 25.0 or 10.0 < box2 would already compile because the compiler would be injecting implicit conversions from double to Box. (That is, they would compile provide you defined operator<() as a nonmember function, but we'll return to this distinction later in this chapter.) However, box1 < 25.0 would then again not be comparing the volume of box1 with 25.0, but instead with the volume of a cubic Box with dimensions 25 × 25 × 25, or 15,625. Clearly, this Box constructor really does need to be `explicit`, just like we concluded before! Since you cannot rely on implicit conversions here to facilitate comparisons between Box objects and numbers, you'll have to put in some extra work to support such expressions.

You can easily support these possibilities for comparing Box objects by adding overloads for operator<(). We'll first add a function for < where the first operand is a Box object and the second operand is of type double. We'll define it as an `inline` function with the definition outside the class in this instance, just to show how it's done. You need to add the following member specification to the public section of Box class definition:

```
bool operator<(double value) const;               // Compare Box volume < double value
```

The Box object that is the left operand will be accessed in the function via the implicit pointer `this`, and the right operand is `value`. Implementing this is as easy as the first operator function; there's just one statement in the function body:

```
// Compare the volume of a Box object with a constant
inline bool Box::operator<(double value) const
{
  return volume() < value;
}
```

This definition can follow the class definition in Box.h. An `inline` function should not be defined in a .cpp file because the definition of an `inline` function must appear in every source file that uses it. If you put the definition of an `inline` member in a separate source file, it will be in a separate translation unit, and you will get linker errors.

Dealing with an expression such as 10.0 < box2 isn't harder; it's just different. A *member* operator function always provides the this pointer as the left operand. In this case, the left operand is type double, so you can't implement the operator as a member function. That leaves you with two choices: to implement it as an ordinary operator function or to implement it as a `friend` function. Because you don't need to access private members of the class, you can implement it as an ordinary function:

```
// Function comparing a constant with volume of a Box object
inline bool operator<(double value, const Box& aBox)
{
  return value < aBox.volume();
}
```

This is an `inline` function, so you can put it in `Box.h`. You now have three overloaded versions of the `<` operator for Box objects to support all three less-than comparison possibilities. Let's see that in action. We'll assume you have modified `Box.h` as described.

Here's a program that uses the new comparison operator functions for Box objects:

```cpp
// Ex12_02.cpp
// Using the overloaded 'less-than' operators for Box objects
#include <iostream>
#include <vector>
#include "Box.h"

// Display box dimensions
void show(const Box& box)
{
  std::cout << "Box " << box.getLength()
            << 'x' << box.getWidth()
            << 'x' << box.getHeight() << std::endl;
}

int main()
{
  std::vector<Box> boxes {Box {2.0, 2.0, 3.0}, Box {1.0, 3.0, 2.0},
                          Box {1.0, 2.0, 1.0}, Box {2.0, 3.0, 3.0}};
  const double minVolume{6.0};
  std::cout << "Objects with volumes less than " << minVolume << " are:\n";
  for (const auto& box : boxes)
    if (box < minVolume) show(box);

  std::cout << "Objects with volumes greater than " << minVolume << " are:\n";
  for (const auto& box : boxes)
    if (minVolume < box) show(box);
}
```

You should get this output:

```
Objects with volumes less than 6 are:
Box 1x2x1
Objects with volumes greater than 6 are:
Box 2x2x3
Box 2x3x3
```

The `show()` function that is defined preceding `main()` outputs the details of the Box object that is passed as an argument. This is just a helper function for use in `main()`. The output shows that the overloaded operators are working. Again, if you want to see when they are called, put an output statement in each definition. Of course, you don't need separate functions to compare Box objects with integers. When this occurs, the compiler will insert an implicit cast to type `double` before calling one of the existing functions.

Implementing All Comparison Operators in a Class

We have implemented < for the Box class, but there's still ==, <=, >, >=, and != . Of course, we could plow on and define all the others in the class. There would be nothing wrong with that. But there is an alternative: we could get some help from the Standard Library. The utility header defines templates in the rel_ops namespace that define the operators <=, >, >=, and != for any type T in terms of T's less-than and equality operators (< and ==). So, all you have to do is define < and ==, and the templates from the utility header will be used by the compiler to generate the other comparison operators when required.

Suppose, for the sake of argument, that the single defining characteristic of a Box is its volume. Then defining a corresponding test for the equality of Box objects is easy enough:

```
bool operator==(const Box& aBox) const { return volume() == aBox.volume(); }
```

If you add this definition for operator==() to the Box class from Ex12_02, you can use it to try some of the templates in the rel_ops namespace with the following program:

```cpp
// Ex12_03.cpp
// Using the templates for overloaded comparison operators for Box objects
#include <iostream>
#include <string_view>
#include <vector>
#include <utility>       // For the std::rel_ops utility function templates
#include "Box.h"

using namespace std::rel_ops;

void show(const Box& box1, std::string_view relationship, const Box& box2)
{
  std::cout << "Box " << box1.getLength() << 'x' << box1.getWidth() << 'x' << box1.getHeight()
            << relationship
            << "Box " << box2.getLength() << 'x' << box2.getWidth() << 'x' << box2.getHeight()
            << std::endl;
}

int main()
{
  const std::vector<Box> boxes {Box {2.0, 2.0, 3.0}, Box {1.0, 3.0, 2.0},
                                Box {1.0, 2.0, 1.0}, Box {2.0, 3.0, 3.0}};
  const Box theBox {3.0, 1.0, 3.0};

  for (const auto& box : boxes)
    if (theBox > box) show(theBox, " is greater than ", box);

  std::cout << std::endl;

  for (const auto& box : boxes)
    if (theBox != box) show(theBox, " is not equal to ", box);

  std::cout << std::endl;
```

```
  for (size_t i {}; i < boxes.size() - 1; ++i)
    for (size_t j {i+1}; j < boxes.size(); ++j)
      if (boxes[i] <= boxes[j])
        show(boxes[i], " less than or equal to ", boxes[j]);
}
```

The output from this program is as follows:

```
Box 3x1x3 is greater than Box 1x3x2
Box 3x1x3 is greater than Box 1x2x1

Box 3x1x3 is not equal to Box 2x2x3
Box 3x1x3 is not equal to Box 1x3x2
Box 3x1x3 is not equal to Box 1x2x1
Box 3x1x3 is not equal to Box 2x3x3

Box 2x2x3 less than or equal to Box 2x3x3
Box 1x3x2 less than or equal to Box 2x3x3
Box 1x2x1 less than or equal to Box 2x3x3
```

There's a different version of the show() helper function; it now outputs a statement about two Box objects. You can see that main() makes use of the >, !=, >=, and <= operators with Box objects. All these are created from the templates that are defined in the utility header. The output shows that the three operators are working.

Notice the using statement before main(). This is necessary because the templates for comparison functions are defined in the std::rel_ops namespace, named from relational operators. Without this using statement, the compiler would not be able to match the operator function names it deduces, such as operator>(), with the names of the templates. The using statement is in effect from the point at which it appears to the end of the source file. You could also put the using statement in the body of main(), in which case its effect would be restricted to main().

As it stands, our alternative to explicitly defining all operators has one downside: it hinges on the users of the Box class knowing about the utility header, its various helper templates, and how to use them. It would be much better if after including Box.h, you could simply use the >, !=, <=, and >= operators out of the box (pun intended), without the need for additional #include and using statements. The obvious solution, of course, is to put both the #include directive for the utility header and the using statement for the std::rel_ops namespace into the Box.h header file itself.

■ **Note** Adding using statements to a header file is generally considered bad practice. The consequence of doing so is that names become available without qualification throughout every source file that includes this header file. In general, this can have undesirable effects. Remember, these names were normally put in a namespace for a good reason: to avoid name clashes with other functions. Adding a using namespace std::rel_ops statement seems like a safe enough exception to this guideline, though. This namespace only contains the templates for the four comparison operators, nothing more, and if any of these operators would already be defined specifically for some type, the compiler would always call the existing function rather than create a new instance from the std::rel_ops templates.

Operators That Can Be Overloaded

Most operators can be overloaded. Although you can't overload every single operator, the restrictions aren't particularly oppressive. Notable operators that you cannot overload include, for instance, the conditional operator (?:) and sizeof. Nearly all other operators are fair game, though, which gives you quite a bit of scope. Table 12-1 lists all operators that you can overload.

Table 12-1. *Operators That Can Be Overloaded*

Operators	Symbols	Nonmember
Binary arithmetic operators	+ - * / %	Yes
Unary arithmetic operators	+ -	Yes
Bitwise operators	~ & | ^ << >>	Yes
Logical operators	! && ||	Yes
Assignment operator	=	No
Compound assignment operators	+= -= *= /= %= &= |= ^= <<= >>=	Yes
Increment/decrement operators	++ --	Yes
Comparison operators	== != < > <= >=	Yes
Array subscript operator	[ ]	No
Function call operator	( )	No
Conversion-to-type-T operator	T	No
Address-of and dereferencing operators	& * -> ->*	Yes
Comma operator	,	Yes
Allocation and deallocation operators	new new[] delete delete[]	Only
User-defined literal operator	"" _	Only

Most operators can be overloaded either as a class member function or as a nonmember function outside of a class. These operators are marked with Yes in the third column of Table 12-1. Some can be implemented only as a member function, though (marked with No), whereas others can be implemented only as nonmember functions (marked with Only).

In this chapter, you will learn when and how to overload nearly all of these operators, all except the bottom four categories in the table. The address-of and dereferencing operators are mostly used to implement pointer-like types such as the std::unique_ptr<> and std::shared_ptr<> smart pointer templates you encountered earlier. In part because the Standard Library already offers excellent support for such types, you will not often have to overload these operators yourself. The other three categories of operators that we won't be discussing are overloaded even less frequently.

Restrictions and Key Guideline

While operator overloading is flexible and can be powerful, there are some restrictions. In a way, the name of the language feature already gives it away: operator *overloading*. That is, you can only *overload existing* operators. This implies the following:

- You *cannot invent new* operators such as ?, ===, or <>.

- You *cannot change* the number of operands, associativity, or precedence of the existing operators, nor can you alter the order in which the operands to an operator are evaluated.[1]

- As a rule, you *cannot override* built-in operators, and the signature of an overloaded operator will involve at least one class type. We will discuss the term *overriding* in more detail in the next chapter, but in this case it means you cannot modify the way existing operators operate on fundamental types or array types. In other words, you cannot, for instance, make integer addition perform multiplication. While it would be great fun to see what would happen, we're sure you'll agree that this is a fair restriction.

These restrictions notwithstanding, you have quite some freedom when it comes to operator overloading. But it's not because you *can* overload an operator that it necessarily follows that you *should*. When in doubt, always remember the following key guideline:

▓ **Tip**   The main purpose of operator overloading is to increase both the ease of writing and the readability of code that uses your class and to decrease the likelihood of defects. The fact that overloaded operators make for more compact code should always come second. Compact yet incomprehensible or even misleading code is no good to anyone. Making sure your code is both easy to write and easy to understand is what matters. One consequence is that you should, at all costs, avoid overloaded operators that do not behave as expected from their built-in counterparts.

Obviously, it's a good idea to make your version of a standard operator reasonably consistent with its normal usage, or at least intuitive in its meaning and operation. It wouldn't be sensible to produce an overloaded + operator for a class that performed the equivalent of a multiplication. But it can be more subtle than that. Reconsider, if you will, the equality operator we defined earlier for Box objects:

```
bool Box::operator==(const Box& aBox) const { return volume() == aBox.volume(); }
```

While this might have seemed sensible at the time, this unconventional definition could easily lead to confusion. Suppose, for example, that we create these two Box objects:

```
Box oneBox { 1, 2, 3 };
Box otherBox { 1, 1, 6 };
```

---

[1]The latter is new in C++17. Prior to C++17, compilers were free to choose in which order to evaluate the operands of overloaded operator functions. As of C++17, however, they have to follow the same rules as their built-in counterparts.

Would you then consider these two boxes "equal"? Most likely the answer is that you don't. After all, they have significantly different dimensions. If you order a box with dimensions 1 × 2 × 3, you would not be pleased if you receive one with dimensions 1 × 1 × 6. Nevertheless, with our definition of operator==(), the expression oneBox == otherBox would evaluate to true. This could easily lead to misunderstandings and therefore bugs.

The way most programmers would expect an equality operator for Box to be defined is like this:

```
bool Box::operator==(const Box& aBox) const
{
  return width == aBox.width
      && length == aBox.length
      && height == aBox.height;
}
```

This new definition of equality has one slight disadvantage. You then can no longer use the std::rel_ops operator templates for <= and >=, as it would be more natural if these operators still compare volumes. You'll have to define these operator functions explicitly yourself. Of course, which definition you use will depend on your application and how you expect Boxes to be used. But in this case, we believe it is best to stick with our second, more intuitive definition of operator==(). The reason is that it probably leads to the least number of surprises. When programmers see ==, they think "is equal to," not "has same volume as." If need be, you can always introduce a member function hasSameVolumeAs() to check for equal volumes. Yes, hasSameVolumeAs() involves more typing than ==, but it does ensure your code remains readable and predictable—and that is far more important! A modified version of Ex12_03 based on these ideas is available as Ex12_03A.

Most of the remainder of this chapter is about teaching you similar conventions regarding operator overloading. Deviating from these conventions should be done only if you have a good reason.

■ **Caution** One concrete consequence of our key guideline for operators is that you should never overload the logical operators && or | |. If you want logical operators for objects of your class, overloading & and | instead is generally preferable.

The reason is that overloaded && and | | will never behave quite like their built-in counterparts. Recall from Chapter 4 that if the left operand of the built-in && operator evaluates to false, its right operand does not get evaluated. Similarly, for the built-in | | operator, the right-side operand is never evaluated if the left-side operand evaluates to true. You can never obtain this so-called *short-circuit evaluation* with overloaded operators.[2] As we will see shortly, an overloaded operator is essentially equivalent to a regular function. This implies that all operands to an overloaded operator are always evaluated concretely. Like with any other function, all arguments are always evaluated before entering the function's body. For overloaded && and | | operators, this means that both the left and right operands will always be evaluated. Because users of any && and | | operator will always expect the familiar short-circuit evaluation, overloading them would thus easily lead to some subtle bugs. When overloading & and | instead, you make it clear not to expect short-circuit evaluation.

---

[2]Prior to C++17, it was not even guaranteed that the left operand of an overloaded && or | | operator would be evaluated before the right operand like it is for the built-in operators. That is, the compiler was allowed to evaluate the right operand before it even started evaluating the left operand. This would have made for another potential source of subtle bugs. This was also the reason that prior to C++17 overloading the comma operator (,) was generally discouraged.

Operator Function Idioms

The remainder of this chapter is all about introducing commonly accepted patterns and best practices regarding the when and how of operator overloading. There are only a few real restrictions for operator functions. But with great flexibility comes great responsibility. We will teach you when and how to overload various operators and the various conventions C++ programmers typically follow in this context. If you adhere to these conventions, your classes and their operators will behave predictably, which will make them easy to use and thus reduce the risk of bugs.

All the binary operators that can be overloaded always have operator functions of the form that you've seen in the previous section. When an operator, Op, is overloaded and the left operand is an object of the class for which Op is being overloaded, the member function defining the overload is of the following form:

```
Return_Type operator Op(Type right_operand);
```

In principle, you are entirely free to choose Return_Type or to create overloads for any number of parameter Types. It is also entirely up to you to choose whether you declare the member function as const. Other than the number of parameters, the language imposes nearly no constraints on the signature or return types of operator functions. For most operators, though, there are certain accepted conventions, which you should as much as possible try to respect. These conventions are nearly always motivated by the way the default built-in operators behave. For comparison operators such as <, >=, and !=, for instance, ReturnType is typically bool (although you could use int). And because these operators normally do not modify their operands, they usually are defined as const members that accept their argument either by value or by const reference—but never by non-const reference. Besides convention and common sense, however, there is nothing stopping you from returning a string from operator<() or from creating a != operator that doubles a Box's volume when used, or even one that causes a typhoon halfway around the world. You'll learn more about the various conventions throughout the remainder of this chapter.

You can implement most binary operators as nonmember functions as well, using this form:

```
Return_Type operator Op(Class_Type left_operand, Type right_operand);
```

Class_Type is the class for which you are overloading the operator. Type can be any type, including Class_Type. As can be read from Table 12-1, the only binary operator for which this is not allowed is the assignment operator, operator=().

If the left operand for a binary operator is of class Type, and Type is not the class for which the operator function is being defined, then the function must be implemented as a global operator function of this form:

```
Return_Type operator Op(Type left_operand, Class_Type right_operand);
```

We'll give you some further guidelines for choosing between the member and nonmember forms of operator functions later in this chapter.

You have no flexibility in the number of parameters for operator functions—either as class members or as global functions. You *must* use the number of parameters specified for the particular operator. Unary operators defined as member functions don't usually require a parameter. The post-increment and post-decrement operators are exceptions, as you'll see. The general form of a unary operator function for the operation Op as a member of the Class_Type class is as follows:

```
Class_Type& operator Op();
```

Naturally, unary operators defined as global functions have a single parameter that is the operand. The prototype for a global operator function for a unary operator Op is as follows:

```
Class_Type& operator Op(Class_Type& obj);
```

We won't go through examples of overloading every operator, as most of them are similar to the ones you've seen. However, we will explain the details of operators that have particular idiosyncrasies when you overload them. We'll start with by far the most common family of overloads for the << operator, because it will quickly prove useful in later examples.

Overloading the << Operator for Output Streams

Up until now we have been defining specific functions to output Boxes to std::cout. In this chapter, for instance, we have defined several functions called show(), which were then used in statements such as this:

```
show(box);
```

or this:

```
show(theBox, " is greater than ", box);
```

Now we know how to overload operators; however, we could make the output statements for Box objects feel more natural by overloading the << operator for output streams. This would then allow us to simply write this:

```
std::cout << box;
```

and this:

```
std::cout << theBox << " is greater than " << box;
```

But, how to overload this << operator? Before we go there, let's first revise exactly how the second statement works. As a first step, let's add parentheses to clarify the associativity of the << operator:

```
((std::cout << theBox) << " is greater than ") << box;
```

The innermost << expression will be evaluated first. So, the following is equivalent:

```
auto& something = (std::cout << theBox);
(something << " is greater than ") << box;
```

Naturally, the only way this could ever work is if something, the result of the innermost expression, is again a reference to a stream. To clarify things further, we can also use function-call notation for operator<<() as follows:

```
auto& stream1 = operator<<(std::cout, theBox);
(stream1 << " is greater than ") << box;
```

Using a few more similar rewrite steps, we can easily spell out every step the compiler takes to evaluate the entire statement:

```
auto& stream0 = std::cout;
auto& stream1 = operator<<(stream0, theBox);
auto& stream2 = operator<<(stream1, " is greater than ");
auto& stream3 = operator<<(stream2, box);
```

While this is quite verbose, it makes clear the point we wanted to make. This particular overload of operator<<() takes two arguments: a reference to a stream object (left operand) and the actual value to output (right operand). It then returns a fresh reference to a stream that can be passed along to the next call of operator<<() in the chain. This is an example of what we called *method chaining* in Chapter 11.

Once you understand this, deciphering the function definition that overloads this operator for Box objects should be straightforward:

```
std::ostream& operator<<(std::ostream& stream, const Box& box)
{
  stream << "Box(" << std::setw(2) << box.getLength() << ','
    << std::setw(2) << box.getWidth() << ','
    << std::setw(2) << box.getHeight() << ')';

  return stream;
}
```

The first parameter identifies the left operand as an ostream object, and the second specifies the right operand as a Box object. The standard output stream, cout, is of type std::ostream, as are other output streams that you'll meet later in the book. We can, of course, not add the operator function to the definition of std::ostream, so we have to define it as an ordinary function. Because the dimensions of a Box object are publically available, we do not have to use a friend declaration. The value that is returned is, and always should be, a reference to the same stream object as referred to by the operator's left operand.

To test this operator, you can add its definition to the Box.h header of Ex12_03A. In the main() function of Ex12_03A then, you can replace expressions such as show(theBox, " is greater than ", box) with equivalent expressions that use the << operator:

```
std::cout << theBox << " is greater than " << box << std::endl;
```

You'll find the resulting program in Ex12_04.

■ **Note** The << and >> operators of the stream classes of the Standard Library are prime examples of the fact that overloaded operators do not always have to be equivalent to their built-in counterparts—recall that the built-in << and >> operators perform bitwise shifts of integers! Another nice example is the convention to use the + and += operators to concatenate strings, something you have already used repeatedly with std::string objects. The fact that until now you may not have given it much thought yet on how and why such expressions work just proves that, if used judiciously, overloaded operators can lead to very natural coding.

Overloading the Arithmetic Operators

We'll explain how you overload the arithmetic operators by looking at how you might overload the addition operator for the Box class. This is an interesting example because addition is a binary operation that involves creating and returning a new object. The new object will be the sum (whatever you define that to mean) of the two Box objects that are its operands.

What might the sum of two Box objects mean? There are several possibilities we could consider, but because the primary purpose of a box is to hold something, its volumetric capacity is of primary interest, so we might reasonably presume that the sum of two boxes was a new box that could hold both. Using this assumption, we'll define the sum of two Box objects to be a Box object that's large enough to contain the two original boxes stacked on top of each other. This is consistent with the notion that the class might be used for packaging because adding several Box objects together results in a Box object that can contain all of them.

You can implement the addition operator in a simple way, as follows. The length member of the new object will be the larger of the length members of the objects being summed, and a width member will be determined in a similar way. If the height member is the sum of the height members of the operands, the resultant Box object can contain the two Box objects. By modifying the constructor, we'll arrange that the length member of an object is always greater than or equal to the width member.

Figure 12-2 illustrates the Box object that will be produced by adding two Box objects. Because the result of this addition is a new Box object, the function implementing addition must return a Box object. If the function that overloads the + operator is to be a member function, then the declaration of the function in the Box class definition can be as follows:

```
Box operator+(const Box& aBox) const;        // Adding two Box objects
```

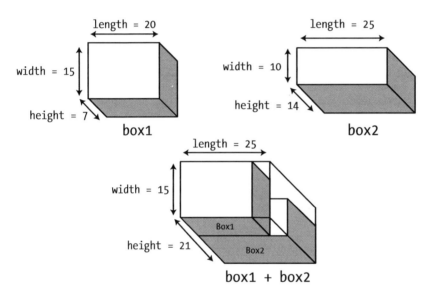

Figure 12-2. *The object that results from adding two Box objects*

The aBox parameter is const because the function won't modify the argument, which is the right operand. It's a const reference to avoid unnecessary copying of the right operand. The function itself is specified as const because it doesn't alter the left operand. The definition of the member function in Box.h will be as follows:

```
// Operator function to add two Box objects
inline Box Box::operator+(const Box& aBox) const
{
  // New object has larger length and width, and sum of heights
  return Box{ std::max(length, aBox.length),
            std::max(width, aBox.width),
            height + aBox.height };
}
```

As is conventional for an arithmetic operator, a local Box object is created, and a *copy* of it is returned to the calling program. Of course, as this is a new object, returning it by reference must never be done. The box's dimensions are computed using std::max(), which simply returns the maximum of two given arguments. It is instantiated from a function template in the algorithm header. This template works for any argument type that supports operator<(). Of course, an analogous std::min() function template to compute the minimum of two expressions exists as well.

We can see how the addition operator works in an example. For brevity, we'll start from the Box class from Ex12_03 again:

```
// Box.h
#ifndef BOX_H
#define BOX_H
#include <iostream>
#include <iomanip>
#include <algorithm>                 // For the min() and max() function templates

class Box
{
private:
  double length {1.0};
  double width {1.0};
  double height {1.0};

public:
  // Constructors
  Box(double lv, double wv, double hv)
            : length {std::max(lv,wv)}, width {std::min(lv,wv)}, height {hv} {}

  Box() = default;                            // No-arg constructor

  double volume() const                       // Function to calculate the volume
  {
    return length*width*height;
  }

  // Accessors
  double getLength() const { return length; }
  double getWidth() const  { return width; }
  double getHeight() const { return height; }

  bool operator<(const Box& aBox) const;      // Less-than operator
  bool operator<(double value) const;         // Compare Box volume < double value

  Box operator+(const Box& aBox) const;       // Function to add two Box objects
};

// Definitions of all operators (member and non-member functions) like before.
// Also include the << operator from Ex12_04,
// and of course the definition of the new operator+() member function...
```

The first important difference is the first constructor, which uses std::min() and max() to ensure a Box's length is always larger than its width. The second is the addition of the declaration of operator+(). The inline definition of this member function shown earlier in this section goes in Box.h as well, immediately following the declaration of the Box class.

Here's the code to try it:

```cpp
// Ex12_05.cpp
// Using the addition operator for Box objects
#include <iostream>
#include <vector>
#include <cstdlib>        // For basic random number generation
#include <ctime>          // For time function
#include "Box.h"

// Function to generate integral random box dimensions from 1 to max_size
inline double random(double max_size)
{
  return 1 + static_cast<int>(std::rand() / (RAND_MAX / max_size + 1));
}

int main()
{
  const double limit {99.0};       // Upper limit on Box dimensions
  // Initialize the random number generator
  std::srand(static_cast<unsigned>(std::time(nullptr)));

  const size_t boxCount {20};      // Number of Box object to be created
  std::vector<Box> boxes;          // Vector of Box objects

  // Create 20 Box objects
  for (size_t i {}; i < boxCount; ++i)
    boxes.push_back(Box {random(dimLimit), random(dimLimit), random(dimLimit)});

  size_t first {};                          // Index of first Box object of pair
  size_t second {1};                        // Index of second Box object of pair
  double minVolume {(boxes[first] + boxes[second]).volume()};

  for (size_t i {}; i < boxCount - 1; ++i)
  {
    for (size_t j {i + 1}; j < boxCount; j++)
    {
      if (boxes[i] + boxes[j] < minVolume)
      {
        first = i;
        second = j;
        minVolume = (boxes[i] + boxes[j]).volume();
      }
    }
  }
}
```

```
    std::cout << "The two boxes that sum to the smallest volume are: "
              << boxes[first] << " and " << boxes[second];
    std::cout << "\nThe volume of the first box is " << boxes[first].volume();
    std::cout << "\nThe volume of the second box is " << boxes[second].volume();
    std::cout << "\nThe sum of these boxes is " << (boxes[first] + boxes[second]);
    std::cout << "\nThe volume of the sum is " << minVolume << std::endl;
}
```

We got the following output:

```
The two boxes that sum to the smallest volume are: Box(17,14,11) and Box(63,15,13)
The volume of the first box is 2618
The volume of the second box is 12285
The sum of these boxes is Box(63,15,24)
The volume of the sum is 22680
```

You should get a different result each time you run the program. Just to emphasize what we have said previously, the rand() function is OK when you don't care about the quality of the random number sequence, but when you need something better, use the pseudorandom number generation facilities provided by the random Standard Library header.

The main() function generates a vector of 20 Box objects that have arbitrary dimensions from 1.0 to 99.0. The nested for loops then test all possible pairs of Box objects to find the pair that combines to the minimum volume. The if statement in the inner loop uses the operator+() member to produce a Box object that is the sum of the current pair of objects. The operator<() member is then used to compare this resultant Box object with the value of minVolume. The output shows that everything works at it should. We suggest you instrument the operator functions and the Box constructors just to see when and how often they are called.

Of course, you can use the overloaded addition operator in more complex expressions to sum Box objects. For example, you could write this:

```
Box box4 {box1 + box2 + box3};
```

This calls the operator+() member twice to create a Box object that is the sum of the three, and this is passed to the copy constructor for the Box class to create box4. The result is a Box object box4 that can contain the other three Box objects stacked on top of each other.

Implementing One Operator in Terms of Another

One thing always leads to another. If you implement the addition operator for a class, you inevitably create the expectation that the += operator will work too. If you are going to implement both, it's worth noting that you can implement + in terms of += very economically.

First, we'll define += for the Box class. Because assignment is involved, convention dictates that the operator function returns a reference:

```
// Overloaded += operator
inline Box& Box::operator+=(const Box& aBox)
{
  // New object has larger length and width, and sum of heights
  length = std::max(length, aBox.length);
```

```
  width  = std::max(width, aBox.width);
  height += aBox.height;
  return *this;
}
```

This is straightforward. You simply modify the left operand, which is *this, by adding the right operand according to the definition of addition for Box objects. You can now implement operator+() using operator+=(), so the definition of operator+() simplifies to the following:

```
// Function to add two Box objects
inline Box Box::operator+(const Box& aBox) const
{
  Box copy{*this};
  copy += aBox;
  return copy;
}
```

The first line of the function body calls the copy constructor to create a copy of the left operand to use in the addition. The operator+=() function is then called to add the right operand object, aBox, to the new Box object. This object is then returned.

If you feel comfortable doing so, you could also compress this function body into a one-liner:

```
return Box{*this} += aBox;
```

The convention to return a reference-to-this from compound assignment operators is motivated by the fact that it enables statements such as this, that is, statements that use the result of an assignment expression in a bigger expression. To facilitate this, most operators that modify their left operand by convention return either a reference-to-this or, if implemented as a nonmember function, a reference to the first argument. You already saw this in action for the << stream operator, and you will encounter it again when we discuss the overloading of increment and decrement operators.

Ex12_06 contains a Box.h header that started from that of Ex12_05, but with the addition operators implemented as described in this section. With this new definition of Box, you can easily modify the main() function of Ex12_05 as well to try the new += operator. In Ex12_06.cpp, for instance, we did this as follows:

```
int main()
{
  // Generate boxCount random Box objects as before in Ex12_05...

  Box sum{0, 0, 0};                 // Start from an empty Box
  for (const auto& box : boxes)     // And then add all randomly generated Box objects
    sum += box;

  std::cout << "The sum of " << boxCount << " random Boxes is " << sum << std::endl;
}
```

▓ **Tip**   Always implement the *op*() operator in terms of *op=*(), not the other way around. In principle, it would be equally easy to implement operator+=() in terms of operator+() as follows:

```
inline Box& Box::operator+=(const Box& aBox)
{
  *this = *this + aBox;        // Creates a temporary Box object
  return *this;
}
```

We'll explain later this chapter why the assignment in this function's body works. For now, just notice that if you are implementing operator+=() this way, a new temporary object is created on the right side of the assignment. That is, the assignment statement is essentially equivalent to this:

```
  Box newBox = *this + aBox;
  *this = newBox;
```

This may not give optimal performance. An operator+=() should simply modify the left operand (this), without first creating a new object. If you are lucky, especially in this simple case, the compiler will optimize this temporary object away after inlining. But why take the risk?

Member vs. Nonmember Functions

Both Ex12_05 and Ex12_06 define operator+() as a member function of the Box class. You can, however, just as easily implement this addition operation as a nonmember function. Here's the prototype of such a function:

```
Box operator+(const Box& aBox, const Box& bBox);
```

Because the dimensions of a Box object are accessible through public member functions, no friend declarations are required. But even if the values of the member variables were inaccessible, you could still just define the operator as a friend function, and that begs the question, which of these options is best? A member function? A nonmember function? Or a friend function?

Of all your options, a friend function is generally seen as the least desirable. While there is not always a viable alternative, friend declarations undermine data hiding and should therefore be avoided when possible.

The choice between a member function and a nonfriend nonmember function, however, is not always as clear-cut. Operator functions are fundamental to class capability, so we mostly prefer to implement them as class members. This makes the operations integral to the type, which puts this right at the core of encapsulation. Your default option therefore should probably be to define operator overloads as member functions. But there are at least two cases where you should implement them as nonmember functions instead.

First, there are circumstances where you have no choice but to implement them as nonmember functions, even if this means you have to resort to friend functions. These include overloads of binary operators for which the first argument is either a fundamental type or a type different from the class you are currently writing. We have already seen examples of both categories:

```
bool operator<(double value, const Box& box);        // double cannot have member functions
ostream& operator<<(ostream& stream, const Box& box);  // you cannot add ostream members
```

> ■ **Note** Once one of the overloads of an operator needs to be a nonmember function, you might decide to turn all other overloads of that same operator into nonmember functions as well for consistency. You might consider this, for instance, for the operator<() of the Box class. Even though only the first overload of the following list really needs to be nonmember, turning one or both of the other operator overloads into nonmember functions as well allows you to nicely group these declarations together in the header file:
>
> ```
> bool operator<(double, const Box&);       // Must be non-member function
> bool operator<(const Box&, double);       // Symmetrical case often done for consistency
> bool operator<(const Box&, const Box&); // Box-Box case sometimes as well for consistency
> ```

A second reason you might sometimes prefer nonmember functions over member functions is when implicit conversions are desired for a binary operator's left operand. We'll discuss this case in its own little subsection next.

Operator Functions and Implicit Conversions

As noted earlier in this and previous chapters, allowing implicit conversions from double to Box is not a good idea. Because such conversions would lead to unpleasant results, the corresponding single-argument constructor for Box should really be explicit. But this is not the case for all single-argument constructors. The Integer class you worked on earlier during the exercises of Chapter 11, for instance, provides a good example. At its essence, this class looked like this:

```
class Integer
{
private:
  int n;
public:
  Integer(int m = 0) : n{m} {}
  int getValue() const { return n; }
  void setValue(int m) { n = m; }
};
```

For this class, there is no harm in allowing implicit conversions. The main reason is that Integer objects are much closer to ints than Boxes are to doubles. Other examples of harmless (and convenient!) implicit conversions you already know about are those from string literals to std::string objects or T values to std::optional<T> objects.

For classes that allow implicit conversions, the general guideline for overloading operators as member functions typically changes. Consider the Integer class. Naturally, you'd like binary arithmetic operators such as operator+() for Integer objects. And, of course, you'd like them to work also for additions of the form Integer + int and int + Integer. Obviously, you could still define three operator functions like we did for the + operator of Box—two member functions and one nonmember one. But there is an easier option. All you need to do is define one single nonmember operator function as follows:

```
Integer operator+(const Integer& one, const Integer& other)
{
  return one.getValue() + other.getValue();
}
```

Put this function together with our simple class definition of Integer in a file Integer.h. Add similar functions for -, *, /, and %. Because int values implicitly convert to Integer objects, these five operator functions then suffice to make the following test program work. Without relying on implicit conversions, you would've needed no less than 15 function definitions to cover all possibilities!

```
// Ex12_07.cpp
// Implicit conversions reduce the number of operator functions
#include <iostream>
#include "Integer.h"

int main()
{
  const Integer i{1};
  const Integer j{2};
  const auto result = (i * 2 + 4 / j - 1) % j;
  std::cout << result.getValue() << std::endl;
}
```

The reason you need to use nonmember functions to allow implicit conversions for either operand is that the compiler never performs conversions for the left operand of member functions. That is, if you'd define operator/() as a member function, an expression such as 4 / j would no longer compile.

■ **Tip**   Operator overloads mostly should be implemented as member functions. Only use nonmember functions if a member function cannot be used or if implicit conversions are desired for the first operand.

■ **Caution**   The operator templates from the std::rel_ops namespace do not allow for implicit conversions. This means you always have to define all six comparison operators yourself if you want comparisons between operands of different types. With some careful copying and pasting, this shouldn't be all that much work, though.

Overloading Unary Operators

So far, we have only seen examples of overloading binary operators. There are quite some unary operators as well. For the sake of illustration, assume a common operation with boxes is to "rotate" them in the sense that their width and length are swapped. If this operation is indeed frequently used, you could be tempted to introduce an operator for it. Because rotation involves only a single Box—no additional operand is required—you'd have to pick one of the available unary operators. Viable candidates are +, -, ~, !, &, and *. From these, operator~() seems like a good pick. Just like binary operators, unary operators can be defined either as a member function or as a regular function. Starting again from the Box class from Ex12_04, the former possibility would look like this:

```
class Box
{
private:
  double length {1.0};
  double width {1.0};
  double height {1.0};
```

```
public:
  // Constructors
  Box(double lv, double wv, double hv) : length{lv}, width{wv}, height{hv} {}

  // Remainder of the Box class as before...

  Box operator~() const
  {
    return Box{width, length, height};        // width and length are swapped
  }
};
#endif
```

As convention dictates, operator~() returns a new object, just like we saw for the binary arithmetic operators that do not modify their left operand. Defining the Box "rotation" operator as a nonmember function should come easy by now as well:

```
Box operator~(const Box& box)
{
  return Box{ box.getWidth(), box.getLength(), box.getHeight() };
}
```

With either of these operator overloads in place, you could write code like the following:

```
Box someBox{ 1, 2, 3 };
std::cout << ~someBox << std::endl;
```

You can find this example in Ex12_08. If you run that program, you'll get this result:

```
Box( 2, 1, 3)
```

> ■ **Note** Arguably, this operator overload violates our key guideline from earlier in this chapter. While it clearly leads to very compact code, it does *not* necessarily make for natural, readable code. Without looking at the class definition it is doubtful that any of your fellow programmers would ever guess what the expression ~someBox is doing. So, unless the notation ~someBox is commonplace in the world of packaging and boxes, you may be better off defining a regular function here instead, such as rotate() or GetRotatedBox().

Overloading the Increment and Decrement Operators

The ++ and -- operators present a new problem for the functions that implement them for a class because they behave differently depending on whether they prefix the operand. You need two functions for each operator: one to be called in the prefix case and the other for the postfix case. The postfix form of the operator function for either operator is distinguished from the prefix form by the presence of a dummy parameter of type int. This parameter only serves to distinguish the two cases and is not otherwise used. The declarations for the functions to overload ++ for an arbitrary class, MyClass, will be as follows:

```
class MyClass
{
public:
  MyClass& operator++();                  // Overloaded prefix increment operator

  const MyClass operator++(int);          // Overloaded postfix increment operator

// Rest of MyClass class definition...
};
```

The return type for the prefix form normally needs to be a reference to the current object, *this, after the increment operation has been applied to it. Here's how an implementation of the prefix form for the Box class might look:

```
inline Box& Box::operator++()
{
  ++length;
  ++width;
  ++height;
  return *this;
}
```

This just increments each of the dimensions by 1 and then returns the current object.

For the postfix form of the operator, you should create a copy of the original object *before* you modify it; then return the *copy* of the original after the increment operation has been performed on the object. Here's how that might be implemented for the Box class:

```
inline const Box Box::operator++(int)
{
  auto copy{*this};   // Create a copy of the current object
  ++(*this);          // Increment the current object using the prefix operator...
  return copy;        // Return the unincremented copy
}
```

In fact, the previous body could be used to implement any postfix increment operator in terms of its prefix counterpart. While optional, the return value for the postfix operator is sometimes declared const to prevent expressions such as theObject++++ from compiling. Such expressions are inelegant, confusing, and inconsistent with the normal behavior of the operator. If you don't declare the return type as const, such usage is possible.

The Ex12_09 example, part of the online download, contains a small test program that adds the prefix and postfix increment and decrement operators to the Box class of Ex12_04 and then takes them for a little test-drive in the following main() function:

```
int main()
{
  Box theBox {3.0, 1.0, 3.0};

  std::cout << "Our test Box is " << theBox << std::endl;

  std::cout << "Postfix increment evaluates to the original object: "
            << theBox++ << std::endl;
  std::cout << "After postfix increment: " << theBox << std::endl;

  std::cout << "Prefix decrement evaluates to the decremented object: "
            << --theBox << std::endl;
  std::cout << "After prefix decrement: " << theBox << std::endl;
}
```

The output of this test program is as follows:

```
Our test Box is Box( 3, 1, 3)
Postfix increment evaluates to the original object: Box( 3, 1, 3)
After postfix increment: Box( 4, 2, 4)
Prefix decrement evaluates to the decremented object: Box( 3, 1, 3)
After prefix decrement: Box( 3, 1, 3)
```

▥ **Note**   The value returned by the postfix form of an increment or decrement operator should always be a copy of the original object, before it was incremented or decremented; the value returned by the prefix form should always be a reference to the current (and thus incremented or decremented) object. The reason is that this is precisely how the corresponding built-in operators behave with fundamental types.

Overloading the Subscript Operator

The subscript operator, [ ], provides very interesting possibilities for certain kinds of classes. Clearly, this operator is aimed primarily at selecting one of a number of objects that you can interpret as an array, but where the objects could be contained in any one of a number of different containers. You can overload the subscript operator to access the elements of a sparse array (where many of the elements are empty), an associative array, or even a linked list. The data might even be stored in a file, and you could use the subscript operator to hide the complications of file input and output operations.

The Truckload class from Ex11_15 in Chapter 11 is an example of a class that could support the subscript operator. A Truckload object contains an ordered set of objects, so the subscript operator could provide a means of accessing these objects through an index value. An index of 0 would return the first object in the list, an index of 1 would return the second, and so on. The inner workings of the subscript operator would take care of iterating through the list to find the object required.

The operator[]() function for the Truckload class needs to accept an index value as an argument that is a position in the list and to return the pointer to the Box object at that position. The declaration for the member function in the TruckLoad class is as follows:

```
class Truckload
{
private:
  // Members as before...

public:
  SharedBox operator[](size_t index) const;          // Overloaded subscript operator
// Rest of the class as before...
};
```

You could implement the function like this:

```
SharedBox Truckload::operator[](size_t index) const
{
  size_t count {};                                // Package count
  for (Package* package{pHead}; package; package = package->pNext)
  {
    if (index == count++)                         // Up to index yet?
      return package->pBox;                       // If so return the pointer to Box
  }
  return nullptr;
}
```

The for loop traverses the list, incrementing the count on each iteration. When the value of count is the same as index, the loop has reached the Package object at position index, so the smart pointer to the Box object in that Package object is returned. If the entire list is traversed without count reaching the value of index, then index must be out of range, so nullptr is returned. Let's see how this pans out in practice by trying another example.

This example will use any Box class that includes the operator<<(), which makes outputting Boxes to std::cout easier. We can remove the listBoxes() member of Truckload as well and add an overload for the << operator for outputting Truckload objects to a stream, analogous to that of the Box class. If you use the Truckload class you created for Exercise 11-6, which contains the nested Iterator class, you can implement this operator function without the need for a friend declaration. The definition for it is as follows:

```
std::ostream& operator<<(std::ostream& stream, const Truckload& load)
{
  size_t count {};
  auto iterator = load.getIterator();
  for (auto box = iterator.getFirstBox(); box; box = iterator.getNextBox())
  {
    std::cout << *box;
    if (!(++count % 5)) std::cout << std::endl;
  }
  if (count % 5) std::cout << std::endl;
  return stream;
}
```

You can use this to replace the listBoxes() member function of the old Truckload class. The code is similar to that for listBoxes() except that now only public functions are used instead of directly working with the Packages in the list. The function makes use of the operator<<() function of the Box class. Outputting a Truckload object will now be very simple—you just use << to write it to cout.

If you add both the array subscript operator and the stream output operators to the Truckload class, you can use the following program to exercise these new operators:

```cpp
// Ex12_10.cpp
// Using the subscript operator
#include <iostream>
#include <memory>
#include <cstdlib>                          // For random number generator
#include <ctime>                            // For time function
#include "Truckload.h"

// Function to generate integral random box dimensions from 1 to max_size
inline double random(double max_size)
{
  return 1 + static_cast<int>(std::rand() / (RAND_MAX / max_size + 1));
}

int main()
{
  const double dimLimit {99.0};             // Upper limit on Box dimensions
  // Initialize the random number generator
  std::srand(static_cast<unsigned>(std::time(nullptr)));
  Truckload load;
  const size_t boxCount {20};               // Number of Box object to be created

  // Create boxCount Box objects
  for (size_t i {}; i < boxCount; ++i)
    load.addBox(std::make_shared<Box>(random(limit), random(limit), random(limit)));

  std::cout << "The boxes in the Truckload are:\n";
  std::cout << load;

  // Find the largest Box in the Truckload
  double maxVolume {};
  size_t maxIndex {};
  size_t i {};
  while (load[i])
  {
    if (load[i]->volume() > maxVolume)
    {
      maxIndex = i;
      maxVolume = load[i]->volume();
    }
    ++i;
  }
```

```
  std::cout << "\nThe largest box is: ";
  std::cout << *load[maxIndex] << std::endl;

  load.removeBox(load[maxIndex]);
  std::cout << "\nAfter deleting the largest box, the Truckload contains:\n";
  std::cout << load;
}
```

When we ran this example, it produced the following output:

```
The boxes in the Truckload are:
 Box(26,68,23) Box(89,60,94) Box(46,82,27) Box(22, 2,29) Box(98,23,90)
 Box(25,81,55) Box(52,64,28) Box(98,33,40) Box(83,14,80) Box(91,78,94)
 Box(28,54,50) Box(57,79,18) Box(91,89,99) Box(26,39,57) Box(26,42,35)
 Box(15,29,74) Box(10,17,21) Box(91,86,68) Box(94, 5,30) Box(87,10,94)

The largest box is:  Box(91,89,99)

After deleting the largest box, the Truckload contains:
 Box(26,68,23) Box(89,60,94) Box(46,82,27) Box(22, 2,29) Box(98,23,90)
 Box(25,81,55) Box(52,64,28) Box(98,33,40) Box(83,14,80) Box(91,78,94)
 Box(28,54,50) Box(57,79,18) Box(26,39,57) Box(26,42,35) Box(15,29,74)
 Box(10,17,21) Box(91,86,68) Box(94, 5,30) Box(87,10,94)
```

The main() function now uses the subscript operator to access pointers to Box objects from the Truckload object. You can see from the output that the subscript operator works, and the result of finding and deleting the largest Box object is correct. Output of Truckload and Box objects to the standard output stream now works the same as for fundamental types.

▓ **Caution**   In the case of Truckload objects, the subscript operator masks a particularly inefficient process. Because it's easy to forget that each use of the subscript operator involves traversing at least part of the list from the beginning, you should think twice before adding this operator in production code. Especially if the Truckload object contains a large number of pointers to Box objects, using this operator too often could be catastrophic for performance. It is because of this that the authors of the Standard Library decided not to give their linked-list class templates, std::list<> and std::forward_list<>, any subscript operators either. Overloading the subscript operator is best reserved for those cases where it can be backed by an efficient element retrieval mechanism.

To solve this performance problem of the Truckload array subscript operator, you should either omit it or replace the linked list of Truckload::Packages with a std::vector<SharedBox>. The only reason we used a linked list in the first place was for educational purposes. In real life, you should probably never use linked lists. A std::vector<> is almost always the better choice. We'll postpone implementing this version of Truckload until the exercises of Chapter 19 because you haven't actually seen yet how to remove elements from a vector.

Modifying the Result of an Overloaded Subscript Operator

You'll encounter circumstances in which you might want to overload the subscript operator and use the object it returns, for instance, on the left of an assignment or call a function on it. With your present implementation of operator[]() in the Truckload class, a program compiles but won't work correctly if you write either of these statements:

```
load[0] = load[1];
load[2].reset();
```

This will compile and execute, but it won't affect the items in the list. What you want is that the first pointer in the list is replaced by the second and that the third is reset to null, but this doesn't happen. The problem is the return value from operator[](). The function returns a *temporary copy* of a smart pointer object that points to the same Box object as the original pointer in the list but is *a different pointer*. Each time you use load[0] on the left of an assignment, you get a *different* copy of the first pointer in the list. Both statements operate but are just changing *copies* of the pointers in the list, which are copies that won't be around for very long.

This is why the subscript operator normally returns a reference to the actual values inside a data structure and not copies of these values. Doing this for the Truckload class, however, poses one significant challenge. You can no longer return nullptr from operator[]() in the Truckload class because you cannot return a reference to nullptr. Obviously, you must never return a reference to a local object in this situation either. You need to devise another way to deal with an invalid index. The simplest solution is to return a SharedBox object that doesn't point to anything and is permanently stored somewhere in global memory.

You could define a SharedBox object as a static member of the Truckload class by adding the following declaration to the private section of the class:

```
static SharedBox nullBox;                    // Pointer to nullptr
```

As you saw in Chapter 11, you initialize static class members outside the class. The following statement in Truckload.cpp will do it:

```
SharedBox Truckload::nullBox {};             // Initialize static class member
```

Now we can change the definition of the subscript operator to this:

```
SharedBox& Truckload::operator[](size_t index)
{
  size_t count {};                           // Package count
  for (Package* package{pHead}; package; package = package->pNext)
  {
    if (index == count++)                    // Up to index yet?
      return package->pBox;                  // If so return the pointer to Box
  }
  return nullBox;
}
```

It now returns a reference to the pointer, and the member function is no longer const. Here's an extension of Ex12_10 to try the subscript operator on the left of an assignment. We have simply extended main() from Ex12_10 to show that iterating through the elements in a Truckload list still works:

```
// Ex12_11.cpp
// Using the subscript operator on the left of an assignment
#include <iostream>
#include <memory>
#include <cstdlib>                    // For random number generator
#include <ctime>                      // For time function
#include "Truckload.h"

// Function to generate integral random box dimensions from 1 to max_size
inline double random(double max_size)
{
  return 1 + static_cast<int>(std::rand() / (RAND_MAX / max_size + 1));
}

int main()
{
  // All the code from main() in Ex12_10 here...

  load[0] = load[1];                   // Copy 2nd element to 1st
  std::cout << "\nAfter copying the 2nd element to the 1st, the list contains:\n";
  std::cout << load;

  load[1] = std::make_shared<Box>(*load[2] + *load[3]);
  std::cout << "\nAfter making the 2nd element a pointer to the 3rd plus 4th,"
                                                " the list contains:\n";
  std::cout << load;
}
```

The first part of the output is similar to the previous example, after which the output is as follows:

```
After copying the 2nd element to the 1st, the list contains:
 Box(65,31, 6) Box(65,31, 6) Box(75, 4, 4) Box(40,18,48) Box(32,67,21)
 Box(78,48,72) Box(22,71,41) Box(36,37,91) Box(19, 9,71) Box(98,78,30)
 Box(85,54,53) Box(98,13,66) Box(50,57,39) Box(56,80,88) Box(17,60,23)
 Box(85,42,41) Box(51,31,61) Box(41, 9, 8) Box(75,79,43)

After making the 2nd element a pointer to the sum of 3rd and 4th, the list contains:
 Box(65,31, 6) Box(75,18,52) Box(75, 4, 4) Box(40,18,48) Box(32,67,21)
 Box(78,48,72) Box(22,71,41) Box(36,37,91) Box(19, 9,71) Box(98,78,30)
 Box(85,54,53) Box(98,13,66) Box(50,57,39) Box(56,80,88) Box(17,60,23)
 Box(85,42,41) Box(51,31,61) Box(41, 9, 8) Box(75,79,43)
```

The first block of new output shows that the first two elements point to the same Box object, so the assignment worked as expected. The second block results from assigning a new value to the second element in the Truckload object; the new value is a pointer to the Box object produced by summing the third and fourth Box objects. The output shows that the second element points to a new object that is the sum of the next two. Just to make it clear what is happening, the statement that does this is equivalent to the following:

```
load.operator[](1).operator=(
  std::make_shared<Box>(load.operator[](2)->operator+(*load.operator[](3))));
```

That's much clearer, isn't it?

▦ **Caution**   The workaround used in this section to deal with invalid indexes to a subscript operator—returning a reference to a special "null object"—has one critical flaw. Perhaps you can already guess what this is? Hint: if supplied with an invalid index, the `operator[]()` function returns a *non-const reference* to `nullBox`. Exactly. The fact that this reference is non-`const` implies that there is nothing preventing the caller from modifying `nullBox`. In general, allowing the user to modify the objects that are accessed through the operator is exactly what we set out to do. But for the special `nullBox` object, this exposes a grave risk. It allows a careless caller to assign a non-null value to the `nullBox` pointer, which would essentially cripple the subscript operator! The following illustrates how things could go wrong:

```
Truckload load(std::make_shared<Box>(1, 2, 3));   // Create a load containing a single box
...
load[10] = std::make_shared<Box>(6, 6, 6);        // Oops: assigning a value to nullBox...
...
auto secondBox = load[100];                       // Access non-existing Box...
if (secondBox)                                    // Reference to nullBox no longer null!
{
   std::cout << secondBox->volume() << std::endl; // Prints 216 (volume of our "nullBox")
}
```

As this example shows, one accidental assignment to a nonexistent 11th element causes unexpected and undesirable behavior. The `Truckload` now appears to have a box with dimensions {6, 6, 6} at index 100. (Note that this will even break the subscript operator for all `Truckload` objects at once. Because `nullBox` is a static member of `Truckload`, it is shared between all objects of this class.)

Because of this dangerous loophole, you should never use the technique we used here in real programs. In Chapter 15 you will learn about a more appropriate mechanism for dealing with invalid function arguments: exceptions. Exceptions will allow you to return from a function without having to invent a return value.

Function Objects

A *function object* is an object of a class that overloads the function call operator, which is (). A function object is also called a *functor*. The operator function in a class looks like a misprint. It is `operator()()`. A function object can be passed as an argument to a function, so it provides yet another way to pass functions around. The Standard Library uses function objects quite extensively, particularly in the functional header. We'll show you how function objects work with an example.

Suppose we define a Volume class like this:

```
class Volume
{
public:
  double operator()(double x, double y, double z) { return x*y*z; }
};
```

We can use a Volume object to calculate a volume:

```
Volume volume;                        // Create a functor
double room { volume(16, 12, 8.5) };  // Room volume in cubic feet
```

The volume object represents a function, one that can be called using its function call operator. The value in the braced initializer for room is the result of calling operator()() for the volume object, so the expression is equivalent to volume.operator()(16, 12, 8.5). Of course, you can define more than one overload of the operator()() function in a class:

```
class Volume
{
public:
  double operator()(double x, double y, double z) { return x*y*z; }

  double operator()(const Box& box) { return box.volume(); }
};
```

Now a Volume object can return the volume of a Box object:

```
Box box{1.0, 2.0, 3.0};
std::cout << "The volume of the box is " << volume(box) << std::endl;
```

Surely, this example is not enough to convince you of the usefulness of function objects. In Chapter 18, though, we'll show you why representing callable functions as objects is a powerful concept indeed. In later chapters, you'll use functors extensively in combination with, for instance, Standard Library algorithms.

▓ **Note**   Unlike most operators, function call operators must be overloaded as member functions. They cannot be defined as regular functions. The function call operator is also the only operator that can have as many parameters as you want and that can have default arguments.

Overloading Type Conversions

You can define an operator function as a class member to convert from the class type to another type. The type you're converting to can be a fundamental type or a class type. Operator functions that are conversions for objects of an arbitrary class, MyClass, are of this form:

```
class MyClass
{
 public:
   operator Type() const;                          // Conversion from MyClass to Type
// Rest of MyClass class definition...
};
```

Type is the destination type for the conversion. Note that no return type is specified because the target type is always implicit in the function name, so here the function must return a Type object.

As an example, you might want to define a conversion from type Box to type double. For application reasons, you could decide that the result of this conversion would be the volume of the Box object. You could define this as follows:

```
class Box
{
public:
   operator double() const  { return volume(); }

// Rest of Box class definition...
};
```

The operator function would be called if you wrote this:

```
Box box {1.0, 2.0, 3.0};
double boxVolume = box;            // Calls conversion operator
```

This causes an implicit conversion to be inserted by the compiler. You could call the operator function explicitly with this statement:

```
double total { 10.0 + static_cast<double>(box) };
```

You can prevent implicit calls of a conversion operator function by specifying it as explicit in the class. In the Box class you could, and probably should, write this:

```
explicit operator double() const { return volume(); }
```

Now the compiler will not use this member for implicit conversions to type double.

▓ **Note**   Unlike most operators, conversion operators must be overloaded as member functions. They cannot be defined as regular functions.

Potential Ambiguities with Conversions

When you implement conversion operators for a class, it is possible to create ambiguities that will cause compiler errors. You have seen that a constructor can also effectively implement a conversion—a conversion from type Type1 to type Type2 can be implemented by including a constructor in class Type2 with this declaration:

```
Type2(const Type1& theObject);            // Constructor converting Type1 to Type2
```

This can conflict with this conversion operator in the Type1 class:

```
operator Type2();                         // Conversion from type Type1 to Type2
```

The compiler will not be able to decide which constructor or conversion operator function to use when an implicit conversion is required. To remove the ambiguity, declare either or both members as explicit.

Overloading the Assignment Operator

You have already encountered several instances where one object of a nonfundamental type is seemingly overwritten by another using an assignment operator, like so:

```
Box oneBox{1, 2, 3};
Box otherBox{4, 5, 6};
...
oneBox = otherBox;
...
std::cout << oneBox.volume() << std::endl;     // Outputs 120 (= 4 x 5 x 6)
```

But how exactly does this work? And how do you support this for your own classes?

You know that the compiler (sometimes) supplies default constructors, copy constructors, and destructors. This is not all the compiler provides, though. Similar to a default copy constructor, a compiler also generates a default *copy assignment operator*. For Box, this operator has the following prototype:

```
class Box
{
public:
    ...
    Box& operator=(const Box& right_hand_side);
    ...
};
```

Like a default copy constructor, the default copy assignment operator simply copies all the member variables of a class one by one (in the order they are declared in the class definition). You can override this default behavior by supplying a user-defined assignment operator, as we'll discuss next.

Implementing the Copy Assignment Operator

The default assignment operator copies the members of the object to the right of an assignment to those of the object of the same type on the left. For a Box, this default behavior is just fine. But this is not the case for all classes. Consider a simple Message class that, for whatever reason, stores the text of its message in a std::string that is allocated in the free store. You then already know to implement a destructor that explicitly reclaims that memory. A definition for such a class might look like this:

```
class Message
{
public:
  explicit Message(std::string_view message = "") : pText{new std::string(message)} {}
  ~Message() { delete pText; }
  std::string_view getText() const { return *pText; }
private:
  std::string* pText;
};
```

You call its (default) assignment operator when you write the following:

```
Message message;
Message beware {"Careful"};
message = beware;                      // Call the assignment operator
```

This snippet will compile and run. But now think about what the default assignment operator of the Message class does exactly during this last statement. It copies the pText member from the beware Message into that of the message object. This member is just a raw pointer variable, though, so after the assignment we have two different Message objects whose pText pointer refers to the same memory location. Once both Messages go out of scope, the destructors of both objects will therefore apply delete on the same location! It's impossible to tell what the result of this second delete—which will be the one inside the destructor of message—will be. In general, it is undefined what will happen. One likely outcome, though, is a program crash.

So, clearly, the default assignment operator will not do for classes such as Message, that is, classes that themselves manage dynamically allocated memory. You thus have no other option but to redefine the assignment operator for Message.

■ **Note** The assignment operator cannot be defined as a regular function. It is the only binary operator that must always be overloaded as a class member function.

An assignment operator should return a reference, so in the Message class it would look like this:

```
  Message& operator=(const Message& message);     // Assignment operator
```

The parameter should be a reference-to-const and the return type a reference-to-non-const. As the code for the assignment operator will just transfer data from the members of the right operand to the members of the left operand, you may wonder why it has to return a reference—or indeed, why it needs to return anything. Consider how the assignment operator is applied in practice. With normal usage you can write this:

```
message1 = message2 = message3;
```

These are three objects of the same type, so this statement makes message1 and message2 copies of message3. Because the assignment operator is right associative, this is equivalent to the following:

```
message1 = (message2 = message3);
```

The result of executing the rightmost assignment is evidently the right operand for the leftmost assignment, so you definitely need to return something. In terms of operator=(), this statement is equivalent to the following:

```
message1.operator=(message2.operator=(message3));
```

You have seen this several times before. This is called method chaining! Whatever you return from operator=() can end up as the argument to another operator=() call. The parameter for operator=() is a reference to an object, so the operator function must return the left operand, which is the object that is pointed to by this. Further, to avoid unnecessary copying of the object that is returned, the return type must be a reference.

One option for duplicating the right operand is to simply leverage the assignment operator of std::string as follows:

```
Message& operator=(const Message& message)
{
  *pText = *message.pText;      // Copy the std::string object
  return *this;                 // Return the left operand
}
```

While this is probably the more recommended approach, this variant does not teach you anything about the perils of overloading an assignment operator. It just relies on the fact that the implementors of the Standard Library knew how to implement a correct assignment operator—which they most probably did. So, suppose, for argument's sake, that you decided to call the copy constructor of std::string instead. Then this would be a reasonable first go at such an assignment operator:

```
Message& operator=(const Message& message)
{
  delete pText;                             // Delete the previous text
  pText = new std::string(*message.pText);  // Duplicate the object
  return *this;                             // Return the left operand
}
```

The this pointer contains the address of the left argument, so returning *this returns the object. The function looks OK, and it appears to work most of the time, but there is one serious problem with it. Suppose someone writes this:

```
message1 = message1;
```

The likelihood of someone writing this explicitly is very low, but self-assignment could occur indirectly. The result of this statement is that you first apply delete on the pText pointer of message1, after which you dereference that same pointer in an attempt to copy it. Remember, inside the operator=() function, message and *this both refer to the same object: message1! It is, in other words, as if you were executing this:

```
delete message1.pText;
message1.pText = new std::string(*message1.pText);  // Reference reclaimed memory!
return message1;
```

485

Because the pText member you are dereferencing now points to reclaimed free store memory, it is not unlikely that this results in a fatal error. Swapping the first lines in the operator=() function body won't help either by the way. Suppose you did that; then the assignment operator would first copy the string pointed to by pText into itself, only to immediately delete this newly made copy! Let's inline that as well to make this variation clearer:

```
message1.pText = new std::string(*message1.pText); // Memory leak!
delete message1.pText;
return message1;                                    // Returning message with deleted pText!
```

Of course you'd again never write this, but this is effectively what would happen during the assignment operator after swapping its first two lines. Not only would this variant leak memory—delete was never applied on the original pText!—you'd also end up with a Message object whose pText points to memory that has already been reclaimed. So, yet again, your program would almost certainly crash at some point later.

The correct solution is to check for identical left and right operands:

```
Message& operator=(const Message& message)
{
  if (this != &message)
  {
    delete pText;                          // Delete the previous text
    pText = new std::string(*message.pText);  // Duplicate the object
  }
  return *this;                            // Return the left operand
}
```

Now if this contains the address of the argument object, the function does nothing and just returns the same object. Therefore:

■ **Tip**   Every user-defined copy assignment operator should start by checking for self-assignment. Forgetting to do so may lead to fatal errors when accidentally assigning an object itself.

If you put this in the Message class definition, the following code will show it working:

```
// Ex12_12.cpp
// Defining a copy assignment operator
#include "Message.h"

int main()
{
  Message beware {"Careful"};
  Message warning;

  warning = beware;                         // Call assignment operator

  std::cout << "After assignment beware is: " << beware.getText() << std::endl;
  std::cout << "After assignment warning is: " << warning.getText() << std::endl;
}
```

The output will demonstrate that everything works as it should and that the program does not crash!

■ **Note** You'll encounter a more realistic example of a user-defined copy assignment operator in Chapter 16, where you'll work on a bigger example of a `vector`-like class that manages an array of dynamically allocated memory. Based on that example, we'll also introduce the standard technique for implementing a correct, safe assignment operator: the so-called copy-and-swap idiom. Essentially, this C++ programming pattern dictates to always reformulate the copy assignment operator in terms of the copy constructor and a `swap()` function.

Copy Assignment vs. Copy Construction

The copy assignment operator is called under different circumstances than the copy constructor. The following snippet illustrates this:

```
Message beware {"Careful"};
Message warning;
warning = beware;                  // Call assignment operator
Message otherWarning{warning};     // Calls the copy constructor
```

On the third line, you *assign* a new value to a previously contructed object. This means that the *assignment* operator is used. On the last line, however, you *construct* an entirely new object as a copy of another. This is thus done using the copy *constructor*. If you do not use the uniform initialization syntax, the difference is not always that obvious. It is also legal to rewrite the last line as follows:

```
Message otherWarning = warning;    // Still calls the copy constructor
```

Programmers sometimes wrongly assume that this form is equivalent to a copy assignment to an implicitly default-constructed `Message` object. But that's not what happens. Even though this statement contains an equal sign, the compiler will still use the copy contructor here, not an assignment. Assignment operators come into play only when assigning to existing objects that were already constructed earlier.

Notice that, of course, the default copy constructor for the `Message` class will cause the same problem as the default copy assignment operator. That is, applying this default copy constructor results in a second object with the same pText pointer. Any class that has problems with the default assignment operator will also have problems with the copy constructor, and vice versa. If you need to implement one, you also need to implement the other. `Ex12_12A` contains an augmented version of `Ex12_12` where a correct copy constructor was added.

In Chapter 17, we'll return in more detail to the discussion of when and how you must override default-generated members. For now just remember this guideline:

■ **Tip** If a class manages members that are pointers to free store memory, you must never use the copy constructor and assignment operator as is; and if it has members that are raw pointers, you must always define a destructor.

Assigning Different Types

You're not limited to overloading the assignment operator just to copy an object of the same type. You can have several overloaded versions of the assignment operator for a class. Additional versions can have a parameter type that is different from the class type, so they are effectively conversions. In fact, you have even already seen objects being assigned values of a different type:

```
std::string s{"Happiness is an inside job."};
...
s = "Don't assign anyone else that much power over your life.";    // Assign const char[] value
```

Having reached the end of this chapter on operator overloading, we are positive that you can figure out how to implement such assignment operators on your own. Just remember, by convention any assignment operator should return a reference to *this!

Summary

In this chapter, you learned how to add functions to make objects of your own data types work with the basic operators. What you need to implement in a particular class is up to you. You need to decide the nature and scope of the facilities each class should provide. Always keep in mind that you are defining a data type—a coherent entity—and that the class needs to reflect its nature and characteristics. You should also make sure that your implementation of an overloaded operator doesn't conflict with what the operator does in its standard form.

The important points from in this chapter include the following:

- You can overload any number of operators within a class to provide class-specific behavior. You should do so only to make code easier to read and write.

- Overloaded operators should mimic their built-in counterparts as much as possible. Popular exceptions to this rule are the << and >> operators for Standard Library streams and the + operator to concatenate strings.

- Operator functions can be defined as members of a class or as global operator functions. You should use member functions whenever possible. You should resort to global operator functions only if there is no other way or if implicit conversions are desirable for the first operand.

- For a unary operator defined as a class member function, the operand is the class object. For a unary operator defined as a global operator function, the operand is the function parameter.

- For a binary operator function declared as a member of a class, the left operand is the class object, and the right operand is the function parameter. For a binary operator defined by a global operator function, the first parameter specifies the left operand, and the second parameter specifies the right operand.

- Functions that implement the overloading of the += operator can be used in the implementation of the + function. This is true for all op= operators.

- To overload the increment or the decrement operator, you need two functions that provide the prefix and postfix form of the operator. The function to implement a postfix operator has an extra parameter of type int that serves only to distinguish the function from the prefix version.

- To support customized type conversions, you have the choice between conversion operators or a combination of conversion constructors and assignment operators.

EXERCISES

The following exercises enable you to try what you've learned in this chapter. If you get stuck, look back over the chapter for help. If you're still stuck after that, you can download the solutions from the Apress website (www.apress.com/book/download.html), but that really should be a last resort.

Exercise 12-1. Define an operator function in the Box class from Ex12_05 that allows a Box object to be post-multiplied by an unsigned integer, n, to produce a new object that has a height that is n times the original object. Demonstrate that your operator function works as it should.

Exercise 12-2. Define an operator function that will allow a Box object to be premultiplied by an unsigned integer n to produce the same result as the operator in Exercise 12-1. Demonstrate that this operator works.

Exercise 12-3. Take another look at your solution of Exercise 12-2. If it's anything like our model solution, it contains two binary arithmetic operators: one to add two Boxes and one overloaded operator to multiply Boxes by numbers. Remember that we said that one thing always leads to another in the world of operator overloading? While subtracting Boxes does not work well, surely if you have operators to multiply with an integer, you'd also want operators to divide by one? Furthermore, each binary arithmetic operator *op*() creates the expectation of a corresponding compound assignment operator *op* =(). Make sure to implement all requested operators using the canonical patterns!

Exercise 12-4. Create the necessary operators that allow Box objects to be used in if statements such as these:

```
if (my_box) ...
if (!my_other_box) ...
```

A Box is equivalent to true if it has a nonzero volume; if its volume is zero, a Box should evaluate to false. Create a small test program that shows your operators work as requested.

Exercise 12-5. Implement a class `Rational` that represents a rational number. A rational number can be expressed as the quotient or fraction n / d of two integer numbers, an integral numerator n, and a nonzero, positive integral denominator d. Do not worry about enforcing that the denominator is nonzero, though. That's not the point of the exercise. Definitely create an operator that allows a rational number to be streamed to `std::cout`. Beyond that, you are free to choose how many and which operators you add. You could create operators to support multiplication, addition, subtraction, division, and comparison of two `Rational` numbers and of `Rational` numbers and integers. You could create operators to negate, increment, or decrement `Rational` numbers. And what about converting to a `float` or a `double`? There really is a huge amount of operators you could define for `Rationals`. The `Rational` class in our model solution supports well over 20 different operators, many overloaded for multiple types. Perhaps you come up with even more rational (as in: sensible) operators for your `Rational` class? Do not forget to create a program to test that your operators actually work.

Exercise 12-6. Take another look at the `Truckload` class from `Ex12_11`. Isn't there an operator missing? The class has two raw pointers called `pHead` and `pTail`. What will the default assignment operator do with these two raw pointers? Clearly, it will not do what you want, so the `Truckload` class is in dire need of a custom assignment operator. Add the assignment operator to the `Truckload` class, and modify the `main()` function to exercise your freshly written assignment operator.

CHAPTER 13

▓ ▓ ▓

Inheritance

In this chapter, you'll look at a topic that lies at the heart of object-oriented programming: *inheritance*. Inheritance is the means by which you can create new classes by reusing and expanding on existing class definitions. Inheritance is also fundamental to making *polymorphism* possible. We'll discuss polymorphism in the next chapter, so what you'll learn there is an integral part of what inheritance is all about. There are subtleties in inheritance that we'll tease out using code that shows what is happening.

In this chapter, you'll learn:

- How inheritance fits into the idea of object-oriented programming
- What base classes and derived classes are and how they're related
- How to define a new class in terms of an existing class
- The use of the `protected` keyword as an access specification for class members
- How constructors behave in a derived class and what happens when they're called
- What happens with destructors in a class hierarchy
- The use of `using` declarations within a class definition
- What multiple inheritance is
- How to convert between types in a class hierarchy

Classes and Object-Oriented Programming

We'll begin by reviewing what you've learned so far about classes and explain how that leads to the ideas we'll introduce in this chapter. In Chapter 11, we explained the concept of a class and that a class is a type that you define to suit your own application requirements. In Chapter 12 you learned how you can overload the basic operators so that they work with objects of your class types. The first step in applying object-oriented programming to solve a problem is to identify the types of entities to which the problem relates and to determine the characteristics for each type and the operations that will be needed to solve the problem. Then you can define the classes and their operations, which will provide what you need to program the solution to the problem in terms of instances of the classes.

Any type of entity can be represented by a class—from the completely abstract such as the mathematical concept of a complex number to something as decidedly physical as a tree or a truck. A class definition characterizes a *set* of entities, which share a common set of properties. So, as well as being a data type, a class can also be a definition of a set of real-world objects, or at least an approximation that is sufficient for solving a given problem.

© Ivor Horton and Peter Van Weert 2018
I. Horton and P. Van Weert, *Beginning C++17*, https://doi.org/10.1007/978-1-4842-3366-5_13

In many real-world problems, the *types* of the entities involved are related. For example, a dog is a special kind of animal. A dog has all the properties of an animal plus a few more that characterize a dog. Consequently, classes that define the Animal and Dog types should be related in some way. As a dog is a specialized kind of animal, you can say that any Dog *is* also an Animal. You would expect the class definitions to reflect this. A different sort relationship is illustrated by an automobile and an engine. You can't say that an Automobile *is* an Engine, or vice versa. What you can say is that an Automobile *has* an Engine. In this chapter you'll see how the *is a* and *has a* relationships are expressed by classes.

Hierarchies

In previous chapters, we defined the Box class to represent a rectilinear box. The defining properties of a Box object were just the three orthogonal dimensions. You can apply this basic definition to the many different kinds of rectangular boxes that you find in the real world: cardboard cartons, wooden crates, candy boxes, cereal boxes, and so on. All these have three orthogonal dimensions, and in this way they're just like generic Box objects. However, each of them has other properties such as the things they're designed to hold, the material from which they're made, or the labels printed on them. You could describe them as specialized kinds of Box objects.

For example, a Carton class could have the same properties as a Box object—namely, the three dimensions—plus the additional property of its composite material. You could then specialize even further by using the Carton definition to describe a FoodCarton class, which is a special kind of Carton that is designed to hold food. A FoodCarton object will have all the properties of a Carton object and an additional member to model the contents. Of course, a Carton object has the properties of a Box object, so a FoodCarton object will have those too. Figure 13-1 shows the connections between classes that express these relationships.

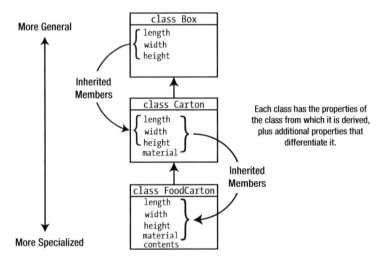

***Figure 13-1.** Classes in a hierarchy*

The Carton class is an extension of the Box class. You might say that the Carton class is *derived* from the Box class. In a similar way, the FoodCarton class has been derived from the Carton class. It's common to indicate this relationship diagrammatically by using an arrow pointing toward the more general class in the hierarchy. This notation is used also by the Unified Modeling Language (UML), the de facto standard way for visualizing the design of object-oriented software programs. Figure 13-1 is a simplified UML *class diagram*, with some additional annotations to clarify.

In specifying one class in terms of another, you're developing a hierarchy of interrelated classes. One class is derived from another by adding extra properties—in other words, by *specialization*—making the new class a specialized version of the more general class. In Figure 13-1, each class in the hierarchy has *all* the properties of the Box class, which illustrates precisely the mechanism of class inheritance. You could define the Box, Carton, and FoodCarton classes quite independently of each other, but by defining them as related classes, you gain a tremendous amount. Let's look at how this works in practice.

Inheritance in Classes

To begin with, we'll introduce the terminology that is used for related classes. Given a class A, suppose you create a new class B that is a specialized version of A. Class A is the *base* class, and class B is the *derived* class. You can think of A as being the "parent" and B as being the "child." A base class is sometimes referred to as a *superclass* of a class that is derived from it, and the derived class is a *subclass* of its base. A derived class automatically contains all the member variables of its base class and (with some restrictions that we'll discuss) all the member functions. A derived class *inherits* the member variables and member functions of its base class.

If class B is a derived class defined *directly* in terms of class A, then class A is a *direct base class* of B. Class B is *derived from* A. In the preceding example, the Carton class is a direct base class of FoodCarton. Because Carton is defined in terms of the Box class, the Box class is an *indirect base class* of the FoodCarton class. An object of the FoodCarton class will have inherited members from Carton, including the members that the Carton class inherits from the Box class. Figure 13-2 illustrates the way in which a derived class inherits members from a base class.

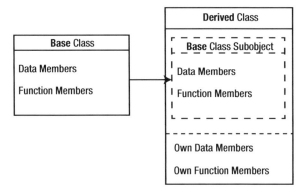

Figure 13-2. *Derived class members inherited from a base class*

As you can see, the derived class has a complete set of member variables and functions from the base class, plus its own member variables and functions. Thus, each derived class object contains a complete base class subobject, plus its own members.

Inheritance vs. Aggregation

Class inheritance isn't just a means of getting members of one class to appear in another. There's an important idea that underpins the whole concept: derived class objects should be sensible specializations of base class objects. To decide whether this is the case in a specific instance, you can apply the *is a* test, which is that any derived class object *is a* base class object. In other words, a derived class should define a subset of the objects that are represented by the base class. We explained earlier that a Dog class might be derived from

493

an Animal class because a dog *is an* animal; more precisely, a Dog object is a reasonable representation of a particular kind of Animal object. On the other hand, a Table class shouldn't be derived from the Dog class. Although Table and Dog objects share a common attribute in that they both usually have four legs, a Table object can't really be considered to be a Dog in any way, or vice versa.

The *is a* test is an excellent first check, but it's not infallible. For example, suppose you define a Bird class that among other things reflects the fact that most birds can fly. Now, an ostrich *is a* bird, but it's nonsense to derive a class Ostrich from the Bird class because ostriches can't fly! The problem arises because of a poor definition for Bird objects. You really need a base class that doesn't have the ability to fly as a property. You can then derive two subclasses, one for birds that can fly and the other for birds that can't. If your classes pass the *is a* test, you should double-check by asking whether there is anything we can say about (or demand of) the base class that's inapplicable to the derived class. If there is, then the derivation probably isn't sound. Deriving Dog from Animal is sensible, but deriving Ostrich from Bird as we described it, isn't.

If classes fail the *is a* test, then you probably shouldn't use class derivation. In this case, you could check the *has a* test. A class object passes the *has a* test if it contains an instance of another class. You can accommodate this by including an object of the second class as a member variable of the first. The Automobile and Engine classes that we mentioned earlier are an example. An Automobile object would have an Engine object as a member variable; it may well have other major subassemblies as member variables of types such as Transmission and Differential. This type of relationship is called *aggregation*.

If the child object contained in a parent object cannot exist independently of its parent, their relation is called *composition* instead of aggregation. An example of composition would be the relation between a House and a Room, if Rooms cannot exist without a House. If you delete a House, all its Rooms are typically deleted as well. An example of aggregation is the relation Class–Student. Students generally do not cease to exist if their Class is cancelled.

Of course, what is appropriate to include in the definition of a class depends on the application. Sometimes, class derivation is used simply to assemble a set of capabilities so that the derived class is an envelope for packaging a given set of functions. Even then, the derived class generally represents a set of functions that are related in some way. Let's see what the code to derive one class from another looks like.

Deriving Classes

Here's a simplified version of the Box class from Chapter 12:

```
// Box.h - defines Box class
#ifndef BOX_H
#define BOX_H
#include <iostream>                        // For standard streams
#include <iomanip>                         // For stream manipulators

class Box
{
private:
  double length {1.0};
  double width  {1.0};
  double height {1.0};

public:
  // Constructors
  Box(double lv, double wv, double hv) : length {lv}, width {wv}, height {hv} {}
  Box() = default;                         // No-arg constructor
```

```
  double volume() const { return length*width*height; }

  // Accessors
  double getLength() const { return length; }
  double getWidth()  const { return width; }
  double getHeight() const { return height; }
};

// Stream output for Box objects
inline std::ostream& operator<<(std::ostream& stream, const Box& box)
{
  stream << " Box(" << std::setw(2) << box.getLength() << ','
                    << std::setw(2) << box.getWidth()  << ','
                    << std::setw(2) << box.getHeight() << ')';
  return stream;
}
#endif
```

We can define a Carton class based on the Box class. A Carton object will be similar to a Box object but with an extra member variable that indicates the material from which it's made. We'll define Carton as a derived class, using the Box class as the base class:

```
// Carton.h - defines the Carton class with the Box class as base
#ifndef CARTON_H
#define CARTON_H
#include <string>
#include <string_view>
#include "Box.h"

class Carton : public Box
{
private:
  std::string material;

public:
  explicit Carton(std::string_view mat = "Cardboard") : material{mat} {}  // Constructor
};
#endif
```

The #include directive for the Box class definition is necessary because it is the base class for Carton. The first line of the Carton class definition indicates that Carton is derived from Box. The base class name follows a colon that separates it from the derived class name, Carton in this case. The public keyword is a base class access specifier that determines how the members of Box can be accessed from within the Carton class. We'll discuss this further in a moment.

In all other respects, the Carton class definition looks like any other. It contains a new member, material, which is initialized by the constructor. The constructor defines a default value for the string describing the material of a Carton object so that this is also the no-arg constructor for the Carton class. Carton objects contain all the member variables of the base class, Box, plus the additional member variable, material. Because they inherit all the characteristics of a Box object, Carton objects are also Box objects. There's a glaring inadequacy in the Carton class in that it doesn't have a constructor defined that permits the values of inherited members to be set, but we'll return to that later. Let's first see how these class definitions work in an example:

```cpp
// Ex13_01.cpp
// Defining and using a derived class
#include <iostream>
#include "Box.h"                  // For the Box class
#include "Carton.h"               // For the Carton class

int main()
{
  // Create a Box object and two Carton objects
  Box box {40.0, 30.0, 20.0};           /
  Carton carton;
  Carton chocolateCarton {"Solid bleached paperboard"};
  // Check them out - sizes first of all
  std::cout << "box occupies " << sizeof box << " bytes" << std::endl;
  std::cout << "carton occupies " << sizeof carton << " bytes" << std::endl;
  std::cout << "candyCarton occupies " << sizeof chocolateCarton << " bytes" << std::endl;

  // Now volumes...
  std::cout << "box volume is " << box.volume() << std::endl;
  std::cout << "carton volume is " << carton.volume() << std::endl;
  std::cout << "chocolateCarton volume is " << chocolateCarton.volume() << std::endl;

  std::cout << "chocolateCarton length is " << chocolateCarton.getLength() << std::endl;

  // Uncomment any of the following for an error...
  // box.length = 10.0;
  // chocolateCarton.length = 10.0;
}
```

We get the following output:

```
box occupies 24 bytes
carton occupies 56 bytes
chocolateCarton occupies 56 bytes
box volume is 24000
carton volume is 1
chocolateCarton volume is 1
chocolateCarton length is 1
```

The main() function creates a Box object and two Carton objects and outputs the number of bytes occupied by each object. The output shows what you would expect—that a Carton object is larger than a Box object. A Box object has three member variables of type double; each of these occupies 8 bytes on nearly every machine, so that's 24 bytes in all. Both of the Carton objects are the same size: 56 bytes. The additional memory occupied by each Carton object is down to the member variable material, so it's the size of a string object that contains the description of the material. The output of the volumes for the Carton objects shows that the volume() function is indeed inherited in the Carton class and that the dimensions have the default values of 1.0. The next statement shows that the accessor functions are inherited too and can be called for a derived class object.

Uncommenting either of the last two statements results in an error message from the compiler. The member variables that are inherited by the Carton class were private in the base class, and they are still private in the derived class, Carton, so they cannot be accessed from outside the class. There's more, though. Try adding this function to the Carton class definition as a public member:

```
double carton_volume() const { return length*width*height; }
```

This won't compile. The reason is that although the member variables of Box are inherited, they are inherited as private members of the Box class. The private access specifier determines that members are totally private to the class. Not only can they not be accessed from outside the Box class, they also cannot be accessed from inside a class that inherits them.

Access to inherited members of a derived class object is not only determined by their access specification in the base class but by *both* the access specifier in the base class and the access specifier of the base class in the derived class. We'll go into that a bit more next.

protected Members of a Class

The private members of a base class being only accessible to member functions of the base class can be, to say the least, inconvenient. Often you want the members of a base class to be *accessible* from within the derived class but nonetheless *protected* from outside interference. In addition to the public and private access specifiers for class members, you can declare members as protected. Within the class, the protected keyword has the same effect as the private keyword. protected members cannot be accessed from outside the class except from functions that have been specified as friend functions. Things change in a derived class, though. Members of a base class that are declared as protected are freely accessible in member functions of a derived class, whereas the private members of the base class are not.

We can modify the Box class to have protected member variables:

```
class Box
{
protected:
  double length {1.0};
  double width {1.0};
  double height {1.0};

public:
  // Rest of the class as before...
};
```

Now the member variables of Box are still effectively private in that they can't be accessed by ordinary global functions, but they're now accessible within member functions of a derived class. If you now try compiling Carton with the carton_volume() member uncommented and the Box class members specified as protected, you'll find that it compiles without a problem.

▨ **Tip**   Member variables should normally always be private. The previous example was just to indicate what is possible. In general, protected member variables introduce similar issues as public member variables, only to a lesser extent. We'll explore this in more detail in the next section.

The Access Level of Inherited Class Members

In the Carton class definition, we specified the Box base class as public using the following syntax: class Carton : public Box. In general, there are three possibilities for the base class access specifier: public, protected, or private. If you omit the base class access specifier in a class definition, the default is private (in a struct definition, the default is public). For example, if you omit the specifier altogether by writing class Carton : Box at the top of the Carton class definition in Ex13_01, then the private access specifier for Box is assumed. You already know that the access specifiers for class members come in three flavors as well. Again, the choice is the same: public, protected, or private. The base class access specifier affects the access status of the inherited members in a derived class. There are nine possible combinations. We'll cover all possible combinations in the following paragraphs, although the usefulness of some of these will only become apparent in the next chapter when you learn about polymorphism.

First let's consider how private members of a base class are inherited in a derived class. Regardless of the base class access specifier (public, protected, or private), a private base class member *always* remains private to the base class. As you have seen, inherited private members are private members of the derived class, so they're inaccessible outside the derived class. They're also inaccessible to member functions of the derived class because they're private to the base class.

Now, let's look into how public and protected base class members are inherited. In all the remaining cases, inherited members can be accessed by member functions of the derived class. The inheritance of public and protected base class members works like this:

1. When the base class specifier is public, the access status of the inherited members remains unchanged. Thus, inherited public members are public, and inherited protected members are protected in a derived class.

2. When the base class specifier is protected, both public and protected members of a base class are inherited as protected members.

3. When the base class specifier is private, inherited public and protected members become private to the derived class, so they're accessible by member functions of the derived class but cannot be accessed if they're inherited in another derived class.

This is summarized in Figure 13-3. Being able to change the access level of inherited members in a derived class gives you a degree of flexibility, but remember that you can only make the access level more stringent; you can't relax the access level that is specified in the base class.

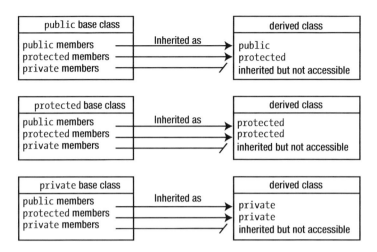

Figure 13-3. *The effect of the base class specifier on the accessibility of inherited members*

Access Specifiers and Class Hierarchies

Figure 13-4 shows how the accessibility of inherited members is affected only by the access specifiers of the members in the base class. Within a derived class, `public` and `protected` base class members are always accessible, and `private` base class members are never accessible. From outside the derived class, only `public` base class members may be accessed, and this is the case only when the base class is declared as `public`.

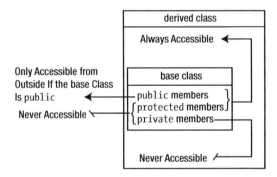

Figure 13-4. *The effect of access specifiers on base class members*

If the base class access specifier is `public`, then the access status of inherited members remains unchanged. By using the `protected` and `private` base class access specifiers, you are able to do two things:

- You can prevent access to `public` base class members from outside the derived class—either specifier will do this. If the base class has `public` member functions, then this is a serious step because the class interface for the base class is being removed from public view in the derived class.

- You can affect how the inherited members of the derived class are inherited in another class that uses the derived class as its base.

Figure 13-5 shows how the public and protected members of a base class can be passed on as protected members of another derived class. Members of a privately inherited base class won't be accessible in any further derived class. In the majority of instances, the public base class access specifier is most appropriate with the base class member variables declared as either private or protected. In this case, the internals of the base class subobject are internal to the derived class object and are therefore not part of the public interface for the derived class object. In practice, because the derived class object *is a* base class object, you'll want the base class interface to be inherited in the derived class, and this implies that the base class must be specified as public.

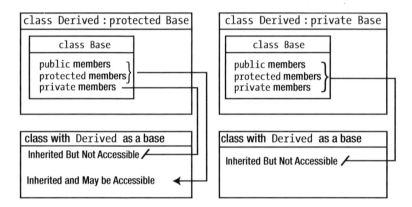

Figure 13-5. *Affecting the access specification of inherited members*

Constructors are not normally inherited for very good reasons, but you'll see later in this chapter how you can cause constructors to be inherited in a derived class.

Choosing Access Specifiers in Class Hierarchies

You have two aspects to consider when defining a hierarchy of classes: the access specifiers for the members of each class and the base class access specifier in each derived class. The public members of a class define the external interface to the class, and this shouldn't normally include any member variables. In fact:

▨ **Tip** As a rule, member variables of a class should always be private. If code outside of the class requires access to member variables, you should add public or protected getter and/or setter functions.

(This guideline commonly does not extend to structures. structs mostly do not encapsulate any member functions at all; the only members they typically have are public member variables.)

This widely accepted guideline is motivated by the data hiding principle explained in Chapter 11. If you recall, there were at least four good reasons to only access or modify member variables through a set of well-defined interface functions. Briefly, these were the following:

- Data hiding allows you to preserve the integrity of an object's state.

- It reduces coupling and dependencies with external code, thus facilitating evolution and changes either in a class's internal representation or in the concrete implementation of its interface functions.

- It allows you to inject extra code to be executed for every access and/or modification of member variables. Beyond validity and sanity checks, this may include logging and debugging code, for instance, or change notification mechanisms.

- It facilitates debugging, as most development environments support putting so-called debugging breakpoints on function calls. Putting breakpoints on getters and setters makes it much easier to track which code reads or writes to member variables and when.

Most programmers therefore abide by the rule to avoid `public` member variables at all times. What is often forgotten, though, is that `protected` member variables have many of the same disadvantages as `public` ones:

- There is nothing stopping a derived class from invalidating an object's state, which may for instance invalidate so-called *class invariants*—properties of an object's state that should hold at all times—counted on by code in the base class.

- Once derived classes directly manipulate the member variables of a base class, changing its internal implementation becomes impossible without changing all of the derived classes as well.

- Any extra code added to public getter and setter functions in the base class becomes void if derived classes can bypass it.

- Breaking a debug session when member variables are modified becomes, at the least, more difficult if derived classes can access them directly, breaking when they're read impossible.

Therefore, always make member variables `private`, unless you have a good reason not do so.

■ **Note**   To keep our code samples short, we will at times use `protected` member variables in this book. Such shortcuts have no place in professional-quality code, though.

Member functions that aren't part of the `public` interface of a class should not be directly accessible from outside the class either, which means that they should be `private` or `protected`. Which access specification you choose for a particular function then depends on whether you want to allow access from within a derived class. If you do, use `protected`; otherwise, use `private`.

Changing the Access Specification of Inherited Members

You might want to exempt a particular base class member from the effects of a `protected` or `private` base class access specification. This is easier to understand with an example. Suppose you derive the `Carton` class from the `Box` class in `Ex13_01` but with `Box` as a `private` base class. All members inherited from `Box` will now be `private` in `Carton`, but you'd like the `volume()` function to remain `public` in the derived class, as it is in the base class. You can restore the `public` status for a particular inherited member that was `public` in the base class with a `using` declaration.

This is essentially the same as the `using` declaration for namespaces. You can force the `volume()` function to be `public` in the derived class by defining the `Carton` class like this:

```
class Carton : private Box
{
private:
  std::string material;

public:
  using Box::volume;                                              // Inherit as public
  explicit Carton(std::string_view mat = "Cardboard") : material {mat} {}    // Constructor
};
```

The class definition defines a scope, and the `using` declaration within the class definition introduces a name into that class scope. The member access specification applies to the `using` declaration, so the volume name is introduced into the public section of the `Carton` class so it overrides the `private` base class access specification for the `volume()` member of the base class. The function will be inherited as `public` in the `Carton` class, not as `private`. `Ex13_01A` in the code download shows this working.

There are several points to note here. First, when you apply a `using` declaration to the name of a member of a base class, you must qualify the name with the base class name, because this specifies the context for the member name. Second, note that you don't supply a parameter list or a return type for a member function—just the qualified name. This implies that overloaded functions always come as a package deal. Third, the `using` declaration also works with inherited member variables in a derived class.

You can use a `using` declaration to override an original `public` or `protected` base class access specifier in a base class. For example, if the `volume()` function was `protected` in the Box base class, you could make it `public` in the derived `Carton` class with the same `using` declaration in a `public` section of `Carton`. However, you can't apply a `using` declaration to relax the specification of a `private` member of a base class because `private` members cannot be accessed in a derived class.

Constructors in a Derived Class

If you put output statements in the constructors for the `Carton` class and the `Box` class and rerun the example, you'll see what happens when a `Carton` object is created. You'll need to define the default Box and Carton class constructors to include the output statements. Creating each Carton object always results in the default no-arg Box constructor being called first, followed by the Carton class constructor.

Derived class objects are always created in the same way, even when there are several levels of derivation. The most base class constructor is called first, followed by the constructor for the class derived from that, followed by the constructor for the class derived from that, and so on, until the constructor for the most derived class is called. This makes sense if you think about it. A derived class object has a complete base class object inside it, and this needs to be created before the rest of the derived class object. If that base class is derived from another class, the same applies.

Although in `Ex13_01` the default base class constructor was called automatically, this doesn't have to be the case. You can call a particular base class constructor in the initialization list for the derived class constructor. This will enable you to initialize the base class member variables with a constructor other than the default. It will also allow you to choose a particular base class constructor, depending on the data supplied to the derived class constructor. Let's see it working in another example.

Here's a new version of the Box class:

```
class Box
{
protected:
  double length {1.0};
  double width {1.0};
  double height {1.0};

public:
  // Constructors
  Box(double lv, double wv, double hv) : length{lv}, width{wv}, height{hv}
  { std::cout << "Box(double, double, double) called.\n"; }

  explicit Box(double side) : Box{side, side, side}
  { std::cout << "Box(double) called.\n"; }

  Box() { std::cout << "Box() called.\n"; }    // No-arg constructor

  double volume() const { return length * width * height; }

  // Accessors
  double getLength() const { return length; }
  double getWidth()  const { return width; }
  double getHeight() const { return height; }
};
```

There are now three Box constructors, and they all output a message when they are called.
operator<<() is defined as in Ex13_01.
     The Carton class looks like this:

```
class Carton : public Box
{
private:
  std::string material {"Cardboard"};

public:
  Carton(double lv, double wv, double hv, std::string_view mat)
    : Box{lv, wv, hv}, material{mat}
  { std::cout << "Carton(double,double,double,string_view) called.\n"; }

  explicit Carton(std::string_view mat) : material{mat}
  { std::cout << "Carton(string_view) called.\n"; }

  Carton(double side, std::string_view mat) : Box{side}, material{mat}
  { std::cout << "Carton(double,string_view) called.\n"; }

  Carton() { std::cout << "Carton() called.\n"; }
};
```

This class has four constructors, including a no-arg constructor. You must define this here because if you define any constructor, the compiler will not supply a default no-arg constructor. As always, we declare our single-argument constructor to be explicit to avoid unwanted implicit conversions.

Here's the code to exercise this class:

```
// Ex13_02.cpp
// Calling base class constructors in a derived class constructor
#include <iostream>
#include "Carton.h"                    // For the Carton class

int main()
{
  // Create four Carton objects
  Carton carton1;                              std::cout << std::endl;
  Carton carton2 {"Thin cardboard"};           std::cout << std::endl;
  Carton carton3 {4.0, 5.0, 6.0, "Plastic"};   std::cout << std::endl;
  Carton carton4 {2.0, "paper"};               std::cout << std::endl;

  std::cout << "carton1 volume is " << carton1.volume() << std::endl;
  std::cout << "carton2 volume is " << carton2.volume() << std::endl;
  std::cout << "carton3 volume is " << carton3.volume() << std::endl;
  std::cout << "carton4 volume is " << carton4.volume() << std::endl;
}
```

The output is as follows:

```
Box() called.
Carton() called.

Box() called.
Carton(string) called.

Box(double, double, double) called.
Carton(double,double,double,string) called.

Box(double, double, double) called.
Box(double) called.
Carton(double,string) called.

carton1 volume is 1
carton2 volume is 1
carton3 volume is 120
carton4 volume is 8
```

The output shows which constructors are called for each of the four Carton objects that are created in main():

- Creating the first Carton object, carton1, results in the no-arg constructor for the Box class being called first, followed by the no-arg constructor for the Carton class.

- Creating carton2 calls the no-arg Box constructor followed by the Carton constructor with a string_view parameter.

- Creating the carton3 object calls the Box constructor with three parameters followed by the Carton constructor with four parameters.

- Creating carton4 causes two Box constructors to be called because the Box constructor with a single parameter of type double that is called by the Carton constructor calls the Box constructor with three parameters in its initialization list.

This is all consistent, with constructors being called in sequence from the most base to the most derived.

■ **Note**   The notation for calling the base class constructor is the same as that used for initializing member variables in a constructor. This is perfectly consistent with what you're doing here, because essentially you're initializing the Box subobject of the Carton object using the arguments passed to the Carton constructor.

Although inherited member variables that are not private to the base class can be *accessed* from a derived class, they can't be *initialized* in the initialization list for a derived class constructor. For example, try replacing the first Carton class constructor in Ex13_02 with the following:

```
// Constructor that won't compile!
Carton::Carton(double lv, double wv, double hv, std::string_view mat)
  : length{lv}, width{wv}, height{hv}, material{mat}
  { std::cout << "Carton(double,double,double,string_view) called.\n"; }
```

You might expect this to work because length, width, and height are protected base class members that are inherited publicly, so the Carton class constructor should be able to access them. However, the compiler complains that length, width, and height are *not* members of the Carton class. This will be the case even if you make the member variables of the Box class public. If you want to initialize the inherited member variables explicitly, you could do it in the *body* of the derived class constructor. The following constructor definition would work:

```
// Constructor that will compile!
Carton::Carton(double lv, double wv, double hv, std::string_view mat) : material{mat}
{
  length = lv;
  width = wv;
  height = hv;
  std::cout << "Carton(double,double,double,string_view) called.\n";
}
```

By the time the body of the Carton constructor begins executing, the base part of the object has been created. In this case, the base part of the Carton object is created by an implicit call of the no-arg Box class constructor. You can subsequently refer to the names of the non-private base class members without a problem. Still, if possible, it is always best to forward constructor arguments to an appropriate base class constructor and have the base class deal with initializing the inherited members.

The Copy Constructor in a Derived Class

You already know that the copy constructor is called when an object is created and initialized with another object of the same class type. The compiler will supply a default copy constructor that creates the new object by copying the original object member by member if you haven't defined your own version. Now let's examine the copy constructor in a derived class. To do this, we'll add to the class definitions in Ex13_02. First, we'll add a copy constructor to the base class, Box, by inserting the following code in the public section of the class definition:

```
// Copy constructor
Box(const Box& box) : length{box.length}, width{box.width}, height{box.height}
{ std::cout << "Box copy constructor" << std::endl; }
```

■ **Note**   You saw in Chapter 11 that the parameter for the copy constructor *must* be a reference.

This initializes the member variables by copying the original values and generates some output to track when the copy constructor is called.

Here's a first attempt at a copy constructor for the Carton class:

```
// Copy constructor
Carton(const Carton& carton) : material {carton.material}
{ std::cout << "Carton copy constructor" << std::endl; }
```

Let's see if this works (it won't!):

```
// Ex13_03
// Using a derived class copy constructor
#include <iostream>
#include "Carton.h"                    // For the Carton class

int main()
{
  // Declare and initialize a Carton object
  Carton carton(20.0, 30.0, 40.0, "Glassine board");
  std::cout << std::endl;

  Carton cartonCopy(carton);           // Use copy constructor
  std::cout << std::endl;

  std::cout << "Volume of carton is " << carton.volume() << std::endl
            << "Volume of cartonCopy is " << cartonCopy.volume() << std::endl;
}
```

This produces the following output:

```
Box(double, double, double) called.
Carton(double,double,double,string_view) called.

Box() called.
Carton copy constructor

Volume of carton is 24000
Volume of cartonCopy is 1
```

All is not as it should be. Clearly the volume of cartonCopy isn't the same as carton, but the output also shows the reason for this. To copy the carton object, you call the copy constructor for the Carton class. The Carton copy constructor should make a copy of the Box subobject of carton, and to do this it *should* call the Box copy constructor. However, the output clearly shows that the *default* Box constructor is being called instead.

The Carton copy constructor won't call the Box copy constructor if you don't tell it to do so. The compiler knows that it has to create a Box subobject for the object carton, but if you don't specify how, the compiler won't second-guess your intentions—it will just create a default base object.

▓ **Caution**   When you define a constructor for a derived class, you are responsible for ensuring that the members of the derived class object are properly initialized. This includes all the directly inherited member variables, as well as the member variables that are specific to the derived class. Moreover, this applies to any constructor, including copy constructors.

The obvious fix for this is to call the Box copy constructor in the initialization list of the Carton copy constructor. Simply change the copy constructor definition to this:

```
Carton(const Carton& carton) : Box{carton}, material{carton.material}
{ std::cout << "Carton copy constructor" << std::endl; }
```

The Box copy constructor is called with the carton object as an argument. The carton object is of type Carton, but it is also a perfectly good Box object. The parameter for the Box class copy constructor is a reference to a Box object, so the compiler will pass carton as type Box&, which will result in only the base part of carton being passed to the Box copy constructor. If you compile and run the example again, the output will be as follows:

```
Box(double, double, double) called.
Carton(double,double,double,string_view) called.
Box copy constructor
Carton copy constructor
Volume of carton is 24000
Volume of cartonCopy is 24000
```

The output shows that the constructors are called in the correct order. In particular, the Box copy constructor is called to create the Box subobject of carton before the Carton copy constructor. By way of a check, you can see that the volumes of the carton and cartonCopy objects are now identical.

The Default Constructor in a Derived Class

You know that the compiler will not supply a default no-arg constructor if you define one or more constructors for a class. You also know that you can tell the compiler to insert a default constructor in any event using the default keyword. You could replace the definition of the no-arg constructor in the Carton class definition in Ex13_02 with this statement:

```
Carton() = default;
```

Now the compiler will supply a definition, even though you have defined other constructors. The definition that the compiler supplies for a derived class calls the base class constructor, so it looks like this:

```
Carton() : Box{} {};
```

This implies that if the compiler supplies the no-arg constructor in a derived class, a non-private no-arg constructor *must* exist in the base class. If it doesn't, the code will not compile. You can easily demonstrate this either by removing the no-arg constructor from the Box class in Ex13_02 or by making it private. With the compiler-supplied default constructor specified for the Carton class, the code will no longer compile. Every derived class constructor calls a base class constructor. If a derived class constructor does not explicitly call a base constructor in its initialization list, the no-arg constructor will be called.

Inheriting Constructors

Base class constructors are not normally inherited in a derived class. This is because a derived class typically has additional member variables that need to be initialized, and a base class constructor would have no knowledge of these. However, you can cause constructors to be inherited from a direct base class by putting a using declaration in the derived class. Here's how a version of the Carton class from Ex13_02 could be made to inherit the Box class constructors:

```
class Carton : public Box
{
using Box::Box;                              // Inherit Box class constructors

private:
  std::string material {"Cardboard"};

public:
  Carton(double lv, double wv, double hv, std::string_view mat)
    : Box{lv, wv, hv}, material{mat}
    { std::cout << "Carton(double,double,double,string_view) called.\n"; }
};
```

If the Box class definition is the same as in Ex13_02, the Carton class will inherit two constructors: Box(double, double, double) and Box(double). The constructors in the derived class will look like this:

```
Carton(double lv, double, wv, double hv) : Box {lv, wv, hv} {}
explicit Carton(double side) : Box{side} {}
```

Each inherited constructor has the same parameter list as the base constructor and calls the base constructor in its initialization list. The body of each constructor is empty. You can add further constructors to a derived class that inherits from its direct base, as the Carton class example illustrates.

Unlike regular member functions, (non-`private`) constructors are inherited using the same access specifier as the corresponding constructor in the base class. So, even though the `using Box::Box` declaration is part of the implicitly `private` section of the `Carton` class, the constructors inherited from `Box` are both `public`. If the `Box` class would've had `protected` constructors, these would've been inherited as `protected` constructors in `Carton` as well.

Notice that one constructor of `Box` is flagrantly missing from the list of inherited constructors: the default constructor. That is, the `using` declaration did not cause a default constructor of the following form to be inherited:

```
Carton() : Box{} {}
```

Default constructors are never inherited. And because `Carton` explicitly defines a constructor (inherited constructors do not count here, by the way), the compiler did not generate a default default constructor either. Technically speaking, copy constructors are not inherited either, but you won't notice this as the compiler mostly generates a default copy constructor anyway. You could try this by modifying `Ex13_02` to create the following objects in `main()`:

```
// Carton cart;                          // Does not compile: default constructor is not inherited!
  Carton cube{4.0};                          // Calls inherited constructor
  Carton cartcopy { cube };                  // Calls default copy constructor
  Carton carton {1.0, 2.0, 3.0};             // Calls inherited constructor
  Carton candyCarton (50.0, 30.0, 20.0, "Thin cardboard"); // Calls Carton class constructor
```

The resulting program is available online as `Ex13_04`. The output statements in the `Box` constructors will show that they are indeed called to create the first three objects. Of course, if you want `Carton` to have a default constructor, you could always instruct the compiler to generate one using the `default` keyword.

Destructors Under Inheritance

Destroying a derived class object involves both the derived class destructor *and* the base class destructor. You can demonstrate this by adding destructors with output statements in the `Box` and `Carton` class definitions. You can amend the class definitions in the correct version of `Ex13_03`. Add the destructor definition to the `Box` class:

```
// Destructor
~Box() { std::cout << "Box destructor" << std::endl; }
```

And for the `Carton` class:

```
// Destructor
~Carton()
{
  std::cout << "Carton destructor. Material = " << material << std::endl;
}
```

Of course, if the classes allocated free store memory and stored the address in a raw pointer, defining the class destructor would be essential to avoid memory leaks. The Carton destructor outputs the material so you can tell which Carton object is being destroyed by assigning a different material to each. Let's see how these classes behave in practice:

```
// Ex13_05.cpp
// Destructors in a class hierarchy
#include <iostream>
#include "Carton.h"                              // For the Carton class

int main()
{
  Carton carton;
  Carton candyCarton{50.0, 30.0, 20.0, "Thin cardboard"};

  std::cout << "carton volume is " << carton.volume() << std::endl;
  std::cout << "candyCarton volume is " << candyCarton.volume() << std::endl;
}
```

Here's the output:

```
Box() called.
Carton() called.
Box(double, double, double) called.
Carton(double,double,double,string_view) called.
carton volume is 1
candyCarton volume is 30000
Carton destructor. Material = Thin cardboard
Box destructor
Carton destructor. Material = Cardboard
Box destructor
```

The point of this exercise is to see how the destructors behave. The output from the destructor calls indicates two aspects of how objects are destroyed. First, you can see the order in which destructors are called for a particular object, and second, you can see the order in which the objects are destroyed. The destructor calls recorded by the output correspond to the following actions:

Destructor Output	Object Destroyed
Carton destructor. Material = Thin cardboard.	candyCarton object
Box destructor.	Box subobject of candyCarton
Carton destructor. Material = Cardboard.	carton object
Box destructor.	Box subobject of carton

This shows that the objects that make up a derived class object are destroyed in the *reverse* order from which they were created. The carton object was created first and destroyed last; the candyCarton object was created last and destroyed first. This order is chosen to ensure that you never end up with an object in an illegal state. An object can be used only after it has been defined—this means that any given object can only contain pointers (or references) that point (or refer) to objects that have already been created. By destroying a given object *before* any objects that it might point (or refer) to, you ensure that the execution of a destructor can't result in any invalid pointers or references.

510

The Order in Which Destructors Are Called

The order of destructor calls for a derived class object is the reverse of the constructor call sequence for the object. The derived class destructor is called first, and then the base class destructor is called, just as in the example. Figure 13-6 illustrates the case of a three-level class hierarchy.

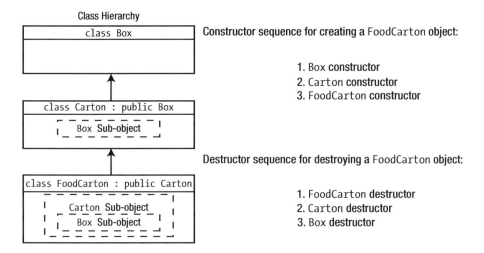

Figure 13-6. *The order of destructor calls for derived class objects*

For an object with several levels of derivation classes, this order of destructor calls runs through the hierarchy of classes, starting with the most derived class destructor and ending with the destructor for the most base class.

Duplicate Member Variable Names

It's possible that a base class and a derived class each have a member variable with the same name. If you're really unlucky, you might even have names duplicated in the base class and in an indirect base. Of course, this is confusing, and you should never deliberately set out to create such an arrangement in your own classes. However, circumstances or oversights may make that this is how things turn out. So, what happens if member variables in the base and derived classes have the same names?

Duplication of names is no bar to inheritance, and you can differentiate between identically named base and derived class members. Suppose you have a class Base, defined as follows:

```
class Base
{
public:
  Base(int number = 10) : value{number} {}          // Constructor

protected:
  int value;
};
```

This just contains a single member variable, value, and a constructor. You can derive a class Derived from Base as follows:

```
class Derived : public Base
{
public:
  Derived(int number = 20) : value{number} {}        // Constructor
  int total() const;                                 // Total value of member variables

protected:
  int value;
};
```

The derived class has a member variable called value, and it will also inherit the value member of the base class. You can see that it's already starting to look confusing! We'll show how you can distinguish the two members with the name value in the derived class by writing a definition for the total() function. Within the derived class member function, value by itself refers to the member declared within that scope, that is, the derived class member. The base class member is declared within a different scope, and to access it from a derived class member function, you must qualify the member name with the base class name. Thus, you can write the total() function as follows:

```
int Derived::total() const
{
  return value + Base::value;
}
```

The expression Base::value refers to the base class member, and value by itself refers to the member declared in the Derived class.

Duplicate Member Function Names

What happens when base class and derived class member functions share the same name? There are two situations that can arise in relation to this. The first is when the functions have the same name but different parameter lists. Although the function signatures are different, this is *not* a case of function overloading. This is because overloaded functions must be defined within the same scope, and each class, base or derived, defines a separate scope. In fact, scope is the key to the situation. A derived class member function will *hide* an inherited member function with the same name. Thus, when base and derived member functions have the same name, you must introduce the qualified name of the base class member function into the scope of the derived class with a using declaration if you want to access it. Either function can then be called for a derived class object, as illustrated in Figure 13-7.

```
class Base
{
public:                          By default the derived class function doThat( ) would hide
  void doThat(int arg);          the inherited function with the same name. The using
  ...                            declaration introduces the base class function name,
};                               doThat, into the derived class's scope, so both versions of
                                 the function are available within the derived class. The
                                 compiler can distinguish them in the derived class because
class Derived: public Base       they have different signatures.
{
public:                          Derived object;
  void doThat(double arg);       object.doThat(2);    // Call inherited base function
  using Base::doThat;            object.doThat(2.5);  // Call derived function
  ...
};
```

Figure 13-7. *Inheriting a function with the same name as a member function*

The second possibility is that both functions have the same function signature. You can still differentiate the inherited function from the derived class function by using the class name as a qualifier for the base class function:

```
Derived object;              // Object declaration
object.Base::doThat(3);      // Call base version of the function
```

However, there's a lot more to this latter case than we can discuss at this point. This subject is closely related to polymorphism, which is explored in much more depth in the next chapter.

Multiple Inheritance

So far, your derived classes have all been derived from a *single* direct base class. However, you're not limited to this structure. A derived class can have as many direct base classes as an application requires. This is referred to as *multiple inheritance* as opposed to *single inheritance*, in which a single base class is used. This opens vast new dimensions of potential complexity in inheritance, which is perhaps why multiple inheritance is used much less frequently than single inheritance. Because of the complexity, it is best used judiciously. We'll just explain the basic ideas behind how multiple inheritance works.

Multiple Base Classes

Multiple inheritance involves two or more base classes being used to derive a new class, so things are immediately more complicated. The idea of a derived class being a specialization of its base leads in this case to the notion that the derived class defines an object that is a specialization of two or more different and independent class types concurrently. In practice, multiple inheritance is rarely used in this way. More often, multiple base classes are used to add the features of the base classes together to form a composite object containing the capabilities of its base classes, sometimes referred to as *mixin* programming. This is usually for convenience in an implementation rather than to reflect any particular relationships between objects. For example, you might consider a programming interface of some kind—for graphics programming, perhaps. A comprehensive interface could be packaged in a set of classes, each of which defines a self-contained interface that provides some specific capability, such as drawing two-dimensional shapes. You can then use several of these classes as bases for a new class that provides precisely the set of capabilities you need for an application.

To explore some of the implications of multiple inheritance, we'll start with a hierarchy that includes the Box and Carton classes. Suppose you need a class that represents a package containing dry contents, such as a carton of cereal. It's possible to do this by using single inheritance, deriving a new class from the Carton class, and adding a member variable to represent contents, but you could also do it using the hierarchy illustrated in Figure 13-8.

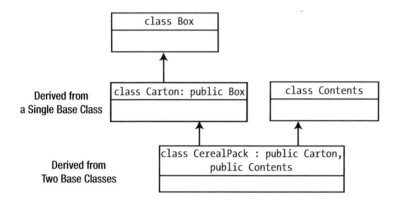

Figure 13-8. *An example of multiple inheritance*

The definition of the CerealPack class looks like this:

```
class CerealPack : public Carton, public Contents
{
  // Details of the class...
};
```

Each base class is specified after the colon in the class header, and the base classes are separated by commas. Each base class has its own access specifier, and if you omit the access specifier, private is assumed, the same as with single inheritance. The CerealPack class will inherit *all* the members of *both* base classes, so this will include the members of the indirect base, Box. As in the case of single inheritance, the access level of each inherited member is determined by two factors: the access specifier of the member in the base class and the base class access specifier. A CerealPack object contains two subobjects, a Contents subobject and a Carton subobject that has a further subobject of type Box.

Inherited Member Ambiguity

Multiple inheritance can create problems. We'll put together an example that will show the sort of complications you can run into. The Box class is the same as in Ex13_05, but we'll extend the Carton class from that example a little:

```
class Carton : public Box
{
protected:
  std::string material {"Cardboard"};
  double thickness {0.125};               // Material thickness inches
  double density {0.2};                   // Material density in pounds/cubic inch
```

```
public:
  // Constructors
  Carton(double lv, double wv, double hv, std::string_view mat)
    : Box{lv, wv, hv}, material{mat}
  {
    std::cout << "Carton(double,double,double,string_view) called.\n";
  }

  explicit Carton(std::string_view mat)
    : material{mat}
  { std::cout << "Carton(string_view) called.\n"; }

  Carton(double side, std::string_view mat)
    : Box{side}, material{mat}
  {
    std::cout << "Carton(double,string_view) called.\n";
  }

  Carton()
  {
    std::cout << "Carton() called.\n";
  }

  Carton(double lv, double wv, double hv, std::string_view mat, double dense, double thick)
    : Carton{lv, wv, hv, mat}
  {
    density = dense;
    thickness = thick;
    std::cout << "Carton(double,double,double,string_view,double,double) called.\n";
  }

  // Copy constructor
  Carton(const Carton& carton) : Box{carton}, material{carton.material}
  {
    std::cout << "Carton copy constructor" << std::endl;
  }

  // Destructor
  ~Carton()
  {
    std::cout << "Carton destructor. Material = " << material << std::endl;
  }

  // "Get carton weight" function
  double getWeight() const
  {
    return 2.0*(length*width + width*height + height*length)*thickness*density;
  }
};
```

We've added two member variables that record the thickness and density of the material from which the Carton object is made; a new constructor that allows all member variables to be set; and a new member function, getWeight(), which calculates the weight of an empty Carton object. The new constructor calls another Carton class constructor in its initialization list, so it is a delegating constructor, as you saw in Chapter 11. A delegating constructor cannot have further initializers in the list, so the values for density and thickness have to be set in the constructor body.

The Contents class will describe an amount of a dry product, such as breakfast cereal, that can be contained in a carton. The class will have three member variables: name, volume, and density (in pounds per cubic inch). In practice, you would probably include a set of possible cereal types, complete with their densities, so that you could validate the data in the constructor, but we'll ignore such niceties in the interest of keeping things simple. Here's the class definition along with the preprocessing directives that you need in the header file, Contents.h:

```cpp
// Contents.h - Dry contents
#ifndef CONTENTS_H
#define CONTENTS_H
#include <string>
#include <string_view>
#include <iostream>

class Contents
{
protected:
  std::string name {"cereal"};        // Contents type
  double volume {};                   // Cubic inches
  double density {0.03};              // Pounds per cubic inch

public:
  Contents(std::string_view name, double dens, double vol)
    : name {name}, density {dens}, volume {vol}
  { std::cout << "Contents(string_view,double,double) called.\n"; }

  Contents(std::string_view name) : name {name}
  { std::cout << "Contents(string_view) called.\n"; }

  Contents() { std::cout << "Contents() called.\n"; }

  // Destructor
  ~Contents()
  {
    std::cout << "Contents destructor" << std::endl;
  }

  // "Get contents weight" function
  double getWeight() const
  {
    return volume * density;
  }
};
#endif
```

In addition to the constructors and the destructor, the class has a `public` member function, `getWeight()`, to calculate the weight of the contents. Note how the `name` member is initialized in the member initializer list with the parameter value that has the same name. This is just to illustrate that this is possible—not a recommended approach. We'll define the `CerealPack` class with the `Carton` and `Contents` classes as `public` base classes:

```
// Cerealpack.h - Class defining a carton of cereal
#ifndef CEREALPACK_H
#define CEREALPACK_H
#include <iostream>
#include "Carton.h"
#include "Contents.h"

class CerealPack : public Carton, public Contents
{
public:
  CerealPack(double length, double width, double height, std::string_view cerealType)
    : Carton {length, width, height, "cardboard"}, Contents {cerealType}
  {
    std::cout << "CerealPack constructor" << std::endl;
    Contents::volume = 0.9 * Carton::volume();            // Set contents volume
  }

  // Destructor
  ~CerealPack()
  {
    std::cout << "CerealPack destructor" << std::endl;
  }
};
#endif
```

This class inherits from both the `Carton` and `Contents` classes. The constructor requires only the external dimensions and the cereal type. The material for the `Carton` object is set in the `Carton` constructor call, in the initialization list. A `CerealPack` object will contain two subobjects corresponding to the two base classes. Each subobject is initialized through constructor calls in the initialization list for the `CerealPack` constructor. Note that the `volume` member variable of the `Contents` class is zero by default, so, in the body of the `CerealPack` constructor, the value is calculated from the size of the carton. The reference to the `volume` member variable inherited from the `Contents` class must be qualified here because it's the same as the name of the function inherited from `Box` via `Carton`. You'll be able to trace the order of constructor and destructor calls from the output statements here and in the other classes.

Let's try creating a `CerealPack` object and calculate its volume and weight with the following simple program:

```
// Ex13_06 - doesn't compile!
// Using multiple inheritance
#include <iostream>
#include "CerealPack.h"                  // For the CerealPack class
```

```
int main()
{
  CerealPack cornflakes {8.0, 3.0, 10.0, "Cornflakes"};

  std::cout << "cornflakes volume is " << cornflakes.volume() << std::endl
            << "cornflakes weight is " << cornflakes.getWeight() << std::endl;
}
```

Unfortunately, there's a problem. The program won't compile. The difficulty is that we have foolishly used some nonunique function names in the base classes. The name volume is inherited as a function from Box and as a member variable from Contents, and the getWeight() function is inherited from Carton and from Contents in the CerealPack class. There's more than one ambiguity problem.

Of course, when writing classes for use in inheritance, you should avoid duplicating member names in the first instance. The ideal solution to this problem is to rewrite your classes. If you are unable to rewrite the classes—if the base classes are from a library of some sort, for example—then you would be forced to qualify the function names in main(). You could amend the output statement in main() to get the code to work:

```
  std::cout << "cornflakes volume is " << cornflakes.Carton::volume() << std::endl
            << "cornflakes weight is " << cornflakes.Contents::getWeight() << std::endl;
```

With this change, the program will compile and run, and it will produce the following output:

```
Box(double, double, double) called.
Carton(double,double,double,string_view) called.
Contents(string_view) called.
CerealPack constructor
cornflakes volume is 240
cornflakes weight is 6.48
CerealPack destructor
Contents destructor
Carton destructor. Material = cardboard
Box destructor
```

You can see from the output that this cereal will give you a solid start to the day—a single packet weighs more than six pounds. You can also see that the constructor and destructor call sequences follow the same pattern as in the single inheritance context: the constructors run down the hierarchy from most base to most derived, and the destructors run in the opposite order. The CerealPack object has subobjects from both legs of its inheritance chain, and all the constructors for these subobjects are involved in the creation of a CerealPack object.

An alternative way of making Ex13_06 compile, by the way, is by adding casts to a reference to either of the base classes (we cast to a reference and not the class type itself to avoid the creation of a new object):

```
  std::cout << "cornflakes volume is " << static_cast<Carton&>(cornflakes).volume()
            << std::endl
            << "cornflakes weight is " << static_cast<Contents&>(cornflakes).getWeight()
            << std::endl;
```

A working version along these lines is in the code download as Ex13_06A.

But, wait, we're not done yet! There's yet another way of ensuring that this compiles—one that is definitely worth mentioning as well. Clearly it is inconvenient that users of your CerealPack class always have to disambiguate the volume() and getWeight() members. Luckily, you can typically prevent this from happening. Suppose we insist in the insanity that a CerealPack's volume should always be computed using the volume() member of Carton and its weight using the getWeight() member of Contents. Then you could stipulate this property as such in the definition of its class (see Ex13_06B) as follows:

```
class CerealPack : public Carton, public Contents
{
public:
  // Constructor and destructor as before...

  using Carton::volume;
  using Contents::getWeight;
};
```

Earlier this chapter you encountered a similar use of the using keyword to inherit constructors from the base class. In this case you use it to cherry-pick from which base class a multiply inherited member function needs to be inherited. Now CerealPack users—or breakfast eaters, as they are more commonly known as—can simply write this:

```
std::cout << "cornflakes volume is " << cornflakes.volume() << std::endl
          << "cornflakes weight is " << cornflakes.getWeight() << std::endl;
```

Clearly this last option is thus preferred whenever there is a clear answer as to which multiply inherited members should be used. If you disambiguate the inheritance already in the class definition, it saves the users of your class the hassle of fighting against the compiler errors that would otherwise surely follow.

Repeated Inheritance

The previous example demonstrated how ambiguities can occur when member names of base classes are duplicated. Another ambiguity can arise in multiple inheritances when a derived object contains multiple versions of a subobject of one of the base classes. You must not use a class more than once as a direct base class, but it's possible to end up with duplication of an *indirect* base class. Suppose the Box and Contents classes in Ex13_06 were themselves derived from a class Common. Figure 13-9 shows the class hierarchy that is created.

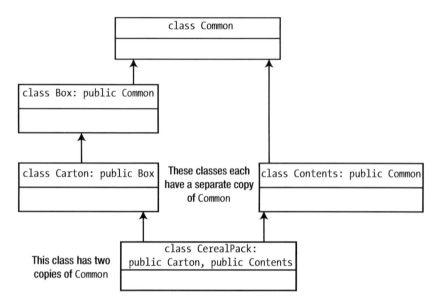

Figure 13-9. *Duplicate base classes in a derived class*

The CerealPack class inherits all the members of both the Contents and Carton classes. The Carton class inherits all the members of the Box class, and both the Box and Contents classes inherit the members of the Common class. Thus, as Figure 13-9 shows, the Common class is duplicated in the CerealPack class. The effect of this on objects of type CerealPack is that every CerealPack object will have two subobjects of type Common. The complications and ambiguities that arise from such repeated inheritance are often referred to as the *diamond problem*—named after the shape of inheritance diagrams such as Figure 13-9.

It is conceivable that you actually want to *allow* the duplication of the Common class. In this case, you must qualify each reference to the Common class member so that the compiler can tell which inherited member you're referring to in any particular instance. In this case, you can do this by using the Carton and Contents class names as qualifiers because each of these classes contains a unique subobject of type Common. Of course, to call the Common class constructors when you're creating a CerealPack object, you would also need qualifiers to specify which of the two base objects you were initializing. More typically, though, you would want to *prevent* the duplication of a base class, so let's see how to do that.

Virtual Base Classes

To avoid duplication of a base class, you must identify to the compiler that the base class should appear only once within a derived class. You do this by specifying the class as a *virtual base class* using the virtual keyword. The Contents class would be defined like this:

```
class Contents : public virtual Common
{
  ...
};
```

The Box class would also be defined with a `virtual` base class:

```
class Box : public virtual Common
{
  ...
};
```

Now any class that uses the Contents and Box classes as direct or indirect bases will inherit the other members of the base classes as usual but will inherit only one instance of the Common class. The derived CerealPack class would inherit only a single instance of the Common base class. Because there is no duplication of the members of Common in the CerealPack class, no qualification of the member names is needed when referring to them in the derived class.

Converting Between Related Class Types

Every derived class object has a base class object inside it waiting to get out. Conversions from a derived type to its base are always legal and automatic. Here's a definition of a Carton object:

```
Carton carton{40, 50, 60, "fiberboard"};
```

We have already seen two ways this object can be converted to a base class object of type Box. The first is by means of a copy constructor:

```
Box box{carton};
```

And the second is a copy assignment:

```
Box box;
box = carton;
```

Both convert the carton object to a new object of type Box and store a copy of it in box. The assignment operator that is used is the default assignment operator for the Box class. Of course, only the Box subobject part of carton is used; a Box object has no room for the Carton-specific member variables. This effect is called *object slicing*, as the Carton specific portion is sliced off, so to speak, and discarded.

■ **Caution**   Object slicing is something to beware of in general because it can occur when you don't want a derived class object to have its derived members sliced off. In the next chapter, you will learn about the mechanism that allows working with pointers or references to base class objects, while preserving the members and even behavior of the derived class.

Conversions up a class hierarchy (that is, toward the base class) are legal and automatic as long as there is no ambiguity. Ambiguity can arise when two base classes each have the same type of subobject. For example, if you use the definition of the CerealPack class that contains two Common subobjects (as you saw in the previous section) and you initialize a CerealPack object, cornflakes, then the following will be ambiguous:

```
Common common{cornflakes};
```

The compiler won't be able to determine whether the conversion of cornflakes should be to the Common subobject of Carton or to the Common subobject of Contents. The solution here would be to cast cornflakes to either Carton& or Contents&. Here's an example:

```
Common common{static_cast<Carton&>(cornflakes)};
```

You can't obtain automatic conversions for objects down a class hierarchy—that is, toward a more specialized class. A Box object contains no information about any class type that may be derived from Box, so the conversion doesn't have a sensible interpretation. In the next chapter, you'll see that pointers and references are different. A pointer or reference to a base class type can store the address of a derived class object, in which case you can cast it to one for the derived class type.

Summary

In this chapter, you learned how to define a class based on one or more existing classes and how class inheritance determines the makeup of a derived class. Inheritance is a fundamental characteristic of object-oriented programming, and it makes polymorphism possible (polymorphism is the subject of the next chapter). The important points to take from this chapter include the following:

- A class may be derived from one or more base classes, in which case the derived class inherits members from all of its bases.

- Single inheritance involves deriving a class from a single base class. Multiple inheritance involves deriving a class from two or more base classes.

- Access to the inherited members of a derived class is controlled by two factors: the access specifier of the member in the base class and the access specifier of the base class in the derived class declaration.

- A constructor for a derived class is responsible for initializing all members of the class, including the inherited members.

- Creation of a derived class object always involves the constructors of all of the direct and indirect base classes, which are called in sequence (from the most base through to the most direct) prior to the execution of the derived class constructor.

- A derived class constructor can, and often should, explicitly call constructors for its direct bases in the initialization list for the constructor. If you don't call one explicitly, the base class's default constructor is called. A copy constructor in a derived class, for one, should always call the copy constructor of all direct base classes.

- A member name declared in a derived class, which is the same as an inherited member name, will hide the inherited member. To access the hidden member, use the scope resolution operator to qualify the member name with its class name.

- You can use using not only for type aliases but also to inherit constructors (always with the same access specification as in the base class), to modify the access specifications of other inherited members, or to inherit functions that would otherwise be hidden by a derived class's function with the same name but different signature.

- When a derived class with two or more direct base classes contains two or more inherited subobjects of the same class, the duplication can be prevented by declaring the duplicated class as a virtual base class.

EXERCISES

The following exercises enable you to try what you've learned in this chapter. If you get stuck, look back over the chapter for help. If you're still stuck, you can download the solutions from the Apress website (www.apress.com/source-code), but that really should be a last resort.

Exercise 13-1. Define a base class called Animal that contains two private member variables: a string to store the name of the animal (e.g., "Fido" or "Yogi") and an integer member called weight that will contain the weight of the animal in pounds. Also include a public member function, who(), that outputs a message giving the name and weight of the Animal object. Derive two classes named Lion and Aardvark, with Animal as a public base class. Write a main() function to create Lion and Aardvark objects ("Leo" at 400 pounds and "Algernon" at 50 pounds, say) and demonstrate that the who() member is inherited in both derived classes by calling it for the derived class objects.

Exercise 13-2. Change the access specifier for the who() function in the Animal class to protected, but leave the rest of the class as before. Now modify the derived classes so that the original version of main() still works without alteration.

Exercise 13-3. In the solution to the previous exercise, change the access specifier for the who() member of the base class back to public, and implement the who() function as a member of each derived class so that the output message also identifies the name of the class. Change main() to call the base class and derived class versions of who() for each of the derived class objects.

Exercise 13-4. Define a Person class containing member variables for age, name, and gender. Derive an Employee class from Person that adds a member variable to store a personnel number. Derive an Executive class from Employee. Each derived class should define a member function who() that displays information about what it is. Think carefully about proper data hiding and access specifiers in this exercise. In this particular application, privacy concerns prohibit the exposure of personal details, except for the information printed by an object's who() member. Each class can decide explicitly what to expose there. (Name and type will do—something like "Fred Smith is an Employee.") Furthermore, people also aren't allowed to change name or gender, but they are allowed to have birthdays. Write a main() function to generate a vector of five executives and a vector of five ordinary employees and display information about them. In addition, display the information on the executives by calling the member function inherited from the Employee class.

CHAPTER 14

■ ■ ■

Polymorphism

Polymorphism is such a powerful feature of object-oriented programming that you'll use it in the majority of your C++ programs. Polymorphism requires you to use derived classes, so the content of this chapter relies heavily on the concepts related to inheritance in derived classes that we introduced in the previous chapter.

In this chapter, you'll learn:

- What polymorphism is and how you get polymorphic behavior with your classes

- What a virtual function is

- What function overriding is and how this differs from function overloading

- How default parameter values for virtual functions are used

- When and why you need virtual destructors

- How you cast between class types in a hierarchy

- What a pure virtual function is

- What an abstract class is

Understanding Polymorphism

Polymorphism is a capability provided by many object-oriented languages. In C++, polymorphism always involves the use of a pointer or a reference to an object to call a member function. Polymorphism only operates with classes that share a common base class. We'll show how polymorphism works by considering an example with more boxes, but first we'll explain the role of a pointer to a base class because it's fundamental to the process.

Using a Base Class Pointer

In the previous chapter, you saw how an object of a derived class type contains a subobject of the base class type. In other words, you can regard every derived class object as a base class object. Because of this, you can always use a pointer to a base class to store the address of a derived class object; in fact, you can use a pointer to any direct or indirect base class to store the address of a derived class object. Figure 14-1 shows how the Carton class is derived from the Box base class by single inheritance, and the CerealPack class is derived by multiple inheritances from the Carton and Contents base classes. It illustrates how pointers to base classes can be used to store addresses of derived class objects.

© Ivor Horton and Peter Van Weert 2018
I. Horton and P. Van Weert, *Beginning C++17*, https://doi.org/10.1007/978-1-4842-3366-5_14

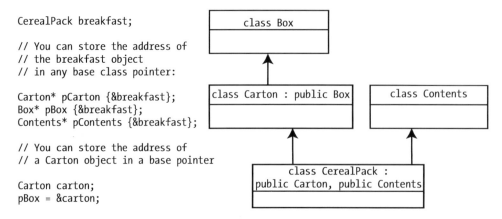

```
CerealPack breakfast;

// You can store the address of
// the breakfast object
// in any base class pointer:

Carton* pCarton {&breakfast};
Box* pBox {&breakfast};
Contents* pContents {&breakfast};

// You can store the address of
// a Carton object in a base pointer

Carton carton;
pBox = &carton;
```

Figure 14-1. *Storing the address of a derived class object in a base class pointer*

The reverse is *not* true. For instance, you can't use a pointer of type Carton* to store the address of an object of type Box. This is logical because a pointer type incorporates the type of object to which it can point. A derived class object is a specialization of its base—it *is a* base class object—so using a pointer to the base to store its address is reasonable. However, a base class object is definitely *not* a derived class object, so a pointer to a derived class type cannot point to it. A derived class always contains a complete subobject of each of its bases, but each base class represents only part of a derived class object.

We'll look at a specific example. Suppose you derive two classes from the Box class to represent different kinds of containers, Carton and ToughPack. Suppose further that the volume of each of these derived types is calculated differently. For a Carton made of cardboard, you might just reduce the volume slightly to take the thickness of the material into account. For a ToughPack object, you might have to reduce the usable volume by a considerable amount to allow for protective packaging. The Carton class definition could be of the following form:

```
class Carton : public Box
{
  // Details of the class...

public:
  double volume() const;
};
```

The ToughPack class could have a similar definition:

```
class ToughPack : public Box
{
  // Details of the class...

public:
  double volume() const;
};
```

Given these class definitions (the function definitions follow later), you can declare and initialize a pointer as follows:

```
Carton carton {10.0, 10.0, 5.0};
Box* pBox {&carton};
```

526

The pointer pBox, of type pointer to Box, has been initialized with the address of carton. This is possible because Carton is derived from Box and therefore contains a subobject of type Box. You could use the same pointer to store the address of a ToughPack object because the ToughPack class is also derived from Box:

```
ToughPack hardcase {12.0, 8.0, 4.0};
pBox = &hardcase;
```

The pBox pointer can contain the address of any object of any class that has Box as a base. The type of the pointer, Box*, is called its *static type*. Because pBox is a pointer to a *base* class, it also has a *dynamic type*, which varies according to the type of object to which it points. When pBox is pointing to a Carton object, its dynamic type is a pointer to Carton. When pBox is pointing to a ToughPack object, its dynamic type is a pointer to ToughPack. When pBox points to an object of type Box, its dynamic type is the same as its static type. The magic of polymorphism springs from this. Under conditions that we'll explain shortly, you can use the pBox pointer to call a function that's defined both in the base class and in each derived class and have the function that is actually called selected at runtime on the basis of the dynamic type of pBox. Consider these statements:

```
double vol {};
vol = pBox->volume();                          // Store volume of the object pointed to
```

If pBox contains the address of a Carton object, then this statement calls volume() for the Carton object. If it points to a ToughPack object, then this statement calls volume() for ToughPack. This works for any classes derived from Box, provided of course the aforementioned conditions are met. If they are, the expression pBox->volume() can result in different behavior depending on what pBox is pointing to. Perhaps more importantly, the behavior that is appropriate to the object pointed to by pBox is selected automatically at runtime.

Polymorphism is a powerful mechanism. Situations arise frequently in which the specific type of an object cannot be determined in advance—not at design time or at compile time. Situations, in other words, in which the type can be determined only at runtime. This can be handled easily using polymorphism. Polymorphism is commonly used with interactive applications, where the type of input is up to the whim of the user. For instance, a graphics application that allows different shapes to be drawn—circles, lines, curves, and so on—may define a derived class for each shape type, and these classes all have a common base class called Shape. A program can store the address of an object the user creates in a pointer, pShape, of type Shape* and draw the shape with a statement such as pShape->draw(). This will call the draw() function for the shape that is pointed to, so this one expression can draw any kind of shape. Let's take a more in-depth look at how inherited functions behave.

Calling Inherited Functions

Before we get to the specifics of polymorphism, we need to explain the behavior of inherited member functions a bit further. To help with this, we'll revise the Box class to include a function that calculates the volume of a Box object, and another function that displays the resulting volume. The new version of the class definition in Box.h and Box.cpp will be as follows:

```
// Box.h
#ifndef BOX_H
#define BOX_H
#include <iostream>
```

```
class Box
{
protected:
  double length {1.0};
  double width {1.0};
  double height {1.0};

public:
  Box() = default;
  Box(double lv, double wv, double hv) : length {lv}, width {wv}, height {hv} {}

  // Function to show the volume of an object
  void showVolume() const
  { std::cout << "Box usable volume is " << volume() << std::endl; }

  // Function to calculate the volume of a Box object
  double volume() const { return length * width * height; }
};
#endif
```

We can display the usable volume of a Box object by calling the showVolume() function for the object. The member variables are specified as protected, so they can be accessed by the member functions of any derived class.

We'll also define the ToughPack class with Box as a base. A ToughPack object incorporates packing material to protect its contents, so its capacity is only 85 percent of a basic Box object. Therefore, a different volume() function is needed in the derived class to account for this:

```
// ToughPack.h
#ifndef TOUGHPACK_H
#define TOUGHPACK_H

#include "Box.h"

class ToughPack : public Box
{
public:
  // Constructor
  ToughPack(double lv, double wv, double hv) : Box {lv, wv, hv} {}

  // Function to calculate volume of a ToughPack allowing 15% for packing
  double volume() const { return 0.85 * length * width * height; }
};
#endif
```

Conceivably, you could have additional members in this derived class, but for the moment, we'll keep it simple, concentrating on how the inherited functions work. The derived class constructor just calls the base class constructor in its member initializer list to set the member variable values. You don't need any statements in the body of the derived class constructor. You also have a new version of the volume()

function to replace the version from the base class. The idea here is that you can get the inherited function showVolume() to call the derived class version of volume() when you call it for an object of the ToughPack class. Let's see whether it works:

```cpp
// Ex14_01.cpp
// Behavior of inherited functions in a derived class
#include "Box.h"                          // For the Box class
#include "ToughPack.h"                    // For the ToughPack class

int main()
{
  Box box {20.0, 30.0, 40.0};            // Define a box
  ToughPack hardcase {20.0, 30.0, 40.0}; // Declare tough box - same size

  box.showVolume();                       // Display volume of base box
  hardcase.showVolume();                  // Display volume of derived box
}
```

When we run the program, we get this rather disappointing output:

```
Box usable volume is 24000
Box usable volume is 24000
```

The derived class object is supposed to have a smaller capacity than the base class object, so the program is obviously not working as intended. Let's try to establish what's going wrong. The second call to showVolume() in main() is for an object of the derived class, ToughPack, but evidently this is not being taken into account. The volume of a ToughPack object should be 85 percent of that of a basic Box object with the same dimensions.

The trouble is that when the volume() function is called by the showVolume() function, the compiler sets it once and for all as the version of volume() defined in the base class. No matter how you call showVolume(), it will never call the ToughPack version of the volume() function. When function calls are fixed in this way before the program is executed, it is called *static resolution* of the function call, or *static binding*. The term *early binding* is also commonly used. In this example, a particular volume() function is bound to the call from the function showVolume() when the program is compiled and linked. Every time showVolume() is called, it uses the base class volume() function that's bound to it.

▨ **Note**　The same kind of resolution would occur in the derived class ToughPack. If you add a showVolume() function that calls volume() to the ToughPack class, the volume() call resolves statically to the derived class function.

What if you call the volume() function for the ToughPack object directly? As a further experiment, let's add statements in main() to call the volume() function of a ToughPack object directly and also through a pointer to the base class:

```cpp
std::cout << "hardcase volume is " << hardcase.volume() << std::endl;
Box *pBox {&hardcase};
std::cout << "hardcase volume through pBox is " << pBox->volume() << std::endl;
```

529

Place these statements at the end of main(). Now when you run the program, you'll get this output:

```
Box usable volume is 24000
Box usable volume is 24000
hardcase volume is 20400
hardcase volume through pBox is 24000
```

This is quite informative. You can see that a call to volume() for the derived class object, hardcase, calls the derived class volume() function, which is what you want. The call through the base class pointer pBox, however, is resolved to the base class version of volume(), even though pBox contains the address of hardcase. In other words, both calls are resolved statically. The compiler implements these calls as follows:

```
std::cout << "hardcase volume is " << hardcase.ToughPack::volume() << std::endl;
Box *pBox {&hardcase};
std::cout << "hardcase volume through pBox is " << pBox->Box::volume() << std::endl;
```

A static function call through a pointer is determined solely by the pointer type and not by the object to which it points. In other words, it is determined by the static type rather than the dynamic type. The pointer pBox has a static type pointer to Box, so any static call using pBox can only call a member function of Box.

■ **Note**   Any call to a function through a base class pointer that is resolved statically calls a base class function.

What we want is for the volume() function that is to be called in any given instance to be resolved when the program executes. So, if showVolume() is called for a derived class object, we want the derived class volume() function to be called, not the base class version. When the volume() function is called through a base class pointer, we want the volume() function that is appropriate to the object pointed to in order to be called. This sort of operation is referred to as *dynamic binding* or *late binding*. To make this work, we have to tell the compiler that the volume() function in Box and any overrides in the classes derived from Box are special, and calls to them are to be resolved dynamically. We can obtain this effect by specifying that volume() in the base class is a *virtual function*, which will result in a *virtual function call* for volume().

Virtual Functions

When you specify a function as virtual in a base class, you indicate to the compiler that you want dynamic binding for function calls in any class that's derived from this base class. A virtual function is declared in a base class by using the keyword virtual, as shown in Figure 14-2. Describing a class as *polymorphic* means that it is a derived class that contains at least one virtual function.

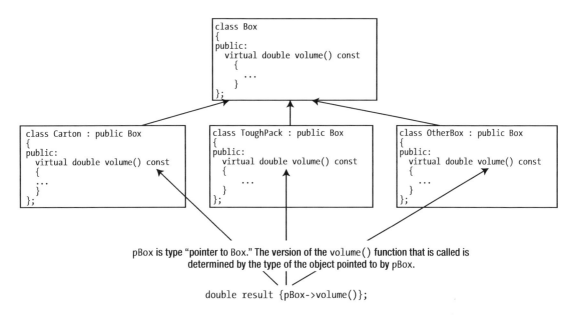

Figure 14-2. *Calling a virtual function*

A function that you specify as virtual in a base class will be virtual in all classes that are directly or indirectly derived from the base. This is the case whether or not you specify the function as virtual in a derived class. To obtain polymorphic behavior, each derived class may implement its own version of the virtual function (although it's not obliged to—we'll look into that later). You make virtual function calls using a variable whose type is a pointer or a reference to a base class object. Figure 14-2 illustrates how a call to a virtual function through a pointer is resolved dynamically. The pointer to the base class type is used to store the address of an object with a type corresponding to one of the derived classes. It could point to an object of any of the three derived classes shown or, of course, to a base class object. The type of the object to which the pointer points when the call executes determines which volume() function is called.

Note that a call to a virtual function using an object is *always* resolved statically. You *only* get dynamic resolution of calls to virtual functions through a pointer or a reference. Storing an object of a derived class type in a variable of a base type will result in the derived class object being sliced, so it has no derived class characteristics. With that said, let's give virtual functions a whirl. To make the previous example work as it should, a very small change to the Box class is required. We just need to add the virtual keyword to the definition of the volume() function:

```
class Box
{
  // Rest of the class as before...

public:
  // Function to calculate the volume of a Box object
  virtual double volume() const { return length * width * height; }
};
```

> ■ **Caution** If a member function definition is outside the class definition, you must *not* add the `virtual` keyword to the function definition; it would be an error to do so. You can only add `virtual` to declarations or definitions inside a class definition.

To make it more interesting, let's implement the volume() function in a new class called Carton a little differently. Here is the class definition:

```
// Carton.h
#ifndef CARTON_H
#define CARTON_H
#include <string>
#include <string_view>
#include "Box.h"

class Carton : public Box
{
private:
  std::string material;

public:
  // Constructor explicitly calling the base constructor
  Carton(double lv, double wv, double hv, std::string_view str="cardboard")
       : Box{lv,wv,hv}, material{str}
  {}

  // Function to calculate the volume of a Carton object
  double volume() const
  {
    const double vol {(length - 0.5)*(width - 0.5)*(height - 0.5)};
    return vol > 0.0? vol : 0.0;
  }
};
#endif
```

The volume() function for a Carton object assumes the thickness of the material is 0.25, so 0.5 is subtracted from each dimension to account for the sides of the carton. If a Carton object has been created with any of its dimensions less than 0.5 for some reason, then this will result in a negative value for the volume, so in such a case, the carton's volume will be set to zero.

We'll also use the ToughPack class from Ex14_01. Here's the code for the source file containing main():

```
// Ex14_02.cpp
// Using virtual functions
#include <iostream>
#include "Box.h"                    // For the Box class
#include "ToughPack.h"              // For the ToughPack class
#include "Carton.h"                 // For the Carton class
```

```
int main()
{
  Box box {20.0, 30.0, 40.0};
  ToughPack hardcase {20.0, 30.0, 40.0};        // A derived box - same size
  Carton carton {20.0, 30.0, 40.0, "plastic"};  // A different derived box

  box.showVolume();                             // Volume of Box
  hardcase.showVolume();                        // Volume of ToughPack
  carton.showVolume();                          // Volume of Carton

  // Now using a base pointer...
  Box* pBox {&box};                             // Points to type Box
  std::cout << "\nbox volume through pBox is " << pBox->volume() << std::endl;
  pBox->showVolume();

  pBox = &hardcase;                             // Points to type ToughPack
  std::cout << "hardcase volume through pBox is " << pBox->volume() << std::endl;
  pBox->showVolume();

  pBox = &carton;                              // Points to type Carton
  std::cout << "carton volume through pBox is " << pBox->volume() << std::endl;
  pBox->showVolume();
}
```

The output that is produced should be as follows:

```
Box usable volume is 24000
Box usable volume is 20400
Box usable volume is 22722.4

box volume through pBox is 24000
Box usable volume is 24000
hardcase volume through pBox is 20400
Box usable volume is 20400
carton volume through pBox is 22722.4
Box usable volume is 22722.4
```

Notice that we have not added the virtual keyword to the volume() functions of either the Carton or ToughPack class. The virtual keyword applied to the function volume() in the base class is sufficient to determine that all definitions of the function in derived classes will also be virtual. You can optionally use the virtual keyword for your derived class functions as well, as illustrated in Figure 14-2. Whether or not you do is a matter of personal preference. We'll return to this choice later in this chapter.

The program is now clearly doing what we wanted. The call to showVolume() for the box object calls the base class version of volume() because box is of type Box. The next call to showVolume() is for the ToughPack object hardcase. It calls the showVolume() function inherited from the Box class, but the call to volume() in showVolume() is resolved to the version defined in the ToughPack class because volume() is a virtual function. Therefore, you get the volume calculated appropriately for a ToughPack object. The third call of showVolume() for the carton object calls the Carton class version of volume(), so you get the correct result for that too.

Next, you use the pointer pBox to call the volume() function directly and also indirectly through the nonvirtual showVolume() function. The pointer first contains the address of the Box object box and then the addresses of the two derived class objects in turn. The resulting output for each object shows that the appropriate version of the volume() function is selected automatically in each case, so you have a clear demonstration of polymorphism in action.

Requirements for Virtual Function Operation

For a function to behave "virtually," its definition in a derived class must have the same signature as it has in the base class. If the base class function is const, for instance, then the derived class function must therefore also be const. Generally, the return type of a virtual function in a derived class must be the same as that in the base class as well, but there's an exception when the return type in the base class is a pointer or a reference to a class type. In this case, the derived class version of a virtual function may return a pointer or a reference to a more specialized type than that of the base. We won't be going into this further, but in case you come across it elsewhere, the technical term used in relation to these return types is *covariance*.

If the function name and parameter list of a function in a derived class are the same as those of a virtual function declared in the base class, then the return type must be consistent with the rules for a virtual function. If it isn't, the derived class function won't compile. Another restriction is that a virtual function can't be a template function.

In standard object-oriented programming terms, a function in a derived class that redefines a virtual function of the base class is said to *override* this function. A function with the same name as a virtual function in a base class only overrides that function if the remainder of their signatures match exactly as well; if they do not, the function in the derived class is a new function that *hides* the one in the base class. The latter is what we saw in the previous chapter when we discussed duplicate member function names.

This of course implies that if you try to use different parameters for a virtual function in a derived class or use different const specifiers, then the virtual function mechanism won't work. The function in the derived class then defines a new, different function—and this new function will therefore operate with static binding that is established and fixed at compile time.

You can test this by deleting the const keyword from the definition of volume() in the Carton class and running Ex14_02 again. The volume() function signature in Carton no longer matches the virtual function in Box, so the derived class volume() function is not virtual. Consequently, the resolution is static so that the function called for Carton objects through a base pointer, or even indirectly through the showVolume() function, is the base class version.

■ **Note** static member functions cannot be virtual. As their name suggest, calls of static functions are always resolved statically. Even if you call a static member function on a polymorphic object, the member function is resolved using the static type of the object. This gives us yet another reason to always call static member functions by prefixing them with the class name instead of that of an object. That is, always use MyClass::myStaticFunction() instead of myObject.myStaticFunction(). This makes it crystal clear not to expect polymorphism.

Using override

It's easy to make a mistake in the specification of a virtual function in a derived class. If you define Volume()—note the capital V—in a class derived from Box, it will not be virtual because the virtual function in the base class is volume(). This means that calls to Volume() will be resolved statically, and the virtual volume() function in the class will be inherited from the base class. The code may still compile and execute but not correctly. Similarly, if you define a `volume()` function in a derived class but forget to specify `const`, this function will overload instead of override the base class function. These kinds of errors can be difficult to spot. You can protect against such errors by using the `override` specifier for every virtual function declaration in a derived class, like this:

```
class Carton : public Box
{
  // Details of the class as in Ex14_02...

public:
  double volume() const override
  {
    // Function body as before...
  }
};
```

The `override` specification, like the `virtual` one, only appears within the class definition. It must not be applied to an external definition of a member function. The `override` specification causes the compiler to verify that the base class declares a class member that is virtual and has the same signature. If it doesn't, the compiler flags the definition here as an error (give it a try!).

▨ **Tip**   Always add an `override` specification to the declaration of a virtual function override. First, this guarantees that you have not made any mistakes in the function signatures at the time of writing. Second, and perhaps even more important, it safeguards you and your team from forgetting to change any existing function overrides if the signature of the base class function needs to be changed.

If you add the `override` keyword to every function declaration that overrides a base class's virtual function, some argue it's clear already to anyone reading it that this is a virtual function and that there's therefore no need to apply the `virtual` keyword in derived classes. Other style guides insist to always add `virtual` nonetheless because it makes it even more apparent that it concerns a virtual function. There is no right answer. In this book, we'll limit the use of the `virtual` keyword to base class functions and apply the `override` specification to all virtual function overrides in derived classes. But you should feel free to include the `virtual` keyword to function overrides as well if you feel it helps.

Using final

Sometimes you may want to prevent a member function from being overridden in a derived class. This could be because you want to limit how a derived class can modify the behavior of the class interface, for example. You can do this by specifying that a function is `final`. You could prevent the `volume()` function in the `Carton` class from being overridden by definitions in classes derived from `Carton` by specifying it like this:

```
class Carton : public Box
{
  // Details of the class as in Ex14_02...

public:
  double volume() const override final
  {
```

```
    // Function body as before...
  }
};
```

Attempts to override volume() in classes that have Carton as a base will result in a compiler error. This ensures that only the Carton version can be used for derived class objects. The order in which you put the override and final keywords does not matter—so both override final and final override are correct—but both have to come after const or any other part of the function signature.

▓ Note   In principle you could declare a member function that is both virtual and final even if it does not override any base class member. This would be self-contradictory, though. You add virtual to allow function overrides, and you add final to prevent them. Note that there is no contradiction in combining override and final. This just states that you disallow any further overrides of the function you are overriding.

You can also specify an entire class as final, like this:

```
class Carton final : public Box
{
  // Details of the class as in Ex14_02...

public:
  double volume() const override
  {
    // Function body as before...
  }
};
```

Now the compiler will not allow Carton to be used as a base class. No further derivation from the Carton class is possible. Note that this time it is perfectly sensible to use final on a class that does not have any base class of its own. What does not make sense, though, is to introduce new virtual functions in a final class, that is, virtual functions that do not override a base class function.

▓ Note   final and override are not keywords because making them keywords could break code that was written before they were introduced. This means you could use final and override as variable or even class names in your code. This doesn't mean you should, though; it only creates confusion.

Virtual Functions and Class Hierarchies

If you want your function to be treated as virtual when it is called using a base class pointer, then you must declare it as virtual in the base class. You can have as many virtual functions as you want in a base class, but not all virtual functions need to be declared within the most basic base class in a hierarchy. This is illustrated in Figure 14-3.

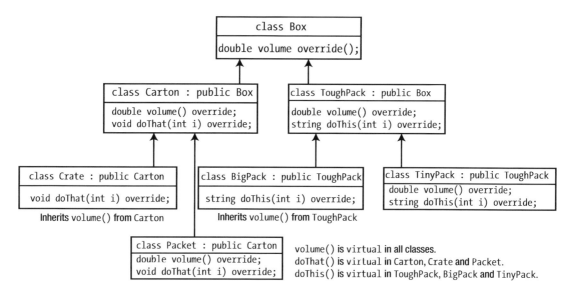

Figure 14-3. *Virtual functions in a hierarchy*

When you specify a function as virtual in a class, the function is virtual in all classes derived directly or indirectly from that class. All of the classes derived from the Box class in Figure 14-3 inherit the virtual nature of the volume() function, even if they do not repeat the virtual keyword. You can call volume() for objects of any of these class types through a pointer of type Box* because the pointer can contain the address of an object of any class in the hierarchy.

The Crate class doesn't define volume(), so the version inherited from Carton would be called for Crate objects. It is inherited as a virtual function and therefore can be called polymorphically.

A pointer pCarton, of type Carton*, could also be used to call volume(), but only for objects of the Carton class and the two classes that have Carton as a base: Crate and Packet.

The Carton class and the classes derived from it also contain the virtual function doThat(). This function can also be called polymorphically using a pointer of type Carton*. Of course, you cannot call doThat() for these classes using a pointer of type Box* because the Box class doesn't define the function doThat().

Similarly, the virtual function doThis() could be called for objects of type ToughPack, BigPack, and TinyPack using a pointer of type ToughPack*. Of course, the same pointer could also be used to call the volume() function for objects of these class types.

Access Specifiers and Virtual Functions

The access specification of a virtual function in a derived class can be different from the specification in the base class. When you call the virtual function through a base class pointer, the access specification in the base class determines whether the function is accessible, regardless of the type of object pointed to. If the virtual function is public in the base class, it can be called for any derived class through a pointer (or a reference) to the base class, regardless of the access specification in the derived class. We can demonstrate this by modifying the previous example. Modify the ToughPack class definition from Ex14_02 to make the volume() function protected, and add the override keyword to its declaration to make absolutely sure it indeed overrides a virtual function from the base class:

```
class ToughPack : public Box
{
public:
  // Constructor
  ToughPack(double lv, double wv, double hv) : Box {lv, wv, hv} {}

protected:
  // Function to calculate volume of a ToughPack allowing 15% for packing
  double volume() const override { return 0.85 * length * width * height; }
};
```

The main() function changes very slightly with a commented-out statement added:

```
// Ex14_03.cpp
// Access specifiers and virtual functions
#include <iostream>
#include "Box.h"                               // For the Box class
#include "ToughPack.h"                         // For the ToughPack class
#include "Carton.h"                            // For the Carton class

int main()
{
  Box box {20.0, 30.0, 40.0};
  ToughPack hardcase {20.0, 30.0, 40.0};       // A derived box - same size
  Carton carton {20.0, 30.0, 40.0, "plastic"}; // A different derived box

  box.showVolume();                            // Volume of Box
  hardcase.showVolume();                       // Volume of ToughPack
  carton.showVolume();                         // Volume of Carton

// Uncomment the following statement for an error
// std::cout << "hardcase volume is " << hardcase.volume() << std::endl;

  // Now using a base pointer...
  Box* pBox {&box};                            // Points to type Box
  std::cout << "\nbox volume through pBox is " << pBox->volume() << std::endl;
  pBox->showVolume();

  pBox = &hardcase;                            // Points to type ToughPack
  std::cout << "hardcase volume through pBox is " << pBox->volume() << std::endl;
  pBox->showVolume();

  pBox = &carton;                              // Points to type Carton
  std::cout << "carton volume through pBox is " << pBox->volume() << std::endl;
  pBox->showVolume();
}
```

It should come as no surprise that this code otherwise produces the same output as the last example. Even though volume() is declared as protected in the ToughPack class, you can still call it for the hardcase object through the showVolume() function that is inherited from the Box class. You can also call it directly through a pointer to the base class, pBox. However, if you uncomment the line that calls the volume() function directly using the hardcase object, the code won't compile.

538

What matters here is whether the call is resolved dynamically or statically. When you use a class object, the call is determined statically by the compiler. Calling `volume()` for a ToughPack object calls the function defined in that class. Because the `volume()` function is protected in ToughPack, the call for the hardcase object won't compile. All the other calls are resolved when the program executes; they are polymorphic calls. In this case, the access specification for a virtual function in the base class is inherited in all the derived classes. This is regardless of the explicit specification in the derived class; the explicit specification only affects calls that are resolved statically.

So, access specifiers determine whether a function can be called based on the *static* type of an object. The consequence is that changing the access specifier of a function override to a more restricted one than that of the base class function is somewhat futile. This access restriction can easily be bypassed by using a pointer to the base class. This is shown by the `showVolume()` function of ToughPack in Ex14_03.

▓ **Tip**   A function's access specifier determines whether you can *call* that function; it plays no role whatsoever, though, in determining whether you can *override* it. The consequence is that you can *override a* `private` `virtual` *function* of a given base class. In fact, it is often recommended that you declare your virtual functions private.

In a way, private virtual functions give you the best of two worlds. On one hand, the function is private, meaning it cannot be called from outside your class. On the other hand, the function is virtual, allowing derived classes to override and customize its behavior. In other words, even though you facilitate polymorphism, you are still in perfect control where and when such a `private` `virtual` member function is called. This function could be a single step in a more complex algorithm, a step that is to be executed only once all previous steps of the algorithm have already been correctly performed. Or it could be a function that must to be called only after acquiring a particular resource, for instance after performing the necessary thread synchronization.

The fundamental idea behind this is the same as with data hiding. The more you restrict access to members, the easier it becomes to ensure that they aren't used incorrectly. Some classic object-oriented design patterns—most prominently the so-called *template method* pattern—are best implemented using `private` `virtual` functions. These patterns are a bit too advanced for us too go into in more detail here. Just understand that access specifiers and overriding are two orthogonal concepts, and always keep in mind that declaring your virtual functions private is a viable option.

Default Argument Values in Virtual Functions

Default argument values are dealt with at compile time, so you can get unexpected results when you use default argument values with virtual function parameters. If the base class declaration of a virtual function has a default argument value and you call the function through a base pointer, you'll always get the default argument value from the base class version of the function. Any default argument values in derived class versions of the function will have no effect. We can demonstrate this quickly by altering the previous example to include a parameter with a default argument value for the `volume()` function in all three classes. Change the definition of the `volume()` function in the Box class to the following:

```
virtual double volume(int i=5) const
{
  std::cout << "Box parameter = " << i << std::endl;
  return length * width * height;
}
```

539

In the Carton class it should be as follows:

```
double volume(int i = 50) const override
{
  std::cout << "Carton parameter = " << i << std::endl;
  double vol {(length - 0.5)*(width - 0.5)*(height - 0.5)};
  return vol > 0.0 ? vol : 0.0;
}
```

Finally, in the ToughPack class, you can define volume() as follows and make it public once more:

```
public:
  double volume(int i = 500) const override
  {
    std::cout << "ToughPack parameter = " << i << std::endl;
    return 0.85 * length * width * height;
  }
```

Obviously, the parameter serves no purpose here other than to demonstrate how default values are assigned.

Once you've made these changes to the class definitions, you can try the default parameter values with the main() function from the previous example, in which you uncomment the line that calls the volume() member for the hardcase object directly. The complete program is in the download as Ex14_04. You'll get this output:

```
Box parameter = 5
Box usable volume is 24000
ToughPack parameter = 5
Box usable volume is 20400
Carton parameter = 5
Box usable volume is 22722.4
ToughPack parameter = 500
hardcase volume is 20400
Box parameter = 5

box volume through pBox is 24000
Box parameter = 5
Box usable volume is 24000
ToughPack parameter = 5
hardcase volume through pBox is 20400
ToughPack parameter = 5
Box usable volume is 20400
Carton parameter = 5
carton volume through pBox is 22722.4
Carton parameter = 5
Box usable volume is 22722.4
```

In every instance of when volume() is called except one, the default parameter value output is that specified for the base class function. The exception is when you call volume() using the hardcase object. This is resolved statically to volume() in the ToughPack class, so the default parameter value specified in the ToughPack class is used. All the other calls are resolved dynamically, so the default parameter value specified in the base class applies, even though the function executing is in a derived class.

Using References to Call Virtual Functions

You can call a virtual function through a reference; reference parameters are particularly powerful tools for applying polymorphism, particularly when calling functions that use pass-by-reference. You can pass a base class object or any derived class object to a function with a parameter that's a reference to the base class. You can use the reference parameter within the function body to call a virtual function in the base class and get polymorphic behavior. When the function executes, the virtual function for the object that was passed as the argument is selected automatically at runtime. We can show this in action by modifying Ex14_02 to call a function that has a parameter of type reference to Box:

```
// Ex14_05.cpp
// Using a reference parameter to call virtual function
#include <iostream>
#include "Box.h"                          // For the Box class
#include "ToughPack.h"                    // For the ToughPack class
#include "Carton.h"                       // For the Carton class

// Global function to display the volume of a box
void showVolume(const Box& rBox)
{
  std::cout << "Box usable volume is " << rBox.volume() << std::endl;
}

int main()
{
  Box box {20.0, 30.0, 40.0};                       // A base box
  ToughPack hardcase {20.0, 30.0, 40.0};            // A derived box - same size
  Carton carton {20.0, 30.0, 40.0, "plastic"};      // A different derived box

  showVolume(box);                        // Display volume of base box
  showVolume(hardcase);                   // Display volume of derived box
  showVolume(carton);                     // Display volume of derived box
}
```

Running this program should produce this output:

```
Box usable volume is 24000
Box usable volume is 20400
Box usable volume is 22722.4
```

The class definitions are the same as in Ex14_02. There's a new global function that calls volume() using its reference parameter to call the volume() member of an object. main() defines the same objects as in Ex14_02 but calls the global showVolume() function with each of the objects to output their volumes. As you see from the output, the correct volume() function is being used in each case, confirming that polymorphism works through a reference parameter.

Each time the showVolume() function is called, the reference parameter is initialized with the object that is passed as an argument. Because the parameter is a reference to a base class, the compiler arranges for dynamic binding to the virtual volume() function.

Polymorphic Collections

Polymorphism becomes particularly interesting when working with so-called polymorphic or heterogeneous collections of objects—both fancy names for collections of base class pointers that contain objects with different dynamic types. Examples of collections include plain C-style arrays, but also the more modern and powerful std::array<> and std::vector<> templates from the Standard Library.

We'll demonstrate this concept using the Box, Carton, and ToughPack classes from Ex14_03 and a revised main() function:

```
// Ex14_06.cpp
// Polymorphic vectors of smart pointers
#include <iostream>
#include <memory>                          // For smart pointers
#include <vector>                          // For vector
#include "Box.h"                           // For the Box class
#include "ToughPack.h"                     // For the ToughPack class
#include "Carton.h"                        // For the Carton class

int main()
{
  // Careful: this first attempt at a mixed collection is a bad idea (object slicing!)
  std::vector<Box> boxes;
  boxes.push_back(Box{20.0, 30.0, 40.0});
  boxes.push_back(ToughPack{20.0, 30.0, 40.0});
  boxes.push_back(Carton{20.0, 30.0, 40.0, "plastic"});

  for (const auto& p : boxes)
    p.showVolume();

  std::cout << std::endl;

  // Next, we create a proper polymorphic vector<>:
  std::vector<std::unique_ptr<Box>> polymorphicBoxes;
  polymorphicBoxes.push_back(std::make_unique<Box>(20.0, 30.0, 40.0));
  polymorphicBoxes.push_back(std::make_unique<ToughPack>(20.0, 30.0, 40.0));
  polymorphicBoxes.push_back(std::make_unique<Carton>(20.0, 30.0, 40.0, "plastic"));

  for (const auto& p : polymorphicBoxes)
    p->showVolume();
}
```

The output from this example is as follows:

```
Box usable volume is 24000
Box usable volume is 24000
Box usable volume is 24000

Box usable volume is 24000
Box usable volume is 20400
Box usable volume is 22722.4
```

The first part of the program shows how *not* to create a polymorphic collection. If you assign objects of derived classes in a vector<> of base class objects by value, as always, object slicing will occur. That is, only the subobject corresponding to that base class is retained. The vector in general has no room to store the full object. The dynamic type of the object also gets converted into that of the base class. If you want polymorphism, you know you must always work with either pointers or references.

For our proper polymorphic vector in the second part of the program we could've used a vector<> of plain Box* pointers—that is, a vector of type std::vector<Box*>—and store pointers to dynamically allocated Box, ToughPack, and Carton objects in there. The downside of that would've been that we'd have had to remember to also delete these Box objects at the end of the program.

You already know that the Standard Library offers so-called smart pointers to help with this. Smart pointers allow us to work safely with pointers without having to worry all the time about deleting the objects.

In the polymorphicBoxes vector, we therefore store elements of type std::unique_ptr<Box>, which are smart pointers to Box objects. The elements can store addresses for objects of Box or any class derived from Box, so there's an exact parallel with the raw pointers you have seen up to now. Fortunately, as the output shows, polymorphism remains alive and well with smart pointers. When you are creating objects in the free store, smart pointers still give you polymorphic behavior while also removing any potential for memory leaks.

▓ **Tip**   To obtain memory-safe polymorphic collections of objects, you can store standard smart pointers such as std::unique_ptr<> and shared_ptr<> inside standard containers such as std::vector<> and array<>.

Destroying Objects Through a Pointer

The use of pointers to a base class when you are working with derived class objects is very common because that's how you can take advantage of virtual functions. If you use pointers or smart pointers to objects created in the free store, a problem can arise when derived class objects are destroyed. You can see the problem if you add destructors to the various Box classes that display a message. Start from the files from Ex14_06, and add a destructor to the Box base class that just displays a message when it gets called:

```
class Box
{
protected:
  double length {1.0};
  double width {1.0};
```

```
  double height {1.0};

public:
  Box() = default;
  Box(double lv, double wv, double hv) : length {lv}, width {wv}, height {hv} {}

  ~Box() { std::cout << "Box destructor called" << std::endl; }

  // Remainder of the Box class as before...
};
```

Do the same for the ToughPack and Carton classes. That is, add destructors of the following form:

```
  ~ToughPack() { std::cout << "ToughPack destructor called" << std::endl; }
```

and

```
  ~Carton() { std::cout << "Carton destructor called" << std::endl; }
```

You'll need to include the <iostream> header into files where it's not already included. There is no need to change the main() function. The complete program is present in the code download as Ex14_07. It produces output that ends with the following dozen or so lines (the output that you'll see before this corresponds to the various Box elements being pushed and sliced into the first vector<>; but this is not the part we want to dissect here):

```
...
Box usable volume is 24000
Box usable volume is 24000
Box usable volume is 24000

Box usable volume is 24000
Box usable volume is 20400
Box usable volume is 22722.4
Box destructor called
Box destructor called
Box destructor called
Box destructor called
Box destructor called
Box destructor called
```

Clearly we have a failure on our hands. The same base class destructor is called for all six objects, even though four of them are objects of a derived class. This occurs even for the objects stored in the polymorphic vector. Naturally, the cause of this behavior is that the destructor function is resolved statically instead of dynamically, just like with any other function. To ensure that the correct destructor is called for a derived class, we need dynamic binding for the destructors. What we need is virtual destructor functions.

▓ **Caution**   You might think that for objects of classes such as ToughPack or Carton calling the wrong destructor is no big deal because their destructors are basically empty. It's not like the destructors of these derived classes perform any critical cleanup task or anything, so what's the harm if they aren't called? The fact of the matter is that the C++ standard specifically states that applying delete on a base class pointer to an object of a derived class results in undefined behavior, unless that base class has a virtual destructor. So while calling the wrong destructor may appear to be harmless, even during program execution, in principle anything might happen. If you're lucky, it's benign, and nothing bad happens. But it might just as well introduce memory leaks (perhaps only the memory for the base class subobject is freed) or even crash your program.

Virtual Destructors

To ensure that the correct destructor is always called for objects of derived classes that are allocated in the free store, you need *virtual class destructors*. To implement a virtual destructor in a derived class, you just add the keyword virtual to the destructor declaration in the base class. This signals to the compiler that destructor calls through a pointer or a reference parameter should have dynamic binding, so the destructor that is called will be selected at runtime. This makes the destructor in every class derived from the base class virtual, in spite of the derived class destructors having different names; destructors are treated as a special case for this purpose.

You can see this effect by adding the virtual keyword to the destructor declaration in the Box class of Ex14_07:

```
class Box
{
protected:
  double length {1.0};
  double width {1.0};
  double height {1.0};

public:
  Box() = default;
  Box(double lv, double wv, double hv) : length {lv}, width {wv}, height {hv} {}

  virtual ~Box() { std::cout << "Box destructor called" << std::endl; }

  // Remainder of the Box class as before...
};
```

The destructors of all the derived classes will automatically be virtual as a result of declaring a virtual base class destructor. If you run the example again, the output will confirm that this is so.

If it weren't for the output message we added for illustration purposes, the function body would have been an empty {} block. Instead of using such an empty block, though, we recommend you declare the destructor using the default keyword. This makes it much more visible that a default implementation is used. For our Box class, you would then write the following:

```
virtual ~Box() = default;
```

The default keyword can be used for all members the compiler would normally generate for you. This includes destructors but also, as you saw earlier, constructors and assignment operators. Note that compiler-generated destructors are never virtual, unless you explicitly declare them as such.

▪ **Tip**   When polymorphic use is expected (or even just possible), your class must have a virtual destructor to ensure that your objects are always properly destroyed. This implies that as soon as a class has at least one virtual member function, its destructor should be made virtual as well. (The only time you do not have to follow these guidelines is if the nonvirtual destructor is either protected or private, but these are rather exceptional cases.)

Converting Between Pointers to Class Objects

You can implicitly convert a pointer to a derived class to a pointer to a base class, and you can do this for both direct and indirect base classes. For example, let's first define a smart pointer to a Carton object:

```
auto pCarton{ std::make_unique<Carton>(30, 40, 10) };
```

You can convert the pointer that is embedded in this smart pointer implicitly to a pointer to Box, which is a direct base class of Carton:

```
Box* pBox {pCarton.get()};
```

The result is a pointer to Box, which is initialized to point to the new Carton object. You know from examples Ex14_05 and Ex14_06 that this also works with references and smart pointers, respectively. A reference to Box, for instance, could be obtained from pCarton as follows:

```
Box& box {*pCarton};
```

▪ **Note**   As a rule, everything we discuss in this section about pointers applies to references as well. We will not always explicitly repeat this, though, nor will we always give analogous examples for references.

Let's look at converting a pointer to a derived class type to a pointer to an indirect base. Suppose you define a CerealPack class with Carton as the public base class. Box is a direct base of Carton, so it is an indirect base of CerealPack. Therefore, you can write the following:

```
CerealPack* pCerealPack{ new CerealPack{ 30, 40, 10, "carton" } };
Box* pBox {pCerealPack};
```

This statement converts the address in pCerealPack from type pointer to CerealPack to type pointer to Box. If you need to specify the conversion explicitly, you can use the static_cast<>() operator:

```
Box* pBox {static_cast<Box*>(pCerealPack)};
```

The compiler can usually expedite this cast because Box is a base class of CerealPack. This would not be legal if the Box class was inaccessible or was a virtual base class.

The result of casting a derived class pointer to a base pointer type is a pointer to the subobject of the destination type. It's easy to get confused when thinking about casting pointers to class types. Don't forget that a pointer to a class type can only point to objects of that type or to objects of a derived class type and not the other way round. To be specific, the pointer pCarton could contain the address of an object of type Carton (which could be a subobject of a CerealPack object) or an object of type CerealPack. It cannot contain the address of an object of type Box because a CerealPack object is a specialized kind of Carton, but a Box object isn't. Figure 14-4 illustrates the possibilities between pointers to Box, Carton, and CerealPack objects.

Despite what we have said so far about casting pointers up a class hierarchy, it's sometimes possible to make casts in the opposite direction. Casting a pointer down a hierarchy from a base to a derived class is different; whether or not a cast works depends on the type of object to which the base pointer is pointing. For a static cast from a base class pointer such as pBox to a derived class pointer such as pCarton to be legal, the base class pointer must be pointing to a Box subobject of a Carton object. If that's not the case, the result of the cast is undefined. In other words, bad things will happen.

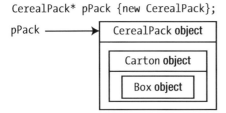

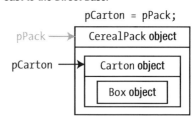

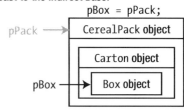

Figure 14-4. *Casting pointers up a class hierarchy*

Figure 14-5 shows static casts from a pointer, pBox, that contains the address of a Carton object. The cast to type Carton* will work because the object is of type Carton. The result of the cast to type CerealPack*, on the other hand, is undefined because no object of this type exists.

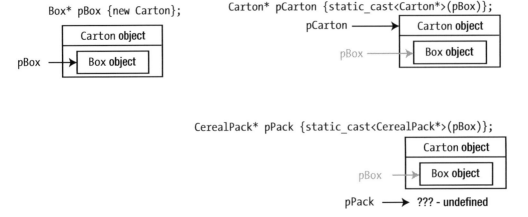

Figure 14-5. Casting pointers down a class hierarchy

If you're in any doubt about the legitimacy of a static cast, you shouldn't use it. The success of an attempt to cast a pointer down a class hierarchy depends on the pointer containing the address of an object of the destination type. A static cast doesn't check whether this is the case, so if you attempt it in circumstances where you don't know what the pointer points to, you risk an undefined result. Therefore, when you want to cast down a hierarchy, you need to do it differently—in a way in which the cast can be checked at runtime.

Dynamic Casts

A *dynamic cast* is a conversion that's performed at runtime. The dynamic_cast<>() operator performs a dynamic cast. You can only apply this operator to pointers and references to polymorphic class types, which are class types that contain at least one virtual function. The reason is that only pointers to polymorphic class types contain the information that the dynamic_cast<>() operator needs to check the validity of the conversion. This operator is specifically for the purpose of converting between pointers or references to class types in a hierarchy. Of course, the types you are casting between must be pointers or references to classes within the same class hierarchy. You can't use dynamic_cast<>() for anything else. We'll first discuss casting pointers dynamically.

Casting Pointers Dynamically

There are two kinds of dynamic cast. The first is a "cast down a hierarchy," from a pointer to a direct or indirect base type to a pointer to a derived type. This is called a *downcast*. The second possibility is a cast across a hierarchy; this is referred to as a *crosscast*. Figure 14-6 illustrates these.

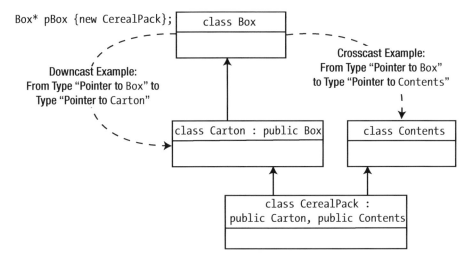

Figure 14-6. *Downcasts and crosscasts*

For a pointer, pBox, of type Box* that contains the address of a CerealPack object, you could write the downcast shown in Figure 14-6 as follows:

```
Carton* pCarton {dynamic_cast<Carton*>(pBox)};
```

The dynamic_cast<>() operator is written in the same way as the static_cast<>() operator. The destination type goes between the angled brackets following dynamic_cast, and the expression to be converted to the new type goes between the parentheses. For this cast to be legal, the Box and Carton classes must contain virtual functions, either as declared or inherited members. For the previous cast to work, pBox must point to either a Carton object or a CerealPack object because only objects of these types contain a Carton subobject. If the cast doesn't succeed, the pointer pCarton will be set to nullptr.

The crosscast in Figure 14-6 could be written as follows:

```
Contents* pContents {dynamic_cast<Contents*>(pBox)};
```

As in the previous case, both the Contents class and the Box class must be polymorphic for the cast to be legal. The cast can succeed only if pBox contains the address of a CerealPack object because this is the only type that contains a Contents object and can be referred to using a pointer of type Box*. Again, if the cast doesn't succeed, nullptr will be stored in pContents.

Using dynamic_cast<>() to cast down a class hierarchy may fail, but in contrast to the static cast, the result will be nullptr rather than just "undefined." This provides a clue as to how you can use this. Suppose you have some kind of object pointed to by a pointer to Box and you want to call a nonvirtual member function of the Carton class. A base class pointer only allows you to call the virtual member functions of a derived class, but the dynamic_cast<>() operator can enable you to call a nonvirtual function. If surface() is a nonvirtual member function of the Carton class, you could call it with this statement:

```
dynamic_cast<Carton*>(pBox)->surface();
```

This is obviously hazardous and in fact little or no better than using static_cast<>(). You need to be sure that pBox is pointing to a Carton object or to an object of a class that has the Carton class as a base. If this is not the case, the dynamic_cast<>() operator returns nullptr, and the outcome of the call again becomes undefined. To fix this, you can use the dynamic_cast<>() operator to determine whether what you intend to do is valid. Here's an example:

```
Carton* pCarton {dynamic_cast<Carton*>(pBox)}
if (pCarton)
  pCarton->surface();
```

Now you'll only call the surface() function member if the result of the cast is not nullptr. Note that you can't remove const-ness with dynamic_cast<>(). If the pointer type you're casting from is const, then the pointer type you are casting to must also be const. If you want to cast from a const pointer to a non-const pointer, you must first cast to a non-const pointer of the same type as the original using the const_cast<>() operator. Recall that using const_cast<>() is rarely recommended, though. Most of the time there is a good reason you have only a const pointer or reference at your disposal, meaning that side-stepping const-ness using const_cast<> often leads to unexpected or inconsistent states.

▓ **Caution**   A common mistake is to resort to dynamic casts too often, especially in those cases where polymorphism would be more appropriate. If at any time you find code of the following form, know then that you may have to rethink the class design:

```
Base* base = ...;                                    // Start from a pointer-to-Base

auto derived1 = dynamic_cast<Derived1*>(base);   // Try to dynamic_cast Base* to
auto derived2 = dynamic_cast<Derived2*>(base);   // any number of derived types...
...
auto derivedN = dynamic_cast<DerivedN*>(base);
if (derived1)                                        // A chain of if-else statements...
  derived1->DoThis();
else if (derived2)
  derived2->do_this();
...
else if (derivedN)
  derivedN->doThat();
```

More often than not, such code should be replaced with a solution based on polymorphism. In our fictional example, you should probably create a function doThisOrThat() in the Base class and override it in any derived class that warrants a different implementation. This entire block of code then collapses to this:

```
Base* base = ...;

base->doThisOrThat();
```

Not only is this much shorter, this will even keep working if at some point yet another DerivedX is derived from Base. This is precisely the power of polymorphism. Your code does not need to know about all possible derived classes, now or in the future. All it needs to know about is the interface of the base class. Any attempt to mimic this mechanism using dynamic casts is bound to be inferior.

While our previous example was clearly fictional, unfortunately we do see such patterns emerge all too often in real code. So, we do advise you to be very cautious about this!

A related symptom of dynamic_cast misuse we sometimes encounter, albeit less frequently, is a dynamic cast of a this pointer. Such ill-advised code might, for instance, look something like this:

```
void Base::DoSomething()
{
  if (dynamic_cast<Derived*>(this))          // NEVER DO THIS!
  {
     /* do something else instead... */
     return;
  }
  ...
}
```

The proper solution here is to make the DoSomething() function virtual and override it in Derived. Downcasting a this pointer is never a good idea, so please don't ever do this! The code of a base class has no business referring to derived classes. Any variation of this pattern should be replaced with an application of polymorphism. Tip: In general, leveraging polymorphism may involve you splitting a function into multiple functions, some of which you can then override. If you're interested, this is again related to the so-called *template method* design pattern. You can find more information online or in other books about this and other standard patterns.

Converting References

You can apply the dynamic_cast<>() operator to a reference parameter in a function to cast down a class hierarchy to produce another reference. In the following example, the parameter to the function doThat() is a reference to a base class Box object. In the body of the function, you can cast the parameter to a reference to a derived type:

```
double doThat(Box& rBox)
{
  ...
  Carton& rCarton {dynamic_cast<Carton&>(rBox)};
  ...
}
```

This statement casts from type reference to Box to type reference to Carton. Of course, it's possible that the object passed as an argument may not be a Carton object, and if this is the case, the cast won't succeed. There is no such thing as a null reference, so this fails in a different way from a failed pointer cast. Execution of the function stops, and an exception of type std:bad_cast is thrown (this exception class is defined in the typeinfo header of the Standard Library). You haven't met exceptions yet, but you'll find out what this means in the next chapter.

So, applying a dynamic cast to a reference blind is obviously risky, but there's an easy alternative. Simply turn the reference into a pointer and apply the cast to the pointer instead. Then you can again check the resulting pointer for nullptr:

```
double doThat(Box& rBox)
{
  ...
  Carton* pCarton {dynamic_cast<Carton*>(&rBox)};
  if (pCarton)
  {
    ...
  }
  ...
}
```

Calling the Base Class Version of a Virtual Function

You've seen that it's easy to call the derived class version of a virtual function through a pointer or reference to a derived class object—the call is made dynamically. However, what do you do when you actually want to call the base class function for a derived class object?

If you override a virtual base class function in a derived class, you'll often find that the latter is a slight variation of the former. An excellent example of this is the volume() function of the ToughPack class you've been using throughout this chapter:

```
// Function to calculate volume of a ToughPack allowing 15% for packing
double volume() const override { return 0.85 * length * width * height; }
```

Obviously, the length * width * height part of this return statement is exactly the formula used to compute the volume() in the base class, Box. In this case, the amount of code you had to retype was limited, but this won't always be the case. It would therefore be much better if you could simply call the base class version of this function instead.

A plausible first attempt to do so in our example case might be this:

```
double volume() const override { return 0.85 * volume(); }    // infinite recursion!
```

If you write this, however, the volume() override is simply calling itself, which would then be calling itself again, which would then be calling itself again.... You get the idea; this would result in what we called infinite recursion in Chapter 8 and therefore a program crash. The solution is to explicitly instruct the compiler to call the base class version of the function (you can find a ToughPack.h with this modification in Ex14_07A):

```
double volume() const override { return 0.85 * Box::volume(); }
```

Calling the base class version from within a function override like this is common. In some rare cases, though, you may also want to do something similar elsewhere. The Box class provides an opportunity to see why such a call might be required. It could be useful to calculate the loss of volume in a Carton or ToughPack object; one way to do this would be to calculate the difference between the volumes returned from the base and derived class versions of the volume() function. You can force the virtual function for a base class to be called statically by qualifying it with the class name. Suppose you have a pointer pBox that's defined like this:

```
Carton carton {40.0, 30.0, 20.0};
Box* pBox {&carton};
```

You can calculate the loss in total volume for a Carton object with this statement:

```
double difference {pBox->Box::volume() - pBox->volume()};
```

The expression pBox->Box::volume() calls the base class version of the volume() function. The class name, together with the scope resolution operator, identifies a particular volume() function, so this will be a static call resolved at compile time.

You can't use a class name qualifier to force the selection of a particular derived class function in a call through a pointer to the base class. The expression pBox->Carton::volume() won't compile because Carton::volume() is not a member of the Box class. A call of a function through a pointer is either a static call to a member function of the class type for the pointer or a dynamic call to a virtual function.

Calling the base class version of a virtual function through an object of a derived class can be done analogously. You can calculate the loss in volume for the carton object with this statement:

```
double difference {carton.Box::volume() - carton.volume()};
```

Calling Virtual Functions from Constructors or Destructors

Ex14_08 illustrates what happens when you call virtual functions from inside constructors and destructors. As always, we start from a Box class with the necessary debugging statements in its relevant members:

```
// Box.h
#ifndef BOX_H
#define BOX_H
#include <iostream>

class Box
{
private:
  double length {1.0};
  double width {1.0};
  double height {1.0};

public:
  Box(double lv, double wv, double hv)
    : length {lv}, width {wv}, height {hv}
  {
    std::cout << "Box constructor called for a Box of volume " << volume() << std::endl;
  }
  virtual ~Box()
```

```
  {
    std::cout << "Box destructor called for a Box of volume " << volume() << std::endl;
  }

  // Function to calculate volume of a Box
  virtual double volume() const { return length * width * height; }

  void showVolume() const
  {
    std::cout << "The volume from inside Box::showVolume() is "
              << volume() << std::endl;
  }
};
#endif
```

We also need a derived class, one that overrides Box::volume():

```
// ToughPack.h
#ifndef TOUGH_PACK_H
#define TOUGH_PACK_H
#include "Box.h"

class ToughPack : public Box
{
public:
  ToughPack(double lv, double wv, double hv)
    : Box{lv, wv, hv}
  {
    std::cout << "ToughPack constructor called for a Box of volume "
              << volume() << std::endl;
  }
  virtual ~ToughPack()
  {
    std::cout << "ToughPack destructor called for a Box of volume "
              << volume() << std::endl;
  }

  // Function to calculate volume of a ToughPack allowing 15% for packing
  double volume() const override { return 0.85 * Box::volume(); }
};
#endif
```

The actual program is trivial. All it does is create an instance of the derived class ToughPack and then show its volume:

```
// Ex14_08.cpp
// Calling virtual functions from constructors and destructors
#include "Box.h"
#include "ToughPack.h"
```

```
int main()
{
  ToughPack toughPack{1.0, 2.0, 3.0};
  toughPack.showVolume();     // Should show a volume equal to 85% of 1x2x3, or 5.1
}
```

This is the resulting output:

```
Box constructor called for a Box of volume 6
ToughPack constructor called for a Box of volume 5.1
The volume from inside Box::showVolume() is 5.1
ToughPack destructor called for a Box of volume 5.1
Box destructor called for a Box of volume 6
```

Let's first focus our attention on the middle line of this output, which is the product of the `toughPack.showVolume()` function call. ToughPack overrides `volume()`, so if you call `volume()` on a ToughPack object, you expect the version of ToughPack to be used, even if this call originates from inside a base class function such as `Box::showVolume()`. The output clearly shows that this is also what happens. `Box::showVolume()` prints out a volume of `0.85 * 1 * 2 * 3`, or `5.1`, as expected.

Now let's see what happens if you call `volume()` not from a regular base class member function such as `showVolume()` but from a base class constructor. The first line in the output shows you that `volume()` then returns 6. So, it's clearly the original function of Box that gets called, not the overridden version of ToughPack! Why is that? You'll recall from the previous chapter that when an object is constructed, all its subobjects are constructed first, including the subobjects of all its base classes. While initializing such a subobject—for instance, the Box subobject of our ToughPack—the object of the derived class will therefore at most be partially initialized. It would in general be extremely dangerous to call member functions on an object whose subobjects have not yet been fully initialized. This is why all function calls from inside a constructor, including those of virtual members, are always resolved statically.

Conversely, when destructing an object, all its subobjects are destructed in the reverse order in which they were constructed. So, by the time the destructor of the base class subobject is called, the derived class is already partially destructed. It would thus again be a bad idea to call members of this derived object. So, all function calls in destructors are thus resolved statically as well.

■ **Caution** Virtual function calls made from inside a constructor or a destructor are always resolved statically. If you in rare cases do need polymorphic calls during initialization, you should do so from within an `init()` member function—often virtual itself—that you then call *after* the construction of the object has completed. This is called the *dynamic binding during initialization* idiom.

The Cost of Polymorphism

As you know, there's no such thing as a free lunch, and this certainly applies to polymorphism. You pay for polymorphism in two ways: it requires more memory, and virtual function calls result in additional overhead. These consequences arise because of the way that virtual function calls are typically implemented in practice.

For instance, suppose two classes, A and B, contain identical member variables, but A contains virtual functions, whereas B's functions are all nonvirtual. In this case, an object of type A requires more memory than an object of type B.

■ **Note**   You can create a simple program with two such class objects and use the `sizeof` operator to see the difference in memory occupied by objects with and without virtual functions.

The reason for the increase in memory is that when you create an object of a polymorphic class type, a special pointer is created in the object. This pointer is used to call any of the virtual functions in the object. The special pointer points to a table of function pointers that gets created for the class. This table, usually called a *vtable*, has one entry for each virtual function in the class. Figure 14-7 illustrates this.

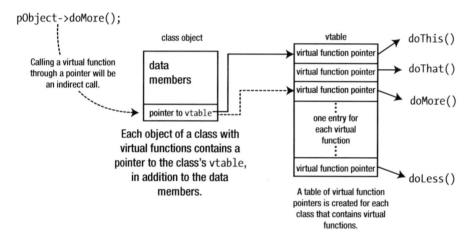

Figure 14-7. *How polymorphic function calls work*

When a function is called through a pointer to a base class object, the following sequence of events occurs:

1. The pointer to the vtable in the object pointed to is used to find the beginning of the vtable for the class.

2. The entry for the function to be called is found in the vtable, usually by using an offset.

3. The function is called indirectly through the function pointer in the vtable. This indirect call is a little slower than a direct call of a nonvirtual function, so each virtual function call carries some overhead.

However, the overhead in calling a virtual function is small and shouldn't give you cause for concern. A few extra bytes per object and slightly slower function calls are small prices to pay for the power and flexibility that polymorphism offers. This explanation is just so you'll know why the size of an object that has virtual functions is larger than that of an equivalent object that doesn't.

■ **Note**   The only time you should even debate whether the overhead of a virtual function table pointer is worth it is when you have to manage millions and millions of objects of the corresponding type. Suppose you have a Point3D class that represents a point in 3D space. If your program manipulates millions and millions of such points—a Microsoft Kinect, for instance, produces up to 9 million points per second—then avoiding virtual functions in Point3D can save you a significant amount of memory.

Determining the Dynamic Type

Suppose you have a reference to an object of a polymorphic class—which as you recall is a class with at least one virtual function. Then you can determine the dynamic type of this object using the typeid() operator. This standard operator returns a reference to a std::type_info object that encapsulates the actual type of its operand. Similar in use to the sizeof operator, the operand to the typeid() operator can be either an expression or a type. Concretely, the semantics of the typeid() operator is more or less as follows:

- If its operand is a type, typeid() evaluates to a reference to a type_info object representing this type.

- If its operand is any expression that evaluates to a reference to a polymorphic type, this expression is *evaluated*, and the operand returns the *dynamic type* of the value referred to by the outcome of this evaluation.

- If its operand is any other expression, the expression is *not evaluated*, and the result is the *static type* of the expression.

The reason we introduce this already more advanced operator to you is because typeid() can be a useful learning or debugging aid. It enables you to easily inspect the type of various expressions or to observe the difference between an object's static and dynamic type.

Let's create a program to see this operator in action. We'll again use the Box and Carton classes of Ex14_06. Of course, by now you know that any base class should have a virtual destructor, so naturally we have given the Box class a defaulted virtual destructor this time. But this small change is not that relevant in this example. Here, we'll use the Box classes to illustrate typeid()'s behavior with polymorphic classes.

■ **Note**   To use the typeid() operator, you always first have to include the typeinfo header from the Standard Library. This makes the std::type_info class available, which is the type of the object returned by the operator. Note that there is an underscore in the name of the type but not in that of the header. Go figure!

```
// Ex14_09.cpp
// Using the typeid() operator
#include <iostream>
#include <typeinfo>          // For the std::type_info class
#include "Box.h"
#include "Carton.h"

// Define trivial non-polymorphic base and derived classes:
class NonPolyBase {};
class NonPolyDerived : public NonPolyBase {};
```

```cpp
Box& GetSomeBox();              // Function returning a reference to a polymorphic type
NonPolyBase& GetSomeNonPoly();  // Function returning a reference to a non-polymorphic type

int main()
{
  // Part 1: typeid() on types and == operator
  std::cout << "Type double has name " << typeid(double).name() << std::endl;
  std::cout << "1 is " << (typeid(1) == typeid(int)? "an int" : "no int") << std::endl;

  // Part 2: typeid() on polymorphic references
  Carton carton{ 1, 2, 3, "paperboard" };
  Box& boxReference = carton;

  std::cout << "Type of carton is "       << typeid(carton).name()       << std::endl;
  std::cout << "Type of boxReference is " << typeid(boxReference).name() << std::endl;
  std::cout << "These are " << (typeid(carton) == typeid(boxReference)? "" : "not ")
            << "equal" << std::endl;

  // Part 3: typeid() on polymorphic pointers
  Box* boxPointer = &carton;
  std::cout << "Type of &carton is "     << typeid(&carton).name()     << std::endl;
  std::cout << "Type of boxPointer is "  << typeid(boxPointer).name()  << std::endl;
  std::cout << "Type of *boxPointer is " << typeid(*boxPointer).name() << std::endl;

  // Part 4: typeid() with non-polymorphic classes
  NonPolyDerived derived;
  NonPolyBase& baseRef = derived;

  std::cout << "Type of baseRef is " << typeid(baseRef).name() << std::endl;

  // Part 5: typeid() on expressions
  const auto& type_info1 = typeid(GetSomeBox());        // function call evaluated
  const auto& type_info2 = typeid(GetSomeNonPoly());    // function call not evaluated
  std::cout << "Type of GetSomeBox() is " << type_info1.name() << std::endl;
  std::cout << "Type of GetSomeNonPoly() is "     << type_info2.name() << std::endl;
}

Box& GetSomeBox()
{
  std::cout << "GetSomeBox() called..." << std::endl;
  static Carton carton{ 2, 3, 5, "duplex" };
  return carton;
}
NonPolyBase& GetSomeNonPoly()
{
  std::cout << "GetSomeNonPoly() called..." << std::endl;
  static NonPolyDerived derived;
  return derived;
}
```

A possible output of this program looks as follows:

```
Type double has name double
1 is an int
Type of carton is class Carton
Type of boxReference is class Carton
These are equal
Type of &carton is class Carton *
Type of boxPointer is class Box *
Type of *boxPointer is class Carton
Type of baseRef is class NonPolyBase
GetSomeBox() called...
Type of GetSomeBox() is class Carton
Type of GetSomeNonPoly() is class NonPolyBase
```

Don't panic if for you the results look different. The names returned by the name() member function of type_info are not always quite so human readable. With some compilers, the type names that are returned are so-called *mangled names*, which are the names that the compiler uses internally. If that's the case, your results might look more like this:

```
Type double has name d
1 is an int
Type of carton is 6Carton
Type of boxReference is 6Carton
These are equal
Type of &carton is P6Carton
Type of boxPointer is P3Box
Type of *boxPointer is 6Carton
Type of baseRef is 11NonPolyBase
GetSomeBox() called...
Type of GetSomeBox() is 6Carton
Type of GetSomeNonPoly() is 11NonPolyBase
```

You can consult your compiler's documentation on how to interpret these names or possibly even on how to convert them to a human-readable format. Normally the mangled names themselves should already carry sufficient information for you to follow this discussion.

The Ex14_09 test program consists of five parts, each illustrating a particular aspect of using the typeid() operator. We'll discuss each of them in turn.

In the first part, we apply typeid() on a hard-coded type name. In itself, this is not that interesting, at least not until you compare the resulting type_info to the result of applying typeid() to an actual value or expression, as shown in the second statement of main(). Note that the compiler does not perform any implicit conversions with type names. That is, typeid(1) == int is not legal C++; you have to explicitly apply the typeid() operator, as in typeid(1) == typeid(int).

The second part of the program demonstrates that typeid() can indeed be used to determine the dynamic type of an object of a polymorphic type—the main topic of this section. Even though the static type of the boxReference variable is Box&, the program's output should reflect that typeid() correctly determines the object's dynamic type: Carton.

The third part of the program shows you that typeid() does not work with pointers in quite the same way as it does with references. Even though boxPointer points to a Carton object, the result of typeid(boxPointer) does not represent Carton*; instead, it simply reflects the static type of boxPointer: Box*. To determine the dynamic type of the object pointed to by a pointer, you therefore have to dereference the pointer first. The outcome of typeid(*boxPointer) shows that this indeed works.

The program's fourth part illustrates that there is no way to determine the dynamic type of objects of nonpolymorphic types. To test this, we quickly defined two simple classes, NonPolyBase and NonPolyDerived, both trivially nonpolymorphic. Even though baseRef is a reference to an object of dynamic type NonPolyDerived, typeid(baseRef) evaluates to the static type of the expression instead, which is NonPolyBase. You can see the difference if you turn NonPolyBase into a polymorphic class, such as by adding a defaulted virtual destructor like this:

```
class NonPolyBase { public: virtual ~NonPolyBase() = default; };
```

If you then run the program again, the output should show that typeid(baseRef) now resolves to the type_info value for the NonPolyDerived type.

■ **Note**   To determine the dynamic type of an object, the typeid() operator needs so-called runtime type information (RTTI for short), which is normally accessed through the object's vtable.[1] Because only objects of polymorphic types contain a vtable reference, typeid() can determine the dynamic type only for objects of polymorphic types. (This, by the way, is also why dynamic_cast<> works only for polymorphic types.)

In the fifth and final part, you learn that the expression passed as an operand to typeid() is evaluated if and only if it has a polymorphic type; from the program's output, you should be able to read that the GetSomeBox() got called, but GetSomeNonPoly() did not. In a way, this is logical. In the former case, typeid() needs to determine the dynamic type because GetSomeBox() evaluates to a reference to a polymorphic type. Without executing the function, the compiler has no way of determining the dynamic type of its result. The GetSomeNonPoly() function, on the other hand, evaluates to a reference to a nonpolymorphic type. In this case, all the typeid() operator needs is the static type, which is something the compiler already knows at compile time simply by looking at the function's return type.

■ **Caution**   Because this behavior of typeid() can be somewhat unpredictable—sometimes its operand is evaluated, sometimes it is not[2]—we advise you to never include function calls in the operand to typeid(). If you only apply this operator to either variable names or types, you will avoid any nasty surprises.

---

[1]Some compilers don't enable runtime type identification by default, so if this doesn't work, look for a compiler option to switch it on.

[2]With some popular compilers, we kid you not, you may even notice that typeid() evaluates its operand *twice*. In our example, that means that the line GetSomeBox() called... might appear twice in the output. This is a bug, of course. But still it's all the more reason never to apply typeid() to a function call.

Pure Virtual Functions

There are situations that require a base class with a number of classes derived from it and a virtual function that's redefined in each of the derived classes, but where there's no meaningful definition for the function in the base class. For example, you might define a base class, Shape, from which you derive classes defining specific shapes, such as Circle, Ellipse, Rectangle, Hexagon, and so on. The Shape class could include a virtual function area() that you'd call for a derived class object to compute the area of a particular shape. The Shape class itself, though, cannot possibly provide a meaningful implementation of the area() function, one that caters, for instance, for both Circles and Rectangles. This is a job for a *pure virtual function*.

The purpose of a pure virtual function is to enable the derived class versions of the function to be called polymorphically. To declare a pure virtual function rather than an "ordinary" virtual function that has a definition, you use the same syntax but add = 0 to its declaration within the class.

If all this sounds confusing in abstract terms, you can see how to declare a pure virtual function by looking at the concrete example of defining the Shape class we just alluded to:

```
// Generic base class for shapes
class Shape
{
protected:
  Point position;                   // Position of a shape

  Shape(const Point& shapePosition) : position {shapePosition} {}

public:
  virtual ~Shape() = default;     // Remember: always use virtual destructors for base classes!

  virtual double area() const = 0;      // Pure virtual function to compute a shape's area
  virtual void scale(double factor) = 0; // Pure virtual function to scale a shape

  // Regular virtual function to move a shape
  virtual void move(const Point& newPosition) { position = newPosition; };
};
```

The Shape class contains a member variable of type Point (which is another class type) that stores the position of a shape. It's a base class member because every shape must have a position, and the Shape constructor initializes it. The area() and scale() functions are virtual because they're qualified with the virtual keyword, and they are pure because the = 0 following the parameter list specifies that there's no definition for these functions in this class.

A class that contains at least one pure virtual function is called an *abstract class*. The Shape class contains two pure virtual functions—area() and scale()—so it is most definitely an abstract class. Let's look a little more at exactly what this means.

Abstract Classes

Even though it has a member variable, a constructor, and even a member function with an implementation, the Shape class is an incomplete description of an object because the area() and scale() functions are not defined. Therefore, you're not allowed to create instances of the Shape class; the class exists purely for the purpose of deriving classes from it. Because you can't create objects of an abstract class, you cannot pass it by value to a function; a parameter of type Shape will not compile. Similarly, you cannot return a Shape by value from a function. However, pointers or references to an abstract class can be used as parameter or return types, so types such as Shape* and Shape& are fine in these settings. It is essential that this should be the case to get polymorphic behavior for derived class objects.

This raises the question, "If you can't create an instance of an abstract class, then why does the abstract class contain a constructor?" The answer is that the constructor for an abstract class is there to initialize its member variables. The constructor for an abstract class will be called by a derived class constructor, implicitly or from the constructor initialization list. If you try to call the constructor for an abstract class from anywhere else, you'll get an error message from the compiler.

Because the constructor for an abstract class can't be used generally, it's a good idea to declare it as a protected member of the class, as we have done for the Shape class. This allows it to be called in the initialization list for a derived class constructor but prevents access to it from anywhere else. Note that a constructor for an abstract class must not call a pure virtual function; the effect of doing so is undefined.

Any class that derives from the Shape class must define both the area() function and the scale() function. If it doesn't, it too is an abstract class. More specifically, if any pure virtual function of an abstract base class isn't defined in a derived class, then the pure virtual function will be inherited as such, and the derived class will also be an abstract class.

To illustrate this, you could define a new class called Circle, which has the Shape class as a base:

```
// A macro defining the mathematical constant π
#define PI 3.14159265358979323846264338327950288

// Class defining a circle
class Circle : public Shape
{
protected:
  double radius;         // Radius of a circle

public:
  Circle(const Point& center, double circleRadius) : Shape{center}, radius{circleRadius} {}

  double area() const override { return radius * radius * PI; }

  void scale(double factor) override { radius *= factor; }
};
```

The area() and scale() functions are defined, so this class is not abstract. If either function were not defined, then the Circle class would be abstract. The class includes a constructor, which initializes the base class subobject by calling the base class constructor.

Of course, an abstract class can contain virtual functions that it does define and functions that are not virtual. An example of the former was the move() function in Shape. It can also contain any number of pure virtual functions.

Let's look at a working example that uses an abstract class. We'll define a new version of the Box class with the volume() function declared as a pure virtual function. As a polymorphic base class, it of course needs a virtual destructor as well:

```
class Box
{
protected:
  double length {1.0};
```

```
    double width {1.0};
    double height {1.0};

    Box(double lv, double wv, double hv) : length {lv}, width {wv}, height {hv} {}
public:
    virtual ~Box() = default;            // Virtual destructor
    virtual double volume() const = 0;   // Function to calculate the volume
};
```

Because Box is now an abstract class, you can no longer create objects of this type. This would not have been possible even if we hadn't made the constructor protected. Because these constructors are only intended for use in derived classes, however, it makes sense to declare them protected. The Carton and ToughPack classes in this example are the same as in Ex14_06. They both define the volume() function, so they aren't abstract, and we can use objects of these classes to show that the virtual volume() functions are still working as before:

```
// Ex14_10.cpp
// Using an abstract class
#include <iostream>
#include "Box.h"                         // For the Box class
#include "ToughPack.h"                   // For the ToughPack class
#include "Carton.h"                      // For the Carton class

int main()
{
    ToughPack hardcase {20.0, 30.0, 40.0};        // A derived box - same size
    Carton carton {20.0, 30.0, 40.0, "plastic"};  // A different derived box

    Box* pBox {&hardcase};                         // Base pointer - derived address
    std::cout << "hardcase volume is " << pBox->volume() << std::endl;

    pBox = &carton;                                // New derived address
    std::cout << "carton volume is " << pBox->volume() << std::endl;
}
```

This generates the following output:

```
hardcase volume is 20400
carton volume is 22722.4
```

Declaring volume() to be a pure virtual function in the Box class ensures that the volume() function members of the Carton and ToughPack classes are also virtual. Therefore, you can call them through a pointer to the base class, and the calls will be resolved dynamically. The output for the ToughPack and Carton objects shows that everything is working as expected. The Carton and ToughPack class constructors still call the Box class constructor that is now protected in their initialization lists.

> ■ **Note** You can now no longer implement the volume() member of the ToughPack class like we did in Ex14_09:

```
double volume() const override { return 0.85 * Box::volume(); }
```

> The Box::volume() is now a pure virtual function, and you can never call pure virtual function using static binding (it has no function body!). Because no base implementation is provided anymore, you'll again have to spell out length * width * height here.

Abstract Classes as Interfaces

Sometimes an abstract class arises simply because a function has no sensible definition in the context of the class and has a meaningful interpretation only in a derived class. However, there is another way of using an abstract class. An abstract class that contains only pure virtual functions—no member variables or other functions—can be used to define what in object-oriented terminology is often called an *interface*. It would typically represent a declaration of a set of related functions that supported a particular capability—a set of functions for communications through a modem, for example. While other programming languages such as Java and C# have specific class-like language constructs for this, in C++ one defines an interface using an abstract class consisting solely of pure virtual functions. As we've discussed, a class that derives from such an abstract base class must define an implementation for each virtual function, but the way in which each virtual function is implemented is specified by whoever is implementing the derived class. The abstract class fixes the interface, but the implementation in the derived class is flexible.

Because the abstract Shape and Box classes from the previous section have member variables, they're not really interface class. An example of an interface would be the following Vessel class, defined in Vessel.h. All it does is specify that any Vessel has a volume, which may be obtained from its (pure virtual) volume() member function:

```
// Vessel.h Abstract class defining a vessel
#ifndef VESSEL_H
#define VESSEL_H

class Vessel {
public:
  virtual ~Vessel() = default;       // As always: a virtual destructor!
  virtual double volume() const = 0;
};
#endif
```

There could be any number of classes implementing the Vessel interface. All would implement the interface's volume() function in their own way. Our first Vessel class will be, naturally, our trusty old Box class:

```
class Box : public Vessel
{
protected:
  double length {1.0};
  double width {1.0};
  double height {1.0};
```

```
public:
  Box() = default;
  Box(double lv, double wv, double hv) : length {lv}, width {wv}, height {hv} {}

  double volume() const override { return length * width * height; }
};
```

This makes any classes derived from Box valid Vessels as well. You can, for instance, use the Carton and ToughPack classes from Ex14_09 (although you can and should again call Box::volume() now from within its ToughPack override since now this base class function is no longer pure virtual).

Of course, you can also add another class derived from Vessel. One example would be a class that defines a can. Here is a class definition you can place in Can.h:

```
// Can.h Class defining a cylindrical can of a given height and diameter
#ifndef CAN_H
#define CAN_H
#include "Vessel.h"

// A macro defining the mathematical constant π
#define PI 3.14159265358979323846264338327950288

class Can : public Vessel
{
protected:
  double diameter {1.0};
  double height {1.0};

public:
  Can(double d, double h) : diameter {d}, height {h} {}

  double volume() const override { return PI * diameter * diameter * height / 4.0; }
};
#endif
```

This defines Can objects that represent regular cylindrical cans, such as a beer can. The class uses the same PI macro we discussed earlier. Note that it might be better to define such constants in a separate header, say math_constants.h, instead. This would then allow you to reuse these constants in multiple header and source files.

You can find the program that glues everything together in Ex14_11.cpp:

```
// Ex14_11.cpp
// Using an interface class and indirect base classes
#include <iostream>
#include <vector>                // For the vector container
#include "Box.h"                 // For the Box class
#include "ToughPack.h"           // For the ToughPack class
#include "Carton.h"              // For the Carton class
#include "Can.h"                 // for the Can class
```

```
int main()
{
  Box box {40, 30, 20};
  Can can {10, 3};
  Carton carton {40, 30, 20, "Plastic"};
  ToughPack hardcase {40, 30, 20};

  std::vector<Vessel*> vessels {&box, &can, &carton, &hardcase};

  for (const auto* vessel : vessels)
    std::cout << "Volume is " << vessel->volume() << std::endl;
}
```

This generates the following output:

```
Volume is 24000
Volume is 235.619
Volume is 22722.4
Volume is 20400
```

This time around, we used a vector of raw pointers to Vessel objects to exercise the virtual functions. The output shows that all the polymorphic calls of the volume() function work as expected.

You have a three-level class hierarchy in this example, as shown in Figure 14-8.

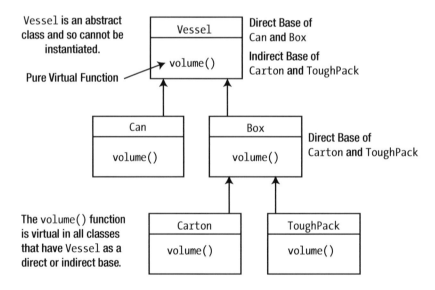

Figure 14-8. *A three-level class hierarchy*

Recall that if a derived class fails to define a function that's declared as a pure virtual function in the base class, then the function will be inherited as a pure virtual function, and this will make the derived class an abstract class. You can demonstrate this effect by removing the const declaration from either the Can or the Box class. This makes the function different from the pure virtual function in the base class, so the derived class inherits the base class version, and the program won't compile.

Summary

In this chapter, we covered the principal ideas involved in using inheritance. These are the fundamentals that you should keep in mind:

- Polymorphism involves calling a (virtual) member function of a class through a pointer or a reference and having the call resolved dynamically. That is, the particular function to be called is determined by the object that is pointed to or referenced when the program is executing.

- A function in a base class can be declared as `virtual`. All occurrences of the function in classes that are derived from the base will then be virtual too.

- You should always declare the destructor of classes intended to be used as a base class as `virtual` (often this can be done in combination with `= default`). This ensures correct selection of a destructor for dynamically created derived class objects. It suffices to do so for the most base class, but it does not hurt to do it elsewhere either.

- You should use the `override` qualifier with each member function of a derived class that overrides a virtual base class member. This causes the compiler to verify that the functions signatures in the base and derived classes are, and forever remain, the same.

- The `final` qualifier may be used on an individual virtual function override to signal that it may not be overridden any further. If an entire class is specified to be `final`, no derived classes can be defined for it anymore.

- Default argument values for parameters in virtual functions are assigned statically, so if default values for a base version of a virtual function exist, default values specified in a derived class will be ignored for dynamically resolved function calls.

- The `dynamic_cast<>` operator is generally used to cast from a pointer-to-a-polymorphic-base-class to a pointer-to-a-derived-class. If the pointer does not point to an object of the given derived class type, `dynamic_cast<>` evaluates to `nullptr`. This type check is performed dynamically, at runtime.

- A pure virtual function has no definition. A virtual function in a base class can be specified as pure by placing `= 0` at the end of the member function declaration.

- A class with one or more pure virtual functions is called an *abstract class*, for which no objects can be created. In any class derived from an abstract class, all the inherited pure virtual functions must be defined. If they're not, it too becomes an abstract class, and no objects of the class can be created.

EXERCISES

The following exercises enable you to try what you've learned in this chapter. If you get stuck, look back over the chapter for help. If you're still stuck after that, you can download the solutions from the Apress website (www.apress.com/source-code), but that really should be a last resort.

Exercise 14-1. Define a base class called Animal with two member variables: a string member to store the name of the animal (e.g., "Fido") and an integer member, weight, that will contain the weight of the Animal in pounds. Also include a public member function, who(), that returns a string object containing the name and weight of the Animal object, as well as a pure virtual function called sound() that in a derived class should return a string representing the sound the animal makes. Derive at least three classes—Sheep, Dog, and Cow—with the class Animal as a public base, and implement the sound() function appropriately in each class.

Define a class called Zoo that can store the addresses of any number of Animal objects of various types in a vector<> container. Write a main() function to create a random sequence of an arbitrary number of objects of classes derived from Animal and store pointers to them in a Zoo object. To keep things simple, work with std::shared_ptr<> pointers to transfer and store Animals into the Zoo. (Later, in Chapter 17, we'll teach you about move semantics, which will allow you to use unique_ptr<> smart pointers for this as well.) The number of objects should be entered from the keyboard. Define a member function of the Zoo class that outputs information about each animal in the Zoo, including the text of the sound they all make.

Exercise 14-2. Start from the solution of Exercise 14-1. Because Cows are notoriously self-conscious about their weight, the result of the who() function of this class must no longer include the weight of the animal. Sheep, on the other hand, are whimsical creatures. They tend to prefix their name with "Woolly"—that is, for a Sheep called "Pete" who() should return a string containing "Woolly Pete". Besides that, it should also reflect a Sheep's true weight, which is its total weight (as stored in the Animal base object) minus that of its wool (known by the Sheep itself). Say that a new Sheep's wool by default weighs 10 percent of his total weight.

Exercise 14-3. Can you think of a way to implement the requirements of Exercise 14-2 without overriding who() in the Sheep class? (Hint: Perhaps Animal::who() could call polymorphic functions to obtain the name and weight of an Animal.)

Exercise 14-4. Add a function herd() to the Zoo class you made for Exercises 14-2 or 14-3 that returns a vector<Sheep*> with pointers to all Sheep in the Zoo. The Sheep remain part of the Zoo. Define a function shear() for Sheep that removes their wool. The function returns the weight of the wool after correctly adjusting the weight members of the Sheep object. Adjust the program of Exercise 14-2 such that it gathers all Sheep using herd(), collects all their wool, and then outputs information in the Zoo again.

Hint: To extract an Animal* pointer from a given shared_ptr<Animal>, you call the get() function of the std::shared_ptr<> template.

Extra: In this chapter, you learned about two different language mechanisms that could be used to herd() Sheep, that is, two techniques to differentiate Sheep* from other Animal* pointers. Try both (leaving one commented out).

Exercise 14-5. You may have wondered why for the herd() function in Exercise 14-4 we asked you to switch from using Animal shared_ptr<>s to raw Sheep* pointers. Shouldn't that have been shared_ptr<Sheep> instead? The main problem is that you cannot simply cast a shared_ptr<Animal> to a shared_ptr<Sheep>. These are unrelated types as far as the compiler is concerned. But you are correct; it probably would've been better to use shared_ptr<Sheep>, and we were probably underestimating your capabilities there. All you really need to know is that to cast between shared_ptr<Animal> and shared_ptr<Sheep> you mustn't use the built-in dynamic_cast<> and static_cast<> operators, but instead the std::dynamic_pointer_cast<> and std::static_pointer_cast<> Standard Library functions defined in the <memory> header. For instance, let shared_animal be a shared_ptr<Animal>. Then dynamic_pointer_cast<Sheep>(shared_animal) results in a shared_ptr<Sheep>. If shared_animal points to a Sheep, the resulting smart pointer will refer to that Sheep; if not, it will contain nullptr. Adapt the solution of Exercise 14-4 to properly use smart pointers everywhere.

Exercise 14-6. Start from the Shape and Circle classes we used earlier to introduce abstract classes. Create one more Shape derivative, Rectangle, that has a width and a height. Introduce an extra function perimeter() that computes a shape's perimeter. Define a main() program that starts by filling a polymorphic vector<> with a number of Shapes (a hard-coded list of Shapes is fine; there's no need to generate them randomly). Next, you should print out the total sum of their areas and perimeters, scale all Shapes with a factor 1.5, and then print out these same sums again. Of course, you haven't forgotten what you learned in the first half of this book, so you shouldn't put all code inside main() itself. Define the appropriate amount of helper functions!

Hint: For a circle with radius r, the perimeter (or circumference) is computed using the formula $2\pi r$.

CHAPTER 15

▩ ▩ ▩

Runtime Errors and Exceptions

Exceptions are used to signal errors or unexpected conditions in a program. While other error-handling mechanisms do exist, exceptions generally lead to simpler, cleaner code, in which you are less likely to miss an error. Particularly in combination with the *RAII principle* (short for "resource acquisition is initialization"), we will show that exceptions form the basis of some of the most effective programming patterns in modern C++.

In this chapter, you'll learn:

- What an exception is and when you should use exceptions

- How you use exceptions to signal error conditions

- How you handle exceptions in your code

- What happens if you neglect to handle an exception

- What RAII stands for and how this idiom facilitates writing exception-safe code

- When to use the noexcept specifier

- Why to be extra careful when using exceptions inside destructors

- What types of exceptions are defined in the Standard Library

Handling Errors

Error handling is a fundamental element of successful programming. You need to equip your program to deal with potential errors and abnormal events, and this can often require more effort than writing the code that executes when things work the way they should. Every time your program accesses a file, a database, a network location, a printer, and so on, something unexpected could go wrong—a USB device is unplugged, a network connection is lost, a hardware error occurs, and so on. Even without external sources of errors, your code is likely not-bug free, and most nontrivial algorithms do fail at times for ambiguous or unexpected inputs. The quality of your error-handling code determines how robust your program is, and it is usually a major factor in making a program user-friendly. It also has a substantial impact on how easy it is to correct errors in the code or to add functionality to an application.

Not all errors are equal, and the nature of the error determines how best to deal with it. You don't usually use exceptions for errors that occur in the normal use of a program. In many cases, you'll deal with such errors directly where they occur. For example, when data is entered by the user, mistakes can result in erroneous input, but this isn't really a serious problem. It's usually quite easy to detect such errors, and the most appropriate course of action is often simply to discard the input and prompt the user to enter the data again. In this case, the error-handling code is integrated with the code that handles the overall input process. Generally, exceptions should be used if the function that notices the error cannot recover from this. A primary advantage of using exceptions to signal errors is that the error-handling code is separated completely from the code that caused the error.

Key is that the name *exception* is aptly chosen. Exceptions should be used only to signal exceptional conditions that you do not expect to occur in the normal course of events and that require special attention. You should definitely never use exceptions during the nominal execution of a program—for instance, to return a result from a function. Also, if a certain error occurs frequently and in most cases can be ignored, you could consider returning an error code of sorts instead of raising an exception, but only do that if you in fact want your program to regularly ignore an error condition. If the error needs further attention from the program or if the program should not continue after an error occurred, exceptions remain the recommended error-handling mechanism.

Understanding Exceptions

An *exception* is a temporary object, of any type, that is used to signal an error. An exception can in theory be of a fundamental type, such as `int` or `const char*`, but it's usually and more appropriately an object of a class type. The purpose of an exception object is to carry information from the point at which the error occurred to the code that is to handle the error. In many situations, more than one piece of information is involved, so this is best done with an object of a class type.

When you recognize that something has gone wrong in the code, you can signal the error by *throwing* an exception. The term *throwing* effectively indicates what happens. The exception object is tossed to another block of code that *catches* the exception and deals with it. Code that may throw exceptions must be within a special block called a `try` block if an exception is to be caught. If a statement that is not within a `try` block throws an exception or a statement within a `try` block throws an exception that is not caught, the program terminates. We'll discuss this further a little later in this chapter.

A `try` block is followed immediately by one or more `catch` blocks. Each `catch` block contains code to handle a particular kind of exception; for this reason, a `catch` block is sometimes referred to as an exception *handler*. All the code that deals with errors that cause exceptions to be thrown is within `catch` blocks that are completely separate from the code that is executed when everything works as it should.

Figure 15-1 shows a `try` block, which is a normal block between braces that is preceded by the `try` keyword. Each time the `try` block executes, it may throw any one of several different types of exception. Therefore, a `try` block can be followed by several `catch` blocks, each of which handles an exception of a different type. A `catch` block is a normal block between braces preceded by the `catch` keyword. The type of exception that a `catch` block deals with is identified by a single parameter between parentheses following the `catch` keyword.

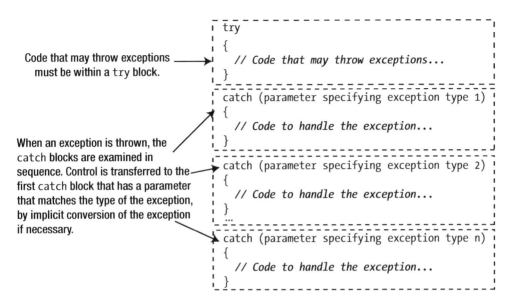

Figure 15-1. *A try block and its catch blocks*

The code in a catch block executes only when an exception of a matching type is thrown. If a try block doesn't throw an exception, then none of the catch blocks following the try block is executed. A try block always executes beginning with the first statement following the opening brace.

Throwing an Exception

It's high time you threw an exception to find out what happens when you do. Although you should always use class objects for exceptions (as you'll do later in the chapter), we'll begin by using basic types because this will keep the code simple while we explain what's going on. You throw an exception using a *throw expression*, which you write using the throw keyword. Here's an example:

```
try
{
  // Code that may throw exceptions must be in a try block...

  if (test > 5)
    throw "test is greater than 5";        // Throws an exception of type const char*

  // This code only executes if the exception is not thrown...
}
catch (const char* message)
{
  // Code to handle the exception...
  // ...which executes if an exception of type 'char*' or 'const char*' is thrown
  std::cout << message << std::endl;
}
```

If the value of test is greater than 5, the throw statement throws an exception. In this case, the exception is the literal "test is greater than 5". Control is immediately transferred out of the try block to the first handler for the type of the exception that was thrown: const char*. There's just one handler here, which happens to catch exceptions of type const char*, so the statement in the catch block executes, and this displays the exception.

■ **Note** The compiler ignores the const keyword when matching the type of an exception that was thrown with the catch parameter type. We'll examine this more thoroughly later.

Let's try exceptions in a working example that will throw exceptions of type int and const char*. The output statements help you see the flow of control:

```
// Ex15_01.cpp
// Throwing and catching exceptions
#include <iostream>

int main()
{
  for (size_t i {}; i < 7; ++i)
  {
    try
    {
      if (i < 3)
        throw i;

      std::cout << "i not thrown - value is " << i << std::endl;

      if (i > 5)
        throw "Here is another!";

      std::cout << "End of the try block." << std::endl;
    }
    catch (size_t i)          // Catch exceptions of type size_t
    {
      std::cout << "i caught - value is " << i << std::endl;
    }
    catch (const char* message)    // Catch exceptions of type char*
    {
      std::cout << "message caught - value is \"" << message << '"' << std::endl;
    }
    std::cout << "End of the for loop body (after the catch blocks)"
              << " - i is " << i << std::endl;
  }
}
```

This example produces the following output:

```
i caught - value is 0
End of the for loop body (after the catch blocks) - i is 0
i caught - value is 1
End of the for loop body (after the catch blocks) - i is 1
i caught - value is 2
End of the for loop body (after the catch blocks) - i is 2
i not thrown - value is 3
End of the try block.
End of the for loop body (after the catch blocks) - i is 3
i not thrown - value is 4
End of the try block.
End of the for loop body (after the catch blocks) - i is 4
i not thrown - value is 5
End of the try block.
End of the for loop body (after the catch blocks) - i is 5
i not thrown - value is 6
message caught - value is "Here is another!"
End of the for loop body (after the catch blocks) - i is 6
```

The try block within the for loop contains code that will throw an exception of type size_t if i (the loop counter) is less than 3, and an exception of type const char* if i is greater than 5. Throwing an exception transfers control out of the try block immediately, so the output statement at the end of the try block executes only if no exception is thrown. The output shows that this is the case. You only get output from the last statement when i has the value 3, 4, or 5. For all other values of i, an exception is thrown, so the output statement is not executed.

The first catch block immediately follows the try block. All the exception handlers for a try block must immediately follow the try block. If you place any code between the try block and the first catch block or between successive catch blocks, the program won't compile. The first catch block handles exceptions of type size_t, and you can see from the output that it executes when the first throw statement is executed. You can also see that the next catch block is not executed in this case. After this handler executes, control passes directly to the last statement at the end of the loop.

The second handler deals with exceptions of type char*. When the exception "Here is another!" is thrown, control passes from the throw statement directly to this handler, skipping the previous catch block. If no exception is thrown, neither of the catch blocks is executed. You could put this catch block before the previous handler, and the program would work just as well. On this occasion, the sequence of the handlers doesn't matter, but that's not always the case. You'll see examples of when the order of the handlers is important later in this chapter.

The statement that identifies the end of a loop iteration in the output is executed whether a handler is executed. Throwing an exception that is caught doesn't end the program—unless you want it to, of course—in which case you terminate the program in the catch block. If the problem that caused the exception can be fixed within the handler, then the program can continue.

The Exception-Handling Process

From the example, you should have a fairly clear idea of the sequence of events when an exception is thrown. Some other things happen in the background, though; you might be able to guess some of them if you think about how control is transferred from the try block to the catch block. The throw/catch sequence of events is illustrated conceptually in Figure 15-2.

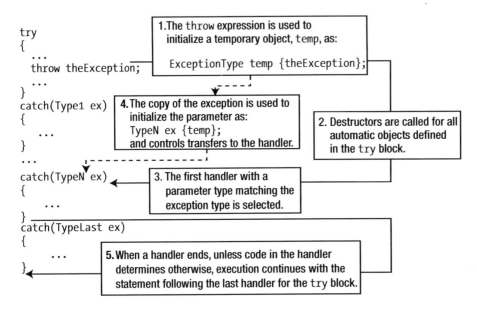

Figure 15-2. *The mechanism behind throwing and catching an exception*

Of course, a try block is a statement block, and you know that a statement block defines a scope. Throwing an exception leaves the try block immediately, so at that point all the automatic objects that have been defined within the try block prior to the exception being thrown are destroyed. The fact that none of the automatic objects created in the try block exists by the time the handler code is executed is most important; it implies that you must not throw an exception object that's a pointer to an object that is local to the try block. It's also the reason why the exception object is copied in the throw process.

▓ **Caution**   An exception object must be of a type that can be copied. An object of a class type that has a private, protected, or deleted copy constructor can't be used as an exception.

Because the throw expression is used to initialize a temporary object—and therefore creates a copy of the exception—you can throw *objects* that are local to the try block but not *pointers* to local objects. The copy of the object is used to initialize the parameter for the catch block that is selected to handle the exception.

A catch block is also a statement block, so when a catch block has finished executing, all automatic objects that are local to it (including the parameter) will be destroyed. Unless you transfer control out of the catch block using, for instance, a return statement, execution continues with the statement immediately following the last catch block for the try block. Once a handler has been selected for an exception and control has been passed to it, the exception is considered handled. This is true even if the catch block is empty and does nothing.

Code That Causes an Exception to Be Thrown

At the beginning of this discussion we said that `try` blocks enclose code that may throw an exception. However, this doesn't mean that the code that throws an exception must be physically between the braces bounding the `try` block. It only needs to be logically within the `try` block. If a function is called within a `try` block, any exception that is thrown and not caught within that function can be caught by one of `catch` blocks for the `try` block. An example of this is illustrated in Figure 15-3. Two function calls are shown within the `try` block: `fun1()` and `fun2()`. Exceptions of type `ExceptionType` that are thrown within either function can be caught by the `catch` block following the `try` block. An exception that is thrown but not caught within a function may be passed on to the calling function the next level up. If it isn't caught there, it can be passed one up to the next level; this is illustrated in Figure 15-3 by the exception thrown in `fun3()` when it is called by `fun1()`. There's no `try` block in `fun1()`, so exceptions thrown by `fun3()` will be passed to the function that called `fun1()`. If an exception reaches a level where no further `catch` handler exists and it is still uncaught, then the program is typically terminated (we'll discuss what happens after an uncaught exception in more detail later).

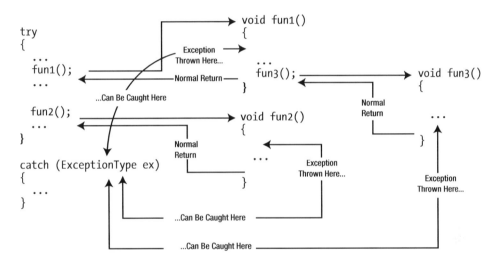

Figure 15-3. *Exception thrown by functions called within a try block*

Of course, if the same function is called from different points in a program, the exceptions that the code in the body of the function may throw can be handled by different `catch` blocks at different times. You can see an example of this situation in Figure 15-4.

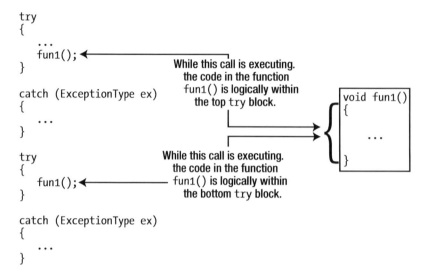

```
try
{
    ...
    fun1();
}

catch (ExceptionType ex)
{
    ...
}

try
{
    fun1();
}

catch (ExceptionType ex)
{
    ...
}
```

Figure 15-4. *Calling the same function from within different try blocks*

As a consequence of the call in the first try block, the catch block for that try block handles any exceptions of type ExceptionType thrown by fun1(). When fun1() is called in the second try block, the catch handler for that try block deals with any exception of type ExceptionType that is thrown. From this you should be able to see that you can choose to handle exceptions at the level that is most convenient to your program structure and operation. In an extreme case, you could catch all the exceptions that arose anywhere in a program in main() just by enclosing the code in main() in a try block and appending a suitable variety of catch blocks.

Nested try Blocks

You can nest a try block inside another try block. Each try block has its own set of catch blocks to handle exceptions that may be thrown within it, and the catch blocks for a try block are invoked for exceptions thrown only within that try block. This process is shown in Figure 15-5.

```
try
{               // outer try block
    ...

    try
    {           // inner try block
        ...
    }
    catch (ExceptionType1 ex)          This handler catches ExceptionType1
    {                                  exceptions thrown in the inner try block.
        ...
    }

    ...

}
catch (ExceptionType2 ex)          This handler catches ExceptionType2
{                                  exceptions thrown in the outer try block, as
    ...                            well as uncaught exceptions of that type from
}                                  the inner try block.
```

Figure 15-5. *Nested try blocks*

Figure 15-5 shows one handler for each `try` block, but in general there may be several. The `catch` blocks catch exceptions of different types, but they could catch exceptions of the same type. When the code in an inner `try` block throws an exception, its handlers get the first chance to deal with it. Each handler for the `try` block is checked for a matching parameter type, and if none matches, the handlers for the outer `try` block have a chance to catch the exception. You can nest `try` blocks in this way to whatever depth is appropriate for your application.

When an exception is thrown by the code in the outer `try` block, that block's `catch` handlers handle it, even if the statement originating the exception precedes the inner `try` block. The `catch` handlers for the inner `try` block can never be involved in dealing with exceptions thrown by code within the outer `try` block. The code within both `try` blocks may call functions, in which case the code within the body of the function is logically within the `try` block that called it. Any or all of the code within the body of the function could also be within its own `try` block, in which case this `try` block would be nested within the `try` block that called the function.

It all sounds rather complicated in words, but it's much easier in practice. We'll put together a simple example in which an exception is thrown and then see where it ends up. Once again, we're going for explanation rather than gritty realism, so we'll throw exceptions of type `int` and type `long` rather than objects of a class type. The code for this example demonstrates nested `try` blocks and throwing an exception within a function:

```cpp
// Ex15_02.cpp
// Throwing exceptions in nested try blocks
#include <iostream>

void throwIt(int i)
{
  throw i;                           // Throws the parameter value
}

int main()
{
  for (int i {}; i <= 5; ++i)
  {
    try
    {
      std::cout << "outer try:\n";
      if (i == 0)
        throw i;                     // Throw int exception

      if (i == 1)
        throwIt(i);                  // Call the function that throws int

      try
      {                              // Nested try block
        std::cout << "inner try:\n";
        if (i == 2)
          throw static_cast<long>(i); // Throw long exception
```

```
        if (i == 3)
          throwIt(i);                    // Call the function that throws int
      }                                  // End nested try block
      catch (int n)
      {
        std::cout << "Catch int for inner try. " << "Exception " << n << std::endl;
      }

      std::cout << "outer try:\n";
      if (i == 4)
        throw i;                         // Throw int
      throwIt(i);                        // Call the function that throws int
    }
    catch (int n)
    {
      std::cout << "Catch int for outer try. " << "Exception " << n << std::endl;
    }
    catch (long n)
    {
      std::cout << "Catch long for outer try. " << "Exception " << n << std::endl;
    }
  }
}
```

This produces the following output:

```
outer try:
Catch int for outer try. Exception 0
outer try:
Catch int for outer try. Exception 1
outer try:
inner try:
Catch long for outer try. Exception 2
outer try:
inner try:
Catch int for inner try. Exception 3
outer try:
Catch int for outer try. Exception 3
outer try:
inner try:
outer try:
Catch int for outer try. Exception 4
outer try:
inner try:
outer try:
Catch int for outer try. Exception 5
```

How It Works

The throwIt() function throws its parameter value. If you were to call this function from outside a try block, it would immediately cause the program to end (as explained in detail later). All the exceptions are thrown within the for loop. Within the loop, you determine when to throw an exception and what kind of exception to throw by testing the value of the loop variable, i, in successive if statements. At least one exception is thrown on each iteration. Entry to each try block is recorded in the output, and because each exception has a unique value, you can easily see where each exception is thrown and caught.

The first exception is thrown from the outer try block when the loop variable, i, is 0. You can see from the output that the catch block for exceptions of type int that follows the outer try block catches this exception. The catch block for the inner try block has no relevance because it can only catch exceptions thrown in the inner try block.

The next exception is thrown in the outer try block when i is 1 as a result of calling throwIt(). This is also caught by the catch block for int exceptions that follows the outer try block. The next two exceptions, however, are thrown in the inner try block. The first is an exception of type long. No catch block for the inner try block for this type of exception exists, so it propagates to the outer try block. Here, the catch block for type long handles it, as you can see from the output. The second exception is of type int and is thrown in the body of the throwIt() function. No try block exists in this function, so the exception propagates to the point where the function was called in the inner try block. The exception is then caught by the catch block for exceptions of type int that follows the inner try block.

When a handler for the inner try block catches an exception, execution continues with the remainder of the outer try block. Thus, when i is 3, you get output from the catch block for the inner try block, plus output from the handler for int exceptions for the outer try block. The latter exception is thrown as a result of the throwIt() function call at the end of the outer try block. Finally, two more exceptions are thrown in the outer try block. The handler for int exceptions for the outer try block catches both. The second exception is thrown within the body of throwIt(), and because it is called in the outer try block, the catch block following the outer try block handles it.

Even though these examples clearly show the mechanics of throwing and catching exceptions and what happens with nested try blocks, the exceptions they use are not particularly realistic. Exceptions in real programs are invariably class objects. Let's therefore move on to take a closer look at exceptions that are objects.

Class Objects as Exceptions

You can throw any type of class object as an exception. However, keep in mind that the idea of an exception object is to communicate information to the handler about what went wrong. Therefore, it's usually appropriate to define a specific exception class that is designed to represent a particular kind of problem. This is likely to be application-specific, but your exception class objects almost invariably contain a message of some kind explaining the problem and possibly some sort of error code. You can also arrange for an exception object to provide additional information about the source of the error in whatever form is appropriate.

Let's define a simple exception class. We'll do so in a header file with a fairly generic name, MyTroubles.h, because we'll be adding to this file later:

```
// MyTroubles.h Exception class definition
#ifndef MYTROUBLES_H
#define MYTROUBLES_H
#include <string>
#include <string_view>
```

```cpp
class Trouble
{
private:
  std::string message;
public:
  Trouble(std::string_view str = "There's a problem") : message {str} {}
  std::string_view what() const { return message; }
};
#endif
```

Objects of the Trouble class simply store a message indicating a problem and are thus ideally suited as simple exception objects. A default message is defined in the parameter list for the constructor, so you can use the default constructor to get an object that contains the default message. Whether you should be using such default messages is another matter entirely, of course. Remember, the idea is usually to provide information regarding the cause of the problem to aid with problem diagnosis. The what() member function returns the current message. To keep the logic of exception handling manageable, your functions should ensure that member functions of an exception class don't throw exceptions. Later in this chapter, you'll see how you can explicitly signal that a member function will never throw exceptions.

Let's find out what happens when a class object is thrown by throwing a few. As in the previous examples, we won't bother to create errors. We'll just throw exception objects so that you can follow what happens to them under various circumstances. We'll exercise the exception class with a simple example that throws some exception objects in a loop:

```cpp
// Ex15_03.cpp
// Throw an exception object
#include <iostream>
#include "MyTroubles.h"

void trySomething(int i);

int main()
{
  for (int i {}; i < 2; ++i)
  {
    try
    {
      trySomething(i);
    }
    catch (const Trouble& t)
    {
      // What seems to be the trouble?
      std::cout << "Exception: " << t.what() << std::endl;
    }
  }
}
```

```
void trySomething(int i)
{
  // There's always trouble when 'trying something' here...
  if (i == 0)
    throw Trouble {};
  else
    throw Trouble {"Nobody knows the trouble I've seen..."};
}
```

This produces the following output:

```
Exception: There's a problem
Exception: Nobody knows the trouble I've seen...
```

Two exception objects are thrown by trySomething() during the for loop. The first is created by the default constructor for the Trouble class and therefore contains the default message string. The second exception object is thrown in the else clause of the if statement and contains a message that is passed as the argument to the constructor. The catch block catches both exception objects.

The parameter for the catch block is a reference. Remember that an exception object is always copied when it is thrown, so if you don't specify the parameter for a catch block as a reference, it'll be copied a second time—quite unnecessarily. The sequence of events when an exception object is thrown is that first the object is copied to create a temporary object and the original is destroyed because the try block is exited and the object goes out of scope. The copy is passed to the catch handler—by reference if the parameter is a reference. If you want to observe these events taking place, just add a copy constructor and a destructor containing some output statements to the Trouble class.

Matching a Catch Handler to an Exception

We said earlier that the handlers following a try block are examined in the sequence in which they appear in the code, and the first handler whose parameter type matches the type of the exception will be executed. With exceptions that are basic types (rather than class types), an exact type match with the parameter in the catch block is necessary. With exceptions that are class objects, implicit conversions may be applied to match the exception type with the parameter type of a handler. When the parameter type is being matched to the type of the exception that was thrown, the following are considered to be a match:

- The parameter type is the same as the exception type, ignoring const.

- The type of the parameter is a direct or indirect base class of the exception class type, or a reference to a direct or indirect base class of the exception class, ignoring const.

- The exception and the parameter are pointers, and the exception type can be converted implicitly to the parameter type, ignoring const.

The possible type conversions listed here have implications for how you sequence the catch blocks for a try block. If you have several handlers for exception types within the same class hierarchy, then the most derived class type must appear first and the most base class type last. If a handler for a base type appears before a handler for a type derived from that base, then the base type is always selected to handle the derived class exceptions. In other words, the handler for the derived type is never executed.

Let's add a couple more exception classes to the header containing the Trouble class and use Trouble as a base class for them. Here's how the contents of the header file MyTroubles.h will look with the extra classes defined:

```
// MyTroubles.h Exception classes
#ifndef MYTROUBLES_H
#define MYTROUBLES_H
#include <string>
#include <string_view>

class Trouble
{
private:
  std::string message;
public:
  Trouble(std::string_view str = "There's a problem") : message {str} {}
  virtual ~Trouble() = default;     // Base classes must always have a virtual destructor!

  virtual std::string_view what() const { return message; }
};

// Derived exception class
class MoreTrouble : public Trouble
{
public:
  MoreTrouble(std::string_view str = "There's more trouble...") : Trouble {str} {}
};

// Derived exception class
class BigTrouble : public MoreTrouble
{
public:
  BigTrouble(std::string_view str = "Really big trouble...") : MoreTrouble {str} {}
};

#endif
```

Note that the what() member and the destructor of the base class have been declared as virtual. Therefore, the what() function is also virtual in the classes derived from Trouble. It doesn't make much of a difference here, but it would in principle allow derived classes to redefine what(). Remembering to declare a virtual destructor in a base class *is* important, though. Other than different default strings for the message, the derived classes don't add anything to the base class. Often, just having a different class name can differentiate one kind of problem from another. You just throw an exception of a particular type when that kind of problem arises; the internals of the classes don't have to be different. Using a different catch block to catch each class type provides the means to distinguish different problems. Here's the code to throw exceptions of the Trouble, MoreTrouble, and BigTrouble types, as well as the handlers to catch them:

```
// Ex15_04.cpp
// Throwing and catching objects in a hierarchy
#include <iostream>
#include "MyTroubles.h"
```

```cpp
int main()
{
  Trouble trouble;
  MoreTrouble moreTrouble;
  BigTrouble bigTrouble;

  for (int i {}; i < 7; ++i)
  {
    try
    {
      if (i == 3)
        throw trouble;
      else if (i == 5)
        throw moreTrouble;
      else if (i == 6)
        throw bigTrouble;
    }
    catch (const BigTrouble& t)
    {
      std::cout << "BigTrouble object caught: " << t.what() << std::endl;
    }
    catch (const MoreTrouble& t)
    {
      std::cout << "MoreTrouble object caught: " << t.what() << std::endl;
    }
    catch (const Trouble& t)
    {
      std::cout << "Trouble object caught: " << t.what() << std::endl;
    }
    std::cout << "End of the for loop (after the catch blocks) - i is " << i << std::endl;
  }
}
```

Here's the output:

```
End of the for loop (after the catch blocks) - i is 0
End of the for loop (after the catch blocks) - i is 1
End of the for loop (after the catch blocks) - i is 2
Trouble object caught: There's a problem
End of the for loop (after the catch blocks) - i is 3
End of the for loop (after the catch blocks) - i is 4
MoreTrouble object caught: There's more trouble...
End of the for loop (after the catch blocks) - i is 5
BigTrouble object caught: Really big trouble...
End of the for loop (after the catch blocks) - i is 6
```

How It Works

After creating one object of each class type, the for loop throws one of them as an exception. Which object is selected depends on the value of the loop variable, i. Each of the catch blocks contains a different message, so the output shows which catch handler is selected when an exception is thrown. In the handlers for the two derived types, the inherited what() function still returns the message. Note that the parameter type for each of the catch blocks is a reference, as in the previous example. One reason for using a reference is to avoid making another copy of the exception object. In the next example, you'll see another, more crucial reason why you should always use a reference parameter in a handler.

Each handler displays the message contained in the object thrown, and you can see from the output that each handler is called to correspond with the type of the exception thrown. The ordering of the handlers is important because of the way the exception is matched to a handler and because the types of your exception classes are related. Let's explore that in a little more depth.

Catching Derived Class Exceptions with a Base Class Handler

Exceptions of derived class types are implicitly converted to a base class type for the purpose of matching a catch block parameter, so you could catch all the exceptions thrown in the previous example with a single handler. You can modify the previous example to see this happening. Just delete or comment out the two derived class handlers from main() in the previous example:

```
// Ex15_05.cpp
// Catching exceptions with a base class handler
#include <iostream>
#include "MyTroubles.h"

int main()
{
  Trouble trouble;
  MoreTrouble moreTrouble;
  BigTrouble bigTrouble;

  for (int i {}; i < 7; ++i)
  {
    try
    {
      if (i == 3)
        throw trouble;
      else if (i == 5)
        throw moreTrouble;
      else if (i == 6)
        throw bigTrouble;
    }
    catch (const Trouble& t)
    {
      std::cout << "Trouble object caught: " << t.what() << std::endl;
    }
    std::cout << "End of the for loop (after the catch blocks) - i is " << i << std::endl;
  }
}
```

The program now produces this output:

```
End of the for loop (after the catch blocks) - i is 0
End of the for loop (after the catch blocks) - i is 1
End of the for loop (after the catch blocks) - i is 2
Trouble object caught: There's a problem
End of the for loop (after the catch blocks) - i is 3
End of the for loop (after the catch blocks) - i is 4
Trouble object caught: There's more trouble...
End of the for loop (after the catch blocks) - i is 5
Trouble object caught: Really big trouble...
End of the for loop (after the catch blocks) - i is 6
```

The catch block with the parameter of type const Trouble& now catches all the exceptions thrown in the try block. If the parameter in a catch block is a reference to a base class, then it matches any derived class exception. So, although the output proclaims "Trouble object caught" for each exception, the output actually corresponds to objects of other classes that are derived from Trouble.

The dynamic type is retained when the exception is passed by reference. To verify this is indeed so, you could obtain the dynamic type and display it using the typeid() operator. Just modify the code for the handler to the following:

```
catch (const Trouble& t)
{
  std::cout << typeid(t).name() << " object caught: " << t.what() << std::endl;
}
```

Remember, the typeid() operator returns an object of the type_info class, and calling its name() member returns the class name. With this modification to the code, the output shows that the derived class exceptions still retain their dynamic types, even though the reference in the exception handler is to the base class. For the record, the output from this version of the program looks like this:

```
End of the for loop (after the catch blocks) - i is 0
End of the for loop (after the catch blocks) - i is 1
End of the for loop (after the catch blocks) - i is 2
class Trouble object caught: There's a problem
End of the for loop (after the catch blocks) - i is 3
End of the for loop (after the catch blocks) - i is 4
class MoreTrouble object caught: There's more trouble...
End of the for loop (after the catch blocks) - i is 5
class BigTrouble object caught: Really big trouble...
End of the for loop (after the catch blocks) - i is 6
```

■ **Note** If your compiler's version of the typeid() operator results in mangled names, the names of the exception classes in your program's output may look less pleasing to the eye. This was discussed in Chapter 14. For illustration's sake, we will always show the results in an unmangled, human-readable format.

Try changing the parameter type for the handler to Trouble so that the exception is caught by value rather than by reference:

```
catch (Trouble t)
{
  std::cout << typeid(t).name() << " object caught: " << t.what() << std::endl;
}
```

This version of the program produces the output:

```
End of the for loop (after the catch blocks) - i is 0
End of the for loop (after the catch blocks) - i is 1
End of the for loop (after the catch blocks) - i is 2
class Trouble object caught: There's a problem
End of the for loop (after the catch blocks) - i is 3
End of the for loop (after the catch blocks) - i is 4
class Trouble object caught: There's more trouble...
End of the for loop (after the catch blocks) - i is 5
class Trouble object caught: Really big trouble...
End of the for loop (after the catch blocks) - i is 6
```

Here, the Trouble handler is still selected for the derived class objects, but the dynamic type is not preserved. This is because the parameter is initialized using the base class copy constructor, so any properties associated with the derived class are lost. Only the base class subobject of the original derived class object is retained. This is an example of *object slicing*, which occurs because the base class copy constructor knows nothing about derived objects. As explained in Chapter 13, object slicing is a common source of error caused by passing objects by value. This leads us to the inevitable conclusion that you should *always* use reference parameters in catch blocks:

■ **Tip**   The golden rule for exceptions is to always *throw by value and catch by reference* (reference-to-const, normally). In other words, you mustn't throw a new'ed exception (and definitely no pointer to a local object), nor should you ever catch an exception object by value. Obviously, catching by value would result in a redundant copy, but that's not the worst of it. Catching by value may slice off parts of the exception object! The reason this is so important is that exception slicing might just slice off precisely that valuable piece of information that you need to diagnose which error occurred and why!

Rethrowing Exceptions

When a handler catches an exception, it can *rethrow* it to allow a handler for an outer try block to catch it. You rethrow the current exception with a statement consisting of just the throw keyword:

```
throw;                          // Rethrow the exception
```

This rethrows the existing exception object without copying it. You might rethrow an exception if a handler that catches exceptions of more than one derived class type discovers that the type of the exception requires it to be passed on to another level of try block. You might want to register or log the point in the program where an exception was thrown, before rethrowing it. Or you may need to clean up some resources—release some memory, close a database connection, etc.—before rethrowing the exception for handling in a caller function.

Note that rethrowing an exception from the inner try block doesn't make the exception available to other handlers for the inner try block. When a handler is executing, any exception that is thrown (including the current exception) needs to be caught by a handler for a try block that *encloses* the current handler, as illustrated in Figure 15-6. The fact that a rethrown exception is not copied is important, especially when the exception is a derived class object that initialized a base class reference parameter. We'll demonstrate this with an example.

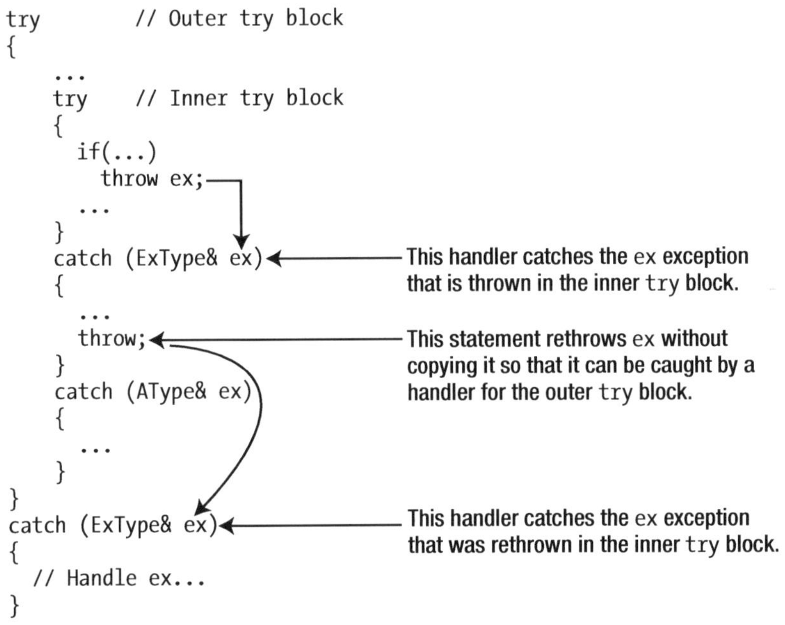

```
try         // Outer try block
{
    ...
    try     // Inner try block
    {
        if(...)
            throw ex;───┐
        ...             │
    }                   ▼
    catch (ExType& ex)◄─────────────── This handler catches the ex exception
    {                                   that is thrown in the inner try block.
        ...
        throw;◄─────────────────────── This statement rethrows ex without
    }                                   copying it so that it can be caught by a
    catch (AType& ex)                   handler for the outer try block.
    {
        ...
    }
}
catch (ExType& ex)◄─────────────────── This handler catches the ex exception
{                                       that was rethrown in the inner try block.
    // Handle ex...
}
```

Figure 15-6. *Rethrowing an exception*

This example throws Trouble, MoreTrouble, and BigTrouble exception objects and then rethrows some of them to show how the mechanism works:

```
// Ex15_06.cpp
// Rethrowing exceptions
#include <iostream>
#include "MyTroubles.h"
```

```cpp
int main()
{
  Trouble trouble;
  MoreTrouble moreTrouble;
  BigTrouble bigTrouble;

  for (int i {}; i < 7; ++i)
  {
    try
    {
      try
      {
        if (i == 3)
          throw trouble;
        else if (i == 5)
          throw moreTrouble;
        else if (i == 6)
          throw bigTrouble;
      }
      catch (const Trouble& t)
      {
        if (typeid(t) == typeid(Trouble))
          std::cout << "Trouble object caught in inner block: " << t.what() << std::endl;
        else
          throw;                         // Rethrow current exception
      }
    }
    catch (const Trouble& t)
    {
      std::cout << typeid(t).name() << " object caught in outer block: "
              << t.what() << std::endl;
    }
    std::cout << "End of the for loop (after the catch blocks) - i is " << i << std::endl;
  }
}
```

This example displays the following output:

```
End of the for loop (after the catch blocks) - i is 0
End of the for loop (after the catch blocks) - i is 1
End of the for loop (after the catch blocks) - i is 2
Trouble object caught in inner block: There's a problem
End of the for loop (after the catch blocks) - i is 3
End of the for loop (after the catch blocks) - i is 4
class MoreTrouble object caught in outer block: There's more trouble...
End of the for loop (after the catch blocks) - i is 5
class BigTrouble object caught in outer block: Really big trouble...
End of the for loop (after the catch blocks) - i is 6
```

The for loop works as in the previous example, but this time there is one try block nested inside another. The same sequence of exception objects as the previous example objects is thrown in the inner try block, and all the exception objects are caught by the matching catch block because the parameter is a reference to the base class, Trouble. The if statement in the catch block tests the class type of the object passed and executes the output statement if it is of type Trouble. For any other type of exception, the exception is rethrown and therefore available to be caught by the catch block for the outer try block. The parameter is also a reference to Trouble so it catches all the derived class objects. The output shows that it catches the rethrown objects and they're still in pristine condition.

You might imagine that the throw statement in the handler for the inner try block is equivalent to the following statement:

```
throw t;                            // Rethrow current exception
```

After all, you're just rethrowing the exception, aren't you? The answer is no; there's a crucial difference. If you make this modification to the program code and run it again, you'll get this output:

```
End of the for loop (after the catch blocks) - i is 0
End of the for loop (after the catch blocks) - i is 1
End of the for loop (after the catch blocks) - i is 2
Trouble object caught in inner block: There's a problem
End of the for loop (after the catch blocks) - i is 3
End of the for loop (after the catch blocks) - i is 4
class Trouble object caught in outer block: There's more trouble...
End of the for loop (after the catch blocks) - i is 5
class Trouble object caught in outer block: Really big trouble...
End of the for loop (after the catch blocks) - i is 6
```

The statement with an explicit exception object specified is throwing a new exception, not rethrowing the original one. This results in the orginal exception object being copied, using the copy constructor for the Trouble class. It's that vexing object slicing problem again! The derived portion of each object is sliced off, so you are left with just the base class subobject in each case. You can see from the output that the typeid() operator identifies all the exceptions as type Trouble. Therefore:

▓ **Tip**   Always throw by value, catch by reference, and rethrow using a throw; statement.

Unhandled Exceptions

If a thrown exception is not caught, either directly or indirectly (that is, it does not have to be caught within the same function, as we discussed earlier), then the program is terminated instantly. And you really should expect such a termination to be fairly abrupt. Destructors for static objects will not get called anymore, for one; there is even no guarantee that the destructors of any objects still allocated on the call stack will be executed. In other words, the program essentially instantly *crashes*.

■ **Note**   In actuality, if an exception goes uncaught, the Standard Library function `std::terminate()` is called (declared in the `exception` header), which in turn by default calls `std::abort()` (declared in `cstdlib`), which then terminates the program. This sequence of events for an uncaught exception is shown in Figure 15-7.

It is technically possible to override the behavior of `std::terminate()` by passing a function pointer to `std::set_terminate()`. However, this is rarely recommended and should be reserved for exceptional (pun intended…) cases. There is also not that much you are allowed to do in a terminate handler. Acceptable uses include making sure that certain critical resources are properly cleaned up or writing a so-called *crash dump* that your customers can then send to you for further diagnosis. These topics are too advanced for this book to warrant further discussion. One thing you must never do is attempt to keep your program running after `std::terminate()` is called! `std::terminate()`, by definition, is called after an *irrecoverable error*; any attempt to recover results in undefined behavior. Your terminate handler must always end with one of two function calls: either `std::abort()` or `std::_Exit()`.[1] Both functions end the program without performing any further cleanup (the difference between the two is that with the latter you can decide which error code the process returns to the environment).

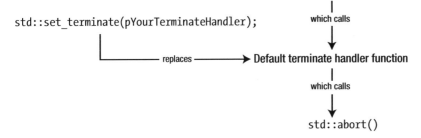

Figure 15-7. Uncaught exceptions

Terminating the program after an uncaught exception may sound harsh, but what other alternative is there really? Remember, you normally throw an exception if something unexpected and unrecoverable has happened that needs further attention. If it then turns out that there is no code in place to appropriately deal with this error, what other course of action is there? The program is inherently in some unexpected, erroneous state, so carrying on as if nothing had happened would generally just lead to more, and potentially far worse, errors. Such secondary errors may furthermore be much harder to diagnose. The only sensible course of action is therefore to halt the execution.

---

[1] You shouldn't even call `std::exit()` from a terminate handler because that again may result in undefined behavior. Consult your Standard Library if you want to know the subtle differences between the various program termination functions.

Catching All Exceptions

You can use an ellipsis (...) as the parameter specification for a catch block to indicate that the block should handle any exception:

```
try
{
  // Code that may throw exceptions...
}
catch (...)
{
  // Code to handle any exception...
}
```

This catch block handles an exception of any type, so a handler like this must always be last in the sequence of handlers for a try block. Of course, you have no idea what the exception is, but at least you can prevent your program from terminating because of an uncaught exception. Note that even though you don't know anything about it, you can still rethrow the exception as you did in the previous example.

You can modify the previous example to catch all the exceptions for the inner try block by using an ellipsis in place of the parameter:

```
// Ex15_07.cpp
// Catching any exception
#include <iostream>
#include <typeinfo> // For use of typeid()
#include "MyTroubles.h"

int main()
{
  Trouble trouble;
  MoreTrouble moreTrouble;
  BigTrouble bigTrouble;

  for (int i {}; i < 7; ++i)
  {
    try
    {
      try
      {
        if (i == 3)
          throw trouble;
        else if (i == 5)
          throw moreTrouble;
        else if (i == 6)
          throw bigTrouble;
      }
      catch (const BigTrouble& bt)
      {
        std::cout << "Oh dear, big trouble. Let's handle it here and now." << std::endl;
        // Do not rethrow...
      }
```

```
      catch (...)          // Catch any other exception
      {
        std::cout << "We caught something else! Let's rethrow it. " << std::endl;
        throw;             // Rethrow current exception
      }
    }
    catch (const Trouble& t)
    {
      std::cout << typeid(t).name() << " object caught in outer block: "
                << t.what() << std::endl;
    }
    std::cout << "End of the for loop (after the catch blocks) - i is " << i << std::endl;
  }
}
```

This produces the following output:

```
End of the for loop (after the catch blocks) - i is 0
End of the for loop (after the catch blocks) - i is 1
End of the for loop (after the catch blocks) - i is 2
We caught something else! Let's rethrow it.
class Trouble object caught in outer block: There's a problem
End of the for loop (after the catch blocks) - i is 3
End of the for loop (after the catch blocks) - i is 4
We caught something else! Let's rethrow it.
class MoreTrouble object caught in outer block: There's more trouble...
End of the for loop (after the catch blocks) - i is 5
Oh dear, big trouble. Let's handle that here and now.
End of the for loop (after the catch blocks) - i is 6
```

The last catch block for the inner try block has an ellipsis as the parameter specification, so any exception that is thrown but not caught by any of the other catch blocks of the same try block will be caught by this catch block. Every time an exception is caught there, a message displays, and the exception is rethrown to be caught by the catch block for the outer try block. There, its type is properly identified, and the string returned by its what() member is displayed. Exceptions of class BigTrouble will be handled by the corresponding inner catch block; as they are not rethrown there, they do not reach the outer catch block.

▧ **Caution**   If your code will throw exceptions of different types, it may be tempting to use a catch-all block to catch them all at once. After all, it's less work than enumerating catch blocks for every possible exception type. Similarly, if you're calling functions that you're less familiar with, quickly adding a catch-all block is much easier than researching which exception types these functions may throw. This is rarely the best approach, though. A catch-all block risks catching exceptions that need more specific handling or sweeping unexpected, dangerous errors under the rug. They also do not allow for much error logging or diagnosis. Still, all too often we encounter patterns such as this in code:

```
try
{
    DoSomething();
}
catch (...)
{
    // Oops. Something went wrong... Let's ignore it and cross our fingers...
}
```

The comments usually don't actually contain the part about ignoring the error and crossing your fingers, but they might as well. The motivation behind such patterns is generally "Anything is better than uncaught exceptions." The truth of the matter is that this is mostly just a symptom of a lazy programmer. There is no substitute for proper, thought-through error-handling code when it comes to delivering stable, fault-tolerant programs. And like we said in the introduction of this chapter, writing error handling and recovery code will take time. So while catch-all blocks may be tempting shortcuts, it's usually preferred to explicitly check which exception types may be raised by the functions that you call and for each consider whether you should either add a catch block and/or leave it to a calling function to handle the exception. Once you know the exception type, you can usually extract more useful information from the object (like with the what() function of our Trouble class) and use this for proper error handling and logging. Note also that, especially during development, a program crash is often preferable over a catch-all. Then at least you learn about potential errors, instead of blindly ignoring them, and can adjust your code to properly prevent them or recover from them. Make no mistake, we do not mean to say that catch-all blocks should never be used—they certainly have their uses. Catch-alls that rethrow after some logging or cleanup, for instance, can be particularly useful. We just want to caution you against using them as an easy, subpar substitute for more targeted error handling.

Functions That Don't Throw Exceptions

In principle, any function can throw an exception, including regular functions, member functions, virtual functions, overloaded operators, and even constructors and destructors. So, each time you call a function somewhere, anywhere, you should learn to think about the potential exceptions that might come out and whether you should handle them with a try block. Of course, this does not mean every function call needs to be surrounded by a try block. As long as you are not working in main(), it is often perfectly acceptable to delegate the responsibility of catching the exception to the callees of the function.

Sometimes, though, you know full well that the function you are writing won't ever throw an exception. Some types of functions should even never throw an exception at all. This section briefly discusses these situations and the language facilities C++ provides for them.

The noexcept Specifier

By appending the noexcept keyword to the function header, you specify that a function will never throw exceptions. For instance, the following specifies that the doThat() functions will never throw:

```
void doThat(int argument) noexcept;
```

If you see a noexcept in a function's header, you can be sure that this function will never throw an exception. The compiler will make sure of it. If a noexcept function *does* unwittingly throw an exception and that exception is not caught within the function, the exception will not be propagated to the calling function. Instead, the C++ program will treat this as an irrecoverable error and call std::terminate(). As discussed earlier in this chapter, std::terminate() always results in an abrupt termination of the process.

Note that this does not mean that no exceptions are allowed to be thrown within the function itself; it only means that no exception will ever escape the function. That is, if an exception is thrown during the execution of a noexcept function, it must be caught somewhere within that function and not rethrown. For example, an implementation of doThat() of the following form would be perfectly legal:

```
void doThat(int argument) noexcept
{
  try
  {
    // Code for the function...
  }
  catch (...)
  {
    // Handles all exceptions and does not rethrow...
  }
}
```

The noexcept specifier may be used on all functions, including member functions, constructors, and destructors. You will encounter concrete examples later in this chapter.

In later chapters, you'll even encounter several types of functions that should always be declared as noexcept. This includes swap() functions (discussed in Chapter 16) and move members (discussed in Chapter 17).

▓ **Note**   Prior to the C++17 language standard, you could specify a list of exception types a function could throw by appending throw(type1, ..., typeN) to a function header. Because such specifications were not effective, they are now no longer supported. The C++17 standard only retains throw() (with an empty list) as a deprecated synonym for noexcept.

Exceptions and Destructors

Starting with C++11, destructors are mostly implicitly noexcept. Even if you define a destructor without a noexcept specification, the compiler will normally add one implicitly. This means that should the destructor of the following class be executed, the exception will never leave the destructor. Instead, std::terminate() shall always be called (in accordance with the implicit noexcept specifier added by the compiler):

```
class MyClass
{
public:
  ~MyClass() { throw std::exception{}; }
};
```

It is in principle possible to define a destructor from which exceptions may be thrown. You could do so by adding an explicit noexcept(false) specification. But since you should normally never do this,[2] we won't discuss or consider this possibility any further in this book.

■ **Tip** Never allow an exception to leave a destructor. All destructors are normally[3] noexcept, even if not specified as such explicitly, so any exception they throw will trigger a call to std::terminate().

Exceptions and Resource Leaks

Making sure all exceptions are caught prevents catastrophic program failure. And catching them with properly positioned and sufficiently fine-grained catch blocks allows you to properly handle all errors. The result is a program that, at all times, either presents the desired result or can inform the user precisely what went wrong. But this is not the end of the story! A program that appears to be functioning robustly from the outside may still contain hidden defects. Consider, for instance, the following example program (it uses the same MyTroubles.h as Ex15_07):

```
// Ex15_08.cpp
// Exceptions may result in resource leaks!
#include <iostream>
#include <cmath>                        // For std::sqrt()
#include "MyTroubles.h"

double DoComputeValue(double);          // A function to compute a single value
double* ComputeValues(size_t howMany);  // A function to compute an array of values

int main()
{
  try
  {
    double* values = ComputeValues(10000);
    // unfortunately, we won't be making it this far...
    delete[] values;
  }
  catch (const Trouble&)
  {
    std::cout << "No worries: I've caught it!" << std::endl;
  }
}
```

---

[2]If you're not careful, throwing from a noexcept(false) may very well still trigger a call to std::terminate(). Details are again out of scope. Bottom line: unless you really know what you're doing, never throw exceptions from a destructor!

[3]Concretely, the compiler implicitly generates the noexcept specification for a destructor without an explicit noexcept(...) specification unless the type of one of the subobjects of its class has a destructor that is not noexcept.

```
double* ComputeValues(size_t howMany)
{
  double* values = new double[howMany];
  for (size_t i = 0; i < howMany; ++i)
    values[i] = DoComputeValue(i);
  return values;
}

double DoComputeValue(double value)
{
  if (value < 100)
    return std::sqrt(value);    // Return the square root of the input value
  else
    throw Trouble{"The trouble with trouble is, it starts out as fun!"};
}
```

If you run this program, a Trouble exception is thrown as soon as the loop counter in ComputeValues()
reaches 100. Because the exception is caught in main(), the program does not crash. It even reassures the
user that all is well. If this was a real program, you could even inform the user about what exactly went wrong
with this operation and allow the user to continue. But that does not mean you are out of the woods! Can you
spot what else has gone wrong with this program?

The ComputeValues() function allocates an array of double values in the free store, attempts to fill them,
and then returns the array to its caller. It is the responsibility of the caller—in this case main()—to deallocate
this memory. However, because an exception is thrown halfway through the execution of ComputeValues(),
its values array is never actually returned to main(). Therefore, the array is never deallocated either. In other
words, we have just leaked an array of 10,000 doubles!

Assuming DoComputeValue() inherently leads to the occasional Trouble exception, the only place
where we can fix this leak is in the ComputeValues() function. After all, main() never even receives a pointer
to the leaked memory, so there is little that can be done about it there. In the spirit of this chapter thus far, a
first obvious solution would therefore be to add a try block to ComputeValues() as follows (you can find this
solution in Ex15_08A):

```
double* ComputeValues(size_t howMany)
{
  double* values = new double[howMany];
  try
  {
    for (size_t i = 0; i < howMany; ++i)
      values[i] = DoComputeValue(i);
    return values;
  }
  catch (const Trouble&)
  {
    std::cout << "I sense trouble... Freeing memory..." << std::endl;
    delete[] values;
    throw;
  }
}
```

Notice that `values` has to be defined outside the `try` block. Otherwise, the variable would be local to the `try` block, and we could not refer to it anymore from within the `catch` block. If you redefine `ComputeValues()` like this, no further changes are required to the rest of the program. It will also still have a similar outcome, except that this time the `values` array is not leaked:

```
I sense trouble... Freeing memory...
No worries: I've caught it!
```

While this `ComputeValues()` function with the `try` block makes for a perfectly correct program, it is not the most recommended approach. The function's code has become about twice as long and about twice as complicated as well. The next section introduces better solutions that do not suffer these shortcomings.

Resource Acquisition Is Initialization

One of the hallmarks of modern C++ is the so-called *RAII idiom*, short for "resource acquisition is initialization." Its premise is that each time you acquire a resource you should do so by initializing an object. Memory in the free store is a resource, but other examples include file handles (while holding these, other processes often may not access a file), mutexes (used for thread synchronization, as we'll discuss in a later chapter), network connections, and so on. As per RAII, *every* such resource should be managed by an object, either allocated on the stack or as a member variable. The trick to avoid resource leaks is then that, by default, the destructor of that object makes sure the resource is always freed.

Let's create a simple RAII class to demonstrate how this idiom works:

```cpp
class DoubleArrayRAII final
{
private:
  double* resource;
public:
  DoubleArrayRAII(size_t size) : resource{ new double[size] } {}
  ~DoubleArrayRAII()
  {
    std::cout << "Freeing memory..." << std::endl;
    delete[] resource;
  }

  // Delete copy constructor and assignment operator
  DoubleArrayRAII(const DoubleArrayRAII&) = delete;
  DoubleArrayRAII& operator=(const DoubleArrayRAII&) = delete;

  // Array subscript operator
  double& operator[](size_t index) noexcept { return resource[index]; }
  const double& operator[](size_t index) const noexcept { return resource[index]; }

  // Function to access the encapsulated resource
  double* get() const noexcept { return resource; }
```

```
// Function to instruct the RAII object to hand over the resource.
// Once called, the RAII object shall no longer release the resource
// upon destruction anymore. Returns the resource in the process.
double* release() noexcept
{
  double* result = resource;
  resource = nullptr;
  return result;
}
};
```

The resource—in this case the memory to hold a double array—is acquired by the constructor of the RAII object and released by its destructor. For this RAII class, it's critical that the resource, the memory allocated for its array, is released only once. This implies that we mustn't allow copies to be made of an existing DoubleArrayRAII; otherwise, we end up having two DoubleArrayRAII objects pointing to the same resource. You accomplish this by deleting *both* copy members (as shown in Chapter 12).

An RAII object often mimics the resource it manages by adding the appropriate member functions and operators. In our case, the resource is an array, so we define the familiar array subscript operators. Besides these, additional functions typically exist to access the resource itself (our get() function) and often also to release the RAII object of its responsibility of freeing the resource (the release() function).

With the help of this RAII class, you can safely rewrite the ComputeValues() function as follows:

```
double* ComputeValues(size_t howMany)
{
  DoubleArrayRAII values{howMany};
  for (size_t i = 0; i < howMany; ++i)
      values[i] = DoComputeValue(i);
  return values.release();
}
```

If anything goes wrong now during the computation of the values (that is, if an exception is thrown by DoComputeValue(i)), the compiler guarantees that the destructor of the RAII object is called, which in turn guarantees that the memory of the double array is properly released. Once all values have been computed, we again hand over the double array to the caller as before, along with the responsibility of deleting it. Notice that if we hadn't called release() prior to returning, the destructor of the DoubleArrayRAII object would still be deleting the array.

■ **Caution**   The destructor of the DoubleArrayRAII object is called regardless of whether an exception occurs or not. Therefore, if we were calling get() instead of release() at the last line of the ComputeValues() function, we would still be deleting the array that is being returned from the function. In other applications of the RAII idiom, the idea is to always release the acquired resources, even in case of success. For instance, when performing file input/output (I/O), you normally want to release the file handle at the end, irrespective of whether the I/O operations succeeded or failed.

The resulting program is available as Ex15_08B. Its outcome demonstrates that even though we have not added any complicated exception-handling code to ComputeValues(), the memory is still freed:

```
Freeing memory...
No worries: I've caught it!
```

■ **Tip**   Even if your program does not work with exceptions, it remains recommended to always use the RAII idiom to safely manage your resources. Leaks due to exceptions can be harder spot, true, but resource leaks can manifest themselves just as easily within functions with multiple return statements. Without RAII, it is simply too easy to forget to release all resources prior to every return statement, especially, for instance, if someone who did not write the function originally returns to the code later to add an extra return statement.

Standard RAII Classes for Dynamic Memory

In the previous section, we created the DoubleArrayRAII class to help illustrate how the idiom works. Also, it is important that you know how to implement an RAII class yourself. You will almost certainly want to create one several times in your career to manage application-specific resources.

Nevertheless, there are of course Standard Library types that perform the same job as DoubleArrayRAII. In practice, you would therefore never write an RAII class to manage arrays.

A first such type is std::unique_ptr<T[]>. If you include the <memory> header, you can write ComputeValues() as follows:

```
double* ComputeValues(size_t howMany)
{
  auto values = std::make_unique<double[]>(howMany);  // type unique_ptr<double[]>
  for (size_t i = 0; i < howMany; ++i)
      values[i] = DoComputeValue(i);
  return values.release();
}
```

In fact, with std::unique_ptr<>, an even better option would be to write it like this:

```
std::unique_ptr<double[]> ComputeValues(size_t howMany)
{
  auto values = std::make_unique<double[]>(howMany);
  for (size_t i = 0; i < howMany; ++i)
      values[i] = DoComputeValue(i);
  return values;
}
```

If you return the unique_ptr<> itself from ComputeValues(), you will of course have to slightly adjust the main() function accordingly. If you do, you'll notice that you no longer need the delete[] statement anymore there. That's yet another potential source of memory leaks eliminated! Unless you are passing a resource to, for instance, a legacy function, there is rarely any need to release a resource from its RAII object. Just pass along the RAII object itself!

▓ **Note** Analogously, returning an object of our DoubleArrayRAII type in ComputeValues() won't compile because of its deleted copy constructor. But the copy constructor of std::unique_ptr<> is deleted as well, of course—for the same reason. So, clearly that's not what makes it work for unique_ptr<>. To be able to return a DoubleArrayRAII from a function, you need to enable *move semantics* for this class. We explain this further in Chapter 17.

Because the resource we are working with here is a dynamic array, you of course know that you could simply use a std::vector<> instead as well:

```
std::vector<double> ComputeValues(size_t howMany)
{
   std::vector<double> values;
   for (size_t i = 0; i < howMany; ++i)
      values.push_back( DoComputeValue(i) );
   return values;
}
```

In this case, a vector<> is probably the most appropriate choice. After all, a vector<> is specifically designed to manage and manipulate dynamic arrays. Whichever you prefer, the main message of this section remains as follows:

▓ **Tip** All dynamic memory should be managed by an RAII object. The Standard Library offers both smart pointers (such as std::unique_ptr<> and shared_ptr<>) and dynamic containers (such as std::vector<>) for this purpose. In the case of smart pointers, make_unique() and make_shared() should always be used instead of new / new[] as well. One important consequence of these guidelines is therefore that the new, new[], delete, and delete[] operators generally have no place anymore in a modern C++ program. Be safe: always, always use an RAII object!

Standard Library Exceptions

Quite a few exception types are defined in the Standard Library. They're all derived from the std::exception class that is defined in the exception header, and they all reside in the std namespace. For reference, the hierarchy for the standard exception classes is shown in Figure 15-8.

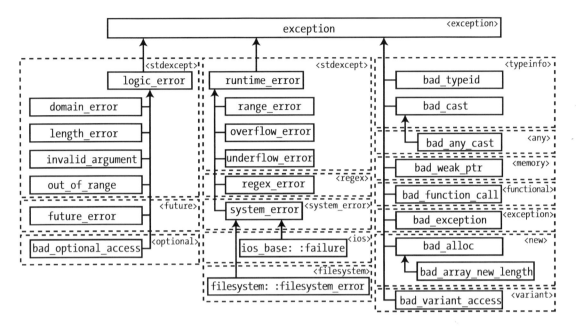

Figure 15-8. *Standard exception class types and the headers they are defined in*

Many of the standard exception types fall into two groups, with each group identified by a base class that is derived from exception. Both these base classes, logic_error and runtime_error, are defined in the stdexcept header. For the most part, Standard Library functions do not throw logic_error or runtime_exception objects directly, only objects of types derived from these. The exceptions that derive from them are listed in the first two columns of Figure 15-8. The rules for categorizing types in either branch of the exception hierarchy are as follows:

- The types that have logic_error as a base are exceptions thrown for errors that could (at least in principle) have been detected before the program executed because they are caused by defects in the program logic. Typical situations in which logic_errors are thrown include calling a function with one or more invalid arguments or calling a member function on an object whose state doesn't meet the requirements (or *preconditions*) for that particular function. You'll see concrete examples of both these situations shortly with std::out_of_range and std::bad_optional_access, respectively. You can avoid these types of errors in your program by explicitly checking the validity of the arguments or the object's state prior to the function call.

- The other group, derived from runtime_error, is for errors that are generally data dependent and can only be detected at runtime. Exceptions derived from system_error, for instance, generally encapsulate errors originating from calls onto the underlying operating system, such as failing file input or output. File access, as any interaction with hardware, can always fail in ways that cannot a priori be predicted (think disk failures, unplugged cables, network failures, and so on).

There are a lot of exception types in Figure 15-8; and we are not going to grind through where they all originate. Your library documentation will identify when a function throws an exception. We only mention some exception types here that are thrown by the operations that you're already familiar with:

- The typeid() operator throws a std::bad_typeid exception if applied on a dereferenced null pointer to a polymorphic type.

- A std::bad_cast exception is thrown by a dynamic_cast<T&>(expr) operation if expr cannot be cast to T&. An exception can occur only when casting to a reference type T&. When failing to cast to a pointer type T*, dynamic_cast<T*>(expr) simply evaluates to nullptr instead.

- A std::bad_alloc exception may be thrown by the operators new and new[]. This occurs when memory allocation fails, such as because of a lack of available memory. By extension, any operation that requires dynamic memory allocation may throw this exception as well. Notable examples of such operations include, for instance, copying or adding elements to std::vector<> or std::string objects.

- Calling the value() member of a std::optional<> object that doesn't hold a value will throw a bad_optional_access exception. The * and -> operators of optional<> never throw exceptions, though. Using these on an optional<> without a value results in undefined behavior. In practice, this means you will read junk data.

- The std::out_of_range exception type is used when accessing array-like data structures with an invalid index (usually defined as lying outside the valid range [0, size-1]). Various member functions of std::string throw this exception, as do the at() accessor functions of, for instance, std::vector<> and std::array<>. For the latter, the corresponding overloaded operator—the array access operator[]()— does not perform bounds checking on the index. Passing an invalid index to these operators leads to undefined behavior.

The Exception Class Definitions

You can usefully use a standard exception class as a base class for your own exception class. Since all the standard exception classes have std::exception as a base, it's a good idea to understand what members this class has because they are inherited by all the other exception classes. The exception class is defined in the exception header like this:

```
class exception
{
public:
  exception() noexcept;                          // Default constructor
  exception(const exception&) noexcept;          // Copy constructor
  exception& operator=(const exception&) noexcept; // Assignment operator
  virtual ~exception();                          // Destructor
  virtual const char* what() const noexcept;     // Return a message string
};
```

This is the `public` class interface specification. A particular implementation may have additional non-`public` members. This is true of the other standard exception classes too. The `noexcept` that appears in the declaration of the member functions specifies that they do not throw exceptions, as we discussed earlier. The destructor is `noexcept` by default. Notice that there are no member variables. The null-terminated string returned by `what()` is defined within the body of the function definition and is implementation dependent. This function is declared as `virtual`, so it will be `virtual` in any class derived from `exception`. If you have a virtual function that can deliver a message that corresponds to each exception type, you can use it to provide a basic, economical way to record any exception that's thrown.

A `catch` block with a base class parameter matches any derived class exception type, so you can catch any of the standard exceptions by using a parameter of type `exception&`. Of course, you can also use a parameter of type `logic_error&` or `runtime_error&` to catch any exceptions of types that are derived from these. You could provide the `main()` function with a `try` block, plus a `catch` block for exceptions of type `exception`:

```
int main()
{
  try
  {
    // Code for main...
  }
  catch (const std::exception& ex)
  {
    std::cerr << typeid(ex).name() << " caught in main: " << ex.what() << std::endl;
    return 1;  // Return a non-zero value to indicate failure
  }
}
```

The `catch` block catches all exceptions that have `exception` as a base and outputs the exception type and the message returned by the `what()` function. Thus, this simple mechanism gives you information about any exception that is thrown and not caught anywhere in a program. If your program uses exception classes that are not derived from `exception`, an additional `catch` block with ellipses in place of a parameter type catches all other exceptions, but in this case you'll have no access to the exception object and no information about what it is. Making the body of `main()` a `try` block is a handy fallback mechanism, but more local `try` blocks are still preferred because they provide a direct way to localize the source code that is the origin of an exception when it is thrown.

The `logic_error` and `runtime_error` classes each only add two constructors to the members they inherit from `exception`. Here's an example:

```
class logic_error : public exception
{
public:
  explicit logic_error(const string& what_arg);
  explicit logic_error(const char* what_arg);

private:
// ... (implementation specifics)
};
```

`runtime_error` is defined similarly, and all the subclasses except for `system_error` also have constructors that accept a `string` or a `const char*` argument. The `system_error` class adds a member variable of type `std::error_code` that records an error code, and the constructors provide for specifying the error code. You can consult your library documentation for more details.

Using Standard Exceptions

There is no reason why you shouldn't make use of the exception classes defined in the Standard Library in your code and a few very good reasons why you should. You can use the standard exception types in two ways: you can either throw exceptions of standard types in your code or use a standard exception class as a base for your own exception types.

Throwing Standard Exceptions Directly

Obviously, if you are going to throw standard exceptions, you should only throw them in circumstances consistent with their purpose. This means you shouldn't be throwing bad_cast exceptions, for instance, because these have a specific role already. Throwing an object of type std::exception is also less interesting as it is far too generic; it does not provide a constructor you can pass a descriptive string to. The most interesting standard exception classes are those defined in the stdexcept header, derived from either logic_error or runtime_error. To use a familiar example, you might throw a standard out_of_range exception in a Box class constructor when an invalid dimension is supplied as an argument:

```
Box::Box(double lv, double wv, double hv) : length {lv}, width {wv}, height {hv}
{
  if (lv <= 0.0 || wv <= 0.0 || hv <= 0.0)
    throw std::out_of_range("Zero or negative Box dimension.");
}
```

The body of the constructor throws an out_of_range exception if any of the arguments are zero or negative. Of course, the source file would need to include the stdexcept header that defines the out_of_range class. The out_of_range type is a logic_error and is therefore well suited for this particular use. Another candidate here would be the more generic std::invalid_argument exception class. If none of the predefined exception classes suits your need, though, you can derive an exception class yourself.

Deriving Your Own Exception Classes

A major point in favor of deriving your own classes from one of the standard exception classes is that your classes become part of the same family. This makes it possible for you to catch standard exceptions as well as your own exceptions within the same catch blocks. For instance, if your exception class is derived from logic_error, then a catch block with a parameter type of logic_error& catches your exceptions as well as the standard exceptions with that base. A catch block with exception& as its parameter type always catches standard exceptions—as well as yours, as long as your classes have exception as a base.

You could incorporate the Trouble exception class and the classes derived from it into the standard exception family quite simply, by deriving it from the exception class. You just need to modify the class definition as follows:

```
class Trouble : public std::exception
{
public:
  Trouble(std::string_view errorMessage = "There's a problem");
  virtual const char* what() const noexcept override;

private:
  std::string message;
};
```

This provides its own implementation of the virtual what() member defined in the base class. Because it is a redefinition of a base class member, we added override to the declaration of what(). Our version of what() displays the message from the class object, as before. We've also added noexcept specifications to signal that no exception will be thrown from this member. In fact, we have to because any function override of a noexcept function must be noexcept as well. It is also worth mentioning that noexcept must always be specified after const and before override. The definition for the member function must include the same exception specification that appears for the function in the class definition. The what() function thus becomes the following (virtual or override must not be repeated):

```
const char* Trouble::what() const noexcept { return message.c_str(); }
```

▨ **Note**   We purposely did not add the noexcept specifier to the constructor of Trouble. This constructor, inevitably, has to copy the given error message into the corresponding std::string member variable. This, in turn, inevitably involves the allocation of a character array. And memory allocation can always, at least in principle, go awry and throw a std::bad_alloc exception.

For a more concrete example, let's return once more to the Box class definition. For the constructor defined in the previous section, it could be useful to derive an exception class from std::range_error to provide the option of a more specific string to be returned by what() that identifies the problem causing the exception to be thrown. Here's how you might do that:

```
#ifndef DIMENSION_ERROR_H
#define DIMENSION_ERROR_H
#include <stdexcept>          // For derived exception classes such as std::out_of_range
#include <string>             // For std::to_string() and the std::string type

class dimension_error : public std::out_of_range
{
private:
  double value;
public:
  explicit dimension_error(double dim)
    : std::out_of_range{"Zero or negative dimension: " + std::to_string(dim)}
    , value{dim} {}

  // Function to obtain the invalid dimension value
  double getValue() const noexcept { return value; }
};
#endif
```

The constructor provides for a parameter that specifies the dimension value that caused the exception to be thrown. It calls the base class constructor with a new string object that is formed by concatenating a message and dim. The to_string() function is a template function that is defined in the string header; it returns a string representation of its argument, which can be a value of any numeric type. The inherited what() function will return whatever string is passed to the constructor when the dimension_error object is created. This particular exception class also adds a member variable to store the invalid value, as well as a public function to retrieve it, such as to use it in a catch block.

Here's how this exception class could be used in the Box class definition:

```cpp
// Box.h
#ifndef BOX_H
#define BOX_H
#include <algorithm>              // For std::min() function template
#include "Dimension_error.h"

class Box
{
private:
  double length {1.0};
  double width {1.0};
  double height {1.0};

public:
  Box(double lv, double wv, double hv) : length {lv}, width {wv}, height {hv}
  {
    if (lv <= 0.0 || wv <= 0.0 || hv <= 0.0)
      throw dimension_error{ std::min({lv, wv, hv}) };
  }

  double volume() const { return length*width*height; }
};
#endif
```

The Box constructor throws a dimension_error exception if any of the arguments are zero or negative. The constructor uses the min() template function from the algorithm header to determine the dimension argument that is the minimum of those specified—that will be the worst offender. Note the use of a so-called initializer list to find the minimum of three elements. The resulting expression std::min({lv, wv, hv}) is certainly more elegant than std::min(lv, std::min(wv, hv)), wouldn't you agree?

The following is an example to demonstrate the dimension_error class in action:

```cpp
// Ex15_09.cpp
// Using an exception class
#include <iostream>
#include "Box.h"                          // For the Box class
#include "Dimension_error.h"             // For the dimension_error class

int main()
{
  try
  {
    Box box1 {1.0, 2.0, 3.0};
    std::cout << "box1 volume is " << box1.volume() << std::endl;
    Box box2 {1.0, -2.0, 3.0};
    std::cout << "box2 volume is " << box2.volume() << std::endl;
  }
  catch (const std::exception& ex)
  {
    std::cout << "Exception caught in main(): " << ex.what() << std::endl;
  }
}
```

The output from this example is as follows:

```
box1 volume is 6
Exception caught in main(): Zero or negative dimension: -2.000000
```

The body of main() is a try block, and its catch block catches any type of exception that has std::exception as a base. The output shows that the Box class constructor is throwing a dimension_error exception object when a dimension is negative. The output also shows that the what() function that dimension_error inherits from out_of_range is outputting the string formed in the dimension_error constructor call.

▓ **Tip**   When throwing exceptions, always throw objects, never fundamental types. And the class of these objects should always derive from std::exception, either directly or indirectly. Even if you declare your own application-specific exception hierarchies—which often is a good idea—you should use std::exception or one of its derived classes as the base class. Many popular C++ libraries already follow this same guideline. Using only a single, standardized family of exceptions makes it much easier to catch and handle these exceptions.

Summary

Exceptions are an integral part of programming in C++. Several operators throw exceptions, and you've seen that they're used extensively within the Standard Library to signal errors. Therefore, it's important that you have a good grasp of how exceptions work, even if you don't plan to define your own exception classes. The important points that we've covered in this chapter are as follows:

- Exceptions are objects that are used to signal errors in a program.

- Code that may throw exceptions is usually contained within a try block, which enables an exception to be detected and processed within the program.

- The code to handle exceptions that may be thrown in a try block is placed in one or more catch blocks that must immediately follow the try block.

- A try block, along with its catch blocks, can be nested inside another try block.

- A catch block with a parameter of a base class type can catch an exception of a derived class type.

- A catch block with the parameter specified as an ellipsis will catch an exception of any type.

- If an exception isn't caught by any catch block, then the std::terminate() function is called, which immediately aborts the program execution.

- Every resource, including dynamically allocated memory, should always be acquired and released by an RAII object. This implies that, as a rule, you should normally no longer use the keywords new and delete in modern C++ code.

- The Standard Library offers various RAII types you should use consistently; the ones you already know about include std::unique_ptr<>, shared_ptr<>, and vector<>.

- The noexcept specification for a function indicates that the function does not throw exceptions. If a noexcept function does throw an exception it does not catch, std::terminate() is called.

- Even if a destructor does not have an explicit noexcept specifier, the compiler will almost always generate one for you. This implies that you must never allow an exception to leave a destructor; otherwise, std::terminate() will be triggered.

- The Standard Library defines a range of standard exception types in the stdexcept header that are derived from the std::exception class that is defined in the exception header.

EXERCISES

The following exercises enable you to try what you've learned in this chapter. If you get stuck, look back over the chapter for help. If you're still stuck after that, you can download the solutions from the Apress website (www.apress.com/source-code/), but that really should be a last resort.

Exercise 15-1. Derive your own exception class called CurveBall from the std::exception class to represent an arbitrary error, and write a function that throws this exception approximately 25 percent of the time. One way to do this is to generate a random integer between 0 (inclusive) and 100 (exclusive) and, if the number is less than 25, throw the exception. Define a main() function to call this function 1,000 times, while recording the number of times an exception was thrown. At the end, print out the final count. Of course, if all went well, this number should fluctuate somewhere around 250.

Exercise 15-2. Define another exception class called TooManyExceptions. Then throw an exception of this type from the catch block for CurveBall exceptions in the previous exercise when the number of exceptions caught exceeds ten. Observe what happens if you neglect to catch the exception.

Exercise 15-3. Remember our conundrum with Ex12_11 in Chapter 12? In the Truckload class of that example we were challenged with defining an array subscript operator (operator[]) that returned a Box& reference. The problem was that we had to return a Box& reference even if the index provided to the function was out of bounds. Our ad hoc solution involved "inventing" a special null object, but we already noted that this solution was severely flawed. Now that you know about exceptions, you should be able to finally fix this function once and for all. Choose an appropriate Standard Library exception type and use it to properly reimplement Truckload::operator[]() from Ex12_11. Write a small program to exercise this new behavior of the operator.

Exercise 15-4. Create a function readEvenNumber() intended to read an even integer from the std::cin input stream. About 25 percent of the time something really odd happens inside readEvenNumber(), resulting in a CurveBall exception. You can simply reuse code from Exercise 15-1 for this. Normally, however, the function verifies the user input and returns an even number if the user enters one correctly. If the input is not valid, however, the function throws one of the following exceptions:

- If any value is entered that is not a number, it throws a NotANumber exception.

- If the user enters a negative number, a NegativeNumber exception is thrown.

- If an odd number is entered, the function throws an OddNumber exception.

You should derive these new exception types from `std::domain_error`, one of the Standard exception types defined in the `<stdexcept>` header. Their constructors should compose a string containing at least the incorrectly entered value and then forward that string to the constructor of `std::domain_error`.

Hint: After attempting to read an integer number from `std::cin`, you can check whether parsing that integer succeeded by using `std::cin.fail()`. If that member function returns `true`, the user entered a string that is not a number. Note that once the stream is in such a failure state, you cannot use the stream anymore until you call `std::cin.clear()`. Also, the non-numeric value the user had entered will still be inside the stream—it is not removed when failing to extract an integer. You could, for instance, extract it using the `std::getline()` function defined in `<string>`. Putting this all together, your code might contain something like this:

```
if (std::cin.fail())
{
  std::cin.clear();  // Reset the failure state
  std::string line;  // Read the erroneous input and discard it
  std::getline(std::cin, line);
  ...
```

Once the `readEvenNumber()` helper is ready, use it to implement `askEvenNumber()`. This function prints user instructions to `std::cout` and then calls `readEvenNumber()` to handle the actual input and input verification. Once a number is read correctly, `askEvenNumber()` politely thanks the user for entering the number (the message should contain the number itself). For any `std::exception` that `readEvenNumber()` throws, `askEvenNumber()` should at least output `e.what()` to `std::cerr`. Any `exception` that is not a `domain_error` is to be rethrown, and `askEvenNumber()` has no idea how to handle these. If the exception is a `domain_error`, however, you should retry asking for an even number, unless the exception is a `NotANumber`. If a `NotANumber` occurs, `askEvenNumber()` stops asking for numbers and simply returns.

Finally, write a `main()` function that executes `askEvenNumber()` and catches any `CurveBalls` that may come out. If it catches one, it should output "...hit it out of the park!" because that's what you do when life throws you a curveball!

Exercise 15-5. The `Exer15_05` directory contains a small program that calls upon a C interface to a fictitious database system (the interface is actually a simplified version of the C interface of MySQL). As is common with C interfaces, our database interface returns so-called handles to various resources—resources that need to be freed again explicitly once you're done using them by calling another interface function. In this case, there are two such resources: the connection to the database and the memory allocated to store the result of a SQL query. Carefully read the interface specification in `DB.h` to learn how the interface should be used. As this is an exercise, in the program of `Exer15_05` these resources may leak under certain conditions. Can you spot any conditions under which the resources are leaked? Since this is an exercise in a chapter on exceptions, these conditions will of course mostly involve exceptions.

Hint: To appreciate how subtle error handling can be, ever wondered what `std::stoi()` does when passed a string that does not contain a number? Check a Standard Library reference—or write a small test program—to find out. Suppose you have customers living at number 10B or 105/5. What will happen in our program? And what if a Russian customer lives at к2, that is, a house whose official address has a street "number" starting with a letter? Similarly, what if for some customers the house number is not filled in? That is, what if the house number stored in the database is an empty string?

To fix the resource leaks in our program, you could add explicit resource cleaning statements, add some more `try-catch` blocks, and so on. For this exercise, however, we'd like you to create and use two small RAII classes instead: one that ensures an active database connection is always disconnected and one that releases the memory allocated for a given query result. Note that if you add cast operators to the RAII classes to implicitly convert to the handle types they encapsulate (and/or to a Boolean), you may not even have to change much of the remainder of the code!

Note: With the approach we suggested for this exercise, the main program still uses the C interface, only now it does so while immediately storing all resource handles in RAII objects. This is certainly a viable option, one that we have used in real-life applications. An alternative approach, though, is to use the so-called *decorator* or *wrapper* design pattern. You then develop a set of C++ classes that encapsulates the entire database and its query functionalities. Only these decorator classes are then supposed to call upon the C interface directly; the remainder of the program simply employs the members of the C++ decorator classes. The interface of these decorator classes is then designed such that memory leaks are not possible; all resources that the program can ever access shall always be managed by an RAII object. The C resource handles themselves are normally never accessible for the rest of the program. Working out this alternative approach would take us too far from the main topic of this chapter (exceptions), but it is one to keep in mind if ever you have to integrate a C interface within a larger C++ program.

CHAPTER 16

■ ■ ■

Class Templates

You learned about templates that the compiler uses to create functions in Chapter 9; this chapter is about templates the compiler can use to create classes. Class templates are a powerful mechanism for generating new class types automatically. A significant portion of the C++ Standard Library is built entirely on the ability to define templates. Both function and class templates are used extensively throughout the Library to provide versatile, generic utilities, algorithms, and data structures.

With this chapter, we are nearing the end of our series of chapters on defining your own classes. Besides introducing the basics of class templates, we will therefore also include a few slightly off-topic sections with somewhat more advanced reasonings on coding style. With these sidebars we intend to incite you to reason about aspects of your code that go beyond mere functional correctness. We will advocate that writing code should become more than just making sure it computes the correct values. Your code should be easy to read and maintain, it should be robust against unexpected conditions and exceptions, and so on. Of course, we will give you a few standard techniques to help you accomplish these fundamental nonfunctional requirements.

In this chapter, you learn:

- What a class template is and how it is defined

- What an instance of a class template is and how it is created

- How to define templates for member functions of a class template outside the class template definition

- How type parameters differ from nontype parameters

- How static members of a class template are initialized

- What a partial specialization of a class template is and how it is defined

- How a class can be nested inside a class template

- Why it pays to invest in high-quality code that is not just correct but also easy to maintain and robust against failure

- How to use the idiom we call "const-and-back-again" to avoid duplicate member function definitions

- What the "copy-and-swap" idiom is and how to use it to write exception-safe code

© Ivor Horton and Peter Van Weert 2018

I. Horton and P. Van Weert, *Beginning C++17*, https://doi.org/10.1007/978-1-4842-3366-5_16

Understanding Class Templates

Class templates are based on the same idea as function templates. A class template is a *parameterized type*; it's a recipe for creating a family of class types using one or more parameters. When you define a variable that has a type specified by a class template, the compiler uses the template to create a definition of a class using the template arguments that you use in the type specification. The argument for each parameter is typically (but not always) a type. You can use a class template to generate any number of different classes. It's important to keep in mind that a class template is not a class but just a recipe for creating classes because this is the reason for many of the constraints on how you define class templates.

A class template has a name, just like a regular class, and one or more template parameters. A class template must be unique within a namespace, so you can't have another template with the same name and parameter list in the namespace in which the template is defined. A class *definition* is generated from a class template when you supply an argument for each of the template's parameters. This is illustrated in Figure 16-1.

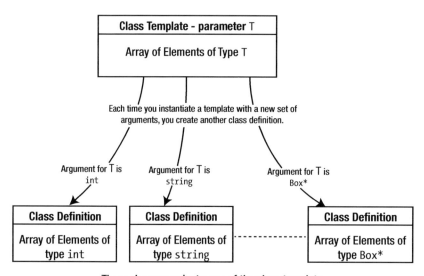

Figure 16-1. Instantiating a template

Each class that the compiler generates from a template is called an *instance* of the template. When you define a variable using a template type for the first time, you create an instance of the template; variables of the same type defined subsequently will use the first instance created. You can also cause instances of a class template to be created without defining a variable. The compiler does not process a class template in a source file in any way if the template is not used to generate a class.

There are many applications for class templates, but they are perhaps most commonly used to define *container classes*. These are classes that can contain sets of objects of a given type, organized in a particular way. In a container class, the organization of the data is independent of the type of objects stored. Of course, you already have experience instantiating and using std::vector<> and std::array<> class templates that define containers where the data is organized sequentially. In this chapter, you will learn how to define your own class templates.

Defining Class Templates

Class template definitions tend to look more complicated than they really are, largely because of the notation used to define them and the parameters sprinkled around the statements in their definitions. Class template definitions are similar to those of ordinary classes, but like so many things, the devil is in the details. A class template is prefixed by the `template` keyword followed by the parameters for the template between angled brackets. The template class definition consists of the `class` keyword followed by the class template name, with the body of the definition between braces. Just like a regular class, the whole definition ends with a semicolon. The general form of a class template looks like this:

```
template <template parameter list>
class ClassName
{
  // Template class definition...
};
```

ClassName is the name of this template. You write the code for the body of the template just as you'd write the body of an ordinary class, except that some of the member declarations and definitions will be in terms of the template parameters that appear between the angled brackets.

Template Parameters

A template parameter list can contain any number of parameters that can be of two kinds—*type parameters* and *nontype parameters*. The argument corresponding to a type parameter is always a type, such as `int`, `std::string`, or `Box*`. The argument for a nontype parameter can be a literal of an integral type such as 200, an integral constant expression, a pointer or reference to an object, or a pointer to a function or a pointer that is null. Type parameters are much more commonly used than nontype parameters, so we'll explain these first and defer discussion of nontype parameters until later in this chapter.

▨ **Note** There's a third possibility for class template parameters. A parameter can also be a *template* where the argument must be an instance of a class template. A detailed discussion of this possibility is a little too advanced for this book.

Figure 16-2 illustrates the options for type parameters. You can write type parameters either using the `class` keyword or using the `typename` keyword preceding the parameter name (typename T in Figure 16-2, for example). In this context, `typename` and `class` are synonyms. By default, you should use `typename` because `class` tends to connote a class type, and in most cases the type argument doesn't have to be a `class` type. If you follow this guideline, you could then reserve the use of the `class` keyword for those type parameters that should effectively only be assigned class types as an argument.

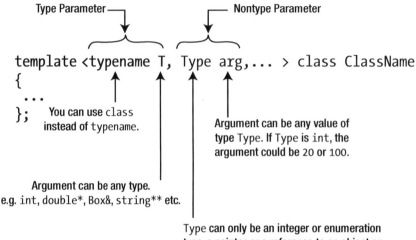

Figure 16-2. *Class template parameters*

T is often used as a type parameter name (or T1, T2, and so on, when there are several type parameters) because it's concise, but you can use whatever name you want. It is often recommended, especially if there are multiple type parameters, to use more descriptive names. Conventionally, type parameter names start with a capital letter to distinguish them from regular variable names, but this is not required.

A Simple Class Template

Let's take an example of a class template for arrays that will do bounds checking on index values to make sure that they are legal. The Standard Library provides a comprehensive implementation of an array template, but building a limited array template is an effective basis from which you can learn how templates work. You already have a clear idea of how arrays work, so you can concentrate on the template specifics.

This template just has a single type parameter, so in outline, its definition will be as follows:

```
template <typename T>
class Array
{
  // Definition of the template...
};
```

The Array template has just one type parameter, T. You can tell that it's a type parameter because it's preceded by the keyword typename. Whatever is "plugged in" for the parameter when you instantiate the template—int, double*, string, or whatever—determines the type of the elements stored in an object of the resultant class. As this obviously does not necessarily have to be a class type, we have used the keyword typename rather than class.

The definition in the body of the template will be much the same as a class definition, with member variables and functions that are specified as public, protected, or private, and it will typically have constructors and a destructor. You can use T to define member variables or to specify the parameters or return types for member functions, either by itself or in types such as T* or T&&. You can use the template name with its parameter list—Array<T>, in this case—as a type name when specifying member variables and functions.

The very least we need by way of a class interface is a constructor, a copy constructor (because the space for the array will need to be allocated dynamically), an assignment operator (because the compiler will supply an unsuitable version if there isn't one defined), an overloaded subscript operator, and finally a destructor. With this in mind, the initial definition of the template looks like this:

```
template <typename T>
class Array
{
private:
  T* elements;                              // Array of type T
  size_t size;                              // Number of array elements

public:
  explicit Array<T>(size_t arraySize);      // Constructor
  Array<T>(const Array<T>& array);          // Copy constructor
  ~Array<T>();                              // Destructor
  T& operator[](size_t index);              // Subscript operator
  const T& operator[](size_t index) const;  // Subscript operator-const arrays
  Array<T>& operator=(const Array<T>& rhs); // Assignment operator
  size_t getSize() const { return size; }   // Accessor for size
};
```

The body of the template looks much like a regular class definition, except for the type parameter T, in various places. For example, it has a member variable, elements, which is of type *pointer to* T (equivalent to *array of* T). When the template is instantiated to produce a specific class definition, T is replaced by the actual type used to instantiate the template. If you create an instance of the template for type double, elements will be of type double* or *array of* double. The operations that the template needs to perform on objects of type T will obviously place requirements on the definition of type T when T is a class type.

The first constructor is declared as explicit to prevent its use for implicit conversions. The subscript operator has been overloaded on const. The non-const version of the subscript operator applies to non-const array objects and can return a non-const reference to an array element. Thus, this version can appear on the left of an assignment. The const version is called for const objects and returns a const reference to an element; obviously this can't appear on the left of an assignment.

The assignment operator function parameter is of type const Array<T>&. This type is *const reference to* Array<T>. When a class is synthesized from the template—with T as type double, for example—this is a const reference to the class name for that particular class, which would be const Array<double>, in this case. More generally, the class name for a specific instance of a template is formed from the template name followed by the actual type argument between angled brackets. The template name followed by the list of parameter names between angled brackets is called the *template ID*.

It's not essential to use the full template ID within a template definition. Within the body of the Array template, Array by itself will be taken to mean Array<T>, and Array& will be interpreted as Array<T>&, so we can simplify the class template definition:

```
template <typename T>
class Array
{
private:
  T* elements;                              // Array of type T
  size_t size;                              // Number of array elements
```

```
public:
  explicit Array(size_t arraySize);          // Constructor
  Array(const Array& array);                  // Copy constructor
  ~Array();                                   // Destructor
  T& operator[](size_t index);                // Subscript operator
  const T& operator[](size_t index) const;    // Subscript operator-const arrays
  Array& operator=(const Array& rhs);         // Assignment operator
  size_t getSize() const { return size; }     // Accessor for size
};
```

■ **Caution**   You *must* use the template ID to identify the template outside the body of the template. This will apply to member functions of a class template that are defined outside the template.

It's desirable that the number of elements in an Array<T> object can be determined, so the getSize() member provides this. The assignment operator allows one Array<T> object to be assigned to another, which is something you can't do with ordinary arrays. If you wanted to inhibit this capability, you should declare the operator=() function with =delete in the declaration to prevent the compiler from supplying the default (as shown in Chapter 12). The getSize() member is implemented within the class template, so it's inline by default, and no external definition is necessary.

Defining Member Functions of a Class Template

If you include the definitions for the member functions of a class template within its body, they are implicitly inline in any instance of the template, just like in an ordinary class. However, you'll want to define members outside of the template body from time to time, especially if they involve a lot of code. The syntax for doing this is a little different from what applies for a normal class.

The clue to understanding the syntax is to realize that external definitions for member functions of a class template are themselves templates. This is true even if a member function has no dependence on the type parameter T, so getSize() would need a template definition if it was not defined inside the class template. The parameter list for the template that defines a member function must be identical to that of the class template.

All the member function definitions that you'll write in this section are templates that are inextricably bound to the class template. They are *not* function definitions; they're templates to be used by the compiler when the code for one of the member functions of the class template needs to be generated, so they need to be available in any source file that uses the template. For this reason, you almost always put all the definitions of the member functions for a class template in the header file that contains the class template itself.

Let's start by defining the constructors for the Array template.

Constructor Templates

When you're defining a constructor outside a class template definition, its name must be qualified by the class template name in a similar way to a member function of an ordinary class. However, this isn't a function definition; it's a *template* for a function definition, so that has to be expressed as well. Here's the definition of the constructor:

```
template <typename T>                  // This is a template with parameter T
Array<T>::Array(size_t arraySize) : elements {new T[arraySize]}, size {arraySize}
{}
```

The first line identifies this as a template and also specifies the template parameter as T. Splitting the template function declaration into two lines, as we've done here, is only for illustrative purposes and isn't necessary if the whole construct fits on one line. The template parameter is essential in the qualification of the constructor name because it ties the function definition to the class template. Note that you *don't* use the typename keyword in the qualifier for the member name; it's only used in the template parameter list. Also, you don't need a parameter list after the constructor name; you need it only in the parameter ID that precedes it. When the constructor is instantiated for an instance of the class template—for type double, for example—the type name replaces T in the constructor qualifier, so the qualified constructor name for the class Array<double> is instantiated as Array<double>::Array().

In the constructor, you must allocate memory in the free store for an elements array that contains size elements of type T. If T is a class type, a public default constructor must exist in the class T; otherwise, the instance of this constructor won't compile.

The copy constructor has to create an array for the object being created that's the same size as that of its argument and then copy the latter's member variables to the former. Here's the code to do that:

```
template <typename T>
Array<T>::Array(const Array& array) : Array{array.size}
{
  for (size_t i {}; i < size; ++i)
    elements[i] = array.elements[i];
}
```

This assumes that the assignment operator works for type T. This demonstrates how important it is to always define the assignment operator for classes that allocate memory dynamically. If the class T doesn't define it, the default copy assignment operator for T is used, with undesirable side effects if creating a T object involves allocating memory dynamically. Without seeing the code for the template before you use it, you may not realize the dependency on the assignment operator.

The Destructor Template

In many cases a default destructor will be OK in a class generated from a template, but this is not the case here. The destructor must release the memory for the elements array, so its definition will be as follows:

```
template <typename T>
Array<T>::~Array()
{
  delete[] elements;
}
```

We are releasing memory allocated for an array, so we must use the delete[] form of the operator. Failing to define this template would result in all classes generated from the template having major memory leaks.

Subscript Operator Templates

The operator[]() function is quite straightforward, but we must ensure illegal index values can't be used. For an index value that is out of range, we can throw an exception:

```
template <typename T>
T& Array<T>::operator[](size_t index)
{
  if (index >= size)
    throw std::out_of_range {"Index too large: " + std::to_string(index)};

  return elements[index];
}
```

We could define an exception class to use here, but it's easier to borrow the out_of_range class type that's already defined in the stdexcept header. This is thrown if you index a string, vector<>, or array<> object with an out-of-range index value, for example, so the usage here is consistent with that. An exception of type out_of_range is thrown if the value of index is not between 0 and size-1. An index can already not be less than zero because it is of type size_t, which is an *unsigned* integer type, so all we need to check for is that the given index is not too large. The argument that is passed to the out_of_range constructor is a message that includes the erroneous index value to make tracking down the source of the problem a little easier.

In a first, natural implementation, the const version of the subscript operator function would be almost identical to the non-const version:

```
template <typename T>
const T& Array<T>::operator[](size_t index) const
{
  if (index >= size)
    throw std::out_of_range {"Index too large: " + std::to_string(index)};

  return elements[index];
}
```

However, introducing such duplicate definitions for the const and non-const overloads of a member function is considered bad practice. It is a particular instance of what is typically referred to as *code duplication*. Because avoiding code duplication is key in making sure your code remains maintainable, we'll contemplate this a bit more before we continue with class templates.

CODE DUPLICATION

Writing the same or similar code more than once is rarely a good idea. Not only is it a waste of time, such so-called duplicated code is undesirable for a number of reasons—most notably because it undermines the maintainability of your code base. Requirements evolve, new insights are gained, and bugs are discovered. So, more often than not, your code will need to be adjusted several times after it is written. So if you have duplicated code snippets, this means you have to remember to always adjust all individual copies of the same code. Believe us when we say that this is a maintenance nightmare! The principle of avoiding code duplication is also sometimes called the *Don't Repeat Yourself* (DRY) principle.

CHAPTER 16 ■ CLASS TEMPLATES

Even if the duplicated code is just a few lines it is often already worthwhile rethinking it. Consider, for instance, the duplicated `operator[]()` member definitions we wrote for the `Array<>` template. Now imagine that at some point later you want to change the type of exception thrown or change the message passed to the exception. Then you would have to change it in two places. Not only is this tedious, but it would be really easy to forget either one of these duplicates. This unfortunately occurs a lot in practice; changes or bug fixes to duplicated code are made in only some of the duplicates, while other duplicates live on containing the original, now-incorrect version. If you only have each piece of logic in one single place in your code base, this cannot happen!

The good news is that you already know most of the tools you need to battle code duplication. Functions are reusable blocks of computations and algorithms, templates instantiate functions or classes for any number of types, a base class encapsulates all that is common to its derived classes, and so on. All these mechanisms were created precisely to make sure you do not have to repeat yourself!

The traditional approach to eliminate the code duplication between the `const` and non-`const` overloads of a member function is to implement the non-`const` version in terms of its `const` twin. While this sounds simple enough in principle, the resulting code may, nay *will*, seem daunting at first. Prepare yourself. For our `operator[]()` member, for instance, the classical implementation of this idiom looks as follows:

```
template <typename T>
T& Array<T>::operator[](size_t index)
{
  return const_cast<T&>(static_cast<const Array<T>&>(*this)[index]);
}
```

Ouch! We warned you that it would get scary, didn't we? The good news is that C++17 has introduced a little helper function, `std::as_const()`, that makes this code already a bit more bearable:

```
template <typename T>
T& Array<T>::operator[](size_t index)
{
  return const_cast<T&>(std::as_const(*this)[index]);
}
```

That's quite a bit shorter and more readable already. Still, since this is your first encounter with the idiom, let's first rewrite that still nonobvious `return` statement into some smaller steps. That will help us explain what is going on:

```
template <typename T>
T& Array<T>::operator[](size_t index)
{
 Array<T>& nonConstRef = *this;                      // Start from a non-const ref
 const Array<T>& constRef = std::as_const(nonConstRef); // Convert to const ref
 const T& constResult = constRef[index];             // Obtain the const result
 return const_cast<T&>(constResult);                 // Convert to non-const result
}
```

Because this template generates non-const member functions, the this pointer has a pointer-to-non-const type. So in our case, dereferencing the this pointer gives us a reference of type Array<T>&. The first thing we need to do is add const to this type. As of C++17, this can be done using the std::as_const() function defined in the <utility> header of the Standard Library. Given a value of type T&, this function template evaluates to a value of type const T&. (If your implementation does not contain this C++17 utility yet, you need to use an equivalent static_cast<const T&> as shown earlier.)

Next, we simply call the same function again, with the same set of arguments—an operator function with a single size_t argument index in our case. The only difference is that this time we call the overloaded function on the reference-to-const variable, which means that the const overload of the function—operator[](size_t) const—gets called. If we hadn't first added const to the type of *this, we'd simply be calling the same function again, which would trigger infinite recursion.

Because we now call the function on a const object, it also means that it typically returns a const reference. If it didn't, it would break const correctness. What we need, however, is a reference to a non-const element. In a final step, we must therefore strip away the constness of the result before returning it from the function. And, as you know, the only way to remove const is by using a const_cast<>.

Paraphrasing J. R. R. Tolkien, we propose to call this idiom "const-and-back-again." You first go from non-const to const (using std::as_const) and then back again to non-const (using a const_cast<>). Note that this idiom is one of the few cases where it is actually recommended to use a const_cast<>. In general, casting away constness is considered bad practice. But eliminating code duplication using the const-and-back-again idiom is a widely accepted exception to this rule:

■ **Tip** Use the const-and-back-again idiom to avoid code duplication between the const and non-const overloads of a member function. In general, it works by implementing the non-const overload of a member in terms of its const counterpart using the following pattern:

```
ReturnType Class::Function(Arguments)
{
  return const_cast<ReturnType>(std::as_const(*this).Function(Arguments));
}
```

The Assignment Operator Template

There's more than one possibility for how the assignment operator works. The operands must be of the same Array<T> type with the same T, but this does not prevent the size members from having different values. You could implement the assignment operator so that the left operand retains the same value for its elements member whenever possible. That is, if the right operand has fewer elements than the left operand, you could just copy sufficient elements from the right operand to fill parts of the array for the left operand. You could then either leave the excess elements at their original values or set them to the value produced by the default T constructor.

To keep it simple, however, we'll just make the left operand allocate a new elements array always, even if the previous array would be large enough already to fit a copy of the elements of the right operand. To implement this, the assignment operator function must release any memory allocated in the destination object and then do what the copy constructor did. To make sure the assignment operator does not delete[] its own memory, it must first check that the objects are not identical. Here's the definition:

```
template <typename T>
Array<T>& Array<T>::operator=(const Array& rhs)
{
  if (&rhs != this)                  // If lhs != rhs...
  {                                  // ...do the assignment...
    delete[] elements;               // Release any free store memory

    size = rhs.size;                 // Copy the members of rhs into lhs
    elements = new T[size];
    for (size_t i {}; i < size; ++i)
      elements[i] = rhs.elements[i];
  }
  return *this;                      // ... return lhs
}
```

Remember, checking to make sure that the left operand is not identical to the right is essential; otherwise, you'd free the memory for the elements member of the object pointed to by this and then attempt to copy it to itself when it no longer exists! Every assignment operator of this form must start with such a safety check. When the operands are different, you release any free store memory owned by the left operand before creating a copy of the right operand.

EXCEPTION SAFETY

The assignment operator for our Array<> class template will work perfectly in the nominal case. But what if something goes wrong? What if an error occurs during its execution and an exception is thrown? Can you perhaps locate the two places in the function's code where this might happen? Try to do so before reading on.

The two potential sources of exceptions inside our function's body are annotated in the following code snippet:

```
template <typename T>
Array<T>& Array<T>::operator=(const Array& rhs)
{
  if (&rhs != this)
  {
    delete[] elements;

    size = rhs.size;
    elements = new T[size];          // may throw std::bad_alloc
    for (size_t i {}; i < size; ++i)
      elements[i] = rhs.elements[i];  // may throw any exception (depends on type T)
  }
  return *this;
}
```

623

The first is operator `new[]`. In the previous chapter, you learned that it throws a `std::bad_alloc` exception if free store memory cannot be allocated for some reason. While unlikely, especially on today's computers, this can certainly happen. Perhaps `rhs` is a very large array that doesn't fit twice in the available memory.

■ **Note** Free store memory allocation is a rare occurrence these days because physical memory is large and because virtual memory is very large. So, checking for or considering `bad_alloc` is omitted in most code. Nevertheless, given that in this case we are implementing a class template whose sole responsibility is managing an array of elements, properly handling memory allocation failures does seem appropriate here.

The second potential source of exceptions is the `elements[i]` = `rhs.elements[i]` assignment expression. Since the `Array<T>` template can be used with any type `T`, it might just be instantiated for a type `T` whose assignment operator throws an exception if the assignment fails. One likely candidate already is again a `std::bad_alloc`. As witnessed by our own assignment operator, an assignment often involves memory allocation. But in general this could be any exception type. It all depends on the definition of the assignment operator of the type `T`.

■ **Tip** As a rule, you should assume that *any* function or operator you call might throw an exception and consequently consider how your code should behave if and when this occurs. The only exceptions to this rule are functions annotated with the `noexcept` keyword and most destructors, as these are generally implicitly `noexcept`.

Once you have identified all potential sources of exceptions, you must analyze what would happen if exceptions are in fact thrown there. It would again be good practice for you to do so now, before reading on. Ask yourself, what exactly would happen to the `Array<>` object if an exception occurs in either of these two locations?

If the `new[]` operator in our example fails to allocate new memory, the `elements` pointer of the `Array<>` object becomes what is known as a *dangling pointer*—a pointer to memory that has been reclaimed. The reason is that right before the failing `new[]`, `delete[]` was already applied on `elements`. This means that even if the caller catches the `bad_alloc` exception, the `Array<>` object has become unusable. Worse, actually, its destructor is almost certainly going to cause a fatal crash because it'll again apply `delete[]` on the now-dangling `elements` pointer.

Note that assigning `nullptr` to `elements` after the `delete[]` like we recommended earlier would in this case only be a small patch on the wound. As none of the other `Array<>` member functions—for instance, `operator[]`—checks for `nullptr`, it would again only be a matter of time before a fatal crash occurs.

If one of the individual assignments performed inside the `for` loop fails, we are only slightly better off. Supposing the culprit exception is eventually caught, you are left with an `Array<>` object where only the first some `elements` have been assigned a correct new value, while the rest is still default-constructed. And there is no way of knowing how many have succeeded.

When you call a member function that modifies an object's state, you typically want one of two things to happen. Ideally, of course, the function fully succeeds and brings the object into its desired new state. As soon as any error prevents a complete success, however, what you really do not want is to be left with an object in some unpredictable halfway state. Leaving a function's work half-finished mostly means that the object becomes unusable. Once anything goes wrong, you instead prefer the object to remain or revert to its initial state. For our assignment operator, this means that if the assignment fails to allocate and assign all elements, the end result should be that the Array<> object still points to the same elements array as it did prior to the assignment attempt.

Like we said in Chapter 15, writing code that is correct might be only half of the work. Making sure that it behaves reliably and robustly when faced with unexpected errors can be at least as hard. Of course, proper error handling always starts from a cautious attitude. That is, always be on the lookout for possible sources of errors, and make sure you understand what the consequences would be of such errors. Luckily, once you have located and analyzed the problem areas—and you'll get better at spotting these over time—there exist standard techniques to make your code behave correctly after an error. Let's see how this might be done for our example.

The programming pattern that can be used to guarantee the desired all-or-nothing behavior for our assignment operator is called the *copy-and-swap idiom*. The idea is simple. If you have to modify the state of one or more objects and any of the steps required for this modification may throw, then you should follow this simple recipe:

1. Create a *copy* of the objects.

2. Modify this copy instead of the original objects. The latter still remain untouched!

3. If all modifications succeed, replace—or *swap*—the originals with the copies.

However, if anything goes wrong either during the copy or any of the modification steps, simply abandon the copied, half-modified objects and let the entire operation fail. The original objects then remain as they were.

While this idiom can be applied to virtually any code, it is often used within a member function. For an assignment operator, the application of this idiom often looks like this:

```
template <typename T>
Array<T>& Array<T>::operator=(const Array& rhs)
{
  if (this != &rhs)
  {
    Array<T> copy{rhs};     // Copy...         (could go wrong and throw an exception)
    swap(copy);             // ... and swap!   (noexcept)
  }
  return *this;
}
```

The main thing to note is that we have rewritten the assignment in terms of the copy constructor. The self-assignment test is now no longer strictly required, but there is no harm in adding it either. Still, if you omit it, you can rewrite the copy assignment operator to make it even shorter:

```
template <typename T>
Array<T>& Array<T>::operator=(Array rhsCopy) // Copy...  (could throw an exception)
{
  swap(rhsCopy);               // ... and swap!  (noexcept)
  return *this;
}
```

Copy construction now occurs when the operator's right side is passed to the function by value.

In a way, this is actually a degenerate instance of the copy-and-swap idiom. In general, the state of the copied object may need any number of modifications between the copy and the swap stages of the idiom. Of course, these modifications are then always applied to the copy, never directly to the original object (*this, in our case). If either the copy step itself or any of the additional modification steps that may follow throw an exception, the stack-allocated copy object is automatically reclaimed, and the original object (*this) remains unchanged.

Once you are done with updating copy, you swap its member variables with those of the original object. The copy-and-swap idiom hinges on the assumption that this final step, the swapping, can be done without any risk for exceptions. That is, it must not be possible that an exception occurs with some members already swapped and others not. Luckily, implementing a noexcept swap function is almost always trivial.

By convention, the function to swap the contents of two objects is called swap() and is implemented as a nonmember function in the same namespace as the class whose objects it is swapping. (We know, in our Array<> template that it is a member function as well. Be patient, though, we're getting to that!) The Standard Library <utility> header also offers the std::swap<>() function template that can be used to swap values or objects of any copyable data type. For now, you can think of this template as if it was implemented like this:[1]

```
template <typename T>
void swap(T& one, T& other) noexcept
{
  T copy(one);
  one = other;
  other = copy;
}
```

Applying this template to Array<> objects would not be particularly efficient. All the elements of the objects being swapped would be copied several times. Besides, we could never use it to swap *this and copy in our copy assignment operator—do you see why?[2] We'll therefore create our own, more effective swap() function for Array<> objects. Similar specializations of std::swap<>() exist for many Standard Library types.

---

[1]The actual swap<>() template is different in two aspects. First, it moves the objects if possible using move semantics. You'll learn all about move semantics in the next chapter. Second, it is only conditionally noexcept. Concretely, it is noexcept if its arguments can be moved without exceptions. Conditional noexcept specifications are a more advanced language feature we do not cover in this book.

[2]The reason we cannot use the std::swap() from within our copy assignment operator is that std::swap() in turn would use the copy assignment operator. In other words, calling std::swap() here would result in infinite recursion!

Because the member variables of Array<> are private, one option is to define swap() as a friend function. Here, we'll take a slightly different approach, one that is also followed by standard container templates such as std::vector<>. The idea is to first add an extra member function swap() to Array<> as follows:

```
template <typename T>
void Array<T>::swap(Array& other) noexcept
{
  std::swap(elements, other.elements);   // Swap two pointers (not their contents!)
  std::swap(size, other.size);           // Swap both sizes
}
```

You then use that to implement the conventional nonmember swap() function:

```
template <typename T>
void swap(Array<T>& one, Array<T>& other) noexcept
{
  one.swap(other);       // Forward to public member function
}
```

You can find the full source code of the improved Array<> template in Ex16_01A.

■ **Tip** Implement the assignment operator in terms of the copy constructor and a noexcept swap() function. This basic instance of the copy-and-swap idiom will ensure the desired all-or-nothing behavior for your assignment operators. While swap() can be added as a member function, convention dictates that making objects swappable involves defining a nonmember swap() function. Following this convention also ensures that the swap() function gets used by various algorithms of the Standard Library.

The copy-and-swap idiom can be used to make any nontrivial state modification exception safe, either inside other member functions or simply in the middle of any code. It comes in many variations, but the idea is always the same. First copy the object you want to change, then perform any number (zero or more) of risky steps onto that copy, and only once they all succeed commit the changes by swapping the state of the copy and the actual target object.

Instantiating a Class Template

The compiler instantiates a class template as a result of a definition of an object that has a type produced by the template. Here's an example:

```
Array<int> data {40};
```

When this statement is compiled, two things happen. The definition for the Array<int> class is created so that the type is identified, and the constructor definition is generated because it must be called to create the object. This is, all that the compiler needs to create the data object, so this is the only code that it provides from the templates at this point.

The class definition that'll be included in the program is generated by substituting int in place of T in the template, but there's one subtlety. The compiler compiles *only* the member functions that your program *uses*, so you do not necessarily get the entire class that would be produced by a simple substitution for the template parameter. On the basis of just the definition for the object, data, it is equivalent to the following:

```
class Array<int>
{
private:
  int* elements;                        // Array of type int
  size_t size;                          // Number of array elements

public:
  explicit Array(size_t arraySize);     // Constructor
  ~Array();                             // Destructor
};
```

You can see that the only member functions are the constructor and destructor. The compiler won't create instances of anything that isn't required to create or destruct the object, and it won't include parts of the template that aren't needed in the program. This implies that there can be coding errors in a class template, and a program that uses the template may still compile, link, and run successfully. If the errors are in parts of the template that aren't required by the program, they won't be detected by the compiler because they are not included in the code that is compiled. Obviously, you are almost certain to have other statements in a program besides the declaration of an object that use other member functions—for instance, you'll always need the destructor to destroy the object—so the ultimate version of the class in the program will include more than that shown in the preceding code. The point is that what is finally in the class generated from the template will be precisely those parts that are actually used in the program, which is not necessarily the complete template.

■ **Caution**   Of course, this implies that you must take care when testing your own class templates to ensure that all the member functions are generated and tested. You also need to consider what the template does across a range of types, so you need to test a template with pointers and references as the template type argument.

The instantiation of a class template from a definition is referred to as an *implicit instantiation* of the template because it arises as a by-product of declaring an object. This terminology is also to distinguish it from an *explicit instantiation* of a template, which we'll get to shortly and which behaves a little differently.

As we said, the declaration of data also causes the constructor, Array<int>::Array(), to be called, so the compiler uses the function template that defines the constructor to create a definition for the constructor for the class:

```
Array<int>::Array(size_t arraySize) : elements {new int[arraySize]}, size {arraySize}
{}
```

Each time you define a variable using a class template with a different type argument, a new class is defined and included in the program. Because creating the class object requires a constructor to be called, the definition of the appropriate class constructor is also generated. Of course, creating objects of a type that you've created previously doesn't necessitate any new template instances. The compiler uses any previously created template instances as required.

When you use the member functions of a particular instance of a class template—by calling functions on the object that you defined using the template, for example—the code for each member function that you use is generated. If you have member functions that you don't use, no instances of their templates are created. The creation of each function definition is an implicit template instantiation because it arises out of the use of the function. The template itself isn't part of your executable code. All it does is enable the compiler to generate the code that you need automatically. This process is illustrated in Figure 16-3.

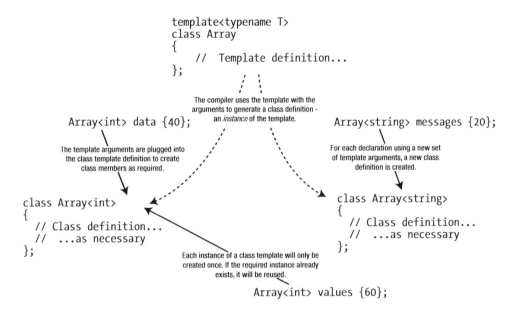

Figure 16-3. *Implicit instantiation of a class template*

Note that a class template is only implicitly instantiated when an object of the specific template type needs to be created. Declaring a pointer to an object type won't cause an instance of the template to be created. Here's an example:

```
Array<std::string>* pObject;                          // A pointer to a template type
```

This defines pObject as type *pointer to type* Array<string>. No object of type Array<string> is created as a result of this statement, so no template instance is created. Contrast this with the following statement:

```
Array<std::string*> pMessages {10};
```

This time the compiler does create an instance of the class template. This defines an Array<std::string*> object, so each element of pMessages can store a pointer to a std::string object. An instance of the template defining the constructor is also generated.

It's high time we tried out the Array template in a working example. You can put the class template and the templates defining the member functions of the template all together in a header file Array.h:

```
// Array class template definition
#ifndef ARRAY_H
#define ARRAY_H
#include <stdexcept>            // For standard exception types
#include <string>               // For std::to_string()
#include <utility>              // For std::as_const()
```

```
// Definition of the Array<T> template...

// Definitions of the templates for member functions of Array<T>...
#endif
```

To use the class template, you just need a program that'll declare some arrays using the template and try them. The example will create an Array of Box objects; you can use this definition for the Box class:

```
// Box.h
#ifndef BOX_H
#define BOX_H

class Box
{
private:
  double length {1.0};
  double width {1.0};
  double height {1.0};

public:
  Box(double lv, double wv, double hv) : length {lv}, width {wv}, height {hv} {}
  Box() = default;

  double volume() const { return length * width * height; }
};
#endif
```

We'll use some out-of-range index values in the example, just to show that it works:

```
// Ex16_01.cpp
// Using a class template
#include "Box.h"
#include "Array.h"
#include <iostream>
#include <iomanip>

int main()
{
  try
  {
    const size_t numValues {50};
    Array<double> values {numValues};              // Class constructor instance created

    for (unsigned i {}; i < numValues; ++i)
      values[i] = i + 1;                           // Member function instance created

    std::cout << "Sums of pairs of elements:";
    size_t lines {};
    for (size_t i {numValues - 1}; i >= 0; --i)
    {
      std::cout << (lines++ % 5 == 0 ? "\n" : "")
```

```
                    << std::setw(5) << values[i] + values[i - 1];
    }
  }
  catch (const std::out_of_range& ex)
  {
    std::cerr << "\nout_of_range exception object caught! " << ex.what() << std::endl;
  }

  try
  {
    const size_t nBoxes {10};
    Array<Box> boxes {nBoxes};                       // Template instance created
    for (size_t i {} ; i <= nBoxes ; ++i)            // Member instance created in loop
      std::cout << "Box volume is " << boxes[i].volume() << std::endl;
  }
  catch (const std::out_of_range& ex)
  {
    std::cerr << "\nout_of_range exception object caught! " << ex.what() << std::endl;
  }
}
```

This example will produce the following output:

```
Sums of pairs of elements:
   99   97   95   93   91
   89   87   85   83   81
   79   77   75   73   71
   69   67   65   63   61
   59   57   55   53   51
   49   47   45   43   41
   39   37   35   33   31
   29   27   25   23   21
   19   17   15   13   11
    9    7    5    3
out_of_range exception object caught! Index too large: 4294967295
Box volume is 1
Box volume is 1
Box volume is 1
Box volume is 1
Box volume is 1
Box volume is 1
Box volume is 1
Box volume is 1
Box volume is 1
Box volume is 1

out_of_range exception object caught! Index too large: 10
```

The main() function creates an object of type Array<double> that implicitly creates an instance of the class template with a type argument of double. The number of elements in the array is specified by the argument to the constructor, numValues. The compiler will also create an instance of the template for the constructor definition.

Next, the elements of the values object are initialized with values from 1 to numValues in a first for loop. The expression values[i] results in an instance of the subscript operator function being created. This instance is called implicitly by this expression as values.operator[](i). Because values is not const, the non-const version of the operator function is called. If you used the const-and-back-again idiom, this will in turn call the const overload of the operator.

A second for loop in the try block then outputs the sums of successive pairs of elements, starting at the end of the array. The code in this loop also calls the subscript operator function, but because the instance of the function template has already been created, no new instance is generated. Clearly, the expression values[i-1] has an illegal index value when i is 0, so this causes an exception to be thrown by the operator[]() function. The catch block catches this and outputs a message to the standard error stream. The what() function for the out_of_range exception returns a null-terminated string that corresponds to the string object passed to the constructor when the exception object was created. You can see from the output that the exception was thrown by the overloaded subscript operator function and that the index value is very large. The value of the index suggests that it originated by decrementing an unsigned zero value. When the exception is thrown by the subscript operator function, control is passed immediately to the handler, so the illegal element reference is not used, and nothing is stored at the location indicated by the illegal index. Of course, the loop also ends immediately at this point.

The next try block defines an object that can store Box objects. This time, the compiler generates an instance of the class template, Array<Box>, which stores an array of Box objects because the template has not been instantiated for Box objects previously. The statement also calls the constructor to create the boxes object, so an instance of the function template for the constructor is created. The constructor for the Array<Box> class calls the default constructor for the Box class when the elements member is created in the free store. Of course, all the Box objects in the elements array have the default dimensions of $1 \times 1 \times 1$.

The volume of each Box object in boxes is output in a for loop. The expression boxes[i] calls the overloaded subscript operator, so again the compiler uses an instance of the template to produce a definition of this function. When i has the value nBoxes, the subscript operator function throws an exception because an index value of nBoxes is beyond the end of the elements array. The catch block following the try block catches the exception. Because the try block is exited, all locally declared objects will be destroyed, including the boxes object.

Class Template Argument Deduction

You'll recall from Chapter 9 that for function templates, more often than not, the compiler automatically deduces all function template arguments from the types of the arguments passed to the function instance. You saw function template argument deduction in action in Ex9_01:

```
template<typename T> T larger(T a, T b);    // Function template prototype

int main()
{
  std::cout << "Larger of 1.5 and 2.5 is " << larger(1.5, 2.5) << std::endl;
  ...
```

You did not have to explicitly specify the template argument using larger<double>(1.5, 2.5). The compiler conveniently deduces that the type argument T of the function template larger<> needs to be double for you.

For a long time, no type deduction existed for class template arguments. These arguments always had to be specified explicitly. Of course, sometimes there is no other choice. Consider the variable definition you encountered in Ex16_01:

```
const size_t numValues {50};
Array<double> values {numValues};              // Class constructor instance created
```

Obviously, the compiler cannot possibly deduce the template argument double from this variable definition. All it has is a size_t argument passed to the constructor. So, it's only fair that you have to specify the template argument double in such cases.

Consider, however, the following variable definition that uses the initializer list constructor of our Array<> template:

```
Array<double> values{ 1.0, 2.0, 3.0, 4.0, 5.0 };
```

Clearly, an intelligent compiler could deduce the template argument here simply by looking at the type of the constructor argument. Starting with C++17, compilers should be capable of doing exactly that. In other words, as of C++17, you are allowed to simply write the following:

```
Array values{ 1.0, 2.0, 3.0, 4.0, 5.0 };
```

Class template deduction will save you some typing when constructing values of either your own types or any number of Standard Library types such as std::pair, std::tuple, std::vector, and so on. Detailing the precise built-in deduction rules or explaining how to override them with so-called user-defined deduction guides would lead us too far for this basic introduction. The good news is that mostly the built-in rules work just fine.

■ **Note** Class template argument deduction is deliberately not enabled for the popular smart pointer types std::unique_ptr<> and shared_ptr<>. That is, you cannot write the following:

```
std::unique_ptr smartBox{ new Box{1.0, 2.0, 3.0} };       // Will not compile!
```

The motivation is that in general the compiler cannot deduce whether a value of type Box* points to either a single Box or an array of Boxes. As you'll recall, pointers and arrays are closely related and can mostly be used interchangeably. When constructed with a Box*, the compiler therefore has no way of knowing whether to deduce either unique_ptr<Box> or unique_ptr<Box[]>. To initialize smart pointer variables, the recommended approach thus remains the use of std::make_unique<>() and std::make_shared<>(). Here's an example:

```
auto smartBox{ std::make_unique<Box>(1.0, 2.0, 3.0) };
```

Nontype Class Template Parameters

A nontype parameter looks like a function parameter—a type name followed by the name of the parameter. Therefore, the argument for a nontype parameter is a value of the given type. However, you can't use just any type for a nontype parameter in a class template. Nontype parameters are intended to be used to define values that might be useful in specifying a container, such as array dimensions or other size specification, or possibly as upper and lower limits for index values.

A nontype parameter can only be an integral type, such as `size_t` or `long`; an enumeration type; a pointer or a reference to an object, such as `string*` or `Box&`; a pointer or a reference to a function; or a pointer to a member of a class. You can conclude from this that a nontype parameter *can't* be a floating-point type or any class type, so types `double`, `Box`, and `std::string` are not allowed, and neither is `std::string**`. Remember that the primary rationale for nontype parameters is to allow sizes and range limits for containers to be specified. Of course, the argument corresponding to a nontype parameter *can* be an object of a class type, as long as the parameter type is a reference.

A nontype parameter is written just like a function parameter, with a type name followed by a parameter name. Here's an example:

```
template <typename T, size_t size>
class ClassName
{
  // Definition using T and size...
};
```

This template has a type parameter, `T`, and a nontype parameter, `size`. The definition is expressed in terms of these two parameters and the template name. If you need it, the *type name* of a type parameter can also be the *type* for a nontype parameter:

```
template <typename T,              // T is the name of the type parameter
          T value>                 // T is also the type of this non-type parameter
class ClassName
{
  // Definition using T and value...
};
```

This template has a nontype parameter, `value`, of type `T`. The parameter `T` must appear before its use in the parameter list, so `value` couldn't precede the type parameter `T` here. Note that using the same symbol with the type and nontype parameters implicitly restricts the possible arguments for the type parameter to the types permitted for a nontype argument.

To illustrate how you could use nontype parameters, suppose you defined the class template for arrays as follows:

```
template <typename T, T value>
class Array
{
  // Definition using T and value...
};
```

You could now use the nontype parameter, value, to initialize each element of the array in the constructor:

```
template <typename T, T value>
Array<T, value>::Array(size_t arraySize) : elements {new T[arraySize]}, size {arraySize}
{
  for (size_t i {} ; i < size ; ++i)
    elements[i] = value;
}
```

This is not a very intelligent approach to initializing the members of the array. This places a serious constraint on the types that are legal for T. Because T is used as the type for a nontype parameter, it is subject to the constraints on nontype parameter types. As you know, a nontype parameter can only be an integral type, a pointer, or a reference, so you can't create Array objects to store double values or Box objects, so the usefulness of this template is somewhat restricted.

To provide a more credible example, we'll add a nontype parameter to the Array template to allow flexibility in indexing the array:

```
template <typename T, int startIndex>
class Array
{
private:
  T* elements;                              // Array of type T
  size_t size;                              // Number of array elements

public:
  explicit Array(size_t arraySize);         // Constructor
  Array(const Array& array);                // Copy Constructor
  ~Array();                                 // Destructor
  T& operator[](int index);                 // Subscript operator
  const T& operator[](int index) const;     // Subscript operator-const arrays
  Array& operator=(const Array& rhs);       // Assignment operator
  size_t getSize() const { return size; }   // Accessor for size
  void swap(Array& other) noexcept;
};
```

This adds a nontype parameter, startIndex, of type int. The idea is that you can specify that you want to use index values that vary over a given range. For example, if you dislike that array indexes in C++ start at 0 and not at 1, you should instantiate Array<> classes for which startIndex equals 1. You could even create Array<> objects that allows index values from -10 to +10. You would then specify the array with the nontype parameter value as –10 and the argument to the constructor as 21 because the array would need 21 elements. Index values can now be negative, so the parameter for the subscript operator functions has been changed to type int. Notice that the size of the array will still always be a positive number, so the type of the size member can remain size_t—this will become important later.

Because the class template now has two parameters, the templates defining the member functions of the class template must have the same two parameters. This is necessary even if some of the functions aren't going to use the nontype parameters. The parameters are part of the identification for the class template, so to match the template, they must have the same parameter list. Let's complete the set of function templates that you need for this version of the Array class.

Templates for Member Functions with Nontype Parameters

Because you've added a nontype parameter to the class template definition, the code for the templates for all member functions needs to be changed. The template for the constructor is as follows:

```
template <typename T, int startIndex>
Array<T, startIndex>::Array(size_t arraySize)
  : elements{new T[arraySize]}, size{arraySize}
{}
```

The template ID is now Array<T, startIndex>, so this is used to qualify the constructor name. This is the only change from the original definition apart from adding the new template parameter to the template.
For the copy constructor, the changes to the template are similar:

```
template <typename T, int startIndex>
Array<T, startIndex>::Array(const Array& array)
  : Array{array.size}
{
  for (size_t i {} ; i < size ; ++i)
    elements[i] = array.elements[i];
}
```

Of course, the external indexing of the array doesn't affect how you access the array internally; it's still indexed from zero here.
The destructor only needs the extra template parameter:

```
template <typename T, int startIndex>
Array<T, startIndex>::~Array()
{
  delete[] elements;
}
```

The template definition for the const subscript operator function now becomes as follows:

```
template <typename T, int startIndex>
const T& Array<T, startIndex>::operator[](int index) const
{
  if (index < startIndex)
    throw std::out_of_range {"Index too small: " + std::to_string(index)};

  if (index > startIndex + static_cast<int>(size) - 1)
    throw std::out_of_range {"Index too large: " + std::to_string(index)};

  return elements[index - startIndex];
}
```

More significant changes have been made here. The index parameter is of type int to allow negative values. The validity checks on the index value now verify that it's between the limits determined by the nontype template parameter and the number of elements in the array. Index values can only be from startIndex to startIndex+size-1. Because size_t is an unsigned integer type, you must explicitly cast it to int; if you don't, the other values in the expression will be implicitly converted to size_t, which will produce a wrong result if startIndex is negative. The choice of message for the exception and the expression selecting it has also been changed.

Finally, you need to alter the template for the non-const version of the subscript operator and the assignment operator functions, but only the template parameter list and the template ID that qualifies these operator names need to be modified. The type of the index parameter for the non-const operator[] also has to be int instead of size_t because the indices for this version of the Array can be negative.

```cpp
template <typename T, int startIndex>
T& Array<T, startIndex>::operator[](int index)
{
  // Use the 'const-and-back-again' idiom to avoid code duplication:
  return const_cast<T&>(std::as_const(*this)[index]);
}

template <typename T, int startIndex>
Array<T, startIndex>& Array<T, startIndex>::operator=(const Array& rhs)
{
    // Exactly the same as before...
}
```

Notice that if we hadn't used the const-and-back-again idiom for operator[](), we would again have had to duplicate the implementation of the operator overload function.

There are restrictions on how you use a nontype parameter within a template. In particular, you must not modify the value of a parameter within the template definition. Consequently, a nontype parameter cannot be used on the left of an assignment or have the increment or decrement operator applied to it. In other words, it's treated as a constant. All parameters in a class template must always be specified to create an instance unless there are default values for them. We'll discuss the use of default argument values for class template parameters later in the chapter.

You must always keep in mind that nontype parameter arguments in a class template are part of the type of an instance of the template. Every unique combination of template arguments produces another class type. As we indicated earlier, the usefulness of the Array<T,int> template is very restricted compared to the original. You can't assign an array of ten values of a given type to another array of ten values of the same type if the starting indexes for the arrays are different—the arrays will be of different types. Later in this chapter we'll discuss a much more effective version of the Array template where the start index is passed as an extra constructor parameter. You should always think twice about using nontype parameters in a class template to be sure that they're really necessary. Often you'll be able to use an alternative approach that will provide a more flexible template and more efficient code.

In spite of these shortcomings of the Array template with a nontype parameter, let's see it in action in a working example. You just need to assemble the definitions for the member function templates into a header file together with the Array template definition with the nontype parameter. The following example will exercise the new features using Box.h from Ex16_01:

```cpp
// Ex16_02.cpp
// Using a class template with a non-type parameter
#include "Box.h"
#include "Array.h"
#include <iostream>
#include <iomanip>
#include <typeinfo>      // For use of typeid()

int main()
{
  try
  {
```

```
    try
    {
      const size_t size {21};                              // Number of array elements
      const int start {-10};                               // Index for first element
      const int end {start + static_cast<int>(size) - 1};  // Index for last element

      Array<double, start> values {size};                  // Define array of double values

      for (int i {start}; i <= end; ++i)                   // Initialize the elements
        values[i] = i - start + 1;

      std::cout << "Sums of pairs of elements: ";
      size_t lines {};
      for (int i {end}; i >= start; --i)
      {
        std::cout << (lines++ % 5 == 0 ? "\n" : "")
                  << std::setw(5) << values[i] + values[i - 1];
      }
    }
    catch (const std::out_of_range& ex)
    {
      std::cerr << "\nout_of_range exception object caught! " << ex.what() << std::endl;
    }

    const int start {};
    const size_t size {11};

    Array<Box, start - 5> boxes {size};                    // Create array of Box objects

    for (int i {start - 5}; i <= start + static_cast<int>(size) - 5; ++i)
      std::cout << "Box[" << i << "] volume is " << boxes[i].volume() << std::endl;
  }
  catch (const std::exception& ex)
  {
    std::cerr << typeid(ex).name() << " exception caught in main()! "
      << ex.what() << std::endl;
  }
}
```

This displays the following output:

```
Sums of pairs of elements:
   41   39   37   35   33
   31   29   27   25   23
   21   19   17   15   13
   11    9    7    5    3
out_of_range exception object caught! Index too small: -11
Box[-5] volume is 1
Box[-4] volume is 1
```

```
Box[-3] volume is 1
Box[-2] volume is 1
Box[-1] volume is 1
Box[0] volume is 1
Box[1] volume is 1
Box[2] volume is 1
Box[3] volume is 1
Box[4] volume is 1
Box[5] volume is 1
class std::out_of_range exception caught in main()! Index too large: 6
```

The entire body of main() is enclosed in a try block that catches any uncaught exceptions that have std::exception as a base class. The nested try block starts by defining constants that specify the range of index values and the size of the array. The size and start variables are used to create an instance of the Array template to store 21 values of type double. The second template argument corresponds to the nontype parameter and specifies the lower limit for the index values of the array. The size of the array is specified by the constructor argument.

The for loop that follows assigns values to the elements of the values object. The loop index, i, runs from the lower limit start, which will be –10, up to and including the upper limit end, which will be +10. Within the loop the values of the array elements are set to run from 1 to 21.

Next the sums of pairs of successive elements are output starting at the last array element and counting down. The lines variable is used to output the sums five to a line. As in the earlier example, sloppy control of the index value results in the expression values[i-1] causing an out_of_range exception to be thrown. The handler for the nested try block catches it and displays the message you see in the output.

The statement that creates an array to store Box objects is in the outer try block that is the body of main(). The type for boxes is Array<Box,start-5>, which demonstrates that expressions are acceptable as argument values for nontype parameters in a template instantiation. The type of such an expression must either match the type of the parameter, or at least be convertible to the appropriate type by means of an implicit conversion. You need to take care if such an expression includes the > character. Here's an example:

```
Array<Box, start > 5 ? start : 5> boxes{42};    // Will not compile!
```

The intent of the expression for the second argument that uses the conditional operator is to supply a value of at least 5, but as it stands, this won't compile. The > in the expression is paired with the opening angled bracket and closes the parameter list. Parentheses are necessary to make the statement valid:

```
Array<Box, (start > 5 ? start : 5)> boxes{42};  // OK
```

Parentheses are also likely to be necessary for expressions for nontype parameters that involve the arrow operator (->) or the shift right operator (>>).

The next for loop throws another exception, this time because the index exceeds the upper limit. The exception is caught by the catch block for the body of main(). The parameter is a reference to the base class, and the output shows that the exception is identified as type std::out_of_range, thus demonstrating there is no object slicing occurring with a reference parameter. There's a significant difference between the ways the two exceptions were caught. Catching the exception in a catch block for the body of main() means that the program ends at this point. The previous exception was caught in the catch block for the nested try block, so it was possible to allow program execution to continue.

```
                        CODE READABILITY
```

It's time for another sidebar on code quality. For Ex16_02, we used the following implementation of operator[]() for our Array<> class template:

```cpp
template <typename T, int startIndex>
const T& Array<T, startIndex>::operator[](int index) const
{
  if (index < startIndex)
    throw std::out_of_range {"Index too small: " + std::to_string(index)};

  if (index > startIndex + static_cast<int>(size) - 1)
    throw std::out_of_range {"Index too large: " + std::to_string(index)};

  return elements[index - startIndex];
}
```

While there is nothing functionally wrong with this code, chances are fairly high that you had to think at least twice to convince yourself that the conditions in the if statements were in fact correct, in particular that of the second one. If so, you may find the following version easier to understand:

```cpp
template <typename T, int startIndex>
const T& Array<T, startIndex>::operator[](int index) const
{
  // Subtract startIndex to obtain the actual index into the elements array
  const int actualIndex = index - startIndex;

  if (actualIndex < 0)
    throw std::out_of_range {"Index too small: " + std::to_string(index)};

  if (actualIndex >= size)
    throw std::out_of_range {"Index too large: " + std::to_string(index)};

  return elements[actualIndex];
}
```

By first computing actualIndex, we have greatly simplified the logic in both if conditions. All that remains is comparing actualIndex with the actual bounds of the elements array. In other words, all that remains is to check that actualIndex lies in the half-open interval [0, size), which is something any C++ programmer is much more accustomed to than working with a startIndex. It follows that it now becomes much more apparent that the conditions are correct.

The second if condition now uses >=, so we do not need to subtract 1 from size anymore. This also removes the need for a static_cast.

While, admittedly, this may not yet have been the most convincing example, the lesson we want to convey here is that professional coding is about much more than simply writing correct code. Writing readable, understandable code is at least as important. In fact, doing so already goes a long way toward avoiding bugs and keeping your code base maintainable.

■ **Tip**   Once you have written a piece of code, small or big, you should get into the habit of taking a step back and placing yourself in the shoes of a person who has to read and understand your code later. This could be a colleague tasked with fixing a bug or making a small change, or it could be you in a year or two (trust us, more than likely, you will not remember writing it anymore!). Ask yourself, can I not rewrite the code to make it more readable? Easier to understand? Should I not clarify things by adding some more code comments? At first, you may find this difficult and time-consuming or even fail to see the point. But believe us, after a while, this will become a second nature, and at some point you will find yourself mostly writing high-quality code already from the start.

Arguments for Nontype Parameters

An argument for a nontype parameter that is not a reference or a pointer must be a compile-time constant expression. This means you can't use an expression containing a non-const integer variable as an argument, which is a slight disadvantage, but the compiler will validate the argument, which is a compensating plus. For example, the following statements won't compile:

```
int start {-10};
Array<double, start> values{ 21 };          // Won't compile because start is not const
```

The compiler will generate a message to the effect that the second argument here is invalid. Here are correct versions of these two statements:

```
const int start {-10};
Array<double, start> values{ 21 };          // OK
```

Now that start has been declared as const, the compiler can rely on its value, and both template arguments are now legal. The compiler applies standard conversions to arguments when they are necessary to match the parameter type. For example, if you had a nontype parameter declared as type const size_t, the compiler converts an integer literal such as 10 to the required argument type.

Nontype Template Arguments vs. Constructor Arguments

Besides the fact that template arguments have to be compile-time constants, there are some other serious disadvantages to the definition of Array<> we have been using throughout this section:

```
template <typename T, int startIndex>
class Array;
```

A consequence of adding the startIndex template parameter is that different values for the argument generate different template instances. This means that an array of double values indexed from 0 will be a different type from an array of double values indexed from 1. If you use both in a program, two independent class definitions will be created from the template, each with whatever member functions you use. This has at least two undesirable consequences. First, you'll get a lot more compiled code in your program than you might have anticipated (a condition known as *code bloat*); second (and far worse), you won't be able to intermix elements of the two types in an expression. The following code would not compile, for instance:

```
Array<double, 0> indexedFromZero{10};
Array<double, 1> indexedFromOne{10};
indexedFromOne = indexedFromZero;
```

▨ **Note**   In principle, you could resort to advanced techniques such as adding member function templates to our `Array<>` class template to facilitate intermixing related instantiations of the `Array<>` template. These are templates for member functions that add extra template parameters—such as a different start index—on top of the two existing template parameters of the class. Explaining this in detail would lead us a bit too far for an introductory level book, though, especially since in this case a much simpler solution exists.

It would be much better to provide flexibility for the range of index values by adding a parameter to the constructor rather than using a non-type template parameter. Here's how that would look:

```cpp
template <typename T>
class Array
{
private:
  T* elements;                                   // Array of type T
  size_t size;                                   // Number of array elements
  int start;                                     // Starting index value

public:
  explicit Array(size_t arraySize, int startIndex=0); // Constructor
  Array(const Array& array);                     // Copy Constructor
  ~Array();                                      // Destructor
  T& operator[](int index);                      // Subscript operator
  const T& operator[](int index) const;          // Subscript operator-const arrays
  Array& operator=(const Array& rhs);            // Assignment operator
  size_t getSize() const { return size; }        // Accessor for size
  void swap(Array& other) noexcept;
};
```

The extra member, `start`, stores the starting index for the array specified by the second constructor argument. The default value for the `startIndex` parameter is 0, so normal indexing is obtained by default. Of course, you would have to update the copy constructor and the `swap()` method to take this extra member into account.

Default Values for Template Parameters

You can supply default argument values for both type and nontype parameters in a class template. This works in a similar way to default values for function parameters. If a given parameter has a default value, then all subsequent parameters in the list must also have default values specified. If you omit an argument for a template parameter that has a default value specified, the default is used, just like with default parameter values in a function. Similarly, when you omit the argument for a given parameter in the list, all subsequent arguments must also be omitted.

The default values for class template parameters are written in the same way as defaults for function parameters—following an = after the parameter name. You could supply defaults for both the parameters in the version of the Array template with a nontype parameter. Here's an example:

```cpp
template <typename T = int, int startIndex = 0>
class Array
{
  // Template definition as before...
};
```

642

You don't need to specify the default values in the templates for the member functions; the compiler will use the argument values used to instantiate the class template.

You could omit all the template arguments to declare an array of elements of type int indexed from 0.

```
Array<> numbers {101};
```

The legal index values run from 0 to 100, as determined by the default value for the nontype template parameter and the argument to the constructor. You must still supply the angled brackets, even though no arguments are necessary. The other possibilities open to you are to omit the second argument or to supply them all, as shown here:

```
Array<std::string, -100> messages {200};   // Array of 200 string objects indexed from -100
Array<Box> boxes {101};                     // Array of 101 Box objects indexed from 0
```

If a class template has default values for any of its parameters, they only need to be specified in the first declaration of the template in a source file, which usually will be the definition of the class template.

Explicit Template Instantiation

So far in this chapter, instances of a class template have been created *implicitly* as a result of defining a variable of a template type. You can also *explicitly* instantiate a class template without defining an object of the template type. The effect of an explicit instantiation of a template is that the compiler creates the instance determined by the parameter values that you specify.

You have already seen how to explicitly instantiate *function* templates in Chapter 9. To instantiate a class template, just use the template keyword followed by the template class name and the template arguments between angled brackets. This statement explicitly creates an instance of the Array template:

```
template class Array<double, 1>;
```

This creates an instance of the template that stores values of type double, indexed from 1. Explicitly instantiating a class template generates the class type definition, and it instantiates all of the member functions of the class from their templates. This happens regardless of whether you call the member functions, so the executable may contain code that is never used.

■ **Tip**   You can use explicit instantiation to quickly test whether a new class template and all its members instantiates for one or multiple types. It saves you the trouble of writing code that calls all the member functions!

Class Template Specialization

You'll encounter many situations where a class template definition won't be satisfactory for every conceivable argument type. For example, you can compare string objects by using overloaded comparison operators, but you can't do this with null-terminated strings. If a class template compares objects using the comparison operators, it will work for type string but not for type char*. To compare objects of type char*, you need to use the comparison functions that are declared in the cstring header. One option to deal with situations like this is to define a *class template specialization*, which provides a class definition that is specific to a given set of arguments for the template parameters.

Defining a Class Template Specialization

A class template specialization is a class definition, not a class template. Instead of using the template to generate the class from the template for a particular type, char* say, the compiler uses the specialization you define for that type instead. Thus, a class template specialization provides a way to predefine instances of a class template to be used by the compiler for specific sets of argument for the template parameters.

Suppose it was necessary to create a specialization of the first version of the Array<> template for type const char*. Perhaps because you'd like to initialize the elements of the array with pointers to the empty string ("") rather than null pointers. You'd write the specialization of the class template definition as follows:

```
template <>
class Array<const char*>
{
  // Definition of a class to suit type const char*...
};
```

This definition of the specialization of the Array template for type const char* must be preceded by the original template definition or by a declaration for the original template. Because all the parameters are specified, it is called a *complete specialization* of the template, which is why the set of angle brackets following the template keyword is empty. The compiler will always use a class definition when it is available, so there's no need for the compiler to consider instantiating the template for type const char*.

It may be that just one or two member functions of a class template need to have code specific to a particular type. If the member functions are defined by separate templates outside the class template, rather than within the body of the class template, you can just provide specializations for the function templates that need to be different.

Partial Template Specialization

If you were specializing the version of the template with two parameters, you may only want to specify the type parameter for the specialization, leaving the nontype parameter open. You could do this with a *partial specialization* of the Array<> template that you could define like this:

```
template <int start>            // Because there is a parameter...
class Array<const char*, start> // This is a partial specialization...
{
  // Definition to suit type const char*...
};
```

This specialization of the original template is also a template. The parameter list following the template keyword must contain the parameters that need to be specified for an instance of this template specialization—just one in this case. The first parameter is omitted because it is now fixed. The angled brackets following the template name specify how the parameters in the original template definition are specialized. The list here must have the same number of parameters as appear in the original, unspecialized template. The first parameter for this specialization is const char*. The other parameter is specified as the corresponding parameter name in this template.

Apart from the special considerations you might need to give to a template instance produced by using const char* for a type parameter, it may well be that pointers in general are a specialized subset that need to be treated differently from objects and references. For example, to compare objects when a template is instantiated using a pointer type, pointers must be dereferenced; otherwise, you are just comparing addresses, not the objects or values stored at those addresses.

For this situation, you can define another partial specialization of the template. The parameter is not completely fixed in this case, but it must fit within a particular pattern that you specify in the list following the template name. For example, a partial specialization of the Array template for pointers would look like this:

```
template <typename T, int start>
class Array<T*, start>
{
  // Definition to suit pointer types other than const char*...
};
```

The first parameter is still T, but the T* between angle brackets following the template name indicates that this definition is to be used for instances where T is specified as a pointer type. The other two parameters are still completely variable, so this specialization will apply to any instance where the first template argument is a pointer.

Choosing Between Multiple Partial Specializations

Suppose both the partial specializations of the Array template that we just discussed were defined—the one for type const char* and the one for any pointer type. How can you be sure that the version for type const char* is selected by the compiler when this is appropriate for any particular instantiation? For example, consider this declaration:

```
Array<Box*, -5> boxes {11};
```

Clearly, this only fits with the specialization for pointers in general, but both partial specializations fit the declaration if you write this:

```
Array<const char*, 1> messages {100};
```

In this case, the compiler determines that the const char* partial specialization is a better fit because it is more specialized than the alternative. The partially specialized template for const char* is determined to be more specialized than the specialization for pointers in general because although anything that selects the const char* specialization—which happens to be just const char*—also selects the T* specialization, the reverse is not the case.

One specialization is more specialized than another when every argument that matches the given specialization matches the other, but the reverse is not true. Thus, you can consider a set of specializations for a template to be ordered from most specialized to least specialized. When several template specializations may fit a given declaration, the compiler will select and apply the most specialized specialization from them.

Using static_assert() in a Class Template

You can use static_assert() to cause the compiler to output a message and fail compilation when a type argument in a class template is not appropriate. static_assert() by default has two arguments; when the first argument is false, the compiler outputs the message specified by the second argument. If the second argument is omitted, a default message will be generated by the compiler.

To protect against misuse of a class template, the first argument to static_assert() will use one or more of the templates from the type_traits header. These test the properties of types and classify types in various ways. There are a lot of templates in the type_traits header, so we'll just mention a few in the following table to give you an idea of the possibilities and leave you to explore the rest in your Standard Library documentation. These templates are all defined in the std namespace.

Template	Result
is_default_constructible_v<T>	Is only true if type T is default constructible, which means for a class type that the class has a no-arg constructor
is_copy_constructible_v<T>	Is true if type T is copy constructible, which means for a class type that the class has a copy constructor
is_assignable_v<T>	Is true if type T is assignable, which means for a class type that it has an assignment operator function
is_pointer_v<T>	Is true if type T is a pointer type and false otherwise
is_null_pointer_v<T>	Is true only if type T is of type std::nullptr_t
is_class_v<T>	Is true only if type T is a class type

It's easy to get confused about what is happening with these templates. Keep in mind that these templates are relevant at *compile time*. An example should make it clear how you use these. Let's amend Ex16_01 to show this in operation. First, comment out the line in the Box class definition in Box.h that generates the default constructor:

```
class Box
{
private:
  double length {1.0};
  double width {1.0};
  double height {1.0};

public:
  Box(double lv, double wv, double hv) : length {lv}, width {wv}, height {hv} {}
// Box() = default;
  double volume() const { return length * width * height; }
};
```

Next, add an #include directive for the type_traits header to Array.h and add one statement following the opening brace in the body of the Array template:

```
#include <stdexcept>          // For standard exception types
#include <string>             // For to_string()
#include <utility>            // For std::as_const()
#include <type_traits>

template <typename T>
class Array
{
  static_assert(std::is_default_constructible_v<T>, "A default constructor is required.");

// Rest of the template as before...
};
```

You can now recompile the example, which will fail, of course. The first argument to static_assert() is the is_default_constructible_v<T> value for the current type argument for T. When T is type Box, this value will be false, triggering the message you'll see in the output from your compiler, and the compilation will fail. Removing the commenting out of the Box default constructor will allow the compilation to succeed. The complete example is in the code download as Ex16_03.

■ **Note** If the Box class does not have a default constructor, the example will fail to compile regardless of whether the static_assert() is added inside the Array<> template. After all, the instantiated code attempts to use a default constructor that is not defined. However, C++ compilers are notorious for producing intricate diagnostic messages when the compilation of a template instantiation fails. It will be instructive to try this yourself, so please comment out both the Box() default constructor and the static_assert() and then recompile. If the user of your class is likely to use unsupported template arguments, it is considered common courtesy to employ static_assert() declarations to improve compilation diagnostics. Note that the static_assert() declarations also double as code documentation, conveying usage intent to the person reading the code.

Friends of Class Templates

Because a class can have friends, you won't be surprised to learn that a class template can also have friends. Friends of a class template can be classes, functions, or other templates. If a class is a friend of a class template, then all its member functions are friends of every instance of the template. A function that is a friend of a template is a friend of any instance of the template, as shown in Figure 16-4.

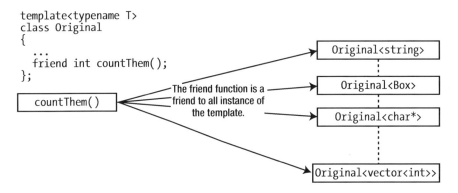

Figure 16-4. A friend function of a class template

Templates that are friends of a template are a little different. Because they have parameters, the parameter list for the template class usually contains all the parameters to define the friend template. This is necessary to identify the instance of the friend template that is the friend of the particular instance of the original class template. However, the function template for the friend is instantiated only when you use it in your code. In Figure 16-5, getBest() is a function template.

```
template<typename T>
class Original
{
    ...
    friend Original<T>* getBest(Original<T>* pObjects);
};
```

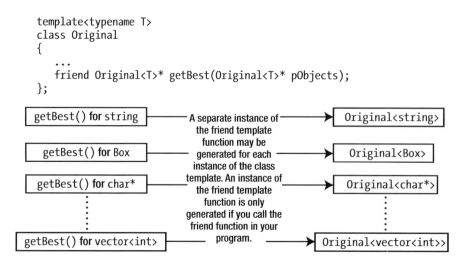

Figure 16-5. *A function template that is a friend of a class template*

Although each class template instance in Figure 16-5 could potentially have a unique friend template instance, this is not necessarily the case. If the class template has some parameters that aren't parameters of the friend template, then a single instance of the friend template may service several instances of the class template.

Note that an ordinary class may have a class template or a function template declared as a friend. In this case, all instances of the template are friends of the class. With the example in Figure 16-6, every member function of every instance of the Thing template is a friend of the Box class because the template has been declared as a friend of the class.

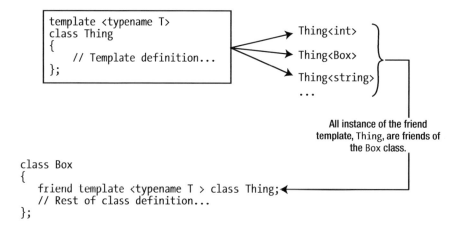

Figure 16-6. *A class template that is a friend of a class*

The declaration in the Box class is a *template* for a friend declaration, and this effectively generates a friend declaration for each class generated from the Thing template. If there are no instances of the Thing template, then the Box class has no friends.

Class Templates with Nested Classes

A class can contain another class nested inside its definition. A class template definition can also contain a nested class or even a *nested class template*. A nested class template is independently parameterized, so inside another class template it creates a two-dimensional ability to generate classes. Dealing with templates inside templates is outside the scope of this book, but we'll introduce aspects of a class template with a nested class.

Let's take a particular example. Suppose you want to implement a stack, which is a "last in, first out" storage mechanism. A stack is illustrated in Figure 16-7. It works in a similar way to a plate stack in a self-service restaurant. It has two basic operations. A *push operation* adds an item at the top of a stack, and a *pop operation* removes the item at the top of the stack. Ideally a stack implementation should be able to store objects of any type, so this is a natural job for a template.

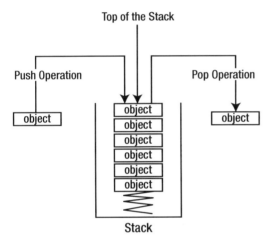

Figure 16-7. *The concept of a stack*

The parameter for a Stack template is a type parameter that specifies the type of objects in the stack, so the initial template definition will be as follows:

```
template <typename T>
class Stack
{
  // Detail of the Stack definition...
};
```

If you want the stack's capacity to grow automatically, you can't use fixed storage for objects within the stack. One way of providing the ability to automatically grow and shrink the stack as objects are pushed on it or popped off it is to implement the stack as a linked list. The nodes in the linked list can be created in the free store, and the stack only needs to remember the node at the top of the stack. This is illustrated in Figure 16-8.

A Stack object only needs to store a pointer to the node at the top.

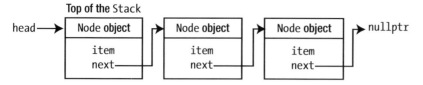

In an empty stack, the pointer to the top of the
stack will be null, because no nodes exist.

```
head = nullptr;
```

Figure 16-8. *A stack as a linked list*

When you create an empty stack, the pointer to the head of the list is `nullptr`, so you can use the fact
that it doesn't contain any Node objects as an indicator that the stack is empty. Of course, only the Stack
object needs access to the Node objects that are in the stack. The Node objects are just internal objects used to
encapsulate the objects that are stored in the stack, so there's no need for anyone outside the Stack class to
know that type Node exists.

A nested class that defines nodes in the list is required in each instance of the Stack template, and
because a node must hold an object of type T, the Stack template parameter type, you can define it as a
nested class in terms of T. We can add this to the initial outline of the Stack template:

```
template <typename T>
class Stack
{
private:
    // Nested class
    class Node
    {
      public:
        T item {};                          // The object stored in this node
        Node* next {};                      // Pointer to next node

        Node(const T& item) : item {item} {} // Create a node from an object
    };

  // Rest of the Stack class definition...
};
```

The Node class is declared as `private`, so we can afford to make all its members `public` so that they're
directly accessible from member functions of the Stack template. A Node object stores an object of T by
value. The constructor is used when an object is pushed onto the stack. The parameter to the constructor is a
`const` reference to an object of type T, and a copy of this object is stored in the `item` member of the new Node
object. The rest of the Stack class template to support the linked list of Node objects shown in Figure 16-8 is
as follows:

```
template <typename T>
class Stack
```

```
{
  private:
    // Nested Node class definition as before...

    Node* head {};                              // Points to the top of the stack

  public:
    Stack() = default;                          // Default constructor
    Stack(const Stack& stack);                  // Copy constructor
    ~Stack();                                   // Destructor
    Stack& operator=(const Stack& rhs);         // Copy assignment operator

    void push(const T& item);                   // Push an object onto the stack
    T pop();                                    // Pop an object off the stack
    bool isEmpty() const;                       // Empty test
    void swap(Stack& other) noexcept;
};
```

As we explained earlier, a Stack<> object only needs to "remember" the top node so it has only one member variable, head, of type Node*. There's a default constructor, a copy constructor, a destructor, and a copy assignment operator function. The destructor and copy members are essential here because nodes will be created dynamically using new and their addresses stored in raw pointers. The push() and pop() members will transfer objects to and from the stack, the isEmpty() function will return true if the Stack<> object is empty, and the swap() function will be used to implement the copy-and-swap idiom for the assignment operator. We'll discuss the definitions of all member function templates for the Stack<> type in the next subsection.

Function Templates for Stack Members

We'll start with the constructors. The default constructor is defaulted within the class template, so the compiler shall generate one for you if and when needed. The copy constructor must replicate a Stack<T> object, which can be done by walking through the nodes and copying them one by one as follows:

```
template <typename T>
Stack<T>::Stack(const Stack& stack)
{
  if (stack.head)
  {
    head = new Node {*stack.head};              // Copy the top node of the original
    Node* oldNode {stack.head};                 // Points to the top node of the original
    Node* newNode {head};                       // Points to the node in the new stack

    while (oldNode = oldNode->next)             // If next was nullptr, the last node was copied
    {
      newNode->next = new Node{*oldNode};       // Duplicate it
      newNode = newNode->next;                  // Move to the node just created
    }
  }
}
```

This copies the stack represented by the stack input argument to the current Stack object, which is assumed to be empty (the head member variable starts out initialized to nullptr). It does this by replicating the head of the argument object, then walking through the sequence of Node objects, copying them one by one. The process ends when the Node object with a null next member has been copied.

The isEmpty() function simply checks whether the head member points to an actual Node or is nullptr:

```
template <typename T>
bool Stack<T>::isEmpty() const
{
  return head == nullptr;
}
```

The swap() function is implemented as follows:

```
template <typename T>
void Stack<T>::swap(Stack& other) noexcept
{
  std::swap(head, other.head);
}
```

The assignment operator then uses this swap() function to implement the familiar copy-and-swap idiom (see Chapter 15):

```
template <typename T>
Stack<T>& Stack<T>::operator=(const Stack& stack)
{
  auto copy{rhs};       // Copy...      (could go wrong and throw an exception)
  swap(copy);           // ... and swap! (noexcept)
  return *this;
}
```

The template for the push() operation is fairly easy as well:

```
template <typename T>
void Stack<T>::push(const T& item)
{
  Node* node{new Node(item)};          // Create the new node
  node->next = head;                   // Point to the old top node
  head = node;                         // Make the new node the top
}
```

The Node object encapsulating item is created by passing the reference to the Node constructor. The next member of the new node needs to point to the node that was previously at the top. The new Node object then becomes the top of the stack, so its address is stored in head.

The pop() operation is slightly more involved, though. The first question you need to answer is, what should happen if pop() is invoked on an empty stack? Because the function returns a T object by value, you can't easily signal an error through the return value. One obvious solution is to throw an exception in this case, so let's do that.

Once this possible corner case is taken care of, you know that the function has to perform at least the following three actions:

1. Return the T item stored in the current head.

2. Make head point to the next Node in the linked list.

3. Delete the old head Node that is no longer required now.

It takes some figuring out in which order these actions should be performed. If you're not careful, you may even run into crashes. Here is a working solution, though:

```
template <typename T>
T Stack<T>::pop()
{
  if (isEmpty())                          // If it's empty
    throw std::logic_error {"Stack empty"};  // Pop is not valid so throw exception

  auto* next {head->next};                // Save pointer to the next node
  T item {head->item};                    // Save the T value to return later
  delete head;                            // Delete the current head
  head = next;                            // Make head point to the next node
  return item;                            // Return the top object
}
```

Key is that you mustn't delete the old head without first extracting all information from it that you still need—in this case both its next pointer (which is to become the new head) and its T item (the value that you have to return from the pop() function). Once you realize this, the rest writes itself.

In the destructor you face a similar problem (remember this for later!). Clearly, it needs to release all dynamically allocated Node objects belonging to the current Stack object. From the pop() template, you know not to delete any Nodes without first copying what you still need from it:

```
template <typename T>
Stack<T>::~Stack()
{
  while (head)
  {                                  // While current pointer is not null
    auto* next = head->next;         // Get the pointer to the next
    delete head;                     // Delete the current head
    head = next;                     // Make head point to the next node
  }
}
```

Without the temporary pointer next to hold the address stored in head->next, you couldn't move head along anymore to the next Node in the list. At the end of the while loop, all Node objects belonging to the current Stack object will have been deleted and head will be nullptr.

That's all the templates you need to define the stack. If you gather all the templates into a header file, Stack.h, you can try it with the following code:

```
// Ex16_04.cpp
// Using a stack defined by nested class templates
#include "Stack.h"
#include <iostream>
#include <string>
#include <array>                    // for std::size()
```

```
int main()
{
  std::string words[] {"The", "quick", "brown", "fox", "jumps"};
  Stack<std::string> wordStack;              // A stack of strings

  for (size_t i {}; i < std::size(words); ++i)
    wordStack.push(words[i]);

  Stack<std::string> newStack{wordStack};    // Create a copy of the stack

  // Display the words in reverse order
  while(!newStack.isEmpty())
    std::cout << newStack.pop() << ' ';
  std::cout << std::endl;

  // Reverse wordStack onto newStack
  while(!wordStack.isEmpty())
    newStack.push(wordStack.pop());

  // Display the words in original order
  while (!newStack.isEmpty())
    std::cout << newStack.pop() << ' ';
  std::cout << std::endl;

  std::cout << std::endl << "Enter a line of text:" << std::endl;
  std::string text;
  std::getline(std::cin, text);              // Read a line into the string object

  Stack<const char> characters;              // A stack for characters

  for (size_t i {}; i < text.length(); ++i)
    characters.push(text[i]);                // Push the string characters onto the stack

  std::cout << std::endl;
  while (!characters.isEmpty())
    std::cout << characters.pop();           // Pop the characters off the stack

  std::cout << std::endl;
}
```

Here's an example of the output:

```
jumps fox brown quick The
The quick brown fox jumps

Enter a line of text:
Never test for errors that you don't know how to handle.

.eldnah ot woh wonk t'nod uoy taht srorre rof tset reveN
```

You first define an array of five objects that are `strings`, initialized with the words shown. Then you define an empty `Stack` object that can store `string` objects. The `for` loop then pushes the array elements onto the stack. The first word from the array will be at the bottom of the `wordStack` stack and the last word at the top. You create a copy of `wordStack` as `newStack` to exercise the copy constructor.

In the next `while` loop, you display the words in `newStack` in reverse order by popping them off the stack and outputting them in a `while` loop. The loop continues until `isEmpty()` returns `false`. Using the `isEmpty()` function member is a safe way of getting the complete contents of a stack. `newStack` is empty by the end of the loop, but you still have the original in `wordStack`.

The next `while` loop retrieves the words from `wordStack` and pops them onto `newStack`. The pop and push operations are combined in a single statement, where the object returned by `pop()` for `wordStack` is the argument for `push()` for `newStack()`. At the end of this loop, `wordStack` is empty, and `newStack` contains the words in their original sequence—with the first word at the top of the stack. You then output the words by popping them off `newStack`, so at the end of this loop, both stacks are empty.

The next part of `main()` reads a line of text into a `string` object using the `getline()` function and then creates a stack to store characters:

```
Stack<const char> characters;                 // A stack for characters
```

This creates a new instance of the `Stack` template, `Stack<const char>`, and a new instance of the constructor for this type of stack. At this point, the program contains two classes from the `Stack` template each with a nested `Node` class.

You peel off the characters from `text` and push them onto the new stack in a `for` loop. The `length()` function of the `text` object is used to determine when the loop ends. Finally, the input string is output in reverse by popping the characters off the stack. You can see from the output that our input was not even slightly palindromic, but you could try, "Ned, I am a maiden" or even "Are we not drawn onward, we few, drawn onward to new era."

A BETTER STACK?

In this chapter we have already illustrated a few times that you should not necessarily be satisfied with your code just because it is correct. We have advised you to shun code duplication, to be on the lookout for code that throws exceptions, and to always strive for readable code. With this in mind, let's review the `Stack<>` class template we wrote in this section and see whether we can improve it. More specifically, let's review the implementation of the destructor. Is there anything there that strikes you as suboptimal there?

We already noted the similarities between the destructor and `pop()` earlier, didn't we? That is, both had to set aside a temporary `next` pointer, `delete` the head, and then move the `head` along to the next node. This is code duplication as well! You can eliminate this using the following, alternative implementation of the destructor template that leverages the existing `isEmpty()` and `pop()` functions instead of directly manipulating the pointers itself:

```
template <typename T>
Stack<T>::~Stack()
{
  while (!isEmpty()) pop();
}
```

Because this is trivially readable and therefore far less prone to errors, you should definitely prefer this new version. In case you are worried about performance, today's optimizing compilers will likely generate the same code for both versions—after inlining the isEmpty() and pop() function calls, it becomes trivial for a compiler to rework the code to exactly what we wrote in the original version. You can find this implementation in Ex16_04A.

We understand that initially it will not always be easy to improve your code like this. And, at first, doing so may seem to take up a lot of your time. Unfortunately, we also cannot give you a fixed set of rules that dictate when code is good, bad, or good enough. But with sufficient practice, you will see that this will come more and more naturally. In the long run, applying the principles you learn about here will improve your productivity as a programmer substantially. You will find yourself consistently producing elegant, readable code, which will therefore contain less bugs and which will be easier to maintain and adapt as well.

We would now like to conclude these digressions on producing high-quality code with one of our favorite quotes, from one of the pioneers of computer science, Donald E. Knuth:

> *Computer programming is an art, [...] because it requires skill and ingenuity, and especially because it produces objects of beauty. A programmer who subconsciously views himself as an artist will enjoy what he does and will do it better.*

Disambiguating Dependent Names

When referring to nested types, you regularly run into one of the more annoying idiosyncrasies of the C++ programming language. To introduce it, we'll use this minimal example of a nested class:

```
template <typename T>
class Outer
{
public:
  class Nested { /* ... */ };

  Nested getNested() const;
};
```

Given a class template definition of this form, anyone with basic knowledge of class templates naturally attempts to define the template for its getNested() member function as follows:

```
template <typename T>
Outer<T>::Nested Outer<T>::getNested() const
{
  return Nested{ /* ... */ };
}
```

Unfortunately, though, this function definition is not valid in C++ and will not compile. You could give it a try for yourself by attempting to compile Ex16_05.cpp. The compiler error you see will most likely contain the term *dependent*. The name of a member of a class template is said to be *dependent* on the template parameters of the class template. In the expression Outer<T>::Nested, the name of the nested type Nested is thus dependent on the type parameter T. When a compiler encounters a dependent name such as the one in our example, the C++ standard says it should assume it is the name of a static member variable. Your compiler will therefore interpret Outer<T>::Nested as the name of some nonexistent variable Nested and not as a type. To fix the problem, you have to explicitly tell the compiler that Outer<T>::Nested is the name of a type by putting the typename keyword in front of it:

```
template <typename T>
typename Outer<T>::Nested Outer<T>::getNested() const
{
  return Nested{ /* ... */ };
}
```

This requirement is not limited to the return type of member function templates. In the following nonmember function template, for instance, you also have to add typename to indicate to the compiler that Outer<MyTemplateParam>::Nested is the name of a type (although auto would be far easier here, of course):

```
template <typename MyTemplateParam>
void foo(/* ... */)
{
  Outer<MyTemplateParam> outer;
  typename Outer<MyTemplateParam>::Nested nested = outer.getNested();
}
```

There is no need for adding typename if the template argument to Outer<> is a known type—only if Nested depends on another template type parameter. In other words, if you would use Outer<int>::Nested somewhere, there is no need to prepend it with typename. The compiler will then instantiate the Outer<> template for the concrete type int and deduce that Nested is a type.

It's also not required if the dependent name is part of the current template instantiation. That is, the following alternative definition of getNested() will compile, even though Outer<T>::Nested in the function body is not preceded with typename:

```
template <typename T>
typename Outer<T>::Nested Outer<T>::getNested() const
{
  Outer<T>::Nested nested{ /* ... */ };
  // ...
  return nested;
}
```

Confused? That's perfectly understandable. Most C++ developers struggle with this. We'd much prefer it if we didn't even have to explain this, but fact is that at some point you'll run into this quirk of the C++ language. As a rule of thumb, it is easiest to remember that whenever you're allowed to simply write Nested, you won't have to disambiguate the dependent name Outer<T>::Nested either. For our latest code snippet, you'll remember from before that you're also allowed to simply write Nested in the template function body:

```
template <typename T>
typename Outer<T>::Nested Outer<T>::getNested() const
{
  Nested nested{ /* ... */ };
  // ...
  return nested;
}
```

As the compiler clearly knows all about Nested in this context, there's no need for a typename disambiguator either. We've also told you before that for the return type the Outer<T>:: specifier *is* required. Our rule of thumb therefore says that the typename specifier is required there as well.

Summary

If you understand how class templates are defined and used, you'll find it easy to understand and apply the capabilities of the Standard Library. The ability to define class templates is also a powerful augmentation of the basic language facilities for defining classes. The essential points we've discussed in this chapter include the following:

- A class template defines a family of class types.

- An instance of a class template is a class definition that is generated by the compiler from the template using a set of template arguments that you specify in your code.

- An implicit instantiation of a class template arises out of a definition for an object of a class template type.

- An explicit instantiation of a class template defines a class for a given set of arguments for the template parameters.

- An argument corresponding to a type parameter in a class template can be a fundamental type, a class type, a pointer type, or a reference type.

- The type of a nontype parameter can be an integral or enumeration type, a pointer type, or a reference type.

- A partial specialization of a class template defines a new template that is to be used for a specific, restricted subset of the arguments for the original template.

- A complete specialization of a class template defines a new type for a specific, complete set of parameter arguments for the original template.

- A friend of a class template can be a function, a class, a function template, or a class template.

- An ordinary class can declare a class template or a function template as a friend.

EXERCISES

The following exercises enable you to try what you've learned in this chapter. If you get stuck, look back over the chapter for help. If you're still stuck after that, you can download the solutions from the Apress website (www.apress.com/source-code/), but that really should be a last resort.

Exercise 16-1. The Array<> template of Ex16_01A is in many ways similar to std::vector<>. One obvious shortcoming is that the size of an Array<T> needs to be fixed at construction time. Let's remedy that and add a push_back() member function that adds a single element of type T after all existing elements (even if those were default-constructed). In reality, this is not quite how std::vector<> works, but to keep things simple, your version of push_back() could first allocate a new, larger array that holds size + 1 elements and then copy all existing elements as well as the new element into that new array. Also, add a default constructor to create an empty Array<>. Write a small program to exercise the new functionality.

Extra: It shouldn't be hard to make push_back() have an all-or-nothing behavior. That is, if any operation during push_back() should go wrong and throw an exception, make sure that no memory is leaked and the original Array<> is left as is, discarding the new element. So, identify the potential sources of exceptions and then make sure the function is robust. One option is to use one of the programming idioms you learned about in this chapter.

Note: If you think you can use some more exercise with try/catch blocks (slightly off-topic), perhaps you can attempt an all-or-nothing implementation of push_back() as well using raw C-style arrays. Even though this approach is not really recommended, it might be instructive to implement it at least once (if only to see the difference with other approaches).

Exercise 16-2. Define a template for classes that represent pairs of values of possibly different types. The values can be accessed using public first and second member variables. (While usually we'd advise against public member variables, we turn a blind eye in this exercise because the standard std::pair<> template also uses these same public members.) A pair of an int and a std::string can then be created and used as follows:

```
auto my_pair = Pair<int, std::string>(122, "abc");
++my_pair.first;
std::cout << "my_pair equals (" << my_pair.first
          << ", " << my_pair.second << ')' << std::endl;
```

Also, define a default constructor, as well as the primary comparison operators == and <. Both operators are defined in terms of the same operators of the template's type arguments. The less-than operator < should implement a so-called *lexicographical* comparison. That is, pairs should be ordered using the same logic as used when sorting two-letter words, except that now the words do not consist of two letters but two different values. Suppose you have the following three pairs:

```
auto pair1 = Pair<int, std::string>(  0, "def");
auto pair2 = Pair<int, std::string>(123, "abc");
auto pair3 = Pair<int, std::string>(123, "def");
```

Then the expressions pair1 < pair2 and pair2 < pair3 should both evaluate to true. The first because 0 < 123; the second because "abc" < "def". The second values of the Pairs are looked at only if the first ones compare equal using ==.

Create a small program to make sure your Pair class works as required. You could, for instance, use the snippets we've provided in this exercise assignment.

Exercise 16-3. Create a << operator template to stream the Pairs of Exercise 16-2 to an output stream. Adjust the test program as well to make use of this operator.

Exercise 16-4. Define a template for one-dimensional sparse arrays that will store objects of any type so that only the elements stored in the array occupy memory. The potential number of elements that can be stored by an instance of the template should be virtually unlimited. The template might be used to define a sparse array containing pointers to elements of type double with the following statement:

```
SparseArray<double> values;
```

Define the subscript operator for the template so that element values can be retrieved and set just like in a normal array. If an element doesn't exist at an index position, the subscript operator should add a default-constructed object to the sparse array at the given index and return a reference to this newly added object. Because this subscript operator modifies the object, there cannot really be a const overload of this operator. Similar to various Standard Library containers, you should therefore define an at(size_t) member function as well, overloaded on const, that instead of adding a default-constructed value throws an appropriate exception if no value exists for the given index. Because it would still be nice to know in advance whether an element exists at a given index, also add an element_exists_at() member to check for this.

There are many ways to represent a sparse array, some more efficient than others. But since this is not the essence of the exercise, we propose you keep things simple. Don't worry about performance yet; you'll learn about more efficient data structures and algorithms offered by the Standard Library in later chapters—including even container types that are nearly equivalent to your SparseArray<>, namely, std::map<> and std::unordered_map<>. For now, we therefore propose you simply represent the sparse array as an unsorted vector<> of index–value pairs. For the individual pairs, you can use the Pair<> class template defined in the previous exercise (or the similar std::pair<> from the <utility> header, of course, should you prefer).

Take the SparseArray template for a spin with a main() function that stores 20 random element values of type int at random index positions within the range 32 to 212 in a sparse array with an index range from 0 to 499 and output the values of element that exist along with their index positions.

Exercise 16-5. Define a template for a linked list type that allows the list to be traversed in both directions, meaning backward from the end of the list as well as forward from the beginning. Naturally, you should use the iterator design pattern you learned about in Chapter 11 for this (see also Exercises 11-6 and 11-7). To keep things simple, elements stored in the list cannot be modified while traversing the list. Elements can be added using push_front() and push_back() to use member names analogous to those of Standard Library containers. Also add functions clear(), empty(), and size() that do the same as those of standard containers (see Chapter 5). Apply the template in a program that stores individual words from some arbitrary prose or poetry as std::string objects in a linked list and then displays them five to a line in sequence and in reverse order.

Exercise 16-6. Use the linked list and sparse array templates to produce a program that stores words from a prose or poetry sample in a sparse array of up to 26 linked lists, where each list contains words that have the same initial letter. Output the words, starting each group with a given initial letter on a new line.

CHAPTER 17

■ ■ ■

Move Semantics

This chapter complements and completes several key topics discussed in the middle parts of the book. In Chapters 11 and 12, for instance, you gained insight into the mechanics behind the copying of objects, that is, copy constructors and assignment operators. And from Chapter 8 you know to prefer pass-by-reference over pass-by-value to avoid undue copying of parameters. And for a long time, that was basically all you needed to know. C++ offered facilities to copy objects, and if you wanted to avoid costly copies, then you simply used either references or pointers. Starting with C++11, however, there is a powerful new alternative. You can no longer only copy objects; you can now also *move* them.

In this chapter, we'll show you how *move semantics* allows you to efficiently transfer resources from one object into another, without *deep copying*. We also wrap up our treatment of the *special class members*—of which you already know the default constructor, destructor, copy constructor, and copy assignment constructor.

In this chapter, you will learn:

- What the difference is between lvalues and rvalues

- That there's another kind of references: rvalue references

- What it means to move an object

- How to provide so-called move semantics for objects of your own types

- When objects are moved implicitly and how to explicitly move them

- How move semantics leads to code that is both elegant and efficient

- What impact move semantics has on various best practices regarding defining your own functions and types

- The "rule of five" and "rule of zero" guidelines

© Ivor Horton and Peter Van Weert 2018
I. Horton and P. Van Weert, *Beginning C++17*, https://doi.org/10.1007/978-1-4842-3366-5_17

Lvalues and Rvalues

Every single expression is either an *lvalue* or an *rvalue* (sometimes written *l-value* and *r-value* and pronounced like that). An lvalue evaluates to some persistent value with an address in memory in which you can store something on an ongoing basis; an rvalue evaluates to a result that is stored only transiently. Historically, lvalues and rvalues are so called because an *l*value expression typically appears on the *left* of an assignment operator, whereas an *r*value could appear only on the *r*ight side. If an expression is not an lvalue, it is an rvalue.[1] An expression that consists of a single variable name is always an lvalue.

■ **Note**   Despite their names, lvalues and rvalues are classifications of *expressions*, not of values.

Consider the following statements:

```
int a {}, b {1}, c {-2};
a = b + c;
double r = std::abs(a * c);
auto p = std::pow(r, std::abs(c));
```

The first statement defines variables a, b, and c as type int and initializes them to 0, 1, and -2, respectively. From then on, the names a, b, and c are all lvalues.

In the second statement, at least in principle, the result of evaluating the expression b + c is briefly stored somewhere, only to copy it into the variable a right after. When execution of the statement is complete, the memory holding the result of b + c is discarded. The expression b + c is therefore an rvalue.

The presence of transient values becomes far more apparent once function calls are involved. In the third statement, for instance, a * c is evaluated first and kept somewhere in memory as a temporary value. This temporary then is passed as an argument to the std::abs() function. This makes that a * c is an rvalue. The int that is returned by std::abs() itself is transient as well. It exists only for an instant, just long enough to be implicitly converted into a double. Similar reasonings apply for the return values of both function calls in the fourth statement—the value returned by std::abs(), for instance, clearly exists only momentarily to serve as an argument to std::pow().

■ **Note**   Most function call expressions are rvalues. Only function calls that return a reference are lvalues. One indication for the latter is that function calls that return a reference can appear on the left side of a built-in assignment operator just fine. Prime examples are the subscript operators (operator[]()) and at() functions of your typical container. If v is a vector<int>, for example, both v[1] = -5; and v.at(2) = 132; would make for perfectly valid statements. v[1] and v.at(2) are therefore clearly lvalues.

---

[1]The C++ standard actually defines three additional expression categories with the names glvalue, prvalue, and xvalue. Formally, lvalue and rvalue are then defined in terms of these. But trust us, you really do not need to know all these gory details. Our brief, more informal discussion here will serve you just fine!

When in doubt, another good guideline to decide whether a given expression is either an lvalue or an rvalue is the following. If the value that it evaluates to persists long enough for you to take and later use its address, then that value is an lvalue. Here's an example:

```
int* x = &(b + c);          // Error!
int* y = &std::abs(a * d);  // Error!
int* z = &123;              // Error!
int* w = &a;                // Ok!
int* u = &v.at(2);          // Ok!   (u contains the address of the third value in v)
```

The memory that stores the result of the expressions b + c and std::abs() is reclaimed immediately after the surrounding statements have finished executing. If they were allowed to exist, the pointers x and y would therefore already be dangling before anyone even had the opportunity to look at them. This indicates that these expressions are rvalues. The example also illustrates that all numeric literals are rvalues. The compiler will never allow you to take the address of a numeric literal.

Granted, for expressions of fundamental types, the distinction between lvalue and rvalue rarely matters. This distinction only becomes relevant for expressions of class types and even then only when, for instance, passed to functions that have overloads specifically defined to accept the result of an rvalue expression or when storing objects in containers. The only way for you to truly appreciate these little theory lessons is therefore to bear with us until the next section. There's just one more concept left to introduce first.

Rvalue References

A reference is a name that you can use as an alias for something else. That much you already know from Chapter 6. What you don't know yet—how could you?—is that there are actually two kinds of references: *lvalue references* and *rvalue references*.

All references that you've worked with thus far are *lvalue references*. Normally, an lvalue reference is an alias for another variable; it is called an lvalue reference because it normally refers to a persistent storage location in which you can store data so it can appear on the left of an assignment operator. We say "normally" because C++ does allow reference-to-const lvalue references—so variables of type const T&—to be bound to temporary rvalues as well. We established as much in Chapter 8 already.

An *rvalue reference* can be an alias for a variable, just like an lvalue reference, but it differs from an lvalue reference in that it can also reference the outcome of an rvalue expression, even though this value is generally transient. Being bound to an rvalue reference extends the lifetime of such a transient value. Its memory will not be discarded as long as the rvalue reference is in scope. You specify an rvalue reference type using *two* ampersands following the type name. Here's an example:

```
int count {5};
int&& rtemp {count + 3};            // rvalue reference
std::cout << rtemp << std::endl;    // Output value of expression
int& rcount {count};                // lvalue reference
```

This code will compile and execute, but of course it is definitely *not* the way to use an rvalue reference, and you should never code like this. This is just to illustrate what an rvalue reference is. The rvalue reference is initialized to be an alias for the result of the rvalue expression count + 3. The output from the next statement will be 8. You cannot do this with an lvalue reference—at least not unless you add a const qualifier. Is this useful? In this case, no, indeed it is not recommended at all; but in a different context, it is very useful. It's high time you found out when and why, don't you agree?

Moving Objects

In the running example of this chapter you'll be working with an Array<> class template similar to that of Ex16_01A. Not unlike std::vector<>, it's a template for classes that encapsulate and manage dynamically allocated memory. The main difference is that the number of elements that an Array<> object will store always needs to be fixed at construction time, whereas a vector<> has the ability to grow as you add more elements. The definition of this Array<> class template looks like this:

```
template <typename T>
class Array
{
private:
  T* elements;                                   // Array of type T
  size_t size;                                   // Number of array elements

public:
  explicit Array(size_t arraySize);              // Constructor
  Array(const Array& array);                     // Copy constructor
  ~Array();                                      // Destructor
  Array& operator=(const Array& rhs);            // Copy assignment operator
  T& operator[](size_t index);                   // Subscript operator
  const T& operator[](size_t index) const;       // Subscript operator-const arrays
  size_t getSize() const noexcept { return size; } // Accessor for size
  void swap(Array& other) noexcept;              // noexcept swap function
};
```

The implementation of all members can remain the same as in Ex16_01A. For now the only thing we add is an extra debug output statement in the copy constructor to track when an Array<> is being copied:

```
// Copy constructor
template <typename T>
inline Array<T>::Array(const Array& array)
  : Array{array.size}
{
  std::cout << "Array of " << size << " elements copied" << std::endl;
  for (size_t i {}; i < size; ++i)
    elements[i] = array.elements[i];
}
```

Because the Array<> template of Ex16_01A employs the copy-and-swap idiom, this single output statement also covers the cases where a given Array<> is copied through its copy assignment operator. To refresh your memory, the following is a possible definition of this copy-and-swap assignment operator template. It rewrites copy assignment in terms of the copy construction and a noexcept swap() function:

```
// Copy assignment operator
template <typename T>
inline Array<T>& Array<T>::operator=(const Array& rhs)
{
  Array<T> copy(rhs);      // Copy ...       (could go wrong and throw an exception)
  swap(copy);              // ... and swap!  (noexcept)
  return *this;            // Return lhs
}
```

Using this Array<> class template, we now compose a first example to underline the cost of copying:

```cpp
// Ex17_01.cpp - Copying objects into a vector
#include "Array.h"
#include <string>
#include <vector>

// Construct an Array<> of a given size, filled with some arbitrary string data
Array<std::string> buildStringArray(const size_t size)
{
  Array<std::string> result{ size };
  for (size_t i = 0; i < size; ++i)
    result[i] = "You should learn from your competitor, but never copy. Copy and you die.";
  return result;
}

int main()
{
  const size_t numArrays{ 10 };                  // Fill 10 Arrays with 1,000 strings
  const size_t numStringsPerArray{ 1000 };

  std::vector<Array<std::string>> vectorOfArrays;
  vectorOfArrays.reserve(numArrays);   // Inform the vector<> how many Arrays we'll be adding

  for (size_t i = 0; i < numArrays; ++i)
  {
    vectorOfArrays.push_back(buildStringArray(numStringsPerArray));
  }
}
```

■ **Note** This example uses a member function of std::vector<> that you haven't encountered yet: reserve(size_t). Essentially, it tells the vector<> object to allocate sufficient dynamic memory to accommodate for the given number of elements. These elements will be added, for instance, using push_back().

The program in Ex17_01.cpp constructs a vector<> of 10 Arrays, each containing 1,000 strings. The output of a single run normally looks as follows:

```
Array of 1000 elements copied
Array of 1000 elements copied
Array of 1000 elements copied
... (10 times in total)
```

▨ **Note** It is possible that your output shows that the Array<> is copied no less than 20 times. The reason is that during each execution of buildStringArray() your compiler might first create the variable result that is defined locally in that function's body and then copy that Array<> for the first time into the object that is returned by the function. After that, this temporary return value is then copied a second time into an Array<> that is allocated by the vector<>. Most optimizing compilers, however, implement the so-called (named) return value optimization that eliminates the former copy. We'll discuss this optimization further later in this chapter.

▨ **Tip** If Ex17_01 does perform 20 copies for you, the most likely cause is that your compiler is set to use a nonoptimizing, so-called Debug configuration. If so, switching to a fully optimizing Release configuration should resolve the issue. Consult your compiler documentation for more information.

The for loop of the main() function calls buildStringArray() 10 times. Each call returns an Array<string> object filled with 1,000 string objects. Clearly, buildStringArray() is an rvalue, as the object it returns is transient. In other words, your compiler arranges for this object to be stored temporarily (almost certainly somewhere on the stack) before it passes it on to the push_back() function of vectorOfArrays. Internally, the push_back() member of this vector<> then uses the Array<string> copy constructor to copy this rvalue into an Array<string> object inside the dynamic memory managed by the vector<>. In doing so, all 1,000 std::strings the Array<string> contains get copied as well. That is, for each of the 10 times that such a transient Array<> is copied into vectorOfArrays, the following happens:

1. The Array<> copy constructor allocates a new block of dynamic memory to hold 1,000 std::string objects.

2. For each of the 1,000 string objects this copy constructor has to copy, it calls the std::string copy assignment operator. Each of these 1,000 assignments in turn allocates one additional block of dynamic memory in which it copies all 73 characters (chars) from the source string.

In other words, your computer has to perform 10 times 1,001 dynamic memory allocations and a fair amount of character copying. In itself this is not a disaster, but it surely feels like all this copying ought to be avoidable. After all, once push_back() returns, the temporary Array<> that buildStringArray() had returned gets deleted and together with it all the strings it used to contain. This means that in total we have copied no less than 10 Arrays and 10,000 string objects and 730,000 characters, only to throw away the originals an instant later!

Imagine being forced to manually copy a 10,000-sentence book—say one of the thicker *Harry Potter* novels—only to watch someone burn the original immediately afterward. What a total waste of effort! If no one needs the original anymore, why not simply reuse the original instead of creating a copy? To wrap up the *Harry Potter* analogy, why not give the book a shiny new cover and then pretend that you copied all the pages?

What you need, in other words, is a way to somehow "move" the original strings from inside the transient Array<> into the newly created Array<> object that is held by the vector<>. What you need is a specific "move" operation that does not involve any excessive copying. And if the original Array<> object is to be torn down in the process, so be it. We know it to be a transient object anyway, destined for a *Harry Potter* bonfire. Before we present you with the modern, now highly recommended solution, we'll first talk about the programming patterns that were used to avoid such needless memory allocations and copying in pre-C++11 code.

Traditional Workarounds

In older code, one would often use an output parameter to output large objects instead of a return value. We first introduced the concept of output parameters in Chapter 8. For our example, this would mean redefining buildStringArray() as follows:

```
void buildStringArray(Array<std::string>& out);
```

Note that there's then no need for the size parameter anymore now. This size had to be provided already when the output Array<> was constructed (and can be obtained from its getSize() member). This approach has a few problems, though:

- As argumented in Chapter 8, mixing input and output parameters makes your code harder to understand. What you want is for all function output to be part of the function return value. In modern C++, function parameters should thus mostly be input parameters.

- Output arguments do not only lead to code that is less clear, they also make calling a function and using its output rather cumbersome. To illustrate, inside the for loop of Ex17_01.cpp, you'd now need these three lines instead of just one:

  ```
  Array<std::string> string_array(numStringsPerArray);
  buildStringArray(string_array);
  vectorOfArrays.push_back(string_array);
  ```

  You always first need to define the output variable—which also precludes the use of auto by the way!—and cannot embed the function call into the argument list of another function anymore either.

- As witnessed by the previous three lines of code, simply reworking the function to use output parameters does not yet eliminated the copy that is being made when entering the Array<> into the vector<>. More changes would be needed. The traditional solution would have you first create all Array<>s in the vector<>— using resize() instead of reserve(), for instance—and then use calls of the form buildStringArray(vectorOfArrays[i]) to fill them with strings. For this to work here, however, we'd first have to rework the Array<> template to no longer require a size at construction time.

But let's not dwell on this approach any further! The main message should be clear by now. While extra copies and allocations can mostly be avoided using output parameters, the problem is that doing so typically involves a rather awkward coding style. What you really want is code that is clear and intuitive—as close as possible to that of Ex17_01.cpp, ideally—but that at the same time avoids all the expensive copying.

Another traditional workaround is to allocate all Array<> objects in the free store. With this approach, the outline of your code already comes much closer to what you want. Using a C++11 smart pointer, it looks as follows:

```
std::unique_ptr<Array<std::string>> buildStringArray(const size_t size);
```

However, even if we ignore the extra dynamic allocations, this approach clearly comes with a hefty syntactical overhead. For starters, you'd need a variable of type std::vector<std::unique_ptr<Array<std::string>>>, which is quite the impressive type name already. Also, you'd constantly have to dereference the Array<> pointers through their * and -> operators. Surely there must be a better, more elegant way, right?

Defining Move Members

Thankfully, modern C++ offers precisely what you want. C++11's move semantics allows you to program in a natural, intuitive style, while at the same time avoiding any unnecessary, costly copy operations. You even do not have to alter the code of Ex17_01.cpp at all. Instead, you extend the Array<> template to ensure that the compiler knows how to instantly *move* a transient Array<> object into another Array<>, without effectively copying its elements.

For this, we'll take you back to our earlier example, Ex17_01.cpp. There you studied the following statement:

```
vectorOfArrays.push_back(buildStringArray(numStringsPerArray));
```

Given a statement such as this, any C++11 compiler is, of course, well aware that copying the result of buildStringArray() is just silly. After all, the compiler knows full well that it's a temporary object that is passed to push_back() here and is an object that is scheduled to be deleted right after. So, the compiler *knows* that you'd prefer not to copy the pushed Array<>. Clearly that's not the problem. Rather, the problem is that the compiler has no other option but to copy this object. After all, all it has to work with is a copy constructor. The compiler cannot just magically "move" a temporary Array<> object into a new Array<> object—it needs to be told how.

Since the code to construct a *copy* of an object is defined by the *copy constructor* of its class (see Chapter 11), it's only natural that the code to construct a new object from a *moved* object is defined by a constructor as well. We'll discuss how you can define one next.

■ **Note**   Under the right circumstances, the move members that we're about to introduce will be generated by the compiler, though clearly not for our Array<> template. For the Array<> template you need to define them yourself explicitly. We'll explain why that is later in this chapter.

Move Constructors

Here is, one last time, the familiar template for the Array<> copy constructor:

```
// Copy constructor
template <typename T>
inline Array<T>::Array(const Array& array)
  : Array{array.size}
{
  std::cout << "Array of " << size << " elements copied" << std::endl;
  for (size_t i {}; i < size; ++i)
    elements[i] = array.elements[i];
}
```

It's an instance of this constructor template that the push_back() function uses in Ex17_01, which is why each evaluation of this statement involves 1,001 dynamic memory allocations and a whole lot of string copying:

```
vectorOfArrays.push_back(buildStringArray(numStringsPerArray));
```

The goal is to write precisely this same line of code but have push_back() use some different constructor instead—one that does not copy the Array<> and its std::string elements. Instead, this new constructor should somehow *move* all these strings into the new object, without actually copying them. Such a constructor is aptly called a *move constructor*, and for the Array<> template you can declare one as follows:

```
template <typename T>
class Array
{
private:
  T* elements;                      // Array of type T
  size_t size;                      // Number of array elements

public:
  explicit Array(size_t arraySize);   // Constructor
  Array(const Array& array);          // Copy constructor
  Array(Array&& array);               // Move constructor

  // ... other members like before
}
```

The type of the move constructor's parameter, Array&&, is an rvalue reference. This makes sense; after all, you want this parameter to bind with temporary rvalue results—something regular lvalue references will not do. An lvalue-reference-to-const parameter would, but its const-ness precludes moving anything out of it. When choosing between overloaded functions or constructors, your compiler will always prefer to bind an rvalue argument to an rvalue reference parameter. So whenever an Array<> is constructed with an Array<> rvalue as the only argument (such as our buildStringArray() call), the compiler will call the move constructor rather than the copy constructor.

All that remains now is to actually implement the move constructor. For Array<>, you might do so using this template:

```
// Move constructor
template <typename T>
Array<T>::Array(Array&& moved)
  : size{moved.size}, elements{moved.elements}
{
  std::cout << "Array of " << size << " elements moved" << std::endl;
  moved.elements = nullptr;   // Otherwise destructor of moved would delete[] elements!
}
```

When this constructor is called, moved will be bound to the outcome of an rvalue, in other words, a value that is typically about to be deleted. In any case, the calling code definitely no longer needs the contents of the moved object anymore. And since no one needs it anymore, there's certainly no harm in you prying the elements array out of the moved object to reuse it for the newly constructed Array<> object. That saves both you and your computer the hassle of copying all the T values.

You thus begin by copying the size and the elements members in the member initializer list. Key here is that you realize that elements is nothing but a pointer of type T*. That is, it's a variable containing the address of a dynamically allocated array of T elements. And copying such a pointer is not the same as copying the entire array and all its elements. Far from it. Copying a single pointer is of course much, much cheaper than copying an entire array of T values!

669

> ■ **Note** This is the difference between what is called a *shallow copy* and a *deep copy*. A *shallow copy* simply copies all members of an object one by one, even if these members are pointers to dynamic memory. A *deep copy*, on the other hand, copies all dynamic memory referred to by any of its pointer members as well.

Simply performing a member-by-member shallow copy of the moved object is rarely enough for a move constructor. In the case of Array<>, you probably already guessed why. Having two objects point to the same dynamically allocated memory is rarely a good idea, as we explained at length in Chapter 6. The following assignment statement in the body of the Array<> move constructor is therefore of the utmost importance as well:

```
moved.elements = nullptr;    // Otherwise destructor of moved would delete[] elements!
```

If you wouldn't set moved.elements to nullptr, you'd have two different objects pointing to the same elements array. This includes your newly constructed object, clearly, but the transient Array<> moved object still points to that array as well. That would put you right in the middle of the highly volatile minefield that we cautioned you about in Chapter 6, complete with dangling pointers and multiple deallocations! By setting the elements pointer of the moved object to null, the destructor of the temporary object bound to moved will effectively perform delete[] nullptr, which as you know is harmless. Phew! Mines defused.

You should plug this move constructor into the Array<> template of Ex17_01 and then run the program again (the resulting program is available in Ex17_02). The output then normally becomes as follows:

```
Array of 1000 elements moved
Array of 1000 elements moved
Array of 1000 elements moved
... (10 times in total)
```

Instead of 10,000 string objects and three-quarters of a million char values, only ten pointers and ten size_t values have now been copied. As performance improvements go, that's not too shabby! Certainly it's well worth the effort of defining a few extra lines of code, wouldn't you agree?

Move Assignment Operators

Just like a copy constructor is normally accompanied by a copy assignment operator (see Chapter 12), a user-defined move constructor is typically paired with a user-defined *move assignment operator*. Defining one for Array<> should be easy enough for you at this point:

```
// Move assignment operator
template <typename T>
Array<T>& Array<T>::operator=(Array&& rhs)
{
  std::cout << "Array of " << rhs.size << " elements moved (assignment)" << std::endl;

  if (this != &rhs)              // prevent trouble with self-assignments
  {
    delete[] elements;          // delete[] all existing elements
```

```
    elements = rhs.elements;    // copy the elements pointer and the size
    size = rhs.size;

    rhs.elements = nullptr;    // make sure rhs does not delete[] elements
  }
  return *this;                // return lhs
}
```

The only new thing here is the rvalue reference parameter rhs, designated using the double ampersands: &&. The operator's body itself simply contains a mix of elements that you've already seen before, either in the copy assignment operators of Chapter 12 or in the move constructor of Array<>.

If present, the compiler will use this assignment operator rather than the copy assignment operator whenever the object on the right side of the assignment is a temporary Array<> object. One case where this would occur is in the following snippet:

```
Array<std::string> strings { 123 };
strings = buildStringArray(1'000);           // Assign an rvalue
```

The Array<std::string> object returned by buildStringArray() is again clearly a temporary object, so the compiler realizes that you'd prefer not to copy it and will therefore pick the move assignment over the copy assignment operator. You can see this assignment operator in action if you add it to the Array<> template of Ex17_02 and use that together with this program:

```
// Ex17_03.cpp - Defining and using a move assignment operator
#include "Array.h"
#include <string>

// Construct an Array<> of a given size, filled with some arbitrary string data
Array<std::string> buildStringArray(const size_t size);

int main()
{
  Array<std::string> strings { 123 };
  strings = buildStringArray(1'000);                // Assign an rvalue to strings

  Array<std::string> more_strings{ 2'000 };
  strings = more_strings;                           // Assign an lvalue to strings
}
```

You can use the same definition of the buildStringArray() function as in Ex17_01 and Ex17_02. The output of this program should reflect that assigning an rvalue to the strings variable indeed results in a call to the move assignment operator, whereas assigning the lvalue more_strings to the same variable results in a call to the copy assignment:

```
Array of 1000 elements moved (assignment)
Array of 2000 elements copied
```

Explicitly Moved Objects

The main() function of Ex17_03.cpp ended with the following two statements:

```
...
Array<std::string> more_strings{ 2'000 };
strings = more_strings;                  // Assign an lvalue to strings
}
```

Running Ex17_03 revealed that this final assignment resulted in the more_strings Array<> being copied. The reason, of course, is that more_strings is an lvalue. A variable name always is (remember this, it's important!). In this case, however, the fact that more_strings gets copied is actually quite unfortunate. The culprit assignment is the very last statement of the function, so there's clearly no need for more_strings to persist. And even if the main() function would have continued beyond this point, it would still be perfectly plausible that this assignment would be the last statement to ever reference more_strings. In fact, it is fairly common for a named variable such as more_strings to no longer be needed once its contents have been handed over to another object or to some function. It would be a real shame if "handing over" a variable such as more_strings could be done only by copying just because you gave the variable a name?

C++11 foresees a solution for this: you can turn any lvalue into an rvalue reference simply by applying one of C++11's most vital Standard Library functions: std::move().[2] To see its effect, you should first replace the final two lines of main() in Ex17_03.cpp with the following and then run the program again (you can find this variant in Ex17_04):

```
...
Array<std::string> more_strings{ 2'000 };
strings = std::move(more_strings);       // Move more_strings into strings
}
```

If you do, you will notice that more_strings is indeed no longer copied:

```
Array of 1000 elements moved (assignment)
Array of 2000 elements moved (assignment)
```

Move-Only Types

No discussion of std::move() is complete without an honorary mention of std::unique_ptr<>—undoubtedly the type whose variables you'll be moving the most in modern C++ programming. As explained in Chapter 6, and again in Chapter 12, there must never be two unique_ptr<> smart pointers pointing to the same address in memory. Otherwise, both would delete (or delete[]) the same raw pointer twice, which is a perfect

---

[2]Technically, std::move() is defined in the <utility> header. In practice, though, you'll rarely have to explicitly include this header to make use of std::move().

way to initiate a tragic failure of your program. It is thus only fortunate that neither of the two lines that are commented out at the end of the following code snippet compiles:

```
std::unique_ptr<int> one = std::make_unique<int>(123);

std::unique_ptr<int> other;
// other = one;                               /* Error: copy assignment operator is deleted!
*/

//std::unique_ptr<int> yet_another{ other };  /* Error: copy constructor is deleted! */
```

What would compile, however, are these two lines:

```
other = std::move(one);                            // Move assignment operator is defined
std::unique_ptr<int> yet_another{ std::move(other) }; // Move constructor is defined
```

That is, while both copy members of std::unique_ptr<> are deleted (as explained in Chapter 12), both its move assignment operator and its move constructor are present. This is an outline of how you'd normally accomplish this:

```
namespace std
{
  template <typename T>
  class unique_ptr
  {
    ...
    // Prevent copying:
    unique_ptr(const unique_ptr&) = delete;
    unique_ptr& operator=(const unique_ptr&) = delete;

    // Allow moving:
    unique_ptr(unique_ptr&& source);
    unique_ptr& operator=(unique_ptr&& rhs);
    ...
  };
}
```

To define a move-only type, you always start by deleting its two copy members (like we taught you in Chapter 12). By doing so, you implicitly delete the move members as well (more on this later), so to allow uncopiable objects to be moved, you must explicitly define the move members. Often, but not in the case of unique_ptr<>, it would suffice to use = default to define the two move members and have the compiler generate them for you.

Extended Use of Moved Objects

An lvalue expression by definition evaluates to a persistent value, which is a value that remains addressable after the execution of the lvalue's parent statement. This is why the compiler normally prefers to copy the value of an lvalue expression. We just told you, however, how you can overrule this preference with std::move(). That is, you can force the compiler to pass any object to a move constructor or move assignment operator, even if it's not a temporary. This raises the question, what happens if you keep using an object after it has been moved? Here's an example (if you want, you can try this in Ex17_04):

```
...
Array<std::string> more_strings{ 2'000 };
strings = std::move(more_strings);              // Move more_strings into strings

std::cout << more_strings[101] << std::endl;   // ???
}
```

In this specific case, you of course already know what will happen. After all, you've written the code for the move assignment operator of Array<> yourself. Once moved, an Array<> object will contain an elements pointer that is set to nullptr. Any further use of a moved Array<> then would trigger a null pointer dereference, which, as always, is destined to end in the tragic, gruesome death of your program. This example therefore nicely underlines the rationale behind this guideline:

■ **Caution**   As a rule, you should only move an object if you are absolutely sure it is no longer required. Unless otherwise specified, you're not supposed to keep on using an object that was moved. By default, any extended use of a moved object results in undefined behavior (read: it'll result in fatal crashes).

This guideline applies for objects of Standard Library types as well. Completely analogous to Arrays, for instance, you must never simply keep using a moved std::vector<>. Doing so could very well end equally badly. You might hope that a moved vector<> is equivalent to an empty one. And while this may be so for some implementations, in general the C++ standard does not specify at all in which state a moved vector<> should be. What is (implicitly) allowed, however, and which is something that not too many developers will know, is this:

■ **Tip**   If need be, you can safely revive a move()'d vector<> by calling its clear() member. After calling clear(), the vector<> is guaranteed to be equivalent to an empty vector<> and thus safe to use again.

In the rare cases where you do want to reuse moved Standard Library objects, you should thus always check the specification of their move members. When a std::optional<T> object that contains a T value is moved, for instance, it will still contain a T value—a T value that is now moved (we covered std::optional<> in Chapter 8). Similar to a vector<>, the optional<> can safely be reused after calling its reset() member. Smart pointers are a scarce exception:

■ **Tip**   The Standard Library specification clearly stipulates that you may continue using smart pointers of type std::unique_ptr<> and std::shared_ptr<> after moving out the raw pointer, and this without first calling reset(). For both types, move operations must always set the encapsulated raw pointer to nullptr.

A Barrel of Contradictions

Many find move semantics confusing at first, and understandably so. We hope this section can somewhat spare you from this fate, as it aims to alleviate some of the most common sources of confusion.

std::move() Does Not Move

Make no mistake, std::move()does not move anything. All this function does is turn a given lvalue into an rvalue reference. std::move() is effectively nothing more than a type conversion, not at all unlike built-in cast operators static_cast<>() and dynamic_cast<>(). In fact, you could almost implement your own version of the function simply like so (somewhat simplified):

```
template <typename T>
T&& move(T& x) noexcept { return static_cast<T&&>(x); }
```

Clearly, this moves nothing. What it does do, however, is make a persistent *lvalue* eligible for binding with the *rvalue* reference parameter of a move constructor or assignment operator. It's these member functions then that are supposed to move the members of the former lvalue into another. std::move() only performs a type cast to make the compiler pick the right function overload.

If no function or constructor overload exists with an rvalue reference parameter, an rvalue will happily bind with an lvalue reference instead. That is, you can move() all you want; but if there's no function overload standing ready to receive the resulting rvalue, it's all in vain. To demonstrate this, we'll again start from Ex17_04.cpp. As you may recall, this latest variant of our running example ended with these statements:

```
...

  Array<std::string> more_strings{ 2'000 };
  strings = std::move(more_strings);              // Move more_strings into strings
}
```

Obviously, the intent of this final statement is to move the 2,000 strings of more_strings into strings. And in Ex17_04 this worked flawlessly. But now see what happens if you remove the declaration and definition of the move assignment operator from its Array<> template. If you then run the main() function of Ex17_04.cpp once more, unaltered, the last line of the output reverts to this:

```
...
Array of 2000 elements copied
```

It does not matter that you still call std::move() in the body of main(). If there's no move assignment operator for Array<> to accept the rvalue, the copy assignment operator will be used instead. So, always remember, adding std::move() is of no consequence if the function or constructor that you are passing a value to has no overload with an rvalue reference parameter!

An Rvalue Reference Is an Lvalue

To be precise, the *name* of a named variable with an rvalue reference type is an lvalue. Let's show what we mean by this, as it turns out that many struggle with this idiosyncrasy at first. We'll keep on milking the same example, naturally, so take Ex17_04 once again (make sure it contains the original Array<> template where the move assignment operator is still defined) and change the last two lines of the program to the following:

```
...

Array<std::string> more_strings{ 2'000 };
Array<std::string>&& rvalue_ref{ std::move(more_strings) };
strings = rvalue_ref;
}
```

Notwithstanding that the rvalue_ref variable clearly has an rvalue reference type, the output of the program will show that the corresponding object is copied:

```
Array of 1000 elements moved (assignment)
Array of 2000 elements copied
```

Every variable name expression is an lvalue, even if the type of that variable is an rvalue reference type. To move the contents of a named variable, you must therefore always add std::move():

```
strings = std::move(rvalue_ref);
```

While you'd normally not create an rvalue reference in the middle of a block of code like rvalue_ref in our latest example, the analogous situation does occur regularly if you define function parameters that are rvalue references. You can find an example of this in the next section.

Defining Functions Revisited

In this section we'll study how move semantics has influenced best-practice guidelines for defining new functions, complementing what you saw earlier in Chapter 8. We'll answer questions such as these: How does move semantics affect the choice between pass-by-reference and pass-by-value? Or, to return an object by value without copying, should I use std::move() or not? You'll find both answers coming up. We kick off with investigating how and when to pass arguments by rvalue reference to regular functions, that is, to functions that are not move constructors or move assignment operators.

Pass-by-Rvalue-Reference

In Exercise 16-1, you were tasked with defining a push_back() member function template for Array<>. If all went well, you created a function similar to this:

```
template <typename T>
void Array<T>::push_back(const T& element)
{
  Array<T> newArray(size + 1);        // Allocate a larger Array<>
  for (size_t i = 0; i < size; ++i)   // Copy all existing elements...
```

```
    newArray[i] = elements[i];

  newArray[size] = element;            // Copy the new one...

  swap(newArray);                      // ... and swap!
}
```

While this is by no means the only way to implement push_back(), it is definitely one of the cleanest and most elegant options. More important, it is 100 percent robust and safe in the face of exceptions. In fact, if this exercise were part of an exam of Chapter 16, this is what we would be grading you on:

1. To avoid redundant copies of the arguments passed to push_back(), you defined the template using a reference-to-const parameter—precisely like we taught you in Chapter 8.

2. In the function body, you used the copy-and-swap idiom to make sure that the push_back() member behaves as desired even if the function body were to throw an exception (std::bad_alloc, for instance, or any other exception that T's copy assignment might throw). We refer you to Chapter 16 for a detailed discussion of copy-and-swap.

The part we'd like to draw your attention to here is the blatant amount of copying that this function performs. First, all existing elements are copied into the new, larger Array<> and then the newly added element as well. While still excusable for a Chapter 16 exam, in your Chapter 17 exam such needless copying will start costing you grades. And in this case it is not because copying on your exam is cheating, but because clearly you should at least try to *move* all these elements instead!

Fixing the loop that copies all existing elements appears easy enough. Simply apply std::move() to turn the lvalue elements[i] into an rvalue, right? Doing so clearly avoids all copies, provided that the template argument type T has an appropriate move assignment operator:

```
for (size_t i = 0; i < size; ++i)        // Move all existing elements...
  newArray[i] = std::move(elements[i]);
```

▨ **Caution**   If the sidebar sections in Chapter 16 taught you anything, however, it's that appearances can be deceiving. Yes, adding std::move() like this works like a charm in the nominal case. But that's not the end of it. In general, this implementation is ever so slightly flawed. We'll reveal what this minor imperfection is later in this chapter. For now this initial version will do its job just fine. Adieu, gratuitous copying!

Now that all existing elements have been move()'d, let's focus our attention on the newly added element. Omitting all irrelevant parts, this is thus the code we will consider next:

```
template <typename T>
void Array<T>::push_back(const T& element)
{
...
  newArray[size] = element;                // Copy the new element...
...
}
```

Your first instinct might be to simply slap another std::move() onto element, like so:

```
template <typename T>
void Array<T>::push_back(const T& element)
{
...
  newArray[size] = std::move(element);    // Move the new element... (???)
...
}
```

This will not work, though, and with good reason. element is a reference to a *const* T, meaning that the caller of the function expects the argument not to be modified. Moving its contents into another object is therefore completely out of the question. This is also why the std::move() type conversion function will never cast a const T or const T& type to T&&. Instead, std::move() converts it to the rather pointless type const T&&—a reference to a transient value that you're not allowed to modify. In other words, because the type of element is const T&, the type of std::move(element) is const T&&, meaning that assigning the latter expression still goes through the copy assignment operator, despite the std::move().

But of course you still want to cater for those cases where the caller does not need the element argument anymore—that is, for those cases where push_back() is called with an rvalue. Luckily, you cannot only use rvalue reference parameters for move constructors and move assignment operators; you can use them for any function you want. And so you could easily add an extra overload of push_back() that accepts rvalue arguments:

```
template <typename T>
void Array<T>::push_back(T&& element)
{
...
  newArray[size] = std::move(element);    // Move the new element...
...
}
```

■ **Caution**   When passing an argument such as element by rvalue reference, never forget that inside the function's body the expression element is again an lvalue. Remember, any named variable is an lvalue, even if the variable itself has an rvalue reference type! In our push_back() example, this means that the std::move() in the function's body is very much required to compel the compiler into choosing T's move assignment operator rather than its copy assignment operator.

The Return of Pass-by-Value

The introduction of move semantics has caused a significant shift in how you can and should define the parameters of certain functions. Before C++11, life was easy. To avoid copies, you simply always passed objects by reference, just like we taught you in Chapter 8. Now that support for move semantics is prevalent, however, pass-by-lvalue-reference is no longer always your best option. In fact, it turns out that passing arguments by value is back on the table, at least in some specific cases. To explain when and why, we'll build further on the same push_back() example as just now.

In the previous subsection, we created two separate overloads of push_back(), one for const T& and one for T&& references. For your convenience, you can find this variant in Ex17_05A. While using two overloads is certainly a viable option, it does imply some tedious code duplication. One way to work around this duplication is to redefine the const T& overload in terms of the T&& one like so:

```
template <typename T>
void Array<T>::push_back(const T& element)
{
  push_back(T{ element });      // Create a temporary, transient copy and push that
}
```

But there is an even better, more compact way, one where one single function definition is all you need. Somewhat surprisingly, this single push_back() definition will use *pass-by-value*. You'd probably never have guessed to replace two *pass-by-reference* overloads with one single definition that uses *pass-by-value*, but once you see it in action, you'll surely appreciate the sheer elegance of this approach. If we again omit the irrelevant, this is what your new push_back() would look like:

```
template <typename T>
void Array<T>::push_back(T element)       // Pass by value (copy of lvalue, or moved rvalue!)
{
...
  newArray[size] = std::move(element);  // Move the new element...
...
}
```

Provided you only use types that support move semantics (such as Standard Library types), this function always does precisely what you want. It does not matter what kind of argument you pass it: lvalue arguments are copied, once, and rvalue arguments are moved. Because the function parameter is of value type T, a new object of type T is created whenever push_back() is called. The beauty is that in order to construct this new T object, the compiler will use a different constructor depending on the kind of argument. If the function's argument is an lvalue, the element argument is constructed using T's copy constructor. If it's an rvalue, however, element will be constructed using T's move constructor.

▓ **Caution**   For a generic container such as Array<>, you probably still want to take into account the possibility that the type T does not provide a move constructor or assignment operator. For such types, the variant that accepts T by value would actually copy any given argument twice. Remember, std::move() does not move unless T has a move assignment operator. If it doesn't, the compiler will quietly revert to the copy assignment operator to evaluate newArray[size] = std::move(element). In real life, a container like Array<> would thus mostly still have both overloads of push_back()—one for lvalues and one for rvalues.

The only reason that using pass-by-value is interesting here is because push_back() always and inevitably copies a given lvalue. Since a copy is thus inevitable anyway, you might as well create this copy already when constructing the input argument. Arguments that do not need to be copied by a function should of course still be passed by reference-to-const!

For nontemplated functions that inherently copy any lvalue input, however, the use of a single function with a pass-by-value parameter is a wonderfully compact alternative. Concrete examples would be functions with signatures such as setNumbers(std::vector<double> values) or add(BigObject bigboy). The traditional reflex would be to use pass-by-reference-to-const, but by passing the arguments by value instead, you can actually kill two birds with one stone. If defined like this, the same single function can handle both lvalues and rvalues with near-optimal performance!

To demonstrate that this effectively works, simply add the push_back(T) function we laid out here into the Array<> template of Ex17_04. Now that Array<> supports push_back(), it also makes sense to give the arraySize parameter of its constructor a default value of zero:

```
template <typename T>
class Array
{
public:
  explicit Array(size_t arraySize = 0);  // Constructor
// ...
  void push_back(T element);              // Add a new element (either copied or moved)
// ...
};
```

All other members can remain as they were in Ex17_04. With this, you can compose the following example program (the definition of buildStringArray() can be taken from Ex17_04 as well):

```
// Ex17_05B.cpp - Use of a pass-by-value parameter to pass by either lvalue or rvalue
#include "Array.h"
#include <string>

// Construct an Array<> of a given size, filled with some arbitrary string data
Array<std::string> buildStringArray(const size_t size);

int main()
{
  Array<Array<std::string>> array_of_arrays;

  Array<std::string> array{ buildStringArray(1'000) };
  array_of_arrays.push_back(array);              // Push an lvalue

  array.push_back("One more for good measure");
  std::cout << std::endl;

  array_of_arrays.push_back(std::move(array));   // Push an rvalue
}
```

In main(), we create an Array of Arrays of strings, aptly named array_of_arrays. We begin by inserting an Array<> of 1,000 strings into this container. This Array<> element, aptly named array, is clearly pushed as an lvalue, so we expect it to be copied. That is a good thing: we still need its contents for the remainder of the program. At the end of the program, we add array a second time, but this time we first convert it into an rvalue by applying std::move() to the variable's name. We do so in the hopes that the

Array<> and its string array will now be moved instead of copied. Running Ex17_05B confirms that this is indeed the case; in total, array is copied only once:

```
Array of 1000 elements copied
Array of 1000 elements moved (assignment)

Array of 1001 elements moved
Array of 1000 elements moved (assignment)
Array of 1001 elements moved (assignment)
```

The various move assignments occur in the body of the push_back() function. In between adding array as an lvalue and adding it again as an rvalue, we inject one extra string into it to be able to differentiate the two Array<> elements in the output. Note that in the process of pushing this additional string none of the 1,000 preexisting string elements inside array are copied either. They are all moved to a larger string Array<> through the move assignment operator of std::string!

In the following tip, we summarize the various guidelines regarding function parameter declarations that you have encountered throughout the book, mainly in Chapter 8 and here:

■ **Tip** For fundamental types and pointers, you can simply use pass-by-value. For objects that are more expensive to copy, you should normally use a const T& parameter. This avoids any lvalue arguments from being copied, and rvalue arguments will bind just fine with a const T& parameter as well. If your function inherently copies its T argument, however, you should pass it by value instead, even when it concerns a large object. Lvalue arguments will then be copied when passed to the function, and rvalue arguments will be moved. The latter guideline presumes that the parameter types support move semantics—as all types should these days. In the less likely case that the parameter type lacks proper move members, you should stick with pass-by-reference. More and more types support move semantics these days, though—not in the least all Standard Library types—so pass-by-value is most certainly back on the table!

Return-by-Value

The recommended way for returning an object from a function has always been to return it by value; even for larger objects such as a vector<>. As we'll discuss shortly, compilers have always been good at optimizing away any redundant copies of objects that you return from a function. The introduction of move semantics therefore doesn't change anything for the best practices. There are many misconceptions in this area (believe us, there are!), however, so it remains well worth reviewing this aspect of defining functions as well.

Many sample programs in this chapter were built around the following function:

```
Array<std::string> buildStringArray(const size_t size)
{
  Array<std::string> result{ size };
  for (size_t i = 0; i < size; ++i)
    result[i] = "You should learn from your competitor, but never copy. Copy and you die.";
  return result;
}
```

681

This function returns an `Array<>` by value. Its last line is a `return` statement with the lvalue expression `result`, the name of an automatic, stack-allocated variable. Performance-conscious developers often get worried when they see this. Won't the compiler use `Array<>`'s copy constructor to copy `result` into the object that is being returned? They need not be worried, at least not in this case. Let's review how a C++17 compiler is supposed to handle return-by-value (slightly simplified, as always):

- In a `return` statement of the form `return name;`, a compiler is *obliged* to treat name *as if it were an rvalue expression*, provided name is either the name of a locally defined automatic variable *or* that of a function parameter.

- In a `return` statement of the form `return name;`, a compiler is *allowed* to apply the so-called *named return value optimization* (NRVO), provided name is the name of a locally defined automatic variable (*not* if it is that of a parameter name).

For our example, NRVO would entail that the compiler stores the `result` object directly in the memory designated to hold the function's return value. That is, after applying NRVO, no memory is set aside anymore for a separate automatic variable named `result`.

The first bullet implies that using `std::move(result)` in our example would be, at the very least, redundant. Even without the `std::move()`, the compiler already treats `result` as if it is an rvalue. The second bullet moreover implies that `return std::move(result)` would prohibit the NRVO optimization. NRVO applies solely to statements of the form `return result;`. By adding `std::move()`, you would instead force the compiler to look for a move constructor. Doing so would introduce two potential issues—the first of which can be very severe indeed:

- If the type of the object that you return has no move constructor, then adding `std::move()` causes the compiler to fall back to the copy constructor! Yes, that's right. Adding *move()* can cause a *copy*, where before the compiler would probably have applied NRVO.

- Even if the returned object can be moved, adding `std::move()` can only make matters worse—never better. The reason is that NRVO generally leads to code that is even more efficient than move construction (move construction typically still involves some shallow copying and/or other statements; NRVO does not).

So, adding `std::move()` at best makes things a little bit slower, and at worst it causes the compiler to *copy* the return value where it otherwise would not! Therefore:

■ **Tip**   If value is either a local variable (with automatic storage duration) or a function parameter, you should never write `return std::move(value);`. Always write `return value;` instead.

Note that for `return` statements such as `return value + 1;` or `return buildStringArray(100);` you never have to worry about adding `std::move()` either. In both these cases you are already returning an rvalue, so adding `std::movc()` would again be redundant.

Does this mean that you should never use `std::move()` when returning a value? Alas, no. Life with C++ is rarely that easy. Mostly, returning by value without `std::move()` is what you want but certainly not always:

- If the variable `value` in `return value;` has *static or thread-local storage duration* (see Chapter 10), you need to add `std::move()` if moving is what you want. This case is rare, though.

- When returning an object's *member variable*, as in `return member_variable;`, `std::move()` is again required if you do not want the member variable to be copied.

- If the return statement contains any other lvalue expression besides the name of a single variable, then NRVO does not apply, nor will the compiler treat this lvalue as if it were an rvalue when looking for a constructor.

Common examples for the latter case are return statements of the form return condition? var1 : var2;. While not obvious, a conditional expression such as condition? var1 : var2 is in fact an lvalue. Because it's clearly no variable name, the compiler forsakes NRVO and will not implicitly treat it as an rvalue either. It will, in other words, look for a copy constructor to create the returned object (either var1 or var2). To avoid this, you have at least three options. Any of the following return statements will at least attempt to move the value that is returned:

```
return std::move(condition? var1 : var2);

return condition? std::move(var1) : std::move(var2);

if (condition)
  return var1;
else
  return var2;
```

Out of these three, the last one is most recommended. The reason is again that it allows a clever compiler to apply NRVO, something that with the former two forms is not allowed.

Defining Move Members Revisited

Now that you are a move semantics expert, we can give some more advice on how to properly define your own move constructors and move assignment operators. Our first guideline—that is, to always declare them as noexcept—is particularly important. Without noexcept, your move members are not nearly as effective. (The noexcept specifier was explained in Chapter 16.)

Always Add noexcept

It is important that all your move members have a noexcept specifier, assuming they do not throw, of course, though in practice move members rarely do. Adding noexcept is so important that we'll even go out of our way to explain why this is so. The reason is that we firmly believe that knowing why a guideline exists makes you remember it all the better!

For this, let's pick up where we left off earlier with Ex17_05B. In this example, you defined the following push_back() function for Array<>:

```
template <typename T>
void Array<T>::push_back(T element)      // Pass by value (copy of lvalue, or moved rvalue!)
{
  Array<T> newArray(size + 1);           // Allocate a larger Array<>
  for (size_t i = 0; i < size; ++i)      // Move all existing elements...
    newArray[i] = std::move(elements[i]);

  newArray[size] = std::move(element); // Move the new one...

  swap(newArray);                        // ... and swap!
}
```

Looks good, right? Running Ex17_05B also confirmed that all redundant copies are gone. So, what's wrong with this definition then? In Chapter 16 we cautioned you to look beyond apparent correctness. For one, we urged you to always consider what happens in case of unexpected exceptions. Any idea as to what could be wrong with push_back()? It might be good for you to reflect on this for a moment.

The answer is that, while unlikely, the move assignment operator of T could in principle throw an exception. This is especially relevant here since the Array<> template should work for any type T. Now consider what happens if such an exception occurred in the middle of the function's for loop, or even while moving the new element?

In a way, adding the std::move() in the for loop has undermined the workings of the copy-and-swap idiom. With this idiom it is crucial that the object you are modifying (*this, typically, in the case of a member function) remains in pristine, untouched condition, right up to the final swap() operation. Any modification prior to the swap() does not get undone in case of an exception. So if an exception occurs inside push_back() while moving one of the objects in the elements array, there's nothing in place to restore any earlier objects that were already moved into newArray.

It turns out that, no matter what you try, if a move member may throw at any time, there is in general no way for you to safely move the existing elements into the new array without copying. If only there was a way for you to know that a given move member never throws any exceptions. After all, if moving never throws, safely moving existing elements into a larger array becomes feasible. But, hang on. Of course, you know of such a way already! It was introduced in Chapter 16: the noexcept specifier. If a function is noexcept, you know for a fact that it will never throw an exception. In other words, what you want to somehow express in push_back() is this:

```
template <typename T>
void Array<T>::push_back(T element)      // Pass by value (copy of lvalue, or moved rvalue!)
{
  Array<T> newArray(size + 1);           // Allocate a larger Array<>
  for (size_t i = 0; i < size; ++i)      // Move all existing elements (copy if not noexcept)...
    newArray[i] = move_assign_if_noexcept(elements[i]);

  newArray[size] = move_assign_if_noexcept(element);   // Move (or copy) the new one...

  swap(newArray);                        // ... and swap!
}
```

The move_assign_if_noexcept() function we need here to accomplish an efficient yet safe push_back() template should act as std::move(), yet only if the move assignment operator of T is specified to be noexcept. If not, move_assign_if_noexcept() should turn its argument in an lvalue reference instead, thus triggering the use of T's copy assignment.

This is where we hit a minor bump in the road:

▨ **Caution**   The Standard Library utility header does provide std::move_if_noexcept(), but reading the fine print reveals that this function is intended to conditionally invoke either a move *constructor* or a copy *constructor* depending on whether the move *constructor* is noexcept. The Standard Library offers no equivalent for conditionally invoking a move assignment operator.

While implementing such a move_assign_if_noexcept() function is certainly possible, it unfortunately requires a technique that is actually way too advanced for a beginner's book; concretely, it requires *template metaprogramming*. Before we go there, here's an important conclusion already:

▦ **Caution**   If nothing else, what the Array<>::push_back() function should teach you is to never give in to the temptation to implement your own container classes, unless this is absolutely necessary (and it rarely is!). Getting them 100 percent right is deceptively hard. Always use containers of the Standard Library instead (or those of other tested and tried libraries if you prefer). Even with the move_assign_if_noexcept() function in place, your Array<> class can hardly be called optimal. You'd need to rework it considerably using rather advanced memory management techniques to even get remotely close to a fully optimized std::vector<>!

The upcoming sidebar briefly explains how you could implement the move_assign_if_noexcept() function required for our exception-safe push_back() member (you can find the result in Ex17_06). It involves template metaprogramming, so it is not for the faint-hearted. So, please feel free to skip straight ahead to the next regular subsection, where we'll demonstrate the effect of adding noexcept to move members when using your types in Standard Library containers.

IMPLEMENTING MOVE_ASSIGN_IF_NOEXCEPT

Template metaprogramming typically involves making decisions based on template arguments (which, as you know, are often type names) to control the code that is generated by a template when it is instantiated by the compiler. In other words, it involves writing code that is evaluated at compile time, whenever the compiler generates a concrete instance of the corresponding template. In the case of move_assign_if_noexcept(), what we essentially need to encode is the equivalent of a regular C++ if-else statement that expresses the following logic for the function's return type:

"If rvalues of type T&& can be assigned without throwing, then the return type should be an rvalue reference (that is, T&&); otherwise, it should be an lvalue reference instead (const T&)."

T here is the template type argument to move_assign_if_noexcept(). Without further ado, this is how you'd convey precisely this logic using some of the template metaprogramming primitives—so-called type traits—provided by the type_traits Standard Library header:

```
std::conditional_t<std::is_nothrow_move_assignable_v<T>, T&&, const T&>
```

To a template metaprogrammer, this reads almost word for word as what we said earlier. It takes some (read: a lot of) getting used to, though, which obviously is something we don't have time for now. We therefore won't dwell on this any further either. The aim of this sidebar, after all, is just to give you a quick first taste of what is possible with template metaprogramming.

With the previous meta-expression, composing a fully functioning move_assign_if_noexcept() function is actually not that hard anymore:

```
template<class T>
std::conditional_t<std::is_nothrow_move_assignable_v<T>, T&&, const T&>
move_assign_if_noexcept(T& x) noexcept
{
  return std::move(x);
}
```

The function body is trivial; all template meta-magic happens in the return type of the function. Depending on the properties of type T—more concretely, depending on whether T&& values can be assigned without throwing—the return type will be either T&& or const T&. Note that in the latter case, it does not matter that the std::move() in the function's body still returns an rvalue reference. If the return type in the template's instantiation for type T is const T&, then the rvalue reference that is returned from the function body gets turned right back into an lvalue reference.

Moving Within Standard Library Containers

Naturally all container types of the Standard Library are optimized to move objects whenever possible, just like you did for the Array<> container template. This means that any implementation of std::vector<> faces challenges analogous to those you faced with push_back(). Namely, how does one guarantee internal integrity in the presence of exceptions when moving existing elements into a newly allocated, larger array? How then does one guarantee the desired all-or-nothing behavior—a behavior the C++ standard normally requires for all container operations?

We can deduce how the Standard Library implementers approached these challenges using the following variant of Ex17_05B:

```
// Ex17_07.cpp - the effect of not adding noexcept to move members
#include "Array.h"
#include <string>
#include <vector>

// Construct an Array<> of a given size, filled with some arbitrary string data
Array<std::string> buildStringArray(const size_t size);

int main()
{
  std::vector<Array<std::string>> v;

  v.push_back(buildStringArray(1'000));

  std::cout << std::endl;

  v.push_back(buildStringArray(2'000));
}
```

Instead of adding the Array<>s to an Array<>, we now add them to a std::vector<>. More concretely, we add two rvalues of type Array<>&& to a single vector<> (the implementation of buildStringArray() is the same as always). One possible sequence of events then is this (provided you started with an Array<> template where the move members do not yet have the necessary noexcept specifiers, that is):

```
Array of 1000 elements moved

Array of 1000 elements copied
Array of 2000 elements moved
```

From this output, you clearly see that when adding the second element (the Array<> with 2,000 elements), the std::vector<> copies the first element (the Array<> with 1,000 strings). Its push_back() member does so while transferring all existing elements to a larger dynamic array, similar to what we did earlier in Array::push_back().

▓ **Note**   The Standard Library specification does not explicitly prescribe when and how often a vector<> should allocate a larger dynamic array as you add more elements. So, it could in principle be that with Ex17_07.cpp you do not yet see the Array<> of 1,000 elements being copied. If so, just add more push_back() statements to add extra Array<>&& elements. Because the Standard Library does require a vector<> to store all its elements in one contiguous dynamic array, eventually the vector<> inevitably has to allocate a larger array and then transfer all its existing elements into that.

The reason that the Array<> is *copied* rather than *moved* is that the compiler deemed moving to be unsafe. That is, it could not deduce that moving is possible without throwing. Naturally, if you now add noexcept to your Array<> move constructor template and run Ex17_07 again, you'll find that the Array<> and its 1,000 strings are no longer copied:

```
Array of 1000 elements moved

Array of 1000 elements moved
Array of 2000 elements moved
```

▓ **Tip**   Standard containers and functions typically only exploit move semantics if the corresponding move members are declared with noexcept. Whenever possible—and it almost always is—it is therefore crucial that all your move constructors and move assignment operators are declared noexcept.

The "Move-and-Swap" Idiom

Before we move on to the final section of this chapter, we'll first revisit the implementation of the `Array<>` move assignment operator. When we defined it earlier, near the beginning of the chapter, you didn't know enough yet to implement this operator in a clean and elegant manner. Going back to this definition, isn't there something that strikes you as suboptimal? We'll throw in the noexcept specifier to get things going, as shown here:

```
// Move assignment operator
template <typename T>
Array<T>& Array<T>::operator=(Array&& rhs) noexcept
{
  std::cout << "Array of " << rhs.size << " elements moved (assignment)" << std::endl;

  if (this != &rhs)              // prevent trouble with self-assignments
  {
    delete[] elements;          // delete[] all existing elements

    elements = rhs.elements;    // copy the elements pointer and the size
    size = rhs.size;

    rhs.elements = nullptr;     // make sure rhs does not delete[] elements
  }
  return *this;                 // return lhs
}
```

What if we told you that you're looking for code duplication?

If you look closely, you'll find that the function in fact contains not one but two accounts of duplication:

- First, it contains the same logic as the destructor to clean up any existing members. In our case this is just a single `delete[]` statement, but in general this could require any number of steps.

- Second, it contains the same logic as the move constructor to copy all members and to set the `elements` member of the moved object to `nullptr`.

In Chapter 16 we told you that it's always good practice to avoid duplication as much as reasonably possible. Any duplication, even that of only one or a couple of lines of code, is just another opportunity for bugs—either now or in the future. Just imagine that one day you add an extra member to `Array<>`; it would then be easy to forget to update all places where they're copied one by one. The fewer places you need to update, the better.

For copy assignment operators, you are already familiar with the standard technique to solve the analogous problem: the copy-and-swap idiom. Fortunately, you can use a similar pattern for move assignment operators as well:

```
// Move assignment operator
template <typename T>
Array<T>& Array<T>::operator=(Array&& rhs) noexcept
{
  Array<T> moved(std::move(rhs)); // move...        (noexcept)
  swap(moved);                    // ... and swap   (noexcept)
  return *this;                   // return lhs
}
```

This move-and-swap idiom eliminates both accounts of duplication. Any existing elements are deleted by the destructor of the automatic variable moved, and the responsibility of copying the members and assigning nullptr is delegated to the move constructor. Key is not to forget the explicit std::move() of rhs in the function body. Remember, and we cannot repeat this enough, a variable name is always an lvalue, even the name of a variable with an rvalue reference type!

Take care not to go too far in weeding out duplication. Given earlier guidelines, you may be tempted to reduce code duplication even more and combine the copy and move assignment operators into one single assignment operator of the following form:

```
// Assignment operator
template <typename T>
Array<T>& Array<T>::operator=(Array rhs)  // Copy or move...
{
  swap(rhs);          // ... and swap!
  return *this;       // Return lhs
}
```

At first sight, this looks like a nice and elegant improvement. Whenever the right side of an assignment is a temporary object, the rhs value argument to this assignment operator will be constructed and initialized using the move constructor. Otherwise, the copy constructor is used. The problem, however, is that it violates another guideline, which is that the move assignment operator should always be noexcept. Otherwise, you risk that the copy assignment is still used by containers and other Standard Library templates that move only when noexcept is present.

The following guideline thus summarizes our advice regarding defining assignment operators:

▓ **Tip** If you define them at all (see later), always define separate copy and move assignment operators. The latter should be noexcept, the former typically not (copying typically risks triggering a bad_alloc exception, at the least). To avoid additional duplication, the copy assignment operator should use the traditional copy-and-swap idiom, and the move assignment operator should use the analogous move-and-swap idiom we introduced here.

Finally, the copy assignment operator should always use pass-by-reference-to-const, not pass-by-value. Otherwise, you risk running into compiler errors because of so-called ambiguous assignments.

Special Member Functions

There are six so-called *special member functions*, and you now know all of them:

- The default constructor (Chapter 11)
- The destructor (Chapter 11)
- The copy constructor (Chapter 11)
- The copy assignment operator (Chapter 12)
- The move constructor
- The move assignment operator

The quality that makes them "special" is that, under the right circumstances, the compiler is kind enough to generate them for you. It's interesting to note what the compiler may provide you with a simple class. Here's a class with just a single data member:

```
class Data
{
  int value {1};
};
```

What you actually get is the following, assuming your compiler conforms to the current language standard:

```
class Data
{
public:
  Data() : value{1} {}                        // Default constructor
  Data(const Data& data) : value{data.value} {}            // Copy constructor
  Data(Data&& data) noexcept : value{std::move(data.value)} {}  // Move constructor

  ~Data() {}                                  // Destructor (implicitly noexcept)

  Data& operator=(const Data& data)           // Copy assignment operator
  {
    value = data.value;
    return *this;
  }
  Data& operator=(Data&& data) noexcept       // Move assignment operator
  {
    value = std::move(data.value);
    return *this;
  }

private:
  int value;
};
```

Default-generated move members are something we haven't discussed yet, so we'll start there. Once they are covered, the remainder of this section then reviews when exactly you should define your own versions of these special functions.

Default Move Members

Analogous to the two default copy members (see Chapters 11 and 12), compiler-generated move members simply move all non-static member variables one by one, in the order in which the member variables are declared in the class definition. If the class has base classes, their move constructors or move assignment operators are called first, again in the order in which the base classes are declared. An implicitly defined move member, finally, is always noexcept, as long as the corresponding member function is noexcept for all base classes and non-static member variables as well.

So, no surprises there. *If* the move members are defined by the compiler, they behave exactly as you'd expect. The main questions we still need to answer are as follows: *When* exactly does the compiler generate these default move members? And, why did it for instance not do so for our Array<> class template? The answer is as follows:

▓ **Tip**   As soon as you declare either any of the four copy or move members or a destructor, the compiler will no longer generate any missing move members.

While this rule may appear fairly restrictive at first, it actually makes a lot of sense. Consider our original Array<> template. The compiler observes that you explicitly defined the destructor, copy constructor, and copy assignment operator. The only sensible reason for you to provide such explicit definitions is, of course, because the compiler-generated defaults would be wrong. From this, the compiler can draw only one sensible conclusion: if it were to generate default move members, they would almost certainly be wrong as well (note that for Array<>, this reasoning is most definitely sound!). When in doubt, generating no default move members at all is clearly always better than generating incorrect ones. After all, the worst that could happen to an object without move members is that it gets copied from time to time; this is a fate that pales in comparison to what might happen to objects with incorrect move members!

The Rule of Five

Naturally, whenever you define a move constructor, you should also define its companion, the move assignment operator—and vice versa. From Chapter 12 you'll recall that the same holds when defining the copy members. These observations are generalized in the so-called rule of five. This best-practice guideline concerns the following five special member functions: the copy constructor, copy assignment operator, move constructor, move assignment constructor, and destructor. In other words, it applies to *all* special member functions except for the default constructor. The rule goes as follows:

▓ **Rule of Five**   As soon as you declare any of the five special member functions other than the default constructor, you should normally declare all five of them.

The motivation, not by chance, is analogous to that in the previous subsection. As soon as you need to override the default behavior for any one of these five special functions, you almost certainly need to do so for the other four as well. For instance, if you need to delete or delete[] a member variable memory in the destructor, it stands to reason that a shallow copy of the corresponding member would be extremely dangerous. The converse is perhaps less obvious but generally holds as well.

Notice that the rule of five does not state that it is required to actually provide explicit *definitions* for all five special member declarations. It is perfectly OK to use = delete at times (for instance when creating uncopiable types—as shown in Chapter 12) or even = default (typically combined with some = delete definitions as well).

The Rule of Zero

The rule of five governs *what* to do if and when you declare your own special member functions. It does not say anything, however, about *when* you should do so. This is where the *rule of zero* comes in:

■ **Rule of Zero** Avoid having to implement any of the special member functions as much as possible.

In a way, the rule of zero is what mathematicians would call a corollary of the rule of five (a *corollary* is a logical consequence of an already proven proposition). After all, the latter rule stipulates that defining any special member function instantly means defining five of them, as well as perhaps a swap() function, as you already know. Even with the copy-and-swap and move-and-swap idioms, defining these five members always involves writing a significant amount of code. And a significant amount of code means a significant number of opportunities for bugs and a significant maintenance overhead.

The usual motivational example is to consider what you'd need to do after adding a new member variable to an existing class. In how many places then do you need to add a line of code? One more line in the member initializer list of the copy constructor? And one in the move constructor as well? And, oh yes, we almost forgot about the extra line in swap()! Whatever the count is, nothing beats zero! That is, in an ideal world, all you'd have to do to add a new member variable is to add the corresponding declaration to the class definition. Nothing more, nothing less.

Fortunately, adhering to the rule of zero is not as hard as it might seem at first. In fact, all you generally need to do is follow the various guidelines regarding containers and resource management that we advocated in earlier chapters:

- All dynamically allocated objects should be managed by a smart pointer (Chapter 4).

- All dynamic arrays should be managed by a std::vector<> (Chapter 5).

- More generally, collections of objects are to be managed by container objects such as those provided by the Standard Library (see also Chapter 19).

- Any other resources that need cleanup (network connections, file handles, and so on) are managed by a dedicated RAII object as well (Chapter 16).

If you simply apply these principles to all member variables of your class, none of these variables should contain so-called raw or naked resources anymore. That normally implies that none of the five special member functions that the rule of five speaks about requires an explicit definition anymore either.

One consequence of respecting the rule of zero is that defining the rule of five member functions becomes reserved almost exclusively for when you define either a custom RAII type or (and this should be even rarer) a custom container type. Afterward, with these custom RAII and container types in place, you can then compose higher-level types that then mostly need no explicit copy, move, or destructor declarations of their own anymore.

There is one special member function we haven't covered yet with the previous guidelines. This is the same one that is not covered by the rule of five: the default constructor. You can typically avoid having to define a default constructor by initializing all member variables in your class definition. We did this, for instance, for the Data class at the beginning of this section:

```
class Data
{
  int value {1};
};
```

Mind you, you'll recall from Chapter 11 that as soon as you declare any constructor, even one that is not a special member function, the compiler will no longer generate a default constructor. The rule of zero therefore most definitely does not preclude defaulting a default constructor like this:

```
class Data
{
public:
  Data() = default;
  Data(int val);

private:
  int value {1};
};
```

Summary

This chapter, in more ways than one, wrapped up that which we started in Chapters 10 and 11. You learned what move semantics is and how it allows for natural, elegant, and—most importantly, perhaps—efficient code. We taught you how to facilitate moving for your own types. The idea of move operations is that since the argument is temporary, the function doesn't necessarily need to copy data members; it can instead steal the data from the object that is the argument. If members of the argument object are pointers, for example, the pointers can be transferred without copying what they point to because the argument object will be destroyed and so doesn't need them.

The important points and best-practice guidelines from this chapter include the following:

- An rvalue is an expression that typically results in a temporary value; an lvalue is one that results in a more persistent value.

- `std::move()` can be used to convert an lvalue (such as a named variable) into an rvalue. Take care, though. Once moved, an object should normally not be used anymore.

- An rvalue reference type is declared using a double ampersand, &&.

- The move constructor and move assignment operator have rvalue reference parameters, so these will be called when the argument is a temporary (or any other rvalue).

- If a function inherently copies one of its inputs, passing this argument by value is preferred, even if this concerns an object of a class type. By doing so, you can cater for both lvalue and rvalue inputs with one single function definition.

- Automatic variables and function parameters should be returned by value and without adding `std::move()` to the `return` statement.

- Move members should normally be `noexcept`; if not, they risk not being invoked by Standard Library containers and other templates.

- The rule of five entails that you either declare all copy members, move members, and the destructor together, or none of them at all. The rule of zero urges you to strive to define none at all. The means to achieve rule of zero compliance you actually already know: always manage dynamic memory and other resources using smart pointers, containers, and other RAII techniques!

EXERCISES

The following exercises enable you to try what you've learned in this chapter. If you get stuck, look back over the chapter for help. If you're still stuck after that, you can download the solutions from the Apress website (http://www.apress.com/book/download.html), but that really should be a last resort.

Exercise 17-1. Define move operators for the Truckload class (the last time you encountered this class was in Exercise 15-3) and provide a small test program to show that it works.

Exercise 17-2. Another class that desperately needs to be upgraded with moving capabilities is the LinkedList<> template you defined for Exercise 16-5. It could even do with more brushing up than just the two special move members. Can you tell what else would be needed for a modern LinkedList<> type? Write a quick program that demonstrates the newly added moving capabilities.

Exercise 17-3. Now that we're digging in the code that you created earlier already, what about the two RAII types you created (or should have created) during Exercise 15-5 when wrapping a C-style API to a fictional database management system? If you recall, one managed a database connection and ensured this connection was always timely severed, whereas the other encapsulated a pointer to the result of a database query whose memory had to be deallocated whenever the user was done inspecting this result. Obviously, you do not want these objects to be copied (why not?). Add the appropriate measures to prevent this.

Exercise 17-4. Like any RAII type (just think of std::unique_ptr<> for an example), the two types you worked on in the previous exercise could surely benefit from move members. Modify the solution of the exercise accordingly, including a few extra lines in the main() function, to prove that your solution works. Is what you did earlier in Exercise 17-3 still needed now? Also, Exercise 15-5 made use of a Customer class. Does this type perhaps need move members as well?

CHAPTER 18

■ ■ ■

First-Class Functions

In C++, you have economy-class functions, business-class functions, and first-class functions, all with varying degrees of comfort, space, privacy, and onboard service...no, of course that's not what the term *first-class* means.[1] We're just kidding. Let's start over:

In computer science, a programming language is said to offer *first-class functions* if it allows you to treat functions like any other variable. In such a language, for instance, you can assign a function as a value to a variable, just like you would an integer or a string. You can pass a function as an argument to other functions or return one as the result of another function. At first sight you may find it difficult to imagine the applicability of such language constructs, but they are immensely useful and powerful.

This chapter introduces what C++ has to offer in this area, ranging from basic first-class functions in the form of function pointers to anonymous functions and closures that are defined by means of lambda expressions (not to worry, all these fancy terms will become clear to you before this chapter is over). The introduction of lambda expressions in C++11 in particular has thoroughly reshaped C++. It lifted the expressivity of the language to a whole new level. This was, in no small part, due to the heavy use of first-class function parameters throughout the Standard Library. The function templates of its generic algorithms library (which is a topic of the next chapter), in particular, are a prime use case for lambda expressions.

In this chapter, you will learn:

- What a function pointer is and what you use it for

- The limitations of function pointers and how to overcome them using standard object-oriented techniques and operator overloading

- What a lambda expression is

- How you define a lambda expression

- What a lambda closure is and why it is more powerful than an anonymous function

- What a capture clause is and how you use it

- How you pass any first-class function as an argument to another function

- How `std::function<>` allows you to represent any first-class function as a variable

---

[1]The term does have a somewhat similar origin. In the 1960s, Christopher Strachey (the same computer language pioneer who first formalized the concepts of lvalues and rvalues, by the way) coined the term when he labeled procedures (functions) as second-class citizens in the programming language ALGOL: "They always have to appear in person and can never be represented by a variable or expression...."

© Ivor Horton and Peter Van Weert 2018

I. Horton and P. Van Weert, *Beginning C++17*, https://doi.org/10.1007/978-1-4842-3366-5_18

Pointers to Functions

You are familiar already with pointers to data, variables that store the address of those regions in memory containing values of other variables, arrays, or dynamically allocated memory. A computer program is more than just data alone, however. Another essential part of the memory allotted to a computer program holds its executable code, consisting of blocks of compiled C++ statements. Naturally, all compiled code belonging to a given function will typically be grouped together as well.

A *pointer to a function* or *function pointer* is a variable that can store the address of a function and therefore point to different functions at different times during execution. You use a pointer to a function to call the function at the address it contains. An address is not sufficient to call a function, though. To work properly, a pointer to a function must also store the type of each parameter as well as the return type. Clearly, the information required to define a pointer to a function will restrict the range of functions to which the pointer can point. It can only store the address of a function with a given number of parameters of specific types and with a given return type. This is analogous to a pointer that stores the address of a data item. A pointer to type int can only point to a location that contains a value of type int.

Defining Pointers to Functions

Here's a definition of a pointer that can store the address of functions that have parameters of type long* and int and return a value of type long:

```
long (*pfun)(long*, int);
```

This may look a little weird at first because of all the parentheses. The name of the pointer variable is pfun. It doesn't point to anything because it is not initialized. Ideally, it would be initialized to nullptr or with the address of a specific function. The parentheses around the pointer name and the asterisk are essential. Without them, this statement would declare a function rather than define a pointer variable because the * will bind to the type long:

```
long *pfun(long*, int);  // Prototype for a function pfun() that returns a long* value
```

The general form of a pointer to a function definition is as follows:

```
return_type (*pointer_name)(list_of_parameter_types);
```

The pointer can only point to functions with the same return_type and list_of_parameter_types as those specified in its definition.

Of course, you should always initialize a pointer when you declare it. You can initialize a pointer to a function to nullptr or with the name of a function. Suppose you have a function with the following prototype:

```
long find_maximum(const long* array, size_t size);    // Returns the maximum element
```

Then you can define and initialize a pointer to this function with this statement:

```
long (*pfun)(const long*, size_t) { find_maximum };
```

The pointer is initialized with the address of some function find_maximum(), which is a function that most likely searches for the largest element of type long in a given array. The second parameter would then be the size of that array. The prototype of this function could thus look like this:

```
long find_maximum(const long* array, size_t size);
```

Using auto will make defining a pointer to this function much simpler:

```
auto pfun = find_maximum;
```

You could also use auto* to highlight the fact that pfun is a pointer:

```
auto* pfun = find_maximum;
```

This defines pfun as a pointer to any function with the same parameter list and return type as find_maximum() and initializes it with the address of find_maximum(). You can store the address of any function with the same parameter list and return type in an assignment. If find_minimum() has the same parameter list and return type as find_maximum(), you can make pfun point to it like this:

```
pfun = find_minimum;
```

■ **Note** Even though the name of a function already evaluates to a value of a function pointer type, you can also explicitly take its address using the address-of operator, &. The following statements, in other words, have the same effect as the earlier ones:

```
auto* pfun = &find_maximum;
pfun = &find_minimum;
```

Some recommend to always add the address-of operator because in doing so you make it jump out more that you're creating a pointer to a function.

To call find_minimum() using pfun, you just use the pointer name as though it were a function name. Here's an example:

```
long data[] {23, 34, 22, 56, 87, 12, 57, 76};
std::cout << "Value of minimum is " << pfun(data, std::size(data));
```

This outputs the minimum value in the data array. As with pointers to variables, you should ensure that a pointer to a function effectively contains the address of a function before you use it to invoke a function. Without initialization, catastrophic failure of your program is almost guaranteed.

To get a feel for these newfangled pointers to functions and how they perform in action, let's try one out in a working program:

```
// Ex18_01.cpp
// Exercising pointers to functions
#include <iostream>

long sum(long a, long b);                    // Function prototype
long product(long a, long b);                // Function prototype

int main()
{
  long(*pDo_it)(long, long) {};              // Pointer to function
```

```
  pDo_it = product;
  std::cout << "3 * 5 = " << pDo_it(3, 5) << std::endl; // Call product thru a pointer

  pDo_it = sum;                                          // Reassign pointer to sum()
  std::cout << "3 * (4+5) + 6 = "
     << pDo_it(product(3, pDo_it(4, 5)), 6) << std::endl;   // Call thru a pointer twice
}

// Function to multiply two values
long product(long a, long b) { return a * b; }

// Function to add two values
long sum(long a, long b) { return a + b; }
```

This example produces the following output:

```
3 * 5 = 15
3 * (4+5) + 6 = 33
```

This is hardly a useful program, but it does show how a pointer to a function is defined, assigned a value, and used to call a function. After the usual preamble, you define and initialize pDo_it as a pointer to a function, which can point to either of the functions sum() or product().

pDo_it is initialized to nullptr, so before using it the address of the function product() is stored in pDo_it. product() is then called indirectly through the pointer pDo_it in the output statement. The name of the pointer is used just as if it were a function name and is followed by the function arguments between parentheses, exactly as they would appear if the original function name were being used. It would save a lot of complication if the pointer were defined and initialized like this:

```
auto* pDo_it = product;
```

Just to show that you can, the pointer is changed to point to sum(). It is then used again in a ludicrously convoluted expression to do some simple arithmetic. This shows that you can use a pointer to a function in the same way as the function to which it points. Figure 18-1 illustrates what happens.

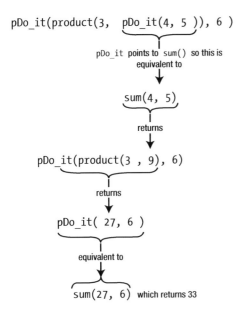

Figure 18-1. *Execution of an expression using a function pointer*

Callback Functions for Higher-Order Functions

Pointer to function is a perfectly reasonable type, which means a function can have a parameter of this type as well. The function can then use its pointer to function parameter to call the function to which the argument points when the function is called. You can specify just a function name as the argument for a parameter that is a "pointer to function" type. A function passed to another function as an argument is referred to as a *callback function*; the function that accepts another function as an argument is a *higher-order function*. Consider the following example:

```
// Optimum.h - a function template to determine the optimum element in a given vector
#ifndef OPTIMUM_H
#define OPTIMUM_H
#include <vector>

template <typename T>
const T* find_optimum(const std::vector<T>& values, bool (*compare)(const T&, const T&))
{
  if (values.empty()) return nullptr;

  const T* optimum = &values[0];
  for (size_t i = 1; i < values.size(); ++i)
  {
    if (compare(values[i], *optimum))
    {
      optimum = &values[i];
    }
  }
  return optimum;
}
#endif // OPTIMUM_H
```

This function template generalizes the find_maximum() and find_minimum() functions we alluded to earlier. The function pointer you pass to the compare parameter determines which "optimum" the function returns. The type of compare forces you to pass a pointer to a function that takes two T values as input and returns a Boolean. This function is expected to compare the two T values it receives and evaluate whether the first one is somehow "better" than the second one. The higher-order find_optimum() then calls the given comparison function through its compare parameter and uses this to determine which out of all the T values in its vector argument is best, or optimal.

The key point is that you, as the caller of find_optimum(), determine what it means for one T value to be better or more optimal than the other. If it's the minimum element you want, you pass a comparison function equivalent to the less-than operator, <; if it's the maximum element you want, the compare callback should behave like the greater-than operator, >. Let's see this in action:

```cpp
// Ex18_02.cpp
// Exercising the use of function pointers as callback functions
#include <iostream>
#include <string>
#include "Optimum.h"

// Comparison prototypes:
bool less(const int&, const int&);
template <typename T> bool greater(const T&, const T&);
bool longer(const std::string&, const std::string&);

int main()
{
  std::vector<int> numbers{ 91, 18, 92, 22, 13, 43 };
  std::cout << "Minimum element: " << *find_optimum(numbers, less) << std::endl;
  std::cout << "Maximum element: " << *find_optimum(numbers, greater<int>) << std::endl;

  std::vector<std::string> names{ "Moe", "Larry", "Shemp", "Curly", "Joe", "Curly Joe" };
  std::cout << "Alphabetically last name: "
            << *find_optimum(names, greater<std::string>) << std::endl;
  std::cout << "Longest name: " << *find_optimum(names, longer) << std::endl;
}

bool less(const int& one, const int& other) { return one < other; }

template <typename T>
bool greater(const T& one, const T& other) { return one > other; }

bool longer(const std::string& one, const std::string& other)
{
  return one.length() > other.length();
}
```

This program prints out these results:

```
Minimum element: 13
Maximum element: 92
Alphabetically last name: Shemp
Longest name: Curly Joe
```

The first two calls to find_optimum() demonstrate that, indeed, this function can be used to find both the minimum and maximum numbers in a given vector. In passing, we illustrate that a function pointer may point to the instantiation of a function template such as greater<>() as well. All you have to do is explicitly instantiate the template by specifying all its template arguments between < and >.

The second half of the example is perhaps even more interesting. The default comparison operators of std::string, as you know, compare strings alphabetically. As in a phone book, Shemp would therefore always appear last. But there are times where you'd prefer to compare strings in a different manner. Adding callback parameters to your sorting or find_optimum() functions facilitates this. We illustrate this capability in Ex18_02 by looking for the longest string instead, by passing a pointer to longer().

This example showcases the tremendous value of higher-order functions and callbacks in your never-ending battle against code duplication. If it weren't for first-class functions, you would have had to write at least three distinct find_optimum() functions already only to make Ex18_02 work: find_minimum(), find_maximum(), and find_longest(). All three would then have contained the same loop to extract the corresponding optimum from a given vector. While for beginners it may be a great exercise to write such loops at least a couple of times, this soon gets old and certainly has no place in professional software development. Luckily, the Standard Library offers a vast collection of generic algorithms similar to find_optimum() that you can reuse instead, and all will accept similar callback functions that allow you to tune them to your needs. We'll discuss this in more detail in the next chapter.

■ **Note** First-class callback functions have plenty more uses beyond serving as the argument to higher-order functions. Callbacks are actively used in day-to-day object-oriented programming as well. Objects often store one or multiple callback functions inside their member variables. Invoking such callbacks can serve any number of purposes. They could constitute a user-configurable step in the logic implemented by one of the object's member functions, or they may be used to signal other objects that some event has occurred. Callback members in all their various forms and manifestations facilitate various standard object-oriented idioms and patterns, most notably perhaps variations on the classical Observer pattern. Discussing object-oriented design falls outside of the scope of this book; there are other excellent books that specialize in this. You can find a basic example of a callback member variable in the exercises at the end of the chapter.

Type Aliases for Function Pointers

As we're sure you will agree, the syntax required to define a function pointer variable is rather horrendous. The less you have to type this syntax, the better. The auto keyword can help, but there are times where you do want to specify the type of a function pointer explicitly when a function pointer is used as a function parameter, for instance, or as an object's member variable. Because "pointer to function" is just a type like any other, however, you can define a type alias for such types using the using keyword (see Chapter 3).

Consider the definition of the callback parameter in the optimum() function template of Ex18_02:

```
bool (*compare)(const T&, const T&)
```

Unfortunately, this type contains a template type parameter, T, which complicates matters a bit. Let's simplify that for a moment and instead start with a concrete instantiation of this type template:

```
bool (*string_comp)(const std::string&, const std::string&)
```

You obtain the type of this variable by copying the entire variable definition and dropping the variable name, `string_comp`:

```
bool (*)(const std::string&, const std::string&)
```

Quite a mouthful this type is, so it's well worth creating an alias for. With the modern syntax based on the `using` keyword, defining an alias for this type is as straightforward as this:

```
using StringComparison = bool (*)(const std::string&, const std::string&);
```

The right side of this assignment-like declaration simply matches the type name; the left side, of course, is a name of your choosing. With this type alias in place, declaring a parameter such as `string_comp` immediately becomes a lot less tedious and a lot more readable:

```
StringComparison string_comp
```

One nice thing about the `using` syntax for type aliases is that it extends gracefully to templated types. To define an alias for the type of the `compare` callback parameter of `Ex18_02`, all you need to do is generalize the `StringComparison` definition in the most natural way; you simply prepend it with the `template` keyword, as always, followed by a template parameter list between angular brackets:

```
template <typename T>
using Comparison = bool (*)(const T&, const T&);
```

This defines an *alias template*, which is a template that generates type aliases. In `Optimum.h`, you could use this template to simplify the signature of `find_optimum()`:

```
template <typename T>
const T* find_optimum(const std::vector<T>& values, Comparison<T> comp);
```

Of course, you can also use it to define a variable with a concrete type:

```
Comparison<std::string> string_comp{ longer };
```

■ **Note**   For historical reference, this is how you would define `StringComparison` using the old `typedef` syntax (see also Chapter 3):

```
typedef bool (*StringComparison)(const std::string&, const std::string&);
```

With the alias name needlessly appearing in the middle, this syntax is again far more complex than the one that uses the `using` keyword. Defining an alias template, moreover, is not even possible with `typedef`. Our conclusion from Chapter 3 thus stands, stronger than ever. To define a type alias, you should always use `using`; `typedef` has no place in modern C++.

Function Objects

Much like pointers to data values, pointers to functions are low-level language constructs that C++ has inherited from the C programming language. And just like raw pointers, function pointers have their limitations, which can be overcome using an object-oriented approach. In Chapter 6 you learned that smart pointers are the object-oriented answer to the inherently unsafe raw pointers. In this section, we introduce a similar technique where objects are used as a more powerful alternative to plain C-style function pointers. These objects are called *function objects* or *functors* (the two terms are synonymous). Like a function pointer, a function object acts precisely like a function; but unlike a raw function pointer, it is a full-fledged class type object—complete with its own member variables and possibly even various other member functions. We'll show you that function objects are hence far more powerful and expressive than plain C-style function pointers.

Basic Function Objects

A *function object* or *functor* is simply an object that can be called as if it were a function. The key in constructing one is to overload the function call operator, as was briefly introduced in Chapter 12 already. To see how this is done, we will define a class of function objects that encapsulate this simple function:

```
bool less(int one, int other) { return one < other; }
```

Quickly recapping what you saw in Chapter 12, here is how you define a class with an overloaded function call operator:

```
// Less.h - A basic class of functor objects
#ifndef LESS_H
#define LESS_H

class Less
{
public:
  bool operator()(int a, int b) const;
};

#endif // LESS_H
```

This basic functor class has only one member: a function call operator. The main thing to remember here is that the function call operator is denoted with operator() and that its actual parameter list is specified only *after* an initial set of empty parentheses. Beyond that, this is just like any other operator function. You can define it in the corresponding source file in the usual manner:

```
// Less.cpp - definition of a basic function call operator
bool Less::operator()(int a, int b) const
{
  return a < b;
}
```

With this class definition, you can create your very first function object and then call it as if it were an actual function like so:

```
Less less;                    // Create a 'less than' functor...
const bool is_less = less(5, 6);   // ... and 'call' it
std::cout << (is_less? "5 is less than 6" : "Huh?") << std::endl;
```

Of course, what is being "called" is not the object itself but rather its function call operator function. If you're into self-harm and code-obscuring, you could thus also write less(5,6) as less.operator()(5,6).

Granted, creating a functor just to call it right after is not very useful at all. Things become a bit more interesting already if you use a functor as a callback function. To demonstrate this, you'll first have to generalize the find_optimum() template of Ex18_02 since currently it only accepts a function pointer for its callback argument. Of course, creating an extra overload specifically for the Less type would defeat the purpose of having a higher-order function with a callback in the first place. And there's also no such thing as one single type that encompasses all function object class types. The most common way to generalize a function such as find_optimum() is therefore to declare a second template type parameter and to use that then as the type of the compare parameter:

```
// Optimum.h - a function template to determine the optimum element in a given vector
#include <vector>

template <typename T, typename Comparison>
const T* find_optimum(const std::vector<T>& values, Comparison compare)
{
  if (values.empty()) return nullptr;

  const T* optimum = &values[0];
  for (size_t i = 1; i < values.size(); ++i)
  {
    if (compare(values[i], *optimum))
    {
      optimum = &values[i];
    }
  }
  return optimum;
}
```

Because Comparison is a template type parameter, you can now invoke find_optimum() with compare arguments of any type you like. Naturally, the template's instantiation will then only compile if the compare argument is a function-like value that can be called with two T& arguments. And you know of two categories of arguments that might fit this bill already:

- Function pointers of type bool (*)(const T&, const T&) (or similar types, such as for instance bool (*)(T, T)). Therefore, if you were to plug this new definition of find_optimum<>() into Ex18_02, this example would still work precisely like before.

- Function objects of a type like Less that have a corresponding function call operator.

Both options are demonstrated in our next example:

```
// Ex18_03.cpp
// Exercising the use of a functor as callback functions
#include <iostream>
#include "Optimum.h"
#include "Less.h"

template <typename T>
bool greater(const T& one, const T& other) { return one > other; }

int main()
{
  Less less;      // Create a 'less than' functor

  std::vector<int> numbers{ 91, 18, 92, 22, 13, 43 };
  std::cout << "Minimum element: " << *find_optimum(numbers, less) << std::endl;
  std::cout << "Maximum element: " << *find_optimum(numbers, greater<int>) << std::endl;
}
```

Standard Function Objects

You can customize many templates of the Standard Library by providing them with a first-class function, similar to what you did with find_optimum<>() in examples Ex18_02 and Ex18_03. For regular functions you can mostly use a plain function pointer, but for built-in operators that is not an option. You cannot create a pointer to a built-in operator. Of course, it's easy to quickly define either a function (as in Ex18_02) or a functor class (Less in Ex18_03) that emulates the operator's behavior, but doing so for every operator all the time would become tedious very fast.

Of course, this did not escape the designers of the Standard Library either. The functional header of the Standard Library therefore defines a series of function object class templates, one for every built-in operator you may want to pass to other templates. The class template std::less<>, for instance, is fundamentally analogous to the Less template of Ex18_03. After adding an #include for the functional header, you could thus replace the definition of the less variable in Ex18_03 with this one:

```
std::less<int> less;      // Create a 'less than' functor
```

■ **Tip** As of C++14, the recommended way to use the function object types of the functional header is actually by omitting the type argument, for instance, as follows:

```
std::less<> less;      // Create a 'less than' functor
```

The templates defined by <functional> employ more advanced template programming techniques to ensure that functors defined without an explicit type argument generally behave precisely like those defined the traditional way, except in specific situations that involve implicit conversions, where a function object of type std::less<> may lead to more efficient code than a function object of type std::less<int> (or, to use a more common example, more efficient than, say, one of type std::less<std::string>). Explaining this in more detail would lead us too far astray, though. Trust us, if you simply always omit the type argument, you're guaranteed that the compiler can generate optimal code under all circumstances. Plus, it saves you some typing; it's a clear win-win!

Table 18-1 lists the complete set of templates. As always, all these types are defined in the std namespace.

Table 18-1. *The Function Object Class Templates Offered by the <functional> Header*

Comparisons	`less<>`, `greater<>`, `less_equal<>`, `greater_equal<>`, `equal_to<>`, `not_equal_to<>`
Arithmetic operations	`plus<>`, `minus<>`, `multiplies<>`, `divides<>`, `modulus<>`, `negate<>`
Logical operations	`logical_and<>`, `logical_or<>`, `logical_not<>`
Bitwise operations	`bit_and<>`, `bit_or<>`, `bit_xor<>`, `bit_not<>`

We could also use `std::greater<>` to replace our `greater<>` function template of Ex18_03. Now isn't that great?

```
std::vector<int> numbers{ 91, 18, 92, 22, 13, 43 };
std::cout << "Minimum element: " << *find_optimum(numbers, std::less<>{}) << std::endl;
std::cout << "Maximum element: " << *find_optimum(numbers, std::greater<>{}) << std::endl;
```

This time we created the `std::less<>` and `greater<>` function objects as temporary objects directly inside the function call expression itself, rather than storing them first in a named variable. You can find this variant of the program in Ex18_03A.

Parameterized Function Objects

Perhaps you've already noticed that, in fact, none of the function objects that you have seen thus far has been more powerful than a plain function pointer. Why go through all the trouble of defining a class with a function call operator if defining a plain function is so much easier? Surely, there must be more to function objects than this?

Indeed there is. Function objects only truly become interesting once you start adding more members—either variables or functions. Building on the same `find_optimum()` example as always, suppose you want to search not for the smallest or largest number but instead for the number that is nearest to some user-provided value. There is no clean way for you to accomplish this using functions and pointers to functions. Think about it, how would the callback's function body ever get access to the value that the user has entered? There is no clean way for you to pass this value along to the function if all you have is a pointer. If you use a function-like object, however, you can pass along any information you want by storing it in the object's member variables. The easiest is if we just show you how you might do this:

```
// Nearer.h
// A class of function objects that compare two values based on how close they are
// to some third value that was provided to the functor at construction time.
#ifndef NEARER_H
#define NEARER_H

#include <cmath>    // For std::abs()

class Nearer
{
public:
  Nearer(int value) : n(value) {}
```

```
  bool operator()(int x, int y) const { return std::abs(x - n) < std::abs(y - n); }
private:
  int n;
};

#endif // NEARER_H
```

Every function object of type Nearer has a member variable n in which it stores the value to compare with. This value is passed in through its constructor, so it could easily be a number that was entered by the user earlier. Of course, the object's function call operator has access to this number as well, which is the part that would not have been possible when using a function pointer as a callback. This program illustrates how to use this functor class:

```
// Ex18_04.cpp
// Exercising a function object with a member variable
#include <iostream>
#include "Optimum.h"
#include "Nearer.h"

int main()
{
  std::vector<int> numbers{ 91, 18, 92, 22, 13, 43 };

  int number_to_search_for {};
  std::cout << "Please enter a number: ";
  std::cin >> number_to_search_for;

  std::cout << "The number nearest to " << number_to_search_for << " is "
            << *find_optimum(numbers, Nearer{ number_to_search_for }) << std::endl;
}
```

A possible session then might go like this:

```
Please enter a number: 50
The number nearest to 50 is 43
```

Lambda Expressions

Ex18_04 clearly demonstrates a couple of things. First, it shows the potential of passing a function object as a callback. Given that it can have any number of members, function objects are certainly much more powerful than plain function pointers. But that's not all that we can learn from Ex18_04. Indeed, if there's one more thing that Ex18_04 clearly exposes, it's that defining a class for a function object requires you to write quite some code. Even a simple callback class such as Nearer—which has only one member variable—quickly takes about ten lines of code already.

This is where *lambda expressions* come in. They offer you a convenient, compact syntax to quickly define callback functions or functors. And not only is the syntax compact, lambda expressions also allow you to define the callback's logic right there where you want to use it. This is often much better than having to define this logic somewhere in the function call operator of some class definition. Lambda expressions thus generally lead to particularly expressive yet still very readable code.

A *lambda expression* has a lot in common with a function definition. In its most basic form, a lambda expression basically provides a way to define a function with no name, an *anonymous function*. But lambda expressions are far more powerful than that. In general, a lambda expression effectively defines a full-blown function object that can carry any number of member variables. The beauty is that there's no need for an explicit definition of the type of this object anymore; this type is generated automatically for you by the compiler.

Practically speaking, you'll find that a lambda expression is different from a regular function in that it can access variables that exist in the enclosing scope where it is defined. Thinking back to Ex18_04, for instance, a lambda expression there would be able to access number_to_search_for, the number that was entered by the user. Before we examine how lambda expressions get access to local variables, though, let's first take one step back again and begin by explaining how you can define a basic *unnamed* or *anonymous function* using a lambda expression.

Defining a Lambda Expression

Consider the following basic lambda expression:

```
[] (int x, int y) { return x < y; }
```

As you can see, the definition of a lambda expression indeed looks very much like the definition of a function. The main differences are that a lambda expression does not specify a return type or function name and that it always starts with square brackets. The opening square brackets are called the *lambda introducer*. They mark the beginning of the lambda expression. There's more to the lambda introducer than there is here—the brackets are not always empty—but we'll explain this in more depth a little later. The lambda introducer is followed by the *lambda parameter list* between round parentheses. This list is exactly like a regular function parameter list (ever since C++14, default parameter values are even allowed). In this case, there's two int parameters, x and y.

■ **Tip** For lambda functions without parameters, you may omit the empty parameter list, (). That is, a lambda expression of form []() {...} may be further shortened to [] {...}. An empty lambda initializer, [], must not be omitted, though. The lambda initializer is always required to signal the start of a lambda expression.

The body of the lambda expression between braces follows the parameter list, again just like a normal function. The body for this lambda contains just one statement, a return statement that also calculates the value that is returned. In general, the body of a lambda can contain any number of statements. The return type defaults to that of the value returned. If nothing is returned, the return type is void.

It's educational to have at least a basic notion of how lambda expressions are compiled. This will aid you later in understanding how more advanced lambda expressions behave. Whenever the compiler encounters a lambda expression, it internally generates a new class type. In the case of our example, the generated class will be similar to the LessThan class you defined in Ex18_03. Slightly simplified, such a class might look something like this:

```
class __Lambda8C1
{
public:
  auto operator()(int x, int y) const { return x < y; }
};
```

A first notable difference is that the implicit class definition will have some unique, compiler-generated name. We picked __Lambda8C1 here, but your compiler could use whatever name it wants. There's no telling what this name will be (at least not at compile time), nor is there any guarantee it will still be the same the next time you compile the same program. This somewhat limits the way in which these function objects can be used, but not by much—as we'll show you in one of the next subsections.

Another point worth noting first is that, at least by default, a lambda expression results in a function call operator() with a return type equal to auto. You first encountered the use of auto as a return type in Chapter 8. Back then, we explained to you that the compiler then attempts to deduce the actual return type from the return statements in the function's body. There were some limitations, though: auto return type deduction requires that all return statements of the function return a value of the same type. The compiler will never apply any implicit conversions—any conversions need to be added by you explicitly. This same limitation therefore applies to the body of a lambda expression as well.

You do have the option to specify the return type of a lambda function explicitly. You could do this to have the compiler generate implicit conversions for the return statements or simply to make the code more self-documenting. While clearly not necessary here, you could supply a return type for the previous lambda like this:

```
[] (int x, int y) -> bool { return x < y; }
```

The return type is specified following the -> operator that comes after the parameter list and is type bool here.

Naming a Lambda Closure

As you know, a lambda expression evaluates to a function object. This function object is formally called a *lambda closure*, although many also refer to it informally as either a *lambda function* or a *lambda*. You don't know a priori what the type of the lambda closure will be; only the compiler does. The only way to store the lambda object in a variable is thus to have the compiler deduce the type for you:

```
auto less{ [] (int x, int y) { return x < y; } };
```

The auto keyword tells the compiler to figure out the type that the variable less should have from what appears on the right of the assignment—in this case a lambda expression. Supposing the compiler generates a type with the name __Lambda8C1 for this lambda expression (as shown earlier), this statement is then effectively compiled as follows:

```
__Lambda8C1 less;
```

Passing a Lambda Expression to a Function Template

You can use less just like the equivalent functor of Ex18_03:

```
auto less{ [] (int x, int y) { return x < y; } };
std::cout << "Minimum element: " << *find_optimum(numbers, less) << std::endl;
```

This works because the callback parameter of the find_optimum() template of Ex18_03 is declared with a template type parameter, which the compiler can substitute with whatever name it picked for the lambda closure's generated type:

```
template <typename T, typename Comparison>
const T* find_optimum(const std::vector<T>& values, Comparison compare);
```

709

Rather than first storing a lambda closure in a named variable, it is at least as common to directly use a lambda expression as a callback argument as follows:

```
std::cout << "Minimum element: "
          << *find_optimum(numbers, [] (int x, int y) { return x < y; }) << std::endl;
```

■ **Tip**   The previous statements would also compile with the find_optimum() function template of Ex18_02, whose callback argument still had to be a function pointer (concretely, the type of the corresponding parameter in that version of find_optimum() was still bool (*)(int,int)). The reason is that the compiler makes sure that a lambda closure that does not capture any variables always has a (nonexplicit) type conversion operator to the equivalent function pointer type. As soon as the lambda closure requires member variables, it can no longer be cast to a function pointer. The next subsection explains how and when lambda closures capture variables into member variables.

Ex18_05 is yet another variant of Ex18_02 and Ex18_03, only this time one that uses lambda expressions to define all its callback functions:

```
// Ex18_05.cpp
// Exercising the use of stateless lambda expressions as callback functions
#include <iostream>
#include <string>
#include <string_view>
#include "Optimum.h"

int main()
{
  std::vector<int> numbers{ 91, 18, 92, 22, 13, 43 };
  std::cout << "Minimum element: "
            << *find_optimum(numbers, [](int x, int y) { return x < y; }) << std::endl;
  std::cout << "Maximum element: "
            << *find_optimum(numbers, [](int x, int y) { return x > y; }) << std::endl;

  // Define anonymous comparison functions for strings:
  auto alpha = [](std::string_view x, std::string_view y) { return x > y; };
  auto longer = [](std::string_view x, std::string_view y) { return x.length() > y.length(); };

  std::vector<std::string> names{ "Moe", "Larry", "Shemp", "Curly", "Joe", "Curly Joe" };
  std::cout << "Alphabetically last name: " << *find_optimum(names, alpha) << std::endl;
  std::cout << "Longest name: " << *find_optimum(names, longer) << std::endl;
}
```

The result will be the same as before. Clearly, if you only need to sort strings on their length once, a lambda expression is more convenient than defining a separate longer() function and definitely far more interesting than defining a Longer functor class.

■ **Tip** If <functional> defines a suitable functor type, using that type is normally far more compact and readable than a lambda expression. std::less<> and std::greater<>, for instance, could readily replace the first three lambda expressions in Ex18_05.cpp (see also Ex18_03A).

The Capture Clause

As we've said before, the lambda introducer, [ ], is not necessarily empty. It can contain a *capture clause* that specifies how variables in the enclosing scope can be accessed from within the body of the lambda. The body of a lambda expression with nothing between the square brackets can work only with the arguments and with variables that are defined locally within the lambda. A lambda with no capture clause is called a *stateless lambda expression* because it cannot access anything in its enclosing scope.

If used in isolation, a *capture default* clause applies to all variables in the scope enclosing the definition of the lambda. There are two capture defaults: = and &. We'll discuss both of them in turn next. The capture clause can contain only one of the capture defaults, never both.

Capturing by Value

If you put = between the square brackets, the body of the lambda can access all automatic variables in the enclosing scope by value. That is, while the values of all variables are made available within the lambda expression, the values stored in the original variables cannot be changed. Here's an example based on Ex18_04:

```cpp
// Ex18_06.cpp
// Using a default capture-by-value clause to access a local variable
// from within the body of a lambda expression.
#include <iostream>
#include "Optimum.h"

int main()
{
  std::vector<int> numbers{ 91, 18, 92, 22, 13, 43 };

  int number_to_search_for {};
  std::cout << "Please enter a number: ";
  std::cin >> number_to_search_for;

  auto nearer { [=](int x, int y) {
    return std::abs(x - number_to_search_for) < std::abs(y - number_to_search_for);
  }};
  std::cout << "The number nearest to " << number_to_search_for << " is "
            << *find_optimum(numbers, nearer) << std::endl;
}
```

The = capture clause allows all the variables that are in scope where the definition of the lambda appears to be accessed by value from within the body of the lambda expression. In Ex18_06 this means that the lambda's body has, at least in principle, access to main()'s two local variables, numbers and number_to_search_for. The effect of capturing local variables by value is rather different from passing arguments by value, though. To properly understand how capturing works, it's again instructive to study the class that the compiler might generate for the lambda expression of Ex18_06:

```
class __Lambda9d5
{
public:
  __Lambda9d5(const int& arg1) : number_to_search_for(arg1) {}

  auto operator()(int x, int y) const
  {
    return std::abs(x - number_to_search_for) < std::abs(y - number_to_search_for);
  }

private:
  int number_to_search_for;
};
```

The lambda expression itself is then compiled as follows:

```
__Lambda9d5 nearer{ number_to_search_for };
```

It should come as no surprise that this class is completely equivalent to the Nearer class we defined earlier in Ex18_04. Concretely, the closure object has one member per local variable of the surrounding scope that is used inside the lambda's function body. We say that these variables are *captured* by the lambda. At least conceptually the member variables of the generated class have the same name as the variables that were captured. That way, the lambda expression's body appears to have access to variables of the surrounding scope, while in reality it is accessing the corresponding member variables that are stored inside the lambda closure.

■ **Note**   Variables that are not used by the lambda expression's body, such as the numbers vector in Ex18_06, are never captured by a default capture clause such as =.

The = clause denotes that all variables are to be captured by value, which is why the number_to_search_for member variable has a value type, in this case, type int. The number_to_search_for member variable contains, in other words, a *copy* of the original local variable with the same name. While this implies that the value of the original number_to_search_for variable is in a sense available during the function's execution, you cannot possibly update its value. Even if updates to this member were allowed, you'd only be updating a copy. To avoid any confusion, the compiler therefore even arranges it so that by default you cannot update number_to_search_for at all from within the lambda's body—not even the copy that is stored in the closure's member variable. It does so by declaring the function call operator, operator(), as const. You'll recall from Chapter 11 that you cannot modify any of the member variables of an object from within one of its const member functions.

■ **Tip**   In the unlikely event that you do want to alter a variable that was captured by value, you can add the keyword mutable to the definition of a lambda expression, right after the parameter list. Doing so causes the compiler to omit the const keyword from the function call operator of the generated class. Remember that you'd still only be updating a *copy* of the original variable. If you want to update the local variable itself, you should capture it by reference. Capturing variables by reference is explained next.

Capturing by Reference

If you put & between the square brackets, all variables in the enclosing scope are accessible by reference, so their values can be changed by the code in the body of the lambda. To count the number of comparisons performed by find_optimum(), for instance, you could use this lambda expression:

```
unsigned count = 0;
auto counter{ [&](int x, int y) { ++count; return x < y; } };
find_optimum(numbers, counter);
```

All variables within the outer scope are available by reference, so the lambda can both use and alter their values. If you plug this code snippet in Ex18_06, for instance, the value of count after the call to find_optimum<>() will be 5.

For completeness, this is a class similar to the one that your compiler would generate for this lambda expression:

```
class __Lambda6c5
{
public:
  __Lambda6c5(unsigned& arg1) : count(arg1) {}
  auto operator()(int x, int y) const { ++count; return x < y; }
private:
  unsigned& count;
};
```

Note that this time the captured variable count is stored in the closure's member variable by reference. The ++count increment in this operator() will therefore compile, even though that member function is declared with const. Any modification to a reference leaves the function object itself unaltered. It is the variable that the count reference refers to that is modified instead. The mutable keyword is therefore not needed in this case.

▓ **Tip**   Although the & capture clause is legal, capturing all variables in the outer scope by reference is not considered good practice because of the potential for accidentally modifying one of them. Similarly, using a = capture default risks introducing costly copies. It's therefore safer to explicitly specify how each individual variable that you need should be captured. We'll explain how you do this next.

Capturing Specific Variables

You can identify specific variables in the enclosing scope that you want to access by listing them in the capture clause. For each variable, you can choose whether it should be captured either by value or by reference. You capture a specific variable by reference by prefixing its name with &. You could rewrite the previous statement as follows:

```
auto counter{ [&count](int x, int y) { ++count; return x < y; } };
```

Here, count is the only variable in the enclosing scope that can be accessed from within the body of the lambda. The &count specification makes it available by reference. Without the &, the count variable in the outer scope would be available by value and not updatable. The lambda expression in Ex18_06, in other words, could also be written as follows:

```
auto nearer { [number_to_search_for](int x, int y) {
  return std::abs(x - number_to_search_for) < std::abs(y - number_to_search_for);
}};
```

■ **Caution**   You mustn't prefix the names of the variables that you want to capture by value with =. The capture clause [=number_to_search_for], for example, is invalid; the only correct syntax is [number_to_search_for].

When you put several variables in the capture clause, you separate them with commas. You can freely mix variables that are captured by value with others that are captured by reference. You can also include a capture default in the capture clause along with specific variable names that are to be captured. The capture clause [=, &counter], for instance, would allow access to counter by reference and any other variables in the enclosing scope by value. Analogously, you could write a capture clause such as [&, number_to_search_for], which would capture number_to_search_for by value and all other variables by reference. If present, the capture default (= or &) must always be the first item in the capture list.

■ **Caution**   If you use the = capture default, you are no longer allowed to capture any specific variables by value; similarly, if you use &, you can no longer capture specific variables by reference. Capture clauses such as [&, &counter] or [=, &counter, number_to_search_for] should therefore trigger a compiler error.

Capturing the this Pointer

In this final subsection on capturing variables, we'll discuss how to use a lambda expression from within the member function of a class. Sadistically beating the find_optimum<>() example to death one last time, suppose you defined this class:

```
// Finder.h - A small class to illustrate the use of lambda expression in member functions
#ifndef FINDER_H
#define FINDER_H

#include <vector>
#include <optional>

class Finder
{
public:
  double getNumberToSearchFor() const;
  void setNumberToSearchFor(double n);
```

```
  std::optional<double> findNearest(const std::vector<double>& values) const;
private:
  double number_to_search_for {};
};
```

```
#endif // FINDER_H
```

A fully functional implementation of the Finder example is available under Ex18_07. The definitions of the getter and setter members are of no particular interest, but to define findNearest() you'd of course like to reuse the find_optimum<>() template you defined earlier. A reasonable first attempt at defining this function might therefore look as follows:

```
// Finder.cpp
#include "Finder.h"
#include "Optimum.h"
```

```
std::optional<double> Finder::findNearest(const std::vector<double>& values) const
{
  if (values.empty())
    return std::nullopt;
  else
    return *find_optimum(values, [number_to_search_for](double x, double y) {
      return std::abs(x - number_to_search_for) < std::abs(y - number_to_search_for);
    });
}
```

Unfortunately, though, your compiler won't be too happy with this yet. The problem is that this time number_to_search_for is the name of a member variable rather than that of a local variable. And member variables cannot be captured, neither by value nor by reference; only local variables and function arguments can. To give a lambda expression access to the current object's members, you should instead add the keyword this to the capture clause, like so:

```
  return *find_optimum(values, [this](double x, double y) {
    return std::abs(x - number_to_search_for) < std::abs(y - number_to_search_for);
  });
```

By capturing the this pointer, you effectively give the lambda expression access to all members that the surrounding member function has access to. That is, even though the lambda closure will be an object of a class other than Finder, its function call operator will still have access to all protected and private members of Finder, including the member variable number_to_search_for, which is normally private to Finder. When we say *all* members, we do mean all members. Next to member variables, a lambda expression thus has access to all member functions as well—either public, protected, or private. Another way to write our example lambda is therefore as follows:

```
  return *find_optimum(values, [this](double x, double y) {
    return std::abs(x - getNumberToSearchFor()) < std::abs(y - getNumberToSearchFor());
  });
```

■ **Note**   Precisely like in the member function itself, there is no need to add `this->` when accessing a member. The compiler takes care of that for you.

Together with the `this` pointer, you can still capture other variables as well. You can combine it with a &
capture default to capture local variables by reference or any sequence of captures of named variables.
The = capture default already implies that the this pointer is captured (by value). So, this would also be valid:

```
return *find_optimum(values, [=](double x, double y) {
  return std::abs(x - getNumberToSearchFor()) < std::abs(y - getNumberToSearchFor());
});
```

■ **Caution**   You are not allowed to combine a = default capture with a capture of `this` (at least not yet in
C++17; C++20 is rumored to relax this restriction). A capture clause of the form [=, this] will thus be flagged
as an error by the compiler. [&, this] is allowed, though, as & does not imply the capture of `this`.

The std::function<> Template

The type of a function pointer is very different from that of a function object or lambda closure. The former is
a pointer, and the latter is a class. At first sight, it might thus seem that the only way to write code that works for
any conceivable callback—that is, either a function pointer, function object, or lambda closure—is to use either
`auto` or a template type parameter. This is what we did for our `find_optimum<>()` template in earlier examples.
The same technique is heavily used throughout the Standard Library, as you will see in the next chapter.
    Using templates does have its cost. It typically implies defining all your code inside the header file,
for one, which is not always very practical. Also, you risk template code bloat, where the compiler has to
generate specialized code for all different types of callbacks, even when it's not required for performance
reasons. It also has its limitations: what if you needed say a vector<> of callback functions—a vector<> that
is potentially filled with a mixture of function pointers, function objects, and lambda closures?
    To cater for these types of scenarios, the `functional` header defines the std::function<> template.
With objects of type std::function<> you can store, copy, move, and invoke any kind of function-like
entity—be it a function pointer, function object, or lambda closure. The following example demonstrates
precisely that:

```
// Ex18_08.cpp
// Using the std::function<> template
#include <iostream>
#include <functional>
#include <cmath>            // for std::abs()

// A global less() function
bool less(int x, int y) { return x < y; }

int main()
{
  int a{ 18 }, b{ 8 };
  std::cout << std::boolalpha;    // Print true/false rather than 1/0
```

```
std::function<bool(int,int)> compare;

compare = less;                          // store a function pointer into compare
std::cout << a << " < " << b << ": " << compare(a, b) << std::endl;

compare = std::greater<>{};              // store a function object into compare
std::cout << a << " > " << b << ": " << compare(a, b) << std::endl;

int n{ 10 };                             // store a lambda closure into compare
compare = [n](int x, int y) { return std::abs(x - n) < std::abs(y - n); };
std::cout << a << " nearer to " << n << " than " << b << ": " << compare(a, b);

// Check whether a function<> object is tied to an actual function
std::function<void(const int&)> empty;
if (empty)                               // Or, equivalently: 'if (empty != nullptr)'
{
  std::cout << "Calling a default-constructed std::function<>?" << std::endl;
  empty(a);
}
}
```

The output looks as follows:

```
18 < 8: false
18 > 8: true
18 nearer to 10 than 8: false
```

In the first part of the program, we define a std::function<> variable compare and assign it three different kinds of first-class functions in sequence: first a function pointer, then a function object, and finally a lambda closure. In between, all three first-class functions are always called. More precisely, they are indirectly invoked through the compare variable's function call operator. A std::function<> itself is, in other words, a function object—one that can encapsulate any other kind of first-class function.

There is only one restriction for the function-like entities that can be assigned to a given std::function<>. They must all have matching return and parameter types. These type requirements are specified between the angular brackets of the std::function<> type template. In Ex18_08, for instance, compare has type std::function<bool(int,int)>. This indicates that compare will only accept first-class functions that can be called with two int arguments and that return a value that is convertible to bool.

▓ **Tip**   A variable of type std::function<bool(int,int)> not only can store first-class functions whose signature is precisely (int, int); it can store any function that is *callable* with two int arguments. There is a subtle difference. The latter implies that functions with signatures such as (const int&, const int&), (long, long), or even (double, double) are acceptable as well. Similarly, the return type must not be exactly *equal* to bool. It suffices that its values can be *converted* into a Boolean. So, functions that return either int or even double* or std::unique_ptr<std::string> would work as well. You can try this by playing with the signature and return type of the less() function in Ex18_08.cpp.

The general form of a `std::function<>` type template instantiation is as follows:

```
std::function<ReturnType(ParamType1, ..., ParamTypeN)>
```

The `ReturnType` is not optional, so to represent functions that do not return a value, you should specify `void` for the `ReturnType`. Similarly, for functions without parameters you must still include an empty parameter type list, `()`. Reference types and `const` qualifiers are allowed for any of the `ParamTypes`, as well as for the `ReturnType`. All in all, it's a most natural way of specifying function type requirement, wouldn't you agree?

A default-constructed `std::function<>` object does not contain any callable first-class function yet. Invoking its function call operator would then result in a `std::bad_function_call` exception. In the last five lines of the program, we show you how you can verify whether a `function<>` is callable. As the example shows, there are two ways: a `function<>` implicitly converts to a Boolean (through a nonexplicit cast operator), or it can be compared to a `nullptr` (even though in general a `function<>` need not contain a pointer).

The `std::function<>` template forms a powerful alternative to the use of `auto` or template type parameters. The prime advantage to these other approaches is that `std::function<>` allows you to name the type of your first-class function variables. Being able to name this type facilitates the use of lambda-enabled callback functions in a much wider range of use cases than just higher-order function templates: `std::function<>` may, for example, be used for function parameters and member variables (without resorting to templates) or to store first-class functions into containers. The possibilities are limitless. You'll find a basic example of such a use in the exercises later.

Summary

This chapter introduced first-class functions in all their forms and flavors—from plain C-style function pointers over object-oriented functors to full-blown closures. We showed that lambda expressions offer a particularly versatile and expressive syntax not just to define anonymous functions but to create lambda closures capable of capturing any number of variables from their surroundings. Like function objects, lambda expressions are much more powerful than function pointers; but unlike function objects, they do not require you to specify a complete class—the compiler takes care of this tedious task for you. Lambda expressions really come into their own when combined, for instance, with the algorithms library of the C++ Standard Library, where many of the higher-order template functions have a parameter for which you can supply a lambda expression as the argument. We'll return to this in the next chapter.

The most important points covered in this chapter are as follows:

- A pointer to a function stores the address of a function. A pointer to a function can store the address of any function with the specified return type and number and types of parameters.

- You can use a pointer to a function to call the function at the address it contains. You can also pass a pointer to a function as a function argument.

- Function objects or functors are objects that behave precisely like a function by overloading the function call operator.

- Any number of member variables or functions can be added to a function object, making them far more versatile than plain function pointers. For one, functors can be parameterized with any number of additional local variables.

- Function objects are powerful but do require quite some coding to set up. This is where lambda expressions come in; they alleviate the need to define the class for each function object you need.

- A lambda expression defines either an anonymous function or a function object. Lambda expressions are typically used to pass a function as an argument to another function.

- A lambda expression always begins with a lambda introducer that consists of a pair of square brackets that can be empty.

- The lambda introducer can contain a capture clause that specifies which variables in the enclosing scope can be accessed from the body of the lambda expression. Variables can be captured by value or by reference.

- There are two default capture clauses: = specifies that all variables in the enclosing scope are to be captured by value, and & specifies that all variables in the enclosing scope are captured by reference.

- A capture clause can specify specific variables to be captured by value or by reference.

- Variables captured by value will have a local copy created. The copy is not modifiable by default. Adding the `mutable` keyword following the parameter list allows local copies of variables captured by value to be modified.

- You can specify the return type for a lambda expression using the trailing return type syntax. If you don't specify a return type, the compiler deduces the return type from the first return statement in the body of the lambda.

- You can use the `std::function<>` template type that is defined in the `functional` header to specify the type of a function parameter that will accept any first-class function as an argument, including a lambda expression. In fact, it allows you to specify a named type for a variable—be it a function parameter, member variable, or automatic variable—that can hold a lambda closure. This is a feat that would otherwise be very hard as the name of this type is known only to the compiler.

EXERCISES

Exercise 18-1. Define and test a lambda expression that returns the number of elements in a `vector<string>` container that begin with a given letter.

Exercise 18-2. Throughout this book you've already defined various sort functions but always to sort elements in ascending order and always according to the evaluation of the < operator. Clearly, a truly generic sorting function would benefit from a comparison callback, completely analogous to the `find_optimum<>()` templates that you worked with throughout this chapter. Take the solution to Exercise 9-6 and generalize its `sort<>()` template accordingly. Use this to sort a sequence of integers in descending order (that is, from large to small); to sort a sequence of characters alphabetically, ignoring the case ('a' must rank before 'B', even though 'B' < 'a'); and a sequence of floating-point values in ascending order but ignoring the sign (5.5 should thus precede -55.2 but not -3.14).

Exercise 18-3. In this exercise, you will compare the performance of two sorting algorithms. Given a sequence of n elements, quicksort should in theory use about $n \log_2 n$ comparisons on average, and bubble sort n^2. Let's see whether you can replicate these theoretical results in practice! Start by recycling the quicksort template from the previous exercise (perhaps rename it to `quicksort()`?). Then you should extract the bubble sort algorithm from `Ex5_09`, and generalize it to work for any element type and comparison callback as well. Next you define an integer comparison functor that counts the number of times it is called (it can sort in any which order you prefer). Use it to count the number of comparisons that both algorithms need to sort, for instance, sequences of 500, 1,000, 2,000, and 4,000 random integer values between 1 and 100. Do these numbers agree, at least more or less, with the theoretical expectations?

Exercise 18-4. Create a generic function that collects all elements of a `vector<T>` that satisfy a given unary callback function. This callback function accepts a `T` value and returns a Boolean value that indicates whether the element should be part of the function's output. The resulting elements are to be collected and returned in another vector. Use this higher-order function to gather all numbers greater than a user-provided value from a sequence of integers, all capital letters from a sequence of characters, and all palindromes from a sequence of strings. A palindrome is a string that reads the same backward and forward (such as, for example, `"racecar"`, `"noon"`, or `"kayak"`).

Exercise 18-5. As noted earlier, callback functions have many more interesting uses beyond serving as the argument to higher-order functions. They are used frequently in more advanced object-oriented designs as well. While creating a full-blown, complex system of intercommunicating objects would lead us too far astray, one basic example of how this could work should get you started. Begin by recovering the `Truckload` class of Example 17-1. Create a `DeliveryTruck` class that encapsulates a single `Truckload` object. Add `DeliveryTruck::deliverBox()` that not only applies `removeBox()` on its `Truckload` but also notifies any interested party that the given `Box` is delivered. It does so, of course, by calling a callback function. In fact, make it so that a `DeliveryTruck` can have any number of callback functions, all of which are to be called whenever a `Box` is delivered (the newly delivered `Box` is then to be passed to these callbacks as an argument). You could store these callbacks in a `std::vector<>` member, for instance. New callbacks are added through a `DeliveryTruck::registerOnDelivered()` member. We'll leave it to you to choose the appropriate types, but we do expect that all known flavors of first-class functions are supported (that is, function pointers, function objects, and lambda closures). In real life, such callbacks could be used by the trucking company to accumulate statistics on delivery times, to send an e-mail to the customer that his `Box` has arrived, and so on. In your case, a smaller test program suffices. It should register at least these callback functions: a global `logDelivery()` function that streams the delivered `Box` to `std::cout` and a lambda expression that counts the number of times any `Box` is delivered.

Note: What you are to implement in this exercise is a variation on the often-used Observer pattern. In the terminology of this classical object-oriented design pattern, the `DeliveryTruck` is called the *observable*, and the entities that are being notified through the callbacks are called the *observers*. The nice thing about this pattern is that the observable does not need to know the concrete type of its observers, meaning that both can be developed and compiled completely independently from each other.

CHAPTER 19

■ ■ ■

Containers and Algorithms

The Standard Library offers an immense number of types and functions, and this number only increases with the release of every new version of the C++ standard. We could not possibly introduce the full range and scope of the Standard Library here in this book. For a contemporary overview of all the possibilities, details, and intricacies of this vast and growing library, we highly recommend *C++ Standard Library Quick Reference* by Peter Van Weert and Marc Gregoire. Good online references exist as well, but these make it harder to quickly get a feeling of every single feature that the Standard Library has to offer.

Nevertheless, no introduction of C++ would be complete without at least a brief discussion of *containers* and *algorithms*, as well as the glue that binds them: *iterators*. Rarely is a program written in C++ without either of these concepts. However, even for these aspects of the Standard Library alone, a gradual yet in-depth coverage would take up an entire book. *Using the C++ Standard Template Libraries* by Ivor Horton is precisely such a book. It provides a much wider and deeper coverage of containers and algorithms than we could possibly offer you in this one chapter. As a companion to this book, it does this in the same style as you've grown accustomed to, meaning a gentle, informal tutorial with many hands-on code samples.

The goal of this chapter is thus to give you a quick, high-level overview of what the containers and algorithms libraries of the Standard Library have to offer. We'll focus on the underlying principles and ideas, as well as standard usage idioms, rather than listing and showcasing every individual function and capability. Our goal is not to provide you with an exhaustive reference; for that we refer you to the aforementioned reference works. Instead, we aim to sufficiently arm you to be able to read, understand, and effectively browse such references. For that, you need to have at least a global idea of what functionality is out there, how to choose between the various options, and what the common pitfalls are in their use.

In this chapter, you will learn:

- What other containers the Standard Library has to offer (beyond `std::vector<>` and `std::array<>`, that is)

- What the differences are between all container types, their advantages and disadvantages, and how to choose between them

- How to traverse the elements of any container using iterators

- What Standard Library algorithms are and how to use them effectively

Containers

We already introduced two of the most commonly used containers in Chapter 5: `std::array<T,N>` and `std::vector<T>`. Of course, not all containers store their elements in an array. There are countless other ways to arrange your data, each tailored to make one or the other operation more efficient. Arrays are great for linearly traversing elements, but they do not necessarily lend themselves to quickly finding a particular

© Ivor Horton and Peter Van Weert 2018
I. Horton and P. Van Weert, *Beginning C++17*, https://doi.org/10.1007/978-1-4842-3366-5_19

element. If you're looking for the proverbial needle in a haystack, linearly traversing all stalks may not be the fastest way to go about it. If you organize your data such that all needles automatically group themselves in a common region, retrieving needles becomes much easier.

Sequence Containers

A *sequence container* is a container that stores its elements sequentially, in some linear arrangement, one element after the other. The order in which the elements are stored is determined entirely by the user of the container. Both std::array<> and std::vector<> are sequence containers, but the Standard Library defines three more such container types. The Standard Library thus offers five sequence containers, each backed by a different data structure. In this section, we'll briefly introduce each of them in turn.

Arrays

Both std::array<T,N> and std::vector<T> are backed by a single built-in array of T elements, precisely the kind you learned to use in Chapter 5. The advantage of using the containers is that they make it easier to use these arrays and near impossible to misuse.

Surely you'll recall that std::array<> is backed by a statically sized array, and std::vector<> is backed by a dynamic array that it allocates for you in the free store. For an array<>, you therefore always need to specify the number of elements at compile time, which somewhat limits the possible use cases of this container. A vector<>, on the other hand, is capable of dynamically growing its array as you add more and more elements. It does this in much the same way as you did inside the push_back() function of our Array<> template in Chapter 17—only using significantly more efficient techniques.

You know both these sequence containers already quite well from Chapter 5, though; there's little more we want to add to this at this point. We will have more to say about std::vector<> later in this chapter. We will show how you can add and delete elements in the middle of the sequence, rather than only at the end. We can only do so, though, after we have first introduced iterators.

Lists

Out of all data structures that are used instead of an array, the simplest undoubtedly is the *linked list*. You already encountered linked lists at least twice in this book, first in Chapter 11 while working on the Truckload class and again while implementing a Stack<> template in Chapter 16. If you recall, a Truckload was essentially a container of Box objects. Internally, it stored each individual Box inside an object of a nested class called Package. Next to a Box, each Package object contained a pointer to the next Package in the list, thus linking together a long chain of tiny Package objects. We refer to Chapter 11 for more details. The Stack<> class of Chapter 16 was essentially analogous, except that it used the more generic term Node instead of Package as the name for its nested class.

The Standard Library forward_list and list headers offer two container types that are implemented in a similar manner:

- std::forward_list<T> stores T values in a so-called singly linked list. The term *singly-linked* refers to the fact that each node in the linked list has only a single link to another node—the next one in the list. This data structure is completely analogous to that of your Truckload and Stack<> types. Looking back, the Truckload class could simply have used a std::forward_list<std::shared_ptr<Box>>, and creating the Stack<T> template would've been much easier with a plain std::forward_list<T>.

- std::list<T> stores T values in a *doubly linked list*, where each node not only has a pointer to the next node but has one to the previous node as well. For Exercise 11-7 you created a Truckload class backed by an analogous data structure.

In theory, the key advantage of these linked list containers compared to the other sequence containers is that they facilitate insertions and removals of elements in the middle of the sequence. If you insert an element in the middle of a vector<>—as said, we'll show you later how to do this—the vector<> clearly first has to move all elements beyond the point of insertion one position to the right. Moreover, if the allocated array is not large enough to hold any more elements, a new larger array will have to be allocated and all elements moved into that one. With a linked list, on the other hand, inserting an element in the middle involves virtually no overhead at all. All you need to do is create a new node and rewire some next and/or previous pointers.

The key disadvantage of linked lists, however, is that they lack the so-called *random access* capability. Both array<> and vector<> are called *random-access containers* because you can instantly jump to any element with a given index. This capability is exposed through the array subscript operator, operator[ ], of both array<> and vector<> (and their at( ) function as well, of course). With a linked list, however, you cannot access any element in the list without first traversing an entire chain of nodes containing other elements (for a forward_list<>, you always have to start at the first node of the list—the so-called *head*; for a list<>, you can start at either end). Being able to efficiently insert in the middle of a list means little if you first have to linearly traverse half of the list to get there!

Another disadvantage is that linked lists typically exhibit particularly poor memory locality. The nodes of a list tend to become scattered around in free store memory, making it much harder for a computer to quickly fetch all elements one by one. Linearly traversing a linked list is therefore much, much slower than linearly traversing an array<> or vector<>.

The combination of these disadvantages makes for this observation:

■ **Tip**   While they make for great practice in programming with pointers and dynamic memory, the need to use linked lists in production code occurs only very rarely. A vector<> is nearly always the better choice. Even when elements need to be inserted in or removed from the middle at times, a vector<> normally remains the more efficient choice (today's computers are good at moving big blocks of memory around!).

In all our years of C++ programming, we have never used linked lists in practice. We will therefore not discuss them any further here.

Deque

The fifth and final sequence container is called std::deque<T>. The term *deque* is short for *double-ended queue* and is pronounced /dɛk/, precisely like the word *deck* (as in a deck of cards). It is somewhat of a hybrid data structure with the following advantages:

- Just like array<> and vector<>, deque<> is a *random access container*, meaning it has constant-time operator[ ] and at( ) operations.

- Just like a list<>, a deque<> allows you to add elements in constant time both at the front and the back of the sequence. A vector<> only supports constant-time additions to the back of the sequence (inserting in the front at least requires all other elements to be moved one position to the right).

- Unlike a vector<>, the elements of a deque<> are never moved to another bigger array when adding to or removing from either the front or the back of the sequence. This means that T* pointers to elements stored inside the container remain valid (provided you do not insert into or remove from the middle of the sequence using the functions explained later in this chapter, that is).

723

In our experience, the latter advantage is mainly what makes a deque<> useful at times in more complex scenarios where other data structures store pointers to data that is stored inside a deque<> (the need to insert at both ends of a sequence occurs surprisingly seldom). For basic use, and this accounts for well over 95 percent of the cases, your go-to sequence container should thus remain std::vector<>.

The following example shows basic use of a deque<>:

```
// Ex19_01.cpp - Working with std::deque<>
#include <iostream>
#include <deque>

int main()
{
  std::deque<int> my_deque;       // A deque<> allows efficient insertions to
  my_deque.push_back(2);          // both ends of the sequence
  my_deque.push_back(4);
  my_deque.push_front(1);

  my_deque[2] = 3;                // A deque<> is a random-access sequence container

  std::cout << "There are " << my_deque.size() << " elements in my_deque: ";

  for (int element : my_deque)    // A deque<>, like all containers, is a range
    std::cout << element << ' ';
  std::cout << std::endl;
}
```

This code should need no further explanation. The output of this example, of course, is this:

```
There are 3 elements in my_deque: 1 2 3
```

Key Operations

All standard containers—not just sequence containers—provide a similar set of functions, with analogous names and behaviors. All containers have empty(), clear(), and swap() functions, and nearly all have a size() function (the only exception is std::forward_list<>!). All containers can be compared using == and !=, and most—including all sequence containers—can be compared by means of <, <=, >, and >= as well. Like we said in the introduction of this chapter, however, it is not our intention to provide you with a detailed and complete reference. For that we already referred you to other sources. What we do want to give you here is a brief overview of the key distinguishing operations of the various sequence containers.

With the exception of the fixed-size std::array<>, you can freely add or remove as many elements as you want to or from the front, the back, or even somewhere in the middle of the sequence. The following table shows some of the most important operations that the five sequence containers—vector<> (**V**), array<> (**A**), forward_list<> (**F**), list<> (**L**), and deque<> (**D**)—offer to insert, remove, or access their elements. If a square is filled, the corresponding container supports the operation.

Operation	V	A	L	F	D	Description
push_front() pop_front()	□	□	■	■	■	Adds an element to, or removes one from, the front of the sequence.
push_back() pop_back()	■	□	■	□	■	Adds an element to, or removes one from, the back of the sequence.
insert() erase()	■	□	■	■	■	Inserts or removes one or multiple elements at arbitrary positions. As explained later in this chapter, you indicate the positions at which to insert or remove elements using iterators. (Note: The corresponding members for forward_list<> are called insert_after() and erase_after().)
front()	■	■	■	■	■	Returns a reference to the first element in the sequence.
back()	■	■	■	□	■	Returns a reference to the last element in the sequence.
operator[] at()	■	■	□	□	■	Returns a reference to the element at a given index.
data()	■	■	□	□	□	Returns a pointer to the start of the underlying array. This is useful to pass to legacy functions or C libraries. Note: In older code, you often see the equivalent &myContainer[0].

Stacks and Queues

This section covers three related class templates: std::stack<>, std::queue<>, and std::priority_queue<>. They are called *container adapters* because they are technically not containers themselves. Instead, they encapsulate one of the five sequential containers (by default either a vector<> or deque<>) and then use that container to implement a specific, very limited set of member functions. For instance, while a stack<> is typically backed by a deque<>, this deque<> is kept strictly private. It will never allow you to add or remove elements from the front of the encapsulated deque<>, nor will it allow you to access any of its elements by index. Container adapters, in other words, employ the data hiding principle of Chapter 11 to force you to use the encapsulated containers only in a very specific way. For these specific yet common use cases of sequential data, using one of the adapters is therefore much safer and less error-prone than directly using the containers themselves.

LIFO vs. FIFO Semantics

A std::stack<T> represents a container with so-called *last-in first-out (LIFO)* semantics—the last T element that goes in will be the first one to come out. You can compare it to a stack of plates in a self-service restaurant. Plates are added at the top, pushing down other plates. A customer takes a plate from the top, which is the last added plate on the stack. You already created your own Stack<> template earlier in Chapter 16.

A std::queue<> is similar to a stack<> but instead has *first-in first-out (FIFO)* semantics. You can compare it to a queue at a nightclub. A person who arrived before you will be allowed to enter before you (provided you do not grease the bouncer, that is—though there's no greasing a queue<>!).

The following example clearly shows the difference between both container adapters:

```cpp
// Ex19_02.cpp - Working with stacks and queues
#include <iostream>
#include <stack>
#include <queue>
```

```
int main()
{
  std::stack<int> stack;
  for (int i {}; i < 10; ++i)
    stack.push(i);

  std::cout << "The elements coming of the top of the stack:     ";
  while (!stack.empty())
  {
    std::cout << stack.top() << ' ';
    stack.pop();                        // pop() is a void function!
  }
  std::cout << std::endl;

  std::queue<int> queue;
  for (int i {}; i < 10; ++i)
    queue.push(i);

  std::cout << "The elements coming from the front of the queue: ";
  while (!queue.empty())
  {
    std::cout << queue.front() << ' ';
    queue.pop();                        // pop() is a void function!
  }
  std::cout << std::endl;
}
```

The program shows canonical use of both adapters, first of a stack and then of a queue. Even though the same ten elements are added to both in the same order, the output confirms that they will be taken out in opposite orders:

```
The elements coming of the top of the stack:     9 8 7 6 5 4 3 2 1 0
The elements coming from the front of the queue: 0 1 2 3 4 5 6 7 8 9
```

There are two things worth noticing about Ex19_02:

- The pop() function does not return any element. You must therefore typically first access these elements using top() or front(), depending on which adapter you use. (Unsurprisingly, the same holds by the way for all pop_front() and pop_back() members of the various sequence containers.)

- Beyond those used in the example, there are actually only a few other member functions that std::stack<> and queue<> provide. Both have the conventional size(), empty(), and swap() functions, but that is about it. Like we said, the interface of these adapters is specifically tailored for one specific use and that use alone.

▓ **Tip**   Container adapters are typically used to manage elements that represent tasks that need to be executed in a setting where executing all tasks at once is unfeasible. If independent or consecutive tasks are scheduled, then a `queue<>` is often the most natural data structure to use. Tasks are then simply executed in the order in which they are requested. If the tasks represent subtasks of other scheduled or suspended tasks, then you normally want all subtasks to finish first before initiating or resuming their parent tasks. A `stack<>` is then the easiest approach (note that this is also how C++ executes functions—using a call *stack*!).

FIFO and LIFO are thus useful for most simple task scheduling applications; for more complex scenarios, priority-based scheduling may be required. This is what `std::priority_queue<>` provides, which is the container adapter that we'll briefly introduce next.

Priority Queues

The final container adapter is `std::priority_queue<>`, defined by the same queue header as `queue<>`. You can compare a priority queue to how a queue works at a *real* night club; that is, certain groups of guests will get in before others. Guests that have a higher priority—VIPs, good-looking ladies, even daft nephews of the nightclub's owner—take precedence over those with lower priority. Another analogy is the queue at your local super market or bus stop, where disabled people and pregnant women can cut the line.

Similar to the other adapters, elements are added to a `priority_queue<>` through `push()` and taken out via `pop()`. To access the next element in the queue, you use `top()`. The order in which elements exit a `priority_queue<T>` is determined by a comparison functor. By default, the `std::less<T>` functor is used (see Chapter 18). You can override this comparison functor with your own. We refer to a Standard Library reference for more details on how to use a priority queue.

▓ **Caution**   In common speech, it is normally the element with the *highest* priority that takes precedence. In a `priority_queue<>`, however, the front (or better yet, the `top()`) of the queue will by default be the element that compares *lowest* using `<`. If you instead want the element with the highest priority to rise to the `top()` first, you can override the default comparison functor by `std::greater<>`.

Sets

In C++ Standard Library speak, a *set* is a container in which each element can appear at most once. Adding a second element equal to any of the elements that is already stored in a set has no effect. It's easiest to show this with a quick example:

```
// Ex19_03.cpp - Working with sets
#include <iostream>
#include <set>              // For the std::set<> container template

void printSet(const std::set<int>& my_set);   // Print the contents of a set to std::cout

int main()
{
  std::set<int> my_set;
```

```
  // Insert elements 1 through 4 in arbitrary order:
  my_set.insert(1);
  my_set.insert(4);
  my_set.insert(3);
  my_set.insert(3);              // The elements 3 and 1 are added twice
  my_set.insert(1);
  my_set.insert(2);

  printSet(my_set);

  std::cout << "The element 1 occurs " << my_set.count(1) << " time(s)" << std::endl;

  my_set.erase(1);              // Remove the element 1 once
  printSet(my_set);

  my_set.clear();              // Remove all elements
  printSet(my_set);
}
void printSet(const std::set<int>& my_set)
{
  std::cout << "There are " << my_set.size() << " elements in my_set: ";
  for (int element : my_set)              // A set, like all containers, is a range
    std::cout << element << ' ';
  std::cout << std::endl;
}
```

Executing this code produces the following output:

```
There are 4 elements in my_set: 1 2 3 4
The element 1 occurs 1 time(s)
There are 3 elements in my_set: 2 3 4
There are 0 elements in my_set:
```

There are no "push" or "pop" members for set containers. Instead, you always add elements through insert() and remove them again through erase(). You can add any number of elements you like, and in any order you like. As Ex19_03 clearly demonstrates, however, adding the same element a second time indeed has no effect. Even though in the example you add the values 1 and 3 to my_set twice, the output clearly shows that both elements are stored only once in the container.

You'll often use these set containers to manage or gather a collection of duplicate-free elements. Beyond that, their main advantage is that sets are very good at quickly checking whether they contain a given element or not. That's much better than, say, a plain unordered vector<>. This is not surprising, given that checking whether an element exists already is precisely what they need to do to weed out all duplicates. To check for yourself whether a given element is contained in a set or not, you either use its count() member or use its find() member. The former is used in Ex19_03 and returns either 0 or 1; the latter returns an iterator. We'll discuss the find() function some more later, after you've had a thorough introduction on iterators.

The Standard Library offers two generic set containers: std::set<> and unordered_set<>. In essence, both set containers provide the same functionality. You could replace the std::set<> in Ex19_03 with a std::unordered_set<>, for instance, and the example will work (nearly) the same. Both containers differ drastically in the way they are implemented. They use very different data structures to organize their data, albeit it both toward the same goal: quickly determining where to insert a new element or, similarly, whether a given element is already present in the container.

Ordered Sets

As the name unordered_set<> already gives away, a regular set<> organizes its elements such that they are always sorted. This is also apparent from Ex19_03. Even though you added the elements 1 through 4 in some arbitrary order, the output clearly corroborates that the container somehow stores them in a sorted order. Searching through a sorted set of data can be done much faster—just imagine how long it would take you to find the definition of *capricious* if all words in your English dictionary were scrambled in some arbitrary order!

■ **Note**   For those who know their data structures, a std::set<> is normally backed by some *balanced tree* data structure (typically a *red-black tree*). Beyond the fact that this gives you logarithmic insert(), erase(), find(), and count() operations, there is normally little need for you to know these implementation details.

By default, a set<> orders all elements using the < operator. For fundamental types, this translates to the built-in < operator; by default, elements of a class type T, though, should thus overload the < operator to be stored in a std::set<T>. We say "by default" since beyond overloading the < operator you could also override the way a set<> orders its elements by specifying which functor it should use. If you, for instance, replace the definition of my_set in Ex19_03 with the following, then its elements become sorted from highest to lowest instead. (To print the set you'll have to update the signature of printSet() accordingly; also, to use std::greater<>, you may have to first include the functional header:)

```
std::set<int, std::greater<>> my_set;
```

The second type argument of std::set<T> is optional (by default it equals std::less<T>). You can specify any functor type whose binary function call operator compares two T elements and returns true if the element passed to its first parameter should precede that passed to the second. Typically, a set<> default constructs a functor of the corresponding type, but if need be, you could pass one yourself to one of the set<> constructors as well. Functors, and std::less<> and greater<> in particular, were discussed in detail in the previous chapter.

■ **Caution**   To decide whether two elements are duplicates, set<> does not use the == operator. For the default < comparison, two elements x and y are considered equal if !(x < y) && !(y < x).

Unordered Sets

An unordered_set<>, naturally, does not order its elements—at least not in any predefined order that is of any particular use to you, the user of the container. Instead, it is backed by a so-called *hash table* or *hash map*. All operations of an unordered_set<> consequently usually run in near-constant time, making them potentially even faster than a regular set<>. For the most commonly used variable types—including all fundamental types, pointers, strings, and smart pointers—an unordered_set<> may be used as a drop-in replacement of std::set<>. A further discussion of this more advanced data structure, however, or how to specify so-called *hash functions* for your own custom types is outside the scope of this brief introduction.

■ **Caution**   The only way to know for sure which is faster for your application, though—a set<> or an unordered_set<>—is to measure its performance on some real, representative input data. For nearly all applications, it does not really matter because both will be more than fast enough.

■ **Tip**   Besides `set<>` and `unordered_set<>`, the Standard Library also offers `std::multiset<>` and `std::unordered_multiset<>`. Unlike set containers, multiset containers (also known as *bags* or *msets*) may contain the same element more than once (that is, for these containers, `count()` might return numbers higher than 1). Their key feature remains that multisets are very fast at determining whether and where a given element is stored in the container.

Maps

A *map* or *associative array* container is best thought of as a generalization of a dictionary or phone book. Given a specific *key* (a word or name of a person), you want to store or quickly retrieve a certain *value* (a definition or phone number). Keys in a map need to be unique; values do not (a dictionary allows for synonyms, and a phone book in principle allows for family members to share the same phone number).

Analogous to set<T> and unordered_set<T>, the Standard Library offers two different map containers: std::map<Key,Value> and std::unordered_map<Key,Value>. Unlike most containers, a map container needs at least two template type arguments, one to determine the type of the keys and one to determine the type of the values. Let's clarify this with a quick example:

```
// Ex19_04.cpp - Basic use of std::map<>
#include <map>
#include <iostream>
#include <string>

int main()
{
  std::map<std::string, unsigned long long> phone_book;
  phone_book["Donald Trump"] = 202'456'1111;
  phone_book["Melania Trump"] = 202'456'1111;
  phone_book["Francis"] = 39'06'6982;
  phone_book["Elizabeth"] = 44'020'7930'4832;

  std::cout << "The president's number is " << phone_book["Donald Trump"] << std::endl;

  for (const auto& [name, number] : phone_book)
    std::cout << name << " can be reached at " << number << std::endl;
}
```

This produces the following result:

```
The president's number is 2024561111
Donald Trump can be reached at 2024561111
Elizabeth can be reached at 4402079304832
Francis can be reached at 39066982
Melania Trump can be reached at 2024561111
```

In Ex19_04, phone_book is defined as a map<> with keys of type std::string and values of type unsigned long long (people rarely have negative phone numbers). It therefore uniquely associates strings with numbers. No two keys can be the same. The example does confirm, though, that no such restriction exists for the values. The same number can be inserted multiple times.

730

The map<> and unordered_map<> containers again offer functionality that is completely analogous. You typically use them in much the same way as an array (or its object-oriented counterpart, a random-access sequential container), that is, through its array subscript operator. Only with maps you do not (necessarily) address the values by contiguous integers (oft-called indices); instead, you can in principle use keys of any type you like.

The difference between the two map types again lies in the way they are implemented. Depending on which map implementation you use, there are some requirements on the types you can use for your keys. These requirements are analogous to those for the values of set<> and unordered_set<>. A map<> again works by ordering its elements; an unordered_map<> is essentially a textbook hash map. The former is witnessed as well by the output of Ex19_04. The four names appear in alphabetical order, even though they were added to the map in a different order.

Elements of a Map

To traverse the elements of its phone_book container, Ex19_04 uses a syntax that you have not yet seen before:

```
for (const auto& [name, number] : phone_book)
  std::cout << name << " can be reached at " << number << std::endl;
```

This syntax has been possible only since C++17. It is instructive to see how you'd express this loop using more familiar C++11 syntax:

```
for (const auto& element : phone_book)
  std::cout << element.first << " can be reached at " << element.second << std::endl;
```

In fact, even more instructive here would be to spell out the type of element:

```
for (const std::pair<std::string, unsigned long long>& element : phone_book)
  std::cout << element.first << " can be reached at " << element.second << std::endl;
```

That is, the elements that are contained in either a std::map<K,V> or unordered_map<K,V> have type std::pair<K,V>. You've briefly encountered the std::pair<> type before during the exercises of Chapter 16. It is a basic class template (defined in the utility header) whose objects each represent a pair of values, possibly of different types. You can access these two values through their public member variables first and second. As of C++17, however, there is a more compact way.

Consider the following snippet of C++17 code, for example:

```
std::pair my_pair{ false, 77.50 };
auto [my_bool, my_number] = my_pair;
```

Prior to C++17, you always had to write this in a much more verbose way (recall from Chapter 16 that C++17 introduced class template argument deduction for constructor invocations as well!):

```
std::pair<bool, double> my_pair{ false, 77.50 };
bool my_bool = my_pair.first;
double my_number = my_pair.second;
```

The loop in Ex19_04 nicely shows that this same C++17 syntax is convenient when traversing the elements of a map container as well. (And also that the auto [] syntax can be combined with const and &, for that matter!)

We'll use this syntax again in the somewhat larger example we explore in the next subsection.

Counting Words

Enough with the tiny toy examples. Let's look at an example use of std::map<> with some more body to it. A possible use case for a map is to count unique words in a string. Let's see how this works with an example based on Ex8_18. We'll use the following type aliases and function prototypes:

```
// Type aliases
using Words = std::vector<std::string_view>;
using WordCounts = std::map<std::string, size_t>;

// Function prototypes
Words extract_words(std::string_view text, std::string_view separators = " ,.!?\"\n");
WordCounts count_words(const Words& words);
void show_word_counts(const WordCounts& wordCounts);
size_t max_word_length(const WordCounts& wordCounts);
```

The extract_words() function is a slight variation of the function with the same name in Ex8_18; you should therefore have no trouble at all defining it on your own. The function extracts all individual words from a given text. A word is defined as any sequence of characters different from the given separators.

Our main point of interest here, though, is the count_words() function. This, as you may have guessed, is to count the amount of times each individual word occurs in the input vector<>. To count all unique words, the function uses a std::map<std::string, size_t>. In the map that the function returns, the words are the keys, and the value associated with each key is the number of times that the corresponding word occurs in the words vector<>. The function thus has to insert a new key/value pair into the map each time a new word is encountered. The same counter needs to be incremented whenever the same word is seen multiple times. Both of these operations can be implemented using a single line of code:

```
WordCounts count_words(const Words& words)
{
  WordCounts result;
  for (auto& word : words)
    ++result[std::string(word)];
  return result;
}
```

The following line does all the work:

```
++result[std::string(word)];
```

To understand this, we need to explain the workings of the array index operator, operator[], of a map container bit better:

- If a value is already associated with the given key, the operator simply returns a reference to that value. Applying the ++ operator to this reference then simply increments the value that was already stored within the map to 2 or higher.

- If no value is associated with the given key yet, though, the operator first inserts a new key/value pair into the map. The value of this new element is zero-initialized (or default constructed, if it concerns an object of a class type). Once the new element is inserted, the operator then returns a reference to this zero-initialized value. In count_words(), we then instantly increment the resulting size_t value to 1.

The max_word_length() function from Ex8_18 needs to be changed slightly, because we want it to use the words stored in the map. For brevity, we'll only output words that appear more than once in the output, so we best ignore these here as well:

```
size_t max_word_length(const WordCounts& wordCounts)
{
  size_t max{};
  for (const auto& [word, count] : wordCounts)
    if (count >= 2 && max < word.length()) max = word.length();
  return max;
}
```

Finally, all the words, including their count, can be output with a show_word_counts() function. As said, we only stream out words that appear more than once:

```
void show_word_counts(const WordCounts& wordCounts)
{
  const size_t field_width{max_word_length(wordCounts) + 1};
  const size_t words_per_line{5};

  size_t words_in_line{};      // Number of words in the current line
  char previous_initial{};
  for (auto& [word, count] : wordCounts)
  {
    if (count < 2) continue;    // Skip words that appear only once

    // Output newline when initial letter changes or after 5 per line
    if (previous_initial &&
        (word[0] != previous_initial || ++words_in_line == words_per_line))
    {
      words_in_line = 0;
      std::cout << std::endl;
    }
    std::cout << std::setw(field_width) << word;        // Output a word
    std::cout << " (" << std::setw(2) << count << ')';  // Output count
    previous_initial = word[0];
  }
  std::cout << std::endl;
}
```

The fact that we used a map<> automatically ensures that all words are sorted in alphabetical order, making it easy for us to print them out alphabetically as well. In particular, show_word_counts() groups words that begin with the same letter on the same line. Beyond this, show_word_counts() does not really contain much you haven't seen several times before already in other, similar output functions. So, we believe we can skip any further explanations and fast-forward to seeing it all working in a complete example:

```
// Ex19_05.cpp - Working with maps
#include <iostream>
#include <iomanip>
#include <map>
#include <string>
#include <string_view>
#include <vector>
```

```
// Type aliases
using Words = std::vector<std::string_view>;
using WordCounts = std::map<std::string, size_t>;

// Function prototypes
Words extract_words(std::string_view text, std::string_view separators = " ,.!?\"\n");
WordCounts count_words(const Words& words);
void show_word_counts(const WordCounts& wordCounts);
size_t max_word_length(const WordCounts& wordCounts);

int main()
{
  std::string text;                                      // The string to count words in

  // Read a string from the keyboard
  std::cout << "Enter a string terminated by *:" << std::endl;
  getline(std::cin, text, '*');

  Words words = extract_words(text);
  if (words.empty())
  {
    std::cout << "No words in text." << std::endl;
    return 0;
  }

  WordCounts wordCounts = count_words(words);
  show_word_counts(wordCounts);
}

// The implementations of the extract_words(), count_words(), show_word_counts(),
// and max_word_length() function as discussed earlier.
```

If you compile and run this program, a possible session could go as follows:

```
Enter a string terminated by *:
It was the best of times, it was the worst of times, it was the age of wisdom, it was the
age of foolishness, it was the epoch of belief, it was the epoch of incredulity, it was the
season of Light, it was the season of Darkness, it was the spring of hope, it was the winter
of despair, we had everything before us, we had nothing before us, we were all going direct
to Heaven, we were all going direct the other way—in short, the period was so far like the
present period, that some of its noisiest authorities insisted on its being received, for
good or for evil, in the superlative degree of comparison only.*
    age ( 2)      all ( 2)
 before ( 2)
 direct ( 2)
  epoch ( 2)
    for ( 2)
  going ( 2)
    had ( 2)
     it ( 9)      its ( 2)
     of (12)
```

```
period ( 2)
season ( 2)
   the (14)   times ( 2)
   was (11)     we ( 4)   were ( 2)
```

Iterators

You first encountered the concept of iterators in Chapter 11, where we employed an iterator to traverse all Boxes of a given Truckload container in a nice and elegant manner. To do so, you simply asked the Truckload object for an Iterator object, after which you could use this iterator's getFirstBox() and getNextBox() members to retrieve all Boxes in a straightforward loop:

```
auto iterator{ my_truckload.getIterator() };
for (auto box { iterator.getFirstBox() }; box != nullptr; box = iterator.getNextBox())
{
  std::cout << *box << std::endl;
}
```

This iterator concept is actually a classical and widely applied object-oriented design pattern. One used extensively by the Standard Library as well, as you'll discover throughout this chapter. Before we go there, however, let's first reflect some more on why an iterator is such an attractive pattern.

The Iterator Design Pattern

Iterators allow you to traverse a set of elements contained within any container-like object in an effective, uniform manner. This approach has several advantages, as discussed next.

The Truckload example from earlier is actually an excellent starting point. If you recall, internally a Truckload object used a so-called *(singly) linked list* to store its Boxes. Concretely, a Truckload stored each individual Box inside its own dedicated instance of a nested class called Package. Next to a Box, each Package object contained a pointer to the next Package in the list. We refer to Chapter 11 for more details, in case you forgot. Or, better yet, do not reach back to Chapter 11 just yet! Our main point here is precisely that you do not need to know anything of a Truckload's internal wiring to iterate over all its Boxes. All you need to learn as a user of the Truckload class is the straightforward public interface of its Iterator class.

Library writers typically define Iterators with analogous interfaces for all their container types. This is the case, for instance, for all containers of the Standard Library, as we'll discuss shortly. With this approach, it thus becomes possible to traverse different containers in precisely the same way—be it an array, linked list, or even some more complex data structure. You then no longer need to know at all how a particular container works internally to inspect its elements! Among other thing, this leads to code that is as follows:

- Easy to write and understand.

- Bug-free and robust. Compared to traversing pointers within potentially complex data structures, there is considerably less room for errors when using an iterator.

- Efficient. For instance, as discussed earlier in this chapter already, one important limitation of a linked list data structure is that you cannot jump to an arbitrary element with a given index without first traversing all other elements prior to this element. In a Truckload, for example, you can only get to the Box you need by following a whole lot of next pointers starting from the head of the list. This means that a loop of the following form would be particularly inefficient:

```
for (size_t i {}; i < my_truckload.getNumBoxes(); ++i)
{
   std::cout << my_truckload[i] << std::endl;
}
```

  In such a loop, each invocation of the array subscript operator [ ] would involve traversing the linked list of the iterator starting from the first Package (the head of the list) all the way until the ith Package. That is, with each iteration of the for loop, obtaining a reference to the ith Box would take longer and longer. An Iterator's getNextBox() function does not suffer from this problem, as it always contains a pointer to the current Package, from which moving to the next can be done in constant time.

- Flexible and maintainable. You can readily change the internal representation of a container without having to worry about breaking any external code traversing its elements. For instance, after this chapter, it should be straightforward to reimplement the Truckload class in terms of a vector<> instead of a custom linked list, while still preserving the same public functions, both for the class itself and for its Iterator class.

- Easy to debug. You could add extra debugging statements and assertions to the iterator's member functions. Typical examples are out-of-bounds checks. Mostly, library writers add such checks conditionally, provided some specific macros are defined (see Chapter 10). None of this would be possible if external code was manipulating the internal pointers or arrays directly.

■ **Note**   It should come as no surprise that iterators share many of these advantages with the concept of data hiding we explained in Chapter 11. Data hiding is precisely what iterators and other object-oriented design patterns do. They hide implementation details from the users of an object behind an easy-to-use public interface.

Another clear advantage of uniform iterators is that they facilitates the creation of function templates that work for iterators of any container type—functions that can operate on any range of elements, irrespective of whether these elements are contained within for instance a vector, a list, or even a set. As all iterators have analogous interfaces, these function templates thus do not need to know about the inner workings of the containers anymore. It's precisely this idea, combined with first-class functions (see Chapter 18), that powers the higher-order functions of the Standard Library's algorithms library that we will discuss in the final part of this chapter.

Iterators for Standard Library Containers

All container types of the Standard Library—and with them those of virtually any third-party C++ library—offer iterators that are completely analogous. No matter which containers you work with, you can always traverse the elements they store in the same manner. You create new iterator objects through member functions with the same name, you access the element an iterator currently refers to in the same manner, and you advance to the next element in the same manner. The public interface of these iterators is slightly different from that of the Truckload Iterators we discussed earlier, but the general idea remains the same.

Creating and Working with Standard Iterators

The most common way to create an iterator for a given container is by invoking its `begin()` member function. Every single standard container provides this function. Here's an example:

```
std::vector<char> letters{ 'a', 'b', 'c', 'd', 'e' };
auto my_iter{ letters.begin() };
```

The type of an iterator for a container of type `ContainerType` is always `ContainerType::iterator`, which is either a concrete type or a type alias. Our `my_iter` variable definition in full would thus be as follows:

```
std::vector<char>::iterator my_iter{ letters.begin() };
```

It's safe to say that container iterator types are a prime example where C++11's auto type deduction truly has made all our lives a lot easier!

Through the magic of operator overloading (see Chapter 12), each and every iterator provided by the Standard Library containers mimics a pointer. For example, to access the element that our `my_iter` iterator currently refers to, you apply its dereference operator:

```
std::cout << *my_iter << std::endl;       // a
```

As `begin()` always returns an iterator that points to the first element in the container, this statement will simply print out the letter `'a'`.

Just like with a pointer, a dereferenced iterator results in a reference to the actual element stored inside the container. In our example, `*my_iter` therefore results in a reference of type `char&`. As this expression is clearly an lvalue reference, you can of course also use it, for instance, on the left side of an assignment:

```
*my_iter = 'x';
std::cout << letters[0] << std::endl;       // x
```

Naturally, you can do more with an iterator than access the first element of the container. As you'll recall from Chapter 6, pointers support the arithmetic operators ++, --, +, -, +=, and -=, which you could use to move from one element in an array to the next (or previous). You work with `vector<>` iterators in precisely the same manner. Here's an example:

```
++my_iter;                                  // Move my_iter to the next element
std::cout << *my_iter << std::endl;         // b

my_iter += 2;
std::cout << *my_iter-- << std::endl;       // d
std::cout << *my_iter << std::endl;         // c  (my_iter was altered using the post-decrement
                                            //     operator in the previous statement)
```

737

```
auto copy{ my_iter };
my_iter += 2;
std::cout << *copy << std::endl;          // c
std::cout << *my_iter << std::endl;       // e
std::cout << my_iter - copy << std::endl; // 2
```

This code, which you can find in its totality in Ex19_06, should really explain itself at this point, as all this is completely analogous to working with pointers. This even applies for the last line in our example, which is perhaps a bit less obvious than the others; that is, subtracting two vector<> iterators results in a value of a signed integer type that reflects the distance between the two iterators.

▒ **Tip**   Iterators also provide a member access operator (informally, arrow operator), ->, to access the member variables or functions of the element they refer to. That is, suppose string_iter is an iterator that refers to an element of a class std::string; then string_iter->length() is short for (*string_iter). length()—again just like it is with a pointer. We will see more concrete examples later in the chapter.

Different Flavors of Iterators

The iterator that we used for the example in the previous subsection is a so-called random-access iterator. Out of all iterator categories, random-access iterators offer the richest set of operations. All iterators returned by standard containers support operators ++, *, and ->, as well as == and !=. But beyond that, there are some differences. Any and all limitations are easily explained from the nature of the data structures behind the various containers:

- The iterators for a std::forward_list<> do not support --, -=, or -. The reason, of course, is that there is no (efficient) way for an iterator to go back to the previous element. Each node in a singly linked list only has a pointer to the next element in the list. Such iterators are referred to as *forward iterators*. Other containers that may only support forward iterators are unordered_set<>, unordered_map<>, and unordered_multimap<>.

- The iterators for a std::list<>, on the other hand, do support the -- decrement operators (both pre- and post-decrement). Going back to the previous node in a double-linked is trivial. Jumping multiple elements at once still cannot be done efficiently, though. To discourage such use, std::list<> iterators do not feature, for instance, the +=, -=, +, or - operators. The iterators for the std::set<>, map<>, and multimap<> containers have the same limitations, as traversing the nodes of the underlying tree data structure is similar to traversing those of a doubly linked list. This category of iterators is termed *bidirectional iterators*—for obvious reasons.

- The only iterators to offer +=, -=, +, and -, as well as the comparison operators <, <=, >, and >=, are *random-access iterators*. The only containers that are required to provide random-access iterators are the random-access sequence containers (or std::vector<>, array<>, and deque<>).

Library reference, most particularly its section on the generic algorithms library that we discuss later in this chapter. The reference of each algorithm template will specify which type of iterators it expects as input, either a forward iterator, bidirectional iterator, or random-access iterator.

Notice that these three iterator categories form a hierarchy. That is, every random-access iterator is also a valid bidirectional iterator, and every bidirectional iterator is also a forward iterator. So to an algorithm that requires, for instance, a forward iterator, you could most certainly pass a random-access iterator as well. For completeness, your Standard Library reference may also employ the terms *input iterator* and *output iterator* in this context. These are more theoretical concepts that refer to iterators with even less requirements than a forward iterator. In practice, every iterator created by a Standard container is thus always a valid input or output iterator.

Note The three container adapters—`std::stack<>`, `queue<>`, and `priority_queue<>`—do not offer any iterators at all—not even forward iterators. Their elements can be accessed only through the `top()`, `front()`, or `back()` functions (whichever is applicable).

Traversing Elements of a Container

From Chapter 6, you know how to traverse an array using pointers and pointer arithmetic. To print out all elements in an array, for instance, you may use the following loop:

```
int numbers[] { 1, 2, 3, 4, 5 };
for (int* pnumber {numbers}; pnumber < numbers + std::size(numbers); ++pnumber)
{
  std::cout << *pnumber << ' ';
}
std::cout << std::endl;
```

You could traverse all elements of a vector in precisely the same manner:

```
std::vector<int> numbers{ 1, 2, 3, 4, 5 };
for (auto iter {numbers.begin()}; iter < numbers.begin() + numbers.size(); ++iter)
{
  std::cout << *iter << ' ';
}
std::cout << std::endl;
```

The problem with this loop is that it uses two operations that are exclusive to random-access iterators: `<` and `+`. This loop would thus not have compiled had numbers been, for instance, of type `std::list<int>` or `std::set<int>`. A more conventional way of expressing this same loop, therefore, is this:

```
for (auto iter {numbers.begin()}; iter != numbers.end(); ++iter)
{
  std::cout << *iter << ' ';
}
```

■ **Tip**   In C++ you normally always use expressions of the form `iter != numbers.end()` rather than `iter <`
`numbers.end()` precisely because forward and bidirectional iterators are not required to support comparisons
by means of `<`.

This new loop is equivalent to the one we used before, only this time it works for any standard
container. Conceptually, iterators returned by a container's end() member point to "one past the last
element." Once an iterator is incremented up to the point that it equals the container's end() iterator. That
is, once an iterator is incremented past the container's last element, you should therefore clearly abort the
loop. While it is undefined what would happen, no good can come from dereferencing an iterator that points
beyond the bounds of the actual container.

The following example uses a loop exactly like this to traverse all elements contained in a list<>:

```cpp
// Ex19_07.cpp
// Iterating over the elements of a list<>
#include <iostream>
#include <list>

int main()
{
  std::cout << "Enter a sequence of positive numbers, "
            << "terminated by a negative number: ";

  std::list<unsigned> numbers;

  while (true)
  {
    signed number{-1};
    std::cin >> number;
    if (number < 0) break;
    numbers.push_back(static_cast<unsigned>(number));
  }

  std::cout << "You entered the following numbers: ";
  for (auto iter {numbers.begin()}; iter != numbers.end(); ++iter)
  {
    std::cout << *iter << ' ';
  }
  std::cout << std::endl;
}
```

A possible session then might go like this:

```
Enter a sequence of positive numbers, terminated by a negative number: 4 8 15 16 23 42 -1
You entered the following numbers: 4 8 15 16 23 42
```

Of course, each container is a range as well, and ranges can be used in range-based for loops (see Chapter 5). The for loop of Ex19_07, for instance, could therefore be replaced by the following much simpler range-based for loop:

```
for (auto number : numbers)
{
  std::cout << number << ' ';
}
```

> ■ **Tip** To iterate over all elements in a container, always use a range-based for loop. You should only use a more verbose and complex iterator-based loop either if you explicitly need access to the iterator for more advanced processing in the loop's body or if you only want to iterator over a subrange of the container's elements.

We will see examples where the loop's body needs access to the iterator later.

Const Iterators

All iterators that we have used thus far have been so-called *mutable* (or *nonconst*) iterators. You can alter the element that a mutable iterator refers to simply by dereferencing it or, for elements of a class type, through its member access operator -> operator. Here's an example:

```
// Ex19_08.cpp
// Altering elements through a mutable iterator
#include <iostream>
#include <vector>
#include "Box.h" // From Ex11_04

int main()
{
  std::vector<Box> boxes{ Box{ 1.0, 2.0, 3.0 } };  // A vector containing 1 Box

  auto iter{ boxes.begin() };
  std::cout << iter->volume() << std::endl;        // 6 == 1.0 * 2.0 * 3.0

  *iter = Box{ 2.0, 3.0, 4.0 };
  std::cout << iter->volume() << std::endl;        // 24 == 2.0 * 3.0 * 4.0

  iter->setHeight(7.0);
  std::cout << iter->volume() << std::endl;        // 42 == 2.0 * 3.0 * 7.0
}
```

There is nothing new or surprising about this example yet. The point we wanted to make is that besides mutable iterators of type ContainerType::iterator (see earlier), each container also offers *const iterators* of type ContainerType::const_iterator. Dereferencing a const iterator results in a reference to a const element (const Box& in our example), and its -> operator only allows you to either access member variables as const or invoke const member functions.

There are two ways you typically obtain a const iterator:

- By calling cbegin() or cend() instead of begin() or end(). The c in the names of these member functions of course refers to const. You can try this by changing begin() to cbegin() in Ex19_08.

- By invoking begin() or end() on a const container. If the container is const, these functions return a const iterator; only if the container itself is mutable will the result be a mutable iterator as well. (You saw in Chapter 11 how to accomplish this effect through function overloading, where one overload of the same function is const and the other is not.) You can give this a try as well by adding the keyword const in front of the declaration of the boxes vector<> in Ex19_08.

If you turn iter in Ex19_08 into a const iterator in either of these two ways, the lines containing the statements *iter = Box{ 2.0, 3.0, 4.0 }; and iter->setHeight(7.0) will no longer compile: altering an element through a const iterator is not possible.

▦ **Tip**   Just like it is good practice to add const to your variable declarations whenever possible, you should also use const iterators whenever applicable. This prevents you or anyone else from accidentally altering elements in contexts where that is not desired or expected.

The for loop in Ex19_07, for instance, simply prints out all elements in the container. This certainly is not supposed to alter these elements. You could therefore write the loop like this:

```
for (auto iter{ numbers.cbegin() }; iter != numbers.cend(); ++iter)
{
  std::cout << *iter << std::endl;
}
```

▦ **Caution**   All standard set and map container types only provide const iterators. For these types, begin() and end() always return const iterators, even when invoked on a non-const container. As always, though, these restrictions are easily explained by the nature of these containers. For example, as you know, a std::set<> always stores all its elements in a sorted order. If you allow a user to alter the value of these elements through an iterator, mid-traversal, maintaining this invariant obviously becomes infeasible.

Inserting in and Erasing from Sequence Containers

In Chapter 5, we already introduced push_back() and pop_back()—functions you can use to add elements to, respectively, remove elements from most sequence containers. There was only one restriction: these functions only allow you to manipulate the very last element of the sequence. Earlier this chapter you also saw push_front() in action, a similar function that some sequence containers provide to add elements to the front of the sequence. This is all well and good, but what if you need to insert or remove elements in or from the middle of the sequence? Shouldn't this be possible as well?

The answer is that of course you can insert in the middle of a sequence or remove whichever element you want! And now that you know about iterators, we are ready to show you how. That is, to indicate where to insert or which elements to remove, you need to provide iterators. All sequence containers except std::array<> offer various insert() and erase() functions that accept either iterators or iterator ranges to this end.

Let's start off with something simple and add a single element to the beginning of a vector:

```
std::vector<int> numbers{ 2, 4, 5 };
numbers.insert(numbers.begin(), 1);    // Add single element to the beginning of the sequence
printVector(numbers);                  // 1 2 4 5
```

The element you provide as insert()'s second argument is inserted *right before* the position referred to by the iterator you provide as its first argument. So, provided the printVector() function indeed lives up to its name, then the output of this snippet of code should be something of the form "1 2 4 5."

Naturally, you can insert() new elements at any position you want. The following, for instance, adds the number 3 right in the middle of our numbers sequence:

```
numbers.insert(numbers.begin() + numbers.size() / 2, 3); // Add in the middle
printVector(numbers);                                    // 1 2 3 4 5
```

The insert() function moreover has a couple of overloads that allow you to add multiple elements at once. One common use of these is to append one vector<> to another:

```
std::vector<int> more_numbers{ 6, 7, 8 };
numbers.insert(numbers.end(), more_numbers.begin(), more_numbers.end());
printVector(numbers);                         // 1 2 3 4 5 6 7 8
```

Like with all overloads of insert(), the first argument again indicates the position *right after* where the new elements are to be added. In this case, we selected the end() iterator, which means we're inserting right before "one past the end" of the current sequence—or, in other words, right after the last element. The two iterators passed to the function's second and third parameters indicate the range of elements to insert. In our example, this range corresponds to the entire more_numbers sequence.

▦ **Note**   Ranges of elements are always indicated using half-open intervals in standard C++. In Chapter 7, you already saw that many member functions of std::string accepted half-open character intervals specified through size_t indexes. Container members such as insert() and erase() (discussed next) similarly work with half-open intervals indicated by means of iterators. If you provide two iterators, from and to, then that range encompasses all elements in the interval [from, to). That is, the range includes the element of the from iterator but not that of the to iterator. Iterator ranges are used by virtually every template function of the Standard Library algorithms library discussed later in this chapter as well.

The opposite of insert() is called erase(). The following sequence of statements removes, one by one, the same elements we added earlier using insert():

```
numbers.erase(numbers.end() - 3, numbers.end());       // Erase last 3 elements
numbers.erase(numbers.begin() + numbers.size() / 2);   // Erase the middle element
numbers.erase(numbers.begin());                        // Erase the first element
printVector(numbers);                   // 2 4 5
```

The overload of erase() with two parameters deletes a range of elements; the one with a single parameter deletes only a single element (remember this distinction; it'll be important again later in this chapter!).

The complete source for the example we used throughout this section can be found in Ex19_09.

■ **Note**   Most containers offer similar insert() and erase() functions (the only exception is std::array<>). Naturally, set and map containers will not allow you to indicate where to insert() an element (only sequence containers do), but they do allow you to erase() the element or elements that correspond to an iterator or iterator range. Consult your Standard Library reference for more details.

Altering Containers During Iteration

In past sections we showed you how to iterate over elements in a container as well as how to insert() and erase() elements. The logical next question is then, what if you insert() or erase() elements *while* you are iterating over a container?

Unless otherwise specified (consult a Standard Library reference for details), any modification to a container is said to *invalidate* all iterators that were ever created for that container. Any further use of an invalidated iterator results in undefined behavior, which, of course, translates to anything from unpredictable results to crashes. Consider the following function template:

```
template <typename NumberContainer>
void removeEvenNumbers(NumberContainer& numbers)     /* Wrong!! */
{
  auto from{ numbers.begin() }, to{ numbers.end() };
  for (auto iter {from}; iter != to; ++iter)
  {
    if (*iter % 2 == 0)
      numbers.erase(iter);
  }
}
```

The intent is to write a template that removes all even numbers from containers of a variety of types—be it vector<int>, deque<unsigned>, list<long>, set<short>, or unordered_set<unsigned>.

The problem is that this template contains two serious yet fairly realistic bugs, both triggered by the erase() in the loop's body. Once you modify a sequence, for instance, through erase(), you should generally stop using any existing iterators. Yet the loop in removeEvenNumbers() ignores that. Instead, it simply soldiers on using both the to and iter iterators, even after invoking erase() on the container to which both these iterators refer. There's therefore no telling what will happen should you execute this code, but it most certainly will not be what you might've hoped for.

More specifically, once you call erase() a first time, the to iterator no longer points "one past the last element," but (at least in principle) "two past the last element." This means that your loop probably dereferences the actual end() iterator, with all its catastrophic consequences. You can solve this rather easily by requesting a new end() iterator after each iteration of the for loop as follows:

```
  for (auto iter {numbers.begin()}; iter != numbers.end(); ++iter)     /* Still wrong! */
  {
    if (*iter % 2 == 0)
      numbers.erase(iter);
  }
```

This new loop is still very wrong, though, as it still continues to use the iter iterator after invoking erase(). This, in general, will end in disaster just as well. For a linked list, for instance, erase() will likely deallocate the node that iter refers to, meaning it becomes highly unpredictable what the upcoming ++iter will do. For a std::set(), an erase() might reshuffle the entire tree to put its elements back nicely in order. Any further iteration then becomes risky business as well.

Does this mean that you cannot remove multiple individual elements from a container without restarting each time from begin()? Fortunately not, as that would be particularly inefficient. It just means that you have to follow this pattern:

```cpp
template <typename NumberContainer>
void removeEvenNumbers(NumberContainer& numbers)     /* Correct!! */
{
  for (auto iter {numbers.begin()}; iter != numbers.end(); )
  {
    if (*iter % 2 == 0)
    {
      iter = numbers.erase(iter);
    }
    else
    {
      ++iter;
    }
  }
}
```

Most erase() and insert() functions return an iterator that you can use to continue the iteration with. This iterator will then refer to one element past the one that was just inserted or erased (or be equal to end(), if the latter concerned the last element in the container).

Caution   Do not deviate from the standard pattern we just laid out. For instance, the iterator returned by either erase() or insert() should itself not be incremented anymore, which is why we moved the for loop's classic ++iter statement into the else branch in the loop's body!

Tip   This pattern is relatively easy to get wrong, and for sequence containers it is even quite inefficient. Later in this chapter we will introduce the *remove-erase* idiom, which you should therefore use instead of such loops whenever possible. To insert() elements while iterating over a sequence, however, or to erase() select elements from either set or map containers, you still need to write the loop explicitly yourself.

The following example takes the removeEvenNumbers() template we just developed for a spin. Even though it does so using a vector<int> container, we could've used any of the aforementioned types as well:

```cpp
// Ex19_10.cpp
// Removing all elements that satisfy a certain condition
// while iterating over a container
#include <vector>
#include <string_view>
#include <iostream>
```

```
std::vector<int> fillVector_1_to_N(size_t N);        // Fill a vector with 1, 2, ..., N
void printVector(std::string_view message, const std::vector<int>& numbers);

// Make sure to include the removeEvenNumbers() template from before as well...

int main()
{
  const size_t num_numbers{20};

  auto numbers{ fillVector_1_to_N(num_numbers) };

  printVector("The original set of numbers", numbers);

  removeEvenNumbers(numbers);

  printVector("The numbers that were kept", numbers);
}

std::vector<int> fillVector_1_to_N(size_t N)    // Fill a vector with 1, 2, ..., N
{
  std::vector<int> numbers;
  for (int i {1}; i <= N; ++i)
    numbers.push_back(i);
  return numbers;
}

void printVector(std::string_view message, const std::vector<int>& numbers)
{
  std::cout << message << ": ";
  for (int number : numbers) std::cout << number << ' ';
  std::cout << std::endl;
}
```

The outcome of this program, of course, is this:

```
The original set of numbers: 1 2 3 4 5 6 7 8 9 10 11 12 13 14 15 16 17 18 19 20
The numbers that were kept: 1 3 5 7 9 11 13 15 17 19
```

Iterators for Arrays

Iterators behave precisely like pointers—so much so that any pointer is a valid iterator as well. To be more precise, any raw pointer may serve as a random-access iterator. This observation will allow the generic algorithm templates we discuss in the next section to iterate over arrays and containers alike. In fact, array pointers can be used in any context where one would otherwise use iterators. Recall the following statements from Ex19_09:

```
std::vector<int> more_numbers{ 6, 7, 8 };
numbers.insert(numbers.end(), more_numbers.begin(), more_numbers.end());
```

Now suppose the more_numbers variable was defined as a built-in array instead. Then one way to append these numbers is by exploiting the array-pointer duality, combined with pointer arithmetic and the std::size() function, as introduced first in Chapter 5:

```
int more_numbers[] { 6, 7, 8 };
numbers.insert(numbers.end(), more_numbers, more_numbers + std::size(more_numbers));
```

While perfectly sound, there is a nicer and more uniform way as well. For that, you use the std::begin() and std::end() function templates that are defined in the Standard Library iterator header:

```
int more_numbers[] { 6, 7, 8 };
numbers.insert(numbers.end(), std::begin(more_numbers), std::end(more_numbers));
```

In fact, these function templates do not only work for arrays; they work for any container as well:

```
std::vector<int> more_numbers{ 6, 7, 8 };
numbers.insert(std::end(numbers), std::begin(more_numbers), std::end(more_numbers));
```

When used with containers, thanks to the way name resolution works in C++ for nonmember functions, you even do not have to explicitly specify the std:: namespace:

```
std::vector<int> more_numbers{ 6, 7, 8 };
numbers.insert(end(numbers), begin(more_numbers), end(more_numbers));
```

Not surprisingly, cbegin() and cend() nonmember functions exist as well, which create the corresponding const iterators for either arrays or containers:

```
std::vector<int> more_numbers{ 6, 7, 8 };
int even_more_numbers[]{ 9, 10 };
numbers.insert(end(numbers), cbegin(more_numbers), cend(more_numbers));
numbers.insert(end(numbers), std::cbegin(even_more_numbers), std::cend(even_more_numbers));
```

The compactness and uniformity of this syntax makes it our preferred way of specifying ranges in the remainder of this chapter (not in the least because compactness rules when fitting examples onto the pages of a book). In practice, many will continue using the begin() and end() member functions for containers, and there is nothing wrong with that!

Algorithms

The generic algorithms of the Standard Library combine the strengths of various concepts explored earlier in this book, such as function templates (Chapter 8), first-class and higher-order functions (Chapter 18), and, of course, iterators (earlier this chapter). You'll find that these algorithms are particularly powerful and expressive when combined with C++11's lambda expressions (Chapter 18).

A First Example

Some of the higher-order functions defined in Chapter 18 actually come close to some of the standard algorithms already. Recall the find_optimum() template? It looked as follows:

```
template <typename T, typename Comparison>
const T* find_optimum(const std::vector<T>& values, Comparison compare)
{
  if (values.empty()) return nullptr;

  const T* optimum = &values[0];
  for (size_t i = 1; i < values.size(); ++i)
  {
    if (compare(values[i], *optimum))
    {
      optimum = &values[i];
    }
  }
  return optimum;
}
```

While already quite generic, this template still has two unfortunate limitations:

- It works only for elements that are stored inside a container of type vector<>.

- It works only if you want to consider all elements of the given collection. Considering only a subset of these elements is not possible yet without copying them all in a new container first.

You can resolve both shortcomings rather easily by generalizing the template even further using iterators:

```
template <typename Iterator, typename Comparison>
Iterator find_optimum(Iterator begin, Iterator end, Comparison compare)
{
  if (begin == end) return end;

  Iterator optimum = begin;
  for (Iterator iter = ++begin; iter != end; ++iter)
  {
    if (compare(*iter, *optimum))
    {
      optimum = iter;
    }
  }
  return optimum;
}
```

This new version does not suffer the two aforementioned issues. After all:

- Iterators can be used to traverse the elements of all container and array types alike.

- The new template readily works with subranges as well by simply passing only part of a complete [begin(), end()) iterator range.

The algorithms header actually offers an algorithm that is implemented in precisely this manner. Only it is not called find_optimum(), but std::max_element(). And where there's a max_element(), there's of course a min_element(), which searches for whichever element in the range is minimal rather than maximal when compared using the relevant callback function. Let's see them both in action by adjusting some of the examples of the previous chapter:

```
// Ex19_11.cpp
// Your first algorithms: std::min_element() and max_element()
#include <iostream>
#include <algorithm>
#include <vector>

int main()
{
  std::vector<int> numbers{ 91, 18, 92, 22, 13, 43 };
  std::cout << "Minimum element: "
            << *std::min_element(begin(numbers), end(numbers)) << std::endl;
  std::cout << "Maximum element: "
            << *std::max_element(begin(numbers), end(numbers)) << std::endl;

  int number_to_search_for {};
  std::cout << "Please enter a number: ";
  std::cin >> number_to_search_for;

  auto nearer { [=](int x, int y) {
    return std::abs(x - number_to_search_for) < std::abs(y - number_to_search_for);
  }};

  std::cout << "The number nearest to " << number_to_search_for << " is "
            << *std::min_element(begin(numbers), end(numbers), nearer) << std::endl;
  std::cout << "The number furthest from " << number_to_search_for << " is "
            << *std::max_element(begin(numbers), end(numbers), nearer) << std::endl;
}
```

A first thing that jumps from this example is that for min_element() and max_element(), the comparison callback function is optional. Both offer an overload without this third parameter—both of which use the less-than operator, <, to compare elements. Besides that, these standard algorithms of course do precisely what you'd expect:

```
Minimum element: 13
Maximum element: 92
Please enter a number: 42
The number nearest to 42 is 43
The number furthest from 42 is 92
```

■ **Tip** The `algorithm` header also provides `std::minmax_element()`, which you can use to obtain both minimum and maximum elements within a given range at once. This algorithm returns a `pair<>` of iterators, with the expected semantics. You could therefore replace the last two statements in `Ex19_11` with this:

```
const auto [nearest, furthest] =
  std::minmax_element(begin(numbers), end(numbers), nearer);

std::cout << "The number nearest to " << number_to_search_for << " is "
        << *nearest << std::endl;
std::cout << "The number furthest from " << number_to_search_for << " is "

        << *furthest << std::endl;
```
We refer to earlier in this chapter for an introduction on the `pair<>` template and `auto []` syntax.

Finding Elements

The Standard Library provides various algorithms to search for elements within a range of elements. In the previous subsection we already introduced `min_element()`, `max_element()`, and `minmax_element()`. The two related algorithms that you'll probably use most often are `std::find()` and `find_if()`. The first, `std::find()`, is used to search a range for an element that equals a given value (it compares values with the `==` operator). The second, `find_if()`, instead expects a first-class callback function as an argument. It uses this callback function to determine whether any given element satisfies the desired characteristics.

To try them, let's reach back to an old favorite again: the Box class. Because `std::find()` needs to compare two Boxes, you'll need a variant of Box with an overloaded `operator==()`. The `Box.h` header from `Ex12_09`, for one, will do just fine:

```
// Ex19_12.cpp - Finding boxes.
#include <iostream>
#include <vector>
#include <algorithm>
#include "Box.h"      // From Ex12_09

int main()
{
  std::vector<Box> boxes{ Box{1,2,3}, Box{5,2,3}, Box{9,2,1}, Box{3,2,1} };

  // Define a lambda functor to print the result of find() or find_if():
  auto print_result = [&boxes] (auto result)
  {
    if (result == end(boxes))
      std::cout << "No box found." << std::endl;
    else
      std::cout << "Found matching box at position "
              << (result - begin(boxes)) << std::endl;
  };
```

```
// Find an exact box
Box box_to_find{ 3,2,1 };
auto result{ std::find(begin(boxes), end(boxes), box_to_find) };
print_result(result);

// Find a box with a volume larger than that of box_to_find
const auto required_volume = box_to_find.volume();
result = std::find_if(begin(boxes), end(boxes),
            [required_volume](const Box& box) {return box.volume() > required_volume; });
print_result(result);
}
```

The output is as follows:

```
Found matching box at position 3
Found matching box at position 1
```

Both find() and find_if() return either an iterator to the found element or the end iterator of the range if no element is found that matches the search criteria.

■ **Caution**   If no element is found, the end iterator of the range to search is returned, not the end iterator of the container. Even though in many cases these are the same (in Ex19_12 they are), this is not always true.

A number of variants are provided by the standard. The following list shows a few of them. Consult a Standard Library reference for more details.

- find_if_not() is similar to find_if(), only it searches for the first element for which the given callback function returns false (rather than true).

- find_first_of() searches a range of elements for the first element that matches any element from another given range.

- adjacent_find() searches for two consecutive elements that are equal or that satisfy a given predicate.

- search() / find_end() search for a range of elements in another range of elements. The former returns the first match, while the latter returns the last match.

- binary_search() checks whether a given element is present in a sorted range. By exploiting the fact that the elements in the input range are sorted, it can find the desired element faster than find(). Elements are compared using either the < operator or a user-provided comparison callback.

■ **Caution**   Earlier in this chapter, we explained that set and map containers are really good at finding elements themselves already. Because they know the internal structure of their data, they can find elements much faster than any generic algorithm ever could. These containers therefore offer a find() member function that you should always use instead of the generic std::find() algorithm. In general, whenever a container offers member functions that are functionally equivalent to an algorithm, you should always use the former. Consult your Standard Library reference for further details.

Outputting Multiple Values

find(), find_if(), find_if_not()—these three algorithms all search for the first element that meets a particular requirement. But what if you're interested in finding all of them instead? If you glance through all algorithms that the Standard Library has to offer, you'll find that there is no algorithm with a name like find_all(). Luckily, there are at least three algorithms that would allow you to obtain all elements in a given range that satisfy a given condition:

- std::remove_if() can be used to remove all elements that do *not* satisfy the condition. We discuss this algorithm later in the next subsection.

- std::partition() rearranges the elements in a range such that those elements that satisfy a callback condition are moved to the front of the range and those that do not are moved to the back. We'll leave this option for you to try later in the exercises.

- std::copy_if() may be used to copy all elements you need to a second output range.

```
// Ex19_13.cpp - Extracting all odd numbers.
#include <iostream>
#include <set>
#include <vector>
#include <algorithm>

std::set<int> fillSet_1_to_N(size_t N);        // Fill a set with 1, 2, ..., N
void printVector(const std::vector<int>& v);   // Print the contents of a vector to std::cout

int main()
{
  const size_t num_numbers{20};

  const auto numbers = fillSet_1_to_N(num_numbers);

  std::vector<int> odd_numbers( numbers.size() );
  auto end_odd_numbers = std::copy_if(begin(numbers), end(numbers), begin(odd_numbers),
                                 [](int n) { return n % 2 == 1; });
  odd_numbers.erase(end_odd_numbers, end(odd_numbers));

  printVector(odd_numbers);
}
```

The printVector() function you can recycle from Ex19_09, and fillSet_1_to_N() is trivially analogous to the fillVector_1_to_N() function of Ex19_10.

Let's focus our attention on the three lines of the program that matter: those that copy all odd numbers in the numbers set<> into the odd_numbers vector<>. Clearly, the first two parameters of std::copy_if() determine the range of elements that potentially need to be copied; the fourth determines which elements are effectively copied. The third parameter of copy_if() is more interesting, though. The first element that copy_if() copies is assigned to this position. The next position that copy_if() assigns to is then obtained by incrementing the target iterator using ++.

It is therefore critical that the target range, the vector<> odd_numbers in Ex19_13, is at least large enough to hold all elements that copy_if() will copy. Because in general you do not know in advance how many elements there will be, you may be forced to allocate a buffer of memory that is larger than required. This is what you see in Ex19_13 as well: odd_numbers is initialized with a dynamic array of num_numbers elements (all zeroes), which is most definitely sufficient to hold all odd numbers. Of course, it will turn out to be twice larger than actually required. For that purpose, the std::copy_if() algorithm returns an iterator that points one past the last element that it copied. You then typically use this iterator to erase all superfluous elements from the target container, precisely like this is done in Ex19_13.

▦ **Caution**   Take care not to forget the second argument to the call to erase()! It must be the end iterator of the container. If you forget this second argument, erase() will just erase the single element pointed to by the iterator passed as the first argument. (In Ex19_13, in other words, only one of the original zeroes would then be erased from odd_numbers!)

Many algorithms copy or move output into a target range analogously to std::copy_if() (std::copy(), move(), replace_copy(), replace_copy_if(), remove_copy()—the list goes on...). All could therefore in principle be using the same idiom. That is, you conservatively allocate an overly large target range, which you then shrink again using the iterator returned by the algorithm.

This pattern, however, while still useful at times, is clearly cumbersome, verbose, and quite error prone. Luckily, there is a better way. For Ex19_13, you could use the following two statements instead (see Ex19_13A):

```
std::vector<int> odd_numbers;
std::copy_if(begin(numbers), end(numbers), std::back_inserter(odd_numbers),
          [](int n) { return n % 2 == 1; });
```

With this technique, there is no need to over-allocate and thus no need to erase() any redundant elements afterward either. Instead, you create a very special "fake" iterator through the std::back_inserter() function, which is defined by the iterator header of the Standard Library. In our case, every time copy_if() dereferences and assigns a value to this iterator, what effectively happens is that the element that is assigned is forwarded to the push_back() function of the container object that you passed to back_inserter() earlier—that is, odd_numbers.

The end result is therefore the same (all odd numbers are added to odd_numbers), but this time you did so with less code and, more importantly, code that is much clearer, and that leaves considerably less room for error. This is the conclusion:

▦ **Tip**   The iterator header defines the back_inserter(), front_inserter(), and inserter() functions that create "fake" iterator objects that trigger, respectively, push_back(), push_front(), and insert() whenever a value is assigned to these iterators after dereferencing. Use these functions whenever an algorithm needs to output multiple values into some container.

The Remove-Erase Idiom

Often you need to delete all elements from a container that satisfy specific conditions. With the removeEvenNumbers() function of Ex19_10 earlier in this chapter, we showed you how you can do this using a rather complex for loop that iterates over all the elements of the container, checks whether an element satisfies the conditions, and calls erase() on the container to remove the element. Implementing it this way is inefficient and error prone, however. Take a vector<> as an example. If you remove an element from the middle of the vector<>, all subsequent elements need to be shifted down to fill the gap of the removed element. Also, when removing elements from the container while you are iterating over that same container, you need to take extra care that the iterator is correctly handled, as discussed earlier. This is prone to errors. Therefore:

▩ **Tip**   Instead of manually iterating over the elements of a sequence container, you should always use the *remove-erase idiom*. With this idiom, discussed next, you use the std::remove() or std::remove_if() algorithm to remove elements that satisfy a certain condition from a container.

The std::remove() and remove_if() algorithms don't really remove the elements from the container; they can't because they only get a range identified by a pair of iterators. They don't have access to the container, so they can't erase elements, even if they wanted to. Instead, these algorithms work by moving all elements that should not be removed to the front of the input range. That way, all elements to be kept are moved toward the beginning of the container, and all elements to be erased are left at the end of the container. Similar to copy_if() and friends (see the previous subsection), remove() and remove_if() then return an iterator to the first element to erase. This iterator can then be used as a first argument to the erase() method of the container to truly erase the elements.

Let's see how the remove-erase idiom works with some actual code. You can use the same program as Ex19_10, only this time you replace the removeEvenNumbers() with this version:

```
void removeEvenNumbers(std::vector<int>& numbers)
{
  // Use the remove_if() algorithm to remove all even numbers
  auto first_to_erase{ std::remove_if(begin(numbers),
    end(numbers), [](int number) { return number % 2 == 0; }) };

  // Erase all elements including and beyond first_to_erase
  numbers.erase(first_to_erase, end(numbers));
}
```

The output of the resulting program (available in Ex19_14) should then remain the same:

```
The original set of numbers: 1 2 3 4 5 6 7 8 9 10 11 12 13 14 15 16 17 18 19 20
The numbers that were kept: 1 3 5 7 9 11 13 15 17 19
```

▩ **Caution**   Take care—and we cannot repeat this enough—not to forget the second argument to the call to erase()! It must be the end iterator of the container. If you forget this second argument, erase() will just erase the single element pointed to by the iterator passed as the first argument. In Ex19_14, in other words, only the number 11 would then be removed.

Sorting

One key operation for arrays and sequence containers is sorting their elements. The std::sort() algorithm is defined in <algorithm> and can be used to sort a range of elements. The first two arguments passed to the algorithm are the begin and end iterators of the range to sort. The third argument passed is an optional comparator. If no comparator is given, the elements are sorted in ascending sequence. That is, if applied to a range of strings, the strings will be sorted lexicographically. The following example sorts a range of strings twice, first lexicographically and then according to the length of each string:

```cpp
// Ex19_15.cpp - Sorting strings
#include <iostream>
#include <string>
#include <vector>
#include <algorithm>

int main()
{
  std::vector<std::string> names{"Frodo Baggins", "Gandalf the Gray", "Aragon",
    "Samwise Gamgee", "Peregrin Took", "Meriadoc Brandybuck", "Gimli",
    "Legolas Greenleaf", "Boromir"};

  // Sort the names lexicographically
  std::sort(begin(names), end(names));
  std::cout << "Names sorted lexicographically:" << std::endl;
  for (const auto& name : names) std::cout << name << ", ";
  std::cout << std::endl << std::endl;

  // Sort the names by length
  std::sort(begin(names), end(names),
    [](const auto& left, const auto& right) {return left.length() < right.length(); });
  std::cout << "Names sorted by length:" << std::endl;
  for (const auto& name : names) std::cout << name << ", ";
  std::cout << std::endl;
}
```

The output is as follows:

```
Names sorted lexicographically:
Aragon, Boromir, Frodo Baggins, Gandalf the Gray, Gimli, Legolas Greenleaf, Meriadoc
Brandybuck, Peregrin Took, Samwise Gamgee,
Names sorted by length:
Gimli, Aragon, Boromir, Frodo Baggins, Peregrin Took, Samwise Gamgee, Gandalf the Gray,
Legolas Greenleaf, Meriadoc Brandybuck,
```

Parallel Algorithms

Some of the most notable additions to the C++17 Standard Library are parallel versions of most generic algorithms. Virtually every computer today has multiple processing cores. Even the most modest of phones has multiple processing cores these days. By default, invoking any of the standard algorithms, however, will use only one of these cores. All other cores risk sitting by idly, waiting until someone throws some work in their direction. That is a real shame. When processing large arrays or containers of data, these algorithms could run so much faster if they'd just divide the work among all available cores. With C++17, doing this becomes easy. All you have to do, for instance, to sort the fellowship in Ex19_15 in parallel is tell the algorithm to use the so-called *parallel execution policy*, like so:

```
std::sort(std::execution::par, begin(names), end(names));
```

The std::execution::par constant is defined by the execution header, so you'll have to include that first. The header defines other execution policies as well, but we won't discuss them here.

Naturally, with only nine elements, you are unlikely to notice any difference. Of course, if Saruman or Sauron were to sort the names of their troops, then parallel execution would make a lot more sense.

Nearly every algorithm can be parallelized this way. It costs you almost nothing, and the gains could be significant. So, always keep this option in mind when processing larger data sets.

■ **Tip** The algorithm header also defines the for_each() algorithm, which you now could use to parallelize many regular range-based for loops. Do take care, though, that each iteration of the loop can execute independently of the other, or you'll run into data races. Data races and other aspects of concurrent programming, however, are outside the scope of this book.

Summary

This chapter provided you with a solid first introduction on three of the most important, most frequently used features of the Standard Library: containers, iterators, and algorithms. Containers organize your data using various data structures, each with their strengths and limitations. A typical container, and sequential containers in particular, do not offer much functionality beyond adding, removing, and traversing elements. More advanced operations to manipulate the data that is stored inside these containers are provided instead in the form of an impressive collection of generic, higher-order function templates, called *algorithms*.

Our goal here was never to make you an expert user of the various container and algorithm templates yet. For that, considerably more pages are required than we had left for this book. To actively start using the features that you learned about in this chapter, you'll therefore need to regularly consult a Standard Library reference—one that lists all member functions of the various containers, as well as the many algorithm templates that exist (there are more than 100 of them in total!), and that specifies the precise semantics of all this powerful functionality. Even the most seasoned C++ developer regularly needs guidance from a good reference book or website.

In this chapter, we therefore aimed to convey a broad bird's-eye overview, focused on general principles, best practices, and common caveats to watch out for, with guidelines on choosing between the rich set of features that the Standard Library has to offer, typical use cases, and standard idioms. In short, it contained everything that you cannot readily extract from a typical reference work. The most important points covered in this chapter are the following:

- Sequence containers store data in a straightforward user-determined linear order, one element after the other.

- Your go-to sequential container should be `std::vector<>`. The practical use for the other sequential containers in real-life applications, and `list<>`, `forward_list<>`, and `deque<>` in particular, is typically limited.

- The three container adapters—`std::stack<>`, `queue<>`, and `priority_queue<>`— all encapsulate a sequential container, which they use to implement a limited set of operations that allow you to inject and later take out elements. Their difference mostly lies in the order in which these elements come out again.

- Sets are duplicate-free containers and are good at determining whether they contain a given element.

- Maps uniquely associate keys with values and allow you to quickly retrieve a value given their keys.

- Both sets and maps come in two flavors: ordered and unordered. The former are particularly interesting if you need a sorted view on your data as well; the latter have the potential to be more efficient but may come with the complexity of having to define an effective hash function first (we did not cover hash functions here, but you can read all about it in your favorite Standard Library reference).

- You—and of course the Standard algorithms as well—can use iterators to enumerate the elements of any given container, without having to know how this data is actually physically organized.

- Iterators in C++ typically make heavy use of operator overloading in order to look and feel like pointers.

- The Standard Library offers more than a 100 different algorithms, most in the `algorithms` header. We made sure that the ones you'll likely use most often are covered either in the main text or in the following exercises.

- All algorithms operate on half-open ranges of iterators, and many accept a first-class callback function. Mostly you'll call an algorithm with a lambda expression if its default behavior does not suit you.

- Algorithms that retrieve a single element from a range (`find()`, `find_if()`, `min_element()`, `max_element()`, and so on) do so by returning an iterator. The end iterator of the range is then always used to denote "not found."

- Algorithms that produce multiple output elements (`copy()`, `copy_if()`, and so on) should normally always be used in conjunction with the `std::back_inserter()`, `front_inserter()`, and `inserter()` utilities provided by the `iterator` header.

- To remove multiple elements from sequence containers, you should use the remove-erase idiom.

- You can take advantage of the extensive multiprocessing capabilities of current hardware by passing the `std::execution::par` execution policy as the first argument to most algorithms.

EXERCISES

The following exercises enable you to try what you've learned in this chapter. If you get stuck, look back over the chapter for help. If you're still stuck after that, you can download the solutions from the Apress website (www.apress.com/book/download.html), but that really should be a last resort.

Exercise 19-1. In practice, we would never recommend you to implement your own linked list data structure to store Boxes in Truckload. At the time it made perfect sense to practice nested classes, as well as working with pointers; but normally you should follow our advice from earlier in this chapter and simply use a vector<> instead (a polymorphic vector<>, to be precise—see Chapter 14). If you need a sequence container, a vector<> is almost always the way to go! Eliminate the linked list from the Truckload class of Exercise 17-1 according to this guideline. Notice how you can now adhere to the rule of zero as well (see Chapter 18)?

Exercise 19-2. Replace both instances of your self-defined Stack<> in Ex16_04A with an instance of std::stack<>.

Exercise 19-3. Rework your solution to Exercise 16-6 by replacing all instances of your SparseArray<> and linked list template types with standard containers. Carefully think about which container types would be most appropriate!

▓ **Note** If you want extra practice, you can do the same for the solutions of Exercises 16-4 and 16-5 as well.

Exercise 19-4. Research the std::partition() algorithm and use it to reimplement the removeEvenNumbers() function of either Ex19_10 or Ex19_14.

Exercise 19-5. Not all Standard Library algorithms are defined by the algorithms header. Some are defined by the numeric header as well. One such example is accumulate(). Research this algorithm and use it to implement an algorithm-like function template that computes the average of a given iterator range. Exercise your newly implemented template with a little test program.

Exercise 19-6. Another algorithm that is defined by the numeric header is the oddly named iota() algorithm, which you can use to fill a given range with values M, M+1, M+2, and so on. Use it to rework the fillVector_1_to_N() function of Ex19_10.

▓ **Note** The name of the iota() algorithm refers to the Greek letter iota, written ι. It is an homage to the classical programming language APL developed by Turing Award winner Kenneth E. Iverson in the 1960s in his influential book *A Programming Language* (this title is where the acronym APL itself stems from). The APL programming language used mathematical symbols to name numeric functions, one of which was ι. In APL, ι3, for instance, would produce the array {1 2 3}.

Exercise 19-7. `erase()` and `erase_if()` are not the only algorithms for which the remove-erase idiom is applicable. Another example is `std::unique()`, which is used to remove duplicates from a presorted range of elements. Write a little program that fills a `vector<>` with a considerably large amount of random integers between 0 and `RAND_MAX`, sorts this sequence, removes the duplicates, and then prints out the amount of remaining elements.

Exercise 19-8. Parallelize your solution to the previous exercise.

Index

© Ivor Horton and Peter Van Weert 2018
I. Horton and P. Van Weert, *Beginning C++17*, https://doi.org/10.1007/978-1-4842-3366-5

▒ U

▒ V

▒ W

▒ X, Y

▒ Z

Get the eBook for only $5!

Why limit yourself?

With most of our titles available in both PDF and ePUB format, you can access your content wherever and however you wish—on your PC, phone, tablet, or reader.

Since you've purchased this print book, we are happy to offer you the eBook for just $5.

To learn more, go to http://www.apress.com/companion or contact support@apress.com.

Apress®

Made in the USA
Lexington, KY
01 June 2019